FRIENDSHIP AND FRATRICIDE

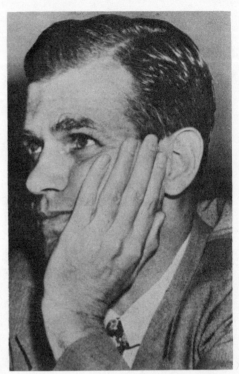

Alger Hiss, 1948

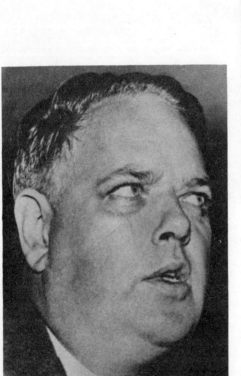

Whittaker Chambers, 1948

FRIENDSHIP
and
FRATRICIDE

AN ANALYSIS OF

Whittaker Chambers AND *Alger Hiss*

BY *Meyer A. Zeligs,* M.D.

NEW YORK / THE VIKING PRESS

First published in 1967 by The Viking Press, Inc.

625 Madison Avenue, New York, N.Y. 10022

Published simultaneously in Canada by

The Macmillan Company of Canada Limited

Library of Congress catalog card number: 66-23822

Printed in U.S.A. by Vail-Ballou Press, Inc.

Grateful acknowledgment is made to Random
House, Inc., for permission to quote extensively
from Witness by Whittaker Chambers. Copyright
1952 by Whittaker Chambers.

Can one man actually destroy another—not by murder, which need involve no metaphysical destruction—but by more refined methods; destroy him in the most delicate and secret places of his soul? Or are limits set to the guilty man's evil instinct, in that he must destroy himself with his victim, more cruelly and more surely even than him whom he would destroy?

FRANZ WERFEL
Introduction to *Class Reunion*
in *Twilight of a World*

Contents

Appendix

I L L U S T R A T I O N S

Preface

IN 1958, when I first began to think about writing this book, I was, as I still am, engaged in the full-time practice of psychoanalysis in a large city. The Hiss case, like any piece of national or political news, was far removed from my work. I had never known or met either Alger Hiss or Whittaker Chambers. I had no political ax to grind. My curiosity about some of the testimony of the protagonists stemmed from the challenge it presented as a fascinating riddle in human behavior. As a political and personal mystery, the case seemed to be settling into one of those unresolved paradoxes of history.

The six years of research and writing, of which this book is the result, represent a project that I undertook without a sponsor and in the spirit of pure inquiry. Now that my task is finished I feel that I owe my readers some explanation as to how a busy psychoanalyst could become so involved in an area seemingly remote from the mainstream of his clinical work and previous medical writings. And so I have turned my thoughts back to the earliest beginnings of my interest in this subject. The organized research on this book did not get under way until the fall of 1959. It was, however, sometime during 1953–54, after I read Chambers' *Witness* and then the Earl Jowitt's *The Strange Case of Alger Hiss*, that my clinical curiosity about the lives of Hiss and Chambers was first stirred. After reading Jowitt's book—a jurist's analysis of the trial record and the conflicting evidence, which even to him was "so baffling"—I was moved by his special appeal to American psychiatrists to help solve the riddle of this important event.

I should be profoundly interested [Jowitt wrote] to hear the opinion of distinguished American psychiatrists on all the new circumstances revealed in *Witness*. I wonder what conclusion they would reach. . . . Surely it should be put to the test.

This challenge must have intrigued me as a psychoanalyst.

Important questions raised by Jowitt, an eminent British jurist, soon after Chambers' autobiography, *Witness,* had been published and was being widely read in this country (it was a Book-of-the-Month Club selection), made the entire matter even more perplexing; and, a few years later, when Chambers' widely publicized revelations of his life were placed in apposition to Hiss's then recently published account—*In the Court of Public Opinion,* 1957—the mystery grew even more intense and the rumors more rampant.

Then, in 1958, still another account, *The Unfinished Story of Alger Hiss* (by Fred J. Cook) appeared, and once again my attention was focused on the riddle of the case. Cook's book was the sixth full-length volume to be published on the subject in as many years since the end of the Hiss trials. I read it, as I had the previous ones, with that degree of interest one keeps up in relation to any long-standing, unresolved mystery. Cook's account was succinct, its easy readability helped disentangle some of the old controversies. It highlighted some new hard facts and lifted them out of the diffuse mass of evidence that beclouded the case. But the human enigma of the case, by far the deepest area of its mystery, remained untouched and unexplored. By 1958, ten years had passed since the hearings and trials. But the Hiss affair remained an unfinished story, the same nagging doubts persisted.

Either Alger Hiss [wrote Cook] was a traitor to his country and remains one of the most colossal liars and hypocrites in history, or he is an American Dreyfus, framed on the highest level of justice for political advantage.

It seemed to me that a comprehensive exploration into the lives of Alger Hiss and Whittaker Chambers was sorely needed. I had no idea how such a study could be accomplished and knew even less in what direction the pursuit of such a project would take me, if I was going to be foolhardy enough to attempt it. A brief account, therefore, of the vicissitudes this study underwent will define my personal posture as a biographer, or as a social or political scientist, to none of which titles I have ever laid claim.

Early in 1959 a chance circumstance sent me into a more active pursuit of this subject. While attending a New York meeting, I happened to meet Dr. Carl Binger, a colleague whom I had known casually over a period of years. Dr. Binger had testified as an expert witness in the second Hiss trial and had alluded to some of Chambers' writings and translations. In the course of his testimony Dr. Binger brought out an unusual fact: twenty years before the Hiss case, in 1929, Chambers had translated from the German a short novel by Franz Werfel, *Der Abituriententag,* titled *Class Reunion* in English. During a period of cross-examination Dr. Binger had pointed out some "extraordinary analogies" of psychological significance in the plot of *Class Reunion* and certain patterns in Chambers' behavior toward Hiss. Since I had then been reading about the case and was curious about the meaning of Dr. Binger's testimony, I asked him if he would be kind enough to lend me his copy of *Class Reunion* as it was long since out of print. Dr. Binger sent both the original German edition and Chambers' translation. After a careful reading of these two books, it was evident that by means of deletions and insertions and translation errors Chambers had effectively altered the original meaning of some of the passages. He had an extraordinary gift for languages; he was well qualified as a writer and translator. I did not regard the alterations as insignificant, nor could I dismiss them as simple academic errors. I felt I was definitely on the track of certain factors in this human equation that had not been examined in the literature on the case.[1] I began to look systematically into Chambers' writings and beyond them into the vast body of facts, assertions, denials, proofs, and disproofs that made up the corpus of the case.

Despite the many recorded accounts, it became evident to me that no one had examined the personal lives of the protagonists or the psychological motives and forces that underlay the legal and political contradictions of the case. Whatever light had been shed illuminated only the periphery. Each book, as it appeared, provided an added perspective, but the mystery remained.

More than seventeen years have passed since the summer of 1948 when Whittaker Chambers, a senior editor of *Time* magazine, a confessed ex-Communist courier and espionage agent, first publicly accused Alger Hiss, president of the Carnegie Endowment for International Peace and a former high official in the State Department, of having belonged to an underground Communist cell in Washington, D.C., during the 1930s. Hiss categorically denied the charge and sued Chambers for libel. Chambers then produced copies of typed State Department documents, which he charged Hiss had turned over to him for transmittal to the Soviets. On the basis of the documentary evidence provided by Chambers, Hiss was indicted by a federal grand jury, after denying that he had passed documents to Chambers and that he had seen Chambers after the year 1936. After two long federal trials Hiss was found guilty of perjury and sentenced to five years' imprisonment in the federal penitentiary at Lewisburg, Pennsylvania. Hiss has long since served his

---

[1] By 1962 the number of full-length accounts of the Hiss-Chambers case had increased to eight: Ralph de Toledano and Victor Lasky, *Seeds of Treason,* 1950. Alistair Cooke, *A Generation on Trial,* 1952. Whittaker Chambers, *Witness,* 1952. The Earl Jowitt, *The Strange Case of Alger Hiss,* 1953. Alger Hiss, *In the Court of Public Opinion,* 1957. Fred J. Cook, *The Unfinished Story of Alger Hiss,* 1957. Bert and Peter Andrews, *A Tragedy of History,* 1962. Richard M. Nixon, *Six Crises,* 1962.

prison sentence and has been released into the obscurity that his conviction and disbarment have forced upon him. And in 1961 Whittaker Chambers died.

Along with those who followed the outcome of this case, I remained perplexed by its parodoxes. And as a psychiatrist who has on occasion been called to testify in court, I was interested in appraising the credibility of witnesses. I felt that a psychoanalytic type of investigation, encompassing all areas of the protagonists' lives, might resolve some of the unanswered questions. The demands of such a research often led me into disciplines outside my competency, into the fields of political science, history, literary criticism, journalism, and the law. These forays were, however, essential to my understanding of the case and served, it may be hoped, to keep my clinical probings in correct perspective.

The printed reports of the congressional hearings and a copy of the transcript of the second trial, *United States* v. *Alger Hiss* (ten volumes), were made available through the courtesy of an interested colleague. Though the lapse of time has subdued the drama of this event, I have become a silent witness to the verbal accusations and denials of the protagonists.

I set out to arrange a series of personal interviews with Hiss and Chambers. Through the help of a colleague I met Alger Hiss for the first time in the spring of 1960. I explained to him my reasons for wanting to write an analytic biography of himself and Whittaker Chambers. He expressed the feeling that his private life had little bearing on the case but agreed to go along with the use of any competent investigative method that might offer some hope of clarifying the entire matter. His case had been legally lost in the courts; any further efforts of appeal on his part in that direction were no longer possible.

I made clear to Hiss at the outset, as I had in similar letters to Chambers and to all the others I planned to interview, that my projected study was to be an analytic biography. It was not my intent to confirm the guilt or establish the innocence of Hiss. I pointed out to Hiss the necessity of having no restrictions in the gathering of background material pertaining to all aspects of his life, private and public, personal and political. Despite a deep-seated aversion to talking about himself, Hiss agreed to these stipulations.

Since May 1960 Hiss and I have spent many hours in discussion of his life. The subjects covered in these talks have been supplemented by correspondence (which now fills a full-sized volume). With Hiss's permission, I also interviewed his past defense counsel and his present attorneys, who made available to me the complete Hiss files. These included all correspondence, confidential memoranda, investigators' reports, legal briefs. Hiss's relatives provided an abundance of anecdotes dating from his childhood. His lawyers contributed their views of Hiss, the person, as well as the problems of the case. Personal physicians, former associates in government, and friends were helpful in more ways than I can describe. Former schoolteachers, professors, and university registrars made available a great deal of information pertaining to Hiss's academic life. And from a cross section of representative informants, ranging from ambassadors and federal court judges to ex-convicts who knew him at Lewisburg, I gathered more material. Most of the ingredients requisite for a portrait in depth were now at hand.

My study of Chambers' life took a different tack. Despite my repeated efforts, Chambers refused to see me. He would not answer my letters or phone calls. Attempts to contact him through mutual friends proved equally unsuccessful. One informant, close to Chambers, wrote me:

While I know Mr. Chambers to be an introspective and somewhat talkative man in some spheres . . . the Hiss-Chambers case is one area he does not like to talk about.

Another intermediary wrote:

I'm afraid I was not able to be of help to you in arranging an interview with Chambers. I've been in contact with two close friends of his who approached him concerning an interview. They were quite unsuccessful. From what I can gather, the Hiss-Chambers case, the subject of Communism, anything in an area relating to the case is strictly taboo.

Even from Chambers' Baltimore attorneys I failed to get a response. Their opinions are therefore absent from this study.

Chambers' silence stands in ironic contrast to the cooperation of Hiss. Chambers' account of his personal life has been widely publicized: in his testimony at many congressional hearings, in the two trials, and in his autobiography; yet he would not speak to me privately. Hiss, who has insisted that the Hiss case is distinct from Hiss, the person, and who has confined his public utterances strictly to legal facts, has willingly related the details of his personal and political life.

After Whittaker Chambers' death on July 9, 1961 (two years after I began my study), many sources of information opened up. Informants, unwilling to relate their past experiences while Chambers was still alive, now provided me with anecdotal and documentary material. I sought out Chambers' friends, former classmates, colleagues, professors, political associates (ex-Communists, fellow travelers, leftists, and rightists); also journalists, editors, physicians, literary associates, and many others. Most related to me freely, and some reluctantly, what they remembered about him. There were those who doubted him and those who believed in him implicitly; many were awed by his literary knowledge and fascinated by his experience and intrigues. He was variously admired, distrusted, held in contempt. But all who had any dealings with him shared a common feeling: Whittaker Chambers was a man of mystery. Even in the minds of the politically astute, he remains to this day a misunderstood figure. Despite the extent of his political and personal intrigues and despite his success as a journalist, Whittaker Chambers led an isolated and secretive existence. This book endeavors to illuminate the interaction between his inner and outer life, a life whose effects are still felt on the present-day American scene.

The task of distinguishing biographical fact from autobiographical fantasy and dissecting out the ingredients of partial truth posed itself as a constant challenge. Chambers' lengthy accounts, like his spoken testimony, were dramatic, emotionalized, and free-flowing. Hiss's utterances were dry, logical, and detached. The juxtaposition of their accounts served as a helpful index in appraising identical events that involved their lives and careers.

But an early realization of the striking oppositeness of their lives and careers made it especially important to maintain a proper equidistance in my investigation and analysis of them. The task of searching out and presenting biographical facts, whether praiseworthy or shameful, could not be compromised. Only in this way, without sacrifice of my own proximity and empathy, could I avoid the danger of bias in so personalized a study. Having appointed myself the biographer of such a unique pair of adversaries, it was incumbent on me to maintain careful analytic neutrality toward them. Though Chambers had been the stanchest public witness in support of his actions and beliefs and had already revealed the gamut of his emotional life to the public in *Witness* and in his testimony, he would not acknowledge this study. This book therefore lacks the added dimension his personal participation would have provided. Conversely, Hiss, who had always been reluctant to discuss his personal life, either as a public witness or in, *In the Court of Public Opinion,* cooperated closely with me in this work. Their opposite attitudes and the effect of Chambers' unexpected death during the course of the work determined to some extent the shape of this book. Whatever imbalance it contains I have carefully left untouched. It remains, I hope, not the measure of my own leanings, but an essential dimension of the analytic biographer in his endeavor to encompass in full scope the deeply contrasting life styles of his two subjects.

MEYER A. ZELIGS

San Francisco
May 1966

I

1

Accusation and Denial

THE NAMES of Alger Hiss and Whittaker Chambers are now inseparable in the American memory. The tragic drama they performed in public fixed the course of their remaining years and, in retrospect, transformed the established images of their past. But the decades that prepared them for that now historic event had made them fundamentally different men, as is evident from the briefest sketch of their careers or the smallest glimpse of their behavior. The differences, indeed, are so marked that their conflict seems almost to be between those essential human contradictions which we all contain: faith against materialism, passion against reason, honesty against cynicism—each of the polarities could apply.

Chambers' multifarious life was beset by passionate but shifting convictions. He was a sometime student at Columbia but left before graduation. In 1925 he joined the Communist Party, with which he remained intermittently and variously associated until 1937–38.[1] At Columbia he made a name for himself as a literary figure, and he later held jobs on the *Daily Worker* and, for a short time, on the *New Masses*. For much of his life he supported himself by doing free-lance translations. It was thought by some that at one time he had been a German spy. Others who seemed to know him well regarded him as a Trotskyist. For more than five years he was, according to his account, a paid functionary of the Communist Party, a member of its underground. When he left the party he underwent a personal revolution that turned him finally into a Quaker and a conservative journalist. Although his literary career did not, in effect, begin until he was nearly forty, he became, a few years thereafter, one of seven senior editors of *Time* magazine.

Hiss's career—as it appeared in the public record—involved no such reversals. It was distinguished and utterly straightforward. He was a gifted law student (Harvard Law School, 1929), secretary to Justice Oliver Wendell Holmes, Jr., a young practicing lawyer, and then from 1933 to 1947 an offi-

[1] The exact date was to become a matter of controversy.

cial in various government agencies. He left his last post—as head of the State Department office in charge of United Nations affairs—to become president of the Carnegie Endowment for International Peace. It was Chambers' charge in 1948 that behind this brilliant record lay a great deception: that Hiss had also been a Communist.

Chambers had first made the charge secretly ten years before, after leaving the Communist Party, in a privately arranged conversation with Assistant Secretary of State Adolf A. Berle, Jr. Hiss knew nothing of Chambers' initial charges or of any investigation of him at that time by the FBI, as no action was taken by them. However, subsequent interrogations by the FBI of Hiss and Chambers made it likely that Chambers' charge might be revived at any moment. And, to be sure, in August 1948, under the auspices of the House Committee on Un-American Activities, which was pursuing alleged Communist infiltration of government, Chambers again named Hiss, among others, as having been a Communist during the 1930s.

The House Committee's investigation led to the celebrated Hiss-Chambers case. Hiss was ultimately convicted of perjury and sentenced to prison. Each man subsequently wrote his own version of the controversy. The accounts are as different as their authors. Chambers' *Witness* is a massive (799 pages), emotional, sometimes mystical work, a testament from the soul. Hiss's *In the Court of Public Opinion* is as dry and detached as the lawyer's brief that, in effect, it is. This study will make abundant use of both documents.

Chambers was subpoenaed to testify before the House Committee on August 3. He recalls, in extraordinary terms, his response to the subpoena:

What I felt was what we see in the eye of a bird or an animal that we are about to kill, which knows that it is about to be killed, and whose torment is not the certainty of death or pain, but the horror of the interval before death comes in which it knows that it has lost light and freedom forever. It is not yet dead. But it is no longer alive.

Like any creature that knows it is meant to die, I simply went inert in an animal sense. I deliberately numbed and blacked out the soul so that only the body could be torn; for the body can endure any agony up to death. But the soul cannot endure the violation I have described, which is probably the most terrible in life, without dissolving in a liquefaction of panic.[2]

The tone of this passage from *Witness* is not atypical. As he is about to kill, he is overwhelmed by his identification with his victim and portrays himself as helpless, alone, victimized. But his aloneness carries with it a certain

[2] The Chambers quotations, unless otherwise cited, are from Whittaker Chambers, *Witness* (New York: Random House, 1952).

sense of specialness as well, even of nobility. He considers refusing to give
any information at all, but then

I could not do it. I believed that I was not meant to be spared from testifying. I
sensed, with a force greater than any fear or revulsion, that it was for this that my
whole life had been lived. For this I had been a Communist, for this I had ceased
to be a Communist. For this the tranquil strengthening years had been granted to
me. This challenge was the terrible meaning of my whole life, of all that I had
done that was evil, of all that I had sought that was good, of my weakness and my
strength. Everything that made me peculiarly myself, and different from all others,
qualified me to testify. My failure to do so, any attempt to evade that necessity,
would be a betrayal that would measure nothing less than the destruction of my
own soul. I felt this beyond any possibility of avoiding it.

And so he decides to testify. His decision is put in the largest terms available to him: his "soul," the "terrible meaning of my whole life." Then his
sense of being hunted is transformed into a sort of compassion for his own
prey, that is, the men he will accuse. He decides to make a compromise: he
will tell, but he will not tell all.

I, unfortunately, was the man who could speak. The necessity seemed clear to me.
My intention was clear, too. I did not wish to harm, more than was unavoidable,
those whom I must testify against, of whose lives in the years since I had left them
I knew next to nothing, many of whom might no longer be Communists. I would
not, therefore, testify to espionage against them.

On Tuesday, August 3, Whittaker Chambers gave his first testimony before the House Committee. Identifying himself as "senior editor of *Time*
magazine" and giving his address as "9 Rockefeller Plaza," he told the committee that he "joined the Communist Party in 1924 and remained a member
until 1937." He then asked for and was given permission to read a prepared
statement in which he testified that for part of that time he had been attached
to a secret underground "apparatus" in Washington. He added some personal
notes, including a description of his terror of the Communist Party, which
confirm the troubled state of mind that he later reported in his autobiography.

For a year I lived in hiding, sleeping by day and watching through the night with
gun or revolver within easy reach. That was what underground Communism could
do to one man in the peaceful United States in the year 1938.
    I had sound reason for supposing that the Communists might try to kill me.
For a number of years I had myself served in the underground, chiefly in Washington, D.C. The heart of my report to the United States Government consisted of a
description of the apparatus to which I was attached. It was an underground organization of the United States Communist Party developed, to the best of my
knowledge, by Harold Ware, one of the sons of the Communist leader known as

Mother Bloor. I knew it at its top level, a group of seven or so men, from among whom in later years certain members of Miss Bentley's organization were apparently recruited. The head of the underground group at the time I knew it was Nathan Witt, an attorney for the National Labor Relations Board. Later, John Abt became the leader. Lee Pressman was also a member of this group, as was Alger Hiss, who, as a member of the State Department, later organized the conferences at Dumbarton Oaks, San Francisco, and the United States side of the Yalta Conference.

The purpose of this group at that time was not primarily espionage. Its original purpose was the Communist infiltration of the American Government. But espionage was certainly one of its eventual objectives. Let no one be surprised at this statement. Disloyalty is a matter of principle with every member of the Communist Party. The Communist Party exists for the specific purpose of overthrowing the Government, at the opportune time, by any and all means; and each of its members, by the fact that he is a member, is dedicated to this purpose.

It is ten years since I broke away from the Communist Party. During that decade I have sought to live an industrious and God-fearing life. At the same time, I have fought Communism constantly by act and written word. I am proud to appear before this committee. The publicity, inseparable from such testimony, has darkened, and will no doubt continue to darken my effort to integrate myself in the community of free men. But this is a small price to pay if my testimony helps to make Americans recognize at last that they are at grips with a secret, sinister and enormously powerful force whose tireless purpose is their enslavement.

At the same time I should like, thus publicly, to call upon all ex-Communists who have not yet disclosed themselves, and all men within the Communist Party whose better instincts have not yet been corrupted and crushed by it, to aid in the struggle while there is still time.

Questioned after his statement, Chambers elaborated on its meaning, naming the leaders of the alleged "apparatus":

The head of the group, as I have said, was at first Nathan Witt. Other members of the group were Lee Pressman, Alger Hiss, Donald Hiss, Victor Perlo, Charles Kramer. . . . Harold Ware was, of course, the organizer.

(All of them, except the Hiss brothers, refused to deny the charges on the grounds of self-incrimination. Donald Hiss appeared before the committee on August 13 and denied all the charges against him. Despite the fact that, if Chambers' story was true, Donald was as guilty as Alger Hiss, the case against Donald was dropped and the case against Alger pursued.)

"These people," Chambers elaborated,

were specifically not wanted to act as sources of information. . . . These people were an elite group, an outstanding group, which it was believed would rise to positions—as, indeed, some of them did—notably Mr. White [3] and Mr. Hiss—in the Government, and their position in the Government would be of very much more service to the Communist Party.

The press reaction to Chambers' statement was immediate and immense. Robert Stripling, the House Committee's chief investigator, said that the hearing "drew perhaps the biggest turnout of reporters and spectators in the history of our inquiries." Before Chambers even took the stand there had been a sensational build-up by the press and radio. The *New York Times* on August 2 had announced Chambers as "tomorrow's witness on the ubject of Russian espionage is Washington." Immediately following Chambers' appearance, Hiss's photograph was prominently displayed in the *New York Herald Tribune*, together with the photographs of two others, under the sensational heading, "Implicated in Yesterday's Testimony on Espionage Ring." [4]

Hiss made immediate denials, to the newspapers and in the setting where the charges had been made. The same day that Chambers testified Hiss sent a telegram to the House Committee:

My attention has been called by representatives of the press to statements made about me before your committee this morning by one Whittaker Chambers. I do not know Mr. Chambers and, so far as I am aware, have never laid eyes on him. There is no basis for the statements about me made to your committee. I would appreciate it if you would make this telegram a part of your committee's records and I would further appreciate the opportunity of appearing before your committee to make these statements formally and under oath. I shall be in Washington on Thursday and hope that it will be a convenient time from the committee's point of view for me to appear.

Hiss appeared before the committee on August 5 and read the following prepared statement:

My name is Alger Hiss. I am here at my own request to deny unqualifiedly various statements about me which were made before this Committee by one Whittaker Chambers day before yesterday. I appreciate the Committee's having promptly granted my request. I welcome the opportunity to answer to the best of my ability any inquiries the members of this Committee may wish to ask me.

I am not and never have been a member of the Communist Party. I do not and never have adhered to the tenets of the Communist Party. I am not and never have been a member of any Communist front organization. I have never followed the Communist Party line directly or indirectly. To the best of my knowledge none of my friends is a Communist.

As a State Department official I have had contacts with representatives of for-

[3] Harry Dexter White, not named as one of the "others" but, along with Henry Collins, called a Communist.
[4] The word "espionage" was prematurely used, of course; Chambers had specifically denied active espionage.

eign governments some of whom undoubtedly have been members of the Communist Party, as for example representatives of the Soviet Government. My contacts with any foreign representative who could possibly have been a Communist have been strictly official.

To the best of my knowledge I never heard of Whittaker Chambers until in 1947 when two representatives of the Federal Bureau of Investigation asked me if I knew him and various other people some of whom I knew and some of whom I did not know. I said I did not know Chambers. So far as I am aware I have never laid eyes on him and I should like to have the opportunity to do so.

I have known Henry Collins since we were boys in camp together. I knew him again when he was at the Harvard Business School, while I was at the Harvard Law School, and have seen him from time to time since I came to Washington in 1933.

Lee Pressman was in my class at the Harvard Law School and we were both on the Harvard Law Review at the same time. We were also both assistants to Judge Jerome Frank on the legal staff of the Agricultural Adjustment Administration. Since I left the Department of Agriculture I have seen him only casually and infrequently.

Witt and Abt were both members of the legal staff of the AAA. I knew them both in that capacity. I believe I met Witt in New York a year or so before I came to Washington. We were both practising law in New York at that time.

Kramer was in another office of the AAA and I met him in that connection. I have seen none of these last three except most infrequently since I left the Department of Agriculture.

I don't believe I ever knew Victor Perlo.

Except as I have indicated, the statements about me made by Mr. Chambers are complete fabrications.

I think my record in the Government and since speaks for itself.

The two men who were destined to be locked in a battle for their public lives had sharply different styles of combat, evident even from these first statements. As the pace of events swiftly increased, Hiss would maintain his icy detachment, his meticulous attention to detail, in seeming oblivion to the spirit of the moment. In his careful manner he would continuously speak of himself anonymously. And Chambers would continue to display his skill for dramatizing his claims, and himself; if there was concealment involved, on his part, it would be of a more complicated kind: his own impulse was to portray himself as a Man of Destiny. These habits, striking and interesting as they are, have, of course, no absolute meaning. They are only the first symptoms that an interested investigator notices.

Chambers was not present at the hearings when Hiss testified on August 5 and expressed the desire to see his accuser face to face. After Hiss read his prepared statement, Representative Karl E. Mundt asked the obvious question—the question that would occur to the general public and that would put the burden of proof on Hiss. What motive could Chambers possibly have for the accusation if Hiss was innocent?

MUNDT: . . . it is extremely puzzling that a man who is senior editor of *Time* magazine, by the name of Whittaker Chambers . . . should come before this committee and discuss the Communist apparatus working in Washington, which he says is transmitting secrets to the Russian Government, and he lists a group of seven people—Nathan Witt, Lee Pressman, Victor Perlo, Charles Kramer, John Abt, Harold Ware, Alger Hiss, and Donald Hiss—

HISS: That is eight.

MUNDT: There seems to be no question about the subversive connections of the six other than the Hiss brothers, and I wonder what possible motive a man who edits *Time* magazine would have for mentioning Donald Hiss and Alger Hiss in connection with those other six.

HISS: So do I, Mr. Chairman. I have no possible understanding of what could have motivated him. There are many possible motives, I assume, but I am unable to understand it. . . .

MUNDT: All we are are trying to do is find the facts.

HISS: I wish I could have seen Mr. Chambers before he testified.[5]

The committee was incredulous that Hiss claimed never to have seen Chambers:

STRIPLING: You say you have never seen Mr. Chambers?

HISS: The name means absolutely nothing to me, Mr. Stripling.

STRIPLING: I have here, Mr. Chairman, a picture which was made last Monday by the Associated Press. I understand from people who knew Mr. Chambers during 1934 and 1935 that he is much heavier today than he was at that time, but I show you this picture, Mr. Hiss, and ask you if you have ever known an individual who resembles this picture.

HISS: I would much rather see the individual. I have looked at all the pictures I was able to get hold of in, I think it was, yesterday's paper which had the pictures. If this is a picture of Mr. Chambers, he is not particularly unusual looking. He looks like a lot of people. I might even mistake him for the chairman of this committee. [Laughter]

Richard Nixon [6] would later make a special point of Hiss's repeated expression: "I have never known a man *by the name of* [italics added] Whittaker Chambers." It should be noted, therefore, that in his private interviews with the committee and in his first day's testimony Chambers did not reveal the fact that Hiss had never known him by the name of Chambers. It was not until his second appearance before the committee on August 7, when Nixon

[5] House Committee on Un-American Activities, *Hearings Regarding Communist Espionage in the United States Government,* 80th Cong. 2d Sess., p. 646. (Hereafter cited as HUAC Hearings.)

[6] Then a freshman Congressman and member of the House Committee on Un-American Activities.

asked Chambers whether Hiss had ever known him by that name, that Chambers stated he had been known to Hiss only under the pseudonym "Carl."

One wonders why, in his puzzlement about Chambers' identity, Hiss did not go over to the office of *Time* and see for himself who his accuser was. He could have done this rather easily after Chambers accused him on August 3, and also after his own appearance before the committee on August 5, when the matter of Chambers' identity was fast becoming an important issue. Why did this simple expedient not occur to him? To this question by the writer, Hiss replied:

It did *indeed* occur to me. I discussed it by telephone with my lawyer, William Marbury, who was in Baltimore and saw no particular disadvantage, and with Foster Dulles [then chairman of the Board of the Carnegie Endowment]. But Dulles was strongly opposed to it as improper, in view of the fact that the House Committee had assumed jurisdiction of the topic of my knowing Chambers as a subject of inquiry, and on the first day Nixon had said a confrontation would be arranged by the Committee.

In the course of the day's hearings Hiss was asked many questions about his life and career, his educational background, and his employment both in and out of government. From the outset he displayed a reluctance to bring in the names of former colleagues, superiors, or friends unless he was specifically asked.

Any number of meanings could be—and were—attached to this reluctance to name his associates.[7] Was it modesty? Or the uncomplicated wish not to involve others in his own problems? Or was it guilt, and the desperate fear of implicating respected figures in his own crime? Some of the committee members felt that Hiss was being evasive, but in general his initial appearance seemed to help his position vis-à-vis the committee.

Hiss was assured that a confrontation between himself and Chambers would be "promptly" arranged. And as the meeting drew to a close Hiss was asked: ". . . do you feel you have had a free and fair and proper hearing this morning?" He replied to Representative McDowell:

I think I have been treated with great consideration by this committee. I am not happy that I didn't have a chance to meet with the committee privately before there was such a great public press display of what I consider completely unfounded charges against me. Denials do not always catch up with charges.

The committee terminated the hearing by saying:

[7] Chambers in *Witness* quotes the testimony and comments with evident irony, though uncertain intent: "Why the long struggle to elicit that one name"—after Hiss mentioned Felix Frankfurter.

The Chair wishes to express the appreciation of the committee for your very co-operative attitude, for your forthright statements, and for the fact that you were first among those whose names were mentioned by various witnesses to communicate with us asking for an opportunity to deny the charges.

Representative Rankin added:

And another thing. I want to congratulate the witness that he didn't refuse to answer the questions on the ground that it might incriminate him, and he didn't bring a lawyer here to tell him what to say.

The committee was aware, as was the press, that they may well have been taken in by Chambers. And the awareness was, it is apparent, no comfort. The committee in many eyes depended for its existence on demonstrating that the Communist threat in government was actual.[8] A *Washington Post* correspondent told Nixon after the hearing: "This case is going to kill the Committee unless you can prove Chambers' story." [9] "In executive session that afternoon," said Stripling, the committee's chief investigator, "you could have cut the gloom with a knife."

Nixon, in *Six Crises,* titles the Hiss case as his "First Crisis." He presents an intimate description of the committee's feeling of defeat, his own concerns, why and how he should pursue the problem:

One Republican member lamented, "We've been had. We're ruined."

Ed Hébert, a Louisiana Democrat, suggested that the only way the Committee could get "off the hook" would be to turn the whole file over to the Department of Justice and hold no more hearings in the case. "Let's wash our hands of the whole mess," he said. That appeared to be the majority view, and if Hébert had put his suggestion in the form of a motion, it would have carried overwhelmingly. I was the only member of the Committee who expressed a contrary view. . . .

Nixon's arguments, however, won out, and as a result he was appointed head of a subcommittee to investigate further. He directed Stripling to issue a subpoena ordering Chambers to appear on August 7.[10] "There was little

[8] The committee's role throughout the hearing has, of course, been frequently criticized, and an impartial reading of the testimony cannot fail to conclude that the committee was, in fact, either biased or reckless. There is the often quoted remark of Representative Mundt on Chambers' first day of testimony before Hiss had appeared: "Certainly there is no hope for world peace under the leadership of men like Alger Hiss."

And Representative Rankin added: ". . . don't you think Mr. Carnegie, the rich Scotchman that developed this foundation, would turn over in his grave if he knew that kind of people were running the foundation?"

These injudicious comments not only represented the mood of the committee but were a measure of the national hysteria that swept the country during the late 1940s and early '50s.

[9] Richard M. Nixon, *Six Crises* (Garden City, N.Y.: Doubleday & Co., 1962), p. 9.

[10] The subcommittee was made up of Representatives Richard M. Nixon, F. Edward Hébert, and John McDowell, with Robert E. Stripling as chief staff investigator. The full committee had as its chairman J. Parnell Thomas, and its other members were Karl E.

optimism," said Stripling, "in our little subcommittee as we rode to New York on the night of August 6, 1948, to confront Chambers with the brunt of Hiss's denial."

They met at 10:30 a.m. on August 7 at the New York Federal Court House in Foley Square. It was a secret session.

At the start we were frankly skeptical of him [Chambers], but he blandly ignored this and began adding a great store of detail to the astonishing story he had told earlier.[11]

Chambers was quizzed extensively about the Hisses' private lives, on the theory that knowledge of this sort would tend to prove his claim of a close relationship between himself and Hiss and, by extension, would corroborate his story that Hiss was a Communist. Chambers offered such details as the Hisses' nicknames for each other, their hobbies (bird-watching: "I recall that they once saw to their great excitement a prothonotary warbler"), their furniture ("the only thing I recall was a small leather cigarette box, leather-covered cigarette box, with gold tooling on it. It seems to me that box was red leather"). In addition he claimed to have been a house guest of the Hisses.

CHAMBERS: I have stayed there as long as a week.
NIXON: A week one time. What would you be doing during that time?
CHAMBERS: Most of the time reading. . . .
MANDEL: What was Mr. Hiss' library devoted to?
CHAMBERS: Very nondescript, as I recall.

And he offered this story of Hiss's disposal of an old car, which was to become an important issue.

NIXON: Did they have a car?
CHAMBERS: Yes; they did. When I first knew them they had a car. Again I am reasonably sure—I am almost certain—it was a Ford and that it was a roadster. It was black and it was very dilapidated. There is no question about that.
    I remember very clearly that it had hand windshield wipers. I remember that because I drove it one rainy day and had to work those windshield wipers by hand.
NIXON: Do you recall any other car?
CHAMBERS: It seems to me in 1936, probably, he got a new Plymouth.
NIXON: Do you recall its type?
CHAMBERS: It was a sedan, a two-seated car.
MANDEL: What did he do with the old car?
CHAMBERS: The Communist Party had in Washington a service station—that is,

---

Mundt, Richard B. Vail, John E. Rankin, H. Hardin Peterson, and John S. Wood. Benjamin Mandel was the director of research for the committee. Donald Appell was an investigator.
[11] Robert Stripling, *Red Plot Against America* (Drexel Hill, Pa.: Bell Publishing Co., 1949), p. 117.

the man in charge or owner of this station was a Communist—or it may have been a car lot.

NIXON: But the owner was a Communist?

CHAMBERS: The owner was a Communist. I never knew who this was or where it was. It was against all the rules of underground organization for Hiss to do anything with his old car but trade it in, and I think this investigation has proved how right the Communists are in such matters, but Hiss insisted that he wanted that car turned over to the open party so it could be of use to some poor organizer in the West or somewhere.

   Much against my better judgment and much against Peters' [12] better judgment, he finally got us to permit him to do this thing. Peters knew where this lot was and he either took Hiss there, or he gave Hiss the address and Hiss went there, and to the best of my recollection of his description of that happening, he left the car there and simply went away and the man in charge of the station took care of the rest of it for him. I should think the records of that transfer would be traceable.

NIXON: Where was that?

CHAMBERS: In Washington, D.C., I believe; certainly somewhere in the District.

NIXON: You don't know where?

CHAMBERS: No; never asked.[13]

   The committee was impressed. They felt, in the words of Stripling, that

Chambers added facts which only an extremely intimate friend of Hiss (or one who had hired dozens of private detectives to compile a report on Hiss) could have provided.

   On the strength of this testimony the committee subpoenaed Hiss once more. Their reasoning ran that if Hiss confirmed Chambers' testimony he would in effect be admitting the fact of a close relationship with Chambers. This was a critical early moment in the Hiss case. By keeping the two men separate, the committee did not take cognizance of the possibility that Hiss had known Chambers but under a different name and in a different context from the one Chambers alleged. This was what Hiss was later to claim.

   Some of Chambers' testimony taken in secret session on August 7 had been leaked to the press.

   As Hiss was riding down to Washington on the train from Vermont on Monday, August 16, on his way to testify a second time, he was reading the news reports. It was at this moment, Hiss claims, that he was first able to put together facts from Chambers' testimony with a past relationship with a person in his life who fitted those facts. He said that one George Crosley, a free-

[12] "Peters" (a code name, more frequently referred to as "J. Peters") was, according to Chambers, the chief of the entire Communist underground apparatus in the United States: He allegedly maintained contact between the Soviet espionage apparatus in Washington, D.C., and the underground of the American Communist Party.

[13] HUAC Hearings, pp. 664, 666–67.

lance writer, last seen by him around 1935 or 1936, came to his mind. The
name, by the end of the day's session, would become crucially important.

In this session Nixon informed Hiss of Chambers' statement that Hiss
had known him only by the name "Carl." Hiss was shown two recent pictures
of Chambers. Looking at the photographs, Hiss stated: "The face has a certain familiarity." A few minutes later Hiss was again shown a large picture of
Chambers, and he reiterated:

If I could see the man face to face, I would perhaps have some inkling as to
whether he ever had known me personally.

Hiss was again asked if he could recognize the photograph of Whittaker
Chambers as that of someone who had stayed in his home for a week. Hiss
said:

Mr. Chairman, I hope you will not think I am being unreasonable when I say I am
not prepared to testify on the basis of a photograph. On the train coming down
this morning I searched my recollection of any possible person that this man could
be confused with or could have got information from about me.

Hiss soon testified:

I have written a name on this pad in front of me of a person whom I knew in 1933
and 1934 who not only spent some time in my house but sublet my apartment.
That man certainly spent more than a week, not while I was in the same apartment. I do not recognize the photographs as possibly being this man. If I hadn't
seen the morning papers with an account of statements that he knew the inside of
my house, I don't think I would even have thought of this name. I want to see
Chambers face to face and see if he can be this individual. I do not want and I
don't think I ought to be asked to testify now that man's name and everything I
can remember about him. I have written the name on this piece of paper. I have
given the name to two friends of mine before I came to this hearing. I can only
repeat, and perhaps I am being over anxious about the possibility of unauthorized
disclosure of testimony, that I don't think in my present frame of mind that it is
fair to my position, my own protection, that I be asked to put down here of record
personal facts about myself which, if they came to the ears of someone who had
for no reason I can understand a desire to injure me, would assist him in that endeavor.[14]

There was a five-minute break in the hearing during which time Hiss was
asked to leave the room. After the recess Hiss suddenly reversed his position
and volunteered the name of Crosley. He later wrote that he did so because
the name had been on his pad at his place; a member of the committee staff
might have seen it.

Nixon pursued the matter:

[14] HUAC Hearings, p. 953.

NIXON: Going back to this man, do you know how many days approximately he stayed with you?

HISS: I don't think more than a couple of times. He may have come back. I can't remember when it was I finally decided it wasn't any use expecting to collect from him, that I had been a sucker and he was a sort of deadbeat; not a bad character, but I think he just was using me for a soft touch.

NIXON: You said before he moved in your apartment he stayed in your house with you and your wife about how many days?

HISS: I would say a couple of nights. I don't think it was longer than that.

NIXON: A couple of nights?

HISS: During the delay of the van arriving.

NIXON: Wouldn't that be longer than two nights?

HISS: I don't think so. I wouldn't swear that he didn't come back again some later time after the lease and say, "I can't find a hotel. Put me up overnight," or something of that sort. I wouldn't swear Crosley wasn't in my house maybe a total of 3 or 4 nights altogether.

NIXON: You don't recall any subjects of conversation during that period?

HISS: We talked backwards and forwards about the Munitions Committee work. He told various stories that I recall of his escapades. He purported to be a cross between Jim Tully, the author, and Jack London. He had been everywhere. . . .

NIXON: Even though he didn't pay his rent you saw him several times?

HISS: He was about to pay it and was going to sell his articles. He gave me a payment on account once. He brought a rug over which he said some wealthy patron gave him. I have still got the damned thing.

NIXON: Did you ever give him anything?

HISS: Never anything but a couple of loans; never got paid back. . . .

NIXON: Would you say this would be sufficient motive to do what Whittaker Chambers has done?

HISS: No, that is why I say I can't believe it was the same man. I can't imagine a normal man holding a grudge because somebody had stopped being a sucker.[15]

Then Hiss was asked questions which would tend to confirm or repudiate Chambers' testimony of August 7. Not all the information checked, but Hiss's answers bore out enough of Chambers' testimony to keep the committee's suspicions alive. There was, for example, the incident of the prothonotary warbler. (Asked if he had ever seen one, Hiss replied with apparent spontaneity: "I have right here on the Potomac. Do you know that place . . . beautiful yellow head, a gorgeous bird.") And the matter of the Ford was also raised.

STRIPLING: What kind of automobile did that fellow have?

HISS: No kind of automobile. I sold him an automobile. I had an old Ford, that I threw in with the apartment, and had been trying to trade it in and get rid of it. I had an old, old Ford we had kept for sentimental reasons. We got it just before we were married in 1929. . . .

---

[15] *Ibid.*, pp. 958–70, *passim.*

STRIPLING: What kind of a bill of sale did you give Crosley?

HISS: I think I just turned over—in the District you get a certificate of title, I think it is. I think I just simply turned it over to him.

STRIPLING: Handed it to him?

HISS: Yes.

STRIPLING: No evidence of any transfer. Did he record the title?

HISS: That I haven't any idea. This is a car which had been sitting on the streets in snows for a year or two. I once got a parking fine because I forgot where it was parked. We were using the other car.[16]

The hearing terminated with arrangements for Hiss to return on August 25, at 1:30 p.m., at which time the long-awaited confrontation between Chambers and Hiss was to take place. Said Chairman Thomas to Hiss, "Thank you for coming and we will see you August 25."

The next morning, August 17, Hiss received a call at his Carnegie office from Donald Appell, a committee investigator, that McDowell would like to see him later in the day for a few minutes. "Was it to be a hearing?" Appell said he did not know what McDowell wanted to see Hiss about. Hiss had met McDowell prior to the hearings and thought it might be something personal. Hiss told Appell that he would be at his office all day.

Chambers, meanwhile, had been resting at his Maryland farm and was preparing to get the train to New York, to return to the *Time* office. However, at the station he was overtaken by some "curious need to go and see the Committee," he wrote later in *Witness,* and instead of going to New York he went to Washington. The committee members were greatly relieved to see him, having been searching for him all morning. They had decided to advance the date of the confrontation.[17]

---

[16] *Ibid.,* p. 959.

[17] The reason for the change in date is controversial. Hiss and others claim that it was because of the sudden death of Harry Dexter White, who had been questioned by the committee the previous Friday. During the questioning Chairman Thomas had implied that White was being evasive in asking for a rest for health reasons and cited White's prowess as an athlete. White's reply to Thomas won applause in the hearing room and sympathy in the press.

> MR. WHITE: I did not intend that this note should be read aloud. I do not know any reason why it should be public that I am ill, but I think probably one of the reasons why I suffered a heart attack was because I played so many sports and so well. The heart attack which I suffered was last year. I am speaking of playing ping-pong, and I was a fair tennis player, and a pretty good ball player, many years prior to that. I hope that clears that up, Mr. Chairman.

White died over the weekend of a heart attack, a tragedy that clearly placed the committee in an unfortunate position with the press. It is the charge of Hiss supporters that the sudden change in confrontation dates was a move to regain the initiative for the committee. Nixon vigorously denies this, saying that "Timing now became especially important," because if Hiss had invented the story of Crosley he would have more time to find facts to make his story more plausible. Nixon's reason is, however, inconsistent

Later that day McDowell wired Hiss: "Leaving for New York immediately. Will call upon arrival at approximately 5:15 p.m." When McDowell called at 5:30 and requested to see him, Hiss asked if he would like to come to his office. No, McDowell said, it would be more convenient if Hiss came to the Hotel Commodore, where, he stated for the first time, Nixon and one other person were waiting. Hiss agreed, but for the first time took along Charles Dollard, then president of the Carnegie Corporation, because, he later remarked, "the manner in which the arrangements had been made had been deliberately less than frank." Some of the testimony given in executive session the previous day had been leaked to the press and, Hiss said, "I wanted at least one friend present who would be able to give his version of any further relations I might have with the Committee."

When Hiss arrived the suite at the Commodore was being set up for a hearing, with quite a few staff members present, in addition to Congressmen Nixon, McDowell, and Thomas. To his surprise, Hiss was told that at this impromptu meeting he would be confronted with his accuser. Chambers was in another room. This was twelve days after Hiss had first testified and nine days before the prearranged meeting was to have taken place.

---

with the committee's having the previous day set the confrontation for August 25. And Chambers' own account of the day confirmed the claim of the Hiss forces, in that he described that a committee member's first act on seeing him was to point silently at the headlines reporting White's death.

2

Confrontation

THE CONFRONTATION REMAINS one of the most confused chapters in the reporting of the entire Hiss-Chambers affair. How does one explain the remarkable behavior of both Hiss and Chambers on this dramatic occasion? Could they have known each other in ways they did not wish to admit? Was Hiss that masterfully evasive person the committee suspected him of being? Or was he, lawyer-like and careful, as he explained, "not inclined on important occasions to make loose statements"? And how much truth could the committee find in the words of an ex-Communist courier, a self-admitted perjurer on former occasions? The officially printed record of this event can hardly convey the drama, the tense emotional atmosphere that prevailed, the demeanor of the principals involved, and the many nuances of meaning subsequently elaborated by Hiss, Chambers, and Nixon in their respective books. Much of this will be considered later. I shall, for the present, introduce the record, without commentary, as a documentary report of the exchanges that took place.

The confrontation began:

NIXON: Sit over here, Mr. Chambers. Mr. Chambers, will you please stand? And will you please stand, Mr. Hiss? Mr. Hiss, the man standing here is Mr. Whittaker Chambers. I ask you now if you have ever known that man before?
HISS: May I ask him to speak? Will you ask him to say something?
NIXON: Yes. Mr. Chambers, will you tell us your name and your business?
CHAMBERS: My name is Whittaker Chambers.

(At this point, Mr. Hiss walked in the direction of Mr. Chambers.)
HISS: Would you mind opening your mouth wider?
CHAMBERS: My name is Whittaker Chambers.
HISS: I said, would you open your mouth. You know what I am referring to, Mr. Nixon.[1] Will you go on talking?
CHAMBERS: I am senior editor of *Time* magazine.

[1] Hiss here referred to the fact that on August 16, when he was testifying about Crosley, Nixon asked Hiss, "How about his teeth?" Nixon was by then aware that Chambers' teeth had been bad during the 1930s and this was what Hiss was "referring to."

18

HISS: May I ask whether his voice, when he testified before, was comparable to this?

NIXON: His voice?

HISS: Or did he talk a little more in a lower key?

McDOWELL: I would say it is about the same now as we heard.

HISS: Would you ask him to talk a little more?

NIXON: Read something, Mr. Chambers. I will let you read from—

HISS: I think he is George Crosley, but I would like to hear him talk a little longer.

McDOWELL: Mr. Chambers, if you would be more comfortable, you may sit down.

HISS: Are you George Crosley?

CHAMBERS: Not to my knowledge. You are Alger Hiss, I believe.

HISS: I certainly am.

CHAMBERS: That was my recollection. (Reading) "Since June—"

NIXON (interposing): Just one moment. Since some repartee goes on between these two people, I think Mr. Chambers should be sworn.

HISS: That is a good idea.

McDOWELL: You do solemnly swear, sir, that the testimony you shall give this committee will be the truth, the whole truth, and nothing but the truth, so help you God?

CHAMBERS: I do.

NIXON: Mr. Hiss, may I say something? I suggested that he be sworn, and when I say something like that I want no interruptions from you.

HISS: Mr. Nixon, in view of what happened yesterday, I think there is no occasion for you to use that tone of voice in speaking to me, and I hope the record will show what I have just said.

NIXON: The record shows everything that is being said here today.

STRIPLING: You were going to read.

CHAMBERS (reading from *Newsweek* magazine): "Tobin for Labor. Since June, Harry S. Truman had been peddling the labor secretaryship left vacant by Lewis B. Schwellenbach's death in hope of gaining the maximum political advantage from the appointment."

HISS: May I interrupt?

McDOWELL: Yes.

HISS: The voice sounds a little less resonant than the voice that I recall of the man I knew as George Crosley. The teeth look to me as though either they have been improved upon or that there has been considerable dental work done since I knew George Crosley, which was some years ago. I believe I am not prepared without further checking to take an absolute oath that he must be George Crosley.

NIXON: May I ask a question of Mr. Chambers?

HISS: I would like to ask Mr. Chambers, if I may.

NIXON: I will ask the questions at this time. Mr. Chambers, have you had any dental work since 1934 of a substantial nature?

CHAMBERS: Yes; I have.

NIXON: What type of dental work?

CHAMBERS: I have had some extractions and a plate.

NIXON: Have you had any dental work in the front of your mouth?

CHAMBERS: Yes.

NIXON: What is the nature of that work?

CHAMBERS: That is a plate in place of some of the upper dentures.

NIXON: I see.

HISS: Could you ask him the name of the dentist that performed these things? Is that appropriate?

NIXON: Yes. What is the name?

CHAMBERS: Dr. Hitchcock, Westminster, Maryland.

HISS: That testimony of Mr. Chambers, if it can be believed, would tend to substantiate my feeling that he represented himself to me in 1934 or 1935 or thereabout as George Crosley, a free-lance writer of articles for magazines. I would like to find out from Dr. Hitchcock if what he has just said is true, because I am relying partly, one of my main recollections of Crosley was the poor condition of his teeth.

NIXON: Can you describe the condition of your teeth in 1934?

CHAMBERS: Yes. They were in very bad shape.

NIXON: The front teeth were?

CHAMBERS: Yes; I think so.

HISS: Mr. Chairman—

NIXON: Excuse me. Before we leave the teeth, Mr. Hiss, do you feel that you would have to have the dentist tell you just what he did to the teeth before you could tell anything about this man?

HISS: I would like a few more questions asked. I didn't intend to say anything about this, because I feel very strongly that he is Crosley, but he looks very different in girth and in other appearances—hair, forehead, and so on, particularly the jowls.[2]

Hiss paid extraordinary attention to the condition of Chambers' teeth and the tonal quality of his voice, so much so that it was thought that he was play-acting. The confrontation took place at a closed, executive session. That evening Nixon gave the press his version of the session, which the press reported; readers were amused and then suspicious of Hiss's request to have Chambers open his mouth in order that he might see the condition of Chambers' teeth. Nixon helped to fortify that impression when at a later confrontation he asked Hiss: "Didn't you ever see Crosley with his mouth closed?" To which Hiss replied: "The striking thing in my recollection about Crosley was not when he had his mouth shut, but when he had his mouth open." The public was not made to understand, it should be said, the fact (which Nixon knew quite well) that Chambers' outstanding physical characteristic until around 1944 was the incredibly bad state of his teeth.

Hiss was next questioned further by Nixon about subleasing his apartment to Crosley and about the Ford car—Hiss had earlier testified that he had

[2] HUAC Hearings, pp. 977–79.

"sold" it to Chambers, "thrown it in" with the apartment since he had another car at that time. It was at about this point in the hearings that serious doubts about the unusualness of Hiss's relationship with Chambers assertedly developed in the minds of the committee members. As Hiss spoke, he recalled further episodes about his relationship with Chambers. He repeated testimony of the 16th that Crosley had given him a rug that he said he'd had from a wealthy patron and that Hiss said he assumed was offered in part payment of the unpaid rent. Hiss proceeded to amplify his memories of the man he called Crosley, with, it seems fair to say, little or no awareness of the unfavorable effect it might have on his audience or his own already endangered position—for each factual detail of their relationship he revealed served only to whet further the suspicions of the committee that he was lying about the central issue.

The session soon returned to the all-important question of identification. Finally Hiss asked and was granted the right to interrogate Chambers directly.

HISS: I saw him at the time I was seeing hundreds of people. Since then I have seen thousands of people. He meant nothing to me except as one I saw under the circumstances I have described.

My recollection of George Crosley, if this man had said he was George Crosley, I would have no difficulty in identification. He denied it right here.

I would like and asked earlier in this hearing if I could ask some further questions to help in identification. I was denied that.

STRIPLING: I think you should be permitted—

HISS: I was denied that right. I am not, therefore, able to take an oath that this man is George Crosley. I have been testifying about George Crosley. Whether he and this man are the same or whether he has means of getting information from George Crosley about my house, I do not know. He may have had his face lifted.

STRIPLING: The witness says he was denied the right to ask this witness questions. I believe the record will show you [Nixon] stated "at this time." I think he should be permitted to ask the witness questions now or any other motion should be granted which will permit him to determine whether or not this is the individual to whom he is referring.

HISS: Right. I would be very happy if I could pursue that. Do I have the Chair's permission?

McDOWELL: The Chair will agree to that.

HISS: Do I have Mr. Nixon's permission?

NIXON: Yes.

McDOWELL: Here is a very difficult situation.

NIXON: The only suggestion I would make in fairness to Mr. Chambers is that he should also be given the opportunity to ask Mr. Hiss any questions.

McDOWELL: Of course.

HISS: I will welcome that.

NIXON: Mr. Chambers, do you have any objection?

HISS: Did you ever go under the name of George Crosley?

CHAMBERS: Not to my knowledge.[3]
HISS: Did you ever sublet an apartment on Twenty-ninth Street [4] from me?
CHAMBERS: No; I did not.
HISS: You did not?
CHAMBERS: No.
HISS: Did you ever spend any time with your wife and child in an apartment on Twenty-ninth Street in Washington when I was not there because I and my family were living on P Street?
CHAMBERS: I most certainly did.
HISS: You did or did not?
CHAMBERS: I did.
HISS: Would you tell me how you reconcile your negative answers with this affirmative answer?
CHAMBERS: Very easily, Alger. I was a Communist and you were a Communist.
HISS: Would you be responsive and continue with your answer?
CHAMBERS: I do not think it is needed.
HISS: That is the answer?
NIXON: I will help you with the answer, Mr. Hiss. The question, Mr. Chambers, is, as I understand it, that Mr. Hiss cannot understand how you would deny that you were George Crosley and yet admit that you spent time in his apartment. How would you explain the circumstances? I don't want to put that until Mr. Hiss agrees that is one of his questions.
HISS: You have the privilege of asking any questions you want. I think that is an accurate phrasing.
NIXON: Go ahead.
CHAMBERS: As I have testified before, I came to Washington as a Communist functionary, a functionary of the American Communist Party. I was connected with the underground group of which Mr. Hiss was a member. Mr. Hiss and I became friends. To the best of my knowledge, Mr. Hiss himself suggested that I go there, and I accepted gratefully.

At this point, Hiss later said, the matter became clear in his mind:

Of course this was Crosley—as I had felt from his entrance—though he chose not to admit the name. The Crosleys, and only the Crosleys, had taken over the apartment when we moved to P Street. Chambers' admission that he and his family had done just this definitely settled the question of identity. He was simply claiming that he had been there not as a tenant but as a fellow conspirator.

Hiss continued:

HISS: Mr. Chairman.
NIXON: Just a moment. How long did you stay there?

[3] On subsequent occasions, during the trials and in his book, Chambers admitted that he "may" have used the name George Crosley when he lived at the Twenty-eighth Street apartment. On cross-examination during the second trial he answered; "I have never been able to remember" what name he used. He was asked if it might have been Crosley and answered, "It may have been." Mrs. Chambers, too, said she had forgotten.
[4] Hiss had forgotten the correct address, which was Twenty-eighth Street.

CHAMBERS: My recollection was about 3 weeks. It may have been longer. I brought no furniture, I might add.

HISS: Mr. Chairman, I don't need to ask Mr. Whittaker Chambers any more questions. I am now perfectly prepared to identify this man as George Crosley.[5]

The session ended with a show of ire on Hiss's part and a challenge to Chambers.

HISS: May I say for the record at this point, that I would like to invite Mr. Whittaker Chambers to make those same statements out of the presence of this committee without their being privileged for suit for libel. I challenge you to do it, and I hope you will do it damned quickly.

Hiss's increasing anger against Chambers moved the committee's senior investigator, Louis J. Russell, to place his hand on Hiss's arm, thereby gently restraining him from any untoward action. Addressing Russell, Hiss said, "I am not going to touch him. You are touching me."

RUSSELL: Please sit down, Mr. Hiss.

HISS: I will sit down when the chairman asks me. Mr. Russell, when the chairman asks me to sit down—

RUSSELL: I want no disturbance.

HISS: I don't—

McDOWELL: Sit down, please.

HISS: You know who started this.[6]

Hiss later wrote of the encounter that he had lost all confidence in the committee's methods and

I felt that the sooner Chambers' charges could be tested in a court, the sooner they would be demonstrated as false.

For his part, Chambers wrote in *Witness:*

Now, as I go over the details, the feeling uppermost in my mind is a resentment close to anger, though it is a detached and impersonal anger. Above all, it is a sense of chill amusement at the preposterousness of the scene as human behavior. I felt resentment and I was aware of the comic by-play at that time, too. But then both feelings were overweighed by my sense of the human disaster of which I was a part and an agent.

The lines, on August 17, 1948, were drawn. Hiss would continue to insist that Chambers was only the man who had called himself George Crosley and was inexplicably trying to frame him. Chambers would insist until his death that Hiss had been his close friend and Communist colleague. Chambers would soon accept the Hiss libel challenge. At a critical moment, Cham-

[5] HUAC Hearings, pp. 985–86.
[6] *Ibid.*, p. 988.

bers would reverse his former position that espionage had not been involved, would accuse Hiss of relaying secret State Department documents to the party. He would produce evidence that purported to prove his claim. Hiss would be indicted and later convicted of perjury.

But doubts about the case would remain, owing partly to Hiss's adamant insistence that he was innocent, and partly to the wealth of mysteries left unresolved in the courts. It is the suggestion of this study that the doubts cannot be resolved, and the case cannot be fully understood, without a psychobiographical investigation into those regions of the protagonists' lives and minds that were beyond the scope of their own counsel and the courts to explore.

The Hiss-Chambers controversy was not just a political event of the late 1940s or a crisis in the political lives of its principals. Earlier writers have thought of it as "a generation on trial," "a tragedy of history." That it was all this no one can dispute; but, as will be seen in the following pages, it was in its inner reaches a profound personal tragedy as well.

II

3

Vivian

SEARCHING FOR an understanding of Whittaker Chambers, we turn naturally to that part of his autobiography that concerns his early years. He calls it "The Story of a Middle-class Family." As an epigraph for his story he quotes a poem he himself wrote in 1926:

> My brother lies in the cold earth,
> A cold rain is overhead.
> My brother lies in the cold earth,
> A sheet of ice is over his head.
>
> The cold earth holds him round;
> A sheet of ice is over his face.
> My brother has no more
> The cold rain to face.

Why he chose this poem about his brother's death (a suicide) to begin the story of his own life must remain, at least for the moment, a mystery. (A clumsy poem at best, it is not a fair introduction to his verse. He wrote far better things.) But whatever his reasons, the poem does serve to introduce one half of a central preoccupation of *Witness*: death. The other half of the theme is birth. On the next page Whittaker Chambers is born, and his remarkably vivid account of his own delivery bears quoting.

I was born in the house of my grandfather, James S. Chambers. I began to come into the world very early in the morning. Snow was falling and soon turned into a blizzard. From her high bed, my mother could look into the whitening world outside the window and see the cemetery across the street. She wondered if, in a day or two, she would be lying under the snow.

The doctor had not been told that I was arriving. He lived several miles away and my grandmother Chambers was waiting for my grandfather to return from his office so that he could go for the doctor. My grandfather, one of the crack political reporters of his day, was then with the Philadelphia *Bulletin* or the *Record*. He reached home, tired from a day's editorial work, some time after one o'clock in the morning. He took one look at my mother, jumped on his bicycle and returned through the snow with the doctor. His prompt action probably saved my mother's life.

Mine was a dry birth and I weighed twelve pounds and measured fourteen inches across the shoulders. I had to be taken with instruments. After this frightful delivery, Dr. Dunning sat for several hours beside my mother, holding together the edges of a torn artery. At one point, he thought that she was certainly dying and asked: "Are you afraid?" My mother said: "Doctor, the Power that brought me here will take me away again." She said "Power" because she belonged to a generation of intellectuals for whom the word God was already a little embarrassing. But the calm with which she accepted the possibility of death was a quality that she transmitted to me; it is part of my heritage from my mother.

My mother overcame her memory sufficiently to bear a second son, my brother, Richard Godfrey. But my terrible birth was fixed indelibly in her mind. Throughout my boyhood and my youth, she repeated to me the circumstances of that ordeal until they were vivid to me. They made me acutely unhappy, and her repetition of them made me even unhappier (for it seemed to imply a reproach). But I never told her so.

This is such a startling passage that I was moved to try to determine the factual accuracy of Chambers' account. Its most extraordinary feature, that at the time of birth he "measured fourteen inches across the shoulders," transcended whatever obstetrical experience I had had as student and intern. But three professors of obstetrics, all eminent specialists in this area, were consulted, and all three declared the story to be hardly believable. "Old wives' tales" was the verdict of those to whom I submitted this matter. The medical records themselves proved to be unavailable; [1] there is no way of determining precisely how difficult the delivery was.

Other aspects of Chambers' curious story were open to inquiry. The ominous cemetery that waited outside his mother's room was indeed present; in fact, there were two nearby.[2] On the other hand, the snow that Chambers explicitly described as part of the forbidding landscape during the night of his birth on April 1, 1901,

. . . snow was falling . . . it soon turned into a blizzard . . . she wondered if she would soon be lying under the snow . . .

[1] Chambers refers to "Dr. Dunning." A Dr. Thomas S. Dunning did indeed practice in Philadelphia at the time when Chambers was born, and his signature appears as the reporting physician on Chambers' birth certificate. Dr. Dunning died in Philadelphia in 1945 (aged ninety-six). The Physicians' Records Section of the American Medical Association informed me that they were unable to locate what medical records Dr. Dunning may have left.

[2] The United American Mechanics Cemetery, started in 1848, was directly across the street from the house at 2232 Diamond Street. The Odd Fellows Cemetery was west of the house and on both the north and south side of Diamond Street. It probably was visible from the marble stoop in front of the three-story red-brick row house. (B. Chardale of *The Evening and Sunday Bulletin,* Philadelphia, to the author, June 18, 1962, via Abe Mellinkoff, city editor of the *San Francisco Chronicle.*)

was, according to the meteorologist in charge of the United States Weather Bureau in Philadelphia, imaginary:

On April 1, 1901, the maximum temperature [in Philadelphia] was 56°; the minimum temperature was 38° and the average temperature was 47°. No precipitation occurred on the above-mentioned date.[3]

What do we make of these inaccuracies? Certainly it is no indictment of a man's honesty that he imagines himself to have been of monstrous size at his birth or that he mistakenly feels that there was a blizzard on the occasion. And perhaps these notions were not originally the product of his own imagination but of his mother's. But it is nevertheless significant that his idea of his birth was, to one extent or another, a grim fantasy that apparently existed in his own mind from boyhood until his last years. This note of fantasy appears early in the autobiography, and, as will be seen, it is not an isolated occurrence. It poses a clear problem in our study of *Witness,* our assessment of his testimony or his other utterances; if there are points which, when checked against outside sources, prove to be imaginative rather than factual, how are we to deal with those other areas of Chambers' experience—such as details of family life—for which he is the only reporter? Our solution must finally be to focus our interest on the reporting itself: for just as it does not matter whether the birth fantasy originated with Chambers or his mother, so later it will not matter whether Chambers' re-creations of extreme moments of emotional tension in the household are "true"—the fact of their existence in our subject's mind is all-important.

Chambers made no secret of the unhappiness of his early years. He clearly felt himself to be an unwelcome child. He felt, quite simply, that he had nearly killed his mother by being born. As for his father:

I was born in Philadelphia on April 1, 1901. When my father, Jay Chambers, who was then a young staff artist on the New York *World,* received the startling news, he crumpled the telegram and threw it into a waste basket. He did not believe it and he did not think that April Fool jokes were in good taste.

Whether this story is wholly accurate matters little; obviously there was some source for the young Vivian's [4] impression that he was unwanted. His parents' circumstances, as he reports them, do indeed seem unfavorable for them to want a child. Laha Whittaker and Jay Chambers were married in New York, but their first home was the Philadelphia house of Jay's family,

[3] From Glenn Stallard, meteorologist in charge of United States Weather Bureau, Philadelphia, Pa., to the author, June 14, 1962.
[4] He was named Jay Vivian Chambers; not until many years later did he change his name to Whittaker. For clarity of presentation, the name Vivian, by which he was known throughout his youth, will be used until that time in the narrative when the actual change of name took place.

where, at the age of thirty, Laha gave birth to Vivian. Jay became almost at once an absentee husband, living much of the time near his New York job. From Chambers' account we gather that this early disaffiliation was symptomatic of deeper trouble; the marriage seems never to have been satisfactory.

Laha was the daughter of a wealthy midwestern family. As a girl she led a privileged life, though she was separated from her parents for much of it—from the age of five she was educated at boarding schools. She seems to have idealized her parents, if Chambers' own account of them may be read as a reflection of her stories to him. Laha's father is pictured as a colorful man of many parts: an adventurer, a soldier, inventor, student of languages, socialite, and world traveler. He led a romantic, venturesome, up-and-down existence. Between 1870 and 1880, says Chambers, "he made and lost several small fortunes."

An eastern college education was planned for Laha, but she was denied it because, Chambers says, her father "lost his last fortune" as Laha came of age. She set out on her own, pursuing a career on the stage with increasing success for seven or eight years. It was during a Philadelphia engagement that she met Jay Chambers, a callow young artist of twenty-two, with a slight build and rather puckish ways. They were soon married, despite their having, according to Chambers, little in common besides an interest in "books, pictures and plays." Laha gave up the theater with her marriage, but not her love of theatricality or her longing for the upper-middle-class life she had known. She soon looked with disdain and disappointment on Jay. Chambers says that she always made him feel "that she had married the cook."

When he was about a year old Vivian's parents moved from his grandparents' home in North Philadelphia into a small house of their own at 4612 Greene Street in the same city. It was here that Vivian's younger brother, Richard Godfrey, was born on September 26, 1903. Shortly thereafter (1904), Laha, Jay, and the two children moved to Lynbrook, New York. They acquired a house at 228 Earle Street, which was spacious but rundown, and Chambers remarks that his father, who had opposed the move, never would make the necessary repairs. He also recalls that it was underfurnished, though hung with pre-Raphaelite prints and Oriental *objets d'art*.

The move made it possible for Jay to commute from home to the city. Nevertheless, he was frequently absent, losing himself in the city or staying in the studio apartments of his artist friends. We see him in the pages of *Witness* as a sullen, preoccupied figure, content, from the earliest times Chambers recalls, to let Laha run the household. But this was apparently only one side of Jay. He was also a quiet prankster and a nonconformist who, on occasion, had his fun. I have been told by an old friend of Jay's that Jay once bet five dollars that he could walk, clad only in pajamas, from his home in Lynbrook to the business center of that town and back without being stopped or causing any undue distraction. And he won the bet.

From another erstwhile friend, a man who for eighteen months during 1915 and 1916 shared a mid-Manhattan apartment with Jay, I learned that the Jay Chambers he knew was an entirely different kind of person from the one he read about in *Witness* years later. "Whittaker Chambers' description of his father didn't tie in with anything that I knew him to be," my informant declared. "Jay was the most friendly, jovial man I knew. . . . He was very kind, avoided arguments, and ran from a fight. He never hurt anybody in his life. But he never would speak of his family."

He told me of an incident that had so moved him he never forgot it. "It was," he said, "one of those rare occasions when Jay had taken Vivian with him to New York." The boy and his father were alone in Jay's studio when he happened by. He recalled with vividness and obvious emotion (forty-five years after it happened) how Jay had that day in 1916 turned to him and exclaimed, "I have no use for that boy. He's just a thick-ankled, good-for-nothing so-and-so!" And, my informant explained:

During the entire time that Jay was carrying on, Vivian sat absolutely silent in a corner of the room, meek and immobile. He just absorbed all this ridicule from his father. It was horrible. The kid just sat there. He was mute, like a big dumb ox.

He continued:

Jay and I were very close friends; we were together almost daily for many years. He never talked to me about his family. You know, Doctor, he never even told me he had a second son! I was amazed when I discovered it many years later when reading *Witness*.

He told me also how boyish Jay was, described his kindliness, generosity, and especially his shyness with women. The tragic part about Jay's life, he explained, was the unhappiness within his family life; it overshadowed everything else.

It was during a period of courtship which preceded my informant's marriage that he had shared his studio-apartment with Jay, who used it as a pied-à-terre and free-lance studio. On the day of his friend's marriage, Jay reacted with shock and disappointment.

He resented the idea of my getting married, felt terribly let down and cried. He had become so dependent on me and didn't want to lose me.

And on this note their friendship ended.

In a sketch published in *The New Yorker* at the time of the Hiss trials,

E. B. White gives a vivid glimpse of the young Jay Chambers, when, after the *World* folded, he was working for an ad agency. White remembers him as a "short, gay, round man . . . the sort of man who never really grows up." He describes Jay's most bizarre quirk, his part-time job ushering in the Metropolitan Opera House, which he had to do on an extended lunch hour:

I never knew just why Jay did this. It might have been that the atmosphere of the Met nourished him and satisfied the craving of a man who was left hungry by the atmosphere of an advertising office. . . . Maybe the mere business of playing hooky amused him. . . . He scampered over to the Met a couple of times a week, donned a maroon uniform, directed people to their seats, and then scampered back. . . . He almost always got back from lunch later than the rest of us, and would glide swiftly to his cell, looking a bit breathless.

The duality of Jay's personality was a secret from both his family and his friends. He kept his two worlds widely apart. The description of Jay in *Witness* is the polar opposite to the jovial, easygoing man his New York friends knew:

. . . my father was a powerful man, even late in life, as I discovered in my one desperate fight with him. . . . Not once in our whole lives did he ever play with me. He was uncommunicative to the point of seeming mute. Occasionally, he took me to New York to his studio or the art museum.

My mother wanted me to call him Papa. But he insisted that my brother and I call him Jay—his given name. For years, that single, colorless syllable was like an insulation between us, as, no doubt, it was intended to be. For me, my father early invented a nickname—"Beadle" [5]—which I found even more distressing than my given name. He never called me anything else, and he would utter the ugly word with four or five different intonations each of which was charged with quiet derision, aimed not at me, but at my mother. For this nickname, I presently came to see, was his revenge for her having named me Vivian. Thus, I was caught between them, as my brother and I were to be caught all our lives.

"Caught" between the two parents, the boys were more immediately affected, of course, by their mother than by their absent father. Like Jay—in one sense—Laha seems to have functioned better outside the home than within its emotional confines. She was active in the community; responsible for much of Lynbrook's early civic and educational progress. With the widow of a prominent local judge (James P. Nieman), then her closest friend, she founded a private library association which later became the Lynbrook Public Library. She organized the first Mother's Association in the Lynbrook public schools and became generally a leader in community life.[6] But from what can

[5] One of the definitions of "beadle" as given by Webster: "An official attendant whose office it is to walk before dignitaries; a mace-bearer, specif. an officer in a university who precedes processions of officers and students. . . ."
[6] Oliver Pilat, "Report on Whittaker Chambers," *New York Post,* June 14, 15, 1949.

be reconstructed of her life at home, it is apparent that Laha was a depriving mother. Chambers' first memories are significant:

Two impressions sum up my earliest childhood world. I am lying in bed. I have been told sternly to go to sleep. I do not want to. Then I become conscious of an extreme silence which the fog always folds over the land. On the branches of the trees the mist has turned to moisture, and, as I listen to its irregular drip, drip pause drip pause, I pass into the mist of sleep.

This "earliest childhood world" suggests the pattern and quality of Laha's mothering by revealing her son's feelings of impoverishment and intense loneliness. The poignant sensibilities of his childhood suffering are sharply remembered. In his metaphoric way Chambers describes how he tried to alleviate his hunger and to fall asleep by drawing into himself all possible external sounds or stimuli. Thus he strove to incorporate whatever sensory "nutriment" his surroundings could supply. In his nocturnal wakefulness Vivian reached out with elongated auditory antennae to absorb the sound of the moist drippings from the tree branches outside the house, and by drinking in the repetitive sounds he enables himself to pass "into the mist of sleep." From this memory one gets an important glimpse into an area of his earliest infantile strivings, his shift of attention away from his "sad" mother onto her surrogate, Mother Nature, the only other available source of supply. In the second of his two earliest memories, Chambers includes his brother. It is a scene so vivid and real, so pervadingly sad, there is little room for doubt about its factual validity:

The other memory is of my brother. He is standing on our front porch, dressed in one of those shapeless wraps children used to be disfigured with. It is raining softly. I am in the house. He wants me to come out to him. I do not want to go. In a voice whose only reproach is a plaintiveness so gentle that it has sounded in the cells of my mind through all the years he calls: "Bro (for brother), it's mainin (raining), Bro." He calls it over and over without raising his voice. He needs me because he knows what no child should know: that the soft rain is sad. I will not understand this knowledge in him until too late when it has ended his life. And so I do not go out onto the porch.

With an empathy born of his own suffering, Chambers feels his brother's loneliness, imbues it with his own misery, and projects the over-all emotion onto the rain—"the soft rain is sad."

Laha, according to Chambers' later speculations, distorted the lives of her children in the hope of recapturing her own idealized youth. In her resolution "to live entirely for her children," she buried herself in the little Long Island village and hoped that some day the children would find their way back to that upper-middle-class world which was, for her, the earthly paradise. But she had a foreboding that this would not happen. And that is why, writes Chambers, she sang in the sad voice from which, as a child, he recoiled:

> "Late, late, too late,
> Ye cannot enter now."

Another of Chambers' memories lends support to his speculation. He portrays her as the genteel mother singing lullabies in French—echoes of her "cultured" heritage—but all the while transmitting her despair to her children. It is a recollection of his mother sitting in the lamplight, in a rocking chair, in front of the parlor stove.

She is holding my brother on her lap. It is bed time and, in a thin sweet voice, she is singing him into drowsiness. I am on the floor, as usual among the chair legs, and I crawl behind my mother's chair because I do not like the song she is singing and do not want her to see what it does to me. She sings:

> "Au clair de la lune,
> Mon ami, Pierrot,
> Prête-moi ta plume,
> Pour écrire un mot."

Then his mother's voice "deepens dramatically, as if she were singing in a theater." It was, he recalls, the part of the song he disliked most, not only because it was sad, but because he knew that his mother was "deliberately . . . making it sadder":

> "Ma chandelle est morte,
> Je n'ai plus de feu;
> Ouvre-moi la porte,
> Pour l'amour de Dieu."

The song, Chambers then thought, was about a little girl who was cold because her candle and fire had gone out and she went to a little boy to ask him to help her, but he said "No." As he listened to the song's sorry end,

I crept farther into the shadows beyond the lamplight and thought how much I disliked my mother's dramatic singing and how happy I would be when my brother fell asleep and she put him to bed.

In this poignant memory, most likely a blending of fact and fantasy, he directly equates his own childhood plight with that of a forlorn little girl; recalls how he skulked beneath the chair, as his mother fondled his brother, and how he waited for him to be put down. Resentment of his brother's presence persists as the central theme of the only two other "earlier" memories he records:

. . . our old kitchen in Lynbrook was only the anteroom of my world. It was from its two back windows that I received the most intense of my earliest impressions—the enfolding beauty of the external world. . . . Imagine a view, unimpeded by house or tree for as many miles as a child's eye could gaze. . . . I would stand at the window for half an hour, staring out in a kind of breathless stupor. Sometimes my brother Richard also stood at the window beside me. . . . He was looking out because I was looking out. He tagged after me everywhere to my great annoyance.

He wants to take in the pleasurable expanse that surrounds him, not to share it with anyone. For to do so would remind him of Richard's intrusive existence. Starved for warmth and affection, he searched with all his senses to the beyonds of Nature for succor and survival. Whatever he could perceive, through his imaginative eyes and ears, was greedily incorporated. The external world became for him a rich and magical reservoir, a frightening power and pleasure which he sought to control in order to insure his self-preservation.

Inland, too, the sea was always around us. Sometimes it came as fog, rolling in suddenly, heavy with the smell of tidal water, softly blotting out the houses and the streets. Sometimes it came as sound—the terrible sound of the surf pouring without pause on the beaches seven miles away. As a boy, I used to hear it while I tried to fall asleep. I would sit up in my bed to listen to it, on winter nights when the cold air brought it in clearly. I was frightened, for it seemed about to pound away the land. It was the sound of inhuman force—the first I knew.

The tides, too, moved through my earliest childhood consciousness. . . . No land ever again has such power over him as that in which a man was once a child.

That Chambers almost fifty years later could still remember the "terrible" sound of surf from "seven miles away" is a measure of his precocious sensibilities and evidences the extent of his withdrawal from the immediate to the remote. His feelings about his family were transmuted into fears about the external world. This fascination with the forces of nature, the sea, the tides—the "inhuman force" that could destroy the earth—echoed the fear of his own extinction.[7]

By the time Vivian was five years old he was beset by diverse fears and specific phobias. Laha and Jay, bent on educating the two boys in areas of their own interest, had little or no regard for the effects their methods might produce on the fragile psyches of their offspring. They very much enjoyed going to the theater and felt that the boys should also be taken as early as possible. Chambers writes how his brother "wailed" at being left home when

[7] Later, as a young adult, in his compelling need to write poetry (write or die), he expressed in words his archaic childhood concern about the destruction of the world.

he (Vivian) was taken to see *Peter Pan*. He describes how the pirates terrified him, as did the crocodile with the ticking clock inside it. Then they tried him out on another "child's play," Maeterlinck's *Bluebird*. Again he was terrified by two scenes, which he never forgot:

Grandfather and grandmother Tyl were sleeping beside their cottage. It was then that I somehow grasped the idea that the dead wake from their sleep only when a living person thinks of them. . . . That thought I stowed carefully away to reflect on later.

The other scene was the land of the unborn children. One side of the stage was space from which came a deep, resonant humming. "That," my mother whispered to me, "is the mother, singing to the babies that are coming to them." On the other side of the stage was a landing platform, where Father Time was shooing into a little boat the unborn children that were going down to earth. Each child hugged a box that contained the deed that he would do during his life. At the back of the platform were two great doors. One child was almost in the boat, when he broke away from Father Time and ran back through the doors. Father Time scolded him.

Puzzled by the scene, Vivian later asked his mother: "Why did the little boy run back?" "Why," she said, "he had forgotten his crime. He had to go back to get the box with the crime that he would commit on earth."

This account, despite its self-mockery, again reveals the little boy's fascination with the phenomena of pregnancy and birth. His guilt about his own birth, the feeling that he should or will be punished for it, and the hope that he might be reborn so as to undo his crime and have a second chance in life are all discernible.

It seems to follow from Laha's commentaries and her son's remembrances that she plied him with many guilt-engendering ideas about birth, life, and death. Young Vivian, in his effort to find himself, identified with the unreality of his surroundings and with his mother's strangely hostile attitude toward him. He hated himself in the cryptic way his mother hated him. Yet he remained gratefully dependent and kindly to her, for she was his only actual source of supply.

His mother, Chambers remarks, "unfitted me for the simple realism of the Lynbrook grammar school yard." The unhappiness of Vivian's schooldays is apparent. His quiet curiosity, shyness, and introversion were clearly remembered by everyone who knew him. One of his elementary schoolteachers recalled him as "the pudgy little boy standing alone at the sidelines of the school playground, silent and observant, never taking part." A high-school classmate said of him: "Vivian didn't care much about his appearance; the boys used to call him 'Stinky.' His hair was never combed. He usually wore dirty sneakers. He was a butterball, soft and effeminate. None of the kids had much use for him." His seventh-grade teacher (at the Atlantic Avenue public school in Lynbrook), Mrs. Chester Talfor, remembered him as being a sissified student, who constantly walked home from school with a little girl named Vermilea.

Vivian revealed nothing of his thoughts or his feelings. He would neither fight nor play games. He was not friendly or even communicative. It is easy to see how he became a scapegoat for his classmates, who frequently ganged up to humiliate him. They teased him especially about his sissy name, "Vivian," the sound of which he despised. He writes that before starting school he wanted to be called "Jay," like his father, but his mother would not hear of it. She insisted that Vivian was his officially recorded name. Furthermore, the name "Vivian" was very dear to her for it was the family surname of one of her earliest childhood schoolmates. She commented that her parents had named her "Lahah" [8] (supposedly a Malay word meaning "princess"), and she had suffered considerable taunting as a young girl. But she had withstood the humiliation all those years and had not considered changing her name. She felt it would be character-strengthening for Vivian to do the same. Besides, she insisted, certain things in life, such as one's given name, just should not be changed.

Throughout his school years his mother engaged him in daily study sessions with assigned readings from literary masters, especially Dickens, Thackeray, and Shakespeare. When the boys were quite young Laha sat them in straight-backed chairs for hour-long sessions of listening to records. She recited poetry (Gray's "Elegy," "Thanatopsis," and modern verse) and taught them French. She spoke French fluently and insisted on their competence in foreign languages.

The psychic development of Richard at this time would be, naturally, of central interest. But it is impossible to reconstruct in detail because Richard virtually disappears from the pages of *Witness* until the period of his suicide. It can be assumed, however, that Richard in these years had an easier time in the world outside the family. He was, in contrast to Vivian, a strikingly good-looking boy, tall and dark—by the age of fifteen he outgrew his brother—and he was a natural athlete. There is no doubt that their early sibling rivalry continued, but Vivian's strategy at this time was apparently to ignore Richard, as he ignored much of the world around him.

"I don't think Vivian ever learned even to play marbles," one of Lynbrook's citizens, a former schoolmate, related years later. "His chief delight

[8] Shortly after Vivian's birth, for some reason, perhaps clerical, the final "h" was dropped, changing "Lahah" to "Laha." (See birth certificate, Registrar, Vital Statistics, Philadelphia.)

was solitary walking in the woods." His thoughts driven deeper into himself, away from his mother's incessant tutelage, young Vivian withdrew and secretly occupied himself with the enrichment of his fantasy life. From the prescribed readings Vivian soon shifted to those of his own choice. He reports, as a moment of memorable importance, discovering a barrel of his grandfather's books in the attic.

By the time he was eleven years old Vivian had read Victor Hugo's *Les Misérables,* Dostoevski's *Crime and Punishment* and *The Possessed*; he came hard under the influence of these two authors. As he read, his emotions vacillated with the shifting moods, the exaltations and abasements, of the characters. Endowed with an intense curiosity, he found solace and excitement in the widening scope of his private world and in the fictional world of his books. At an age when his forlorn image of himself was reaching out for documentation, he read:

So long as there shall exist, by reason of law and custom, a social damnation, which, in the face of civilization, creates hells on earth, and complicates a destiny which is divine with human fatality—

So long as the three problems of the age—the degradation of man by poverty, the ruin of woman by hunger, and the stunting of childhood by physical and spiritual night—are not solved;—

So long as, in certain areas, social asphyxia shall be possible—

So long as ignorance and misery remain on earth, books like this cannot be useless.[9]

He did not understand the meaning of half of the words, Chambers recalls, but was nonetheless overwhelmed; for, when he "read those lines, there moved through my mind a solemn music that is the overtone of justice and compassion. A spirit moved upon the page and through my ignorance I sensed that spirit."

Important developments in Vivian's thinking, especially in regard to his sense of self and the outside world, were taking place as early as his ninth year. Vivian found special meaning in an empathic and spiritual identification with the wretchedness of a bygone world and the misery of its inhabitants. What he read stirred his thoughts and fantasies and took him further away from reality. He read and reread *Les Misérables*. His literary precocity propelled him further into the realm of historical fantasy. With his love for language and early discovery of the magical powers of words and ideas, he kept himself removed from the intolerable reality that surrounded him, lost himself in the times and lives of the fictional characters, whose fate became his own. In this mythical way he fancied himself as a person loved and admired; it was

[9] Foreword to *Les Misérables,* quoted by Chambers in *Witness*.

a refuge from his miserable lonely self. In his living out this personal myth, it was the world that was "sick" and deprived. Moved by a need to save it (himself), he endowed himself with feelings of grandiosity, compassion, courage, and humility.

Les Misérables—The Wretched of the Earth was destined to have a lasting effect on him. Years later he would still turn to it as a source of self-esteem. In its pages he found "the play of forces that carried him into the Communist Party, and the play of forces that carried him out of the Communist Party." The roots of both actions, he writes, were in the same book, which he read devotedly for almost a decade before he ever opened a Bible, and which was, in many respects, "the Bible of my boyhood." Chambers then goes on to relate a much later experience:

One night, in the Union Station, in Washington, I stood in line with J. Peters, the head of the underground section of the American Communist Party, to buy a ticket for New York. I noticed a man watching me closely. As I left the line, he came up to me and explained that he had some kind of special ticket to New York. It was good only for the weekend. It was Sunday night. He wanted to stay over in Washington. Would I exchange my regular ticket for his special ticket? His ticket seemed to be in order. I gave him mine. Peters, who had walked away so as not to be observed, asked me what had happened. I told him. "Bob," he said, "you are a fool." He must have been pondering on the matter, for as we walked out to the train, he suddenly put his hand on my arm and said gently: "The party needs more fools." I would have been surprised if someone had then suggested to me that the Bishop of Digne had handed my ticket to the stranger. J. Peters would have been horrified to think that it was still the invisible Bishop who made him touch my arm and say: "The party needs more fools."

No doubt, the Bishop was invisibly present still when I broke from the Communist Party, though by then I had strayed so far from him that I could no longer hear him saying: "Jean Valjean, my brother, you belong no longer to evil, but to good. It is your soul that I am buying for you. I withdraw it from dark thoughts and the spirit of perdition, and I give it to God."

One is apt to be beguiled by a certain grace in Chambers' use of metaphor, which enables him to resurrect the fictional bishop from the pages of Les Misérables and turn him into a personification of the spirit of goodness in Chambers himself. Thus, with the appearance of humility, he is able to attribute to himself the virtuous quality of Christian charity. But his art does not obscure the apparent psychological fact that Chambers is distorting reality in this recollection. Surely in a normal life so small an act of kindness as exchanging tickets with a stranger would be likely to pass from memory, or, if recalled, would not find a place in one's autobiography. It would not, in any event, take on the significance Chambers finds for it, a symbol of the triumph of good over evil in his life. It would not, that is, unless a similar struggle were still going on, at the time of the writing: for the clear purpose of this passage is to demonstrate the author's moral integrity. That he invests the seemingly minor incident with such cosmic meaning only makes the reader question Chambers' sense of himself, even as a grown man, surveying the course of his life. One can stop short of calling the incident a fantasy, but the invisible presence of the Bishop of Digne in Union Station must be considered as a projection from Chambers' unresolved inner conflict. It is not insignificant that he turns to a book of his childhood as a confirmation of a solidity and continuity in his life, because that sense of confirmation was so pathetically lacking in his day-to-day existence as a child.

During Vivian's early school days, Jay's absences increased. He would slip away from Lynbrook to the city and lose himself in his world of juvenile creativity, sketching or designing match-box models of city blocks and tall Manhattan buildings. It was easier and certainly more pleasurable for him to go back to his accustomed haunts, his understanding artist friends, or his mother. Laha was as blind to Jay's puerile fixations and his defensive discontent as Jay was to her stoic façade of power and strength.

Yet during Jay's absences, especially after she had reproached him, Laha, in her loneliness and guilt, feared that unknown marauders would attack her. To protect herself, she kept an ax in the closet of her bedroom; later she hid it under her bed. "A woman with an axe," Chambers quotes her as saying, "is a match for any man."

One night [Chambers recounts], we heard a woman's terrified screams quivering in the dark, almost under our windows. My mother sat up in bed and screamed in sympathy. "Scream!" she shouted to us and screamed again herself. It was a hold-up. . . .

Vivian, too, developed the habit of taking a knife to bed with him. Though he shared his mother's fear that they might both be attacked by an outsider, the hidden object of his fear was his mother herself. This came in part from his identification with his weak and helpless father who had been driven out of the house by his mother's dominance. The other side of his divided self strove to be like his dominant—but frightened—mother.

Sometimes, in the middle of the night, I would feel to make sure that it [the knife] was still under my pillow. I always put it away carefully in the morning. My mother never knew that I had it.

Chambers' remembrance and his need to remind the reader that as a child his mother never discovered his secret tell us how intense was his fear of losing this protective phallic symbol. We shall see how important such devices were in sustaining not only his sense of masculinity but his very existence.

Jay Chambers, an effeminate and fearful man, estranged and withdrawn from his family, was hardly a model for emulation. Yet, like all sons, Vivian wanted to be close to him. He watched with envy Jay's freedom to come and go, admired his artistic skills and creations.

I loved my father dearly in those days. If he "had to work" and did not get home until late, I would often lie awake listening until I heard him turn the knob of the front door. Only then, sometimes after midnight, would I fall asleep.

When his father is safely home, Vivian's anxiety is relieved, for then his hidden wish to be rid of him cannot come true. And so he is able to fall asleep. Yet, when his father left the house in the morning, "it was as if the sun had come out," and Laha, "quiet and withdrawn" while Jay was home, dominated the house.

But it was not long until Jay fled the household altogether and stayed away for about two years. He usually sent money home for Laha and the boys. But at times he failed to do so. In another childhood memory, which, like almost everything in *Witness,* has to be taken in the cadence of his auto-biographical stride, Chambers describes his mother's way of finessing her financial predicament.

One of my mother's ways of managing was to charge things at the stores. "Charge it," I would say as casually as possible, with increasing embarrassment when I knew that the unpaid bill was big. Sometimes, the baker's wife would whisper with him before letting me have a loaf of bread. Sometimes, a storekeeper would say: "Tell your mother, no credit till the bill is paid." Once an angry woman leaned over the counter and sneered at me: "Your mother is a broken-down stagecoach." In time the bills were always paid, but I knew a great deal about the relations of the poor man and the shopkeeper before I read about them in Karl Marx.

Vivian learned not only about the relations of the poor and the bourgeoisie; he encountered the difference between his mother's assertions and the world's definitions of reality. At home he was imbued with his mother's pseudo-aristocratic sense of entitlement, but in the community he was forced to see himself as a "have-not."

However, life became easier for young Vivian, for, when his father was away, his absence drew Laha more readily to her sons, which served to distort further their prerogatives and identities. When Vivian was eleven or twelve Jay returned home and found that a new emotional climate prevailed. During the interim Vivian had developed physically; in his own mind he had replaced his father.

The hostility and factionalism that divided the Chambers' home were, beyond doubt, real and severe. After Jay's return, writes Chambers, the chill of his presence spread through the house:

On one side were my mother, my brother and I. On the other side was my father. Between the two sides was a pocket of hostility.

In sharing the burden of her unhappiness, Laha revealed to her son that his father had never wanted children, especially not him. This "was like a poisoned knife," which cut the last ties between them.

He [Jay] moved into the big front bedroom (the best room in the house . . .). Soon he was surrounded by . . . his big boxes of paintings, drawings, sketches and all kinds of drawing papers; his collection of bookplates; his miniature theater for which he used to spend hours painting scenery and cutting little figures out of pasteboard; the puppets which he was continually contriving out of glued strips of cloth and cardboard; his collection of toys, jumping-jack bears, wooden dolls, little carts and horses. . . . Once installed, he retired into his den and closed the door upon us. . . .

Before we sat down to eat, I would take his tray of food upstairs. I would knock at his door. In a voice deliberately pitched so low that sometimes I could not hear him, he would say: "Come in." . . . It was a faintly derisive smile, I thought then. . . . Sometimes, if he were feeling humorous (as I thought), my father would make a great show of clearing the heap of artist's materials from the table so that the messenger from afar could set down the tray of food. There is almost nothing that a boy can take less easily than sarcasm. This pathetic by-play of my father's put off for years my understanding of his loneliness. . . .

One Sunday we heard my father quietly leave his room, pad downstairs and out the front door. He was carrying a sickle. . . . With it he began to slash down some rank grass and weeds along the fence. . . .

Later in the day, my mother came in from the yard and, in a voice in which there was a touch of horror, and, what was worse, a touch of fear, asked which of us had cut down the clematis. Neither of us had. . . . The clematis had been hacked in two at the root . . . the massive vine hung dying. My mother said: "Jay must have done this." . . . he had to perpetrate some violence on us or the tensions of his hostile home would have driven him mad.

Reports from former neighbors and other sources of information from the townsfolk of Lynbrook leave little doubt about the turmoil at the Chambers' home.[10]

Jay's anger soon spent itself. By virtue of the revival of an earlier shared interest, the atmosphere in the house shifted into a conciliatory phase. Laha and Jay organized a theatrical group and invited young people from Lynbrook and neighboring villages to participate in putting on amateur shows. They called themselves "The Larks." Rehearsals took place in the Chambers' living room, where they constructed a stage setting. Chambers does not say which parent initiated this last-ditch stand to save their marriage. At any rate, it was short-lived. Their weakly concocted conciliation was disrupted by a violent altercation over the purchase of a costume for a younger member of the cast.

[10] Investigator's report of W. D. Chambers (November 1948)—Hiss Defense Files.

I do not know what years of hoarded bitterness then found release to swell my mother's surges of anger or my father's white-faced, stolid rage. The scene ended when my brother and I hid weeping in one of the unlighted rooms. A tense quiet settled over the house. When I took the tray of food to my father's room, he smiled at me impishly. It was like a wink, and if I had been big enough, I think that I would have knocked him down.

Enraged by this display of callousness, he "sided completely" with his mother, not only because he sensed the suffering his father caused her, but because his father's "acting and theatrical posturings" caused him to lose his respect for his father as a man.

Vivian's anger at the disappointment in his father at a time when he especially needed a masculine figure for emulation, the now undeniable realization that Jay was, in fact, a weak and ineffectual person, comprised but another in a series of blows on his already battered self-image.

Chambers writes of another experience during this period. The Larks were performing the *Rubáiyát,* and he had been assigned a role in which his body represented "a soul invisibly passing through and into the next world." The curtain rose showing the young Vivian, seated on "a globe made of cheesecloth and hoops," with his right arm extended straight up. His body was bare except for a scrap of gauze laid across his middle, "rather an accent than a concealment." Thus poised, he was the object on the stage at whom his mother then directed her lines with "soaring resonance":

> "I sent my soul through the Invisible
> One letter of that After-life to spell,
> And by and by my soul returned to me,
> And answer'd "I Myself am Heaven and Hell.""

The Larks regarded this scene as one of their best. It was, said Chambers, done by them many times, always called forth a number of audible ahs, and brought a great hand. Vivian complained to his parents (but to no avail) about his embarrassment at being so publicly exposed, until

An unexpected ally came to my aid—nature. For at last it became inescapable, even to my father, that his oldest son was on the way to manhood. To my great relief, some younger rival supplanted me as "I sent my Soul through the Invisible."

Though Chambers covers this childhood embarrassment with good humor and a certain self-mockery, what strikes the reader is the callousness and parental unawareness of the boy's feelings. Laha's and Jay's investment in the boy was not in his person but as artists' material for the dramatization of an idea.

Another performance by The Larks, Chambers reports, was a tableau scene taken from *Ali Baba and the Forty Thieves.* In the stage-setting of this one, Vivian and his brother Richard were cast as dead thieves. Inserted bodily into large urns, their limp arms dangling over the top, they were the corpses of two of the thieves who under cover of night had been surprised in their hiding and scalded to death from a pouring of hot oil. In this autobiographical memory of a double death (either correctly remembered or retrospectively distorted), there is depicted the fantasy of union in death, a theme that emerges again and again in his life under various guises.

Not unlike many boys at this developmental period, Vivian felt awkward and ashamed. But he did not find compensating feelings (such as pride in growth) to counterpoise his embarrassments. And so he grew more passive and introspective, isolated himself still further from family and peers. As the shell about him hardened, he used his abject state as demonstrable proof of his unwantedness. During his high-school years he withdrew more completely into his world of private reality, fortifying his self-image as the abandoned one, substantiating his pessimism, and fomenting his jealousy of his brother's physical attractiveness and outgoingness. He became a silent "disruptive force in this disrupted house," underwent a change of disposition—from "even-tempered, cheerful, active," he became "lethargic, moody, irritable"—clearly an autobiographical exaggeration, for he had never been really "cheerful" or "active."

My change was first noticeable in connection with our after-school walks. My mother loved to walk and long afternoon rambles with my brother and me had become one of our rituals. I no longer wanted to go. Sometimes, I would go to the window and watch my mother and brother walk off a little forlornly without me. I felt a little forlorn, too, but I wanted to be by myself, to think my own thoughts, which were beginning to be a little harsh. They became a little harsher as my mother and brother began to form a new separate unit of our family whose interests and intimacy I no longer shared. . . .

I had always been docile and obedient. I became impudent and rebellious, and one of the school mischief-makers . . . and soon my marks tumbled to just above failing. Only in English and Latin did my marks hold up despite myself. . . .

While I was desperately trying not to learn at school, I was doggedly studying by myself. . . . I began to study Arabic, Persian, Hindustani and the Assyrian of the cuneiform inscriptions. . . .[But] one day it occurred to me that, instead of studying languages that at best I could only hope to talk to myself, I might much better be learning German and mastering French.

These studies proved more useful than anything I ever learned in high school. As a German and French translator, I was later able to earn my living.

Chambers' precocious and omnivorous readings, his love of poetry, fiction, and heroics, his fascination with rare and modern languages, all served to enrich his fantasy life and to satisfy the emptiness inside him, which Laha obviously could not. It is significant that in later years, when he was unhappy and destitute, it was his knowledge of languages that provided him with a meager livelihood. It is not fortuitous that his childhood concerns of being unloved and unwanted and his fantasies of impoverishment and death, magically allayed by his discovery of the rich nutriments contained in books, were transformed into an adult need to establish a literary name for himself. His knowledge of languages and his writing skills were his staff of life. Words provided him with the medium for feeling loved; being an editor or translator was his "life preserver."

With the advent of World War I, Vivian began to indulge in a form of play-acting in which live events were converted into situations about which he wove his personal fantasies. He played with the human movements of war as though he were an army general, or as if it were a chess game, substituting symbol for event.

I can still remember the Sunday morning when I picked up the newspaper and saw the headlines about the Battle of the Marne. I felt that I was experiencing an authentic miracle. After that, I lived day by day through the deadlock of the trench war on the Western Front. My grandfather had sent me a big military map of Europe, showing forts and naval bases. It covered almost one wall of my room. I had marked out the fronts with rubber bands. Every night before I went to bed, I moved the bands to correspond with the day's communiqués.

The war was the direct cause of my Russian studies. After the Russian Revolution (which interested me only as it affected Allied strategy), my mother decided that we might be fighting the Russians soon. She urged me to prepare for a career in the military intelligence by studying Russian.

I planned to get into the war as soon as I finished high school—a plan that I did not share with my mother. . . . In New York City, one day, I had passed the British recruiting office and made a careful note of its address. The day after the false armistice, I left a note for my family, saying that I had gone to enlist. I walked into the British recruiting office and offered my services to the Empire. A stiff English officer looked me up and down. "Hell, boy," he said, "the war's over." I slunk home. My family was amused. It should have been the handwriting on the wall.

Just as Laha and Jay used their living room as a stage-setting and their son for a prop, Vivian now used the world and international events, war and armistice, as the theatrical stage on which he acted out the private drama of life. His secret plan to enlist was a thinly veiled scheme to run away from home and manipulate his mother into worrying about him. There is no discernible evidence of a patriotic motive: he chose a British recruiting office, and that only after the armistice was signed.

At that time Vivian's relation to the world was primarily that of a young poet. The existence of a world war provided him with a huge piece of reality for subjugation into his fantasy system (as though he had convinced himself that he wanted to help but circumstances beyond his control—fate—again precluded it). Only after the war was over did it become safe for him to feel he wanted to enlist.. One is reminded here of Laha's oft-repeated phrase: "Too late, too late, ye cannot enter now!"

Chambers feared death in all its forms and to such an extent that any thoughts or experiences he had in this area were either rationalized or denied. Here is how he reports an incident in his youth, when Laha once insisted that he kill a chicken.

The thought of hurting anything so helpless and foolish was too much for me. I said: "I can't." My mother did not even answer me. She took a sharp knife and pressed the handle into my hand. "I will not have any man in this house," she said fiercely, "who is afraid of blood." I knew that she was thinking of my father.

I tied the chicken's legs and hung it, head down, from a nail, and as quickly and as mercifully as I could, severed its head. The knife fell as if gravity had jerked it from my hand. Then I hid.

And while in hiding, after his first act of killing—"one of the decisive moments of my boyhood"—Chambers recalls having had these thoughts:

Something in me . . . knows that it is wrong to kill anything. But there is something else—a necessity—that forces me to kill. I have the strength to overcome the feeling in myself against killing, and I am proud that I have it for it is part of what makes me a man. All right. As a man, I will kill. But I will kill always under duress, by an act of will, in knowing violation of myself, and always in rebellion against that necessity which I do not understand or agree to. Let me never kill unless I suffer that agony, for if I do not suffer it, I will be merely a murderer.

I came out of hiding, cleansed the knife in the ground, took it in the house and laid it down in front of my mother. I have always been grateful to her for handing it to me in the first place. For years, I was the family butcher. My brother never killed anything. I never killed anything, and never kill anything today, without suffering the same ordeal.

Here Chambers first reminds us, through Laha, that she will not have "any man" in her house, like Jay, who was a coward. By elevating into a pseudo-heroic act the killing of a chicken (aided and abetted by his mother), he proves that he was not a weakling like his father. Whether this be fact, fantasy, or a mixture of both, it is a significant autobiographical passage. It is notable, also that Chambers writes that he "cleansed"—rather than "cleaned" —the knife in the ground before laying the symbolic weapon in front of his mother. In this remembered or invented bit of play-action, Chambers converts his fear of death into an act of bravery (murder), thus displaying himself before his mother as a man (stronger than, and worthy of replacing, his father). But his symbolic act of killing has, of course, really not resolved anything—either his fear of killing or his guilt for wanting to be able to kill.

And so he turned away from thoughts of war and killing, which frightened him, and retreated into the peaceful solitude of Nature. He searched in the "underground" of the earth and found solace.

As nobody seemed able to help me, I strove to help myself. I sought refuge in those places where I had always found it. I became a haunter of the woods and fields. I would set out by myself before the family was stirring in the morning and spend whole days in the woods. . . .

I presently discovered that the life below the surface of shallow ponds was as absorbing as the life on their shores. . . . Through the ice I used to watch the watery world below coming back to life after winter, while the toads came down to the lowlands to deposit their masses of jellied eggs or the frogs unwound their slimy ribbons in the shallows. In these pursuits, I could not always take off my shoes in time to follow an exciting specimen. I learned simply to wade in with my shoes on. This habit so impressed one of my schoolmates that he remembered it through the years, and was able to testify to it, as an example of my bizarre behavior, during the first Hiss trial.

If one paraphrases the story of the "schoolmate," Edward Edstrom, who testified during the first Hiss trial, the biographical data assumes a different complexion. Vivian was very much disliked by a majority of the students in his class. On the way home from school there was a trestle twenty to twenty-five feet above the ground, which bridged a shallow brook. All the boys walked over this except Vivian. He was afraid to do so and instead walked underneath, wading through the water, which was up to his knees.

Vivian is now close to eighteen years old. He is in his senior year at high school. His quest for meaning in life has grown deeper. His great search to find himself is evident in his now scattered conceptualizations about life:

I did not understand that the malady of the life around me from which I retreated into the woods, and the malady of the life of my family, from which I was about to retreat into the world, were different manifestations of the same malady—the disorder that overtakes societies and families when a world has lost its soul. For it was not its mind that the life around me had lost, though I thought so as a boy and was to continue to think so for almost twenty years, but its way, because it had lost its soul. I was about to set out from those quiet woods (to which I would return only at the decisive moment of the Hiss Case) on a lifelong quest for that lost way, first in personal, then in revolutionary, then in religious terms.

In his floundering state of mind he denies his own predicament: it is not "I" who am lost, it is the world that is lost, for it "has lost its soul." And it is not "I" who have lost my direction, but the world has lost its way.

At South Side High in Rockville Centre, Long Island,[11] Vivian Cham-

---

[11] Vivian would normally have continued at the Atlantic Avenue school in Lynbrook, but Laha was dissatisfied with its standards. She had both boys transferred to South Side High, a more select school socially and academically, despite having to pay tuition.

bers was a brilliant but uneven pupil. He hated science, was poor in mathematics, and failed geometry. He excelled in English and delighted his teachers
with his impressive knowledge and facility with words. But at the end of his
senior year, 1919, Vivian destroyed whatever favorable impressions he had
earned by his literary excellence with a dramatic rebellious act. The setting for
his prank was the school auditorium, the occasion, graduation exercises. Having been chosen as the class prophet, he included in his forecast the prediction
that one of his classmates (a girl whose parents had considerable community
influence) would become a prostitute. He also made some comments about
President Wilson. The principal of the school, in looking over the written
draft of Chambers' speech some weeks before graduation day, advised him to
delete certain parts of the text. Chambers quietly agreed to the changes and
submitted a revised draft, but on graduation day he simply delivered the
original text. As punishment, Vivian was not handed his diploma along with
the rest of his class. Instead he straggled off, much to the chagrin of his parents.[12]

That summer Laha managed, through a close friend, to get Vivian a job
at the Lynbrook National Bank, three blocks from his home. This was 1919,
and the job became available because many regular employees had not yet
returned from the war. Vivian's mother insisted that he work through the
summer, and in the fall she planned for him to enter college. Vivian did not
like working at the bank and did not get along well with the other employees.
In turn, they showed him no more acceptance than had his classmates in high
school. At the same time a deeper, more oppressive feeling inside him, brewing
since childhood, was coming to the fore. At long last the time was ripe for
him to make his move; he decided to run away from home. Early one morning
he quietly left the house. From home and mother, he headed for the warm,
inviting South. Dressed in his blue serge graduation suit, with ten dollars in
his pocket, he boarded a southbound train. Within a few hours he arrived at
the old Calvert Street railroad station in Baltimore. He rented a room in "an
old flea-bag hotel" opposite the station, where he spent his first night away
from home. Next morning, after a breakfast of coffee and rolls, he felt buoyed
and exhilarated. It was his first cup of coffee, the symbol of his manliness and
freedom; he called it a "declaration of independence." He set about looking
for work. He looked over the work ads in the morning newspaper, presented
himself for hiring as a laborer for the street railway in Washington, D.C. This

[12] Floyd B. Watson, superintendent, South Side High School, Rockville Centre, reported
this incident to the Hiss defense counsel (November 1948). He added that the episode
provoked a visit to the school by Vivian's mother, who vigorously protested the treatment accorded her son, who, she declared, was possessed of an artistic, sensitive temperament.

was his first entry into an experience with what he later termed the "world of the proletariat." Rebuffed at first because of his soft, schoolboy appearance, he was advised by a fellow applicant to muss up his graduation suit, take off his tie, and unbutton his "white collar." Thus he turned his back on the "bourgeois" world and all the white-collar values.

He lost himself in the world of reality just as he had done in the world of fiction. He went to work, hoping to demonstrate to himself by hard manual labor the reality of his identification with masculine men and with the "wretched of the earth." In thus acting out his identity struggle he joined mind and force with the laborer. This entire episode would seem to be more symbolic than real; a shift from an individual to a class identity, from thought to action, from person to idea. More specifically, from Vivian Chambers to Charles Adams (the alias he assumed), from the emptiness of his home life to the wretchedness of humanity. Throughout his life Chambers continued, in a cyclical way, to act out in the external world this struggle within his inner self. In his ordeal of living, he was, in effect, a person come to life from the pages of Hugo and Dostoevski.

Thus Vivian, a few months past his eighteenth birthday, projected himself into an imaginary state of manhood. He describes how he became physically hardened by manual work, outlasting "almost every man" who had come to work with him. During this period of trial-testing, which lasted for several months, he wrote to his family but did not let them know his address. He hid from his parents and assumed that the police were searching for him.

This escapade in the South was, in effect, a game he played with his family. And he was on the winning side. To be lost by staying away from home, countered, in a revengeful way, his feeling of being lost when he was at home. After all, *he* knew who he now was (Charles Adams) and *where* he was; Laha and Jay knew neither. It was *they* who were lost. He kept them in a state of worry. They kept trying to find *him*. And he had abandoned the whole family, just the way his father had done so many times (the eventual result was the same: Vivian, like Jay, always returned home). Thirteen years later (1932) when he allegedly entered the Communist underground, he symbolically re-enacted the same kind of behavior. In those later years, instead of hiding from his parents, he kept the world in the dark as to his identity and his whereabouts.

This runaway episode, a desperate attempt to escape from the throes of his own intolerable identity and undergo a magical transformation, has the clinical features of a serious mental break. From his descriptions, one might paraphrase his thinking: After living under the name of Charles Adams and enduring the vicissitudes of hunger and loneliness, I will be transmuted. I will no longer be Vivian but, instead, the strong, attractive, masculine Richard. I will be loved and accepted. I will have earned the *right* to such an identity because of the ordeal I have put myself through. I will have paid for my new birthright with pain and suffering and will have absolved my guilt (the fantasy of having almost killed his mother during birth and his wish to replace his brother). Then *I* will be the *wanted one* (the prodigal) in place of my brother. I shall no longer be the ugly, effeminate Vivian. I will be both Charles, after my grandfather Charles Whittaker, and Adams, after President John Quincy Adams.[13] I will be the virile son in the lineage of two great sires, instead of the enfeebled offspring of one like Jay Chambers.

Into this need to substitute "Charles" for "Vivian" and "Adams" for "Chambers" many of the determinants that made up his identity conflict were condensed. From this one maneuver, the runaway and change of name at the age of eighteen, one already sees the open manifestation of his struggle for a new identity. The new name "Charles Adams" is clearly a masculine one. It has the hard "d" sound, instead of the soft, feminine "v." This same use of hard consonants is evident in all subsequent names used by Chambers—for example, David, Dwyer, Breen, Cantwell, Carl, Crosley, Kelly, Land, and so on, and, of course, Whittaker Chambers.

Erik Erikson, author of *Young Man Luther,* has termed the major developmental problem of adolescence the "Identity Crisis." Erikson says:

[The identity crisis] occurs in that period of life cycle when each youth must forge for himself some central perspective and direction, some working unity, out of the effective remnants of his childhood and the hopes of his anticipated adulthood. . . . In some young people this crisis will be minimal; in others, [it] will be clearly marked off as a critical period, a kind of "second birth," apt to be aggravated either by widespread neuroticisms or by pervasive ideological unrest. Some young individuals will succumb to this crisis in all manner of neurotic, psychotic or delinquent behavior; others will resolve it through participation in ideological movements passionately concerned with religion or politics, nature or art.[14]

Vivian Chambers provides an excellent example of Erikson's concept of such an endangered young man.

In the throes of his magical wishes, Vivian believes himself to have hardened and matured. Within a few weeks he surpasses in physical stamina all the senior laborers:

[13] Chambers gave this source of his alias, explaining that he admired President Adams. (Deposition of Whittaker Chambers in "The Case of Alger Hiss, plaintiff, *v.* Whittaker Chambers, defendant," in U.S. District Court, for the District of Maryland, Baltimore, Md. Hereafter cited as Baltimore Deposition.)
[14] Erik H. Erikson, *Young Man Luther, A Study in Psychoanalysis and History* (New York: W. W. Norton Co., 1958), p. 14.

In time, my soft hands outlasted almost every man who had come down from Baltimore with me that first day. One by one, they tired of the heat, the work, the food, the boss—something—and drifted on their aimless way. I stuck to become a veteran.

There was one job that every man dreaded. The two third rails hung, just below the surface of the street, in a shallow tunnel. It could not have been more than four feet deep. The concrete in the tunnel had to be chipped out by hand with a cold chisel. I saw men refuse to go into the shallow tunnel and work with the live rails just above them. One day the boss ordered me down. I went. I thought: "I wonder if I will be killed." I had to lie prone on a heap of rubble. The third rails, with the full power of the Capital Transit System flowing through them, were about two inches above my sweat-soaked shoulders. In that cramping position, I had to break concrete. A sudden turn of my head, a slip of the hammer or chisel would have brought me in contact with the rail. It was an invaluable experience. . . .

As I feared, my grandfather Chambers used the facilities of the *Public Ledger* to set the Washington police hunting for me. They did not find me. . . . That night, when I took the train [to New Orleans] detectives were looking for me in the Union Station.

The drama of his life struggle was gaining momentum. Instead of seeking identity by withdrawal into his own inner world or into the solitude of nature, he now turned to aggressive action in the external world.

Vivian arrived in New Orleans with his summer's earnings in his pocket ("I was now a budding capitalist"). He found a "spacious, clean and airy room," but his interval of comfort was short-lived. His money ran out, and he soon moved to a second room, which was "narrow and dark, with filthy, unpapered walls." This move and these two rooms brought "two first-hand discoveries":

1) that the important day in a workingman's life is never a work day, but the day when he finds himself without work; 2) what a crisis at the top of the economic system means to the man at the bottom.

But one remembers that Chambers' predicament was largely self-induced and suspects his generalization of it into a crisis of the national economy as being somewhat irrelevant. Without discounting the knowledge of the lower reaches of society that this adventure afforded him, it is possible to say that he gained no knowledge of himself. He describes trying and failing to find a job, and muses,

If I had been a wiser boy, I might have caught on in a few days and left the South.

Thirty years later, he still fails to acknowledge that there may have been explanations of his behavior other than simply his not being a "wiser boy." It was more likely the disruptive forces within him that, to a large extent, determined his decision to stay on in New Orleans. Having discomforted himself, he regained a feeling of being in the world. Being clean and comfortable was, in a sense, alien to his inner reality.

The streets of New Orleans were overflowing with soldiers just back from the European war theater. A fugitive from himself, Chambers must have been impressed as he looked at the bemedaled, combat-hardened veterans. From the description of his behavior, it is evident that the soldiers in uniform provided images which satisfied his fantasies. His recently acquired masculine image, achieved in his Washington exploits, had already vanished. He relates how he exchanged his graduation suit for a second-hand khaki army uniform and lost himself in the crowd of soldiers. Out of money and with no job, he wandered about aimlessly. A feeling of lethargy soon enveloped him, and he sank into a state of helplessness and immobility. In the throes of an overwhelming force that engulfed him, as though caught in the grip of a powerful undertow, he found himself drawn down into the sordid depths of society.

At his new lodgings he came to know a New Orleans prostitute named "One-Eyed Annie." Chambers' experience with her was not as heterosexual as one might suppose. The real object of his interest and attraction was the man who lived with her and the way he ruled her life.

One-Eyed Annie was as ugly a woman as I have ever seen. Ben doted on her. Whenever she was out of the house, he would prowl around restlessly, always in his undershirt. His shoulders were massive and he was tattooed like a head hunter. He walked noiselessly and he had a caressing softness of voice and an extreme gentleness of gesture that seemed less natural than the result of some conscious constraint that had settled into a habit. If I had known more about the world, I would have placed Ben Santi more quickly. He was a pimp.

Sometimes he would drift down to my room and ply me with the wisdom of the deep slums—a jungle theory of individualism, in which a man was merely a phallic symbol, as strong as his power to attract women, or pull a knife or a gun on the rest of life which was his natural prey. Ben liked to talk to me because I never interrupted him.

Ben Santi served as an object about whom Chambers wove his magical idealizations and debasements, as in childhood when he lost himself in fiction.

Poverty and salvation were inseparably entwined in Chambers' mind. This is how, according to Chambers, his runaway episode to New Orleans culminated:

Jules Radon did not live in the house, but he spent a good part of his days there. He sometimes came in very early in the morning and slept on the bare floors. Like me, he wore a uniform. . . .

My money had run so low that I now made a loaf of bread last for two days, instead of one. The diet began to tell. I was tired and weak, and sometimes in the great heat I found it too much trouble to get up or move around. I felt trapped too. Early one evening, as I lay with my face to the wall, I heard the shutters of my door open. Jules Radon said: "Let's go eat." I was too listless to turn and look at him. I said: "Thanks, I've eaten." I felt him stand there a moment, looking down at me. Then, without saying anything, he went out. When I finally turned over, I found that he had left a fifty-cent piece on my bed.

I had written to my mother several times from New Orleans, concealing my condition. . . . I did not feel up to jumping freights or riding rods, especially in the South. I wrote for money.

My father wired me the price of a ticket to New York and a few dollars more.

This syndrome of self-induced hunger and starvation, lethargy and immobility was a symbolic enactment of his own death. In this dramatized, self-destructive act, Chambers appropriated the actuality of the slums to which he had gravitated, and from their depths effected a miracle of salvation (epitomized by the "fifty-cent piece" which was left him). Overcome with self-pity and nostalgia, he lifted himself from his depression and brought about a reunion with his mother by writing for money for his return home. Having put himself through a symbolic burial in the underground slums of New Orleans and a period of "living death," he has set the stage to inflict upon his mother his suffering and impress her with the depth of his misery. Like a helpless, hungry infant, Vivian had no other recourse but to appeal to his mother, cling to her again, and hope that the fantasied miracle of reunion would happen.

Back at home, he put aside his pseudonym of Charles Adams and shed the soldier's uniform. He had to assume the painful task of being Vivian and face once again the emptiness and strife from which he fled. He had somehow to find a new identity and establish a new existence.

4

The Poet and the Prankster

Laha's relief at the sight of her errant son was soon superseded by her renewed desire for him to enter college. Until the fall, he was to find a job.
At her insistence Jay reluctantly agreed to arrange for Vivian to go to work as
a file clerk at the Frank Seaman Advertising Company in New York, where
Jay was then manager of the art department. Vivian felt encouraged and
warmed by his father's apparent helpfulness. The estrangement and distance
between them seemed to be eased.

But while Vivian recuperated and readied himself for his new job, his
father grew more sullen at the thought of having him underfoot. On the morning they boarded the train to New York, the sight of the boy next to him
stirred Jay's old resentments. There was no doubt that he felt ashamed to be
recognized as the father of this unattractive, inscrutable youth. And Jay's
every hostile look was a familiar signal to which Vivian had long ago been
sensitized. They bristled with disaffection, each silently wanting to be rid of
the other.

The day he was to take me to Frank Seaman's, we rode together on the train to
New York, as usual, in complete silence. As we neared the City, my father leaned
over and said that it might be embarrassing for him if I worked at Frank Seaman's
as his son. People might talk about favoritism. The new warmth I felt for him
froze. I knew that my father's real reason was not talk about favoritism. That was
nonsense. I knew that he was afraid that I might not do a good job. But since he
wanted it that way, I said I would take my grandfather's name: Charles Whittaker.

Vivian had once again been let down by his father. Although the change
in name was presumably suggested by his father, Vivian pressed the idea into
the service of his own needs. By choosing his grandfather's name (once again,
a hard, masculine symbol) he played his father off against his maternal grandfather. He did this for the entire eleven months that he and his father worked
together at the Frank Seaman Company. Thus he also reversed the son-father
relationship, putting himself in a paternal position over his own father.

During the winter, spring, and summer months of 1920, Vivian, alias Charles Whittaker, commuted to New York from Lynbrook and held down his job as a file clerk, while living in Lynbrook under his real name. Vivian soon mastered a way of life in which his assumed identity overshadowed his true one. His double existence became operational. For almost a year, up to the fall of 1920, the pseudonymous role of Charles Whittaker provided the means of a temporary truce between Jay and Vivian. This strange son-father agreement made it easier for them to deny each other's presence, so that each could go his own way. In this awkward conspiracy of silence they had effected a secret pact between them and the outside world.

The daily commuting from Lynbrook to New York, the work at the advertising agency, and a sense of being on his own made Vivian "city-wise." He soon knew his way around lower Manhattan and the Village. Like his father, he spent little time at home. He came in late at night. He paid no attention to his teen-age brother, who by now was left completely alone with Laha. Despite his father's proximity at work, he enjoyed his new independence, his pseudo-identity, and the exhilarating feeling of earned money in his pocket. He did not want to go to college. He enjoyed spending his free time reading in the libraries, browsing in book shops, and exploring the city.

But although he could stay away from Laha's household he could not free himself of her influence. She had her own plans for his education, and during the summer months she made the necessary arrangements for her son's admission to Williams College in the fall. Her choice of the elite New England school was made with little regard for her son's interest or wishes in the matter. It was an expression of her own unrealistic social aspirations.

The life of Charles Whittaker thus abruptly came to an end when Vivian stopped work at Seaman's and made preparations for college. Once again he had to face the intolerable image that he had temporarily cast off and that Laha had reinstated.

Vivian did go to Williams, according to Laha's plans, but he immediately left—before classes even began. Chambers treats this unusual experience in *Witness* in one paragraph.

In the fall of 1920, I entered Williams College. A room was assigned to me and my furniture had been shipped. But one or two days on that beautiful and expensive campus told me that Williams was not the place for me, that my parents could never stand the costs of that little Harvard. I saw that I had a quick and difficult decision to make. I took a night train for New York. The next morning, before going home, I entered Columbia University. There I could live at home and all expenses would be less. Since I lacked certain requirements for entrance, I took a general intelligence test and passed without difficulty. I also used the occasion to rid myself at last of the name, Vivian. In its place, I took my mother's family name: Whittaker.

It is unlikely that Chambers' entrance into Columbia could have been so quickly effected. When, for example, would he have taken the entrance examination he speaks of? It seems more plausible to assume that he had made the requisite arrangements at some earlier date, despite his apparent compliance with his mother's wishes that he go to Williams. In his testimony during the pre-trial preparation for the Hiss libel suit, Chambers gave much the same story, though he said he first used the name "Whittaker Chambers" at Williams, not Columbia, and he estimated his sojourn there as five days, not two. He stressed that his decision to leave was a matter of money.[1]

In the course of the investigations before the first Hiss trial, Edward Mc-Lean,[2] counsel for the defense, located the freshman student, Karl Helfrich, who had been Chambers' roommate those few days at Williams College. In 1949 he was an executive in the Forstmann Woolen Company in Passaic, New Jersey.

On January 19, 1949, Helfrich informed McLean that he had been assigned Whittaker Chambers as a roommate at the beginning of his freshman year at Williams in September 1920. They roomed in Morgan Hall. They both arrived a few days before college opened and furnished their room and made the usual preparations for beginning of college. Helfrich had never seen or heard of Chambers before. He thought that Chambers acted strangely, that he seemed detached and was devoted to reading the Scriptures.

The night that college opened there was a dinner for the freshman class in Currier Hall. Helfrich asked Chambers to go with him to the dinner, but Chambers said that he would not go, that he preferred to stay in his room and read the Bible. Helfrich went to the dinner, and upon his return to his room that evening Chambers told him that a "great light had come to him" and that he proposed to leave Williams that very night to go to Columbia to take a course in journalism. Helfrich said to him that this seemed somewhat abrupt, but Chambers insisted and proceeded to pack up his bag and took the mid-

---

[1] A letter from the Registrar of Columbia regretfully informed me that Chambers' record of admission was no longer available.

A letter from the Registrar of Williams College also regretfully informed me that "our records do not disclose any information with regard to Whittaker Chambers" (Mrs. Nelson S. McGraw to the author, August 13, 1962). And in a letter dated August 15, 1962, my inquiry having been forwarded to the Librarian by the Registrar, I was further notified that "the records here give no information regarding the brief stay of Whittaker Chambers on the campus. . . . I can only suppose, that since he never officially matriculated, the records were destroyed upon his leaving town." (Signed, Wyllis E. Wright, Librarian.)

[2] Counsel of record in both Hiss trials. McLean directed the investigation and other preparatory work for the full trial. He later became a federal district judge.

night train to New York. He asked Helfrich to sell the furniture and to send Chambers a check for half the proceeds, which Helfrich ultimately did.

Thereafter, over a period of some six weeks, Helfrich received a number of very long letters from Chambers, written in longhand and running to over twelve pages each. They described peculiar adventures of Chambers which Helfrich thought at the time must have been invented. He could not remember much about them except one incident in which Chambers told about having been in a mining camp and of having seen "murder at the worst under my nose."

After Chambers had been gone about six weeks, he wrote Helfrich a letter, from New York, asking him to go to the General Delivery window of the local post office in Williamstown and ask for a letter that was addressed to another name (a name Helfrich could not recall). Chambers further asked Helfrich to take this letter out of the post office and redirect it back to him at his New York address.

Helfrich went to the post office and found the letter there. He and his new roommate, George Degener, decided that it might be a criminal offense —tampering with the mails—to send a letter addressed to one person to another person. They decided that they had better consult Dr. Garfield, the president of the college, about it.

Dr. Garfield spoke at some length about whether he should open the letter and finally decided he should. After they had read the letter together, Garfield told them to forget about it and leave everything in his hands and not to answer any further communications from Chambers. The letter in question was one written by Whittaker to himself. Helfrich remembered it as "a weird recital." It dealt, as he recalled, with some mystic communion between Chambers and the Devil. About a week later Helfrich got another letter from Chambers in which Chambers said he was disappointed in Helfrich, that Helfrich was not the man he had supposed Helfrich was, and that Helfrich must have told somebody about the letter because he, Chambers, had received a visit from some postal inspectors. Helfrich did not answer the letter, never heard from Chambers again, and never saw him since the night he left college.

In testifying about this in 1948 and 1949 Chambers gave varying stories regarding the matter of his matriculation, his roommate, and the name he used when he "entered" Williams. The following is an excerpt from the second Hiss trial.

Q. Did you have a roommate there?
A. I did.
Q. What was his name?
A. Carl Helferich [sic].

Q. Under what name did you matriculate at Williams College?
A. Whittaker Chambers, I believe. . . .
Q. Did you ever see Helferich?
A. I have a vague recollection of seeing Helferich.
Q. Did you communicate with Mr. Helferich after you left Williams?
A. I don't recall doing so but I have been told that I did.
Q. Well, have you any doubt but what you did?
A. I should first have to see what I had said, I suppose.
Q. I beg your pardon?
A. I would first have to see some evidence of it.
Q. Well, you had brought your furniture there, hadn't you?
A. That is right.
Q. And you made arrangements with Helferich to sell him your share in the furniture?
A. I have forgotten that too, but it is possible.
Q. Well, did you matriculate there?
A. I don't know whether I formally matriculated or not.
Q. Your present memory is that you think you saw your roommate Carl Helferich?
A. I have a vague recollection of some such person.
Q. I read you your questions and answers at the first trial during cross-examination, page 248, and ask you whether this question was then asked you and if you gave this answer:
"Q. You were at Williams briefly?
"A. Yes.
"Q. Is that right?
"A. I never matriculated.
"Q. You went up there and had a room?
"A. That is right.
"Q. And had a roommate by the name of Helferich?
"A. I don't think I ever saw him."
Were you asked these questions and did you give those answers at the first trial?
A. I did.
Q. Now, after you left did you write some letters to Helferich?
A. As I said, I do not recall it, but I have been told that I did.
Q. Did you write a letter or letters to Helferich and suggest to him that he go to the Post Office and get a letter, open it, and he would find a letter to mail back to you?
A. I do not recall that.
Q. Would you say that you did not?
A. I would simply say that I do not recall it.
Q. Did you write to Helferich telling him that you had been working in the coal mines after you left and you had stared death in the face?
A. I do not recall that either.
Q. Well, you certainly had not, had you?

A. I had not?

Q. Yes.

A. I don't think I did.

Q. I mean you had not worked in any coal mines after you left Williams?

A. No, that is quite so.

Q. Now, after your return from Williams, you entered, as it has appeared, Columbia sometime in September 1920?

A. That is right.[3]

The whole incident was an obvious embarrassment to Chambers and so emotionally painful that his subsequent recall of it was bound to be defective. It would appear that Chambers, then a youth of nineteen, puerile and prankish, was seeking from the world what he had failed to develop from his family life, a secure sense of his own identity. Since his runaway to New Orleans and his return home, his behavior strongly points to that of a desperate young man, searching for meaning and direction in life.

Chambers' outward compliance with his mother's wishes was a conspiracy of silence against her, a struggle between the factions of his divided self. One part acquiesced, while another plotted, rebelled, and betrayed her by running away. Laha had reason to believe him still under her direction, passive and obedient in her presence. Only away from home could he act out his rebelliousness against her, in ways seemingly remote from his direct feelings for her. Chambers' "quick and difficult decision" to leave Williams College was, in fact, the consequence of an already ongoing self-searching process. It culminated, as did the New Orleans escapade, in his return home. In his decision to leave Williamstown and return to Lynbrook, carried out under the guise of its being a practical choice (attend Columbia instead of Williams), there is discernible both his wish to defy his mother's will and his need to cling to her physically.

In his forgotten religious experiences, when he stayed in his room all day reading the Bible, he may ostensibly have been seeking understanding from God. But in the light of our knowledge of his identity conflict, the answer he was searching for may have been more definitive: should he remain a mother's boy (Vivian), do Laha's bidding and stay on at Williams, or should he be a man (Whittaker) and follow his masculine inclinations and leave Williams? His unprecedented turning to God—a new source, for neither Laha nor Jay

---

[3] From pp. 377–79 of the "Transcript of Record, United States of America Against Alger Hiss." This record of the second Hiss trial, consisting of ten volumes (3900 pages), printed in preparation for Hiss's appeal to the U.S. Court of Appeals for the Second Circuit, includes all of the testimony, government and defendant's exhibits, attorneys' summation statements, charge of the Court, and Motions of Defendant for a new trial. Hereafter to be cited as Trial Transcript.

had provided any basis for religious faith [4]—was, not unlike his turning to a new college, part of his quest for an understanding parental figure.

The Williams College incident had other important implications. Chambers stayed two or more nights in the dormitory room with Helfrich. From the content and length of his six or more letters to Helfrich, several of which ran to ten or twelve pages, it would appear that he had developed a sudden infatuation for his roommate, a homosexual temptation from which he panicked and fled. After his departure, when Helfrich refused to go along with his post-office scheme, Chambers felt it as a rejection that called for revenge. In his last letter to Helfrich, Chambers expressed deep feelings of disappointment for what he now knew was an imagined friendship.

The incident of the self-addressed letter is indeed significant, for it heralds in form and plot the schemes he later designed to protect himself from his persecutory fears. The use of this particular device—the "mail-drop"—recurs many times in Chambers' activities. This manipulation by which he hoped to outwit Helfrich and the postal authorities gave Chambers a feeling of omnipotence. Similarly, his romantic letters to Helfrich purported to demonstrate his worldly experiences and personal strength. His colorful fabrications, a composite of play-acting, acting-out, and writing-out, of wishful fantasies, had all the merits of producing excitement and intrigue, a façade to cover the emptiness inside him.

In September 1920 our subject entered Columbia as Whittaker Chambers.[5] It was difficult to gather with chronological accuracy the details of Chambers' years at Columbia. His own account is highly selective, and interviews with close friends and former classmates, though invaluable, had to be individually appraised. Literary colleagues respected his ability as a writer and some regarded him as a budding genius. Others found him merely a prankster and a mystifier. To a few he was a sensitive, if unrealistic poet. By the more conformist and conventional, he was looked upon as an eccentric character, a campus agitator whose company was best avoided.

Chambers was assigned a faculty advisor, Mark Van Doren, then a young instructor in the English Department. Van Doren's poetic spirit and natural kindliness had an important influence on Chambers. They quickly

---

[4] Though Chambers gives no other explanation for his religious crisis in *Witness,* he does refer to it in *Cold Friday,* the posthumous collection of his miscellaneous writings (New York: Random House, 1964). He described a Miss Dorothea Mund Ellen, who, he says, introduced him to Christian Science at about this time: and he also mentions a Methodist minister, father of a classmate, whose services he attended. The omission of these figures from *Witness* is puzzling, particularly that of Miss Ellen, whom Chambers calls "the greatest single influence for good in my life until I met my wife."
[5] By this time, it should be recalled, he had been known by five names: Jay Vivian Chambers, Vivian Chambers, Charles Adams, Charles Whittaker, and Whittaker Chambers.

passed to a first-name basis and developed an understanding that Chambers very much needed. Van Doren encouraged Whittaker in literary efforts, and his friendship during the next two years was a steady source of inspiration. Chambers recalls with deep gratitude how Van Doren instilled in him a "renewed sense of life," which for the next three or four years sustained in him the feeling that writing poetry could be meaningful and respectable as "a way of life."

Whittaker attended classes irregularly.[6] He spent much of his time in the university's libraries, "buried" in the stacks or reading rooms, a fantasy-rich underground. Like the book-filled attic of his boyhood, these were sources of private pleasure. Extracurricular life at Columbia—enhanced by the spirit of intellectual freedom and rebellion of the postwar years—provided him with unprecedented opportunities for both mischief and creativity. Student friendships, and the Columbia student magazine, *The Morningside,* were his forums. He became an informal member of a progressive student clique of highly imaginative, outspoken students, who came together in greater than usual number on the Columbia campus in the early twenties. The class of 1924 at Columbia was an exceptionally gifted one: it included such distinguished names as Lionel Trilling, Herbert Solow, John Gassner, Meyer Schapiro, Nathaniel Ross, David Cort, and many others. Chambers felt buoyed by his friends and surroundings. Away from home he was a free agent. He loved to wander about the campus and its environs or lose himself in Harlem or Greenwich Village.

When he took the train for Lynbrook each evening the Whittaker image was automatically transformed back into Vivian. His campus personality provided him with an inner image of himself comparable to his former personifications of Charles Adams and Charles Whittaker. These pseudo-images facilitated the formation of an alter-image which helped to fill his otherwise empty self with identificatory ingredients. In the New Orleans slums he had tried to draw sustenance from the dry wellsprings of a sick world; at Columbia, in the libraries and from campus life, he found a rich intellectual storehouse. He hated the discipline of undergraduate academic requirements and rebelled against institutional rules just as he had against Laha's demands. Both in New Orleans and at Columbia (as during all of his life), he manipulated either his self-image or the order of things or people about him.

From the fall term of his second year (September 1921) through the summer and fall of 1922 was a more productive period, and a somewhat more integrated one, as judged by the quality of his academic work and lit-

---

[6] Grades for courses taken in his freshman year are not available, due to the fact that during 1921 a new system of record-keeping was introduced.

erary creativity. He no longer commuted from Lynbrook. He was now living at Hartley Hall on the Columbia campus. He had removed himself from the daily tensions and family disaffections that coming home to Lynbrook entailed. His courses that year consisted almost entirely of languages and literature—two courses in English, one in German, one in Italian, and a beginning course in geology, which he took for only one semester and for which he received a C—; the rest of his grades that year were A's and B's, except for Physical Education, for which he received "NM"—no mark.

During the spring of 1922 he was appointed to the board of editors of *Morningside,* and his name appeared on the editorial masthead of the February issue for that year. In the following issue (March 1, 1922) there appeared under his name a short story entitled "The Damn Fool," somewhat imitative in tone and narrative method of Conrad's "Heart of Darkness."

It is a tale of an international adventurer, enlivened by murders, captures, and escapes, of a man who runs away from his home, intending to fight Bolshevism. It is the story of a man who changes his name, gives up his identity, trades his clothes for the filthy rags of another man. He becomes a fanatic, goes off to a foreign war. Although this main character is mollycoddled, he acts as if he were a hero, and the story ends by saying that the man's life is a lie. It is not without autobiographical significance. Its hero is a man in flight whose adventures are seen in the denouement as being an "escape from himself."

The difficulties encountered by the hero, Everett [7] Holmes, in trying to ship out to Russia are reminiscent of those met by Chambers when he tried to get a job in Washington; he is rebuffed and then finally accepted by older, tougher men. And Holmes' flight bears some relationship to a domineering mother.

Burton, it is a tragedy when a passively good boy adores a brainy mother. It wasn't that she spoiled him. Nothing like that. But she had been through so much—her experience—and she could save him so much, and had, all her life. That was her life, that saving him from himself, and the world. . . . " I made up my mind," she told me once, "that I wouldn't have another mollycoddle in the family."

On completing the second semester of his sophomore year (June 1922), Chambers enrolled in the summer session, taking one course in English, in which he received the grade of A.

But Chambers' interests were not entirely literary and hardly academic. He frequented the Columbia gym and played handball with a strong desire to

---

[7] In the course of the story, Everett changes his name to Edward (from the soft "v" to the hard "d"). This is identical with the changes the author made in real life in his own name (e.g., from *V*ivian to *D*avid).

win, though he was not a good player. He loved wrestling as well and trained regularly with the squad during his undergraduate years but never made the team. After he left Columbia he wrestled and worked out in the YMCA gyms in New York and Baltimore. Though he became strong, he never was an effective wrestler, for his stocky build and unusually short limbs prevented him from mastering the various body holds. He always chose to wrestle with men bigger and better than he was; he invited defeat. (His brother, Richard, was a natural wrestler. In their boyhood encounters Whittaker never stood a chance of winning.)

Whittaker's interest in wrestling leads us to an understanding of his unusual actions toward a classmate, David Zablodowsky. Zablodowsky, though short in stature (about five feet two), was a muscular young man and a member of the varsity wrestling team. He was one of a close group of students that included Meyer Schapiro, John Gassner, Jack Schultz, Alvin Barber, and others. From their first meeting Chambers liked him.

One evening, following a late afternoon workout in the gymnasium with the wrestling team, Zablodowsky was having his dinner at the "Q and D" ("Quick and Dirty"), a student hangout just off the Columbia campus. Zablodowsky sat alone, eating a steak sandwich, when Chambers walked in and saw him. With no warning, Chambers walked over to Zablodowsky, picked up a bottle of catsup from the table, and whipped its contents at him, spattering his face and clothes, and then he walked away. Zablodowsky was nonplused. The atmosphere of the "Q and D" became suddenly charged; it seemed that a scuffle was imminent. But the commotion died down as Chambers turned back and, in a suddenly contrite and polite manner, apologized for his impulsive act. He then offered Zablodowsky a dollar bill to pay for the cost of dry cleaning his suit. In relating this incident to me (forty years later), Zablodowsky went on to explain that despite the obvious annoyance and unpleasantness of the incident, it evoked in him a feeling of surprise and curiosity rather than anger. Furthermore, since Chambers within a few moments after his aggressive action was so docile, the whole thing seemed a mistake. Zablodowsky made the point that Chambers had not been drinking. He said that he did not immediately dislike Chambers because of it, but he has wondered about its meaning ever since, especially in the light of some even stranger antics in which Chambers later involved him. As a student, he admired Chambers as a fine young poet; being himself of a conventional and disciplined nature, he was awed by Chambers' rebelliousness and audacity.

Zablodowsky recalled another experience with Chambers not long after the catsup incident. Zablodowsky, Meyer Schapiro, and Jack Schultz shared a dormitory room during one of their years at Columbia. Chambers often visited them there. One day Schultz, whose family lived in nearby West New York, came back to the dormitory with a strangely disturbing story from his father. During the week Mr. Schultz had been visited by three "nice young men" who stated they were students at Columbia. Two had introduced themselves as friends of his son Jack, and the third as "David, his son's roommate." Schultz could not understand what was going on because he knew that David Zablodowsky had not been off campus, and David assured him that he had not met his father or been to his home. Suspecting some ruse, Schultz then questioned his other roommate, Schapiro, who confessed that he and Alvin Barber had made the trip to Schultz's home with Chambers, whose idea it was, and who was the one who posed as Zablodowsky.

Telling the story years later, Zablodowsky speculated that part of Chambers' motivation might had been an inordinate curiosity about Schultz and his relationship with his parents, who were well known for their generosity; Schultz always returned after a visit home with sweets and cakes baked by his mother for him and his roommates. Dr. Jack Schultz has confirmed Chambers' deceitful inquisitiveness:

. . . my father . . . was quite annoyed at having been taken in: the visit had been quite a pleasant one, there had been questions about my friends and activities. What, apparently, as I recall it, most disturbed my father was the intent for whatever reason, to discover my attitudes and what stories I brought home.

This was all consistent with Whittaker's use of people as the artist's material. How Meyer and Alvin Barber came into the picture, I never discovered. I had no interest in pursuing the matter.[8]

Perhaps more interesting is why Chambers went to the trouble of impersonating Zablodowsky. David Zablodowsky did not see Chambers again until many years later (Chambers vanished from the Columbia scene when he joined the Communist Party early in 1925). But the incident at the Schultz home together with the earlier one at the "Q and D," he said, "stuck in my mind." "I could never understand why Whittaker Chambers had posed as 'David' before Mr. Schultz." It is apparent that Chambers must have felt both admiration and deep envy of Zablodowsky, to perform the two ambivalent acts—besmirching him with catsup and assuming his name. Zablodowsky was not only a strong wrestler but an outstanding scholar. He was also an adored son, idolized by his mother. Chambers had on several occasions overheard David's mother proudly exclaim, "What a beautiful boy my David is." (During the course of the Hiss trials it was revealed that Chambers had, since the mid-twenties, often used the name "David Chambers" or "Jay David Cham-

---

[8] Letter to the author, August 28, 1962. Dr. Schultz is Chief of the Department of Genetics at the Cancer Institute, Philadelphia, Pa.

bers" or "Jay David Whittaker Chambers." After almost thirty years of doubt about this, and after another, more sinister incident yet to be described, David Zablodowsky recognized the meaning of Chambers' use of his name as a deeper assumption of his identity, which Chambers coveted.)

Zablodowsky was not the only object of Chambers' pranks. Excitement and escapades provided external fulfillment for his inner emptiness. The show had to go on.[9]

I have been told by at least three of Chambers' classmates about an incident during his sophomore year at Columbia. One morning Chambers, in a defiant mood, apparently had an urge to do something "shocking." He happened to see "Buck" Weaver, a highly regarded teacher of English, and selected him as his target. Chambers stopped Weaver in Hamilton Hall and engaged him in conversation. He first shocked him with a lurid description of some recent escapades in several Harlem brothels, then took a card out of his pocket and showed it to Weaver. It was a laboratory report showing a (false) positive reaction for syphilis (Wassermann test) from a sample of Chambers' blood.

Chambers used many devices to keep himself constantly onstage. In eccentric, clownish ways he drew attention and aroused curiosity. John Gassner, a Columbia classmate, remembers his first meeting with Whittaker Chambers in the gymnasium locker room after a physical education class:

He was conspicuous; all the others were dressing in layers, from their underwear out. His system was different: top to bottom, hat first, then upper clothing complete to necktie and down finally to socks and shoes.

Gassner became one of Whittaker's close friends. He recalls other incidents illustrating Chambers' unusual behavior (as, for example, the time Chambers frightened Jack Schultz by threatening to leap to his death from Schultz's dormitory window). But more important than an abundance of cursory anecdotes are Gassner's illuminating firsthand observations of Chambers during their Columbia years. His account confirms in its own way how Chambers' clownishness helped dispel his inner misery; by acting the fool Chambers transformed inner turmoil into outward jocularity.

[9] The late A. J. Liebling told me of an experience a friend of his had had with Chambers. During the twenties Chambers once invited Charles Wagner (a classmate of Chambers' and later a friend of Liebling's) and another student out to Lynbrook for family dinner. When they got to his house he told them to wait outside while he went in and made sure everything was all right. They waited quite awhile, and then Chambers came out and said that something grave had happened and they couldn't go in. So all three went back on the train to New York, almost an hour's ride. Whatever it was (or was not) that happened remained a mystery, as Chambers never told them. But many years later (in 1948) Wagner still regarded Chambers as a formidable fellow, "who would come around and kill you if he said he would."

He gave me the impression of having suffered much in private life, and of being deeply attached to his mother and to his younger brother, although he also seemed annoyed at him and paternally critical of him. He used to speak of his father as someone remote from the family; he invested him with a romantic aura but spoke of him with considerable aloofness.

The discrepancy between Chambers' inner emotional state and his outer style of behavior comes through convincingly in Gassner's continuing comments:

He loved to play pranks and it seemed to me that he enjoyed baiting and confusing people he found stuffy. He seemed to be sizing up people and silently challenging them, and he implied superiority to them on the basis of deeper knowledge of life, more maturity, and greater earnestness.

At the same time I found him extremely kind, almost tender to people in whom he found sympathy, talent, or fragility. And he had a great talent—an inborn one—for impressing people.

I think he saw himself as a center of interest and as a battleground for momentous struggles. In a penetratingly quiet way he called attention to himself as a man of destiny. He had a talent indeed for dramatizing himself, especially when he was reserved and laconic. I am sure he thought of himself as an important person with a high destiny, possibly as the hero of a tragedy slowly but inevitably taking shape, as a seeker after faith, and as a seeker after knowledge. He thought hard, he studied hard, he was curious about everything; he was impatient with sloth and he scorned mediocrity in any form. He dressed like a derelict but carried himself like a king. I couldn't always disentangle truth from fiction because there was something imaginative and elevated about what he implied about himself, his family, and his adventures. He seemed to take artistic pride and joy in mystification [10] and in an occasional tale.[11]

The Columbia campus of the early twenties provided Chambers with an excellent forum of onlookers and literary admirers. Within a year he changed externally from a seclusive, quietly ruminating youth to a colorful, rampant campus personality. The growth of his anti-socialism is evident from an appraisal of his literary activities during his sophomore and junior years. In the fall of 1922 he began to write vigorously in the current vogue, profanism. He became editor-in-chief of *The Morningside* with the issue of November 1922.

As editor-in-chief, Chambers became a controversial, much talked about figure on the campus. He was aligned with a small coterie of ultraliberal radicals and launched a new, "radical but not extreme," editorial policy advocating profanism. He philosophized about Christ as Man, Christ as God, and the

[10] T. S. Matthews, former managing editor of *Time,* describing his feelings about Chambers, many years later said, "I liked to be around him because he deepened the atmosphere." Matthews to the author, August 30, 1965.
[11] John Gassner (of the Yale University School of Drama) to the author, September 30, November 7, 1962.

Anti-Christ. Onto these theistic and atheistic surrogates he now transferred his conflicted feelings.

Only two years previously, of course, he had been searching the Scriptures for meaning and direction in life. His struggle during those few days at Williams, with its aftermath of continued searching, now evidenced itself in sophisticated caricatures of rebellion.

Chambers' style was dramatic, forthright, and satirical. Early in his career as a writer he espoused radicalism and nonconformism as a protection against his inner fears. The more he was frightened, the greater was his need to attack. Note the blustering denial of maternal dependency in the editorial comment:

Profanism is the healthiest sign of the determination of Columbia men to wipe away the lactic droolings of the late century and accept something more nearly approaching reality than the ethical, religious and materialistic hypocrisy of modern life.[12]

Such vehemence against the "lactic droolings" of his contemporaries betrays his own emptiness and hunger.

In the same issue of *Morningside* that listed Chambers as editor-in-chief, his brief one-act playlet, called *A Play for Puppets,* appeared under the pseudonym of John Kelly. Although hardly sensational by present standards, the play caused a tempest on the Columbia campus. Its opening lines went:

YOUNG C: This Jesus in here was a poor fellow.
OLD C: He was obstinate and proud.
YOUNG C: They say he never lay with a woman.

About the play, Mark Van Doren remarked in a review that appeared in the *Columbia Spectator* on October 23, 1922:

First comes *A Play for Puppets,* by John Kelly (whoever he is), conceived in the purest profanism and dedicated to the Antichrist. The scene is the Sepulchre on the third day, and the idea—but that will come out in the reading, when the question also may be decided whether the author was merely blasphemous or merely brilliant. I think he was brilliant.

The use of John Kelly as a pseudonym in his blasphemy of Christ is indeed significant. Under the cloak of someone else's identity, the author feels brave enough to attack and destroy the omnipotent father or, as in this case, his religious surrogate, Christ. And in doing so he covers his already changed name (Vivian to Whittaker) with still another hard, masculine one—John Kelly. Before Chambers sent the manuscript to the printers he showed it to his

[12] *The Morningside,* Columbia College Literary Magazine, November 1922 (Vol. XI, No. 1), p. 15.

friend and adviser, Mark Van Doren. He wanted to know whether it "was wise" to have the play printed. Van Doren's approval caused considerable furor with the college authorities. Following the appearance of *A Play for Puppets* and the revelation that "John Kelly" was Whittaker Chambers, he was dropped from the editorial staff of *Morningside* in January 1923. The incident made news beyond the campus; accounts in the New York press were widespread:

New York Evening Post, Tuesday, Nov. 7, 1922:

COLUMBIA MAGAZINE PLAY STIRS STRIFE
Little Group of Profanists at War
with the More Conventionally-Minded
    The objectionable article was *A Play for Puppets* and published in the November issue of *Morningside* under the signature of John Kelly a nom-de-plume of Chambers. . . .

New York Times, November 7, 1922:

ASK EDITOR TO RESIGN

New York Tribune, Tuesday, Nov. 7, 1922:

SKETCH ON CHRIST'S LIFE CAUSES EDITOR TO RESIGN
Head of Columbia University's *Morningside*
Steps Out at Student Body's Request.

    The talk did not die down, and the administration decided to take action. A conference between Chambers and Dean Hawkes resulted in a compromise. Chambers was not officially expelled but was invited to leave Columbia. He left under the pressure of this incident; on his record there is the notation that he "voluntarily withdrew."
    Contrary to what one might expect, Chambers' withdrawal produced in him a feeling of elation and freedom. The incident, and Chambers' reaction, have been elaborated by Charles Wagner, who was Sunday editor of the *New York Daily Mirror* when this reminiscence was first published in the Columbia alumni magazine in 1952.

It is 1923 and the weeks toward graduation are running into each other with speed. In my Hartley room . . . the stacks of *Morningside* magazine are piled, ready for the sales job outside Hamilton Hall. . . . Dean Hawkes wants to see you or Chambers or whoever else was responsible for the vile one-act play in *Morningside*. At your earliest convenience. Whittaker says, "I'll go in after my nine o'clock class" and he does and comes out to tell me, "I'm leaving for good. He wants all copies of *Morningside* confiscated and an apology. It can't be done and I'm leaving college."
    We go to a Chinese restaurant on 110th Street to talk things over. But it

seems that all we do is laugh things over. Whittaker was never happier. Something has been released in him and his usual wit has an edge of fire, Promethean fed with Shavian shavings.[13]

It is noteworthy how similar in action and event were the circumstances of his scandalous departure from Columbia and the cloud of dishonor under which he left high school on graduation day three years before. It will be recalled that in the class prophecy he made some cavalier comments about his classmates and about the President of the United States. Three years later, in his *Play for Puppets,* he attacked Christ. Both at South High School in 1919 and at Columbia University in 1922, his aggressiveness was "written out" in literary acts of public defiance.

It is not clear just what Chambers did during the remaining winter and spring months of 1923 after his withdrawal from Columbia in January. He reports only one incident, an attempt to work with the American Friends Service Committee in their relief program for the Russian famine. Originally suggested by Mark Van Doren, the idea of a trip to Russia stirred him intensely, and he immediately went to see J. Barnard Walton, head of the Friends Service Committee. No promises or offers were made, but Chambers felt that he had won the assignment, and this produced in him a state of elation. His anticipatory excitement over distributing food to masses of starving people no doubt sprang in part from his own inner hunger. Let us keep in mind that because of his own self-destructiveness he had created a situation in which he had to withdraw from Columbia. His friends were back in school and he was "cast out." His outward elation was a compensatory cover for his inner melancholia.

Note in the following passage from *Witness* the wide swings from elation to depression (from anticipated acceptance to the reality of rejection). Note also how rationally documented, yet predetermined from within, is the build-up and letdown, eventuating always with the resurgence of the unwanted, negative self-image. The interval of elation passed like a pleasant dream:

When I first withdrew from Columbia College, I felt a renewed sense of life, and a great desire to go somewhere and do something entirely new.

The first Friend I saw was J. Barnard Walton, a pleasant businesslike Quaker who was then, I believe, the head of the Service Committee. I stayed in Philadelphia several days, meeting other Friends and canvassing the possibilities of my going to the Soviet Union. A new and enormously tranquilizing spirit enveloped me. It emanated from those quiet presences whom I met, from the chaste Quaker rooms. . . .

Then the story of my Atheist play reached Friends. There was a horrified

[13] Cited by Ralph de Toledano, *Lament for a Generation* (New York: Farrar, Straus & Cudahy, 1960), pp. 129–30.

reaction. I received one of those letters, such as only Quakers can write, which, in the most restrained language, said in effect, "You are outcast."

It was an invisible turning point in my life. If, at that moment, one Friend had said: "Sit down with me and tell me, what have you in your heart," this book need never have been written. As it was, it took me seventeen years to find my way, unaided, back to that peace.

Chambers was past fifty when he wrote the above (around 1951–52). In his plaintive retrospection we see how his memory of a disappointment thirty years past, recollected as a wish to have had "one Friend" in whom to confide, affirms his lifelong frustration: his childlike appeal for parental warmth and understanding. His reflections about himself in 1951 are really no different from his feelings in 1923. He has gathered no insight through the years; the anguish had existed long before and was destined to continue long after.[14] The "invisible turning point" was a self-deception. Anchored in repression was a much deeper, abiding conflict which might be paraphrased: If my mother had really wanted me (been my one 'Friend'), I would have accepted myself for what I am and would not have envied, hated, and sought to destroy and re-create, or lost my way and joined the Communist Party.

Although he could not go to Europe under the auspices of the Quakers, Chambers made the trip nevertheless, embarking at New York, "as a first-class passenger," on the North German Lloyd Liner "Seydlitz" on June 20, 1923, and landing at Bremerhaven. It is not known who paid for this trip, which lasted three months. Chambers sailed alone but met, by prearrangement, a Columbia classmate and friend, Meyer Schapiro, and another mutual friend from City College, Henry Zolinsky. Since neither Schapiro nor Zolinsky had travel passports (they had shipped over as working members of the crew), they were dependent upon the use of Chambers' passport to travel around Germany or enter another country. For the balance of Schapiro's and Zolinsky's trip, the three remained together. It was apparently an aesthetically rich holiday (a letter to Mark Van Doren emphasized their reading, writing, painting, and "picture-gallerying"), and it was spiced with adventure, including the arrest of one of them in Holland. They shared an apartment in Berlin, where they lived for about a month, then traveled to Belgium and France.

Schapiro and Zolinsky returned to the United States early in September in order to matriculate for the fall term at Columbia. Chambers, under no such pressure, continued alone to Paris. After a short stay he sailed alone from Le Havre, arriving in America in late September.

A week after his return from Europe, on September 28, 1923, Whittaker

---

[14] Seventeen years later, in 1940, after his period in the Communist Party, Chambers, having undergone a religious experience, was baptized.

got a night job at the New York Public Library; he was assigned to the desk in the Newspaper Division. He had a good deal of time for reflection, and it was his intention at this time to produce a collection of poems that would

. . . preserve . . . the beautiful Long Island of my boyhood before it was destroyed forever by the advancing City. I wished to dramatize the continual defeat of the human spirit in our time, by itself and by the environment in which it finds itself. . . . I called the book: *Defeat in the Village*. It was to be an autobiography of mood, but not of factual reality. Each of the poems in it bore some relationship of tone or feeling to the next poem, and all were intended to build up to a climax of despair. Few of the poems were autobiographical in any other sense. Few were based on real occurrences, though some were touched off by them. Many of them were inspired by places, and in the years when I was composing them, I took to wandering a great deal at night, especially around the little Long Island harbor of East Rockaway, where the tides of my childhood still exerted a strong pull, and the mists and the darkness blotted out the ugliness of the present and helped me to recall the Long Island of the past.

In time, I had written a fair-sized book. I submitted it to a national poetry contest where *Defeat in the Village* was just "nosed out" of first place (I was duly informed) by *Chinese White,* a book of poems by the wife of the *Daily Worker* cartoonist, William Gropper.

The metaphoric theme is by now a familiar one. Nature, her new growth and natural beauty, would be invaded and killed by the city. The vague, melancholy tone of Chambers' description of the poems, the forlorn title of the book, and its negative intent ("to build up to a climax of despair") mark this enterprise as another phase in Chambers' cyclical pattern of creation and destruction. Its own defeat in the contest seems almost predestined.[15] What became of the book is unknown; a friend and Columbia classmate did tell me that Chambers once showed him a book of his poems.

During that year (1923–24) Chambers spent much of his free time on the Columbia campus, with his former colleagues and literary friends. Sometimes he would not return to Lynbrook for days. In the fall of 1924 he felt a renewed urge to be readmitted as a regular student. He went to see Dean Hawkes and, after a "heart-to-heart talk" with him, was readmitted to Columbia as a regular undergraduate student with (according to Chambers) his earnest promise to the dean that "he would go and sin no more."

Later that same day, September 15, 1924, Chambers wrote a long letter to Mark Van Doren. It is a remarkably revealing letter. Chambers begins by ironically announcing that he has "unpleasant news":

---

[15] During this trying time Jay was occupied with the building of a miniature world of his own. Out of match-box wood he had fashioned a group of toy models of classical buildings. He had an exhibit of his work at the New York Public Library during the period his son was working there, though Chambers himself makes no mention of this.

I am returning to College. I should have warned you sooner had I known where to reach you.

He then goes on to explain to Van Doren the reasons for his return, of which there were "several":

I went to see the Dean this morning and gave him the minor reasons. They were the desire of my parents to have a graduated child, my own desire to complete what I had begun, and a wish to specialize in history. I lied to him quite simply and told him I wanted to teach history. After all, what he wanted to be sure is that I would stick, and any major reason is none of the Dean's affair.

Much was made of these lines as Chambers' letter was read in court twenty-five years later during the second Hiss trial.[16] It was used to show that Whittaker Chambers was a "pathological liar," for here, at least was a piece of evidence, Chambers' own candid and apparently unabashed statement: "I lied to him quite simply and told him I wanted to teach history." No doubt too much was made of this remark: the prosecution reduced the argument to absurdity, and, by itself, the statement "I lied . . ." shows nothing more than the fact that Chambers' humiliation at returning sheepishly to school was so great that the confession of a lie was no confession at all, only a device for appearing worldly-wise before Van Doren. The letter is full of such posturings; for example: "I have unpleasant news: I am returning to College." The deception may, however, lie deeper than this rather transparent role-playing. Whittaker told Van Doren a "truth" in his admission to him that he lied to Dean Hawkes, but he did not tell the whole truth.

Let us look further into the text of Chambers' letter for his "major" reason for returning to Columbia and observe how, by a simple confession, he involves Van Doren in a little conspiracy by asking him to keep a secret:

Indeed it is a new one [reason] of my own which I am content to have entre nous. I have an unconventional partner in this world for whom I care very much, and it is she who is urging me to this reversal. No need to analyze the basic feminine motive in getting me again in harness where, in a way, she can at once guide and encourage. She argues (and in this I think she is right) that my present job ideally permits me to study. I shall keep it and pay my own way. And I am happy to do what she wishes.

With the expression "unconventional partner," Chambers leaves the reader to his own imaginings, yet implies that he was having a love affair with a girl, to whose wishes he bowed. Our curiosity is piqued about the identity of the girl, especially in view of her apparent power over Whittaker.

There is no other evidence of Whittaker's participation in a liaison at this time, and the story seems to be just another face-saving device. But that does

<hr>

[16] The entire letter appears as Defendant's Exhibit "M," Trial Transcript, p. 383.

history. I lied to him quite
simply and told him I wanted
to teach history. After all, what
he wanted to be sure was that
I would stick, and my major
reason is none of the Paris affair.

Indeed it is a new one of my own,
which I am content to have
entre nous. I have an un-
conventional partner in this
world for whom I care very much,
and it is she who is urging me to
this reversal. No need to analyze
the basic feminine motive in
getting me again in harness
Here, in a way, she can at once
guide and encourage. She agrees
(and in this I think she is
right) that my present job
ideally permits me to study. I
shall keep it and go my own
way. And I am happy to do this

*Portion of letter from Whittaker Chambers to Mark Van Doren,
dated September 15, 1924.*

not mean that the "unconventional partner" is wholly invented. Surely one person who fits the description, whose desire to get him "again in harness where . . . she can . . . guide," would be Laha herself. No doubt, alarmed at the aimless path his life had been taking, she had indeed been arguing with him to return to college. He is content to do her bidding (in the hope that he may get from her the love she did not have to give him). And he tacitly puts the finger of identity on his mother as the unconventional partner who is driving him.

It is psychologically interesting and not insignificant that Chambers, when asked to read the letter aloud to the court because the writing was not legible to counsel, misread his own handwriting twice at this crucial paragraph. For "No" he read "We," and for "argues" he read "agrees." One could attribute the errors to nervousness as his eye encountered a fabrication of twenty-five years previous, and it is likely that the mistakes had some meaning. "We need" was certainly closer to the psychological truth than "no need." And "argues" suggests the forceful Laha rather than an agreeable young girl.

The undisclosed truth to both Dean Hawkes and Van Doren stems from his real dilemma: he wants to be a good boy (so that his mother will not withdraw her love), and yet he doesn't want to appear as himself to his friend, Van Doren, as the helpless truant child who is returning to school because of his mother. And so he combines fact and fantasy, masquerades his domineering mother as an "unconventional" (sexual) partner, and in so doing convinces himself and Van Doren that he is a "man." If the letter is read with this interpretation the internal meaning is consistent. His mention of money ("I shall pay my own way") is for example, more appropriate to his mother, who had been paying his tuition, than to a lover, who wouldn't be expected to. Chambers' use of another expression is enlightening: "the desire of my parents to have a graduated *child*." Though this is rather ordinary student irony, it illustrates the important "man-boy" conflict.

There is clear evidence of Chambers' inner struggle in the next paragraph of the letter:

I tell this as lightly as possible. But you must judge by the facts. It is not pleasant to play inconsistent. I have fewer illusions about colleges than when I left. And fewer about the value of education or even of intelligence. I think the level of culture like the level of folly and evil remains constant in nearly all generations and our endeavor to screw it up wholesale is a wasteful and revolting debacle. I could name on one hand the boys for whom I think the last four years of college have done a real good. It would take more than two to count over those to whom I have seen it do a real harm. I find that very depressing and, with one or two exceptions, I find the faculty as depressing as the students.

At the very moment of announcing his return to college, he is already giving notice that he does so unwillingly and defiantly: he discounts in advance what he wants so much to have. His wish to get an education from Columbia (the alma mater of his choice that has previously rejected him) is symbolically equivalent to his strivings to get love from mother. And so he accedes to what I have interpreted as Laha's wishes and also makes his peace with Columbia, the mother surrogate. His decision to return to Columbia is made at a time when he is hungry and noncreative, and on this depressed note he concludes his letter to Van Doren:

I have written very little for the past month. All my winter's work now seems to me very thin. It is too personal to be amusing and I strive not to believe I was ever so unhappy. So I have put it by. I have seldom felt so eager and so active. Whether or not I write is a minor consideration.

Again his sense of eagerness and activity, suggestive of imminent elation, comes to the fore to rescue him from his deepening depression.

And so, in September 1924, at the age of twenty-four and one-half, after a lapse of almost two years, Chambers re-entered Columbia. He felt buoyed by his readmission and looked forward with renewed expectancy (his second chance) to the resumption of academic life. He signed up for three history courses, advanced Latin, and physical education—a total of eighteen hours. And from 5 to 10 p.m. weekdays and 1 to 10 p.m. Sundays he worked at the New York Public Library. But it was evident from the outset of his return that he had little interest or desire to continue with his courses. He wanted to be free to think and move about on his own, to write poetry and short stories. He was too restive to attend clases. He did not last the semester. He dropped two courses, "withdrew" from two, and received an F in the remaining one. He stopped attending classes altogether by late November or early December of 1924.

On February 17, 1925, Whittaker Chambers joined the Communist Party. A letter to the Van Dorens, postmarked New York, March 8, 1925, established this date:

It was inevitable. On February 17, I joined the Communist Party. Now I am busy from morning till night, and at night too, but I am also happy and healthy with a feeling of singular mental well being.[17]

Q. There is no doubt but what you place the date back in 1925, is there, Mr. Chambers, for your joining the Communist Party, as February 17?
A. That appears to be conclusive.

[17] Only after he had been confronted with the above letter, and after the following colloquy during the second Hiss trial (see Trial Transcript, pp. 386–89), did he realize he had erred by a year.

Q. And so you joined the Communist Party on February 17, 1925?
A. That seems to be the case.
Q. And at the first trial you testified it was January 1924, did you not?
A. I believed that until this moment.

In *Witness,* as in his testimony at the Hiss trial, the moment of decision is dramatized, but the feeling of personal freedom, elation, and literary productivity is forgotten; in its stead Chambers remembers how he made up his mind while sitting on a cold park bench on the Columbia campus. His reasons have shifted to the ideological. Almost all intellectuals of the West, he said years later, are driven to entertain Communism in response to one of two problems: the economic system or war. "I was one of those who was drawn to Communism by war." He then recalls his trip to Europe in the summer of 1923 and describes how deeply moved he had been by the destructive residues of World War I, and he refers to Germany's state of "manic desperation," "the ruins of Northern France." It was for him, he said, "the crisis of history and its dimension."

These retrospective ideological reflections contrast with his clearly expressed interests and concerns reported by him to Mark Van Doren in a letter posted from Brussels on August 30, 1923, shortly before his return to the United States. In it he describes their "escape" [18] to Belgium, their "first frantic day in Brussels," as the "only garish episodes of the summer." The main theme is Chambers' interest in his own writing and his lounging around the quais of Paris after the departure of his two companions:

I ran down to Paris for a few days and had a thoroughly good time. For the first moment since landing in Germany, I was quite alone and I made the most of my opportunity, finishing half a narrative poem in couplets (heroic and lay), lounging around the quais (the best things in the City) and the Louvre and Montmartre. But what a way to see Paris. If I could live there five months, I believe I could know the City inside out. . . .

Europe is certainly not for writing; not with friends, at any rate. Aside from the narrative poem, an experiment and a pleasure, I have done nothing but three poems written on the boat. But then it is not necessary to write in Europe. I will not be hurried, and what comes easily, comes, and what does not, needs [sic] not. After I have control of my media I have still a whole life to live before I can have anything to say. With some sort of stubborn confidence I set about living life, content sometimes to make observations en route. The sickening apotheosis and striving after Art among our American generation is not for me, nor is it for Zukofsky, or Schapiro or Gassner. By the way, I am convinced that the possibilities of the heroic couplet are little short of magnificent. What a form: unity, order, organization; each couplet as perfect as a little sonnet. After a discipline of that sort, one

---

[18] They had got into difficulties with the local authorities in Holland because of the lack of proper passports.

should be able to write blank verse of the kind I have been looking for and not finding.

Have you ever tried Catullian hendeca syllabics? You will find at the back of Coleridge's poems, one of the finest things in English poetry, Coleridge's translation of Schiller's Urilesisches Mahenschen:

> "Hear, my beloved, an old Urilesian Story;
> High, and embosomed in congregated louvres
> Shimmered a temple upon a breezy headland."

I think it surpasses the original, the Schiller has lines hard to beat. What a pity that a mind so great as Coleridge's should have fallen so completely beneath an influence as devastating as Wordsworth's.

It is quite evident from the letter [19] that Chambers' interests at this time were literary. His tone, of course, is self-conscious; he is, to some extent, playing the poet before Van Doren, but this is no indication that his mind was instead on the crisis of history. His Europe is the ageless Europe of the "grand tour." Not only does he fail to mention its postwar condition, but he fails to include that condition among those things the letter "should have been about." He does not mention the destruction of Western Europe wrought by World War I.

One of Chambers' traveling companions confirmed what is evident from the letter. Chambers' interests, he pointed out, were in reading and writing poetry and in European literature. He was unconcerned with politics or world events at that time. Chambers' subsequent expressions about the "sick and dying world," were retrospectively added. "He conflated earlier events in his life with later ones and produced a more rational account." Until the mid-twenties Chambers was a conservative, a would-be aristocrat, interested in the good and plentiful life. Whatever Chambers' essential reasons for joining the Party were, they were apparently not an abiding concern for the world crisis. We will speculate on the function of the Communist Party in Chambers' life later. It is enough to note for the moment the only faintly disguised pleasure with which he reports the clandestine circumstances of his first contacts with the movement.

A stocky young man in a shabby overcoat walked past my desk in the Public Library and studied me. Then he walked back and studied me from another angle. He did this several times. I thought: "He is the man. He is the contact with the Communist Party."

Chambers described him as a man with "glassy eyes" who then asked him his name and did he "want to join?" "Yes," he replied, "I want to join."

[19] From the Hiss Defense Files.

A few nights later, the Communist with the glassy eyes came back. It was the early spring of 1925, and cold. He steered me toward the Hudson River, and we worked our way on foot, against the wind, toward 59th Street. While we walked, he told me that his name was Sam Krieger. "But my name in the party," he said, "is Clarence Miller." . . .

Not far from the Hudson River, somewhere on or near 59th Street, Krieger drew me into a dark doorway. We went up a dirty stairway to a big lighted loft. At the door two or three short, dark men looked us over silently, nodded to Krieger and let us pass. . . . After a few meetings, Krieger proposed me for membership in the Communist Party. . . .

Later on, I went to the Manhattan headquarters of the Workers Party on 14th Street. There I met a fidgety, kindly man who duly issued me, in the name of Whittaker Chambers, a red party book, listing my party number, stamped with the party's rubber seal (a hammer and sickle) and signed by the nervous man's name: Bert Miller. I knew Bert Miller for many years and even worked closely with him in the Communist Party until his expulsion (another "incurable right-wing deviationist") in 1929. In all that time I never knew his real name.[20]

For the next two years, after his entry into the party, Chambers continued to work at the New York Public Library (until April 1927). He involved himself more deeply in the study of Marxian literature. He did menial jobs for the Communist Party, served as a messenger boy, and learned who some of the higher-ups in the party were. It is interesting to note how he mystified some of the young boys who worked with him at the Library with stories about his secret and illegal activities.

A revealing picture of Chambers during this period was given to me by Leon Herald, who worked in the Library with Chambers during that period:

. . . it was during the winter-spring season of 1926–27 when I met Whittaker Chambers in the 42nd St. Library in New York City. I was then working in the stacks with a Mr. Busch, a German, as the boss, and a blond young man perhaps in his early twenties, if that old.

Chambers must have been working in a section adjacent to ours, for, as I remember, he had been coming to see this young man quite regularly during the lunch hours. What was most striking about Chambers, as I remember, was his way of dramatizing the subject he was telling us. Each time, it seems to me, as I approached him while he was talking to this young man whose name I cannot now remember, he began telling us about his being a Communist, or a Young Communist, and his troubles with the authorities of the Library. The subject of these

[20] Almost twenty years later, Chambers goes on to say, he resumed his close acquaintanceship with Bert Miller, but under his real name. Miller was none other than Ben Mandel, "by then the research director of the House Committee on Un-American Activities." An ex-Communist, Mandel was an employee of the House Committee from 1939 to 1951, save for a two-year period toward the close of World War II, when he was with the State Department. Chambers identified Mandel as "the former business manager of the *Daily Worker*," whom he had met "perhaps twice, briefly," between 1939 and 1948. (*Witness*, p. 536.)

stories he was telling us was his persecutions in the hands of the officials and the nature of that persecution was always the opening of his locker when he was not there. It seemed as if his locker was always broken into for the purpose of finding out what sort of Communist propaganda Chambers was carrying on in the Library. . . .

I knew at the time less than nothing about Communism. I couldn't see why he was a Communist or why somebody was against his being a Communist. His intentions were not to educate us in the knowledge of Communism. . . . The meaning he wanted to convey was that he was an important person and therefore he was the subject of persecution. I left the Library in 1927.[21]

It is of interest that Chambers made a point of telling his colleagues that he used his locker—which he shared with the blond young man—as a hiding place for illegal Communist pamphlets and that as a result he was the object of persecution by the Library authorities.

In April 1927 Library detectives did break into Chambers' locker. They were searching for missing books and, according to their report (April 14, 1927), they found them. Continuing their search for additional books, they went to his home in Lynbrook and discovered fifty-six books taken from the Columbia University stacks.

During the Baltimore pre-trial deposition, twenty-one years later, Chambers was questioned about this episode. He repeated his story that he had kept Communist leaflets in his locker:

Q. What was the occasion of your leaving the Library?
A. My locker was forced open in my absence, and in it were found a number of Communist hand-bills, and I believe also evidence that there was a Communist cell working in the Library, as there was, and I was then charged with stealing certain books, which I had not done.

Chambers' immediate superior at the Library, Mr. E. G. Fox, when asked about this incident in 1948, said that Chambers had obtained the books by inducing his page-boy friend, Oscar, to fetch them from the open shelves of the main reading room. Chambers then put them away in their joint locker.

Fox was amazed to hear that Chambers had testified that the investigation was started because of Communist literature contained in his locker. Fox had had a look in the locker when it was opened, and it had contained no Communist pamphlets, in fact nothing other than the stolen books, as the official report substantiated. Fox recalled that the day after the discovery of the stolen books Chambers' father had appeared at the Library and asked the officials not to prosecute his son. Chambers had been discharged from the Library immediately.

To be regarded as a Communist, as Herald has pointed out, made

[21] Leon Herald to the author, February 7, 1963.

Chambers feel important and "in the know." The story of a secret Communist cell and Communist handbills in his locker shows that Chambers was using the Communist Party as a hoax, to satisfy his need to appear important and mystifying, a need that scarcely came from the "crisis of history" but from himself. Chambers' Communist life was of course only beginning. But an understanding of his deepening involvement in the party depends, in part, on a knowledge of events in Lynbrook.

5

Death of a Brother

THE CIRCUMSTANCES surrounding Richard's suicide provide evidence of importance for the decoding of Whittaker's fantasy life. The particular way Richard killed himself explains more than if he had left a written document. In preparation for his final act he drank a quart of whisky. He then arranged himself as though retiring for a night's sleep, with his head on a pillow placed inside the kitchen oven. Thus he inhaled the gas fumes and sank into oblivion, having at last achieved a state of inner fullness and euphoria. But in whatever way one may regard the psychic meaning or the mode of Richard's death, it would be difficult not to discern in it the inner imprint of an erotic act. For the surviving Whittaker, who "refused to take the journey with him," his brother's death seemingly brought him closer to the fulfillment of his childhood wish. "My brother is gone; now *I* will have mother all to myself." We shall see how this inexorable feeling, born of frustration and carried along, reappears as the hidden motive in Chambers' subsequent actions. Until Laha's death in 1958 he was hardly ever away from her for any extended period. Though he later acquired a large country house, wife, and family, Laha and the house at Lynbrook (despite its turmoil and his running away from it) remained his permanent headquarters. He periodically returned there, especially during periods of stress and crisis.

Richard's suicide was the turning point in Whittaker's life, as will become clear from his own consideration of the event, and from the course his life took thereafter.

In defining the relationship between Whittaker and his brother, which made suicide a psychic as well as a physical catastrophe for him, we must rely heavily on reconstruction, because—until the time of his death—Richard is only a minor character in *Witness*. And yet it will be remembered that Whittaker's poem on his brother's death, "My brother lies in the cold earth . . . ,"[1] introduces his "Story of a Middle-Class Family."

[1] See p. 27.

In its prominence, the poem seems to announce Richard's centrality in Whittaker's life; the reader is apt to be puzzled at not being shown the growth of their brotherly ties. When Richard does loom large in the autobiography, suddenly, at the time of his approaching suicide, the puzzlement is not ended. Recalling the occasion of his brother's departure for college, Chambers describes him in ambivalent terms:

. . . he went with a group of his fellow high-school students who were his close friends. Unlike me, he had been very popular, for he was a smiling, candid uncomplicated boy. He had been on the baseball and track teams.

Throughout our early boyhood, my brother had been a shadow that, in the way of older brothers, I tried to shake off. "He worships you," my mother would say, "how can you be so mean to him?" . . . Neither I, nor anyone else, knew how close we were until, when I was about eight years old, I came down suddenly with scarlet fever. My brother was whisked away to Philadelphia. That night, as I became delirious, I repeated over and over: "Where is my brother? I want my brother."

Though Chambers cites the above memory to show how "close and tender" his tie was to his brother, his concern about Richard's whereabouts is revealing of an opposite meaning—the fear that his hidden wish for his brother to be gone may (in his delirium) have come true.

In character, too, he was wholly unlike me—not so good-natured, but much livelier, much more active but not nearly so strong, in all ways more alert, likable, and without that reserve, reflective and observant, that made people react from me. In appearance we were so unlike that people often refused to believe that we were brothers. By the time he left for Colgate we were almost strangers.

This passage can be easily glossed (my brother and I were different sorts, but we shared an unspoken affection), but there is a central confusion. Chambers finds it hard, writing years later, not only to describe his brother but to express the love he professes to feel. His praise of his brother in each instance rebounds to become praise of himself. His brother was "very popular" for (unlike Whittaker) he was an "uncomplicated boy." He was much livelier but "not so good natured." He was "more active but not nearly so strong." He was likable because he didn't have "that reserve, reflective and observant" (that is, intelligence) that supposedly made Whittaker friendless. It is a grudging affection at best that Chambers pays to his brother's memory. This is not to deny the presence of love in the relationship; it is only to acknowledge the presence of resentment.

The ambivalence that can be glimpsed in the passage above was— I submit—actual and deep. Much of what follows is, to repeat, a construct, but as a working hypothesis it will serve to explain Chambers' unusual reaction to the mental crisis that led Richard to suicide and to that event itself.

Richard was born September 26, 1903, when Vivian was two years and six months old. For any youngster that age to try to share his mother with a newly arrived infant is, at best, a losing proposition. If one adds to Vivian's situation the fact of Laha's insufficiency as a mother, it is easy to see why Vivian did not welcome his brother's arrival. From the very day of Richard's birth, his infantile wailings and demands were perceived by Vivian as hostile sounds; they interposed a barrier between Laha and his own hunger for her. Laha was the only reliable person to whom Vivian could cling, and it was Richard who was in the way and singled out as the one to be eliminated.

But if he secretly hated his brother, he was also compelled to admire him: Richard occupied the position he wanted; he wanted, in effect, to be Richard. His envious admiration was abetted by Richard's natural qualities; Richard's athletic physique and affability were in obvious contrast to Vivian's awkward appearance and his sullen withdrawals. As they grew up, Vivian no doubt did treat Richard with indifference, as if he were nonexistent, but it was not out of boredom or contempt. In his deep wish to replace his brother he transferred to him his own self-image of the "unwanted one." This repressed childhood wish to be his brother was fated to return.

A short story published by Chambers in *Morningside* (1924) bears a clear relevance to his relationship with Richard. It concerns a woman and her son, Robert. He is portrayed as an attractive athlete, and the portrayal is strikingly explicit:

What a splendid thing he was. And he stood not quite six foot with one hand on the railing. He was stripped but for short black tights about the groin. His legs were firm and columnar. His knees were small, the muscle not yet completely developed. His thighs were lean with a perpendicular fluting. His stomach was perfectly flat, not a crease over the navel. And his chest that heaved dangled such arms, long, sinewed, brown, joined to the shoulder with plates of ligament.

The hero seems to be a romanticized image of Richard. He shares Richard's talent for wrestling, and a youthful encounter is described that is strongly reminiscent of the bouts between Whittaker and Richard, which the latter always won. Robert's opponent in the scene is not named, nor does he appear again, but he is presumably the hero's brother; the friendly fight takes place in the house, and it is interrupted by the mother.

Much of the tale is told from the mother's point of view—the father is a nebulous figure, suggestive of Jay—and she sees the boy in curiously sensual terms:

A month later she saw him win the camp's light-heavyweight boxing championship at a YMCA exhibit. How he moved, all life! Coordination: one leg out, one back, swinging on the waist; head between his shoulders. And his shifting arms. How he took his blows, staggered once, but never fell. And how he dealt them. Alive. His flesh was alive.

Robert enlists in the army, and there is a tender farewell scene between him and his mother. Chambers describes the reunion of mother and son when Robert comes home on a brief furlough before being sent into combat.

They walked together beneath the grape arbor, down the slope that ran to the creek at the back of their lot. He had taken off his coat. The very blue star grass was still in flower. She liked them he knew. As a child he had always picked them for his mother. The khaki shirt was smooth and tight on the round of her son's back as he stooped to pick one now. They did not talk.

Robert is killed in battle, and his mother's reaction is described in the same understated tone.

The telegram that reported him among the missing did not really shock her. She had so secretly determined that she would not see him again. In his one letter from abroad he had told her of his voyage, of his companions; he had been made sergeant. He was eighteen. He had won another belt. He had never lost a match. His shoulders were developing abnormally,[2] he thought. The men liked him. They were good fellows. . . .
She did not know what killed in battle was like. Her son had crossed the ocean with the other men. He was simply away.

The story ends on a similar note. No violent grief is described; the mother's reaction is rather of total silence, depletion.

There was really no wind. She raised her arm and laid it in her lap as he would never raise his arm again.

This story was written two years before the suicide of Richard Godfrey Chambers. Startlingly enough, it was called "In Memory of R.G." It was alluded to briefly during the Hiss trial:

CROSS: Did you write something "In Memory of R.G."?
CHAMBERS: I presume I did.
CROSS: Who was "R.G."?
CHAMBERS: Robert Garrison.
MURPHY: Are you offering it?
CROSS: No.[3]

There was no Robert Garrison at Columbia at this time; as far as I could determine, there was no such person in any area of Chambers' life. The

---

[2] This rather jarring sentence (Robert is otherwise seen as a model of perfection) recalls Chambers' fantasied account of his own birth: "I measured fourteen inches across the shoulders."
[3] Trial Transcript, p. 418.

fratricidal implications of "In Memory of R.G." seem inescapable. The initials are those of his brother, Richard Godfrey. Chambers creates a heroic figure with his brother's virtues, seen through a mother's eyes, and then kills him. Chambers portrays a "loving mother," identifies with her (that is, unconsciously, with Laha), and endows her with a destructive attachment for her son. She adores her son and yet quietly assumes the inevitability of his death. ("She had so secretly determined that she would not see him again.") In addition, the quality of her love for him is not, in the conventional sense, motherly: with its interest in muscles, boxing, and black belts, it has the sound instead of a homosexual attachment to the hero on the part of the author, which is attributed to the fictional mother. "In Memory of R.G." is in effect a thinly veiled fictionalization of Whittaker's admiration and envy of his brother Richard, culminating in a psychological murder. In its function as an elegy, it represents a mourning process in advance, expiation for the crime Whittaker unconsciously wanted to commit.

The story was written when Richard was presumably away at college, away from home for the first time, in September 1924, at the time Whittaker had himself returned to Columbia in accordance with his mother's wish to have a "graduated child." Neither Laha nor Columbia could satisfy his deep craving for maternal love and understanding—the image of the admired, envied Richard (Robert) always stood between his mother and himself.

By Christmas of that year Richard—if he had indeed ever been the "uncomplicated boy" Chambers describes—was apparently suddenly as complex as Whittaker and in at least as much trouble.

From college, he wrote my mother regularly. He had not been there long when she told me that she was worried about him. He had failed to make a fraternity which his close friend and roommate had made. My mother thought that this had hurt and shocked him in some very deep way. I laughed. It seemed to me incredible that anybody should be upset about a fraternity. . . .

To my surprise, for we never corresponded, I received a letter from him. He was not at the college. He had taken to the road and had got as far as Buffalo. He was rather pleased with himself and his adventures on the way. With a pang, I grasped that he felt that we had much in common. . . .

When my brother got home for the Christmas holidays, I came in one night to find him sitting in the kitchen with my mother—an almost unrecognizably white-faced, taut-lipped boy, arguing desperately, but, with the natural courtesy that almost never failed him, that life is worthless and meaningless, that to be intelligent is to know this and to have courage to end it. His appearance and a few minutes of conversation was enough to tell me that this was not a schoolboy pose, that this crisis was real and terrifying. My mother was frantic. As soon as she could get me alone, she said: "You must talk to him and find out what is wrong. You're the only one who can." . . .

I took him for a long walk. . . . I said: "The Communists have found a way out."

He simply laughed at me. . . ."They're just like the others, only they have invented a new way. There is only one decent way."

In my desperation, I heard myself saying a surprising thing. I said: "The kingdom of God is within you." The phrase came back from my own struggle.

A thorough investigation of Richard's life and personal problems could not be made beyond the establishment of certain facts; the documentary sources about him were too meager. But whatever emotional conflicts under- lay his tragic life, it is significant that Chambers describes them in terms similar to his own life's difficulties. He partially acknowledges this: "The phrase came back from my own struggle." Though he pictures himself as sound, his struggle quelled, it is highly likely that his description of his brother is in fact a projection of his own continuing confusion, his cynicism, his hatreds.

Chambers seems to cross the boundary line between his psychic troubles and Richard's in another instance. He states that his brother left Colgate Uni- versity because "he had failed to make a fraternity which his close friend and roommate had made"; that the shame and disappointment of not being taken into the fraternity disturbed Richard so deeply that he ran away from school, went on a hitchhiking trip, and did not return home for several weeks.

Curious about this, I wrote to the registrar of Colgate University, asking for dates and details of Richard Godfrey Chambers' matriculation and college activities and for specific information about the fraternity incident. The regis- trar wrote back: "I can find no record in our files of Richard Godfrey Cham- bers having enrolled at Colgate University." In the light of this revelation it becomes necessary to reappraise Chambers' entire story about his brother. It is not unlikely that Richard may have attended some other college, but I have been unable to determine which one.[4]

What is most striking, of course, is that Chambers seems to have a vivid memory of the supposed circumstances of his brother's leaving school but is mistaken about the name of the college, a highly improbable confusion of memory. One quite plausible reading of the fraternity-rejection story is as a fictionalized projection onto his brother of Whittaker's own dilemma, a cover for his own life failure to be accepted into the fraternity of childhood, that is, his own family. Richard's "friend and roommate" might represent Laha's ac- ceptance of Richard and his own exclusion from the family. The hidden re-

[4] William J. Evert, Registrar, Colgate University, to the author, personal communication, January 11, 1962.

In his letter of March 8, 1925, to Van Doren, Chambers wrote, "My brother has definitely renounced college, God be praised, and is home again." (Cf. p. 127.)

versal in Chambers' account of the incident then might be paraphrased: "It is not I in my family who failed fraternally at Columbia College and was cast out by both; it was my unfortunate brother." We, of course, cannot hope to know the whole truth about the Colgate story—any more than one can about any past event involving the deep emotions of people; we are analyzing not an event but a memory, a story. Chambers relates that his brother, in despair, exclaimed:

"Look at marriage. Look at Mother and Jay. What fraud! Look at the family. Look at ours! And children! It's a crime to have children."

The cry, identical with many Whittaker himself has made on other occasions, could also have come from him. Although the two sons may have had polar oppositions in their personalities, they derived from the commonality of their deprivations. But what strikes us, on a close reading, is Chambers' habit of insuring his own position in the reader's mind at the subtle expense of his brother. Chambers recounts trying to help Richard, who would not listen. He explains that Richard simply hated the world, while he, though he shared the hatred, was trying to face it with "mind and will." Then he blames himself for not coming to Richard's aid successfully:

I saw that the one person on whom he had counted for understanding was failing him. We were back in that morning of our childhood when he had stood on the porch in the soft rain, calling me, and I did not go. . . .
By the time his vacation was over, he had withdrawn from me, and I, feeling the baffled hopelessness of helping him, had withdrawn from him. He went back to college, not gaily this time.

The effect is to make the sympathetic reader feel that Chambers, ever sensitive, is being too hard on himself. But I do not think it too cynical to say that this effect was precisely the passage's intent. If we accept the hypothesis that Richard's death was Whittaker's unconscious wish, and that these memories are a prelude to that very event, it is evident that Chambers is reconstructing this period in a way that cloaks him in piety. In portraying his brother as beyond help, then solemnly blaming himself for not helping him, Chambers exonerates himself from the deepest implications of this relationship.

Richard's disturbance deepened. Chambers reports that he left college —at about the same time that Whittaker himself left to join the Communist Party. Richard had no such outlet. He struggled to stave off his increasing despondency by busying himself about the house, doing carpentry and general construction work. He repaired and remodeled some of the rooms. He was trying desperately to "put his house in order," a symbolized, reparative effort to reconstruct his disrupted empty self into something physically whole. He hoped both to win favor with the family and to give himself a sense of purpose. Besides the repairs, he built a small house of his own, a workshop with living space, behind the main house. But this activity did not restore him; his crisis, and the family's, worsened.

One day my mother said to me: "Your brother is drinking." I said: "I don't think so." "I know," she said. She told me that he had been drinking for some time, that now it was becoming a habit. She knew how and where he spent his nights, the names of his friends, and that girls were involved. She knew the details of his most intimate life. I was horrified that she should have to hear such things and shocked that he should dream of telling them to her. I saw that he was a man in his actions, but a child in his relations with his mother.

"You must go with him," she said, "and watch over him. I do not know what he is going to do next. But I am afraid that he is going to try to kill himself." She wept. "What have I done that was so wrong?" she said. "Oh, God, what have I done? I only tried to love you both."

Whittaker and Richard apparently began to see more of each other than had been their custom. In *Witness,* Chambers says that he began coming home right after work and that his brother would meet the train. Often they made the rounds of local speakeasies with Richard's friends. These outings were uneasy mixtures of conviviality and hostility, mirroring the continuing ambivalence of Whittaker's feelings toward Richard. Chambers is quick to point out that "My brother was delighted to have me," though his behavior was not congenial to Richard's friends, as is evident from this incident.

One night, when the wine was having its effect, my brother and his friends began to sing songs in turn—chiefly the song of the year: "If You Knew Susie, Like I Knew Susie." When my turn came, I sang the first verse of the "Internationale":

> Arise, ye prisoners of starvation,
> Arise, ye wretched of the earth,
> For justice thunders condemnation,
> A better world's in birth.

[A Rumanian Bolshevik came over to Whittaker and "grasped" his hand.]
Thereafter, while my brother and his friends laughed and canvassed their sexual exploits at their table, I would sit discussing world politics with the Rumanian and the Greeks, who also spoke French and most of whom were sympathetic to Communism.

Chambers, ill at ease in the presence of those who talked about their sexual conquests, fled from this subject to the world of politics, where he exhibited his knowledge of foreign languages and ideologies. Note also his envy of his brother's popularity and friendliness.

On one occasion there was open violence:

When my brother drank the poisonous Prohibition whiskey, he inclined to be fighty. Once standing at the bar in East Rockaway, he began to tell me, for everyone to hear, what he thought about our family. He shouted that our mother and father had ruined their own lives and both of ours, and then dismissed them with a foul expression. I picked up a tumbler of whiskey and threw it in his face. It was an involuntary action. He sprang at me and we fought. . . .

The bad blood seethed between us for the rest of the night. . . . [Later, at a gas station] My brother baited me and again shouted his filthy remark. Again, we grappled and this time crashed to the concrete floor, he underneath. As I tried to extricate myself, he reached up, and, taking careful aim, struck me in the face with the stone set in his ring. The little scar on the bridge of my nose is one of the things he left me to carry permanently through the rest of my life.

Among the other things Richard left Whittaker was, of course, a set of deep and unresolved emotional conflicts. Chambers' hatred shows through even in reminiscence, with its careful assurance that his own action was "involuntary," coupled with the spiteful note that Richard was underneath as they fell to the ground. The subject of the argument is the cause of their life's difficulty, their parents, and Richard's insult infuriates Whittaker because it expresses a truth that he cannot bear, their aggressive feelings toward Laha and Jay. It infuriates him all the more because it comes from Richard, who has (in Whittaker's mind) the maternal love that he craves. Thus Richard seems to be spurning what Whittaker most wants, an unbearable insult, not to Laha and Jay, but to Whittaker.

The passage, however, leaves Whittaker once again in a posture of ostensible humility. He says that he felt he could do his brother no good and, "I began to go my own ways again." The declaration directly precedes an account of Richard's first attempt at suicide and has the effect of dissociating Whittaker from the event in the mind of the reader.

Whittaker was, in point of psychological fact, as inextricably connected with the suicide as if he had been partner to a death pact—which, in some sense, he was. He reports Richard's proposal of a double suicide.

One day I came in and found him lying on the old couch where we had suffered the toothaches of our childhood. His eyes were open and he was staring at something ahead of him. His face was pinched and white. After a while, he raised his arm and pointed to the old print that still hung at the end of the couch: *Il Conforto—Death, The Comforter.*

Then he asked slowly without looking at me: "If I kill myself, will you kill yourself with me?"

I said: "No."

"Why not?" he asked.

"You are not going to kill yourself," I said.

He laughed meanly. "You're a coward, Bro," he said.

This scene was written twenty-six years after his brother's suicide. The possibilities for distortion in Chambers' reporting are obvious. We cannot assume that the dialogue is accurately remembered; we cannot even assume that the conversation actually took place. As it stands, Richard's invitation to Whittaker to join him in death is a disguised invitation to join him in a love pact. In lieu of Laha, Richard has made of his older brother a substitute mother. The wish for a double suicide pact was his disturbed way of testing whether his brother really loved him. Chambers' dialogue seems to imply a challenge on Richard's part, to which Whittaker said "No." And when Richard then asked, "Why not?" Chambers replied, "You are not going to kill yourself," a remark that may well have egged Richard on and had the effect of a dare. Whittaker of course knew that Richard's self-esteem was already badly shaken, that he could not tolerate the idea of appearing as a coward in the eyes of his older brother. This seems evident from Richard's reaction and reply to his brother's refusal: "He laughed meanly and said, *"You*'re [emphasis added] a coward, Bro" [not me!]. I submit that Whittaker may well have seized this opportunity and used this device to nudge his brother closer to death. But, to repeat, the scene may not have happened as it was rendered. The "mean laughter" may be just a novelistic touch—or, indeed, it may have belonged not to Richard but to Whittaker. It is not inconceivable, in view of Whittaker's intense ambivalence, that he may have reversed this conversation: that he could himself have proposed the pact and chided "You're a coward." What actually happened is of great interest but not of great importance: the fact is that in subsequent events Whittaker behaved as if he had helped Richard toward his death.

Richard made two attempts at suicide before he succeeded. On both these occasions Chambers portrays himself as his brother's rescuer.

Late one night I came home and, as I opened the door, the smell of gas struck me. I rushed into the kitchen. All the jets and the oven were turned on in the gas stove. The room was filled with gas. My brother was slumped across a chair. I picked him up and dragged and carried him into another room. I worked his arms across his chest and slapped his cheeks. Very quickly he revived. He sat up. Presently, I made black coffee and gave him some.

"Why did you stop me?" he asked in a voice so pitiful that I wondered if I had not, in fact, committed a sin. Then, as he sipped his coffee, he said: "You're a bastard, Bro. You stopped me this time, but I'll do it yet."

My father had watched all this helplessly. But one night I heard a shout in the kitchen. I hurried down to find my father and brother fighting furiously. My brother was drunk and could not see what he was doing. My father was blind with rage and no longer knew what he was doing. He was pummeling my brother's face which was streaming with blood. My mother was screaming: "He'll kill him!"

I tried to pry my father off and failed. At that, the ulcer of years of anger

8

burst within me—as if my father had not done his part to make my brother what he was. I struck at my father. My brother slid to the floor and lay there prone. Above him, my father and I wrestled and fought. Finally, I flung him against a cabinet. The ferocious strength drained out of him. His face was ashen and twitching. He was an old man, fighting for breath and panting: "He—has been taking girls—into that little house—at night. Your mother—I won't stand for it."

I walked over to my father and put my arms around him. We wept.

Richard's display of sexual activity was a threat to his brother and to his father, and Whittaker's allegiance suddenly shifted from Richard to Jay. He commiserates with his father and finds him in alliance with him against Richard's exhibited sexual potency.

After this encounter with his father Richard sank into a deep depression. His suddenly released anger and hatred quickly subverted into a mute self-reproach. Whittaker, despite his awareness of his brother's remorse and agony, apparently did nothing to arrest its advancing morbidity. His unconscious wish for Richard's death is subtly revealed by a premonition:

One cold night, with the snow lying hard on the ground, I reached home about midnight. Before I went to bed, some instinct, some prescience, something, made me decide to look in the little house in the yard. I had never done so before.

When I opened the door, gas rushed out at me. My brother was lying on the couch. His hands were cold. I dragged him frantically into the yard. I could scarcely manage his dead weight, his heels hit the snow lifelessly as I lugged him into the big house. His face was rigid, and from the fixed, open mouth came the smell of gas and alcohol. He was almost gone but his heart was still beating.

I laid him on the floor, and endlessly raised and lowered his arms as we do to resuscitate a drowning person. I must have worked over him half an hour. Slowly, life came back. It came in a hideous form. He did not regain normal consciousness. Instead, he pulled himself up on all fours and began to drag himself across the floor. He would hook his leg around a chair or table leg, and his muscles were set in such an iron clamp that it took all my strength simply to pry him loose. Then he would drag himself around again and bark like a coyote—a thin, inhuman yelp repeated four or five times. That kept up all night.

When my mother came down in the morning, I went to bed.

Twice Richard tried to destroy himself. He was frankly psychotic. Still no member of his family grasped the clinical severity of his predicament or sought a doctor's help for him. Emotional storms and crises had long since become commonplace, everyday occurrences in the Chambers household; constant worry and an atmosphere charged with strife and disaffection provided an outflow for unbearable inner conflicts. In this setting of drama and daily suffering the recurrent cycle of guilt and futile expiation played on, producing a life pattern in which all members of the family lived at a pitch of tragic excitement. Laha could not assess the gravity of Richard's break or perceive the danger he was in. Alarmed and anguished, she was as insensitive to the meaning of his suicidal attempts as she had been in her lifelong abetment of his emotional conflicts. Whittaker's actions, like his literary descriptions, are outwardly remedial and full of pity. But his ambivalence about Richard's death comes through in his account of the tragic drama—while he portrays himself saving Richard's life, he spares us none of the hideous details of the near-death; we see Richard yelping "like a coyote."

After Richard's recovery from the almost lethal effects of the gas inhalation, he was left to his own devices. Desperate and searching, he again left home. Within the next few weeks he married a girl from the neighborhood whom he had recently met. Richard knew that Laha would certainly disapprove. This was a vengeful act directed against his entire family, but especially aimed at Laha and her social aspirations. A marriage ceremony was performed in a nearby village in the company of a few of Richard's tavern companions. No family members were present. Dorothy, his bride, was a young girl from "the other side of the tracks." Her reputation in the village of Rockville Centre was not good. After a few months together at one of the ocean beaches they separated, and Dorothy went back to her parents. Richard remained alone in their small makeshift apartment on "one of the Long Island inlets." He was working as a surveyor's helper and drinking heavily. Despondent and repentant, Richard occasionally returned home, hoping for compassion and consolation. But he could not communicate his anguish to Laha. She observed his distress, and if she felt his agony, she was incapable of consoling him.

Richard's despondency forced him again to self-destruction. Chambers reconstructs the tragedy:

One night, my brother drove to the station in Lynbrook with a friend from whom I learned the details that follow. They waited for the train I usually came home on. I was not on it. I had stayed in New York, chatting with a Communist college friend. They waited for another train and another. I was not on them. I had failed my brother for the last time.

My brother and his friend drove to a pier from which they could see across a tidal inlet to the lights of the beach where his wife was staying. He sat there for an hour or more, saying nothing, smoking cigarettes and staring across the black water. Then he drove his friend home and went to his own apartment where he now lived alone.

In the morning, I was awakened by the telephone ringing. I heard my mother hurry to answer it. . . . One single, terrible scream swelled through the house. . . .

We drove to the next village and climbed the stairs to the little apartment. The kitchen was crowded with police and people I had never seen before. My brother was lying with his head in the gas oven, his body partly supported by the open door. He had made himself as comfortable as he could. There was a pillow in the oven under his head. His feet were resting on a pile of books set on a kitchen chair. One of his arms hung down rigid. Just below the finger, on the floor, stood an empty quart whiskey bottle.

I picked it up and put it out of sight. "Put that back. Don't touch anything," an officer snapped at me.[5] I pointed to my mother who was sobbing, with her face buried in my brother's chest. Nobody put back the empty bottle.

The last paragraph deserves a brief comment. Laha clings to the body of her dead son. In her grief she feels her loss but remains unaware of her life role in Richard's death. Whittaker's outwardly pious gesture, putting the empty whisky bottle out of sight, intended as a sign of respect to his now dead brother, and as a balm to his mother's feelings, is an evidence of his disingenuousness. In this mixed caricature of kindness and rebellion, his perverted sense of sincerity and his childlike defiance of authority come to the fore.

The hard fact was that Richard was now dead and Whittaker had survived him. The dilemma of Chambers' life now revolved about a suddenly changed reality situation. He found himself with a new set of guilt feelings. He admits to a certain guilt for not preventing the suicide—"I had let my brother down for the last time." But here, as earlier, he is demanding the reader's sympathy by confessing to a nonexistent crime: surely no one can blame him for missing his train. By confessing to a lesser crime, however, he acquits himself of a psychologically greater one. Now caught forever in the coils of this irreversible piece of reality, like Raskolnikov in *Crime and Punishment,* Whittaker's life darkened into a protracted struggle against the fear of death. He was harassed, thereafter, with an intractable persecution complex. Let us keep in mind that Whittaker's early childhood identification with the life of Dostoevski and his fictional characters was an all-absorbing one. Like Raskolnikov, who shrank before the murder because the fatal act was destined to transform his person into his idea, so Chambers struggled with his unresolved guilt and feared destruction by a concealed enemy.[6]

[5] On the police blotter at the Town Hall, Rockville Centre, Sept. 9, 1926, there is registered the death of Richard Godfrey Chambers, aged twenty-two, 52 Randall Avenue, Rockville Centre. "Death caused by inhalation of illuminating gas, self-administered. He was lying on two chairs, face upward with his head resting on a pillow in the oven of a small gas range in the kitchen."

[6] Chambers told newspaperman Oliver Pilat, during the course of the Hiss trials: "Just now I am rereading Dostoevski's *The Possessed.* I've read it six or seven times before." He further stated: "When I get clear of the Hiss tangle, I would like to do a book on Dostoevski." (Pilat, *op. cit.*)

Chambers lived and wrote as if he were Dostoevski. *Witness* is dramatically conceived and written like a novel. In it his life is depicted as a battleground for the forces of Good and Evil. In introducing himself to the reader, Chambers says: "I am leading you, not through cool pine woods but up and up a narrow defile between bare and steep rocks from which in shadow things uncoil and slither away. It will be dark."

Following Richard's suicide, Whittaker fell into a strangely morbid state. He was unable to move physically and experienced what he termed a "paralysis of the will." He was preoccupied with thoughts about death. He wrote about suicide, philosophized in a pessimistic way about the meaning of Life, Death, and God. He wrote several atheistic poems. The most distressing emotions, however, appeared to be neutralized once they were transformed into a poem or story. He wrote out and acted out his feelings in lieu of suffering. His description of his graveyard visits and the poems he composed while leaning on his brother's tombstone contain ingredients of the actor, poet, and poseur.

After his brother's suicide he struggled with a protracted death wish against himself, putting himself through a tortured graveyard identification with his dead brother. He atoned for his brother's death by bringing himself as close to being dead as he could. Hence the prolonged physical and spiritual immobility. The visits to his brother's grave ("every day and night for a month"), climaxed by the poem he composed in his memory, were, in effect, bribes to pay off the demands of his guilty conscience.

Only when my brother was dead did I know how much I loved him.[7] Death had never really touched me before. I had to fight an all-pervading listlessness of the will. I would lie for hours and watch the leaves, heaving gently in the wind. To do anything else, seemed in the face of death, gross and revolting, seemed a betrayal of my brother because any activity implied that life had meaning. . . .

I forced myself to go to work every evening. I sometimes forced myself to go on long rambles during the day. On one of them I composed that dirge that later appeared in *Poetry* magazine, and which was read in court by the Hiss defense to prove something about me that I never quite understood. Its first verse went:

> The moving masses of clouds, and the standing
> Freights on the siding in the sun, alike induce in us
> That despair, which, we, brother, know there is no
> withstanding.

Every day, before going to work, I walked to the graveyard, sometimes with my mother. Every night, when I came back from work, I went to the graveyard alone. I went in rain and snow. I never missed a night.

The thought that tortured me was whether my brother had not been right in that repeated insight: "We are hopeless. We are gentle people. We are too gentle to face the world." My instinct told me that he was right. I thought that he had acted quickly and bravely to destroy his life before the world could destroy it. *But I questioned whether I was not wrong to have let him make the lonely journey alone. That was the question I was seeking an answer to.*

One night, after returning from the graveyard, I went to look inside the little house, where I had once narrowly saved my brother. There I made my decision:

[7] Italics in this passage are the author's.

"No, I will live. There is something in me, there is some purpose in my life which I feel but do not understand. I must go on living until it is fulfilled." I added to myself: "I shall be sorry that I did not go with my brother."

In *Witness,* Chambers gives only the first few lines of the poem. Twenty-three years later, during the Hiss trials, he professed his inability to recognize why the Hiss defense made a point of reading the poem in court and stated that "it was to prove something about me that I never quite understood." Chambers' poem was published in *Poetry* five years after his brother's death. A perusal of the complete poem reveals Chambers' conflict in clear perspective, his apology to his brother for his "lack of love," his exaltation of the meaning of death, and his feeling that he is marking time until the day he will take the same journey.

"OCTOBER 21, 1926" [8]

The moving masses of clouds, and the standing
Freights on the siding in the sun, alike induce in
    us
That despair, which we, brother, know there is no
    withstanding.

Nothing but the moving masses of clouds has any
    meaning
For this tortured world now; or only motionlessness
    as of the cars,
In beings of substances, remains undermeaning.

Only the momentum of the motion of masses,
Being of substance, has any meaning—or their
    cessation
Upon the perfect turn of the experience motion
    amasses.

We see all about us how, in creation,
Flowers from the dark gathering in their roots,
    with one motion,
Thrust themselves perfect, O God, perfect from
    increation.

As you know, brother, it is the same with cessation;
You know how perfect must be the ways of anything
Designing its return to cessation.

You know it is the cessation of the motion in me
    I am waiting:

[8] *Poetry,* February 1931 (Vol. 37, No. 5, p. 258). The title is presumably the date of composition.

> And not lack of love, or love of the sun's generation,
>   and the motion
> Of bodies, or their status, that keeps me—but my
>   perfection for death I am waiting.

Chambers poetically addresses an appeal to his dead brother—bent on convincing him (and himself) of his love and grief, as shown by his incapacity and his willingness to wait for the perfection of death. But in the end his love of self and his decision to go on living prevail. Yet, as we shall see from his subsequent behavior and some uniquely recurring reversals of significant dates, he lived, in a sense, as if he were his brother.

Twenty-three years later, at the Hiss trials, Chambers, in reply to a question during cross-examination by Hiss's counsel, accepted without correction a significant error concerning the date of his brother's death—so significant, that the failure to catch or correct the error calls for an explanation other than mere carelessness, for it was a date fixed in his mind and one that he used on many occasions, both in fact and in fantasy:

Q. Then your brother committed suicide on September 26?
A. That is right, Sir.
Q. 1926?
A. Yes, Sir.
Q. And then you became a fanatical Communist?
A. That is right, Sir.
Q. How long did you remain a fanatical Communist?
A. Until some time in 1937.[9]

September 26 was not the date of his brother's death—it was the date of his brother's birth; Richard died on September 9 (1926). The above error was not an isolated slip. It occurred with remarkable frequency and in varying forms. I shall point up a number of others later on, as they appeared in his sworn testimony, his autobiography, and other documentary sources. Chambers' special manipulation of dates, names, and other symbols included among its many features a magical system of numerical alternates. From an examination into this area, it became evident that Chambers either invented or exchanged real and imagined events. Most striking was the discovery of his unconscious manipulation of birth and death dates. For example, by substituting a birth date for a death date (or vice versa) he restored to life whomever he had earlier destroyed in fantasy. Thus he practiced the magical art of doing and undoing, warded off feelings of guilt, invoked new ideas for the future, or finessed disturbing ones from his past.

Chambers' testimony during the trials was characterized by a kind of al-

[9] Trial Transcript, p. 424. He would later change this date to 1938.

ternating memory for certain events. At times he exhibited gross lapses, at other times he had a remarkable vividness and fullness of recall. Chambers' testimony is full of such cryptic errors:

Q. How long did you live in Philadelphia?
A. I think my parents left Philadelphia shortly after I was born and went to New York.

Here Chambers eliminated an entire period of his brother's childhood existence, including date, place, and fact of his brother's birth. It will be recalled that the Chamberses did not move from Philadelphia until after Richard was born, which would be almost three years after Vivian's birth. It was in relation to his brother's death that Chambers' memory was consistently inaccurate.

On November 4, 1948, in the Baltimore pre-trial deposition (Hiss libel suit), Chambers testified under oath that his brother committed suicide in 1925: it was in 1926. He also recollected Richard's age to have been "about twenty-one or thereabouts" when he died: he was twenty-two, almost twenty-three. In the second Hiss trial Chambers erred again on this same fact. This time he testified that Richard had died on September 19, 1926. Whether Chambers knew it or not (and it is likely that he did), September 19, 1926, was the birth date of Alger Hiss's stepson, Timothy Hobson (an easy "slip" away from September 9, 1926, the actual date of Richard's death). He erred also in remembering the year his father died. He said it was in 1927: it was in 1929.

The serious defect in Chambers' functioning was the fundamental disturbance in his sense of self and in his relations with others. His intolerable image of himself kept alive an envy of those who in mind or body re-evoked the image of his brother. And Chambers' unconscious need was such that he was compelled to replace such figures by destroying them.

Richard's suicide was, in point of fact, a solitary, self-executed act, an event anticipated and consummated by his own mind and hand. Nevertheless, it must also be regarded as representing one half of a double suicide pact in which the inducements and seductions of Whittaker's motives and magical fantasies played their role. Richard's twice rehearsed and hardly surprising suicide brought closer to fruition Whittaker's central wish, one that was destined to alter the course of his life.[10] Though he erased the date of Richard's death from his mind, the underlying shadow of that day could not be lightened. It was the most calamitous event in Whittaker Chambers' life. It

[10] Chambers testified: "My brother's suicide set the seal on my being a Communist. I was a Communist before, but I became a fanatical Communist afterwards." (Trial Transcript, p. 424.)

deprived him of his alter-ego, a piece of reality he most needed. As long as Richard was alive Whittaker could be his mentor and protector and, at the same time, harbor death wishes against him. Following Richard's death, he had to seek out another brother figure as an object for his love/hate.

Richard's suicide was, in effect, like a theft (stealing someone else's life), which haunted him for the rest of his life. The fateful date has remained forever repressed in his mind. At no time, to my knowledge, did Chambers in any context ever mention or recall it, either in his testimony or autobiography. September 9, 1926, may be used as a symbolic key to Chambers' central fantasy system. Within the private world of his magical system Chambers used vital statistics and personal documents of others to establish a new identity for himself. In Chambers' self-created world he interchanged magical thoughts with rational, deliberately planned schemes. A vital statistic (name, place, or date) served as a "piece of hard reality" around which Chambers wove fantasies of birth, death, life, and rebirth. His hated self-image and infantile guilt about the crime of his birth, subsequently transferred to the crime of his brother's death, moved him throughout life from one identity crisis to another. To ward off his anxiety he acted out by changing the "cards of identity." He became adept at falsifying personal or identifying documents, such as birth and death certificates, passports, applications for government employment, life insurance, and so forth.[11] His ostensible purpose (and conscious excuse) for using false documents was, of course, that they were, he claimed, part of his duties as a Communist courier and spy. But he engaged in similar activity many years before he joined the party—and, as we shall see, after his break from the party.

It would appear that Chambers joined the Communist Party at the age of twenty-four not to save the world but to save himself. It provided him with an appropriate milieu, a forum in which he could act out his private fantasies. His main obsession in life centered in the idea of establishing an existence. His concern did not originate as a real threat from external reality (as, for example, his fear of the Soviet Secret Police), but was primarily a fear of loss of sense of self, a manifestation of his identity problem from early childhood. As a defense against his sense of guilt about the death of his brother, he was in constant flight, a fugitive from himself. He felt pursued, hid from secret police, was constantly harassed by what he was convinced was a "concealed enemy." Such a harried existence was for him *less* anxiety-producing than introspectively confronting his fratricidal guilt. These are the paradoxical and costly economics of mental illness.

[11] For examples of these and other records mentioned in the chapter, see illustrations on pp. 327–29.

Chambers had, in early childhood, already sold short the meager rewards of his true identity in favor of his omnipotence in his fantasy world. He indulged in many overtly unnecessary falsifications of reality in situations where no obvious motive or immediate gain could be discerned. For example, on his New York Public Library employment record he gave the date of his birth as April 1, *1900,* instead of April 1, *1901,* thereby making himself into someone born a year earlier. When asked about his brother's age, he stated that Richard was "three and a half" years younger than himself, when actually his brother was two and a half years younger.

Q. You mentioned a brother of yours. What was his name?
A. Richard Godfrey Chambers.
Q. When was he born?
A. He was born September 26, 1903.
Q. Haven't you missed that year?
A. Perhaps I have.
Q. You were born on April 1, 1901?
A. That is right.
Q. And he was three and a half years younger than you, wasn't he?
A. Then it was 1904.
Q. 1904?
A. Yes. [It was, of course, 1903.]
Q. Did he commit suicide?
MURPHY: I object to that, your Honor. There seems to be no relevance to this case at all. What difference does it make whether his brother did or did not commit suicide? What difference does it make whether my brother committed suicide? It makes no difference. I press the objection.
CROSS: Well, I submit that this is foundation psychiatric testimony and only has a bearing on that.
MURPHY: I press the objection.
THE COURT: It is allowed, but it seems remote.
A. He did.
Q. Before he did did he ask you to enter into a suicide pact with him?
A. He did.
Q. Before his death what was your relationship with your brother?
A. Until the period when my brother began to contemplate suicide our relationship had not been very close. He was at school and I was active in the Communist Party and otherwise; but in the period before his death I was set to watch him by my mother and to try to prevent him from such an action, and we became closer.
Q. After his death what effect did it have on you?
A. It had an almost paralyzing effect on me.
Q. And you for two or three months could not even move your limbs, is that correct?
A. I could move my limbs but I had no desire to do anything.
Q. Did you stop working during that time?

A. I don't know whether I stopped working or not. I should have liked to.[12]

Chambers was then working at the night desk at the New York Public Library. The transcript of his work record does not show him to have been absent from his job during this period. He did resign from his job on July 15, 1925, and was reappointed on January 1, 1926. Chambers' recollection of dates and the description of his activities during this, as well as other periods of his life, is emotionally rather than factually determined. His statements are replete with the chronological inaccuracies which are symbolically meaningful in terms of his identity struggle and his unconscious death wishes against his brother and father.

Chambers' brother died on September 9, 1926; his father, three years and seven weeks later (October 29, 1929).[13] In his autobiographical account of these two events, Chambers deals with them in such a proximate way that it seems as if he fused the memory of these two separate events, temporally as well as emotionally, into a single experience. It is striking how he brings together the death of his father with the death of his brother. This is one example of his manipulation of the time factor, a novelistic device used so masterfully by Dostoevski, in which the chronology of an event is displaced so as to heighten its emotional impact and dramatic effect:

Not long after my brother's death, I was living in a cottage on one of the Long Island tidal inlets. I was living with a Communist girl in what was called a "party marriage"—the kind of union that the Communist Party sanctioned and, in fact, favored. My mother knew where I was living, but, of course, never visited us.

It would appear from the above that he took over his brother's way of life. Richard, too, not long before he died, had taken his wife to live in an apartment on one of the Long Island inlets.[14]

One morning, she drove up to my house, breathless and distraught. "Your father is dead," she said. "You will have to come and move his body." He had dropped dead in the bathroom as he prepared to shave.

My father lay huddled in his bathrobe on the sea-blue tiles my brother had laid. His body was still warm. Of the bodies I had lifted in the last years, his was the most inert. I could move him only inch by inch. My mother had to help me raise him to his bed.

Later, the undertakers carried my father downstairs. Without my knowledge, they began the preliminary stages of embalming, in our living room. Unsuspectingly, I walked into the room. My father lay naked on a stretcher. One of his arms was dangling. From this arm, near the shoulder, his blood, the blood that had

[12] Trial Transcript, pp. 422–23. Murphy was attorney for the prosecution; Cross, for the defense.
[13] Asked by counsel in November 1948 (the Baltimore Deposition) when his father had died, Chambers replied, "He died, I believe, in the year 1927."
[14] Cf. p. 92.

A Verified Transcript from the Register of Deaths

Date of Death September 9, 1926 Registered No. 81

Name of Deceased   Richard Godfrey Chambers

Age 22   Years   Months   Days

Single, Married, Widowed or Divorced   Married

Race or Color if other than White

Occupation   Surveyor's Helper

Birthplace   Philadelphia, Pa.

(Length of Stay in this place)

Father's Name Jay Chambers

Mother's Name   Laha Whittaker

Place of Death 52 Randall Ave., Rockville Centre, N.Y.

Cause of } Chief Causes Gas poisoning from inhaling
Death   }   gas (illuminating) from a gas
         } Other Causes range. - Suicide.

Medical Attendant, or other Attestant Edward T. Neu, Justice
                                                    of Peace
Place of Burial Rockville Cemetary, Lynbrook, N.Y.

Undertaker William B. T. Ronald, Lynbrook, N. Y.

I hereby Solemnly Attest, That this is a true transcript from the public Register of Deaths, as kept in the Village of Rockville Centre, County of Nassau, State of New York.

Dated at Rockville Centre, N. Y., the   5th

day of   January   19 62 .

(Signed) *Edith L. Catal*

Registrar Vital Statistics.

Transcript of Richard Godfrey Chambers' death certificate.

given my brother and me life, was pouring, in a thin, dark arc into a battered mop bucket.

We buried my father beside my brother.[15]

This confluence of memory of the two deaths in his family shows their unified meaning. Patricidal and fratricidal fantasies are, in effect, dealt with collectively.

He then goes on to describe his need to replace the family line with "new growth."

Our line seemed to be at an end. Our family was like a burnt-over woods, which nothing can revive and only new growth can replace. The promise of new growth lay wholly within me—in my having children. No need was so strong in me as the need to have children. But by then I agreed with my brother that to repeat the misery of such lives as ours would be a crime against life.

Chambers' loss of strength and inability to move his father's corpse are a resurgence of the same pathological identification with his dead father that he experienced when his brother died. By fusing the memory of their deaths into a single experience he "buries them together," mentally as well as physically. After the denigrating description of the embalming he concludes his chapter, "The Story of a Middle-Class Family," by absolving himself with a compassionate flashback about his father.

My relations with my father softened after my brother's death. . . . We took to meeting in New York for lunch or supper. Then we would ramble aimlessly around the insensible city. We were still almost as silent with each other as in the past, but now my need for silence had become almost as great as my father's.

This novelistic device gives the reader the almost eerie feeling that his father has been resurrected. After invoking this last tribute to his father, he returns to invoke his final memorial for his dead brother. It was a poem composed while leaning against his brother's gravestone "a little before midnight" on the New Year's Eve following his brother's death.

---

[15] During the Hiss trials Chambers testified that his father died of a "heart attack." He repeated this diagnosis through the years, whenever he had to record or testify to such information. The direct cause of Jay Chambers' death, as officially recorded on his death certificate, is "chronic hepatitis," more commonly known as cirrhosis of the liver, frequently found in chronic alcoholics. He had been ill and under the care of his family physician, Dr. S. J. Bradbury. The interval between the onset of his illness and death was recorded as "9 months," from January 8, 1929, to October 27, 1929. Jay Chambers was well known among his artistic cronies as a free and steady drinker.

Whittaker has stressed the fact that after he joined the Communist Party he "never drank." Yet from his own accounts and many sources, it is known that, on occasion, he drank to excess. But he has remained sensitive about revealing his own drinking, his father's, and his brother's. In answer to a form question on his application for insurance in 1944: "To what extent do you use alcoholic beverages?" Cambers wrote "very rarely." And in answer to age of brother at time of death: "24"; he was twenty-two.

It was a very silent night. A wet snow was falling. The raw earth over my brother's grave had begun to settle. A pool of rain and thaw water had collected. A sheet of ice covered it. As I stood looking at it, the year ended.

The poem was "one of the last few . . . that I would ever write." [16] It was the cry, Chambers wrote, with which he overcame the spiritual exhaustion of his long struggle to keep his brother alive. In it, he holds the world (instead of himself) responsible for having taken his brother's life. In words and action he puts himself through a ritualistic death ("Fall on me, snow,/Cover me up;") and consummates his own mystical reunion with his brother.

It is not surprising to learn that shortly after Richard's death Chambers visited several spiritualists and through their medium tried to commune with the spirit of his dead brother. This was told to me by Joseph Freeman, author and former editor of the *New Masses*.[17] Freeman, a friend of Chambers during the twenties and early thirties, described a revelatory incident. It was sometime during 1927, about a year after Richard's death. Chambers and Freeman had been out drinking and talking together one evening at a public bar. During their conversation Chambers decided that he and Freeman ought to be "blood brothers." Whereupon he arose from his chair, took out a pocket knife, opened the blade, and wanted to cut Freeman's wrist in order to obtain some of his blood, which he intended to mix with his own after cutting his own wrist. Freeman drew away in alarm, and after some commotion the bartender came to Freeman's aid, disarmed Chambers, and asked them both to leave. At this point Chambers was quite drunk, and Freeman took him to his own home. Upon arrival, the hour now being quite late, Freeman's sister let them in. Noting that they were both quite drunk she did not restrain her feelings in telling them what a deplorable, disgusting state they were both in. Whereupon Chambers got down on his knees, burst into tears, and apologized abjectly.

All the accumulated bitterness of his life, his need for revenge against Laha and Jay, his guilt about Richard's death, were condensed and converted

[16]
> Blow, whistles, blow,
> Ring out, joyful bells,
> Shout and caper, happy people,
> You have killed him. . . .
> By this stone of death I lean against
> I hold myself upright for life, . . .
> Fall on me, snow,
> Cover me up;
> Cover the houses and the streets.
> Let me see only in the light of another year
> The roofs and the minds that killed him,
> And the earth that holds him,
> Forever dead.

[17] Interview, Joseph Freeman and the author, December 1963.

into becoming an "irreconcilable Communist." His purpose henceforth in life was to redeem his guilt for his brother's death by unconsciously destroying himself or blaming the existing order for that death. This moved him to suspect and then destroy substitute objects, in order that he might himself live. He "never went back" to the graveyard, for his conflict with his brother had now been effectively displaced and absorbed by his on-the-spot conversion into an "irreconcilable" Communist.

The act of joining the Communist Party and his subsequently alleged entry into the "underground," where he became a faceless man and gave up his true identity, had the significance of death, as did also the symptoms of the strange malady (his lethargy and immobility) which overwhelmed him when his brother and father died. Chambers' graveyard dirges may be viewed as magical re-creative acts, prayerful and poetic words invoked to protect himself from his conscience and from the retaliatory fear that his turn would be next. From our knowledge of his precocious readings in the life and writings of Dostoevski it is of more than passing interest to point up the remarkable parallel between Chambers' episodes of lethargy and immobility and the deathlike "absences" from which Dostoevski suffered. Freud's now classic description and notable interpretation of the psychic significance of these clinical states are directly to the point:

We know the meaning of the first attacks from which Dostoyevsky suffered in his early years, long before the incidence of the "epilepsy." These attacks had the significance of death: they were heralded by fear of death and consisted of lethargic, somnolent states. The illness first came over him while he was still a boy, in the form of a sudden, groundless melancholy, a feeling, as he later told his friend Soloviev, as though he were going to die on the spot. And there in fact followed a state exactly similar to real death.

We know the meaning and intention of such deathlike seizures. They signify an identification with a dead person, either with someone who is really dead, or with someone who is still alive and whom the subject wishes dead. The latter case is the more significant. The attack then has the value of a punishment. One has wished another person dead, and now one *is* this other person and is dead oneself.[18]

Chambers dealt with the persisting aftermath of fratricidal guilt in many ways. One way was to be ostensibly pious and charitable. Colleagues on the *Daily Worker,* where he presently found a job, observed that Chambers' demeanor changed. He assumed an air of piety, made a point of letting it be known that he was a very devout Communist. He liked to pose as a martyr and lover of mankind, a father figure who understood frailties. It was in this

[18] Sigmund Freud, "Dostoyevsky and Parricide" (1928), *Collected Papers* (London: The Hogarth Press, 1950), Vol. 5, p. 228.

fatherly role, which he liked to assume to persons in trouble, that Chambers invited an associate at the *Daily Worker,* A. B. Magil, who had just recovered from some acute illness, to rest for a few days at his Long Island home. This was some time in September 1931, about six months after Chambers' marriage to Esther Shemitz. Chambers' wife was away from home at the time. It was while Magil was a guest in Chambers' home that he met a young man there by the name of "Bub," a college student whom Chambers had "adopted" and about whom he had spoken on several occasions in the office. Bub was a freckle-faced, average-looking lad, not especially bright, and, Magil commented, "just what Chambers' interest in him was no one could make out." But Chambers had let it be known to most of his colleagues that after his brother's death he had a need to be charitable to some boy, and he was allegedly sending Bub through college. But no one had any idea how Chambers could possibly afford this.[19] Chambers makes no mention of Bub in *Witness* or elsewhere, and so his relationship with this young man of unknown identity can only be surmised.

And now Chambers turned his absolved self away from his personal conflict and directed his attention to the "sick and dying world." By a process of self-abnegation, Chambers translated himself out of one world and into another. His person gave way to his idea, and he became absorbed in the world of conflict. From now on he roamed in the unconscious externalization of his conflicts.

At this decisive and transitional juncture of his life, the boundaries maintaining his sense of self have given way, and, like gathering stormclouds, the delusional and paranoid symptoms are seen coming to the fore.

[19] For much information on this period, here and in the next chapter, I am indebted to Elinor Ferry (formerly Mrs. George Kirstein), who knew many of the early staff members on the *Daily Worker* and *New Masses* and who interviewed (around 1952–53) Walt Carmon, A. B. Magil, Sender Garlin, and Harry Freeman, former colleagues of Chambers.

6

The Mask of Tragedy

CHAMBERS joined the Communist Party in February 1925 and was assigned menial jobs, such as returning unsold copies of the *Daily Worker* to the office. After his brother's death in September 1926, he transferred to party activities the full force of his energies and emotions.

Professor Meyer Schapiro, who saw a good deal of Chambers during the twenties and thirties, appreciated Chambers' inner feelings as well as anyone I know. He warned me that if anyone hopes to understand the true character of Chambers, he must always keep in mind that, regardless of all else, deep inside himself, Chambers was an intensely militant person, a "true soldier of the revolution." This appraisal has a corollary: Chambers had to maintain an illusory, exalted image of himself as a "Man of Destiny." Just as he lost himself in fiction as a boy, ran away from home as an adolescent, he would continue through his life to follow a pattern of hiding and emergence. His need to escape from his image of himself was, of course, greater than ever following his brother's death. As a "true soldier of the Revolution," he warded off his guilt-inspired fears of death; at the same time, he replaced them with fears of all manner of "enemies" in the world around him.

The American Communist Party at this time was rich in opportunities for such intrigue. The party, between 1927 and 1929, was purged of Trotskyites on the left and Bukharinites (Lovestoneites) on the right. Those party members who remained behind were uneasy; they did not want to take an open ideological stand. Chambers, Schapiro explained, was apparently unhappy with the general trend of party life and events.

The following poem, published in the *News Magazine Supplement* (July 9, 1927),[1] provides a signpost for his feelings during that highly disturbed interval.

---

[1] Exactly thirty-four years, to the day, before Chambers died (July 9, 1961).

BEFORE THE END

Before the end, Comrade, before the end
How many of us alive today will stand
Helpless to press a sentenced comrade's hand
Knowing we look our last upon a friend,
Comrades, before the end?

Comrades, before the end,
How many faithful known to us will fall
Lonely beside some unwindowed prison wall
And be deprived of help or hope or friend
Comrades, before the end?

Before we make an end, a bitter end
How many faces looked upon today
Will our hands be called to make away,
Because a friend treacherous to a friend,
Comrades, before the end?

Comrades, before the end, before the end
How many strong who swore they could defy
Reverse forever will slacken, fall and die?
How many will despair as friend by friend
Passes before the end?

Yet we who struggle on, today alive
Let never for an instant our purpose bend
The clubbed, the maimed, the shot,
Though prison-penned;
But let our merciless steadfastness survive,
Our bodies at the end.

The desperate sentiments are, of course, reflections of his continuing struggle with fratricidal guilt. But his involvement in party affairs was real— even if his role was not so elevated as he would have readers of *Witness* believe. Chambers describes himself as "acting editor" of the *Daily Worker*. Robert Minor was the editor at that time, and Chambers was, in fact, a far lesser functionary. But Chambers never played a political role while on the paper, nor did he have any political theoretical knowledge to speak of. The staff knew him as a literary man in the left wing [2] and respected him for his knowledge of literature, recognizing his talent for writing and his capacity for

[2] Freeman lends confirmation to Chambers' role in the Communist Party as having been that of a "revolutionary poet" rather than a "real proletarian." The struggle between the "revolutionary poets" and the "revolutionary leaders" during the twenties, explains Freeman, was an active and important one. Freeman felt that the Communist movement had to have both leaders and poets, but ". . . the writers themselves were not very clear about their own problems and tasks." (Joseph Freeman, *An American Testament* [London: Victor Gollancz, Ltd., 1938], p. 356.)

hard work. However, Chambers did make a practice of making cracks about various party leaders—Minor and others. Furthermore, his former colleagues said, "Chambers never edited the *Daily Worker,* never was acting editor, although he did sit in the slot at one time." Sender Garlin used to call him the "boy mayor." Chambers' demeanor, described by another staff member on the *Daily Worker,*

amused all of us very much. You would think he was commanding an army. He took it in that way, although the job was considered nowhere near being editor of the paper, and was not involved directly with policy. Sam Darcy had the job—the slot—for a while. Others had it. Nat Gainley sat in the slot for a time. Sender Garlin did, and Harry Freeman.[3]

Despite his relatively minor position, Chambers—with an affinity for absorbing internecine whisperings—was well informed as to what was going on in and about the office. His ear was especially tuned to the noises behind the closed doors of the higher-ups. He enjoyed interposing himself in the personal differences of others, fomenting ordinary experiences into conspiratorial plots in which he himself played a part. This practice soon led him into trouble and caused his temporary estrangement from the party.

The circumstances of the break are not clear. In his pre-trial testimony in the Hiss libel suit, Chambers attributed the break to the factionalism in the party at the time. In response to questions by Hiss's counsel, William Marbury, Chambers stated:

I went to Robert Minor who was chief editor of the *Daily Worker,* and told him, one, that a member of the Browder group had told me that if it were not for its factional effect, they would get rid of that old fool Browder at once, and also that I would like some time to orient myself in this new situation and think matters out.

He told Marbury that Minor went to the Central Control Commission and the next day when Chambers came to work he "discovered that I had achieved an assistant." "Well, now, what did that mean? Did that result in your resignation?" asked Marbury. Chambers replied, "No, I did not resign. I discovered that my assistant was in fact editing the *Daily Worker,* so feeling myself redundant, I got on the bus and went to Chicago and visited a friend who had just been expelled from the Communist Party." [4]

In *Witness* the dispute assumes a more dramatic coloring. In this version it is Minor instead of Browder who is supposedly called the "old fool" by a Browder partisan. Chambers writes:

[3] From memos of interviews by Elinor Ferry, October, 1952.
[4] Baltimore Deposition, p. 92.

The *Daily Worker* had acquired a new writer in the person of Harrison George, the brother-in-law of Earl Browder. . . .

Harrison was a mischievous man whom I at once spotted as a troublemaker. But we got along pleasantly, and he sometimes whispered information to me that was helpful in those dislocated days. . . . He was also the determined enemy of Robert Minor.

One day he sidled up to me confidentially and said: "We'd get that old fool Minor off this paper in a minute if it would not give ammunition to the Lovestoneites." . . .

I walked into Minor's office and closed the door. . . . "We are so much comrades together, Bob," I said, "that they're after your scalp this minute." Then I repeated what Harrison George had just said to me.

Minor jumped out of his chair, red in the face, as he often became, and frightened. "Who told you that?" he shouted. I said that I was sorry, but I could not tell him.

"You *must* tell me, com-rade," he said. "I *must* know." I absolutely refused to tell. He stared at me out of his little elephant's eyes, now filled with anger and fright. I got up and left him.

I knew exactly what "the old fool" was going to do. He was going to the Central Control Commission to force me to tell. I also knew that I would not tell.

After then describing how he had thus put himself in a very awkward position, Chambers goes on to give his version of how he anticipated his expulsion from the Communist Party and therefore unofficially removed himself before this occurred:

Presently, the telephone rang. It was the call I had been expecting. "This is Charles A. Dirba," said a deliberately chilling voice. "Comrade, I would like to talk with you. Tonight." Dirba was the chairman of the Central Control Commission. . . .

From me, there would be no obscene confessions of political error, no public prostration or phony repentance. . . .

I knew that I was putting myself outside the Communist Party. But if a man could remain within the party only by abasing himself, he and the party were better off if he got out. . . .

There was no point in returning to the *Daily Worker* office. I never went back.

I was outside the Communist Party, but not out of it. For during the two years I remained outside it, the party never expelled me. I still considered myself a Communist. . . . I was an independent Communist oppositionist.

However it came about, Chambers' role as an "independent Communist oppositionist" represents a phase in the cyclical struggles which characterized his life. The two years that this phase lasted are (like most of Chambers' activities in the thirties) hard to reconstruct. He had no permanent address but said that he lived much of the time with his mother in Lynbrook, and for short periods in a New York tenement. He took a hitchhiking trip West one summer but was unable to recall which one. We also know that in February 1931 Chambers applied for a job with the Atlas Stores Corporation in New York. But he was not hired, perhaps because of a letter from Dean Hawkes of Columbia, in response to the firm's request for a character reference. Hawkes, who had not seen Chambers for years but had not forgotten him, praised his "literary attainments" but concluded that he was "rather unstable and a difficult person to get along with." Chambers did find work, however, as a translator, an occupation that provided him with a livelihood for many years.

In 1928–29 Chambers prepared the English edition of a German novelette by Franz Werfel, *Class Reunion*. As translator, Chambers was skillful with words but not too accurate in dealing with textual facts. His errors in translating, when viewed in relation to its themes and in the light of our knowledge of what he had recently been living through at home, become highly revealing. Altering, sometimes reversing Werfel's meaning, Chambers translated with an unconscious but significant design. The book, an exciting psychological story, concerns itself with an ambivalent relationship between two young men, Sebastian and Adler. We meet them first late in their lives. Sebastian is magistrate of an Austrian court; Adler, his old schoolfriend, comes before him as a criminal accused of killing a prostitute. Much of the story is a flashback, in which Sebastian recalls their friendship.

His memories are full of guilt. He recounts how he envied Adler when they were in school, and how he brought him to ruin. Adler, as leader of a dramatic society, rebuffed Sebastian. Thereafter Sebastian taunted him with ridicule. He seemed to get some perverse control over Adler, who lost interest in the society and in his schoolwork. Sebastian led him into hooky-playing and other pranks. Adler's grades fell, and he was warned by the faculty. Even as Sebastian destroyed Adler, he continued to admire him and envy his literary ability. Adler was thought to be clumsy, but one night when Sebastian saw him without clothes for the first time, his body was neither thin nor feeble, but firm and symmetrical. Sebastian now marveled at Adler's physical beauty as well as his intellect.

Adler's crisis worsened. He was threatened with expulsion. Sebastian proposed a way out: altering his grades on the record book. They attempted this, and had just begun removing the true grades when a teacher entered the room. They fled to Sebastian's room, where in desperation they decided to commit suicide together. It was Sebastian's idea. They turned on the "illuminating gas," but at the last moment Sebastian changed his mind and helped revive Adler. Then he induced Adler to run away and gave him some money, proceeds of a theft. Adler did run, and because of his flight took the blame for tampering with the grade books. Sebastian was cleared of suspicion.

After this flashback there is a dramatic scene in the judge's office between the two old schoolmates. Sebastian springs at Adler and seizes him in his arms.

It looked as if a life and death struggle were about to begin but Sebastian's arms slid down from Adler's body. Adler caught him as he was falling and supported him by the shoulders like a wounded man.

The parallels between Werfel's story of Sebastian and Adler and Chambers' relationship with his brother Richard are striking: the ambivalent love, the idea of dying together in a suicide. Chambers translated *Class Reunion* within three years of Richard's suicide. His fraternal guilt, about which he wrote with such intensity on other occasions, must certainly have reverberated through his mind as he translated the suicide pact between the two boys, for the subject of psychological guilt is the story's central theme. Werfel, in his brief explanatory Introduction to a later edition of *Class Reunion*,[5] alerts the reader that his story

. . . ventures to raise a frightful, perhaps the most frightful problem of our life on this earth: the problem of guilt. Can one man actually destroy another—not by murder, which need involve no metaphysical destruction—but by more refined methods; destroy him in the most delicate and secret places of his soul? Or are limits set to the guilty man's evil instinct, in that he must destroy himself with his victim, more cruelly and more surely even than him whom he would destroy?

And the consequence of that sense of guilt—its ongoing ambivalence—is best expressed in a plea by Sebastian near the end of the story. His cry might well be Whittaker's:

I plead guilty to ruining your life. But I charge you, too, with ruining mine. When we were boys together, your finer nature made a criminal of me; but when I had driven you away, you robbed me of my soul forever. Now, when death seems ridiculously close to me, I accuse you of ruining my life. For I was fated to love you!

That the full impact of the story's conflict must surely have affected Whittaker in ways he was unaware of, and stirred hidden anxieties that he had to ward off, is clear from a systematic comparison of his translation with the original, and also with Lowe-Porter's version. There is an abundance of revealing errors and alterations of meaning. These range from simple mistakes such as changes of date ("1868" instead of "1878"), amount ("a" dozen instead of "several" dozen), or dimension ("six feet" instead of "ten centimeters") to more obviously significant frequent mistranslation of certain key

[5] *Twilight of a World* (a collection of Werfel's stories), translated by H. T. Lowe-Porter (New York: The Viking Press, 1937). *Class Reunion* was published by Simon & Schuster in 1929.

words, such as "Verbrecher" ("criminal") as "murderer," and "Mord" ("murder") as "crime." Other more serious distortions of words, ideas, and feelings are prevalent. The most significant and oft recurring errors were Chambers' choice of the exact *reverse* word or phrase, transforming the author's thought into an opposite feeling or idea. Errors, of course, may be due to a variety of factors, from ordinary sloppiness to specifically determined psychic reasons. The possibility of sloppiness as such or lack of true mastery of the language being translated must be considered in all of this. No single error can be called significant; only an analysis of the trends of errors has validity.

But a few selected examples [6] will illustrate how Chambers' inner conflict affected the translation. It should be noted that where the German text threatened to expose a repressed idea or coincided with an area of conflict in Chambers' real life, he deviated from the author's original meaning; on other occasions he altered the meaning to express an unconscious personal wish.

Werfel selected a sentence from Goethe's novel *The Elective Affinities* as an epigraph for the title page. In his English translation of this sentence, Chambers added two words. It is particularly impressive how effectively this simple addition reversed not only the intended meaning of Goethe's historic lines, but the basic moral of Werfel's story and the purpose for which the author selected it. The German passage in question is:

> Gegen grosse Vorzüge eines andern gibt
> es kein Rettungsmittel als die Liebe.

Properly translated, the passage should read:

> Against another's great superiorities
> there is no remedy but love.

Chambers translated it:

> Against the superiority of another
> there exists no weapon or remedy save love.

Chambers' insertion of the words "weapon or" may be used as literary evidence of the way he had, in psychological fact, used love as a weapon. Instead of remedying his frustration at another's superiority with love, he turned admiration into destruction. (Instead of benevolently admiring Richard, he wanted to *be* Richard, to replace him.)

Along this same line of thought, it is important to point out Chambers' omission of Werfel's highly revealing subtitle: "Die Geschichte einer

---

[6] All in all, seventeen typed pages of Chambers' translation errors in *Class Reunion* have been compiled and verified.

Jugendschuld"—"The Story of a Youth's Guilt." Whereas in this instance Chambers represses the idea of his guilt, in another he expresses his secret wishes: "Nein, ein Verbrecher könne Adler nicht gewesen sein," should read, "No, Adler could not be a criminal." Chambers translates: ". . . he could never murder anyone."

In another case he avoids his guilt by blunting Werfel's intent. The passage concerns the question of punishment for a partner to a suicide pact who reneges, and thus commits a kind of murder.

(Werfel)

Man kann fast mit Sicherheit annehmen, dass die *Geschworenen* [7] selbst eine mildere Fragestellung mit Nein beantworten.

(Chambers)

One can state almost positively that even the *prisoner's conscience* would say "No" to a milder verdict.

(Should read)

One can almost certainly assume that the *jury* would say "No" to an even milder charge.

And again, in the following example, we see how he wards off his own conflicted feelings by a most revealing translation reversal:

Sebastian says to Adler:

(Werfel)

Bitte, lassen Sie sich *durch den Kopf gehen,* was ich über den versuchten Doppelselbstmord sagte.

(Chambers)

I wish, however, that you'd be good enough to *forget* what I said to you about the double suicide.

(Should read)

Please *think over* what I said about the attempted double suicide.

(Werfel)

. . . wenn nicht das *Ansehen* meines Vaters mir *geholfen.*

(Chambers)

. . . had not the *memory* of my father *urged* me *on.*

(Should read)

. . . had not the *prestige* of my father *helped* me.

(Werfel)

Was für ein *Mord* also liegt vor?

(Chambers)

What could be the motive for such a *crime?*

(Should read)

What sort of *murder* is it then?

[7] Italics the author's.

The similarity of the fictional plot and of the two main characters in *Class Reunion* to Chambers' real-life tragedy with his brother was so striking and so much was made of it during the second Hiss trial that Chambers could hardly bypass mentioning the subject in *Witness*. Were he to have omitted it altogether he would have made it conspicuous by its absence.[8] And so, instead, he attacks the story's literary worth. In his need to nullify its significance and his personal role in translating it (and also to discredit the psychiatrist who pointed it up during the trial), Chambers proceeds to destroy Werfel's story. He seems, for a moment, to lose his temper.

One of the books I translated at that time [9] was Franz Werfel's novel, *Class Reunion*. It was less a novel than an elongated short story. It related how an Austrian attorney [10] supposed that he saw in a prisoner coming up for examination a classmate who [sic], out of jealousy, he had managed to ruin in their youth. Most of the book was a flashback which described the trivial stages of that ruin (one of them, if I remember rightly, consisted in the bad boy's leading on the good boy to stuff himself with tarts). At the time, the novel seemed to me tiresome and over-contrived. It was one of what I call "unnecessary books"—books, that, for any bearing they have on man's mind, man's fate, or even his entertainment, might as well never have been written. Apparently, readers thought so, too, for *Class Reunion* was not a great success.[11] I soon forgot the details of its story, with which, in any case, I had nothing to do but the tiresome labor of translation. I should probably never have remembered them, but for the Hiss Case.

For in *Class Reunion,* Dr. Carl Binger, the psychologist in the Hiss trials,[12] undertook to discover the psychological clue to Chambers' "mysterious motives" in charging that Alger Hiss had once been a Communist. Chambers was the bad boy and Hiss was the good boy of *Class Reunion,* and the novel, unread by me for some twenty years, had put the idea of ruining Hiss in my mind—why I never quite understood, since it always seemed to me that if I had been bent on ruining Alger Hiss from base motives, the idea might well have occurred to me without benefit of Franz Werfel. But to many enlightened minds *Class Reunion* became a book of revelation.

I have always held that anyone who takes the trouble to read *Class Reunion*

---

[8] When being cross-examined during the Hiss trial regarding this translation, Chambers stated: "Of course I did not help Werfel with the writing." Why was there any need to reassure the court of the obvious?

[9] The author attempted to find out if Chambers had sought out the translation job of this particular story. Clifton Fadiman, then editor-in-chief of Simon & Schuster (1928), could only say: "This was thirty-four years ago—how could I remember? I think Whittaker needed money and I knew he knew German, so we put the two facts together, that's all." Fadiman had known Chambers as a student at Columbia. They had worked together on the staff of *Morningside*. In 1938 Fadiman got Chambers the job of translating *Bambi* for Simon & Schuster, for which Chambers was paid five hundred dollars.

[10] Not an attorney but a judge.

[11] Not so. The first European edition, published by Paul Zsolnay in 1928, sold twenty-five thousand copies.

[12] Not a psychologist but a psychoanalyst, a fact that Chambers knew. (Cf. *Witness*, p. 718, where he refers to Dr. Binger as a "psychoanalyst.")

without having made up his mind in advance, can scarcely fail to see that, if there are any similarities at all between the characters, it is Hiss who *superficially* resembles the bad boy and Chambers who *superficially* resembles his victim.[13]

In his need to reduce Werfel's psychological story to a trivial tale about a "good boy and a bad boy," Chambers argued that Hiss superficially resembled the bad boy and Chambers resembled—and now discreetly he does not use his previous adjective "good" but substitutes—"his victim."

Chambers goes to great lengths to derogate the story. His efforts to make a travesty of Werfel's short novel evidence how deeply Chambers identified himself with Sebastian; and, like Sebastian's feelings toward Adler, Chambers, caught in the coils of his own homosexual love, envy, and guilt (toward Richard and Alger), vigorously denied any resemblance between his plight and Sebastian's. When questioned about his translation of *Class Reunion* during the Hiss trial, Chambers avoided the subject as though it were some terrible deed in his past, for it threatened to bring to the surface the repressed memory of the most disrupting experience of his life, the suicide of his brother. Chambers' comment that this book "might as well never have been written" has the ring of desperate devaluation. It is unlikely that he could have translated *Class Reunion* and not been moved by the poignant story of a friendship between two youths in which the elements of love, envy, and guilt and the forces of betrayal were so vividly portrayed.[14]

But beside his translation work, Chambers says that he was struggling to come to terms with the Communist Party. He had failed to influence policy as copy editor of the *Daily Worker*. There was too much factionalism and there were too many cross-currents of opinion in which Chambers himself was too easily lost. His need for personal expression and literary recognition turned him to the writing of political short stories. He tried, he says, "another way than politics to influence policy." He began writing pro-Communist stories for the *New Masses,* stories in which the correct conduct of the Communist would be shown in fictional action and without political comment.[15] The stories concerned the sufferings and heroism of Bolshevik revolutionaries. One, "The Death of the Communists," was a first-person account by one of five Communist prisoners awaiting execution. It is of interest that death is glorified in this tale and is symbolized as a rebirth. The narrator says it is

[13] Italics the author's.
[14] Although, If Chambers had been unaware of the similarity of himself and Werfel's fictional characters (which I do not believe), the explanation of his subsequent behavior would be even more telling clinically, for it would show how effectively he had unconsciously equated reality and fiction.
[15] "Can You Hear Their Voices?" "Our Comrade Munn"; You Have Seen the Heads"; "The Death of the Communists."

"like lying on my back in a small boat . . . and a strong tide carrying me along with no effort on my part."

His creation of this story was like the narration of a dream:

All that I wanted to say fell into place at one stroke in my mind. I wrote through one night and by morning had completed a rather long short story.

A favorable review of his stories appeared in the Russian magazine *International Literature*. This unexpected recognition and moment of praise were enough to turn his head. "Accepted by Moscow," he became disaffected from the American Communist Party. In a state of buoyant excitement he describes how

Moscow reacted to the stories at once. . . . It was the voice of authority. "So," I thought, "my quarrel is not with Moscow or with Comrade Stalin. Raise the line correctly, and Moscow instantly accepts it. My quarrel is with the invincible stupidity and pettiness of the American Communist Party."

After the appearance of his short stories, he states that the party offered him the editorship of the *New Masses,* at a salary of fifteen dollars a week. Since he had "broken with the party" but wanted the job, a quick reconciliation was necessary. Once again, the precise circumstances are a mystery. Chambers says:

First my misunderstanding with the party would have to be adjusted. But there would be no difficulty about that. There was a friendly visit to Alexander Trachtenberg who, as head of International Publishers, was the party's "cultural commissar" and had the *New Masses* and the John Reed Clubs under his wing, and . . . was a member of the Central Control Commission. Trachtenberg arranged an equally friendly talk with Charles A. Dirba, the chairman of the Control Commission. *In fifteen minutes I was back in the Communist Party without ever having, officially, been out of it.*[16]

Both the men mentioned were questioned about this incident. Alexander Trachtenberg was interviewed in 1957 by William Reuben, a newspaper reporter who has done considerable investigation into the life of Whittaker Chambers. Reuben's notes contain the following information:

Trachtenberg told me that, of his own knowledge, he never knew Chambers was a member of the Communist Party.
      . . . although his firm, International Publishers, reprinted a short story of Whittaker Chambers that had appeared in *New Masses,* Trachtenberg himself had no dealings with Chambers in that connection.
      . . . his only contact with Chambers, other than a vague idea of seeing him "around," was in the newspaper room of the New York Public Library. Trachtenberg frequently went there during the middle and late twenties to read the foreign-

[16] Italics the author's.

language newspapers. He remembers Chambers working there as a clerk and occasionally having conversations with him in German. The one vivid memory that Trachtenberg has of Chambers during this period is his utter and complete slovenliness and sloppiness. Trachtenberg said that Chambers' physical appearance was so bad, his clothes were always so dirty and sweaty and soily . . . it is virtually the only vivid memory that Trachtenberg has of Chambers.

Trachtenberg also categorically denied that he had ever had anything to do with Chambers and the party's Central Control Commission. If in fact, said Trachtenberg, Chambers had been out of the party, it was completely impossible for him, Trachtenberg, to intercede in such a manner without having any direct knowledge himself; . . . if in fact there had been a dispute in some group or cell that Chambers had been a member of, the disputants would be a party to whatever went on before the Central Control Commission; and certainly, he, Trachtenberg, a complete outsider, would not step into such a matter. In any event, Trachtenberg, without any qualifications, emphasized that no such incident ever occurred.[17]

Charles A. Dirba, interviewed in 1957 by Mrs. Helen Buttenwieser, was asked about his recollections of his two contacts with Chambers, as described by Chambers. Dirba had no memory of any such event having taken place. He pointed out that he was secretary of the Control Commission, not chairman, and it was impossible for him to have acted as an individual in any matter involving the Commission. After hearing the account which Chambers had given in *Witness* of his reinstatement, Dirba declared that it was impossible for any such event to have happened. Such matters, far from being resolved "in fifteen minutes," were dealt with in formal hearings in which everything was done in writing and subject to careful review. All matters which came before the Commission were acted upon by all members of the Commission and under no circumstances by Dirba alone. Hence Chambers' statement that as a result of these friendly visits with Trachtenberg and Dirba he was "back in the Communist Party . . . in fifteen minutes," was impossible.

Whatever the circumstances of his self-styled break and his uncorroborated reinstatement, Chambers did become one of the editors of the *New Masses* in 1932 and his name appeared on the editorial masthead of the paper, though it was not to stay there for long. Party disputes, conciliations, shifts of allegiance, reconciliations, and further betrayals all provided Chambers with excitement. Like the restive gambler, Chambers was constantly searching for action. The embellishment and dramatization of daily events kept him in the cross-currents of life and in a state of increased emotional intensity. By creating unusual episodes he enlivened the drabness of his empty inner self. By exaggeration or falsification of reality, he distorted mundane

[17] From the investigative files of Chester T. Lane, in a memorandum by William A. Reuben dated May 21, 1957; Chester Lane was the attorney preparing Hiss's appeal for a new trial, after the second Hiss trial.

happenings into illusory, historical events. To Chambers, politics was the "march of history." It created an aura of mystery and intrigue and made him feel grandiose and important.

Chambers' life at this time was changing in nonpolitical ways as well. He had been involved in what he termed "a Communist marriage" with a girl named Ida Dales. The two lived together in New York and for a time with his mother in Lynbrook, and then in a cottage in East Rockaway. Chambers testified:

A. Oh, I think the relationship lasted a year or more.
Q. And then what happened?
A. Then I broke up with her.
Q. You just agreed to go separate ways?
A. Surely.

In an interview with a close relative of Ida Dales', it was determined that the Communist "marriage" arrangement between Whittaker Chambers and Ida Dales lasted more than two years, from 1929 to early 1931. After Jay Chambers died, for most of their "marriage" they lived with his mother at Lynbrook.[18]

Ida told her sister that on several occasions Chambers sat with a shotgun across his knees all night—confiding in Ida that he "expected the worst." It was at the time that Whittaker Chambers' grandmother (Grandma Whittaker) also lived with them. Because she was so mentally disturbed she was kept locked in the attic when Ida Dales was there. Ida, then pregnant, lived in constant apprehension, and she frequently heard shrieks. On one occasion "Granny" managed to get down to the lower floor of the house. The old woman's appearance so unnerved Ida that she was thereafter afraid to stay alone in the house. For this reason, whenever Laha left the house, Ida accompanied her, often on exhausting, day-long auto trips. Her pregnancy ended in a miscarriage. The termination of this illicit Communist "marriage" preceded by a few weeks Chambers' legal marriage to Esther Shemitz. The relationship

---

[18] Chambers confirmed their stay in Lynbrook in his testimony but put the time at "about a month." He also volunteered an explanation as to why his mother permitted the arrangement.

A. My mother had lost one son and was extremely careful not to do anything that might—
Q. Alienate the other?
A. Alienate the other.

Note that Chambers' reference to his "party marriage" in *Witness,* quoted earlier (cf. p. 171), is quite at variance from his trial testimony and from the account obtained independently by the writer. In *Witness,* it will be recalled, Chambers stated that he was living "in a cottage on one of the Long Island tidal inlets," and his mother "knew" where he was living but "never" visited them.

ended quite abruptly, and Ida was dreadfully hurt. She was about twenty-eight, and although it was a conventionally nonconformist, Communist liaison, she had regarded her life with Chambers as a permanent marriage.

Chambers described his courtship and marriage in April 1931 to Esther Shemitz, a dedicated and vigorous revolutionist of Jewish parentage, with dramatic excitement:

Few courtships can have been much stormier than ours. For the Communist Party, too, soon actively interfered. I called one evening to find Esther Shemitz very silent, grave, and evidently distressed. Presently, she blurted through her tears that Comrade Hutchins had paid her an official visit and brought the party's awful command that she was never again to see the "anti-party element, Chambers."

The stage is set once again for the re-enactment of a momentous decision, another choice between life and death. Chambers' impersonation as "the chosen one," his need to interpose himself between Esther Shemitz and the Communist Party, is dramatically acted out:

One evening, I arrived at Esther Shemitz's for supper—a very special occasion in that house of bare cupboards. I knocked. No one answered. I was certain that my future wife was inside. I beat on the door with my fist. At last a small voice said through its tears: "Go away. The party says I cannot see you. We can never meet again."

I went away, very angry. I cooled off by walking around the city streets for hours. . . . I walked back across town through the absolutely empty streets of the sleeping city.

Again, I knocked on the door of the little house. There was no answer. The door stood at the head of a flight of stairs a story above a flagged court. Just beyond the landing stage was a window. It was open a little way because it was supposed that nobody could reach the window from the landing. Ordinarily, no one could. But I am not the first man who, in my mood, has done what he did not know he could do. I looked down at the flagstones (even small heights usually make me dizzy). I swung from the rail of the landing, reached the window ledge, pushed up the window and climbed in.

Sitting beside my astonished girl's bedside in the dawning light, I explained to her that she must make a choice, and that that choice was not between the Communist Party and renegacy, or between any political viewpoint and any other, but between life and death.

Chambers' recurrent crises were re-enactments of his life-and-death fantasies. In this description, which has all the features of a nightmare—his walking the streets all night, then returning and forcing his re-entry into Esther Schemitz's apartment and into her life by dangerously climbing through the window—he symbolically re-enacts the fantasy of his birth and the near-loss of his mother. This is how he starts a new life. After this symbolic return (compare his return home from New Orleans), with renewed spirit he insists that "his future wife" choose not just between him and the party, but between life and death. Once again he withdraws from the (imagined) political problems which just a few hours before had blocked the path of his gnawing hunger for love and affection.

We never quarreled again. In the twenty years that we have been married, we have had a few disagreements, but never again about politics and not very often about anything else.

The couple moved to rural New Jersey, where they lived without charge on a farm belonging to some friends. In lieu of rent the Chamberses remodeled the house. "Few periods of our life," Chambers says, "have been so happy."

Chambers was now thirty years old, newly married, an editor of the *New Masses*. He was living in the country and had within his external grasp the makings of a new and happy life. Within a year, he had forsaken that life for a mysterious, furtive existence that was to last for over five years. He left his job and, with Esther, moved into the city—even though, for him, "entering a city [was like] entering a grave." It is precisely at this point in his narrative that he describes how he entered the Communist underground.

Why did he do it? According to his own account, it was not entirely his decision:

One hot June day in 1932, while I was preparing my third issue of the *New Masses,* I answered the telephone and an unfamiliar voice said quietly "This is Comrade Bedacht. I would like to see you right away." . . .

I knew of Bedacht only as the fatherly Communist "who had kids to the number of acht," as a singularly self-effacing member of the Central Committee, and head of the International Workers Order, a Communist-controlled benefit and insurance society. . . .

Comrade Bedacht was about to summon me into crypts of Communism that I scarcely dreamed existed, into its deep underground, whose door was about to close noiselessly behind me almost as if I had never existed. . . . "For some reason," he said . . . "they want you to go into one of the party's 'special institutions.' " . . . I said that I must have some time to think it over. . . . "You can have until tomorrow morning," he said.

Chambers continues, in *Witness,* to relate that shortly after he made his decision to enter the underground, Max Bedacht introduced him to "someone from the 'special institution.' " He describes it:

We walked to Union Square and down a subway entrance. Under Union Square, the tunnels that connect the B.M.T. and the East Side subways form a small catacomb. "You know the man you are going to meet," Bedacht said. . . . It was John Sherman whom I had last seen crying in the *Daily Worker* office.

Bedacht introduced him formally as if we were strangers. "This is Don," he said. . . .

Then he [Don] told me that at seven o'clock that night, I must meet him on the uptown subway platform at 116th Street. . . . We did not go to 116th Street. Instead, we got off at 110th Street . . . wove our way over to Riverside Drive near Grant's Tomb.[19]

But once again, despite the richness of detail in Chambers' description, there is great confusion about the realities of the event. Max Bedacht, for example, denies that he was the one who "summon [ed Chambers] into crypts of Communism . . . into its deep underground." In a lengthy conference between Chester Lane and Bedacht, held May 14, 1957, Bedacht described his work in the Communist Party and the contacts he had had with Chambers. The notes, taken by Margaret Burton, Lane's secretary, reveal how far apart the versions of Bedacht and Chambers are.

In 1929–31 Bedacht was a member of the Central Committee and was acting secretary of the Communist Party for a few months. Bedacht said he knew Chambers during his secretaryship of the party, not before. In early 1932 Bedacht started his work in the International Workers Order. The *New Masses* sent Whittaker Chambers over to Bedacht's office to discuss an IWO plan. Bedacht commented:

My only clear recollection of ever having had a personal talk with Chambers was when he came in response to my phone call.

In the Baltimore Deposition, taken in 1948, Chambers testified to seeing Bedacht frequently at the time he was first recruited into the underground. At one time he said he had "fortnightly" meetings with Bedacht and then again he said "weekly" meetings. Bedacht's comment was:

I was secretary of the IWO then and believe me it was a job. The idea that I met him every week is fantastic.

Chambers' account of his relationship with Bedacht, in clear contrast to Bedacht's denials, suggests that Chambers used Bedacht as a vehicle for his own romantic fantasies. Bedacht and Chambers are at odds on another incident—minor insofar as Communist history is concerned but probably significant to Chambers' own history. On December 16, 1933, Robert W. Chambers, a well-known novelist, died. Whittaker Chambers, no doubt ready to claim kinship with a writer, attributes the following story to Bedacht:

Max Bedacht had somehow convinced himself that I was the son of Robert W. Chambers, the novelist. . . . When the novelist died, shortly after I came to know Bedacht, he congratulated me on coming into a fat legacy, which I believe he thought was about to be swept into the party's till. When I tried to undeceive him,

[19] In an earlier version of his story, as given in the Baltimore Deposition, Chambers stated the man's name was "Arthur."

his disappointment was so great that at first he insisted that I was covering up, and I had some trouble convincing him that Robert W. Chambers and Whittaker Chambers were really unrelated.

Lane asked Bedacht:

Q. Did you think Chambers was the son of Robert W. Chambers, the great writer?
A. I don't know the famous novelist Chambers.
Q. So you weren't angry with Chambers because he didn't turn over to you his big inheritance?
A. Why would I expect Chambers to turn over money to me?

Lane then asked about Bedacht's role as secret link between the Communist Party and the Soviet Military Intelligence. Bedacht answered:

I never had any contact with any military persons either from the Soviet Union or anywhere. I know nothing about military things. I certainly never had at any time any underground contact with any country in the world, whether American, Russian, or whatever. I had no occasion to carry or convey any information. I was opposed to connecting legal work with illegal work. It is common sense not to connect the two.

Bedacht went on to tell that he had testified several times before grand juries and, in 1949, before the House Committee on Un-American Activities.

At no time when I testified was I asked about Chambers or my relations with him. There were innumerable visits to Jersey from FBI agents, and then immigration authorities started. None asked me about Chambers.

Chambers has dramatized his departure from the *New Masses,* elevating it to a level of high political importance in the Communist Party. He writes in *Witness* that his "disappearance" from the *New Masses* caused such a scandal in the American Communist Party that Earl Browder, then its titular head, was "furious" and "stamped his foot at Bedacht" when the latter broke the news to him. Chambers goes on to describe how Browder, whom, he says, he met just twice and "we disliked each other at sight," then told Bedacht that Chambers must come back and threatened to take the matter higher up.

In letters to the writer Browder stated that he had never met Chambers, did not know him, and had no first-hand knowledge of him. He knew of him only by "hearsay," knew about his leaving the *Daily Worker* but did not even know he was ever on the *New Masses,* and "certainly did not ever protest his leaving it." When years later Browder heard "as a matter of gossip that Chambers was associated with the Russians," he was "mildly surprised" and commented, "It was strange as I had been under the impression that he was a

Trotskyist. That was about 1938 and was the first time I had heard his name since 1930. I never heard of him again until he appeared in the news as a witness before the Un-American Activities Committee."

In response to the writer's query about Chambers' description of him in *Witness,* Browder said:

The quotation shows he did not even know much about me. To say that I was "furious" and that I "stamped my foot" is ridiculous, as I never was "furious" at anything and never "stamped my foot," and no one who ever worked close to me would think of so describing me.[20]

It is impossible to balance these accounts; their significance lies in the fact that no one who knew Chambers at this time gave the same version of why he left the *New Masses* or how (or whether) he entered the underground. Robert Cantwell, a close friend of Chambers at that time, had still another view. He attributed Chambers' actions at that time to the party's wish to "kill off their good men, lest they become too forceful; . . . they removed Chambers from his position on the *New Masses* because as a former editor everyone knew who he was. Then they gave him an ineffectual, menial job as a courier in the underground." [21] Felix Morrow, a prominent ex-Communist, agreed (in a letter to *Esquire* magazine about an article on Chambers) that Chambers' role in the underground was minor and also that he was forced to accept it. But Morrow said that Alex Trachtenberg introduced him to the underground. Trachtenberg, of course, has denied any party contacts with Chambers. Still another version came from Dr. Nathan Adler, now a clinical psychologist on the West Coast; in 1932 he was an aspiring left-wing writer and Chambers' reader on the *New Masses.* Dr. Adler shared his reminiscences about Chambers and made available to me a letter written by Chambers on the occasion of his departure from the *New Masses.* It is an interesting and revealing document, for its contents provide an apparently straightforward explanation by Chambers of his reason for leaving the *New Masses.*[22] Writing in July 1932 on *New Masses* stationery, Chambers told his friend:

I have asked for, and have been granted a release, and am leaving *New Masses* at once. In fact, chronologically speaking, I have already gone. My work is finished here. Certain problems have been settled and, I believe, certain rudiments of policy and conduct laid down. It will be the task of the new Editor to amplify this work. . . .

Then Chambers quite explicitly states:

[20] Earl Browder to the author, October 18, 29, 1963.
[21] Robert Cantwell to the author, May 10, 1963.
[22] Personal interview with Dr. Adler, September 18, 1963.

I shall return to my writing, which is where I belong or at least where I seem to function best. Perhaps in a few months I may be able to accomplish things on [sic] my own field again. . . .

The remainder of his letter is taken up with Chambers' advice to Adler about the latter's own writing career and a friendly admonition to the fledgling writer to avoid "straining after effect" as that is "what can most easily ruin it." He also cautions him not to worry about publication—"I never think of publishing."

He closes on a characteristically ominous note:

We are on the eve of terrible struggles. What they hold for you and for all of us—no one can say, but if you come out of them, you will probably come into your own.

Chambers makes no mention, of course, of entering the underground. The only reason stated for his departure is to devote his time to his own writing. However he did not return to his writing—not for some years—and he did enter, in one way or another, the underground: the letter is perhaps best read as a cover story, and yet it may be a statement of vague intention as well. No one can say with authority, on the strength of Chambers' own conflicting reports and these of others, precisely how or why Chambers went underground. But if the historical determinants are cloudy, I suggest that the psychic determinants are clear—and at least as important.

Chambers could not remain at his country house with a comfortable job and a devoted wife. Peace of mind was alien to his guilty self-image. He had to remain a "soldier of the Revolution"; he needed the external setting of a sick world in which he could act out further episodes of excitement and suffering. Such is the nature of unresolved guilt and its constant consort, the need for self-punishment. It enshadows the rightful pleasures of life, which are felt to be undeserved.

His inner guilt took the form of an intense force, which he wrote about but did not know the meaning of. It drove him on to this act of self-punishment:

A force greater than myself had picked me up and was disposing of me—a force that, in the end, it would all but cost me my life to break away from, and may yet cost my life, for there is more than one way of killing a man, and the story, begun that night, is not ended.

Chambers was clearly possessed with the "furies." His guilt-laden death wishes, again turned against himself, gained ascendancy and directed the course of his actions. He had to save himself from himself by going underground. Thus he symbolically manipulated his own death as a defense against fear of dying.

His dramatic move had its magical effect, but it was, inevitably, short-lived.

As a Communist, I felt a quiet elation at the knowledge that there was one efficient party organization and that it had selected me to work with it. There was also a little electric jab in the thought. In the nature of its work, such an organization could not pick its personnel at random. Therefore, for some time, it must have been watching me. Unknown to me, eyes must have been observing me. For the first time, I did something involuntary that would soon cease to be involuntary, and would become a technique—I glanced back to see if anybody were following me.

Almost immediately the rising parabola of self-enhancement falls and converts into its emotional opposite, the uneasy feeling that somebody was watching and following him.

The paranoid nature of Chambers' flight underground is borne out by his behavior as a spy. Dr. Adler recalls that after Chambers' sudden disappearance from the *New Masses* he learned that "We don't talk about Whittaker Chambers—he's working for the GPU." Dr. Adler didn't see him again for two years. Then:

I suddenly saw Whittaker Chambers walking down 5th Avenue, with a fedora hat, wearing a dark suit—much too baggy. He was all dressed up. He had a roving eye, a paranoid look. "He's making a drop somewhere," I suspected.

One would assume that if people were involved in a conspiracy, they'd be quiet about it. The whole atmosphere at that time, however, was one where the legal and illegal organizations were not hidden from each other. It was a kind of open secret.

That day when I saw him on 5th Avenue, he seemed to be aware he was being followed. We walked by each other without a nod of recognition, as though we were playing the same conspiratorial game.

Spying manners, Adler suggests, were considerably less sophisticated than one would think, but Chambers apparently exceeded even their liberal boundaries. There is no shortage of anecdotes; Chambers cut a memorable figure. Lionel Trilling and others have pointed out that despite the danger he always seemed to be in, Chambers was always reminding everyone that he was a secret Communist agent by going around behaving like a spy. It was enough of an open secret, to those who knew Chambers in the thirties, to enable Trilling to base the main character of a novel on Chambers' bizarre behavior.[23]

One friend said:

[23] Lionel Trilling, *The Middle of the Journey* (New York: The Viking Press, 1947).

During the period he was in "special work," he was theatrically mysterious, so wrapped up in a cloak-and-dagger pose, looking over his shoulder, convinced he was being followed, that I got the idea something was strange and it got so I didn't like to have him around. I began to feel he was a little peculiar. As a matter of fact, that role suited him to perfection. Even *before* he got conspiratorial, he was conspiratorial, if you know what I mean.

A personal experience described to me by Matthew Josephson, a well-known American author, is identical in pattern with other stories. Once again, Chambers' distortion of external events to conform to his inner fantasies is revealed:

I only met Whittaker Chambers once, for about two hours, [the weekend] of March 3rd, 1933, under circumstances rather particular that caused me to remember him and write an account of my meeting in my journal, around 1949, time of the Hiss trial. At the time I lived in the country, but rented the use of a room for one or two days a week in New York at the apartment occupied by my friend Robert Cantwell. All the banks were closing before Roosevelt's inauguration, and I came down to raise some cash for my family needs in the country, so I remember that time of crisis very distinctly.

As I knocked at the door, Cantwell came, but strangely delayed opening it, calling out to someone: "It's all right, its Matty Josephson." I had given my name. This was unusual. Then he opened and I went in. Chambers then came out from the room I rented—which he had been using during my absence—to which he had retreated at my knock. He had gone back to hide himself, and looked embarrassed as he came out to meet me.

Cantwell had (laughingly) mentioned this odd acquaintance once or twice as a "half-baked" young writer for the *New Masses,* who dramatized himself as a desperate sort of secret agent, carried a big revolver with him, and told everyone that U.S. secret service agents (FBI men) were forever trailing him from place to place. I had received therefore an unfavorable impression of a young fellow of about twenty-six who posed as a devilish conspirator, or Russian agent, but was like a lot of Greenwich Village "neurotics" one encountered. Chambers' attitude toward me, an older person, at thirty-three "an established writer," was a mixture of aggressiveness and inferiority. He was shabby and frowsy, with eyes red-rimmed as if he slept badly, bony of figure, though short, and hardly prepossessing. Our talk for an hour or two hours ran on the economic crisis and banking panic. Chambers and Cantwell questioned me, because I was supposed to be knowledgeable in this field, and argued that The Revolution had begun in America. "This is it!" Chambers exclaimed. "The whole financial system has broken down. . . . Barricades in Union Square this week!" I opposed this idea, saying: probably no revolution, but reform measures by the incoming administration, and money-inflation such as I had seen in Germany after the war. Chambers exploded with anger at me, and began shouting me down, calling me a "bourgeois" or a "stooge" for the capitalists. He sounded as if I were snatching his "baby," the Revolution. As he became abusive, I grew angry also and raised my fists; Cantwell intervened and asked Chambers to leave, also apologizing for Chambers' behavior to me.

. . . He reviewed my books several years later in *Time* in hostile and sneering terms as the maunderings of a deluded Leftist, for he had become a political conservative in 1938–40.

Regardless of actual external events, political or nonpolitical, Chambers held himself constantly in the center of privately created conspiracies. He was an early master of the conspiratorial attitude; shadows and subterfuge were the media for the dramatization of life. The need to mystify motivated much of his activities. Guy Endore, a fellow student at Columbia, later a biographer and novelist, relates an amusing and strange personal experience he had with Chambers during the early thirties. Endore had received a free-lance translation job. Knowing Chambers was in need of money, he phoned and asked if he would translate part of the book for him and they would share the proceeds. Whittaker said that he would be glad to do it. Endore asked where and when they should meet. Chambers gave him an address, and they arranged to meet at 5:30 p.m. somewhere in downtown New York at a place unknown to Endore. Endore arrived at their meeting place at the appointed time. It turned out to be a huge, vacant loft of an unused factory building, and Endore walked up to the second floor in accordance with Chambers' instructions. The entire building was empty, and Endore waited there, not knowing what to think. As he looked about he noted broken windows, a splintered floor, and all the signs of disuse and abandonment. It was a cold, wintry evening and it was getting dark and eerie. After waiting for a while he thought he must have made a mistake in the address. Just as he started to leave, Whittaker Chambers showed up. He appeared suddenly as from nowhere and in an apologetic tone said, "Sorry, I'm a little late." Endore was aware that Chambers was in the Communist Party, and, knowing his strange ways, remarked, "Why here? Do you have another little revolution in your vest pocket?" Endore then gave him his part of the book to be translated, and Chambers walked off into the darkness.[24]

Endore, who knew Chambers well during their undergraduate days at Columbia and in the early thirties, commented that it was not unusual for Chambers to search through people's wastepaper baskets for discarded personal notes. He was a psychic scavenger, looking for "pieces of identity." [25]

Chambers' conspiratorial manner also impressed the proprietors of the farm where he lived shortly after his marriage. He acted so mysteriously that if anyone had been interested, his actions would have aroused suspicion. He never took the same bus two days in succession.

[24] Guy Endore to the author, October 6, 1962.
[25] This characteristic trait takes on special significance later in the study in relation to determining the validity of the source of some handwritten memos of Alger Hiss's (note size, 3 × 5), which Chambers claimed Hiss transmitted to him illegally early in 1938.

Michael Gold, a Communist writer, at one time editor of the *New Masses* and a colleague of Chambers, knew Chambers for about four years. Gold remembers him as a shy, closed person with whom it was difficult to make friends.

He was difficult to talk to . . . he had reservations. He could never look you in the eye. He was always looking over your shoulder, as though he were getting ready for flight.

Then he just disappeared suddenly from the movement. I met him once several years after he disappeared. He was walking down one of the Village streets. I said, "Hello." Chambers looked at me as though I were a stranger and replied, "I don't know you." [26]

He never saw Chambers again.

Chambers' paranoid suspiciousness and conspiratorial stance were soon fixed. Let us see how he documents and rationalizes his thoughts to appear "reality-oriented," and how his descent into the underground symbolized his death and rebirth. Chambers attributes the following anecdotes to "Ulrich," a character of the underground.

This curious man [Ulrich], the only Russian who was ever to become my close friend, was not a Communist. He had been a member of the left wing of the Socialist Revolutionary Party which, during the Russian Revolution, had gone over to the Bolsheviks. . . .

Ulrich had been arrested for political activities and was being marched in a mixed convoy of political prisoners and criminals to exile in Siberia. Now and again, the whole convoy had to halt while the snows melted and the roads opened to the east. To while away the time, a group of prisoners decided that each one should write out and read the story of his life. "There was one young student," said Ulrich. "He was just a boy. He had simply been arrested for reading some Marxist book. That was all. *In his whole life, nothing had ever happened to him. But he wrote a long story, and, do you know, it was very interesting.*[27]

"Then there was a criminal. He was a grown man. When his turn came, he said that he had no story. 'Why?' we asked. 'Didn't you agree to tell the story of your life?' 'There is nothing to tell,' he said. 'I killed a man. They sent me to Siberia. In prison, they beat me. With another convict, I escaped. We got lost in the *taiga*. We were starving. I killed my comrade and ate some of his flesh. If I had not killed him, he would have killed me. I went on. I met a bear. He attacked me. I had no knife, so I choked him with my hands. I ate some of the meat. So at last I escaped. What is there to tell?' " . . .

Once, during the civil war, two members of Ulrich's partisan band were captured by the White Guards. They were to be executed on a square in Sebastopol. Troops were posted everywhere, but Ulrich had decided to save his men. Under a guard of soldiers, they were marched out on the square to be shot. Alone, armed only with two revolvers, Ulrich opened fire on the troops. In a scene of truly Rus-

[26] Michael Gold to the author, January 11, 1964.
[27] Italics the author's.

sian confusion, Ulrich and his two friends (for whom he had brought a revolver apiece) shot their way out and escaped.

Ulrich's wife told me that story. Ulrich told me another. In one pitched battle, his partisan forces were wiped out. Ulrich escaped by riding a horse until it foundered. Then he went on on foot. At last, he dropped, exhausted by combat and flight, on the banks of a little river and fell asleep. He awoke just at sunset and found two peasant children watching him. One of them was crying. He asked her why. "Because," she said, "Ilyosha Ulanov has been killed." (He made up another name when he told me the story.)

"Do you know, Bob," he said to me, "it is the strangest feeling to hear from a child that you are dead."

From the content of these stories it is easy to surmise that these are Chambers' own fantasies being spun out.[28] The central theme in each of them deals with the fateful outcome of killing and the retaliatory fear of being killed. These metaphorical accounts depict, in story form, Chambers' life and struggle.

Chambers believed his own fiction to be the truth. When, in the course of psychic development, the fantasy systems of childhood fail to undergo normal maturation, then these imaginary thoughts about death and life are experienced as death and life. This easy interchangeability of a created (literary) experience, in this instance the fictionalization of the Ulrich stories, into a real experience was typical of Chambers' shiftings, his disturbed sense of identity and projection into his own fictional characters. What he did when he *wrote* fiction, or autobiography, was very similar to what he did as a child when he *read* fiction, especially Dostoevski, and also, but to a lesser extent, when he translated fiction. These forms of literary mastery and manipulation were among Chambers' ways of preserving his own identity by hiding it inside someone else's.

I should like now to consider Chambers' reactions to a significant real event that happened during this time—his wife's first pregnancy—as he describes it in *Witness*.

"For one of us to have a child," my brother had said in his agony, "would be a crime against nature!" I longed for children. But I agreed with my brother. There had been enough misery in our line. . . . As an underground Communist, I took it for granted that children were out of the question. . . .

One day, early in 1933, my wife told me that she believed she had conceived. . . . We discussed the matter, and my wife said that she must go at once for a physical check and to arrange for the abortion. . . .

The doctor . . . said there was a child. "She [the doctor] said that I am in good physical shape to have a baby." Very slowly, the truth dawned on me. "Do you mean," I asked, "that you want to have the child?" . . .

[28] Cf. also "The Damn Fool," written in 1924.

A wild joy swept me. Reason, the agony of my family, the Communist Party and its theories, the wars and revolutions of the 20th century, crumbled at the touch of the child. Both of us simply wanted a child. If the points on the long course of my break with Communism could be retraced, that is probably one of them. . . .

The night of October 16, 1933, I reached home late, around eleven o'clock. My wife was dressed, sitting at a table with a clock in front of her. She was waiting for me and quietly clocking the intervals between her first labor pains. We rode the long miles downtown while she gripped my hand during her pangs. When they took her away from me, a terrible despair seized me. I felt sure that my wife would die. I blamed myself and I knew that, without her, I did not wish to live.

All night I tramped the streets, as I had done the night when I climbed through my wife's window. From time to time, I telephoned the hospital. The answer was always the same: my wife was in the delivery room; the baby had not come. At seven o'clock in the morning, the baby still had not come.

I took the ferry to Staten Island. Then I tramped into the open country where I could find the earth that I felt I must be close to in that crisis.

At nine o'clock, I called again from the ferry house at St. George. "The baby has been born," a nurse said. "It is alive. It is a girl." "And my wife?" I asked. "She is all right," said the nurse. It seemed to me that she had hesitated. Again, I was seized with panic that my wife would die.

She was scarcely out of the anaesthetic, and reeking of ether, when I sat beside her bed. As I looked at her white, hollowed face and the deep, leaden circles under her eyes, and felt her feverish fingers, I thought: "What have I done to her?" At that moment, I cared only for my wife and nothing at all for the child.

Chambers' ideas and feelings about his newborn child were a reemergence of the identical fantasies he had about his own birth. He felt responsible for having almost killed his wife ("What have I done to her"), as he felt responsible for what he had done to his mother when he was born. The guilt of his infantile criminal-birth fantasy now returned in relation to the birth of his child; he was momentarily "undone" by the fleeting thought, "At that moment, I cared only for my wife and nothing at all for the child" (I'll sacrifice my child—myself—to redeem my wife—mother). Here again, as in his clinical account of his own birth and Laha's agony in having him, he saw his wife at the brink of death. Then followed the fear that he, as father, would not approve of the child's arrival (echoing Jay's rejection of him when he was born):

My wife kept urging me feebly to go and look at it. She wanted me, of course, to approve and love what had so nearly cost her life (the birth had been terrible). I went into the hall. Through a glass panel, I peered into the antiseptic nursery where the banks of babies lay in baskets. . . . The child had been born long enough to have lost the puckered, red, natal look. Her face was pink, and peaceful. She was sleeping. Her long lashes lay against her cheeks. She was beautiful.

I went back to my wife who was no longer only my wife but the mother of our child—the child we all yearn for, who, even before her birth, had begun invisibly, to lead us out of that darkness, which we could not even realize, toward that light, which we could not even see.

Now that he has in idea and verbal gesture sacrificed himself and absolved his infantile guilt, the birth of his child is experienced as his own rebirth. It is his wish-fulfilled second chance come true, a magical redemption, "the child we all yearn for, who, even before her birth [began] to lead us out of that darkness. . . ."

Chambers feels bolstered by the reality that his wife does not die (is not killed by him) in childbirth. With the birth of his child he exhibits to himself and the world his masculine identity and his sexual power. Thus he goes through the gamut of his childhood neurosis: his wife is his mother, the birth of his child is his own birth (and his brother's), the wish to abort his wife is a duplication of his infantile wish to remove his brother from his mother's womb and take his place. Then he is reborn the attractive, only one (his identification with his beautiful child). The entire sequence of his neurosis is recreated and re-experienced by a real event in a condensed and accelerated way.

In the most intimate family situation or in the external world of the underground, the forces that moved him are the same. Although he speaks of his child's birth as the beginning of his emergence from the "darkness" of the Communist underground, his life in the underground is itself an enactment, a temporary refuge against the darkness of his inner self. It symbolizes a self-punitive act, a period of "self-burial" and an equivalent of death. It is his magical way of expiating his guilt for the psychological murder of his brother. Elusive shifts from a position of known identity to one of anonymity enable him to feel omnipotent and surround him with an aura of mystery. He has everybody guessing and in wonderment about his activities. His political vacillations are merely a leitmotif; the central theme remains fixed. Unaltered is the hard core of his self-image: one driven by hunger, envy, hate, the need to destroy his brother; beset with guilt and deep ambivalence about life and death.

Current political events nurtured the paranoid, conspiratorial, persecutory, and general delusional systems of thinking that Chambers had long utilized as psychological protection. Distortion of his sense of time was reflected in faulty memory of dates and past events and was an essential accompaniment of his falsification of reality. Whenever the hard reality of recorded facts (as, for example, an authentic date or name) threatened to expose a protective fantasy or cause him accurately to remember a painful experience, he consciously shifted the time of the remembered event or fabricated a false document or imagined an event or a series of "covering" events. Chambers magically turned back the calendar of time so that the tragic events of his life —especially his birth—would be undone and redone. This psychic manipulation effecting a temporal change was acted out by him consciously and unconsciously. When hard facts insisted that he was in error, as was the case so often, he sought new covering rationalizations and new ideologies. But his infantile fantasies remained fixed and unchanged in his unconscious mind: his hatred of himself, his wish to be unborn, then reborn as his brother, to live out a surrogate's existence, his desperate guilt when his brother's death fulfilled this desire.

III

7

Death and Disappointment

RICHARD'S SUICIDE was, to be sure, the single, most disrupting event in the life of Whittaker Chambers. And, ironically, the impact of suicide on the Hiss family must be reckoned with as an important determinant in the development of Alger Hiss's life as well. In 1907, when Alger was two and a half years old, his father killed himself. An accurate historical presentation of the circumstances of Charles Alger Hiss's death and the profound impact this event had on the life course of Alger Hiss are basic to our understanding of his character and personality. A brief reconstruction of certain salient facts from the earlier annals of his father's life is essential.

It is a life which, on the surface, hardly suggests its tragic culmination. Charles Hiss was born in Baltimore in 1864, a Civil War baby, and the last of six children. The family was, according to all accounts, unusually close-knit, and—with three sisters old enough to care for him, and two elder brothers—Charles apparently received a full measure of their warmth. He was educated in the public schools of Baltimore. Tall and physically attractive, extroverted and athletic rather than intellectually inclined, he enjoyed sports and outdoor life. He was bent on business success, and after finishing high school he turned directly to finding a job. He was first employed as a salesman for the Troxell Carriage and Harness Company. After a few years (in anticipation of the decline of the harness business) he took a job as an apprentice with a textile firm and was trained in the manufacture of cotton materials. He emerged a few years later as a promising young salesman for one of Baltimore's large wholesale dry-goods stores.

When Charles was twenty-two (1886) his father died; soon thereafter the eldest brother, George, married and moved to North Carolina; a year later John married. Charles remained at home with his mother and two of his three sisters until a year after John's marriage, when he married Mary Lavinia Hughes. "Minnie" Hughes was the daughter of a respected, middle-class Baltimore family, and their marriage was considered a proper match.

Minnie was childless for five years and then bore their first daughter, Anna, on May 11, 1893. Two years later a second daughter was born (Mary Ann, July 30, 1895). Then five more years passed, and in the twelfth year of her marriage Mrs. Hiss gave birth to her first son, Bosley (April 30, 1900), named after his paternal grandmother. Five more years went by and Alger was born (November 11, 1904).[1] Two years later Donald was born (December 15, 1906). Thus, over a period of thirteen years the Hisses had five children.

Meanwhile Charles was doing well in his career. Shortly after his marriage he had joined Daniel Miller and Company, one of Baltimore's largest importers and jobbers of dry goods. After several years of hard work he became an executive and by 1902 a stockholder and voting member of the firm.

He was evidently a good provider, and he was remembered as a jovial and affectionate family man. His memory was especially cherished by his nieces and nephews, for good reason: for much of their lives he served as their father. Their real father, Charles' brother John, died suddenly at the early age of thirty-three.[2] He left behind his widow, Lillian, and six children, the two youngest being just four months and two years old. Charles was in the seventh year of his marriage when his brother died in 1895. That year his eldest daughter, Anna, was two years old; his second child, Mary Ann, was an infant; they were the same age as his brother's two youngest children, Charles Alger and Elizabeth.[3]

Charles Hiss, along with his two sisters, remained closely attached to his dead brother's family. For the next twelve years remaining of his life, Charles cared for them with uncommon devotion. "Uncle Charlie," as he is still referred to by his nieces and nephews, was as much of a father substitute for his bereaved nieces and nephews as any man could be. He served as counselor for his sister-in-law, instructed her in financial matters, helped her with every-day problems. He arranged their holiday trips, accompanied them to and from their destinations. He regularly took the children for jaunts about the city.

[1] It has been conjectured that Alger's father "perpetuated his own father's admiration" for Horatio Alger in naming their son Alger. Hiss dismissed the Horatio Alger fable but said the name "Alger" did indeed perpetuate his grandfather's admiration, but not for *Horatio* Alger. Alger's grandfather had been a friend and admirer of Russell Alexander Alger, who later became Secretary of War under President McKinley.

[2] John Hiss died in bed during the night of April 23, 1895. He had been working intensely (as a salesman) during the days and in the evenings. The death certificate records the immediate cause of death as "angina pectoris" and "duration of last sickness, five minutes."

[3] The significance and consequences of this parallelism between Charles Hiss's own two children and the two youngest children of his dead brother will be elaborated upon later.

John's youngest son, Charles Alger Hiss (named after his uncle), now in his seventies, has written:

Uncle Charlie, my father's brother, felt responsible to assist our family after my father died. As an example, when Mother planned to take the family to Blue Hill, Me., he arranged for transportation and overnite accommodations at a New York hotel on the way north and took us to the N.Y.-Boston-Bangor boat the next day. Being Uncle Charlie's namesake, he gave me a Boston Bull terrier.

The two families lived six city blocks apart. Uncle Charles brought them close together in a happy and affectionate relationship that has endured through the years. The eleven children, as they grew older, became very closely knit and were frequent visitors in each other's homes. John Hiss had been a Methodist, but after he died his children joined their cousins in the young people's activities at the Reformed Episcopal Church on Bolton Street, which Charles Hiss and his family attended regularly.[4]

John's son Charles (Alger's cousin) goes on to say:

My two Aunts, my sister Mary and I went to Uncle Charles' church for perhaps ten years and maybe three times out of four I went to their home for dinner and the afternoon. I was fond of the whole family (and a good dinner) and generally amused the two youngsters, Alger and Donald, by reading stories—the three of us in a big chair—and later, rough-housing with them. Bosley was too old to enter into this.

Among the many early recollections sent to me about Alger Hiss's father was one from a niece, describing how Uncle Charles always accompanied her home after evening church services. After many years, she assured him that this was no longer necessary and he acceded to her wishes. But, as she later found out, he dutifully persisted, by watching her from a distance until he saw her safely home.

After Charles Hiss had established himself with the Daniel Miller Company, he brought Albert Hughes, his wife's younger brother and a personal favorite of hers, into the firm. Albert is remembered as a charming but irresponsible gay blade of extravagant tastes and habits. Alger Hiss has written:

Uncle Albert was considerably younger than my father, and my mother was utterly devoted to him. He was a master showman, and I can still see him dressed as a boulevardier, with a silver-handled stick, spats, and cutaway—very handsome and maybe a little roguish. He was a charmer, and my father, who must have found him appealing, was evidently fond of him.[5]

[4] Charles Alger Hiss was a devout Episcopalian and on the official board of his neighborhood church. Many years after his death his wife transferred to the Presbyterian Church, attracted there by an exceptional minister, and finally in her later years changed to the Unitarian Church.
[5] A word of explanation about the above quote from Alger Hiss as well as the many

Albert advanced rapidly in the firm and in time became the treasurer of the company. However, he tended to get himself involved in imprudent business transactions, and Charles, who had sponsored and introduced him into the firm, felt morally responsible for his actions, as though he were Albert's "big brother."

In 1906 Albert entered into a large financial commitment involving the firm's funds, to which Charles had pledged his financial support and backing. The exact details of the transaction have become dimmed, but in effect Albert did not fulfill his part of the obligation. As a result of Albert's default Charles suffered a considerable loss. Alger's parents were shocked and disappointed by this lack of loyalty. But Charles did not insist that Albert make good his promises, and Albert got away with his default. Because Charles Hiss was not the type to insist that Albert make amends, he was himself forced to sell his shares of stock to the other members of the firms and terminated an eighteen-year association with them. Albert Hughes, however, remained after Charles Hiss left, and even his adoring sister felt this as a kind of disloyalty.

A close account of the vicissitudes which Charles Alger Hiss subsequently underwent has not come to light. It is known, however, that directly after leaving the Daniel Miller Company he developed signs of poor health. He became more and more concerned about his physical state, brooded over the circumstances of his severed relationship with the Daniel Miller Company and the betrayal by his brother-in-law. Charles Hiss was a proud man and had been a good provider. Several months passed and he did not find new employment. A growing concern about his physical health developed along with a deepening melancholia. As the year 1906 came to an end the country was moving into one of the worst financial depressions in its history, the Panic of 1907. Charles' friends advised him to wait until his health improved before committing himself to any new business.

But as a man of strong conscience he felt keenly his responsibilities to his family and his loss of self-esteem. His wife had just given birth to their

---

others which appear throughout the book. Over a period of five years I engaged Mr. Hiss in a close and continuous correspondence in which I put to him every type of question, the responses to which I felt were necessary both for background information or directly quoted documentation. Often my questions were serial ones on a given topic, and many of Mr. Hiss's historical descriptions of himself or his family were obtained from him as direct responses to a systematic series of specific questions (often in questionnaire form). These queries were put to him both in vis-à-vis interviews and in correspondence.

Other direct quotations from Mr. Hiss which I have used were extracted from my notes recorded by hand during the more than one hundred hours of conversation between Mr. Hiss and myself. Only in this way was it possible for me to obtain a first-hand, living picture of him.

fifth child, Donald. Alger was then two years old, Bosley was seven, Mary Ann, twelve, and Anna, fourteen.

In the early spring of 1907, in search of a new business venture, Charles took a trip to Charlotte, North Carolina, to visit his brother, George Bosley Hiss. There the two Hiss brothers entered into a partnership and drew up plans to purchase and manage a large cotton mill, which, according to reports, had been operating successfully for many years. George Hiss was to be president of the company, Charles, vice-president. After deliberating in North Carolina for about a month, Charles came back to his family in apparent good spirits, seemingly buoyed by the expectations of his new business association, a remedy for the fiasco brought on by his brother-in-law. Upon his return home he made several visits to his Baltimore attorney and completed the contractual agreements. His outward demeanor after his return home was, as always, thoughtful and solicitous toward his family, and he spent much time with his children. But he was inwardly concerned over the fact that his new business venture would necessitate moving his family to Charlotte. The enormous sacrifices such a move entailed, leaving friends, family, and the urban pleasures of Baltimore life, all troubled him deeply. When he revealed his plan to his wife it did not meet with her approval. He was caught in the dilemma of his wife's expressed wish not to leave Baltimore (to say nothing of his own disappointment which such a move entailed) and the opportunities the new move offered. He went to see Dr. Taneyhill, his family physician, who unavailingly urged him to enter Shephard-Pratt Hospital.

On Saturday afternoon, four days after his return from North Carolina, he took his five children for a long drive through Druid Hill Park. The next morning, Sunday, April 7, 1907, Charles Hiss killed himself.

The *Baltimore Sun* on April 8, 1907, in a lengthy obituary, stated:

Mr. Charles A. Hiss, until recently a member of the Daniel Miller Company, importers and jobbers of dry goods and notions, cut his throat with a razor at 9:50 a.m. yesterday at his home, 1427 Linden Avenue.

Mr. Hiss . . . asked his wife to telephone for Dr. G. Lane Taneyhill a few minutes before he was found dead. He expressed a desire to undergo a thorough examination to ascertain beyond any doubt if his lungs and other organs were sound.

About 9:30 a.m. he called to Mrs. Hiss and requested her to summon the physician, which she did. Shortly before 10 o'clock Mrs. Hiss, thinking it time for the doctor to arrive, went to her husband's room to call him to breakfast. . . . Mr. Hiss was lying in bed in his night attire with his throat cut almost from ear to ear. The razor was still grasped firmly in his right hand. . . .

Four months ago Mr. Hiss retired from Daniel Miller Company. A marked change in his health was noticed from that time, and he became apprehensive of his condition.

Worrying on this subject resulted in chronic insomnia, from which he suffered three months. For more than a week he appeared extremely melancholy.

· · ·

He seemed to prefer a domestic life, and was said to have been more than ordinarily thoughtful of the members of his family and to have looked after their needs and comforts.

What forces moved Charles Hiss to end his life? From what we know of his earlier life, his character and personality, his diligence as a family pro-vider, his fraternal altruism, it seems that his final act must have been mobi-lized by hidden psychic disturbances far more profound than the anguish caused him by financial irregularities and his subsequent ill health.[6]

Suicide is often a hostile, revengeful act directed against a loved one. It holds the power to injure, for the rest of their lives, those who survive the person who destroys himself. If Charles' suicide was such an act, whom might he have unconsciously wanted to harm? Most obviously, his wife Minnie comes to mind. Certainly some hidden resentment against her might have been exacerbated by her reluctance to join in his new business venture (not to mention her favoritism toward Albert, indirectly responsible for Charles' fi-nancial troubles). And perhaps unconscious hostility against Minnie was re-sponsible in part for Charles' self-destruction. But other possibilities are sug-gested by Charles' history. His tragic death, leaving behind a large family, re-calls the death of his brother John—and there may indeed be a significant psychological link between the two. It will be remembered that John left six children, for whom Charles performed the role of substitute father with ex-traordinary devotion. As to what motivated Charles' self-sacrifice we can only speculate, but it no doubt involved a strong identification with John. This re-lationship perhaps stemmed from the deep fraternal affection of two youngest sons, only a year apart, growing up and living in the same city and following similar occupations. No doubt it was born partly out of the natural envy of a younger brother toward an older brother, enforced by the fact that John had produced six children in the years of his marriage while Charles' marriage was for five years barren.

By the time of John's death, Charles had one child two years old; a month later Minnie bore another child. John's two youngest children at that time were approximately the same age; thus the identification between Charles and his dead brother was enhanced. I suggest that both before and after his brother's death Charles equated his brother's children with his own. Required

---

[6] As a result of his death, Charles Hiss's five children shared the proceeds of a $50,000 life-insurance policy which he had willed to them.

from then on to perform the responsibilities of double parenthood, he did so with generosity and affection—yet one may ask whether the death of his brother, an event that mobilized in him a life of continuing self-sacrifice, may have been inwardly felt by him as a betrayal.

It is significant that at the time of his own death Charles had lived out a marital cycle in many ways equivalent to John's. He had a large family (five as opposed to John's six). His two youngest were approximately the same age as his first two children had been at the time of John's death—and they were the same age (about four months, and two and a half years) as John's two youngest had been when he left them for Charles to care for. Charles had arrived, by April 1907, at a period of his life reminiscent of, hence symbolically interchangeable with, his brother's in 1895.

At this psychologically crucial anniversary Charles found himself betrayed again: this time by his brother-in-law Albert, who had done in fact what John did in psychological effect: betrayed a trust and left him with new, unwanted responsibilities. Finding himself in an equivalent dilemma, he reacted to it by bringing about his own death as a re-enactment of his brother's fate, thus leaving to Albert, as John had left to him, the consequences of the act. In short, his suicide may be viewed as an irrationally directed act of revenge against his brother-in-law.[7] Such actions, evidencing an unconscious identification with the life course and fate of another person, usually a close family member (so-called "anniversary reactions"), are well known clinically.

The circumstances that surrounded Charles Hiss's death remained a divided family secret; for many years the facts were shielded from the younger Hiss children, including Bosley, who was seven at the time. Mary Ann and Anna, twelve and fourteen, whatever knowledge they may have had, never divulged to their younger brothers the circumstances of their father's death. Many years later Alger and Donald overheard some commiserating remarks of neighbors alluding to their father's suicide. Alger angrily went to Bosley, his "authority," seeking the blunt denial he desired to hear. It was then that Bosley went to the files of the *Baltimore Sun* and discovered the facts of his father's death, which he then passed on to his two brothers.

Deeply rooted in the character and subsequent life story of Alger Hiss there will be discernible, in an entirely different set of external circumstances, the echo of Charles Hiss. It is enough to remember for the moment that Alger was two and a half years old at the time of the suicide, and that for any young

[7] The irony and unrealism of Charles Hiss's suicidal act was, of course, that Albert Hughes, lacking the Hiss quality of responsibility, never became the caretaker or assumed any part of the family burden which Charles' death brought about. George Hiss, the eldest brother, took up the reins of financial benefactor and counselor.

child the death of a parent is thought of as a betrayal. Further, this first unconscious impression was not ever to be entirely dissipated—indeed, it would
be confirmed when Alger learned the circumstances of his father's death.

The tragedy had more obvious effects. It left Alger and his siblings with
only a mother, and left the family in altered financial circumstances.
Though they were never to experience poverty, they could no longer afford,
for example, a horse and carriage. Minnie bore the brunt of her loss and met
the challenge of her future life with remarkable adaptiveness and stoicism.
She tapped new sources of energy within herself, carried out both her domestic tasks and new civic activities.

After her husband's death Minnie Hiss played an active part in Balti-
more life for almost half a century. She helped organize Baltimore's first
Mother's Club and became its president. She later served as president of the
Arundel Club, on the boards of the Women's Civic League, League of
Women Voters, and District Federation of Women's Clubs. In later years she
was chairman of social service in the Unitarian Church. During World War II,
when she was in her seventies, she was a captain of USO and active in the
Red Cross.[8]

Despite her activities outside the home Minnie managed the house with
executive efficiency. Alger has recalled:

My mother's energy was fantastic. She did run the house well and checked on our
clothes, manners, health, and eating habits as thoroughly as if she did naught else.
She was always up late at night and early in the morning. She made most of her
own clothes, she mended and darned ours. She was definitely a good manager. We
always had a cook but Mother supervised the shopping, the choice of menus, and
the preparation of meals.

But if her housekeeping was flawless, there were serious defects in her ability
to preside over her large family as a loving parent.

Without a husband, Minnie was a confused person. Gossip about her
husband's suicide threatened to undermine her social status. In her role as
both mother and father, her club life and listening to lectures took on special
significance. It gave her a feeling of being "in the know," of social recognition

[8] She was, in all, a remarkably indestructible woman. At the age of seventy-five she
successfully underwent an operation for carcinoma and lived for sixteen more years. In
her late years she was operated on for cataracts. She lived alone after the marriage of
her sons, with the exception of several winters spent in Texas with Anna; then during the
last ten years of her life she lived with a niece, Lillian Hiss. At the age of eighty she
was a regular member of the Unitarian Church and belonged to fifteen organizations.
Shortly before her death she suffered a fall and, needing more care, stayed in a conva-
lescent home near her relatives. At the time of her death she still belonged to seven or
eight organizations; her interest in their activities never waned. She died in 1958 at
the age of ninety-one.

and self-importance. To be informed and abreast of the times made her feel that she was a capable, "modern" parent.

Forceful in her own right, Minnie Hiss nevertheless leaned heavily on the advice of those she considered authorities. She put much store in the opinions of professors, doctors, and children's experts. Her own role at home became somewhat akin to that of a lecturer. It is clear that she was not a source of adequate love for the boy, but a fountain of opinion, exhortation, and get-ahead inspirational advice, which had to be examined before it was accepted or rejected.

Shorn of her own respectability, she no doubt became determined to see her daughters established in wealthy marriages and her sons in successful professional careers.

She urged them to exhibit their virtues, talents, and knowledge, and to be nice and especially pleasant to important people. For years in advance she planned their college educations. It was this kind of social aggressiveness on his mother's part that stirred the strongest feelings of resentment in her son. Alger felt "it was bad judgment as well as bad taste," the way his mother insisted that he "blow his own horn" for advancement of scholarship.

Hiss tends to speak of his mother (as he tends to speak in general) dispassionately, with reserve, and frequently with a somewhat condescending note. And no doubt that very tone is a reaction against Minnie's unrestrained urgings. In a moment of self-analysis Hiss has remarked:

I now have an attitude, so conditioned as to seem second nature, that exhibitionism is, to say the least, bad taste. In others, it bores me or annoys me except where it is so evidently pathological as to arouse sympathy or curiosity. . . . It just isn't my idea of the civilized man. My admiration (and emulation) are reserved for British understatement and restraint, for absence of display.

But neither the distance in time nor the distance in his voice can conceal a certain sense of deprivation where his mother is concerned. He has said that from the earliest time he can remember he knew it was necessary to resist his mother's will. The success of that resistance, as will be seen, was dubious, but the struggle was doubtless real.

It was not, of course, Alger's struggle alone; his brothers and sisters faced similar problems. Together they helped maintain a sense of balance in the household. The older children, especially Bosley, led the way.

Bosley, Minnie's eldest son, was a romantic and rebellious youth; between thirteen and fifteen he ran away from home several times, on one occasion staying away four or five weeks. But he was also bright and socially adept, and his wit subdued Minnie. According to Alger, Bosley "dispelled her exhortations by his natural charm and the use of a light touch."

Following Bosley's early revolt, Alger and Donald had a less difficult time. "Bosley's successful battle with Mother" says Alger, "had softened her. In any event, she was a few years older, and Donald and I were dealing with a less vigorous person." With Bosley as the central and unifying force, all five children used to band together in lightheartedly poking fun at their mother's rigid views. Bewildered and almost entirely lacking in humor, Mrs. Hiss became an easy prey to the teasing of her children.

Another counterbalancing force in the household—and of special importance to Alger—was the presence of his Aunt Lila (Eliza), who had moved in to help care for the family after her brother died. She was Alger's main source of affection and understanding. Aunt Lila remained for ten years (until Alger was twelve) as "an important fixture" in the Hiss household. Her constancy made up for Minnie's frequent absences and provided a counterbalance for her authoritarianism. Lillian Hiss writes: "Her wisdom and gentle guidance were a great help with the growing adolescents."

Hiss recalls that, in effect, she replaced his mother. Both Aunt Lila and Aunt Lucy (who did not live with the family but was a frequent visitor) were warmer and more responsive, though quite different in temperament, and the children loved them dearly.

The presence of Aunt Lila in the household had the effect of weakening Mrs. Hiss's familial authority. Both Lila and Lucy were older and surer in the reality of their individuality and of their opinions. And in their presence "little Minnie Hughes" was more overawed by them than by anyone else she saw regularly.

To Aunt Lila, Alger confided his interests and goals, for she was sympathetic in a nondemanding way. It is from Aunt Lila, "the quick, intelligent, ethical little woman," that Hiss dates his earliest childhood recollections; they

are of my Aunt Lila reading aloud. I also remember Sunday morning prayers and Bible reading at home, before Sunday School and Church. And so I knew the Bible and Bible stories well.

He traces his childhood desire to be a medical missionary to his Aunt Lila. This, he says, grew very naturally out of his environment:

I don't recall any earlier aim so it must have formed very early. It promised fulfillment of my boyish desires for adventure and for achievement against obstacles. It is now clear that its social acceptability played an unconscious part of considerable importance.

Aunt Lila was scholarly in taste and read aloud to the children. She had a real love of the literary classics and a "decent respect" for music and art. She was the family poet. For amusement, birthdays, or other celebrations she wrote light doggerel. Minnie, on the contrary, had little interest in books; ". . . she pleaded lack of time, but never admitted lack of desire." Minnie's insistence on art classes, music lessons, travel lectures, and so forth, for her children came more from what she was told in her clubs was "best" than from any real appreciation of her own.

In contrast to the clearly defined imprint Minnie and Aunt Lila left on him, Hiss says that "any father figure with whom I may have been consciously identified was 'diffuse.' " This euphemistic expression glossed over a painfully unfulfilled area in Hiss's emotional life—his quest for a father. One of Alger's older cousins, a prudent and reliable person, wrote that she has "always thought of Minnie's children as *bereft* (as were our family of six) by not having a living father to whom to turn for paternal love and guidance. Alger missed a father, as any boy would, but he never dwelt on it."

His father's memory was somewhat glorified by the family, and the factual circumstances that surrounded the suicide were forgotten or softened by family legend.[9] As a protective balm, the image of Charles Hiss as a man of honesty and integrity, which indeed he was, was memorialized. His revered image as a figure of personal charm, magnanimity, and devotion was thus not overtly blemished by his final act. But the event remained a family blot. The psychic aftermath deeply affected Alger, though he has no direct memories about it. He grew up with the idea that his father had "let the family down" and recalls that as a boy he consciously vowed never to do the same thing. The shameful memory of his father's suicide, though dimmed by time, has never been resolved. The ancestral images of his paternal forebears, among others, have been enhanced as an assurance of patriarchal stability.

Valentine Hesse, great-great-great-grandfather of Alger Hiss, came to the American scene about the middle of the eighteenth century. From the few recorded historical facts, together with a bit of family lore, certain qualities of

---

[9] Charles Alger Hiss, nephew and namesake of Alger's father, in response to my inquiry about the date, circumstances, and meaning of his uncle's death, writes: "I believe Uncle Charles died in 1904 or 1905 [it was 1907]. Presumably because of my age I have no recollections of emotional or psychological effects of his death upon the family."

It is significant to note that the date is erroneously recalled and the circumstances forgotten. From the account of another living relative, we can see how family lore, with beneficent distortion, has softened this tragic family event and transformed its history. Mary C. Hiss (Alger's cousin) gave the following brief account of her Uncle Charles' death: "When a friend with whom Uncle Charles often traveled went back on him, he became discouraged and disheartened, since he was out of work and had a family to look after. His brother in North Carolina, who had a small cotton mill, sent for him to come look over a job there. When Uncle Charles saw the simple life that was lived there at that time he knew it would never suit his wife and children. He returned thoroughly discouraged and died soon after."

Lillian Hiss said: "I scarcely remember the shock of Uncle Charles' tragic death because the details were shielded from us, but I think his depression stemmed largely from great disappointment from monetary losses at the hands of trusted friends."

Valentine's character and person are evident. He was an energetic German immigrant, one of the many hardy, eighteenth-century pioneers who emigrated from the "old country" to meet the challenges of the American frontier. During the voyage he befriended a young French girl named Christine Arnault, whom he married soon after their arrival in the port of Baltimore. With his young French wife he became part of the rural community of early Baltimore. He changed his name from Hesse to Hiss. He sired a family, matured, and prospered. He became a successful farmer; God-fearing and church-going, he early established himself as a pillar of the community. In the sixtieth year of his life, so family legend goes, while standing at the well-pump outside his home during an electrical storm, he was struck dead by lightning. From the legendary accounts of this patriarchal figure, handed down through two centuries and five generations, the present-day, clannish progeny of Valentine Hiss still draws pride of family and, as Alger Hiss says, "a feeling of historicity." During these two hundred years the descendants of Valentine Hiss have left some imprints on Maryland. Once rural, now urban, landmarks still stand which bear their name.[10]

---

[10] Jacob Hiss, great-great-grandfather of Alger Hiss, became a man of property and a gentleman farmer. He industriously accumulated further property and became a successful landowner in the newly formed city of Baltimore. He purchased a section of land off the old Harford Road and developed it into a comfortable country estate: he named it "Lavender Hill." He married Elizabeth Gatch, daughter of a well-known Baltimore landowner.

They had eight sons and eight daughters. In the early 1800s, when the city streets of Baltimore were extended to Harford Road and the Hiss estate had been further divided, a public school and thoroughfare (Hiss School and Hiss Avenue) were constructed.

One of the sons of Jacob Hiss was Jesse Lee Hiss (1788–1876), Alger Hiss's great-grandfather. He married Eliza Millemon, the daughter of a Maryland architect (he designed the Maryland University Law School). It would appear that Jesse Hiss inherited more of his father's magnanimity than his money. Jacob Hiss willed most of his accumulated fortune as philanthropic endowments for educational and religious organizations. Eliza Millemon boasted that she and her husband "never had much wealth," but she was as happy as or happier than her other sisters who married into money. Jesse Hiss lived to be eighty-eight, and his wife survived him by several years.

George Millemon Hiss (1822–86), Alger Hiss's grandfather, was born in a period when Baltimore was regarded as the most flourishing commercial town on the American continent. As a young adult he was already integrated into the communal life of early Baltimore and participated in the city's industrial growth. He was largely self-educated and enjoyed a diversity of interests and occupations. As a young adult he read law and prepared himself for the bar but did not practice as an attorney. He dealt in insurance, was a news reporter and editorial writer. In later years he served as a business adviser for a large paper mill and then became the owner and operator of two large mills. In 1846, at the age of twenty-four, George Millemon Hiss married Mary Ann Bosley. The Bosleys boasted an even earlier line of American forebears than the Hisses, claiming ancestry back to the Ark and Dove Expedition.

George Millemon Hiss and Mary Ann Bosley had six children who survived infancy. Of these the eldest three were daughters (Eliza, Lucy, and Worthina) and the next three sons (George Bosley, John Crowther, and Charles Alger).

During Alger's early youth (eight to twelve), he chose several older boys as models for emulation. He admired especially two older cousins, John Bosley Hiss and Charles Alger Hiss (Charles was a middleweight collegiate wrestler at Lehigh and an intercollegiate champion). Since they were several years older than Bosley, they seemed more like adults to Alger than did Bosley in those years. They often came to Alger's home for family dinner, and Alger's family went to theirs.

A more obvious paternal figure was Charles Mann, a patent attorney and friend of the family. He and his family were fairly frequent visitors, and Minnie consulted him on questions relating to the disciplining and education of the children. Minnie made a conscious effort to have men as family friends to make up for her husband's death. Mann took the boys to ball games and outings. Alger still recalls his enjoyment of the occasions when Mann had the boys up to his office during the World Series, so that they could see play-by-play reports of the game electrically flashed on a large board outside the *Baltimore Sun* building.

There were many revered men in Alger's life. As a boy without a father, he had special affinity for paternal figures in whom he found some facet of a father substitute. Duane Wevill, the rector of his church, held Alger's affection for many years.

He was kindly, gentle, gay. He took the boys of his church on Saturday hikes and had the affection and admiration of all of them. I still have the small Bible he presented to me at a Sunday School function with the inscription, "Alger Hiss, for Bible Study, Church of the Redeemer, 14 June, 1914." . . .

I never lost touch with him. He attended my trial and corresponded with me while I was at Lewisburg prison. He looked forward to my visits until his death a few years after I came home.

Another highly significant figure who appeared intermittently in Alger's life was his uncle, George Bosley Hiss. "No doubt Uncle George contributed some to my concepts of man's estate," writes Hiss. Uncle George left Baltimore before Alger was born, and his earliest memory of him is that of a rich uncle in Charlotte, North Carolina.[11]

George Hiss was a colorful, self-made man. After finishing high school in Baltimore he got his first job working for an oil company in the South. Sometime during the 1880s, a period when cotton manufacturing was rapidly developing, George Hiss borrowed enough money to buy some property along the Catawba River in North Carolina. With a partner he started a small cot-

---

[11] It will be recalled that it was George whom Alger's father visited in 1907, following his severance from the Daniel Miller Company.

ton mill. The Southern Power Company eventually bought it from him for a good price.

George Hiss and his wife, Bertha (they were childless), were very public-spirited in their home-town of Charlotte. Their giving was unostentatious, usually anonymous.

Uncle George was the "rich uncle" from Charlotte. Ever since Charles' death in 1907, years before the Rhodes-Hiss Mills had become a success, George regularly sent financial help to Minnie and the children in substantial amounts and welcomed members of the family when they came through Charlotte. He eventually became a millionaire; and until his death in 1928 he was the financial adviser and benefactor of the entire Hiss family, as Charles had been for John's family.[12] His periodic visits to Baltimore were looked forward to with great excitement by everyone. Uncle George was a romantic figure. He was wise, witty, and independent in thought. There was a legend about him that in early manhood he had been a sculptor and a heavy drinker who had taken the Keeley Cure.[13] He was adored by his two sisters, Aunt Lucy and Aunt Lila, though, to be sure, they were rather shocked by his "worldly intellectual values," which they found little short of iconoclastic. Uncle George's free thinking and nonconformist ways had a direct influence on Bosley and, through Bosley, on Alger. In retrospect, Hiss "suspects" that it was because of Bosley's great admiration for and emulation of Uncle George (whom Bosley visited in Charlotte) that he (Alger), as a youngster, shared the same feelings for his uncle.

During Alger's youth, despite his tendency to multiple hero-worship, it was Bosley whom he deeply loved and emulated. Anyone Bosley thought well of must, Alger believed, be worthy of his own admiration. Though Bosley was often away from the house, took little notice of and spent almost no time with Alger during his early childhood, Bosley's free spirit and charming manner fascinated his little brother. Bosley remained a model for Alger until Alger's adulthood. Bosley and his "grown-up" friends were, of course, much older than Alger. He spent summers away from home. He was either at camp or, one summer, out West working as a laborer in the wheat fields of Kansas. In the winters, too, when he was not at school, Bosley's life, filled with friends and activities, kept him away from home a great deal. When he was home, "he was a figure who occasionally took part in games and sports (tennis and

[12] Through inheritance from Uncle George, after his death in 1928, Aunt Lila and Aunt Lucy were eventually able to build a comfortable suburban house. Mary C. Hiss, cousin to Alger, lives there now. It seems that Uncle George helped them while he was still alive by enabling them to buy a less expensive city house several miles from the Hiss's Linden Avenue home.
[13] A secret, once-popular method for the treatment of alcoholism involving the administration of special drugs.

baseball) with good nature and skill" and who was admired by his younger brothers.

Alger's Uncle Albert (Minnie's brother) was the one person in the family Alger never thought much of. Albert visited the Hiss home sporadically after Charles' death, but the children felt no warmth or close feelings toward him. Although he lived very well and had no children, he didn't help the Hisses out at all. He prospered and died young.

8

Search for a Father

THE HISS HOUSE at 1427 Linden Avenue was small and well ordered. Most family activity took place in the medium-sized living room on the second floor. The front room downstairs, a parlor-sitting room with a piano, was reserved for guests, special occasions, and violin and piano practicing.

Life at home centered in the dining room. The dinner hour was the only time all members were gathered together. Table talk was spirited, led in great part by Anna, Mary Ann, and Bosley, with Donald and Alger tagging along. There were lively discussions, mostly about music, books, plays, with easy laughter and joking. Much of the hilarity and heady talk at dinner was over Minnie's head. She was a natural target for the children, as she consistently misnamed books, authors, plays, artists, as well as people she had met. At the family table, to her children she seemed like a puzzled, slightly bewildered, but very conscientious teacher who has just taken over a spirited class whose members constantly quote the prior teacher and other authorities whose views are at variance with the new teacher's sense of correctness.

The difference in ages did not restrain a close relationship among the children. All five were of high intellectual caliber. Bosley, though years younger than his two sisters, had since his early teens been the equal of the older girls in wit and intelligence. Friends of the children and relatives and friends of Mrs. Hiss frequently shared the family table.

Family life in the Hiss household, though basically ordered, allowed many areas of free activity. Certain patterns were fixed and largely unquestioned: the children were expected to be punctual at meals, come in with hair combed, hands washed, and the boys with jackets on. Once a week, at Sunday dinner, each of the children had to report to the rest of the family what he or she had learned during the week. These routine recitals weren't always relished by the group, but they usually acquiesced in good spirit. The boys were free to be out of the house on their own when routine duties were finished.

. . . we accepted the responsibility with a sense of pride in our not being over-supervised. The chores, among other routine jobs, included, in winter, keeping the two Franklin stoves going—shaken down in the early morning, coal carried in scuttles from the basement bin, damping down for the night, and of course the messy job of cleaning out the ashes and restarting the fires whenever they went out on us. We also were responsible for carrying the smaller-sized coal up for the kitchen range and doing marketing errands (with a list) for the maid or for mother.

The three boys also were expected to report regularly to their Grand-mother Hughes (Minnie's stepmother), who lived just down the street, and to run errands for her. Attendance at Sunday school and church at the nearby Reformed Episcopal Church was obligatory. Alger disliked the religious serv-ices and from the time he was ten or eleven protested having to be present at them, but to no avail. "Church meant constraint and boredom, especially dur-ing the sermons," he recalls. It was through the church, however, that Alger became active in the Boy Scouts, an interest he retained for many years. Bible reading at home, in which the children shared in the reading of verses, and Sunday morning prayers, led by Mrs. Hiss, were formal, serious, and highly disciplined. At times, however, the solemnity was broken by bits of mischief and whispers which passed between the boys.

All five children took some kind of music or art lessons. The house was always filled with the sounds of music, either "live" from Bosley's or Donald's violin or the girls' piano playing, or from Bosley's collection of Red Seal rec-ords, for which he saved most of his spending money. Bosley's great interest was music. He chose—and Minnie permitted him—to go to a Presbyterian church because the soloist there was more to his liking. Alger, like his sisters before him, played the piano, but he regards himself as the least musical of the family.

Alger went reluctantly to dancing school during his early teens. He en-joyed sketching and coloring, and from the age of eleven he went every Satur-day morning to a drawing class given by Marjorie Martenette, a well-known local academic painter. In conjunction with the art class and just before it, he took lessons in conversational German with Franklin Hogendorf. To supple-ment these activities, Mrs. Hiss now and then took the children to concerts, travel talks, and art galleries.

But despite this cultural activity, Hiss portrays himself as an active sports-minded child, a sort of super-typical boy.

The overriding importance in my early youth (six to fourteen or even sixteen) was my life outside the house. The urge was to be out of doors the moment meals, chores, studies, family requirements in general, permitted. This had been equally a feature of Bosley's pattern of activity before me and was the accepted attitude of all my peers. . . .

In the city neighborhoods (four or five blocks), the children "lived on the streets," even in winter. We progressed from hopscotch, jumping rope, spinning tops, playing marbles, hide-and-seek, kick-the-can, and tag to roller-skating (including hockey in the streets), bicycle trips, hikes, interminable games of catch with baseballs or footballs (according to season), or just hobnobbing with our friends in talk of children's interests according to our ages.

In his intellectualizing way, Hiss goes on to explain:

The word "streets" is generic in the sense that the smaller children played their games on the sidewalks—cement sidewalks were beginning to replace bricks and made excellent smooth surfaces for drawing hopscotch and other "courts of play" and for beginner skaters. The streets, almost all of which had recently been macadamized, were largely free of automobile traffic and were quite safe for older children to skate in, bicycle on, or even play games of softball or touch football, and hockey played on roller skates. Our bikes, of course, gave us freedom to go to the parks for tennis or baseball or football or simply for the ride. (Scout hikes from twelve on fitted in easily with this pattern.) We also played catch *across* the streets—one stood on one sidewalk, and the other on the opposite sidewalk—and a blank wall anywhere served as the chief ingredient for a handball court or to practice tennis strokes.

Was the author of that passage ever the carefree youth he describes? The question is not frivolous: the quality of Hiss's recollection is an important clue to his life as both a boy and a man. His intellectualized memories clearly do not seem to be those of a child who was joyfully at play; they are rich in information but barren of nostalgia. He compulsively clarifies the meaning of "streets" but avoids the meaning of the experience. We see hopscotch lines and bicycles, but we do not see Alger.

In the foregoing passage—as in many other instances—Hiss seems to be characterizing himself in terms that sound inappropriate, but that does not make the characterization less revealing. His memories must be faithful in one sense to his actual activity as a boy. He was skinny, not very strong, and runty until fifteen or sixteen. As a way of earning some extra pocket money, Alger and his brothers raised pigeons, for sale, on the roof of their house. They called their "business" the BAD (Bosley, Alger, Donald) Hiss Boys. No doubt Alger took a certain pleasure in this risqué pretense or juvenile display of being "bad." It is evidently his concern that we think of him above all as a "normal" youth, with all the activities, interests, and mischief proper to a boy. And it is a safe assumption that this concern is an adult reflection of a strong childhood need, a need for a masculine self-image, born, of course, from the lack at the center of his identity, his need for a father.

This is not to say that these memories are fantasies, only that Hiss in relating them overlooks his motivation and perhaps avoids his actual feelings at the time. No doubt his life out of doors was indeed important to him.

Along with street play, he recalls his summers in the country. During every year of their childhood and early teens the Hiss children spent their summers on the Eastern Shore of Maryland, at the farm of one of Mrs. Hiss's schoolfriends. Until he was twelve years old Alger spent the entire summer vacation there. His earliest memories in the country are happier and more numerous than those in the city. He recalls "the barefoot days, swimming by five years of age, playing at swimming from the very first years"; jumping in the hayloft and wrestling with Donald and his two "cousins," William, a few months older than Donald, and Hastings, two years younger. "My age," Hiss writes in another clearly informative but at the same time concealing note, "gave me, I now realize, prerogatives of leadership, despite William's and Hastings' country lore."

One of his most vivid impressions is of one of the field hands, Cyrenus Caldwell, a Negro with a powerful physique and a kindly spirit. He was clearly another of Alger's many temporary paternal figures.

He strongly influenced my ideals of manly strength, dignity, kindness, self-respect, and fortitude. Cy was powerfully built and spent endless twilit evening hours, after a full day in the fields, batting towering fly balls for my brothers and my "cousins" and me to catch in my summers on the Wrightson farms. Shortly after my early adolescence he passed the federal examinations to become a postal clerk—in itself unheard of for a field hand—and moved to one of the large cities with his own family.

From the time he was twelve years old until he entered college, Alger followed a family pattern and spent two months of almost every summer at camp. The first two years he was on Moosehead Lake in Maine. The next summer was at a hillside farm his mother rented in New Hampshire, just across the Connecticut River from Vermont, where his two sisters had been campers and counselors for years. Bosley spent that summer with them, "but he was away much of the time even then, getting supplies by riding a horse for them, off on canoeing trips, etc." The following two summers Alger spent at a Quaker camp run by the Baltimore Friends School in Northern Pennsylvania. His last two summers were spent as a camp counselor in the Connecticut Valley in Vermont. His description of this period is now familiar: once again, a catalogue of impersonal events in place of emotion.

My camp experiences were formative: . . . new friends from all parts of the country, wilderness skills (canoeing, camping trips, . . . learning to use axes, large knifes, cook out doors, pole rapids, fly-fishing, making balsam beds, etc.).

. . . Nature study was intensive—trees, ferns, wild flowers, animal lore, birds, mosses. . . . We learned something of logging, mountain climbing, following and making trails, preparing and carrying packs and sleeping bags.

It is, of course, impossible to know what emotion did accompany Hiss's boyhood activity, though there is some evidence that in his behavior at the time there were some precursors of the compulsive style he displayed in description. There is, for example, the form that his interest in baseball took: at the age of nine or ten he knew by heart the batting records of the major league players. He studied and admired the individual batting stances, wind-ups, and other characteristics of the top stars. This is hardly startling behavior in itself, of course, but when it is coupled with other early habits, such as his practice of carrying a notebook around with him at all times to note unfamiliar words, it suggests the formation of a style of living that would later become more marked.

Whatever speculation we may make about Hiss's early life, one thing is absolutely certain: Alger Hiss was, in any conventional sense of the phrase, "a good boy." The fact would hardly be worth noting if it weren't for the extraordinary consistency of his deportment. Everyone who knew him seems to share a picture of Alger as a model of good manners. Even allowing for their natural tendency to rally around a friend or relative who had been publicly disgraced, all those who were interviewed offered accounts of his virtues so similar that they cannot be disbelieved.

Edna Hiss, his cousin, remembers Alger as "a boy of an unusual genial and happy nature"; Huntington Cairns,

. . . as a likable, bright boy, [who] . . . played end on our neighborhood scrub football team. We used to play other scrub teams in Druid Hill Park. We had difficulty in enticing Alger into the games, no doubt because he preferred to do other things, but when he appeared he always gave a good account of himself.

Burns Chalmers (now with the American Friends Service Committee in Washington, D.C.), whose family lived in Baltimore during the period 1914–22, knew Alger as one of the boys in the neighborhood and, especially, as a fellow member of a Scout troop in a nearby church. "He was a good member of the troop," Chalmers writes; he remembers Alger

. . . as a boy who was bright and capable, always taking his part in any job to be done, enjoying the whole range of activities involved in a good Scout troop and in building a camp.

Alger's many cousins and relatives remember him as an "outgoing" boy toward friends and family. To more casual friends, Alger appeared more formal and restrained. Hanson Baldwin, later military editor of the *New York*

Times, lived in Baltimore not too far from the Hisses when he was a boy. He used to see Alger occasionally in the neighborhood and at church or Boy Scout functions.

Alger was always viewed as a bright, very polite, quiet boy who was, however, a little bit of a "loner"; at least he did not seem to mix too much with the other boys in my age group in the immediate neighborhood in which I lived. It is true, of course, that Alger was separated by several blocks from the focus of the neighborhood group of which I am speaking, and he may well have had many other friends who knew him much better than my group did.

Mrs. Hartman (daughter of John Hiss) considered Alger "the keenest one in the Hiss family, always eager for knowledge, unusually articulate, even as a child; truly *smart* and eager to share his widening perceptions and experiences with others." Cousin Edna says he was "most obedient, always listening to reason and giving the other fellow an opportunity to speak first." Another close relative has pictured him as heir to Charles Hiss's virtues. "Alger has inherited many of his father's sterling qualities, unselfishness, tolerance, and broad outlook."

It is apparent that Alger as a boy seems hardly ever to have expressed, if he consciously felt, any hostility. His own account of his grammar-school education enforces this impression.

We were blessed with very good teachers who identified with the children. Though the public-school attitude, then the accepted youthful stereotype—and in many ways justified—was of "hating" school and lumping all teachers into an "others" category, this was not the case with little old No. 14. I'm quite sure my own attitude was shared by most of my schoolmates. We liked to go to school; we liked our teachers, and our teachers, we knew, liked us; our lessons were interesting and geared to our comprehension; we did our homework with pleasure and pride; we enjoyed our recesses because of the general school atmosphere, not because they were temporary escapes or respites from boring or distasteful class work.

To understand the motivation of Alger's exemplary behavior, it is necessary to remind ourselves that his home life was organized to encourage precisely this pattern. Minnie, with her prescribed program of chores and culture, was evidently an efficient but not a spontaneously affectionate mother: Alger learned early that rewards came to the obedient child, and he became a model of obedience.

At the same time Alger reserved a great deal of admiration and emulation for his brother Bosley, who took a different route in his relations with his mother. From late childhood through adolescence and young adulthood, Alger patterned himself after Bosley. He was enchanted by almost everything his brother did or said and was filled with awe by him. Not until Alger was in his twenties did his appraisal of Bosley become more realistic. But even through later years Alger has retained a romantic image of his older brother. Bosley's outgoingness, his quick wit and charm, and especially his early emancipation from his mother, "which he managed without strain or disruption of affection," deeply impressed Alger, who was not his brother's equal in these achievements. Though Bosley's individuality and nonconformity posed problems within the family, he always remained his mother's favorite. As Minnie's first son, he had claimed and received most of her attention. As he came of age, Minnie looked up to him as the "man of the house," an image to which she remained completely devoted. This was doubtless a source of resentment for Alger, though he has repressed whatever hostile feelings he may have had toward Bosley. He refers to his sibling position as "comfortable" and acknowledges Bosley's superiority within the family objectively:

. . . he was the bright elder son who claimed and received most of the attention during my earliest years. . . . At times I felt a little overlooked (not neglected), but didn't resent Bosley's status and didn't envy Donald's niche, which I considered babyish. . . .

Alger was unable to compete for affection in Bosley's style, but he consciously emulated and may well have unconsciously envied Bosley's other traits.

Bosley's wide literary and cultural interests served as a guide for Alger. Alger read Bosley's books, admired his grown-up and independent way of life (as it appeared to him then). Like Bosley before him, in his teens Alger immersed himself in poetry, essays, history, philosophy, and many foreign works in translation. Bosley's freely moving way of life left an indelible imprint on his younger brother. His iconoclasm never found overt expression in Alger's character, but this would-be trait is immanent.

It was, of course, because Alger had no father that Bosley held special significance for him. Bosley, four and a half years older than Alger, hardly paid any attention to his "baby brother" until Alger reached his teens. Though they both went to the same elementary school, their difference in age separated them, and they saw little or nothing of each other there. Summers Bosley spent mostly at camp, and in 1917 and 1918 he was away a good deal of the time with the Students Army Training Corps. With no father, and his mother out of the house a great deal, Bosley was largely on his own after school and did not stay around the house, so that he was more a grown-up model than an actual companion to Alger.

Though primarily interested in literature and the arts, when Bosley came

to high-school age, he chose Baltimore Polytechnic, probably, Hiss specu-
lates, because most of his friends were going there. His free-wheeling ways
and adventuresome spirit found poor outlet there. He grew restless and dissatisfied. Because of this, it was decided that he finish his secondary school education at Blair Academy, a private prep school in New Jersey. He felt equally
constrained there, and one holiday period ran away from home for several
weeks, hoping thereby not to have to return to the academy. The winter before entering college he suffered from ill health and spent the year on the
Wrightson farm.

Then in the fall of 1918, after a summer out West working in the wheat
fields of Kansas, Bosley returned to Baltimore to begin his freshman year at
Johns Hopkins University. During the next four years he was more consistently available to lend a helping hand, and Alger's boyish exaltation of him
was enhanced. From then on, Alger's relationship with Bosley grew closer and
more definite, and a warm and mutual affection existed between them, but the
actual time spent in each other's company was minor. During Bosley's college
days he was "available" as counselor and model. Yet, Alger says, "I don't
recall seeking his advice often, but he shared some of his young man's interests and experiences with me."

From the glamour of Bosley's free spirit and conviviality there radiated
an excitement about life which Alger assimilated. Bosley's love of music, art,
literature, travel—all stimulated Alger and intensified his interest in these
areas.

Bosley went to Europe in 1921 and 1922 and brought back fresh impressions that stimulated Alger's own enthusiasm about Europe, its people,
art, music, and literary developments. He brought back firsthand impressions
of art galleries, cathedrals, operas, and "this household familiarity invested
them with more reality and intensity than books or even courses could."

Bosley had a handsome physique (slender, six-foot-one, fair-haired) and
dressed in a tasteful yet casual way. He was proud and rather vain intellectually, slightly snobbish socially. Politically, he was independent, but Democratic in general ("as was true of the family and most Southerners"). He was
a first-class tennis player but would have nothing to do with organized sports.
A delightful conversationalist, he was in constant demand for dinners and
parties. Trailing Bosley by a few years, Alger found many doors of Baltimore
social life open to him by right of being Bosley's younger brother. "Bosley
was for me the model for cultivation, manners, wit, deportment—in a word,
'style,' in the French sense."

Although Bosley was a brilliant young man (Alger felt he was a near genius), he was more the "gentleman scholar" type rather than the serious student. He spent much time and energy filling up countless notebooks with short stories. His peers at Johns Hopkins characterized him as follows:

BOSLEY HISS

. . . Boz is essentially a man of culture, an idealist, a scholar and the possessor of an excellent sense of humor. He radiates complacency and good fellowship; it bubbles out of him in an effervescent stream like water from a volunteer fire company's hose. He likes to play bridge and talk about devilish things, but can't discuss Freud with a clear conscience. However, he knows all about literature, and can recite the works of Tennyson, Boccaccio, and William Jennings Bryan from start to preface.[1]

In September 1917 Alger went on to Baltimore City College, a public high school for boys. Anna and Mary Ann had been sent to a private school in Baltimore and in 1917 were both out of college. Bosley had just finished high school. Donald was attending Friends School.

Both Baltimore City College and Public School 14 were old-fashioned in architecture and equipment, the classrooms equally ill lighted and unaesthetic.

The level of instruction was equally low—the teachers were overworked because of large classes, most of the boys had little home culture and so slight motivation for scholarship. We were in both schools the typical rough-and-tumble public-school kids, with the old-fashioned adversary relationship between pupil and teacher. It was a mark of manhood to cut as many classes as we dared. I saw many nickel movies instead of going to classes. Cheating was rife: the geometry teacher, Dr. Uhrbroch, was a bluff German disciplinarian who smacked our hands with a ruler for disciplinary infractions and who said to those detected in cheating that the punishment was not for cheating but for getting caught.

But it is not Hiss's description of the physical condition of the public schools he attended, or of the vagaries and delinquencies of his fellow classmates, or of the nostalgia of pedagogic pleasantries that strikes one—it is Alger's containment and correctness of behavior ("Slingluff and I were among the few who did not cheat") in the midst of all the "bad things" that were going on about him that is revelatory. His admiration, heightened sensibility, and savoring of those everyday schoolboy improprieties, which he brushed but did not really engage in, left him unrequited, a would-be bad boy. The exhilaration (and fear) that accompanies or follows a real act of mischief was, for Hiss, more vicarious than real.

In addition to Latin, during his high school years, Alger took four years of English; three years of history, French, mathematics, and drawing; two

[1] *Hullabaloo* (Johns Hopkins Year Book for 1922).

years of science and one of physical education; all of which he passed successfully. Studies were not, however, an all-consuming interest to him yet (he graduated with an average of 79+); his main extracurricular activity was track, where he made "most of a mark." [2]

The 1921 issue of the *Greenbag,* the school's yearbook, had this to say:

ALGER HISS

"No lark more blithe than he"

Alger Hiss is one of the best-liked fellows in our merry crew. A witty, happy, optimistical person is never unwelcome, and Alger is not [3] that sort of person. Now, we'll have it understood that Alger is not a senseless, meaningless wit, but if anyone is hard to discourage or sadden this youth is. And there are few, indeed, who would not like to have this trait. Alger has certainly prospered with his happy habits, for his stay at City College has been far more successful than that of the average fellow.

Alger's witty retorts and sayings have at many a time had the class (and nine times out of ten the professor, too) just rocking with laughter.

Alger's size does not correspond with his athletic ability and hence his efforts in this line have been confined to being a star on the Junior track team. In his sophomore year Alger was a member of a crack relay team that won many a race in the lightweight class.

In conclusion, Alger, we've just a few words, rather flattering, but earnest, and directed straight to you. We've all read and heard how in after life one longs for the good old school days. There are different things an alumnus longs for, the athletic, for instance. But, Alger, the happy boyish laughs you caused us to enjoy will be one of the reasons why all '21 men who have known you shall long for the days we are just completing. Alger, you're irresistible!

After graduating from Baltimore City College, Alger spent part of the next year at Powder Point Academy, a private prep school in Duxbury, Massachusetts, and one semester studying art at the Maryland Institute in Baltimore. He says:

My family thought I was young for college. My sister Mary Ann had a comfortable country place in Duxbury where she and her husband expected to stay until November. I had been exclusively to public schools and under all the circumstances it was decided that a year away from home (it was clear that for financial reasons I would spend my four college years at Johns Hopkins, living at home) would be good for me.

His main interest and activities at Powder Point seem to have been sports. He played on the football team (end and quarterback), second base on the "varsity" baseball team, and was a "mediocre guard" on the

[2] From Henry T. Yost, principal of Baltimore City College.
[3] Yost remarked: ". . . the paragraph seems to contain a typographical error: . . . the complete paragraph indicates that the true meaning would be obtained by leaving out the word 'not.' "

basketball team. Hiss's class chose him as art editor for their class yearbook.

During the winter months of 1921–22 Alger returned to Baltimore and "luxuriated" himself by spending all his time at the Maryland Institute of Art. And the year of interruption between high school and college gave him an opportunity to pursue this interest.

Though his one term at the Art Institute proved educational and enjoyable, it stirred no professional ambition in him. His comment about this period is another example of his unusual need to intellectualize his experience at the expense of whatever it was he "consciously felt."

It was a privileged excursion, an unexpected time of refreshment and opportunity for extracurricular experiences, what Gesell calls a nodal period of consolidation and exploration and preparation for a new stage. This is not what I then consciously felt, of course, but it represents what I have since realized that year actually represented for me.

In any case, the freedom of being away from home, the social opportunities which life in Duxbury and Boston offered, together with the few months at the Maryland Institute of Art, no doubt added an important measure of security to his sense of self.

In September 1922 Alger entered Johns Hopkins University as a freshman. Bosley had just graduated and was vacationing on the Eastern Shore of Maryland. That fall he began work as a news reporter for the *Baltimore Sun*. Bosley was now sufficiently removed from his younger brother's life no longer to enshadow him. But in Alger's mind, when he started at Hopkins, he was "Bosley's little brother."

At college Alger quickly became taken up with class work and extracurricular activities. Each year, for three successive years, he received a scholarship based on good grades. "This was my first serious interest in disciplined study, and it was instantaneous with my first exposure." His chief interests were political science, history, literature, and the Romance languages. Johns Hopkins was then a relatively small college, and Hiss made friends easily and informally with graduate students and faculty members. Joseph Ames, dean of the college (later its president), became a friend "to the extent that the difference in generations and his post permitted."

Alger quickly made his mark. His quiet charm and physical attractiveness made him an almost immediate campus success. He was pledged by Alpha Delta Phi, the most highly regarded social fraternity on the campus. A classmate of Alger's described him as "without a doubt the most popular man in his class." Another Hopkins classmate wrote:

I first met Alger in the fall of 1923, when I was a freshman and he was a sophomore. I was tremendously impressed by him from the first, because of the gentle confidence he had in conversation and his all-around knowledge of almost every subject imaginable. I joined the same fraternity, which brought me into even closer contact with him, as did our mutual interest in the theatre.

Alger had a great influence on me; . . . he repeatedly scolded me gently if I used an uncouth word. . . . I found myself trying to emulate him in other ways. I joined the staff of the college paper, at his urging. He later became editor and I managed to rise as high as managing editor. His guidance and patience were invaluable to me in this extracurricular activity, and the experience rewarding.

He was a leading performer in the dramatic club, "The Barnstormers." . . .

His good influence on me did not escape my mother's attention. She was very fond of Alger and appreciative of his help to me. . . . Our close association ended when he went to law school.

Ruth Emerson, sister-in-law of Mary Ann Hiss, wrote:

I know of no one who as a young man more completely exemplified the finest of young Americans. As an older man, Alger possesses those same qualities.

Brinton Stone, a fellow student at Hopkins, prepared an affadavit for the Hiss trials in which he commented:

I knew no finer man at Johns Hopkins than Alger Hiss. He excelled in many activities, but first of all he was a gracious, friendly, dependable, and admirable man. . . . He held the sincere respect and affection of the whole student body.[4]

During his student years at Hopkins, Hiss served as a reserve officer (ROTC) for four years (only two were required). The last two years of military training were voluntary, but, says Hiss, "My decision to stay in ROTC was determined by the $35 monthly stipend and an army uniform, worn twice a week as a saving on clothes." In his senior year he was made cadet commander and spent two weeks at army camp before getting his reserve commission.

During his sophomore year he wrote a column called *Maybe So* (patterned after Heywood Broun's column in the *New York World*) for the Johns Hopkins *News Letter,* the weekly college newspaper. Samplings from his column provide some enlightening revelations of Alger's personality and thinking. His journalistic style is stilted (very unlike Bosley's), though his choice of topics ranges from student deportment, love of theater, the pressures of final examinations, to the problems of sexuality. What is most significant is the strained sense of humor and pedantic sense of righteousness inordinate in a youth of nineteen.

Nov. 6, 1923

In Baltimore alone there must be nearly a million definitions and standards of that most illusory thing—a sense of humor. Another is witty only when his wit agrees with yours.

[4] From a sworn statement by Brinton H. Stone, June 4, 1949.

A widely read New York columnist [Heywood Broun] recently stated that the thinking, producing, art-loving, drama-supporting class of the metropolis is composed of stenographers, almost entirely. A hasty census of stenographers in Baltimore has failed to show any relative dearth here; apparently the few theatres of which we may boast (but do not) should be overrun by typists. Yet within the last week we have been warned that our three legitimate houses may be closed in the next few weeks unless attendance increases. Meanwhile holders of stock in vaudeville and burlesque "theatres" smile with content—the content of the prosperous. . . .

Nov. 13, 1923

Advertisements for the new William Fox picture, *The Temple of Venus,* announce a cast which includes 100 American beauties as alluring mermaids and all the wonders of the "vasty deep."

It seems some young advertising man lost the chance of his life when he didn't substitute "nasty" for "vasty."

Nov. 28, 1923

Vladimir De Pachman, the famous pianist, has our sincerest admiration. De Pachman's statements that De Pachman is the greatest living interpreter of Chopin, have brought on his head a flood of hostile criticism. We are inclined to take his own word—and this in all seriousness.

A glance at his life shows that he has indeed been, in the terms of his press agent, "his own severest critic." After many early triumphs, and a most successful debut in Russia, De Pachman was not satisfied with himself. Before he would again appear in public he spent eight years in study. Most of his critics, in America at least, have berated him for his "lack of modesty" and not for any deficiencies in his musical talent. Surely, after having lived seventy-five years with himself, he should be a more competent critic of De Pachman than any one else.

Jan. 22, 1924

In one of the seldom-read-letters of this paper's *Mailbag,* we struck a description of "the weekly hour with the tutor" in English universities. This hour "has the air of a friendly conversation, a smoke, or perchance it may be a glass of port." We consider this an ideal model for all classes; but show us the American undergraduate that can make a glass of port last for an hour.

March 11, 1924

A most pernicious rumor reached us last week that the Johns Hopkins Library was endeavoring to act as censor to its readers. Havelock Ellis's works on sex psychology, Boccaccio's *Decameron,* and Burton's edition of *The Arabian Nights,* were forbidden to the undergraduate. Jumping to conclusions in true newspaper, pardon, NEWS-LETTER style, we pictured an appropriate article with appropriate headlines—

"Hopkins Library competes with Parent-Teachers' Association"—and the article was to go on showing that Hopkins was slightly ahead of the Huntingdon, W. Va., Parents and Teachers Association for the 1924 Purity Prize. The West Virginians recently passed resolutions forbidding kissing games at children's parties on the ground that such games "might lead to worse."

. . . we sought out various officials who were responsible for the ban. Blooie went the article!

May 20, 1924

"The melancholy days are come, the saddest of the year." With such nicely mournful thoughts during the "seasons of disagreeableness," we managed to fortify ourselves very well in the past. But now this healthy dependence on our martyr complex is denied us . . . "never mind if you are down in your work—the final will save you." If we are to be forbidden the indulgence of a prolonged period of pleasurable melancholia, how, pray tell, are we going to screw our courage to the sticking place? Plainly it's impossible psychology to regard concentrated study as a blessing. Personally, unless we are unhappily conscious of being imposed on, we can't work. We surely can't be expected to take exams gratefully and cheerfully.

Feb. 12, 1924

. . . some thoughtful reader deposited in Box 729 a copy of one of this column's lumbering attempts with each and every pronoun of the first person encircled with a wreath of carmine. Taking this illuminated Ms. seriously, we succeeded in grinding out a *Maybe So* from a purely objective viewpoint. (Viewpoint translated into Eng. Comp.'s desiccated parlance is point of view. Standpoint, we suppose, is treated similarly.) The only result was that three undergraduates who are not flatterers—whether of the unintentional or fraternity-brother type—congratulated us on our "best effort."

We, personally, have always abhorred even a temperate familiarity with the first person pronouns; but space must be filled. Box 729 awaits you, gentlemen . . . but pray heaven such a drastic measure as the elaboration of the *We-Our-Us* complex will not be necessary to continue the production of further "best efforts."

Hiss's pedantic need for accuracy, his careful definition of objectivity, his "abhorrence of familiarity with the first person pronouns," in short, the propriety and containment of his rebelliousness was, at the age of nineteen, clearly a part of his self-image. Although there was a piece of "Bosley" in him which strove to come out, in doing so it became transmuted into near priggishness.

During his senior year Alger was editor-in-chief of the *News Letter*. He was a member of the Tudor and Stuart Club, an honorary literary club, with its library of first editions, where undergraduates studied with graduates and associated with professors. "Tea was poured daily. I read the *New York World* regularly, delighted in Franklin P. Adams, Broun, Woollcott, Laurence Stallings, and Chotzinoff."

In addition, throughout his four years at Johns Hopkins, he took an active part in the Dramatic Club (The Barnstormers), serving as its president during his third and fourth years.

With all his varied activities, his social life was equally important to him.

Here he followed rather closely in Bosley's footsteps by joining Alpha Delta Phi, the elite fraternity on the campus.

Alpha Delta Phi was part of the Baltimore social set, and Alger went to as many of the debutante dances and dinner parties as he could manage. He was, says Dr. Hugh Jewett of Baltimore, another of his former classmates, "a 'gay blade' with the ladies, and was pursued by many of the more attractive belles. Gregarious and entertaining, he was, at the same time reserved and dignified."

He joined the Cane Club, which specialized in periodic "revelries," including an annual dance with members of the chorus of the then current musical comedy as extra guests. But Alger was discreet and utterly proper insofar as any amorous exploits were concerned. And in this respect, it was evident that he had clearly differentiated himself from Bosley.

Though Alger's behavior was tempered and restrained he was not seclusive. He very much enjoyed the Cane Club, which was like a German student drinking society, with its main purpose social conviviality. Despite Prohibition, drinks were always served at its gatherings. "We were 'young-bloods' in those days, a bit foppish and a bit dashing in our own eyes." Alger delighted in this sort of pseudo-aristocratic group exhibitionism. As an annual celebration, the Cane Club paraded through the campus, sporting spats, derbies, and carnations and swinging thin canes.

Among the friends Alger made at Hopkins was Jesse Slingluff. They had both attended Baltimore City College, but their friendship did not begin until they met as freshmen. Alger's extra year at Powder Point brought them into the same class. They immediately became close friends. Slingluff writes:

In the fall of 1922, we struck up a friendship and immediately became very close. We both joined the same fraternity. . . .

In the summer of 1924, Alger and Howard Briggs went to Europe and I joined them in Paris. I had worked my way over and he went on the Holland-American Line on one of the very first student tours. . . . We were both pretty hard up, so in Paris we didn't live in a very elegant hotel. It was on a top floor and in the general neighborhood of the Folies Bergère. We were in Paris together for a month and I remember that we made it a policy to go to the Louvre every morning so that we slowly went through the picture gallery from beginning to end and spent a fair amount of time doing it. We went to the opera seven or eight times. . . . We also saw Argentina and went to the Comédie Français, and several of Molière's plays and one by Racine. We were duly terrified at the Grand Guignol. We went to Versailles, the Eiffel Tower, climbed the Arc de Triomphe, walked to Montmartre, climbed the tower of Notre Dame, saw Sainte Chapelle and did everything one should except go to good restaurants and all night life, probably because we didn't have enough money.

At Christmas time, when we were growing up, we used to go to my Aunt's

(Mrs. William Marbury's) and there various members of the family would put on plays and skits which we had rehearsed ahead of time, and I remember twice during the course of our college careers that Alger took part in the Christmas plays.

It was through Silvine Marbury, Jesse Slingluff's cousin, that Alger met her younger brother, William Marbury.[5] Marbury lived with his family on Lanvale Street near Alger's home on Linden Avenue. Both families attended Memorial Protestant Episcopal Church and had neighboring pews.

Marbury recollects:

My sister, who was a good deal older than I, was particularly fond of Alger; he used to be around the house . . . and I would meet him when I came home from law school. . . . He soon became well known in my family.

I first got to know Alger well during the summer of 1925 or 1926 when we were both on a house party in upper New York State. At that time a warm friendship began, which has lasted to the present time. . . . He entered law school shortly thereafter, and I wrote letters on his behalf to Dean Pound, Professor Frankfurter, and others. While he was at law school, I used to see him from time to time in vacation period, and he gradually became one of my most intimate friends.[6]

Alger's trip to Europe during the summer of 1924 was the first student sailing (Third Class). It was "a gay collection of young people possessed of more than average initiative who enjoyed being innovators." Though his budget was limited to four dollars a day, it did not take away the glow of his being a "young swell."

We did the cathedrals, the art galleries, the Opera, the theatre . . . bought English tweeds from a Scotch tailor in Paris. We acquired walking sticks and an air of elegance on the boulevards and at the Café de le Paix and an infrequent swank restaurant. . . .

We fancied ourselves, with no great effort, as impecunious traveling students, hoping to be mistaken for Europeans. We bicycled throughout Normandy, stopping at simple village inns, wearing berets and with a minimum of gear in haversacks or strapped on the bikes. We sang local songs over local wine in rural cafés, and I was set up once to be mistaken for an Alsatian student. In Paris, in this mood, we frequented the Left Bank . . . sat at the Dome and the Rotonde, danced in the streets on Bastille Day, went to student dance halls and bistros, explored Montmartre, etc.

In England our progress was less romantic but equally rewarding. As in Paris I had notes from Bosley to friends he'd made when he had gone abroad. I dined at a London men's club (White's I believe), strolled the streets with the feeling from literature that I had been there before—Chelsea, the City, Kew Gardens, St. Paul's (and all the Wren churches), the Tower, Hyde Park, St. James's and Green Parks.

[5] Marbury, then a student at Harvard Law School, was destined twenty-four years later to become Hiss's counsel in his libel suit against Whittaker Chambers.
[6] From a personal memorandum dated December 30, 1948.

We traveled . . . to cathedral towns, Stratford, the Lake Country and the Trossachs.

That summer of 1924 was important in a way that was to prove far more enduring than his travel memories. On the ship going over he first met and was infatuated with Priscilla Fansler, whom he was destined to marry five years later. In London, Alger saw to it that Priscilla was "protectively installed" in a house in Kensington. After a sojourn (with Slingluff) in France, he and Priscilla met again briefly in England when he saw her off on an earlier return boat.

Alger returned from his European jaunt in September to begin his junior year at Johns Hopkins. In his sophomore, junior, and senior years he won scholarships. He was elected to Phi Beta Kappa in his junior year. As a senior, he was president of the Student Council (he was on the council each year), where he presented student problems before the faculty. He was instrumental in strengthening the operation of an effective honor system:

I believed strongly in the honor system and took part in its functioning. . . . It certainly was effective and widely respected in our time.[7]

Many campus honors came his way. He was voted into Omicron Delta Kappa honor society, the highest undergraduate honor conferred by the student body. In athletics he was not active, except as a member of the track team. When he had finished college he had a formidable record of achievements.

The 1926 Hopkins yearbook, *Hullabaloo,* had this to say:

ALGER HISS

And what shall we say of Alger? Well, there is this to be said: When a man with a name like that can make a shining success on the campus, such as he has made, he has the real stuff, nothing else can block him.

Alger is the epitome of success, and yet he is not the proverbial rah, rah lad, he is not a Hopkins Babbitt. Rather not. He goes in for culture, and activities are his side line. Judging solely from the extent of his side line, Alger must be the most cultured, learned bozo around this neck of the woods.

Many discussions we have had with Alger, many and various. The topics ranged from Soviets [8] to styles, from liberty to liquor, from Guelphs to Goodnow. And, like Socrates, we admit our ignorance in the face of his irresistible logic and rhetoric.

---

[7] Brinton Stone, a former classmate, stated that Hiss was responsible for "organizing" the honor system at Hopkins during that year.

[8] "There was no significance to the 'soviet.' . . ." This was learned from Henry J. Turnbull, editor of *Hullabaloo,* who added, "I just needed an 's' to match 'style.' If anything, Alger was the most conservative guy on the campus." (Cited by Ralph de Toledano and Victor Lasky, *Seeds of Treason* [New York: published by Funk & Wagnalls Co. for *Newsweek,* 1950], p. 34.

To all of which we add the usual pat on the back, but this time it does not nauseate us to give it; Alger is a nice chappie, in spite of his attainments.

As a child, Alger had wanted to become a medical missionary. In thinking back about this long-forgotten boyhood vision, he has said that this early desire had, through the years, "metamorphosed" into an adult interest in the Consular Service. He was influenced in this decision by James Gustavus Whiteley, honorary consul of Belgium (an American), a neighbor and family friend of the Hisses. Alger and Bosley frequented the Whiteley home (they were both good friends of Whiteley's daughter, Sophie), where the atmosphere was "intellectual, friendly, and spirited." This was Alger's first personal contact with a "diplomat," and Whiteley obviously made a lasting impression upon him. In his undergraduate curriculum at Johns Hopkins, Alger favored those courses which would best prepare him for a diplomatic career.

In March 1926, nearing the time of his graduation, Alger applied for a scholarship as a graduate student at Johns Hopkins in the Department of Political Science. However, after discussing his career plans with Manley Hudson, then professor of International Law at Harvard (a friend of Alger's sister Mary Ann, later appointed a judge of the World Court), Alger changed the course of his educational plan but retained his ultimate goal. Professor Hudson advised Hiss to go first to law school, as this was the soundest preparation for a diplomatic career. And so, toward the end of his senior year, Alger decided to study law. He applied to Harvard Law School and on the basis of his excellent record at Hopkins was promptly accepted.

During Alger's first two years at Hopkins (1922–24), though Bosley lived at home, Alger saw little of him. Bosley was then working as a staff reporter for the *Baltimore Sun*. During the winter of 1922 he fell ill with "influenza." From about this time Bosley's life underwent a rapid physical and emotional deterioration. His career as a writer was short-lived, and despite his brilliance he got no farther than news reporting. He led an erratic life as a journalist, working at night; his hours were late and irregular. He ate and drank unwisely. More rakish than at college, he expended much of his time and affection on socialites.

But [says Alger] I have always considered that I learned even more from Bosley's mistakes in the area of emotional judgment. He was undisciplined, in habits of sleep, diet, and drink and was to my mind too casual in sexual matters. I thought I could see the injury he brought to himself or was storing up and suspected that he was hurting others. His close cronies were more glaring examples of frivolous and destructively living young men.

Bosley's life might have stabilized or followed a course parallel to that of some of his dissolute friends. But fate ironically precluded the possibility of either. During the winter of 1923 Bosley fell victim to a severe form of kidney disease (nephritis). After some weeks there was a subsidence of symptoms. Further clinical study, however, revealed his illness to be a malignant form of Bright's disease. By the spring of 1924 Bosley, not yet twenty-four, was partially invalided by swellings of the legs, generalized weakness, and other evidence of a rapidly progressive impairment of kidney function.

About a year before the first signs of his illness appeared, Bosley had been gaily courting an attractive, wealthy New York socialite with whom he was very much in love. To his disappointment, the affair cooled and soon ended. For about six months during the first year of his illness he remained at home. He was confined to bed much of the time. The heretofore free-spirited Bosley found his physical dependence on Minnie intolerable, and Minnie was not very understanding. Her attendance lacked the compassion which he then very much needed. There was a period of improvement, and Bosley grew increasingly restive. One day, after a harmless but obtuse remark by Minnie ("I'll clean up your room if you'll read me the editorial page of the *Baltimore Sun*"), Bosley, in a moment of pique, packed his clothes and took off for New York. There he resumed an earlier friendship with Margaret Owen, a successful New York interior decorator, a woman twenty years his senior. They took a trip to Florida, where he hoped to complete his convalescence. But instead his illness progressed, and he was forced to spend most of his time in bed. After he had rested for several months in Florida, Margaret brought him to her comfortable home in Rye, New York. Despite excellent care he grew worse. A few more months passed, and he was reduced to a state of physical dependency and almost complete immobility. Under these tragic circumstances, his relations with his family strained, Bosley Hiss married Margaret Owen.

Just after his graduation from Johns Hopkins in June 1926 until he left for Cambridge to enter Harvard in September, Alger was constantly at Bosley's side.

My stay was a family arrangement. . . . I was and regarded myself as the family's deputed representative sent to help one of us who needed just the kind of practical aid I was qualified to supply. I reported regularly to them by letter an account of my stewardship. Bosley's wife had to be in New York daily. He was largely bedridden. I ran the household as a steward or manager would—driving their car to pick up groceries, driving him to the hospital in New York (the old Presbyterian) for treatment . . . reading and talking to him, playing records. . . . His mind and spirit were as vital and dynamic as ever. . . . At times I certainly recognized with grief and sorrow that he was dying; I'm not sure I accepted fully the nearness of his death.

In mid-September, after an arduous summer with Bosley at Rye, Alger left for Cambridge. In late October, Alger received a call from Margaret that

Bosley had taken a turn for the worse. He immediately came down to New York. Donald also came, as did Mary Ann and Minnie. Alger remained close by his brother's side. On November 3, 1926, Bosley died.

Bosley's death was a tragic blow to his family, his friends, and his contemporaries. To Alger, who had been awed since early childhood by his brother's magnetism, charm, and wit, his death was not only a great loss but a shock, for he had not expected it to come so soon in so young a man.

Years after Bosley's death Alger reflected on the meaning of his deep relationship with Bosley:

I have long thought that Bosley was romantically elevated for his peers and within the family. His charm and precocious talents were enhanced and frozen by his lingering illness and early death. To this extent he became, after his death, somewhat "legendary." Each year since Bosley's death Anna [Hiss] writes an anniversary note on April 30 (Bosley's birthdate) to Donald and to me. . . . After his death, I heard for a number of years constant references from his peers . . . about his magnetism, wit, and scintillating bon mots deflating pompous and self-important people.

The "Byronic" element that I saw and see in Bosley is related to his irreverent wit. ("Byronic" is also an overstatement for purposes of emphasis.) He had a somewhat willful, romantic vanity that showed itself in scorn for complacency and hypocrisy . . . [and] was carried to the extreme of liking to shock. What Holmes referred to with relish as "making the monkeys howl," and that is covered by the classic phrase "épater les bourgeois." This quality I did not admire in Bosley.

One of the reasons Hiss so admired William Marbury was his "unromantic, hardheaded analysis," a characteristic Hiss subsumed under the term "objectivity." That term had a special meaning for Hiss. It was, he explained (in this context)

. . . synonymous with the conscious, patient attempt to recognize and accept reality, as distinguished from quixotic, impulsive self-expression. Bosley and Marbury were, in a sense, opposite poles in my developing scale of values: Bosley's spontaneity and ability to relate warmly to many kinds of people struck me as a good in itself; Bill's respect for the reality principle ditto. On basic attitudes, as opposed to aesthetic quests, Bill has been more of a positive and lasting influence than Bosley.[9]

Needless to say, Bosley was a key person in Alger's life. Alger emulated him during his formative years, and his psychological role in Alger's life was eminent. Bosley's influence, his nonconformist, romantic ways, and his untimely death are relevant to an understanding of Alger's overdetermined sense of personal loyalty. This fraternal image of Bosley, despite Hiss's later, more realistic reappraisals of him, persists to the present.

[9] Alger's persistent romantic image of Bosley becomes meaningful when viewed as a substitute for his idealization of his father.

Hiss tells an anecdote about Bosley that provides some enlightening information.

About a year ago [1962] . . . a demure-looking and -speaking man rather diffidently approached me as I was sauntering in the dusk along Third Avenue and asked if I were Bosley Hiss or related to him. He had been a passenger at whose table Bosley had worked as a steward, working his way back from Europe in 1922. He knew press accounts of my case and had from them learned I was from Baltimore and was so struck by the likeness that he thought there must be some connection. . . . He said he thought he had a few letters Bosley had written him, and I gave him my telephone number. This week he called me to say he found one letter (Jan. 1923) but must have mislaid or thrown away any others. I saw him last evening, and we walked about the city after supper and sat in a small park, talking.

During this meeting Bosley's former friend, a Mr. Copeland, gave the letter to Hiss. A few excerpts provide a vignette of Bosley as a young man.

My dear worshipper of Virginity:
   I think I would even rather wait on those impolite Third Class Passengers, always excluding your fiend (I meant to write friend but I suppose the machine knows best) the TANK,[10] I was very much put out to leave the boat without having found out whether you and the TANK had left together. Do write and let me know if she has given up her husband for you. If so the husband owes you his undying gratitude. I would love to see his expression of pain and surprise when she arrives!
   Must stop raving on. I am afraid I won't get up to the wicked city until the middle of February, but certainly hope to see you then. . . . Have you gotten hold of Havelock Ellis's *Psychology of Sex*? It is very sane, especially his ideas on chastity and celibacy (Volume 6, I believe).
   Hoping you agree with his ideas on the subject

Sincerely
Bosley Hiss

The letter, of course, only partially confirms Hiss's memories of Bosley as an urbane wit and suggests again that Hiss's conception of his brother remains idealized. Despite his conscious awareness that he has learned "even more from Bosley's mistakes," Hiss's youthful, romantic image of him seems hardly to have diminished through the years; he passed along the letter and

---

[10] The "TANK" referred to an overweight, peasant war-bride coming to America to join her ex-soldier (American) husband. She always required a number of extra servings of all dishes, a source of annoyance to Bosley as a waiter.
   Hiss has explained that "the reference to Virginity came about as the result of considerable discussion of that subject between the two young men. Mr. Copeland took the Victorian view that virginity, whether of a man or woman, was to be respected and maintained. Bosley took the 'emancipated' attitude (vide his later reference to Havelock Ellis). Bosley admired Havelock Ellis and read quite widely in him." Alger's own early reading of *The Dance of Life* and other of Ellis's writings undoubtedly was due to Bosley's influence.

anecdote partly to "illustrate the striking impression Bosley's personality made on those he met."

The encounter with Mr. Copeland provides another interesting piece of information: that Bosley once aspired to the Consular Service. Hiss has said he has no recollection of this, "though it may well have played some part in my early intention to go into the Foreign Service." It is a mark of Hiss's ambivalent identification with Bosley that he exaggerates his brother's qualities of irreverent charm but has forgotten his interest in the Foreign Service, which may well have stirred the ambitions that dominated much of his own early life.[11]

---

[11] It is interesting to note in this regard how Donald's basic life pattern and educational and professional career (prior to the Hiss trials) followed closely on the heels of his brother's. Donald followed Alger to Harvard and in 1932 served as Holmes' secretary. After that year he went into government service.

To Alger's closest friend who knew the Hiss family well, the memory of Bosley is more mundanely recalled. Of Bosley, Slingluff says: "Alger's elder brother was somewhat of a dilettante, grew up in the early part of the roaring twenties, and I think that had just as much to do with his bad health as anything else. Alger was very devoted to Bosley and admired him tremendously. . . . Alger was and still is an incurable romantic."

9

A Young Lawyer

HISS'S THREE YEARS as a law student at Harvard encompassed his most broadening experiences. Soon after his entry into Harvard he became so taken up with his law courses that "diplomacy as a career was shelved." Under the aegis of Felix Frankfurter, Francis B. Sayre, and Edward Morgan, and influenced by other Harvard faculty members, Alger's cultural values, his social and political convictions—colored until then by a streak of strait-laced conservatism—were destined to undergo considerable change. Most influential was Felix Frankfurter. Along with other top students Hiss was invited to Frankfurter's seminar, where he found new horizons in scholarly discussion of law, government, and social philosophy. The seminars—groups of about a dozen or so law students and graduate students—dealt with the subjects of federal jurisdiction and administrative law.

He went frequently to the Frankfurter home for tea. There he socialized with fellow students, members of the *Harvard Law Review,* met and enjoyed the company of Frankfurter's many house guests, other faculty members, and Boston friends, mostly lawyers and writers.

Many Sunday afternoons were spent at the home of Dr. Harvey Cushing, "where the talk was not of the law at all." He was friendly with Dr. Cushing's three daughters, and the house was full of young men and women of various ages.

Mrs. Cushing presided over the tea table and the talk was sprightly young peoples' talk of books, plays, music, sports, college and law school activities. Dr. Cushing on occasion arrived drawn and fatigued from an emergency operation. Tea and rest revived him and then (as well as on the occasions when he was present from the beginning) the talk near him was more serious—history, medicine, literature, anecdotes of Osler, Welch, Futcher, Kelly, and the other Hopkins greats. He was an extraordinary man, small, intense, beautifully spoken, warmly outgoing to young people. Both the Cushing and the Frankfurter households were notable for the quality of the talk. At the former the tone was more gemütlich, a warm, gay family grouping with small talk and light topics interspersed with weightier topics.

The Cambridge atmosphere influenced Alger's legal and social perspectives. He became interested in the problems of management, the role of government in labor, and labor's point of view. He worked on a "Note" for the *Law Review,* dealing with the constitutionality of yellow-dog contracts,[1] and did a long "Case" on federal jurisdiction of foreign corporations. Governmental issues now began to interest him.

In his second year Alger was appointed to the editorial board of the *Harvard Law Review* and held this position for two years. Others on the *Review* with him were Richard Field, Edward McLean, Lee Pressman, William Hastie, and Harold Rosenwald: men who later became judges, teachers, government officials, and successful lawyers. Erwin N. Griswold, present dean of the Harvard Law School, a class ahead of Alger, was president of the *Law Review* during Alger's second year. This brought them together quite regularly and marked the beginning of a lasting friendship that has remained unmarred through the years.[2]

In the monthly meetings of the editorial board, held at Gannett House, when cases were assigned to the editors for review and comment, Hiss's brilliant discussion stood out. Whether his social and emotional growth kept pace with his intellectual accomplishments is uncertain. He is remembered by at least one of his classmates as both the "most distinguished man in our class and very definitely a dandy." Hiss himself regards this period as a time of personal social progress.

Ideologically I was at college rather a snob, socially and intellectually. I had already at Johns Hopkins lost the somewhat anti-Semitic snobbishness of my mother's background and outlook. I had good friends at Hopkins who were Jewish. At Harvard, I had many Jewish friends. I worked on the *Law Review* with a Negro student without any feeling on my part.

But even in the very precise way that he describes his recollections there is still discernible a tone that echoes the snobbishness of his younger years, for such traits are not so easily shaken. The Harvard years contain in many ways his proudest moments, and not the least of his pride has to do with his intimacy with famous figures. He takes pleasure, for example, in mentioning the marriages of Dr. Cushing's daughters: "Mary, later Mrs. Vincent Astor and now Mrs. James Fosburgh; Betsy, then being courted by James Roosevelt, now Mrs. John Hay Whitney; Barbara, now Mrs. William Paley."

He seems in general at this time to have been almost a stereotype of the precocious student who remains a bit young and impressionable emotionally.

[1] Contracts in which the employee promises not to join a union and can be fired for breach of contract if he does.
[2] "We have maintained contact," Hiss wrote, "as he went on with his career in the Solicitor General's Office and then as Dean."

Nevertheless, he did not forsake that element of compassion which stirred the "caretaker" in him. It was no doubt the force that sparked his friendship with Harold Rosenwald. Rosenwald, a year behind Alger at Harvard Law School, first met Hiss when he was appointed to the *Law Review*. As outwardly shy as he was inwardly brilliant, Rosenwald found himself rather alone in the large classes. And it was during his first year there that he, like Hiss, suffered the loss of an older brother. It happened about a year or so after Bosley's death. A warm friendship sprang up between them. Alger, already prominent on the *Law Review,* took Rosenwald [3] under his fraternal wing.

Stirred by intellectual competition, Hiss rose rapidly and gained the respect of his teachers and classmates. A deeply imbedded altruism and desire to be of service, the vestige of his boyhood wish to be a medical missionary, matured as the measure of his responsibilities increased. His filial, then fraternal avowal not to forsake whoever might be dependent upon him, directed him toward his life goals. This deeply determined need to avoid the tragic life course his father and brother had taken directed him from within with the force of an obsession.

As Hiss's career at Harvard drew near a close, it was darkened by a family tragedy. On May 2, 1929, a month before his graduation, Alger received the shocking news that his sister Mary Ann had committed suicide.

Mary Ann Hiss, at the time of her death at thirty-four, was an attractive, dutiful woman of great charm. As a girl, she had attended the Bryn Mawr School in Baltimore, where she made an excellent record. She then spent four years at Smith College. After graduation she married Elliot Emerson, a Boston stockbroker of social distinction.

Gardner Jackson, a friend and frequent guest of the Emersons at their homes in Duxbury and Cambridge, remembers Alger's sister as a lovely person with a quality of gentle affection and an outgoing nature. In her geniality, said Jackson, she was much more like Bosley than Alger. Richard Field remembers her as "a real charmer."

Alger knew little of the real emotional causation of Mary Ann's suicide. From his answers to my queries about his sister's mental health, it is evident that at the time he had no awareness of psychiatric forces. Mary had been a pretty and much courted girl. Elliot Emerson was the oldest of her suitors; his financial affluence was part of the allure for a girl brought up with little money and considerable family tradition and aspiration. Not long after her marriage he suffered major financial reverses. He had been the generously helpful member of his clan before. The Hiss family helped to some degree (each of the

---

[3] Along with two other *Harvard Law Review* colleagues, Edward C. McLean and Richard Field, Rosenwald was to play an important role in the trials years later.

children had inherited about $10,000 from their father). Mary's portion was swallowed up; $2000 of Alger's share was "invested" by Elliot and came to nothing. Mary's pride was hurt and the shock to her sense of identity must have been great. She was angered that Elliot continued his senseless, extravagant expenditures. For a while Mary taught school in New York. There were periods of separation, but Mary always accepted Elliot's overtures for reconciliation.

While Alger was at law school he saw them weekends at Duxbury and also when they were in Cambridge. The tension he sensed seemed, so far as he was then capable of seeing, to be exclusively a result of the financial fantasy world in which Elliot continued to live. In other respects Mary seemed to have come to accept quite fully her life with him and their two children.

Consequently he was utterly unprepared for her suicide and was shocked and uncomprehending. When he heard the tragic news he rushed down to Duxbury with Dr. Hilbert Day, a close family friend. Everything he knew at the time or learned afterward made him confident that it was a sudden irrational act, without prior warning and without prior periods of depression or of suicidal contemplation. But his lack of awareness as well as his lack of knowledge (for more than thirty years) of the circumstances that surrounded this tragic family event, the fact that he was utterly "uncomprehending" and unprepared for the news of his sister's "sudden, irrational act" (he was then twenty-four years old), are indeed significant. Like his father's suicide more than twenty years before, this tragedy was closeted as a highly private event and became unmentionable in the saga of the closely knit Hiss clan. And around it there grew a protective scar. The historical facts have been strictured and softened with the passage of years. As a result many of the vicissitudes that beset Mary Ann during the nine years of her marital life, which culminated in her suicide, were neither understood by nor disclosed to even close family members.[4]

Insofar as Hiss's own memories and retrospective appraisal of his sister's death in 1929 are essential to the portrayal of his character and image, an account of the psychological forces that determined the course and character of his sister's life (and her death) are relevant and material.

The overriding feeling of shame, which has for decades characterized the Hisses' sense of privacy, covered over the facts and life circumstances surrounding this tragic family event. Mary Ann's disturbed mental state, her wor-

---

[4] After an emotional quarrel with her husband, which occurred in the middle of the night, Mary Ann killed herself by swallowing a liquid caustic (Lysol). For several years prior to her suicide she had on two occasions suffered recurrent periods of mental depression and elation and spent brief periods as a patient at a private sanitarium. This fact was only recently disclosed to Hiss by a close family member.

ries over her husband's repeated financial losses and careless stock transactions (which forced him into bankruptcy during the early months of 1929), echo the circumstances that ushered in her father's depressive illness in 1907), after Albert Hughes' defalcation. During one of her earlier depressive periods (1926), Mary Ann, harassed with morbid fears, anticipated that she would kill herself as her father had done. Her husband, seventeen years older than she, was clearly a paternal substitute. Elliot Emerson was the same age (forty-three) when he married Mary Ann, as her father had been when he died.

Minnie's influence on her daughter's life and her choice of husband should not be minimized. Social position, wealth, a comfortable home, all the ingredients in the quest for security that underlay Mary Ann's marriage to Elliot Emerson, had been imbued in her since childhood. Minnie's wish for social affluence, satisfied by her husband during his lifetime, became a matter of basic necessity after his untimely death. The effects of Minnie's insistent tutelage, despite the reduced family economy, were clearly echoed in the direction and course of Mary Ann's adult life. The image of her father reappeared in Elliot Emerson. Like those of her father, Elliot Emerson's life and values gave Mary Ann a feeling of status. Emerson's materialistic values in life were precisely the diet on which Mary Ann had been brought up. Mary Ann was sent to the Bryn Mawr School, an exclusive private school, and then to Smith College. Minnie kept Mary Ann in schools where she would be in the company of the same girls she would have met if Charles Hiss had lived to be a financial success.[5]

Elliot Emerson was a member of a well-known Boston family, the older brother of one of Mary Ann's college friends. He was a genteel person, had fine manners, a knowledge of rare wines, owned a country house in Duxbury, and drove a Cadillac. But she soon discovered that these were not enduring values. She did not meet her disillusionment with her mother's fortitude. Instead, she reacted in a manner reminiscent of her father.[6]

---

[5] Anna, too, fell under Minnie's influence but in another way. Anna made her own career by launching a fierce fight for women's equality and emancipation. Though by temperament Anna was always a gentle person, she went into physical education, attended Hollins College (Roanoke, Virginia), then Sargent's School in Cambridge (later absorbed by Boston University). Sargent was the first and leading physical education school for women.

[6] To Alger, also, Elliot Emerson has remained a "transient" paternal figure. In the fall of 1963 Emerson died at the age of eighty-six. This event stirred a residue of past memories in Hiss: "I realized while at Elliot's funeral, that is, in the course of the several days devoted to traveling to and from Cataumet and visiting with the Emerson family, that Elliot had to a slight degree and for a brief period been one of my multiple 'father figures.' I put the phrase in quotes because it overstates the actuality but at the same time conveys by shorthand some of the closeness and affection I felt for him during the

Hiss's striking lack of comprehension of his sister's illness, his un-awareness of psychiatric forces at that time, and his belief that her suicide was sudden and unpremeditated are all significant and cannot be glossed over if we are to understand his actions in other areas. His altruism and stoicism in the face of tragedy developed early in childhood as a consequence of the death of his father. His need to disidentify with his father's failure and the childhood trauma of a shattered paternal image took the form of a self-promise that his own life (unlike his father's, Bosley's or Mary Ann's) would *not* end in comparable failure.

Within a month after his sister's death Alger graduated *cum laude* from Harvard Law School. During his last academic year a distinct honor was be-stowed upon him; he was selected, by Felix Frankfurter, to serve as secretary to Supreme Court Justice Oliver Wendell Holmes, Jr. The appointment was a highly coveted one, traditionally offered each year to one of the top students of the senior class. His new position with the Justice would not begin until October, and that summer Alger and his brother Donald took a trip to Europe. They planned to meet Jesse Slingluff and some other friends, but when they arrived in Paris, Donald fell ill and they had to change the plans of their trip:

The itinerary was cut short by Donie's attack of stomach ulcers. He had had an attack or attacks earlier but they had not led us to have any apprehension about undertaking the trip. . . . In Paris, our first stop, it was beastly hot, and Donie got a really severe attack. So severe that he decided he should go home. At just that time the liner *Paris* had burned and the French Line had grabbed all space available on other sailings to take care of those who had had reservations on the west-bound trip of the *Paris*. It was impossible to get prompt bookings or to fore-cast just when return passage would be feasible.

Alger, acting in character, assumed the role of his brother's caretaker. Unable to find return passage, he soon thought of a salutary plan:

I decided to get Donie into the country near Paris to wait for available space. I'd heard of Giverny and it seemed to fill the bill—once an artist's haunt but by then their former lodgings were readily available. By the time space was again available [on a liner] Donie was so much better he decided to stay on—rather on a week-to-week basis. We stayed all summer.

In October, shortly after their return to the States, Alger moved to Washington to begin his secretaryship with Justice Holmes. Holmes, then in his eighty-ninth year, recently bereaved by death of his wife, found Alger's presence and sense of duty both timely and pleasant.

---

year I was at Powder Point and later while I was at law school. He was twenty-five years older than I and so always a member of the older generation."

While secretary to Holmes, Hiss studied legal briefs filed in cases presented before the Supreme Court. He summarized them and reported to Holmes on their contents. He kept Holmes' docket book, assisted him with his personal correspondence, and helped him in any other way that he could.[7]

In addition to his official duties as Holmes' secretary, Alger served as an intellectual companion and filial figure for Holmes in a way reminiscent of his role as Bosley's companion three years previously. This job uniquely fitted Alger's personal capacities, his realistic as well as romantic aspirations. He was, emotionally and literally, an obedient, awe-inspired young disciple in the presence of the venerable Holmes. Almost every day Alger read to him selections from the classics, poetry, philosophy, or recently published novels.

It is understandable that Holmes stirred Hiss as no paternal figure had ever done before or was ever to do after. Holmes provided Hiss with new humanistic values and deeper insights and made his point of view less provincial. The year Hiss spent with Holmes was

. . . like living in a rich segment of past history. It gave me a sense of social and intellectual historicity and continuity I'd never had got otherwise.

Holmes' philosophical skepticism and wide historical vista were, according to Hiss, probably the most important influences of any in shaping Hiss's intellectual standards and maturation. His ideology was humanist "in the largest sense. . . . Nothing human was alien to him."

Holmes was irreligious. Though he was deeply patriotic he believed (philosophically) that man is but a ganglion in a Cosmos. "How can you take man seriously when his mood will change according to whether the wind is in the South or the North."

Other characteristics of Justice Holmes that were particularly striking to Hiss were:

his wit and gift of language, his vast reading and incisive opinions in philosophy and general literature, including the classics (he read Greek, Latin, German, and French), his feeling of intimacy with his European friends and his feeling for the European scene, his taste in art, his knowledge of history and world culture, his courtliness and graciousness of manner, his high standards in intellectual matters and in character and personal conduct. He referred often to the lessons in democracy he had gained from his army experience, which tempered his patrician youthful outlook and gave him an appreciation of the worth of individuals from less privileged origins—their courage, honesty, manliness, dignity. At the same time his most marked quality was his sense of his own worth and personal dignity, his flashing pride. His Civil War experiences had led him to regard the fanaticism of the

[7] Alger Hiss has recently abridged Mark De Wolfe Howe's original edition of the correspondence between Justice Holmes and Harold J. Laski, *The Holmes-Laski Letters* (New York: Atheneum, 1963).

Abolitionists, which he must originally have shared, with distaste when he saw the horrors of the war, the worth of Southerners he met and the complexity of the issues the Abolitionists had simplified in their thinking. This was a chief cause for his skepticism of Grand Causes, of do-gooders, of idealistic programmatic groups. Another cause was his familiarity with philosophy. A friend of William James, Charles Pierce, and other philosophers, he distrusted all closed philosophic systems.

Withal he had a robust spontaneous appetite for life—for people and experience. For example, he was boyishly delighted when I made arrangements for him (then eighty-nine) to see a show of the Marx Brothers, and whenever I daringly brought young people to tea (obviously I didn't overdo it or the delight would not have been so genuine!). He was eager for my accounts of my own doings and for new books brought to his attention.

The greatness of Justice Holmes provided Hiss with all the attributes of an idealized father-figure. What Holmes, in turn, felt toward his young secretary can only be surmised. There is no doubt that he had a fondness for him. He willed to Hiss a large, antique Queen Anne mirror, which had been in the Holmes family for many generations. Since receiving the mirror after the Justice's death in 1935, Hiss has always placed it in a prominent place in his home, and he still regards it as one of his most prized possessions.

Hiss also revered Holmes' successor, Justice Benjamin N. Cardozo. Though Hiss knew Cardozo less intimately than Holmes, there was something personally unique in Hiss's reverence for Cardozo as a paternal figure. Cardozo's father had been a justice of the New York Supreme Court but had been linked with the corruption of Boss Tweed and publicly disgraced. It is supposed that Justice Cardozo had such a strong feeling of family-name loyalty that he early vowed to erase the blot on the family escutcheon by his own conduct and career. He did in fact lead a saintly personal life and achieved a notable career as a jurist in whom, said Hiss, "ethical principles were never subordinated to the mechanical legalisms of a sophist-in-robes."

Hiss had the opportunity of visiting Cardozo at his residence after Hiss returned to Washington in 1933 (Cardozo succeeded Holmes in 1932) and saw him on a number of occasions. Like many other young lawyers, he fell under his "gentle, radiant, wise charm." But more precisely, Hiss points out, the supposed motivation for Cardozo's evident high standards of personal and professional rectitude was comparable to "my own Maryland background, which made respect for one's family a continuing entity. It was an assured and constant support in return for which one was bound to strive to protect and preserve the continuum. The legend of Cardozo's motivation was therefore natural to my values."

But in addition Hiss was conscious of a more personal appeal in the myth of this particular hero. He, too, felt that his father's suicide represented a "blot" and "a failure to fulfill the individual's obligation to the past, present, and future family unit." The blot was not so shameful as that in Cardozo's line, but there was a strong family sense of shame, which, says Hiss, "no doubt affected us even more strongly than I was conscious of. Else why so much mystery about my father's death in my earliest years, why the continuing reticence of my elders about the subject?"

It was evident why Cardozo was a particularly revered figure for Hiss; the rectitude of both their lives was, in a sense, an expiation for their fathers' sins.

On December 11, 1929, two months after Alger began his secretaryship to Holmes, he married Priscilla Fansler Hobson. Since first meeting her aboard ship in June 1924, Alger had felt a romantic fondness for Priscilla, yet his containment was so great it was "never expressed in terms even of calf love." More than five years before, in September 1924, as Priscilla embarked on an earlier sailing from Southampton, Alger had wondered if they would ever meet again. He had been smitten by the pangs of his first romantic attachment, and at parting they promised to think of each other at specific times.

Priscilla, the youngest of six children (four brothers and one sister), grew up on a suburban estate of about thirteen acres near Frazer, Pennsylvania.[8] The children were brought up as strict Presbyterians. Priscilla was sent to the Phoebe Anne Thorne model school run by Bryn Mawr College, and later (1920–24) attended the college itself, majoring in English literature and philosophy. While there she took an active interest in the college Liberal Club. The contacts with Quakers during her school years were to have a lasting influence on her.

In the fall of 1924 Priscilla entered Yale University as a graduate student in literature. Alger, then a junior at Hopkins, corresponded with her during the winter months. During the Easter recess, in April 1925, Priscilla came to Baltimore for a holiday visit and stayed with a family who were also friends of the Hisses. While on their way to a dance in a taxi, along with several others, Priscilla excitedly announced to the group her engagement to Thayer Hobson, a Yale graduate student whom she had recently met in New

---

[8] Priscilla Fansler was the granddaughter of an American frontiersman. Her grandfather had transported his family on a homemade raft down the Tennessee and Ohio Rivers to Cairo, Illinois. There, he sold his raft for passage upriver and went inland. Two years later, her father, Thomas Fansler, was born in a log cabin. Many years later he moved to Evanston, Illinois, where Priscilla was born. Thomas Fansler moved his family East to the Main Line in Pennsylvania shortly after Priscilla's birth on October 13, 1903. There he took up a position with the Northwestern Mutual Life Insurance Company. He was an amateur writer, interested in education, a trustee of Illinois College (his alma mater).

Haven. Shocked and disappointed, Alger became acutely aware of his love for her.

That summer Priscilla and Thayer Hobson were married. After a winter's sojourn in Europe they returned to live in New York, where Thayer began work in a publishing house.

Alger spent the summer of 1925 as a camp counselor and in the fall returned to Johns Hopkins to begin his senior year. He soon became engaged to a girl from New Orleans who was attending school in Baltimore. His courtship extended through the following winter, when he saw her on his visits to Baltimore from Harvard. During the summer of 1927 he visited her family in New Orleans. After this, a gradual divergence of interests, a coolness toward her family, set in. "I realized," said Alger, "that I was not prepared for marriage and broke the engagement before the year was over."

Concurrently Priscilla's life became increasingly turbulent and her marriage to Thayer Hobson foundered. On September 19, 1926, after a year of marriage, she bore a son, Timothy, and shortly thereafter she and her husband separated.[9] Priscilla took a job as "office manager" for Henry Luce and Britton Haddon, editors of *Time* magazine; the news weekly had only recently made its appearance. She served as copy editor as well as supervisor of the then small staff of office personnel.[10] In the fall of 1928 she enrolled as a graduate student at Columbia to complete her studies in literature. The following summer she was awarded an M.A. degree.

In the spring of 1929 Alger was told by a friend that Priscilla was divorced. Stirred by the news, Alger wrote to her and at Eastertime hurried to New York to see her. It was a happy reunion for them both, and the five years' separation came happily to an end. Alger's feelings were rekindled. He visited her in New York, they went to the theater and the opera. It was an exciting experience to renew a relationship he thought had been lost.

And Priscilla was pleased and flattered by Alger's attentions. There was, however, the matter of another suitor, which she made known to him. Though smitten and disappointed, he remained hopeful.

Soon after his graduation from law school Alger and his brother Donald set off for a summer trip to Europe. Before sailing Alger went to Philadelphia

[9] "There was never any real trouble," Thayer Hobson informed me. "Priscilla was an impractical idealist, interested primarily in art, literature, and music. It was just that oil and water don't mix, and we never should have married." They were divorced in January 1929.

[10] By reason of their respective employment at Time, Inc., Priscilla Fansler and Whittaker Chambers both worked under Henry Luce. There was, however, a ten-year gap between the time of their employment. As far as I have been able to determine, though Chambers may well have known this fact, since both he and Priscilla knew Luce well, there was no connection between this historical fact and the subsequent circumstances under which their lives later crossed.

to visit Priscilla, who had returned to Bryn Mawr College to teach a special English course for women workers, and she, in turn, came to New York to see him off. They felt closer than ever before. Then began a courtship by mail. He wrote to her en route and regularly from Europe. Since she had another suitor, he had no idea where he stood with her.

When Alger got back from Europe he phoned her from Baltimore. She informed him that she was free but added that she was about to enter the hospital for a major operation. Would he come and see her when she was out of the hospital? Hiss took off at once for New York. At the hospital he stayed close by, visiting her daily until she left.

It was five years since they had first met. After a long, interrupted courtship Priscilla accepted his suit. But Alger's mother was disappointed and angered by her son's choice. On the eve of the wedding she wired him: "Do not take this fatal step."

From what we know of Alger Hiss's romantic images, especially his role as caretaker, his choice of a wife is consistent with an established pattern. Priscilla was attractive, resourceful, and self-assertive, but she was also a person in need. She was then living in a small New York apartment with her three-year-old son. Since her divorce she had been under considerable emotional strain, and the quality of Alger's support of her is reminiscent of his father's altruistic ways toward his brother John's widow and children and his own wife and family. Did Alger unwittingly pick up the burden of life at that juncture where his father had failed? Was he therefore moved to continue along his own life course in a manner *antithetical* to his father's? Whether this be valid or not, it is impressive that Alger did choose to marry Priscilla at a time when Timothy, her son, was about the same age as Alger had been when his father "betrayed" him and his family by an act of suicide. All of which, known, does not gainsay the fact that his romantic choice may at the same time have been rational, satisfying, and quite autonomous. But in the inner reaches and deeply rooted determinants in Hiss's actions there is discernible what I believe was the nuclear trauma of his life—the memory of his father's failure. In any event, let us keep in mind this cardinal trait in Hiss's character, as a possible key to understanding some of his later actions.

For several months before his marriage Alger lived in Washington, sharing an apartment with Charles H. Willard, a former Harvard classmate. It was there that, in the presence of Priscilla's parents and a small group of Alger's friends, they were married on December 11, 1929. Alger's mother was in Texas with Anna and did not attend. "I felt independent," says Alger. "The wedding," recalls Slingluff, "was a stag affair, except for the bride and her mother." Marbury persuaded them to have a Presbyterian minister perform the ceremony. Donald and a few close friends (Slingluff, Charles Ford Reese, Ridgely Howard, Richard Field, Marbury) were present. "I remember vividly," says Charles Ford Reese,

the evening a group of us motored to Washington to attend Alger's wedding. When the minister got to the part, "speak now or forever hold your peace," I can remember Alger gently waving his hand behind his back as though to quiet his few close friends who were present.

Alger and Priscilla spent their honeymoon weekend at the Wrightson farm on the Eastern Shore.

Alger's adoration of Priscilla was indeed great. He imbued her with much worldliness and sophistication, respected her fine intellect, and admired the fortitude with which she had met the hard realities of her recent years.

In one sense, he undid the tragic fate of his father by becoming Timmie's father and in his own life lived out with his stepson the unfulfilled filial and paternal relationship of which his father's death had deprived him. In this unconscious anniversary reaction, Priscilla herself bore important resemblances (and differences) to Minnie Hiss. Both were active, energetic, ambitious women. Yet her agressiveness, quiet and controlled, was opposite in quality to that so openly displayed by Alger's mother. It seems evident that Alger chose Priscilla on the basis of her oppositeness to his mother. Priscilla was far less positive in her opinions, had a fine sense of discretion and personal privacy, so different from Minnie in these respects. But Minnie and Priscilla resembled each other physically; both were blond, about the same height, and had the same simplicity of dress, manner, and outward gentleness.

Soon after their marriage Priscilla took a job as assistant to the librarian of the Wickersham Commission. That summer Alger and Priscilla rented a cottage in Montserrat, Massachusetts, near Beverly Farms, where Justice Holmes had his summer residence. Marbury visited them for a week at their cottage. Since Alger had to be away most of the day, Marbury spent a good deal of time with Priscilla. She impressed him as being "a rather domineering woman, who had no intention of letting Alger 'steal the show.' "

During his year with Holmes, Hiss was making plans for his future career. He had apparently by this time decided to enter some private law firm, preferably in New York or Boston. A passing anecdote recollected by Huntington Cairns provides a colorful glimpse of Hiss at that time.

During his last year at the Harvard Law School we dined together one night at the Maryland Club. It was summer and he wore a white linen suit and looked very distinguished. We gossiped about the Law School, the faculty, and I remember criticizing a technical piece by Harold Laski which the *Law Review* had printed. I had been some years at the Bar and I asked Alger if he intended to practice in

Baltimore. He smiled and said "No, I don't want to compete with you," a graceful statement which has stuck in my mind.

Hiss looked forward to his entry into private practice and, after many years of subsistence on a meager allowance, to achieving at last financial independence. His interest was in civil and corporate law, and on the basis of his excellent academic record and reputation he hoped to find a position with some well-established law firm. To this end he sought the advice of a few of his close friends, including William Marbury, then practicing law in Baltimore. On Hiss's behalf, Marbury corresponded with some of his colleagues in Boston and secured a position for him at Choate, Hall and Stewart, a highly regarded law firm.

In October 1930, when his year with Justice Holmes came to a close, Alger and Priscilla found an apartment in Cambridge and Alger began work.

During his first year Hiss made rapid strides and was already an important asset to the firm. His main duties were as legal assistant to John Hall on the Gillette Safety Razor Case, a protracted and involved piece of litigation.

Alger was fully and happily involved in his work. Priscilla, however, could not find a comfortable niche in her new surroundings. Timmy, then four years old, required the usual attentions of a child this age. The restriction of Priscilla's accustomed intellectual pursuits by domestic duties did not suit her temperament. Cambridge and Boston, she found, were not an easy place for her to live; nor could she fit herself into the already established group that consisted mostly of Alger's lawyer friends and former Harvard colleagues. "I'm not sure," the wife of one of Alger's close friends recalled, "that anyone knew Priscilla very well." Almost all of "their" friends were his friends. Priscilla felt alone and left out.

Had it not been for Priscilla's personal dissatisfactions and social misgivings about her life in Boston, Alger would have remained there. Priscilla, however, grew more restive. In an endeavor to fill out her life more meaningfully, she tried doing social work. She then applied for, and was awarded, a research grant in the field of fine arts from the Carnegie Corporation, a job that required her to be in New York. It was decided that they would move to New York, and as the time for her to begin work grew closer she became impatient to leave Boston.[11]

Hiss has expressed a firm belief in the equality of men and women. He believes strongly in equal partnership in marriage and comments that if he

[11] The result of the grant was a book titled *Research in Fine Arts in American Colleges and Universities,"* published in December 1934. Priscilla collaborated on the work with her sister-in-law, Roberta Fansler.

were to condone dependence on the part of the woman "I would be helping
the suppression of women, I would be on the side of exploitation of women by
denigrating them." He cites, as an example, one of the conditions he deplored
as a youth: the custom for women to leave the room after dinner, while the
men smoked cigars and told stories. It made the women appear stupid.
"Men," says Hiss of the Southern tradition, "had a real sense of superiority
toward women, a real sense of scorn, so that when they ran into a woman
with intellect they found her unfeminine."

He remembers with distaste the situation of M. Carey Thomas, the first
woman to get a degree from Johns Hopkins University (later she became
president of Bryn Mawr College, was responsible for revitalizing it, and
founded the Bryn Mawr School for Girls in Baltimore). When attending
classes at Johns Hopkins, Miss Thomas had to sit behind a screen, "as though
she were a leper—it was like not accepting Negroes," comments Hiss.

Minnie Hiss was one of M. Carey Thomas's greatest admirers. Alger
grew up following this line of thought and hoped to find an independent
woman, one who would ideally combine both femininity and intellect. This he
felt he had found in Priscilla Fansler.

Though Alger had agreed to give up his association with Choate, Hall
and Stewart and move to New York, the continuing court hearings of an important case (Gillette Company) made it necessary for him to remain in Boston for several more months. Priscilla and Timmie moved down to New York
ahead of Alger and rented an apartment at 180 Claremont Avenue in Morningside Heights. During this interval Alger commuted between Boston and
New York on weekends. During the week he lived with his friends, the Richard Fields.

This was in the fall of 1931, and the effects of the deepening financial
depression were especially apparent in New York. The unemployment and
poverty had spilled over into the city's streets. Priscilla's apartment in Morningside Heights was close by the quarters of the Uptown-Upper Broadway
Section of the Socialist Party. That branch operated a feeding station, and
outside the party's quarters signs were displayed requesting contributions to
help feed the unemployed. Priscilla passed by the Socialist Party office one
day, saw the signs, was appalled by the long bread line, and went in to offer
her services as a volunteer worker for the feeding station. For the next few
months she occasionally came by in the evenings to assist in making and dis-
pensing sandwiches and coffee. She contributed small sums of money to help
buy bread, sandwich filling, and coffee. When, in the spring of 1932, they
moved from Morningside Heights to Central Park West and were no longer in

the vicinity of the uptown feeding station, she gave up her association there, but it was to count against the Hisses in the trials.

When Mr. Thurlow Gordon, a friend of Hiss's and senior member of the New York law firm of Cotton, Franklin, Wright and Gordon, had heard in 1931 of Hiss's availability and contemplated move to New York, he sought Hiss out. Gordon was in need of an assistant with trial experience, was aware of Hiss's ability, and offered him a position with his firm. Hiss accepted and planned to take up his new position as soon as the Gillette case was completed.[12]

In the spring of 1932 Alger was able to leave Boston and went down immediately to join his new firm. He did well and is remembered with affection by his colleagues. Gerard Swope, Jr., who worked alongside him at Cotton and Franklin (from July 1932 to the spring of 1933), writes:

I was immediately attracted to Alger as a very warm, friendly, and particularly intelligent and able fellow. We got on very well together and liked each other. I cannot recall any particular discussions of note, but no doubt we discussed topical subjects, and generally our approach to matters was very similar. I recall no conflicts in our thinking of any importance.[13]

Of his large array of friends, Alger was closest to William Marbury. They visited each other when occasion permitted, in New York or Baltimore, and for many years carried on a personal as well as a professional correspondence, exchanging legal briefs and opinions on subjects of mutual interest, especially labor law.

Alger's interest in the special field of labor law, first stirred during his student years at Harvard, became more realistically oriented during the depression years of 1932–33, when he was working in New York. Together with several others, and at the invitation of Shad Polier, a former Harvard classmate, Hiss joined a group of young New York lawyers interested in civil rights, and labor and agricultural problems. The members of this group, known as the International Juridical Association, met periodically for discussions of civil rights cases, labor law, and the many farm and other emergency problems that confronted the country during the period just before and during the New Deal. Hiss contributed to the small legal periodical they published.[14]

---

[12] The work which Hiss performed during his two years at Choate, Hall and Stewart was not forgotten. Years later, when Hiss was in the State Department, he was repeatedly asked by James Garfield, managing partner of the firm, to return and become a partner, if and when he decided to leave government service.

[13] Personal communication, August 7, 1963.

[14] Many years later the International Juridical Association merged with the Lawyers Guild. The latter organization was, in the forties, cited by the Attorney General's Office as subversive.

We come now to an important turn in Hiss's life. He decided to leave the employ of Cotton and Franklin and enter government service. It was a significant and eventful decision, which brought him from New York to Washington, D.C., at a time of great political ferment. It was a move that ushered in untold opportunities for his legal skills and brought new horizons within sight of his ideological aspirations.

10

New Deal

IN MAY 1933 Jerome Frank, general counsel for the newly created Agricultural Adjustment Administration, offered Hiss a position as his assistant general counsel.[1] Frank's offer came at a time when Hiss was busily occupied with two important cases. He was well established at Cotton and Franklin and did not wish again to disrupt his life. His interest was to remain a lawyer in private practice. Though Hiss had long admired Jerome Frank and his liberal philosophy, he felt that only a major call warranted dropping out of the large-scale responsibilities he had as a lawyer with Cotton and Franklin.

So after consideration I felt I should not leave, thus disrupting the work of that office that I had recently joined and where I had established warm and friendly relations.

But when Hiss received a telegram from Felix Frankfurter stating, "You must accept Jerome Frank offer on basis of national emergency," he changed his mind.

I accepted on the basis of conscience and civic duty. I left Cotton and Franklin, a big Wall Street firm that was doing well. It was like enlisting in time of war.

In May 1933 His moved to Washington and took up his work with the AAA as assistant general counsel to Frank. In June, after Timmie had finished the school year, Priscilla joined him, and they moved into a house at 3411 O Street in Georgetown.

The motivation behind Hiss's entry into government service was brought into question years later during the trials. Another of Frank's assistants was Lee Pressman, who later admitted having been a Communist. Inasmuch as Pressman, along with Hiss and others, was named by Whittaker Chambers as a member of the same Communist cell in Washington, and furthermore, since Pressman and Hiss had been student friends at Harvard (both were on the

---

[1] There were three assistant counsels to Jerome Frank: Alger Hiss, Lee Pressman, and Philip Wenchel.

Law Review), it was presumed by many that Pressman had been instrumental in bringing Hiss into government service or that Hiss had brought in Pressman. According to Arthur Schlesinger, Jr.,

Though coming from contrasting backgrounds and possessing contrasting personalities, the penetrating and sardonic Jew and the handsome, cool, and reserved Anglo-Saxon [i.e., Pressman and Hiss] were intimate friends. As Jerome Frank wrote Charles Brand in the summer of 1933 about Pressman, "I was reluctant to urge him to come to Washington but finally did so at the insistence of Mr. Hiss, who has the highest regard for Mr. Pressman's ability and character." Pressman brought in Witt, and Frank hired Abt, whom he had known in Chicago.[2]

On the other hand, Ralph de Toledano and Victor Lasky have written:

Solidly entrenched in the AAA, Pressman began to bring in his own friends. They were all clever young men, all absolutely loyal to Pressman. Among those he brought in were Nathan Witt, Charles Kramer, and John Abt. And, of course, his close friend, Alger Hiss. Before leaving New York, Pressman had urged Alger to come to Washington with him. When Hiss decided to take the advice, it was Tommy Corcoran who sent him to Jerome Frank, but the ground had already been prepared by Pressman.[3]

In response to my query, "Did Pressman join the AAA before or after you?" Hiss commented:

I'm sure that when I came to Washington, Pressman had already agreed to join Frank, with whom he was associated in New York.[4] His own commitments in New York may have kept him in New York after I went down to Washington, but I can't believe I was instrumental in his acceptance of the job.
The quotation from Frank [cited by Schlesinger] is perplexing to me for Frank and Pressman knew each other well and I met Frank for the first time when I came down at Frankfurter's urging. I would certainly have expressed the opinion of Pressman [that] Frank quotes me as having, but I'm quite sure there was no question of my urging Jerome in that regard, much less insisting. This is the first time I'd been aware of Frank's putting it as he did. . . . Frank was subtle and sometimes used defensive tactics in his dealings with people like Brand and Peek, who were the conservative faction in the AAA, especially when it came to making a written "record" in official memos. He was embattled from the beginning, and I would certainly have been glad to shoulder the responsibility for Lee's presence on the staff, and Lee was indeed a frequent target of the conservative faction. I'm trying to put myself into the climate of infighting that went on. I had little direct part in it but I was well aware of its prevalence and its intensity.

[2] Arthur M. Schlesinger, Jr., *The Coming of the New Deal,* (Boston: Houghton Mifflin Company, 1959), p. 53.
[3] De Toledano and Lasky, *op. cit.,* p. 41.
[4] Since 1930 Lee Pressman had worked as Jerome Frank's legal assistant in the private firm of Chadbourne, Stanchfield and Levy. This was a well-established firm that handled the transactions of large corporations, problems of receiverships, and so forth.

Hiss's reply, to be sure, is not definitive, but it is supported by Pressman's own account. Pressman is quoted by Schlesinger as saying to the House Committee on Un-American Activities in 1950, "In my desire to see the destruction of Hitlerism and an improvement in economic conditions here at home, I joined a Communist group," and then Schlesinger characterizes Hiss and Pressman as "the two best-placed recruits [who] had been classmates at the Harvard Law School." But Schlesinger fails to include the rest of Pressman's statement:

Now, I believe it of interest to comment that I have no knowledge regarding the political beliefs or affiliations of Alger Hiss. . . . I do know, and I can state as a matter of knowledge, that for the period of my participation in that group, which is the only basis on which I can say I have knowledge, Alger Hiss was not a member of the group.

Pressman also denied that he and Hiss had anything to do with each other's entrance to the AAA.

PRESSMAN: Sometime in the spring of 1933 I was called down to Washington by Mr. Jerome Frank, who was then general counsel of the Agricultural Adjustment Administration, and asked whether I would accept employment with the Administration as an assistant general counsel.
   At this point, Mr. Chairman, I would like to take the opportunity, as I will through the course of these proceedings, to lay low, I hope once and for all, many distortions of truth. It has been asserted time and again by some people that I was responsible, for example, for getting Alger Hiss a job in triple A. I state as a fact, and the public records will bear me out, that when I came to Washington to become employed in the Triple A, at that time Alger Hiss was already working with Jerome Frank as assistant in the triple A. I had nothing whatsoever—and when I say nothing whatsoever I mean precisely that—nothing whatsoever to do with the employment of Alger Hiss in the Triple A.
TAVENNER: Let me interrupt you there.
PRESSMAN: May I continue?
TAVENNER: No. I would like to interrupt you at this point. Who endorsed you for the position in the AAA?
PRESSMAN: I just stated that Mr. Jerome Frank asked me to come to Washington to join up with the triple A because I had been working with him, was his assistant, in the law firm from which I came.
TAVENNER: Did anyone else, to your knowledge, endorse you for that position?
PRESSMAN: Not to my knowledge. Is there a suggestion, sir, that there was?
TAVENNER: I am asking if you know.
PRESSMAN: Not to my knowledge. Jerome Frank was the only person [5] I knew in the city of Washington at that time.[6]

[5] Obviously Pressman meant "person of influence" whose endorsement would carry weight. Hiss was not in that category. He himself was in need of influential endorsement.
[6] HUAC Hearings (August-September 1950), Part II, p. 2848.

Regarding the above, Hiss comments, "In general I find my memory of this event doesn't differ from Pressman's, which rings true."

The testimony of Whittaker Chambers that Hiss was slipped into government by the Communist Party is further negated by a review of Hiss's personal correspondence with William Marbury during the period in question. In one letter Hiss asked his conservative (Democratic) friend to help him find appropriate recommendations for his contemplated government job. On May 10, 1933, while still employed by the firm of Cotton and Franklin, Hiss wrote:

If you could get Senator Tydings to write a letter I think it would be helpful. I haven't the remotest idea to whom the letter should be addressed. The circumstances are:

Jerome Frank is slated to be solicitor to the administrator provided for in the pending Farm Bill. He has been in Washington for about a month working hard but without portfolio. He has asked me to be one of his three assistants—there will also be other lawyers under him. He suggested that a letter from a Congressman would be a good idea but until he was himself appointed I saw no reason to hurry. I understand that he expects things to be under way next week and that he has already sent in his list of names for appointments on his staff. Consequently, I judge that if a letter is to have any weight it should go now.[7]

Whereupon Marbury asked Senator Tydings to address a letter of recommendation for Hiss to Jerome Frank at the Department of Agriculture.

Hiss's duties in the AAA extended into diverse areas. He was called upon to write legal opinions, appear before congressional committees, and draft "benefit contracts" (agreements under which farmers were paid to reduce or control their agricultural production in an attempt to prevent surpluses with consequent reduction in the price of farm goods). He led a full and active life, an almost around-the-clock existence. Discussions of issues and problems of work merged with weekend social activities. During the trials Hiss was asked to describe his activities and mode of life during this period.

Q. Were there times when you were associated with the AAA when the various people of that Administration came out to your house and held meetings?
A. There were indeed.
Q. And that included who?
A. Well, at O Street, when we had a house at O Street, I would say that there were a dozen or more officials of the AAA who were very frequently at our house for conferences, for business discussions. They would include Judge Frank himself; various of the other attorneys; Mr. John Lewin of Baltimore; Mr. Pressman, Mr. Witt, Mr. Bachrach; a number of the economists: Mr. Blaisdell, Dr. Ezekiel; various other people interested in what was called the Consumers' Council; Mr. Gardner Jackson, I remember, and Mr. Gardiner Means, who was

[7] From Marbury memorandum, November 1948, Hiss Defense Files.

an adviser to the Secretary of Agriculture; a number of other people. That is perhaps only a few of the total number.[8]

Gardner Jackson was an important figure in the AAA and in Alger's life while he was in the Department of Agriculture. During the twenties Jackson had been a young reporter on the *Boston Globe.* He had become extremely interested in the Sacco-Vanzetti Case and ended by devoting all of his time to it. Hiss first met Jackson at his sister's home in Duxbury, where Jackson also had a summer home. During the many weekends spent with his sister, when he attended Powder Point Academy and when he was at Harvard, Hiss met Jackson quite often. But in those early years he met him only on a casual and social basis.

"When Hiss came to Washington about ten years later, as an important member of the legal staff of the AAA," Jackson has recalled, "he no longer bore the youthful image of Mary Ann Emerson's young brother." Jackson accepted him as an equal, and they saw quite a lot of each other. Through mutual interest in their work at the AAA, their friendship took on a more meaningful, mature character. Of his personal relations with Jackson during the Washington years, Hiss has written:

Pat Jackson was one of the earlier members of the AAA staff, serving in the Consumers' Council. With the background of having known him personally when I was a youngster, I naturally saw a good deal of him. . . . In the early days of the New Deal, Pat was into everything, and his house in Chevy Chase was a center for rabid discussions of politics, economics, and so forth. It was on such an occasion that I first met Alexander Sachs and other "intellectual giants" of the New Deal period. As an ex-newspaperman and an extreme liberal with a moneyed background, Pat knew all kinds of interesting people. The Consumers' Council were very active during the first couple of years of the AAA, and Pat sat in on many of the topics on which I was working.

In July 1934 Hiss was lent to the Nye Committee as legal assistant. A small appropriation for the creation of the committee had been passed by Congress in early 1934, and the committee went into action in the early summer. Its objectives were to investigate the activities of both foreign and American munitions industries.

Gardner Jackson played an important part in the organization of the Nye Committee. He was extremely interested in it and had close connections with Senator Nye and Senator Bone; he was asked by them to help find the proper personnel to staff the newly organized committee.

Jackson was influential in the "loan" of Hiss from the AAA to the Nye Committee. Jackson's firsthand account reveals clearly the forceful, behind-

[8] Trial Transcript, p. 1810.

the-scenes methods of Lee Pressman, whose ideological aggressiveness played a cryptic role in the political events of the early days of the New Deal—and, as will be seen, to some extent in the career of Alger Hiss.

Preparatory to a clear understanding of the role Pressman played in connection with Hiss's loan to the Nye Committee and the events that followed, it is necessary to examine the special relationship that existed between Pressman and Jackson. "Here is how," Jackson explained, "I got to know Lee Pressman":

Before I was swept out of newspapering into the AAA, two fellows came to my house in Chevy Chase. Here were these two fellows, Lee Pressman and Nat Witt, coming on a pilgrimage for *me* and for what I had done for the Sacco-Vanzetti Case. They had come from their law offices to remake the world and wanted me to join AAA. They had committed themselves to Jerome Frank.

Next Sunday, Jerome Frank and Rex Tugwell came out to see me. I was captured by Jerome Frank, a great guy. Lee Pressman was almost explicit—"you and I will make a hell of a team." Lee supplied a lack in me which I needed. He was an absolutely positive person who knew just where he was going. He was highly articulate. The way we got functioning together was through the sharecroppers contracts. I didn't know it was one of the Communists' primary foci. So we collaborated. We traveled together on milk hearings. I enjoyed his cynical positivism and wasn't analytical of what Lee was up to. Jerome Frank deferred to Pressman in all of his strategies. Frank was a greater intellect than Pressman, but Lee dominated him in strategy, when it was a question of whom to choose, when to move, and so forth. Lee figured mightily in the evolution of Alger Hiss in that period in the AAA.

I had been seeing Lee Pressman every day in connection with fights about milk and vegetables, Consumers' Council, fighting on Pressman's side, and Pressman said [one day], "Don't you think it would be a good idea to have Alger become [legal] head of the Nye Committee?" I said, "I don't know." Pressman said, "If Jerome Frank says it's O.K., would you go fix it up so Alger could be loaned to the Nye Committee?" So I talked with Jerome Frank, Bennett Clark, and Bone, but never talked to Alger about it. It was all Lee Pressman's doings. I felt certain that Alger would have known that it was on the basis of Pressman's request that I arranged Alger's transfer to the Nye Committee. I could not understand why Alger never sought me out to thank me afterward.[9]

In December 1948 columnist Tris Coffin described Pressman as "The Big Brain of the radical wing of the New Deal." One of his associates in the early days of the AAA said of him: "Lee attracted many of us to his wing because he knew all the answers. He had a systematic day-to-day plan all mapped out. He was absolutely sure of himself. He used people like a machin-

[9] Personal interview with Gardner Jackson, May 6, 1963.
The author endeavored on repeated occasions, through several close intermediaries, to arrange an interview with Lee Pressman. In a telephone conversation I had with him, he adamantly refused to see me or discuss any aspects of my research.

ist uses tools—when they are broken or worn out he throws them away, coldly and impersonally." [10]

Regarding Pressman, Hiss has told me that he had "always found him warm, outgoing, frank—not polished, and often blunt." Hiss has not seen Pressman for many years, but during a conversation he had with a CIO associate of Pressman's whom he recently met, Hiss was told that Lee "when younger was ideologically ruthless, then he became just ruthless." Hiss's own feelings about Pressman do not reflect those sinister overtones. "The build-up of Lee Pressman," said Hiss, "as a New Deal controller of Destiny is way off, like the Republican myth that *I* told FDR what to do at Yalta."

When I asked Hiss why Pressman wanted him on the Nye Committee, he replied: "I didn't know that he did. I thought Steve Rauschenbush wanted me and the Committee members who were also on the Agricultural Committee (and so knew me) agreed and got Wallace to lend me to the Committee."

Hiss's earlier account as to how he was lent to the Nye Committee is substantially the same:

As Gardner Jackson was in so many different activities and was a very close friend of Jerome Frank's, it is quite possible that Pat had something to do with my being lent to the Nye Committee. He certainly would have been in a good position to know about this, in view of his connection with Nye and Rauschenbush at one end of the transaction and with Jerome Frank and Secretary Wallace at the other end. My own recollection is that the chief consideration which governed the Department of Agriculture in lending my services to the Committee was that two members of the Senate Agriculture Committee (Bone and Pope) were also on the Nye Committee and that it was considered good Congressional relations policy to honor a request from a committee of which those two were members.[11]

When asked during the second trial (November 1949) the circumstances of his transfer to the Nye Committee, Hiss's testimony did not vary from his previous accounts.

Q. When was that Committee created, approximately, if you know?
A. I think the resolution was passed in May or June, somewhere around there, of 1934.
Q. When did you become associated with it?
A. I was detailed to it on July 30, 1934, by Mr. Frank.
Q. By whom?
A. By my superior, Judge Frank. . . .
Q. Who asked you if you would be interested in coming over?
A. My understanding was . . . that the Committee had asked the Department for the loan of my services, and I understand it was primarily Senator Bone and Senator Pope.

[10] Cited by De Toledano and Lasky, *op. cit.,* pp. 38–39.
[11] From a private, pre-trial memo to Hiss legal counsel, dated November 1948.

As legal counsel to the Nye Committee, Hiss passed on legal questions that the committee wanted ruled upon and gave them opinions on matters of law. He gathered evidence relating to the activities of the munitions industries and handled, as an examiner, four or five specific topics assigned to him. The first of these examinations began on September 10, 1934, when he questioned John S. Allard, president of Curtiss-Wright Export Corporation, regarding the manufacture and sale of aircraft to foreign countries. Hiss went on to officials of the DuPont Company, reaching his height in the questioning of Bernard Baruch. Fully equipped beforehand with all the evidence he needed, Hiss was a meticulous cross-examiner. He received acclaim among the New Dealers, the liberals, and left-wingers and angered Baruch and his friends. Hiss soon began making a name for himself and was asked to speak at various clubs and societies regarding the work of the Nye Committee.

It was at about this time (early in 1935) that tensions within the AAA came to a head, resulting in the now historic "purge." Many writers have chronicled this emotionally charged political event, each according to his own perspective or his political or personal bent. I have condensed Hiss's version (replies to my queries) insofar as it helps reflect his personal activities and political philosophy during this period:

In setting up the AAA President Roosevelt attempted to insure balance by putting in important positions men of very different political philosophies. Mr. George Peek of the Moline Plow Company had been a prominent conservative farm leader under the Hoover administration. Peek was made administrator of the AAA. Rexford Tugwell, who was a vigorous New Dealer and believed in intensive government controls, was made Under Secretary of Agriculture. Wallace at that time was regarded as in between the positions of these two men. Instead of preserving balance, this policy tended to cause rival cliques within the AAA and resulted in administrative conflicts. . . . Jerome Frank, undoubtedly on Tugwell's initiative, was appointed general counsel.

When I came to Washington on Jerome Frank's invitation, it was my understanding that Mr. Peek had wanted Fred Lee as his general counsel. Consequently, from the very beginning of the AAA Mr. Peek felt that he was not complete master in his own house. . . . There was continuous and at times actually bitter disagreement on policies, culminating in Peek's forced resignation in December 1933.

Chester Davis, who succeeded Peek, was considerably more liberal than Peek but after a few months tended to take a more conservative position than the Tugwell-Frank group. In the course of the year 1934, the same type of conflict developed and by the end of 1934 and throughout January of 1935 the bitterness between the two points of view was almost as extreme as it had been during the latter part of Peek's administration. Jerome Frank was seeing Chester Davis less and less and was communicating with him by means of numerous memoranda "for the record." Tugwell and Frank were so committed by conviction to the policies they espoused that Davis may well have thought no change in policy would have been effective without change in personnel. And undoubtedly the worsening of personal relations between Davis and Frank encouraged Davis to take the latter course. In any event, the "purge" came suddenly. Apparently Davis issued an ultimatum to Wallace that either he or Frank must go. Davis had long been associated with agricultural matters and had the respect of all the most important Congressional, industrial, and farm groups concerned. Consequently, under such circumstances, Wallace had no choice but to ask Frank to leave.

The immediate occasion of the "purge" was the cotton contract opinion and involved Hiss with Chester Davis. Hiss writes of it:

This opinion dealt primarily with the question of whether benefit payments had to be apportioned among tenants and sharecroppers with checks actually payable in the names of the tenants and sharecroppers or whether payments should be made simply to the landlord or chief operator of the farm with distribution to the other beneficiaries entrusted to him.

Opinions were under my branch of the legal staff, and though I was on detail to the Nye Committee I supervised the drafting of the opinion and signed it. Davis hit the roof. I was genuinely shocked that he so obviously resented it. He called me in and asked me how I could have approved such a "dishonest opinion"—intellectually dishonest, I believe were the words. I was equally furious and resigned on the spot, telling him that I could not act as lawyer for anyone who would question my integrity. He apologized and asked me to stay on. I did not at that time withdraw my resignation but after I had cooled off somewhat and after he had further apologized and said he hadn't meant to question my integrity, that he hadn't meant it as it sounded and had been overexcited, I agreed to stay on, as I had always admired him and had the best of relations with him and as I believed in the sincerity of his own support of the AAA programs. This personal interchange with Davis naturally had some weight in my not being willing to resign when Jerome Frank and the others were "purged." I did not think that the policies which Mr. Davis would carry out were such as would be incompatible with my own convictions and, as a lawyer, was prepared to accept new directions of policy from him.

By February 1935, Hiss had become so taken up with his Nye Committee work that he was preparing to go full time to the committee. As a replacement for Hiss, the AAA needed someone who could draft legislation, get along well with Congressmen in general, and function as liaison man between the AAA and Congress. Telford Taylor was chosen to replace Hiss as legal representative for the Agriculture Department's point of view in Congress. Taylor came to the AAA in September 1934, fresh from a year of legal experience as a clerk for a New York judge.

Taylor, just twenty-four years old, was six or seven years younger than Hiss and that much his junior in terms of experience and status. For about six weeks following the "purge," Hiss, despite his duties with the Nye Committee, spent as much time as he could in helping Taylor in his new job. In this connection Taylor saw a great deal of Hiss and got to know him well. Taylor said:

I admired Alger very much and enjoyed the training. Alger was the closest thing to a case of minor "hero worship" that I ever had. He was suave, more personable, polished, and cultured than most New Deal lawyers. . . . He took me by the hand and taught me my new job. I accompanied him to the capitol and equipped myself to take over his job as soon as possible.[12]

In March 1935, while still on loan to the Nye Committee, Hiss officially resigned from the AAA. He writes:

For some months in the latter part of 1934 and early 1935 as the duration of my loan to the Nye Committee had been stretched out, I felt increasingly reluctant to be receiving my salary from the Department of Agriculture when Bob Mc-Connaughey was doing my work [benefit contracts] but at a lower salary . . . and finally, on March 2, resigned and went on the Nye committee payroll. I had, of course, continued during the period of my Nye Committee service to do a great deal of work for the AAA, and my resignation did not mean any lessening of interest in the agricultural field.

Hiss goes on to say:

Indeed, when the Nye committee increasingly turned its direction to bolstering isolationism by concentrating on World War I financing and the necessity for neutrality legislation, a direction with which I did not sympathize. I immediately turned to the litigation involving the constitutionality of the AAA—the Butler case.

This led Hiss, in May or June of 1935, to apply for a position in the office of Mr. Stanley Reed, Solicitor General of the United States. The Butler case was at that time before the Solicitor General's Office and was soon to go before the Supreme Court. The AAA was anxious to have someone in the Justice Department who had worked on the day-to-day problems of the Act, and Hiss's experience in the AAA made him extremely suitable for such a position. In August, Hiss began work in the Department of Justice:

I went into Mr. Reed's office with the Butler case as my primary duty and with the full blessings of the AAA and the Department of Agriculture.

Nonetheless, he did not entirely discontinue his work with the Nye committee. He continued to give legal advice after he joined the Justice Department (hearings went on until February 1936), and work on final reports continued for still another few months.

It was during this period, extending from 1934 through 1935, while Alger Hiss was actively involved in the work of not one but three government

[12] Telford Taylor to the writer, personal interview, October 17, 1963.

departments, devoting himself completely to the conscientious and successful execution of his assignments, that Whittaker Chambers appeared on the Washington scene. He was there, according to his own account, as an "underground Communist" and, as he would later say, one of his first assignments was to work with "an exceptional Communist" named Alger Hiss.

IV

11

A Kind of Friendship

W E ARE NOW at the most baffling years of our subjects' lives, the years of their controversial relationship, where their conflicting stories about each other begin. A few facts, the evidence that built the circumstantial case against Hiss, are beyond dispute. But around them can be constructed two opposite and, on the surface at least, quite plausible stories.[1]

It was Chambers' claim that he first met Hiss in the spring of 1934 in a Washington restaurant. The purpose of meeting, he said, was to transfer Hiss —already a Communist—to a new "apparatus," under Chambers' direction. He was introduced, he said, only as "Carl," his Communist alias. According to his story, the meeting was the beginning not only of a Communist liaison but of a friendship.

Hiss's story is, of course, entirely different: that he met Chambers not as "Carl," the Communist, but as "George Crosley," a young man purporting to be a free-lance writer, interested in the work of the Nye Committee.

It is known that Chambers, as either Crosley or Carl, stayed several nights in the Hisses' house on P Street and that for nearly two months (May and June of 1935) he lived with his wife and infant in an apartment leased by the Hisses. No records of the arrangement were kept, and in fact, according to both men, no money changed hands. Chambers claimed that it was simply a Communist favor. Hiss said that "Crosley" had offered to sublet the apartment to finish the Hisses' lease and had welched on the payment. Hiss's account was doubted because of the informality of the arrangement and his seeming laxness in dealing with Crosley, to whom, he admitted, he had also made a couple of small loans. But Hiss's explanation that he had no other hope of renting the apartment for such a short time (and thus was taking no

---

[1] This chapter cannot pretend to offer a complete discussion of the evidence. The writer is not an advocate for either of the subjects; his aim is to inform the reader of his own findings or refresh his memory about certain facts and statements in the record. The State Department documents are not dealt with here. They will be considered when they are chronologically appropriate.

real risk) and that he had sublet other places without written agreement seemed to equalize the credibility of his story. It was rather typical of Hiss not to question anyone's good faith, and Chambers was so obviously a man in need that he stirred the "caretaker" in Hiss.

The question of the Ford car and the vicissitudes of its strange transfer to a Mr. Rosen are still a mystery.[2] Hiss originally said he let Chambers have the car, of little cash value, because it was simply sitting in the street, having been replaced with a new Plymouth. Chambers claimed that Hiss had let him use the Ford but had in fact turned it over to a Communist car dealer as a gift, for "some poor organizer in the West or somewhere." The Motor Vehicle Department documents, when they were uncovered, seemed to support Chambers' story. The transfer was not effected until a year after Chambers had left the apartment, in July 1936. (In addition, there is no record that Hiss acquired his Plymouth until after Chambers left the apartment.) The record showed that Hiss had signed the title over to the Cherner Motor Company (it was notarized by an employee of the Department of Justice, a strange lack of precaution for a conspirator), and the car was resold later the same day to one William Rosen. The new title papers, when later discovered by House Committee investigators, were found to be subject to a lien of $25 enabling the Cherner Motor Company to insist on collection of that amount from the new owner. This lien, in one important sense, negates Chambers' story that Hiss transferred the car as a "gift" to the Communist Party.[3]

Hiss was unable to recollect having signed the certificate or having had it notarized by a Justice Department notary, though he did not deny the likelihood that he had done so. He assumed that Chambers, having had the car for some months, simply sent a messenger to his office with the certificate of title, which he signed "in the midst of a busy day."

Another controversial piece of property was a rug that Hiss first mentioned before the House Committee as a gift from Chambers in "part payment" for the apartment. He pointed out that he still had it. Chambers later confirmed that he had given Hiss the rug but said that it was an expression of the Communist Party's appreciation of Hiss's work. Documents were later

---

[2] Rosen, for example, admitted that he had at one time been a Communist but left the party in 1929 (the year Chambers allegedly also "independently" left it). Though the above fact was not revealed in his testimony during the Hiss trial, he did testify that his signature on the title certificate was not his own, a fact that was later substantiated. This was one of the arguments on which the appeal for a rehearing was based. Rosen claimed privilege and simply agreed he was a Communist. ("A Brief for Appellant," *U.S.A. against Alger Hiss,* pp. 82–88.)

[3] Rosen did not testify. He was put on the stand but refused to talk. Thus he was presumed not only to be a Communist (which he was), but to be the person who got title to the car, which is doubtful, since it is *not* his signature on the document.

produced that showed Chambers had purchased four rugs in December 1936, a date after Hiss claimed to have received his rug. But a former maid confirmed Hiss's testimony, with her memory of the rug in the P Street house, from which the Hisses moved in June 1936. The dealer who sold the four rugs was called to testify. But, strangely, the prosecution did not subpoena the rug, nor did the defense produce it.[4]

One evident way for the House Committee and the courts to get at the credibility of the witnesses was to determine whether anyone else had known Chambers as "George Crosley," as Hiss claimed to have. Hiss and his lawyers failed to produce a single witness who would so testify. The former receptionist of the Nye Committee was dead. Others who might (or might not) have remembered the name (such as the janitor of the 28th Street apartment) did not wish to get involved in an "espionage" case. But here again we confront contradiction. Someone did come forward who had known Chambers as Crosley. He was Samuel Roth, a book publisher. Roth had first met Chambers around 1926–27. Chambers' poem "Tandaradei" had appeared in the June 1926 issue of *Two Worlds,* a quarterly magazine published by Roth. Interviewed by Hiss's lawyers, Roth stated that Chambers had used the name "George Crosley" as a pen name for several other poems. In a letter to me Roth stated:

. . . when the accused Mr. Hiss claimed that he had known Chambers only by the name George Crosley, and Chambers denied ever having used that name, I realized that Chambers was lying and Hiss was telling the truth. Among the many poems submitted to me by Chambers in 1925 and 1926, some were signed George Crosley.

Why, then, did the Hiss defense not call Samuel Roth as a witness to present this all-important piece of evidence? Roth had been convicted of violating obscenity laws. The Hiss counsel thought this would tell against their case. It was no doubt one of their worst decisions. Chambers, it should be said, refused to deny entirely his use of this alias. He gave this puzzling testimony:

Alger Hiss has testified that I lived at 28th Street under the name of George Crosley. It is possible, though I have no recollection of it, and I believe that I have recalled all the other names used in the underground without effort.

Hiss and Chambers were also known to have been involved (during 1935–37) in transactions for the same piece of real estate, a farm in Westminster, Maryland, which Chambers eventually bought and owned for the rest

[4] The defense, fearful of the dealer's relationship to Whittaker Chambers, was unwilling to go into the subject. Whether the government felt that its point was made without further proof, or whether the proof did not exist, is not known.

of his life. Chambers said that he and Hiss talked of buying the place, and in *Witness* he later described the occasion of their trip to see it: Hiss showed him an advertisement, and

proposed that he and I drive to Westminster, . . . look at the little house, and, if it were at all livable, buy it. Then my family could spend the summer there, the Hisses could visit us, and both families could be together without the precautions that hampered us in Baltimore or Washington.

He explained that Hiss did leave a deposit in his own name but that Hiss later decided against buying the place because Mrs. Hiss, when she saw it, did not like the location. In the Baltimore Deposition, Chambers told essentially the same story and added that Hiss "had difficulty getting the deposit back from Mr. Case," the real-estate agent. But, he said, "I recall Alger telling me he had written to Case on Department of Justice stationery, and that that fact had been magical, and Case returned the deposit at once."

This story is not in accord with what facts have been uncovered. Chambers' account in *Witness* suggests that he and Hiss were going to see the place for the first time ("Alger proposed that he and I drive to Westminster, look at the little house, and, if it were at all livable, buy it") presumably in the company of the real-estate agent. Mr. Case has sworn, in an affidavit, that Hiss and his wife came to look at the place, not Hiss and Chambers. This account was enforced by Calvin Zepp,[5] business neighbor of Mr. Case, who recalled Hiss's visit and said that Chambers was not with him. Hiss's letters to Case are extant; they are written not on Justice Department stationery but on his own paper. The correspondence raises many other questions.

The Hisses' interest in the farm was first shown not, as Chambers suggests, by a spur-of-the-moment trip on the part of Hiss and himself, but by a letter, written by Mrs. Hiss, on November 5, 1935. Their interest in the place was terminating by early May 1936. This is also at variance with Chambers' description, which seems to place their supposed first trip in full summer; he mentions tall grass and an abundance of birds. The letters further indicate that it was a price difference that was at issue, not Mrs. Hiss's dislike of the location. The letters also mention tools the Hisses left there (confirming that their intention to buy was real). Asked if he recalled these, Chambers said,

[5] Both Case and Zepp expressed resentment of the government's dealings with them. Case was subpoenaed but never called to appear, and his records were taken and never returned. Thus the government "bottled up" an important witness. Though this made it awkward for the Hiss defense to call him, it did not *prevent* Hiss's counsel from legally doing so. In retrospect, it would appear to have been a tactical error on the part of Hiss's lawyers to depend on the government to produce him.

Zepp said that FBI agents and an investigator from the House Committee tried to get him to say that he had seen Hiss and Chambers together in Westminster.

From a personal interview between Edward W. Case, Calvin Zepp, and the author, Westminster, Maryland, May 8, 1962.

No, I don't. It seems unlikely that Alger Hiss ever took tools there. I don't think he ever worked the place.

It should be said at once that Chambers' account before the House Committee, when the matter first came up, seems more plausible, though it is more vague, than his later story. He told the investigators about his trip with Hiss as a sort of afterthought: "I have left out one important thing—I made one trip up there with Alger Hiss." And asked if Mr. Case was with them he replied, "I don't think so." Reconstructing the incident at his leisure, in the writing of *Witness,* he offered the more dubious version.

In any event, Chambers did buy the property a year later. Here again, however, a mysterious aura surrounds the occasion. He bought it, he said, without telling Hiss because of the need for underground secrecy, an odd action if the two were openly planning to buy it together a year before.

These various issues, though they do not bear directly on whether or not Hiss was the underground Communist that Chambers alleged, were used to attempt to establish the degree of intimacy between the two men. Obviously, the truth of any one of these issues would bear crucially on the credibility of the witnesses, and they no doubt influenced the juries a great deal. And these circumstantial issues are of great significance as well to the psychological investigator.

One notices immediately that Chambers continually stressed the closeness of his friendship with Hiss, not just the number of times they were together, but the quality of their association. For example, in recounting the Westminister farm incident in *Witness,* Chambers, despite the many ambiguities involved, cites the day of the supposed trip as one of his most poignant memories of Hiss.

The day that Alger and I inspected it, we also looked at the other piece that had been advertised with it. It was a much bigger, adjoining tract. It had once been a farmstead, but the house had burned and the old barn was collapsing. . . .

There were birds of all kinds, and Alger stood by the brook in front of the barn, identifying them. In a burst . . . a ground robin flashed out of a shrub . . . and sang. "Do you know what he says?" Alger asked me. . . . The bird sang again. "Listen," Alger said, "he says: 'Sweet bird, sing!' " . . . I have no more vivid recollection of Alger Hiss.

At another moment he recounts the beginning of their friendship, points out that it grew despite the rules of the Communist Party, and remarks on what a comfort it was to Hiss.

. . . there began a development of a kind that is not favored in underground work. Alger Hiss became our personal friend in a way that made my relationship with him unlike my relationship with any others in the underground. Organizationally, this was made possible by the fact that I was expecting to go abroad at any moment. Therefore, I relaxed the underground procedures by bringing Hiss and his wife to visit us in Baltimore one night. Another factor entered in, too. His personal connection with us rescued Hiss from his underground isolation. There was a stimulation in driving to Baltimore to visit a hidden family whose address only he knew, in parking his old Ford roadster in the shadows of a side street and walking slowly (to make sure there were no observers) to the house behind whose completely ordinary front was an outpost of the international underground. No one was more amused than Alger by the thought of the WCTU as an underground "cover." [6]

This is a rather surprising passage, on the strength of what we already know of Hiss's public life at this time. In the reconstruction of Hiss's activities during the years 1934–35, one is impressed with the fullness rather than the loneliness of Hiss's life.

Mrs. Constance Ducey, Hiss's secretary at the AAA, wrote me:

Mr. Hiss worked night and day to do the tasks given him to do, although he tried to read one night a week to Justice Holmes while the Justice was still alive; and also saved an afternoon for his stepson when he could. He had to work many Sundays, for he seemed to be the one assigned to draft farm bills; work on setting up Commodity Credit and many other government matters.[7]

Charles Horsky described the year, "starting August 1, 1935," that he spent with Hiss in the Solicitor General's Office of the Department of Justice:

I would see Alger Hiss every day and night too. . . . Sometimes we'd work till 4 or 5 a.m. against a deadline. . . . We worked long hours and we worked holidays. Sometimes we'd get so tired we'd stretch out on a table and work. There was a sense of mission and destiny during those days of the New Deal.[8]

Hiss, however, found time to play tennis regularly with his friends Horsky, Gardner, and Farrand [9] during 1934–35, and he enjoyed an occasional swim. Social functions in Washington often merged indistinguishably with political meetings and discussions. Roy Veatch, a State Department economist, organized Sunday-evening supper parties at which foreign policy would be discussed. Hiss's long-term interest in foreign affairs led naturally to his meet-

[6] Note how Chambers vividly describes Hiss's actions an an "example of underground procedure" and thereby incriminates him in the reader's mind. Yet, when he has need to prove a point against Hiss, on his own authority, he "relaxes" the underground procedure and permits "Hiss and his wife to visit us in Baltimore one night."
[7] Personal communication, November 12, 1962.
[8] Horsky to the author, personal interview, May 7, 1963.
  In 1963, Horsky was serving as a member of the White House staff (presidential adviser in charge of District of Columbia Affairs).
[9] Stephen Farrand (then in the Justice Department, later a Los Angeles attorney) kept a diary of his Washington years, which contained several references to social activities with the Hisses. Farrand made his diary available for Hiss's use during the trials and for this study.

ing and talking to people in the State Department. John Dickey, then assistant
to Assistant Secretary of State Francis Sayre, was one of these men. Laurence
Duggan and Noel Field were others, as were Leroy Stinebower, Edward True-
blood, and Charles Yost. Hiss belonged to the Foreign Policy Association. At
its regular dinner meetings foreign visitors, American correspondents who had
served abroad, scholars, and many others spoke and took part in general discussions.

Another discordant note is struck by Chambers' assertion that the Hisses
knew him only as "Carl" while the Hisses used their full names. He explains
this unusual fact by saying that only the "heads" of underground groups used
pseudonyms and only first names. Be that as it may, for four years—the extent of the alleged close friendship between the two families—Chambers was
known *only* as "Carl"; in public, said Chambers, they would invent a surname
on the spur of the moment. For four years, he further said, the Hisses believed
him to be a European. In the Baltimore Deposition he testified: "Mrs. Hiss
said that she had come to the conclusion that I was not an American, but a
Central or Eastern European of some kind who had somehow, either through
residence here or otherwise, acquired a mastery of English." [10]

Chambers described many outings the families supposedly took together.
During the summer of 1935 the Chamberses had stayed with their friend,
Maxim Lieber, in his cottage on the Delaware. During this period, Chambers
claimed, Mrs. Hiss paid them a ten-day visit.

Q. She visited you at the cottage on the Delaware?
A. Yes.
Q. By herself?
A. Yes. I believe her husband came afterwards. . . .
Q. Did he spend the night there?
A. I am not sure. I don't think I was there. My wife was there.
Q. You mean you don't believe you were there when he came?
A. That is right.
Q. So you don't know what he did. Were you there when Mrs. Hiss was there?
A. Yes, I was there at least some of the time when she was there.
Q. Was Mr. Lieber there?
A. He was, indeed. . . .
Q. [By Marbury] Now, that would have been in August of 1935?
A. That would have been about then, yes.
Q. I think it is right important that we try to place that as nearly as we can.
A. I think you are quite right.

[10] In *Witness*, Chambers says that in the underground it was believed he was a Russian,
and he takes pride in describing the characteristics which gave him away as a foreigner:
"certain turns of expression . . . intonation rather than phrasing to express shades of
meaning." This impression he did nothing to dispel, for "there was almost nothing that
the underground Communists in Washington would not gladly do for me as a Russian."

Q. Mr. Lieber would know, wouldn't he?
A. Yes. Mr. Lieber is a Communist. Mr. Lieber, I am sure, would have a very exact recollection of it. He was very much impressed with Mrs. Hiss.[11]

This close and intimate relationship was not confirmed by Maxim Lieber. On April 26, 1951, after the Hiss trials, Chester Lane, newly appointed counsel for Hiss, sought out Lieber. On Lane's assurance that he did not wish to embarrass Lieber or inquire into his own activities, except as they might involve knowledge of Chambers' movements and his alleged relations with the Hisses, Lieber gave him an account of his relations with Chambers.

At no time throughout his acquaintance with Chambers, said Lieber, did he ever hear the Hisses' name or hear anything said or see anything done that could support Chambers' story of his connection with the Hisses. As Lieber remarked: "I wouldn't know Mrs. Hiss if she were to come in this office and spit in my tea!" With increasing knowledge that the more vivid of Chambers' descriptions appear to be based on imaginary facts, doubts about the validity of Chambers' stories increase correspondingly, and our doubts about his account of his relationship with the Hisses multiply. Let us note once again how rich in emotion are the memories of his friendship with Hiss; it is clearly an ideal brotherly relation in which his feelings for Richard are echoed. In his assessment of Hiss, Chambers writes:

The bond that cemented his friendship and mine went much deeper than any similarities or dissimilarities of mind. It was a profound, tacit esteem of character, increasing as our Communist activity tested us in common. . . . Each of us sensed in the other an unyielding purpose about those things which we held to be decisive, and a resourcefulness and play of imagination in action, which, among the Communists we knew, I sensed to the same degree only in Harold Ware. No other Communist but Alger Hiss understood so quietly, or accepted with so little fuss or question the fact that the revolutionist cannot change the course of history without taking upon himself the crimes of history. That is why I said of him in a broadcast, shortly after the second Hiss trial, "I cannot hate even an enemy who shares with me the conviction that that life is not worth living for which a man is not prepared to dare all and die at any moment." The recognition that, as Communists, we shared that same force of purpose was the deepest bond between us. . . .

All of us shared another more elusive, but very real bond. That was the mutual simplicity of our tastes. . . .

That simplicity is inseparable from a gentleness of character, though life and history may wrench and pervert it almost past recognition. In the Hisses, it found one expression in an absorption in nature, especially in the life of birds. . . . I remember vividly how Alger came in one morning and announced with an excitement that he almost never showed that for the first time he had seen a prothonotary warbler.

[11] Baltimore Deposition, pp. 283–86 *passim.*

At another point he celebrates the friendship again—though in a way that tends to belittle Hiss.

For our friendship was almost entirely one of character and not of the mind. Despite his acknowledged ability in the legal field, which I was not competent to explore with him, Alger Hiss is not a highly mental man. Compared to the minds I had grown up with at Columbia, free-ranging, witty and deeply informed (one has only to think of Clifton Fadiman or Meyer Schapiro), Alger was a little on the stuffy side. Ideas for their own sake did not interest him at all. His mind had come to rest in the doctrines of Marx and Lenin, and even then applied itself wholly to current politics and seldom, that I can remember, to history or to theory.[12]

It is indeed significant to illustrate Chambers' vacillations and how, in his ongoing account, his hatred and destructivity gain dominance over his admiration and love,

I particularly remember Alger's opinion of Shakespeare. In 1936 or 1937, Maurice Evans played *Richard II* in Baltimore. It was the first time that my wife or I had ever seen Shakespeare acted. We were deeply impressed. . . .
A day or so later, I was trying to convey some of that to Alger. "I'm sorry," he said at last, somewhat less graciously than usual, "I just don't like Shakespeare —platitudes in blank verse." [13]

And the friendship that Chambers recalls was not without its strife. Chambers at great length describes his deep personal and emotional involvement with Hiss at still another moment. It is a passage that deserves careful scrutiny, for in its ambience Chambers senses a deep streak of "cruelty" and "savagery" in Hiss, his "closest friend in the Communist Party."

No account of our friendship would be complete without mention of the continual kindnesses of the Hisses to us. . . . In late years, I have sometimes wondered how much of Hiss's solicitude was for ourselves (as we then supposed) and how much was for Carl as the representative of the Communist Party. . . . But I remember the simple pleasure that all of us took simply in being together. . . .

Since Chambers' sense of his own identity was a divided one, he could never be sure to which part of his own image someone else was relating. For this reason also, the pleasurable feeling (fantasy) of "being together" served to unify his sense of self.

The outstanding fact about Alger Hiss was an unvarying mildness. . . . Only very rarely did a streak of wholly incongruous cruelty crop out. From the first, my wife and I had been charmed by Baltimore and sometimes said so. "Baltimore," Alger

[12] At no time during his six-year period of close scrutiny of Mr. Hiss did the author discover any evidence that "his mind had come to rest in the doctrines of Marx and Lenin."
[13] Timothy Hobson recalled to me his recollections of the many evenings Alger and Priscilla read Shakespeare aloud.

once answered, "is the only city in the country so backward that it still lights its streets by gas. It's a city of dying old men and women." He was so unnecessarily savage that, by way of easing matters, I said: "They seem to be pleasant and harmless old people." "Yes," he said, "the horrible old women of Baltimore!" . . . The same strange savagery cropped out in a conversation about Franklin Roosevelt. Hiss's contempt for Franklin Roosevelt as a dabbler in revolution who understood neither revolution nor history was profound. . . . He startled me, and deeply shocked my wife, by the obvious pleasure he took in the most simple and brutal references to the President's physical condition as a symbol of the middle-class breakdown.

Chambers then shifts from his account of Hiss's "strange savagery" about Roosevelt and describes how Hiss directed "that deeply hidden streak" against him. "It came out in connection with the poor condition of my teeth." One night, he writes, Alger gave him a little lecture to the effect that his teeth were not a personal matter, but, as identifying marks for a conspirator, concerned everybody's safety.

He was oddly waspish, mincing no words. . . . The tone surprised, but the action did not offend me. For, toward the Hisses, we felt a tenderness, spontaneous and unquestioning, that is felt for one another by members of an unusually happy family. Nothing in their manner led us to suppose that they did not share the same feeling about us.

Is it conceivable that all of this, this expression of apparently deep emotion, could be a fabrication? I suggest that it is not only conceivable but highly probable. On the basis of material evidence alone, such a conclusion would hardly seem justified. We would prefer to overlook the contradictions and accept the force of Chambers' passionate rhetoric. It is not comfortable to be in the presence (even the literary presence) of a man whose convictions are so deeply felt and to think that he is lying. But when the material evidence is juxtaposed with what we already know of the psychic struggles that directed Chambers' life, and when we bear in mind that his self-created world of reality based on wish-fulfilling memories was, on other occasions, more real to him than factual reality, we are forced toward such a conclusion. We will not call his relationship with Hiss a lie, in the conventional sense, but we will suggest that much of it was a fantasy.

A brief recapitulation of the course of Chambers' infantile neurosis and how it became manifest in his adult thinking and behavior would be helpful. The infantile fantasy induced by his mother was that, in the act of being born, he almost killed her. This image of himself as a criminal since birth was the matrix of his sense of self. Under the aegis of Laha's depriving and unrealistic way of life this infantile fantasy was nurtured. Consequent to this early trauma were later developmental defects resulting from Vivian's conflicted relationship with his father, from whose neurotic pattern he took over the ways and attitudes of a mischievous, puerile, silent, passively hostile "boy-father." Deeply embedded in the ego of our subject but acted out in a more sinister way were his father's prankishness, his sudden appearances and disappearances, his lifelong duality and duplicity of existence. When Vivian was two and a half years old his brother Richard was born, and this event further separated him from his mother. Feeling unwanted and saddened by the presence of his brother, Vivian withdrew deeper into himself. His yearning to be like Richard, the loved one, permeated his thoughts and wishes, precociously mobilized his gifted mind and stirred his fantasies. Poverty and deprivation became the central mood of his life, omnipotence his need. He lost himself in the fictional characters of his early readings, magically sold out his true identity, and escaped from his external reality with reversals of time, place and person. He dreamed of a second chance in life. By pretense and manipulation of time and event, by substitution of idea for person, of document (symbol) for fact (reality), he strove to undo the tragedy of his birth and life. Thus he endeavored to erase from his memory his true identity and to supplant it with a pseudonymous, unreal existence—using real objects, human or documentary, as material for his artistry.

The acting out of his magical fantasy of suicide and rebirth (suffering and salvation), and the ways he used himself and others in his efforts to materialize it, formed the central theme of his conscious and unconscious mental life.

If we examine the passages from *Witness* quoted on the preceding pages, we see that they are enactments of familiar patterns in Chambers' emotional life. Chambers becomes romantically attached to a friend, then envy and resentment set in, followed by contempt. Hiss and Chambers are linked by a deep "bond," a "tacit esteem of character," they share a "simplicity of taste, a gentleness of character." But Hiss is not Chambers' equal, we are to understand, in intellect; not equal to the minds Chambers grew up with, not interested in ideas, not even interested in Shakespeare. Then Hiss's character itself—praised before for its gentleness—comes under attack: it contains a streak of "cruelty" and "savagery." That underlying meanness is turned on Chambers himself: Hiss reproaches Chambers for his uncared-for teeth; Chambers is victimized, and he forgives Hiss. It is evident that this passage, like all of *Witness,* works for Chambers' self-glorification. He portrays himself as noble in spirit: noble, in his generous praise of Hiss's character, in his appreciation of the friendship, and in his tolerance of Hiss's shortcomings (anti-intellectualism and savagery). If we believe Chambers, he cannot lose.

But do we believe him? The pattern is repeated so often that we suspect instead that it comes not out of social reality but out of Chambers' personal world of emotion. His feelings for Hiss are, in pattern, reminiscent of his feelings for many people, but they resemble nothing more than his relationship with the crucial figure in his life, his brother Richard. Both Richard and Alger have "a gentleness of spirit," but in both he finds a hidden streak of meanness and cruelty. Both attack him, and both are forgiven. And both are seen eventually as victims themselves—victims of "history."

"What possible bearing could my brother's suicide have on the Hiss case?" So Chambers implores in *Witness,* in protest against the mention of the tragedy during the trials.[14] The occasion releases a deep wellspring of feeling in Chambers, despite the lapse of time between the trial and the writing of *Witness.* He goes on to attack Hiss's attorney: "Nor could I fathom the gratuitous relish with which Marbury, obviously a man of intelligence and some sensitivity, insisted on referring to my brother by his nickname, Dickie, instead of by his full name." But a check of the record shows that nowhere did Marbury once use the nickname Dickie. Indeed the only use of that name that I can find is by Chambers himself:

Dickie read the French rationalists at a time when he was unprepared to understand them. He came to the conclusion that this was an irrational world and he didn't want to continue in it. You know, there are gentle folk unable to cope with this world, and he was one of them.[15]

The confusion is significant, because Chambers uses Marbury's imaginary insult as evidence that the Hiss partisans were mounting a malicious attack on him, that Marbury was, in effect, accusing him of having had a homosexual relationship with his brother. But Marbury was saying, as the record clearly shows, no such thing.[16]

Chambers himself refutes the self-imposed charge of homosexuality in the most categorical manner.

It was late in the Hiss case before any friend summoned the courage to tell me the slander in which the Hiss partisans had involved me with my brother—a story so inconceivable that it seemed to me that only a mind deformed by some-

[14] However, only a few pages before in the testimony, Chambers himself introduced the fact of his brother's suicide as a justification for his having at first denied to the grand jury (prior to the libel suit) that Hiss had been involved in espionage.

"My no to the Grand Jury stands for all men to condemn. I will say only this about it. No man can have watched his brother die a spiritual death by inches, or have dragged him half-dead across the frozen ground, or have heard his mother scream as she learned that her son was at last dead . . . without feeling for all humanity in its good and evil, an absolving pity that becomes the central mood of his life."
[15] Quoted in De Toledano and Lasky, *op. cit.*
[16] That there were—outside the courtroom—rampant rumors and speculations about the sexual lives of the subjects and their families is well known.

thing more than malevolence could have excreted it. I said only to the woman who told me: "What kind of beasts am I dealing with?" The fact that men and women could be found to credit and spread a lie so disgusting and so cruel remains the measure of the Hiss defense and the pro-Hiss psychosis.

Chambers recoiled, horrified, from any questioning about his brother.

I could not avoid knowing that I was being treated with a blistering condescension, as a kind of human filth. . . . Then, one day, it came back. It was the three boys in the schoolyard of my childhood, who had wet on a lollypop and then offered it to a fourth boy. Only, now, the lollypop was being offered to me.

It was a most revealing outburst. He felt debased by Marbury's questions, as though he were a little boy being sexually exploited. The very thought of the questioning aroused a homosexual memory.

Is the violence of Chambers' protest not symptomatic of his deep unrest on this matter? We have seen that his life was indeed surrounded by an aura of homosexual conflict. Certainly we find in the history of Chambers' friendships a homosexual element. Chambers' lifelong search for identity, his hatred of his effeminate name (Vivian), his many impersonations, and his use of friends' names all attest to his aspirations to be masculine and all powerful. Though the genesis of homosexuality is infinitely varied and complex, Chambers' early background was a clear medium for its development. His father was weak, effeminate, withdrawn, or absent; his mother, cold, driven, unrealistic. The lack of real warmth between Laha and Jay, transmitted from them to their sons, forced the two boys into an unnatural, defensive closeness—a closeness compounded of anger, rivalry, and despair.

We have seen that Chambers' memories of his brother reveal a homosexual attraction to him and concomitant feelings of hatred and guilt. We remember the story "In Memory of R.G.," in which he symbolically killed his brother, whose literary equivalent was described in frankly homosexual terms.

What a splendid thing he was. And he stood not quite six foot with one hand on the railing. He was stripped but for short black tights about the groin. His legs were firm and columnar. His knees were small, the muscle not yet completely developed. His thighs lean with a perpendicular fluting. His stomach was perfectly flat, not a crease above the navel. . . .

And we remember as well the extravagant, guilt-laden grief that followed his brother's death, an event for which he was still attempting psychologically to atone when he entered the underground.

Chambers' homosexual conflict is expressed more than once in his creative work. Three poems, written around the time of his brother's death, are of interest. The first, "Quag-Hole," expresses youth's fear of heterosexuality, ending in betrayal. The second, "Tandaradei," is an erotic literary piece in which sexuality and identity (male or female) are subtly blended. It reveals a man's feminine identification with a woman. In the third, "Lothrop, Montana," heterosexuality is disavowed and the frankly symbolized homosexual struggle is openly portrayed.

QUAG-HOLE [17]

He waited and, as he waited, grew less eager.
He had come first, believing he was anxious.
The quag lay buried in the darkness at his feet.
The village lights shone far between and meager.

He must not whistle here. His nerves grew tauter.
A wind, that rose among the woods behind him,
Dried through the fields. Then silence—broken only
By turtles puddling the invisible bog water.

Then, through a stillness, listening, he heard
Her running on the path, night-terrified
Or eager. And he watched her body slacken
And look for him. She stopped. He never stirred.

But saw how credulously, hour by hour, she stood.
And when, at last, the longing woman went,
He set his face to make the nearest light,
And marched to beat the silence through the wood.

TANDARADEI [18]

All that I can have at all
Is your body; all I can feel,
As our bodies precipitate and fall,
Is the stretch of your body. I would kneel
If I could touch more than the small
Back of the head of the heavy face you conceal.

In my breast,—with its little hard eyes,
Like little hot lead-moulds, pressed
Into the soft of my breast. My straying hand tries
To gather in the mould of the rest—
How the shins taper out of the thighs,
And end in the broad fresh-wedge of the foot at it
        best.

But all my hand can encompass and possess
Is the tiny spinal-coils in your neck, and the ribs
        that drop
So fearfully into the cavity when you press

[17] Published in *The Nation*, December 31, 1924.
[18] This appeared in the quarterly *Two Worlds*, June 1926.

On me your heart that seems, at moments, to make full
    stop,
As your sap drains out into me in excess,
Like the sap from the stems of a tree that they lop.

And, as you draw your limbs like a pale
Effulgence around me, I must
Have them drawn into me,—as you fail
And begin to leave me. You shall be a hand thrust
Into my flesh; your hand thrust into me impale
My flesh forever on yours, driven in thru the body-
    crust.

As you stir the coil of your spine; and you stir to
    collect
Your limbs from me; as we fall
Away bodily; as we are wrecked
On each other; as we call, as we call
To each other unanswered—O I shall never let you
    recollect
Your heavy limbs from mine at all.

Expended,
And the body well
Again; the long superabundant singleness ended.

The old shell
In hand again, mended,
And sound and resonant with the deep iron nerves of a
    bell.

Body—sound,—
With the swell
A bell makes,—ringing out from the glow my body makes
    on the dark around.

Whole-mended
Again, I may sound
The triumph of my ringing flesh that knew to set itself
    free and be mastered expended.

Now I am right
In what I offended,
I may go forth again, again unmastered, into the light.

LOTHROP, MONTANA [19]

The cottonwoods, the boy-trees,
Imberbe—the clean, green, central bodies
Standing apart, freely, freely, but trammeled;

[19] This appeared in *The Nation,* June 30, 1936.

With the branches inter-resting—for support
Never for caressing, except the wind blow.
And yet, leaning so fearfully into one another,
The leaves so pensile, so tremulously hung, as they
    lean toward one another;
Unable to strain farther into one another
And be apart:
Held back where in the earth their secret roots
Wrap one about another, interstruggle and knot; the
    vital filaments
Writhing in struggle; heavy, fibrous, underearthen
    life,
From which the sap mounts filling those trembling
    leaves
Of the boy-trees, the cottonwoods.

But Chambers' homosexual conflict was not enacted only in literature. On at least one occasion it found expression in an overt act. There is this account from a former fellow worker:

It was during the winter-spring season of 1926–27 when I met Whittaker Chambers in the 42nd Street Library in New York City. . . . I moved to Chicago in 1930 and again returned to New York in 1933.

In 1932, I believe it was, there was a convention of the John Reed Clubs throughout the country held in Chicago that winter. I became a delegate from Chicago.

At the first session the Chicago delegates were asked to help find lodging for the outside delegates. Chambers was a delegate from New York. Having known him, I took it upon myself to get him a room in the same lodging house where I myself lived. I felt more pity for him, as I saw him dressed in a filthy suit of clothes. There is no slur intended here, nor is it an exaggeration. The jacket he wore had on its back a full moon-sized, ugly-looking spot. We have all seen poor people in large cities wherever we have lived, in New York, in Chicago, or anywhere. But I, speaking for myself, have never seen anything like it in the Bowery at any time, and subsequently during the Great Depression, anywhere among tens of thousands of indigent people. It was that sight that moved me to find him a place to sleep rather than a sense of acquaintanceship. . . .

I took him along with me to our place at Chicago's near North Side. The hour was late, and we being quite tired after the day's work, I bade him good night and went to my room.

In the middle of the night I suddenly awoke in the midst of having an orgasm. When I saw him laboring at my penis still in his mouth, I pushed him aside, while moving myself away from him. My shock was so great that I could not say a word. . . . Since I was completely dumbfounded, he started asking me to do the same thing to him. This was too much. The only words I could manage to speak were: You get out of here. . . . He left immediately. . . .

I need say no more to indicate my revulsion. . . . Nor did I ever see him from then on to this very day I am writing this statement.[20]

Chambers, then, was capable of at least one overt homosexual act; he was certainly capable of homosexual attractions. The chief source of this ambivalence was, to repeat, his relationship with his brother, a relationship he was compelled to re-enact in various ways throughout his life. We have seen how this occurred with such figures as Karl Helfrich (his Williams roommate) and David Zablodowsky. We have seen how the fraternal theme recurred in his own writing and, notably, in his translation of *Class Reunion*.

If, in 1934, Whittaker Chambers was in search—on whatever level of consciousness—of a new fraternal surrogate, he could hardly have done better than Alger Hiss. My postulation is that this did indeed happen, and though for the moment it is only a postulation, it is consistent with both Chambers' psychological history and the external evidence.

In the summer of 1934 Chambers moved from New York to Baltimore, where he rented a second-floor apartment at 903 St. Paul Street. The first floor of the building was then the headquarters of the WCTU—"a sober address for an underground worker." He was living in Baltimore under the name of Lloyd Cantwell. As an underground Communist agent, Chambers had by now surrounded himself with a reality of his own making. If he really was a member of the underground, he could have used its facilities as a realistic stage-setting in which to act out his unconscious fantasies.

Baltimore, it will be recalled, was the home town of Hiss, who at that time was counsel for the Nye Committee. One of his tasks was to cultivate good relations with the press and public. He had been making rapid strides in government work and accounts of his activities appeared regularly in the *Baltimore Sun* during 1934 as part of the political news of the time. Alger Hiss was an image of the local boy who made good. Chambers was the polar opposite, an anonymous outcast. Hiss—tall, handsome, and dignified—had the quality of a British aristocrat about him, which made him stand out among his colleagues.[21]

---

[20] This account was subsequently repeated to me in two interviews and an extensive correspondence with my informant.

[21] Apropos of Hiss's definite air of being a Britisher, Dr. Nathan Adler recollects what England represented to him and his one-time colleagues on the *New Masses*:

England was to us the real world of culture and we looked up with a kind of awe at the British image. Most of us in the party were poor Jewish kids from the Bronx or the East Side. As literati, we wanted to appear cultured. We put on airs, dressed in tweedy clothes like the English. This represented to us the British stereotype—the worldly, urbane, cultured type. We would go to Bond's store and buy a pepper-and-salt suit for $18.

As part of the group, Chambers got identified with all the immigrants, the Poles,

In February 1934 the *American Magazine* published an article titled "Uncle Sam Grows Younger," written by Beverly Waugh Smith of Baltimore. It included a photograph of Alger Hiss, along with five other New Dealers (Abe Fortas, Louis Bean, Gardiner Means, Dexter Keezer, and Jerome Frank). Beverly Smith had known Alger and Bosley Hiss since boyhood. He wrote:

Washington is the most exciting place in the world today. . . . history is in quantity production every day. Overnight are made decisions . . . which will affect the lives of all of us for years to come. . . .

Here is a new type of man for a new age in politics. They have tremendous enthusiasm, and are working with a fury which threatens many of them with nervous breakdown. Youth is in the saddle, riding hell-bent for victory or a fall.

After describing a series of youthful New Dealers, Smith continued:

As for Alger Hiss, why, the last time I remember seeing him he was roller skating with the other kids on Mosher Street in Baltimore. Now, in his twenties, he is one of the men chiefly responsible for the plan to buy $650,000,000 worth of pork, milk, butter, fruit, and other commodities to feed the unemployed. He has too much spirit for his bodily strength and is in danger of working himself to death.

Sometime after the appearance of this article, according to Hiss, Chambers appeared in his office, posing, significantly, as a writer for the *American Magazine*. The link is not firm, but it is at least possible that Chambers had already developed an unconscious affinity for Hiss on the basis of the publicity Hiss had received in Baltimore, while on a conscious level he decided to supplement his income with a free-lance article on a topic of interest.[22]

Russians, and East Europeans. He was exposed to all of these foreign groups, none of which really knew America—they had only penetrated the thin epidermis of American life, as their contacts did not extend beyond their own few friends and workers in a factory.

But Chambers had an adoration for "true, real culture," and to be like the British was the then left-wing conception of culture. Chambers adored the whole idea. His clothes were always baggy, looked like hand-me-downs. But both he and his wife, Esther, wore pepper-and-salt tweedy suits. (How well I remember that look of adoration Chambers had for his wife.) Esther habitually dressed in an enormous felt hat and a pepper-and-salt tweed suit.

Parenthetically, it might be noted here that during the second trial Mrs. Chambers testified to remembering the pepper-and-salt trousers Timmy used to wear: "I remember Timmy standing on the stairway there in long pepper-and-salt trousers. . . ." (Trial Transcript, p. 967.) Alger Hiss comments: "Timmy never wore pepper-and-salt suits in his life."

[22] Chambers referred to himself as a free-lance writer on several occasions. On October 4, 1937, a letter was sent to the headmaster of the Park School in Baltimore, signed "Jay and Esther Chambers," for the purpose of applying for a scholarship for their four-year-old daughter. It said:

The father, a free-lance writer, and translator, has just changed from educational work with Maxim Lieber's Literary Agency in New York to similar temporary work with

Hiss saw Crosley in his office, or for lunch, "four or five more times" in connection with the latter's proposed article. Hiss said of him:

He spoke knowingly of publishing and of literary matters and appeared perfectly convincing in the role of a free-lance writer. He appeared well read and gave circumstantial accounts of prior free-lance writing exploits. His stories were on the "tall" side (e.g., the Washington Street Railway story which I recall). He said he had traveled extensively in Europe and claimed to know German literature. I remember him as entertaining rather than the reverse; hard-up but not more so than a free-lance writer in the depression years might well be; on the vain side judging by his tall stories; appearing to know something about most any topic that came up. I have a vague impression of boastful hints of sexual exploits but no hint of any unnatural sex interests. His appearance was not striking—short, lightish hair, ordinary features—except for notably neglected teeth. Present appearance familiar but still not clear or vivid reproduction of Crosley due probably to my having no sharp memory of Crosley.[23]

If Chambers did appear, a stranger posing as George Crosley, the man he interviewed must have stirred in him deep unconscious memories. For Hiss was tall and handsome, as Richard had been; he shared Richard's gentleness of bearing; he was busy and popular; and he was about the same age that Richard would have been.

It was at one of these meetings, according to Hiss, that Crosley mentioned his wish to move to Washington for the summer, a wish Hiss was able to satisfy because he was moving from his apartment, whose lease had two months still to run. Hiss testified that when the time came for Crosley and his family to move in, their van had not arrived. They stayed in the Hisses' new house for a period of perhaps three days. Hiss mentioned other favors he did for Crosley: the loan, and eventually the gift, of his old car; two small cash loans.

We have seen the legal ambiguities of this information. But if we accept for a moment Hiss's story, does it not accord with what we know of Chambers' personal life? Chambers claimed deep intimacy with Hiss at this time; he recalled in particular the many times they spent together; he "rescued" Hiss

---

the Railroad Retirement Board. [See p. 251, footnote, and p. 292 ff. for Chambers' government employment.]

Another letter to the Park School, written on October 11, 1937, from 310 Auchentoroly Terrace, applied for the admission of his daughter Ellen. This was signed by Jay Chambers and referred to himself as a writer, stating that his occupation was "National Research Bureau, Washington, D.C."

In his letter to Mr. Edward W. Case, real-estate agent at Westminster, on February 3, 1937, Chambers stated that he wanted to buy some property, explaining that he was a writer and wanted to find a place in which to work.

And finally, on the birth certificate of "Ursula Breen," mythical daughter of "David Breen," in the space for notation of profession of father, is written "Writer."

[23] Pre-trial memorandum by Alger Hiss, "Account of Contacts with George Crosley."

from his underground isolation. But this was at the time when Beverly Smith wrote that Hiss was "in danger of working himself to death," when his secretary recalls his working weekends and trying to find time to spend with his stepson. Surely this claim is a projection of Chambers' situation onto Hiss. Chambers' own plight was loneliness and isolation. He described Hiss's feelings with poignant understanding for, to be sure, these emotions were his own.

In his wish to be Hiss, he reversed their roles. In 1935, when he first walked into Hiss's office, he was, according to his later revelations, a faceless, underground man in need of a "friend." The fear of his own extinction directed his thoughts and actions. As a contrast to Chambers' migratory existence, the integrated, orderly life of the Hisses strengthened the fantasy of an imagined closeness with them. Thus he created and lived out a family romance, a relationship which, for Chambers, contained enough of a core of reality for him to believe it. Hiss, to be sure, did him favors, and his acts of kindness were received as expressions of love.

In the light of Chambers' readiness to insinuate himself into another person's life and literally possess a piece of that identity, it is now understandable that, after having heard Hiss talk about the piece of property he was considering buying, Chambers should fantasize about taking an actual trip there with him; and that a year later he should buy the property himself in a real, yet symbolic act of becoming Hiss by owning something he once wanted.

Chambers' description of this secret event is infused with nearly mystical significance:

Then, in the spring of 1936 or 1937, when the thawing roads were still all but impassable, without saying anything to anyone, not even to my wife, I drove one day to Westminster. That most beautiful countryside had drawn me back. I did not want the real-estate agent to suppose that I knew anything about the old house, so I asked him to show me his list. He took a route through the rutted back roads that brought us at last to the house that Alger and I had looked at. Even in the bare spring, always the test in the country, the old ruin had much charm for me. I had scarcely any good reason or right to buy it. . . . But it was one of those occasions when a man feels: this I am meant to do.

Throughout the Hiss case and later, Chambers clung to his story of intimacy with the Hisses with an unnecessary tenacity: he supplied details of their supposed relationship, some of which were demonstrably false, some highly dubious (though, to be sure, their sheer weight served its purpose in convincing the juries and the public).

During the House Committee hearings, Chambers described Mrs. Hiss as "a birthright Quaker." The fact is that Mrs. Hiss was born and brought up a

Presbyterian. When she attended Bryn Mawr College she came under the influence of the Quakers. Thereafter she used the "plain speech" with her husband and children and frequently with intimate friends and relatives. She was not a member of a Quaker Meeting.

Anyone who had heard her talk in her own house [said Hiss] as Chambers had, and who did not know otherwise, might readily have concluded that she was a Quaker or of Quaker persuasion. Chambers, however, does not hesitate to jump to the conclusion that she was born a Quaker of Quaker parents. He himself joined the Quaker faith and so must know the distinction between a convinced Friend (one by conversion) and a birthright Friend.

From April 1935 to June 1936 the Hisses lived on P Street in Georgetown. They moved to 1245 30th Street in June 1936 and remained there until December 1937. This was the period, according to Chambers, when he and Hiss had a close relationship, and he used the Hiss home as "a kind of informal headquarters." He said that he was there at least once every two weeks and that he frequently stayed overnight. But when asked to describe the 30th Street house, Chambers made several inaccurate statements. He told the House Committee that the dining room "was below the level of the ground, one of those basement dining rooms." [24] To be exact, the dining room was not below, but at ground level. It was below the level of the entrance to the house but at ground level with the backyard onto which it opened.

On November 5, 1948, in the Baltimore Deposition, Chambers was asked:

Q. Would you mind describing the 30th Street house?
A. . . . . I think it was white clapboard. It had little steps I think that came up on both sides of the platform, and it had a railing on the steps. . . .
Q. Do you remember the color of the shutters?
A. No, I do not. I think they were dark green, but I am not sure.
Q. White clapboard and dark green shutters?
A. I think so.

In 1936 the house was bright yellow with vivid blue shutters. It was subsequently painted as Chambers described it, but at a later date than he claimed to have been there, indicating that he could have based his testimony on a more recent look at the house. (In 1942 it was painted gray).[25] Chambers also testified that he had stayed overnight at the house and said that there was an extra bedroom permitting this:

Q. Well, how often do you think you spent the night there?
A. I would not say. It would be pure speculation.

[24] HUAC Hearings, p. 671.
[25] Trial Transcript, p. 1748.

Q. Well, as many as ten times during the whole period?
A. Possibly.
Q. You think so. And you slept in a bedroom to yourself, a separate bedroom?
A. I believe so.[26]

Three months after Chambers gave the above testimony, in February 1949, the FBI arranged interviews between Chambers and two colored maids formerly employed by the Hisses. Claudia (Cleidi) Catlett, who worked for the Hisses in both the P Street and 30th Street houses, as well as at Volta Place, described her interviews with the FBI and Chambers on the witness stand during the second trial:

Well, Mr. Chambers asked me the questions. He asked me about furniture and asked me was it a red rug on the floor at 30th Street, and I told him it wasn't; I told him they had gray rugs on the floor. . . . And he asked me about different pieces of furniture; he asked me about a table which was at P Street and it was broke—he said it was an old broken table. I said no, that wasn't Mrs. Hiss's table; and he asked me about some chairs, and I told him yes, that was Mrs. Hiss's chairs because she moved them, and I told them there was a red rug, and it was in the closet but it wasn't on the floor; they had gray rugs on the floor. He said no, they were yellow, and I said no, no yellow rugs on the floor. . . . He asked me didn't I serve dinner for them on 30th Street, and I told him no, that I never did. He said, "Yes, you are the woman who used to mash potatoes." I said, "No, it wasn't me. Of course, anybody can mash potatoes," just like that. I said, "You was never to dinner on 30th Street," and he never was at P Street for dinner. . . . He said he slept at 30th Street, he stayed there all night, and I told him no, he didn't because they only had two bedrooms, and I asked him where would he sleep; and he said, "I stayed there"; and I said, "No, you didn't, because there wasn't but two bedrooms, and there was a bed in each room," so he couldn't have stayed there.[27]

Thereafter Chambers testified differently regarding the 30th Street house and the nights he had spent there. At the second trial he was cross-examined about the contradictions in his testimony.

CROSS: Did you . . . say to Clidi [sic] Catlett that you had slept and spent a night at the 30th Street house?
CHAMBERS: I do not recall saying so.
CROSS: Would you deny that you said it?
CHAMBERS: No, I would not. I don't recall.
CROSS: Do you recall whether or not she made any remark about there being only two rooms and you could not have slept at the 30th Street house?
CHAMBERS: No, I am inclined to think she did not.
CROSS: Your testimony is, as I understand it, that you did not say to Clidi Catlett that you had spent a night at the 30th Street house?

[26] Baltimore Depositions, pp. 375–77, 379–80, 380–81. Part of the above testimony was later cited by the Hiss defense counsel during the second trial and appears in Trial Transcript, pp. 537–38.
[27] Trial Transcript, pp. 1570–71.

CHAMBERS: I do not think I did.

CROSS: And you have never up to this time on any occasion under oath testified that you had slept at the 30th Street house when the Hisses were living there?

CHAMBERS: I believe I did so testify.

CROSS: And that was before you had this talk with Clidi Catlett?

CHAMBERS: It was.

CROSS: And you found out after you swore that you had stayed at the 30th Street house that there are only two rooms there, two sleeping rooms upstairs.

CHAMBERS: I tried to recollect, and because I could not remember the layout of the 30th Street house I came to the conclusion that I probably had not spent a night there.

CROSS: In thinking that over you found out they only had two bedrooms, did you?

CHAMBERS: I am not at this moment sure how many bedrooms were on the second floor of the 30th Street house.

CROSS: You have never been up there?

CHAMBERS: It is quite probable I have been up there but I don't recall.

CROSS: You have no clear recollection—

CHAMBERS: No, I have no clear recollection.

CROSS: And you cannot tell his Honor and the jury whether or not there are only two bedrooms at the 30th Street house?

CHAMBERS: No, I am not sure.[28]

This is, obviously, quite different from the way he had earlier spoken to the House Committee of his stays at the Hisses'.

Another fact contradicts Chambers' story even in its modified form. On February 19, 1937, while riding his bicycle, Timmy Hobson was struck down by a car and suffered a severe fracture of his leg. He was confined to his bed for about four months in the 30th Street house, with his leg in a cast. This alone would, of course, have made overnight guests in the two-bedroom house unlikely. And certainly the memory of his prolonged convalescence could hardly be forgotten by anyone who visited the Hiss household. Yet Chambers, who alleged that he was an intimate friend of Hiss's and a frequent visitor, could only testify:

CHAMBERS: Whereas I see him [Timmy] very plainly at P Street, I don't recall him on 30th Street so well. But there was a point at which Timmy had some kind of accident, and I think that occurred at the 30th Street house.

MARBURY: What sort of an accident was that?

A. He was riding his bicycle, and either ran into a truck, or was frightened by a truck and fell off and hurt himself. . . .

Q. Do you remember seeing Timmy on the occasion or shortly after his accident?

A. I believe I did.

Q. Well, do you have any definite recollection one way or the other?

[28] *Ibid.,* pp. 469–70.

A. Yes, some part of him was bandaged, as nearly as I recall, but I have forgotten whether he hurt his arm or his leg.

Q. And you recall seeing him at the 30th Street house on some occasion when he had a bandage on?

A. If this occurred in 30th Street, otherwise, it would have been in Volta Place.[29]

Chambers described Timmy as "a puny little boy." And Mrs. Chambers remembered Timmy "in long pepper-and-salt trousers looking very big for his age; . . . I just recall that because he was so much bigger than you would expect a little eleven-year old to be; he was a nice big strapping boy."

As a frequent visitor to the Hiss household, Chambers might be expected to remember some of the furniture and objects he saw around him. But when questioned by Nixon on August 7, 1948, Chambers could recall only a small leather cigarette box.[30] Later, during the second trial, Chambers remembered having seen a "mirror with gilt frame, topped by an eagle, a circular mirror," in the Hiss home (P Street house). Hiss countered with the fact that Chambers did not recall a more striking piece of furniture, referring to the large Queen Anne mirror Justice Holmes had left him. It came into Hiss's possession in the fall of 1935 or winter of 1935–36 and was prominently placed in the P Street entrance hall. From that time on it occupied a conspicuous position in all the Hiss homes. But again Hiss was in the awkward position of trying to use a negative fact to show that Chambers had *not* been in his home (or he *would* have noticed the Holmes mirror) after a certain date.[31]

NIXON: . . . do you recall any pictures on the wall that they might have owned at the time?

CHAMBERS: No; I am afraid I don't.

. . .

STRIPLING: Did Mr. Hiss ever discuss with you his activities or his career at Harvard where he was an outstanding student?

CHAMBERS: No; I don't think he did. He used to talk about the time when he was Justice Holmes' secretary.

STRIPLING: Do you remember anything he ever told you or said to you about his relationship with Justice Holmes?

CHAMBERS: No, I am sorry. . . .[32]

And Chambers did not know that Hiss, during the period of this "close friendship," went regularly one evening a week to read to Justice Holmes. His

[29] Baltimore Deposition, pp. 1231–32.
[30] See p. 12.
[31] In addition to the Holmes mirror, Hiss has commented on several other pieces that Chambers failed to remember: "A handsome old desk of Priscilla's, Timmy's four-poster bed, and a rather large secretary from Priscilla's family would also be likely to be noticed by anyone who was a frequent visitor to our house."
[32] HUAC Hearings, pp. 670, 1261.

vagueness about the pictures the Hisses had in their home is also significant. Since he testified that he was himself "fond of birds," it would seem likely that he would have noticed the Audubon prints that hung in the Hiss home.

Chambers told the committee he had stayed as long as a week at the Hiss home. When asked by Nixon what he did during those frequent visits, it will be recalled that Chambers stated that he spent most of his time reading. Yet when asked about the kind of books Hiss had in his library, Chambers recalled only that they were "very nondescript," a truly remarkable statement for a man of his literary interest and otherwise fine memory. One of Hiss's books was a photostatic copy of Justice Holmes' notebook, a prized possession given to him by the Justice's literary executor, one he still takes pleasure in proudly showing to his friends.[33] It is likely, since Chambers' interest in books was great, that he would have seen and remembered the Holmes notebook if he had been a close friend, as he claimed. Chambers wrote: "I cannot remember Alger Hiss ever drawing my attention to a book, except certain books about birds."

Nixon asked Chambers, "Did they have a piano?" Chambers replied, "I don't believe so. I am reasonably sure they did not." [34] Chambers' alleged story falls down again. Priscilla Hiss played the piano. Timmy took lessons and practiced regularly during the years Chambers claimed to have known Hiss. A piano was, except for a brief period, a standard piece in the Hiss's home. On the night of Timmy's accident, Stephen Farrand has recalled how he helped to dispel the worry by playing the piano for Priscilla in the 30th Street house. Hiss has explained, however, that the P Street house, where Chambers stayed for a few days, was one of the few places they had no piano. When they moved to the 30th Street house they bought a miniature piano. The piano was clearly remembered by Charles Horsky: ". . . when Mrs. Horsky saw the tiny 'Worch' the Hisses owned, she bought one exactly like it, as it was the only piano that could fit into our narrow . . . house."

Abruptly, in the midst of the August 7 hearing, House Committee investigator Benjamin Mandel interposed: "A picture of Hiss shows his hand cupped to his ear." Chambers quickly picked this up. "He is deaf in one ear." He was unable to say which ear. Told about this on August 25, Hiss noted for the benefit of his counsel:

I have always had exceptionally good hearing. One of the reasons for my continuing pleasure in bird watching is that I am able to get calls and sounds that most people miss. In order to shut out noise behind me or concentrate on statements

[33] Stephen Farrand made special mention of the Holmes notebook in his diary and remembered that Hiss had shown it to Farrand's father on election day in 1936.
[34] HUAC Hearings, p. 667.

made orally I frequently cup a hand to one or the other ear. If I am writing notes at the time, I naturally cup my hand to my left ear. I understand that on frequent occasions during the testimony of August 5 I cupped my left hand to my left ear. Obviously, Chambers thought that Mandel was giving him a piece of solid information which he quickly adopted as his own.

Hiss did not let the matter rest there. He went to Dr. William Fowler, an ear specialist, to have his hearing tested. Dr. Fowler examined Hiss carefully and informed him that his hearing was above average. ("Dr. Fowler," wrote Hiss, "said I would qualify for Navy sonar, and hearing in my left ear was better than in the right.")

An illuminating picture of Hiss's meticulousness is afforded by a letter he wrote (but never sent) to an insurance agent in 1930, regarding an application for an insurance policy he had filled out in 1929. The letter was presented as a Defendant's Exhibit during the second trial. It was put in evidence as one of several samples of the typing from Hiss's old Woodstock typewriter. The subject matter was irrelevant to the issue at hand; Hiss was simply correcting some mistakes in the policy. But a few excerpts, demonstrating his compulsive concern for accuracy and clarity of fact, are of interest:

On reading over my policy last week I examined for the first time the photostatic copies of my applications attached to the policy. There are several inaccuracies and ambiguities. . . .

rD The answer should be "Yes." My occupation being stated as "student" I obviously contemplated a permanent change.

6B The answer should be "Yes." I had frequently consulted doctors for colds and had had several general examinations.

9 It is certainly not true that I had not consulted or been treated by any physician for five years prior to January 24, 1929. It would be impossible for me to be sure I could remember "every" such physician but among such were or may have been: Doctors Penrose (I believe he is now dead); Requardt (now dead); Lockhardt; Earle; and Austrian, all of Baltimore. These do not include dentists or oculists or chiropractors and I may have misspelled some names. . . .

I certified that I had had no illness and had not consulted any physician for five years prior to that date. This was inaccurate in the respects noted above and in addition to the doctors consulted prior to January 24, 1929, there should be added Dr. Weems of Washington. As part of this April 14, 1930 application I also stated that my answers to Part II of the January 24, 1929 application "are true." This was incorrect in the particulars referred to above. Furthermore, if "are true" meant as of April 14, 1930 other answers true in 1929 were no longer true because of events occurring after January 24, 1929 and before April 14, 1930.

As I understand the effect of the incontestable clause and of the Massachusetts statute as to the effect of unintentional and immaterial inaccuracies, the points I have set out probably do not affect the validity of the policy even without the company being thus notified through you of the errors. But I do not wish the policy to be kept alive for any such reasons. Therefore will you please take up with your company the points I have raised.

The specimen provides the biographer with a firsthand piece of documentary evidence, the importance of which transcends the typographical to the psychological. It is psychologically as reliable and identifiable a brainprint of Hiss's personality and character as it is an imprint of his Woodstock machine. A similar review of more than a hundred letters written to me in connection with the preparation of this volume reflects the same emphasis on accuracy (fact or idea), the same precision and attention to detail. His feelings are bridled by an overriding need for exactitude and logic, and he leans over backward to be fair. As a policy holder he seems more protective of the insurance company than he is of himself. This exaggeration of a virtue into a defect shows itself in almost everything Hiss does. It is his most characteristic trait, one that he maintains with precious care among his standards of objectivity in human relations. These criteria he regards as his most valuable asset as a human being.

Hiss's compulsive need for exactitude, especially the correction of minutiae, pervaded all of his actions, public and private. It was precisely this characteristic in his personality that stood out above everything else during the hearings, the confrontation, and the two trials. It was clearly the most observable feature of his behavior as a witness. "One gains a firm impression," wrote Robert Carr in 1952, "that the lawyer in Alger Hiss was very strong."

He watched constantly for inaccuracies, correcting Mundt when the latter referred to *seven* members of the alleged apparatus and then named eight; he was careful not to say flatly that he had never known the man who called himself Whittaker Chambers, and he repeatedly answered questions with the qualifying phrase, "Not to the best of my knowledge." [35]

Yet this was the very quality that impressed the committee, especially Nixon, that Hiss was a master spy and a consummate actor.

A further example of Hiss's wariness is seen in the following exchange.

NIXON: Mr. Hiss, did you testify earlier that you did or did not know Mr. Ware?
HISS: I hadn't been asked the question. I did know Mr. Ware while I was in the Department of Agriculture.[36]

The most widely publicized single piece of testimony linking Hiss and Chambers in a close relationship was Chambers' story about the prothonotary warbler. On August 7, 1948, Chambers testified about the Hisses:

[35] Robert K. Carr, *House Committee on Un-American Activities* (Ithaca, N.Y.: Cornell University Press, 1952), p. 102.
[36] HUAC Hearings, p. 652.

They both had the same hobby—amateur ornithologists, bird observers. They used to get up early in the morning and go to Glen Echo, out the canal, to observe birds.

I recall they once saw, to their great excitement a prothonotary warbler. . . .

McDowell asked: "A very rare specimen? And Chambers replied, "I never saw one. I am also fond of birds." [37]

On August 16 the committee sounded Hiss out:

NIXON: What hobby, if any, do you have, Mr. Hiss?
HISS: Tennis and amateur ornithology.
NIXON: Is your wife interested in ornithology?
HISS: I also like to swim and also like to sail. My wife is interested in ornithology, as I am, through my interest. Maybe I am using too big a word to say an ornithologist because I am pretty amateur, but I have been interested in it since I was in Boston. I think anybody who knows me would know that.
McDOWELL: Did you ever see a prothonotary warbler?
HISS: I have right here on the Potomac. Do you know that place?
THE CHAIRMAN: What is that?
NIXON: Have you ever seen one?
HISS: Did you see it in the same place?
McDOWELL: I saw one in Arlington.
HISS: They come back and nest in those swamps. Beautiful yellow head, a gorgeous bird.
    Mr. Collins is an ornithologist, Henry Collins. He is a really good ornithologist, calling them by their Latin names.[38]

Donald Appell, an investigator for the committee, described for me how he, Nixon, and McDowell "set the trap for Hiss," how the question about the prothonotary warbler was "stacked." In a secret hearing Chambers had informed the committee that Hiss had an interest in birds; if Hiss confirmed this fact, the committee felt that it would be further evidence of close association. Since the committee regarded Hiss as a cunning and clever spy, a mastermind who would try to outwit them at every turn, they anticipated that Hiss might remember mentioning a prothonotary warbler to "Carl" and deny having seen one if such a question was put directly to him as part of their interrogation. They decided, therefore, to pose the question in the most casual, off-the-record manner. At a certain moment during a planned break of their interrogation of Hiss, Nixon and Appell excused themselves and McDowell was left alone with Hiss. During this brief interval, just as Nixon and Appell were returning, McDowell, having engaged Hiss in light conversation, casually asked him, "Did you ever see a prothonotary warbler?" Guilelessly, and with ob-

[37] *Ibid.,* p. 666.
[38] HUAC Hearings, pp. 61–62. Collins had also been accused by Chambers. The oddity of Hiss's willingly introducing his name seems not to have been noted by the committee.

vious show of interest, Hiss responded, "I have right here on the Potomac. Do you know that place?"

The cold type of the official record reveals no hint of the tactic related to me by Donald Appell.[39] The committee, in their enthusiastic alliance with Chambers' story, was so convinced that Hiss was a master spy that they felt the need to use such devices.

The press played up the prothonotary warbler and *Time* magazine featured a prominent picture of the bird. The public did not know what to think. How could Chambers have had such "intimate" information if he had not known Hiss well? Hiss later wrote:

We have never been to Glen Echo, an amusement park, to observe birds. I doubt if anyone else has. . . . It was not a special haunt for bird watchers. Prothonotary warblers . . . can only be seen in the vicinity of Washington in a swampy woods in Virginia south of Alexandria. . . . I might certainly have mentioned to anyone with whom I talked about birds that I had seen a prothonotary warbler.

McDowell, himself an ornithologist, unwittingly bears up Hiss's contention that it would not be at all extraordinary for him to boast of what he had seen to friends and acquaintances alike. On August 25 McDowell said:

I would like to point out, Mr. Chairman, that, as you well know, to discover a rare bird or an unusual bird or identify a bird that many other people have seen is a great discovery in the life of an amateur ornithologist. You can usually recall almost everything around it. It is like winning the ball game or the yacht regatta. You can recall the time of day, how high the sun was, and all the other things.[40]

Chambers was asked if Hiss ever went to church. He replied, "He was forbidden to go to church." To Stripling's question, "Do you know whether he was a member of a church?" Chambers replied, "I don't know." Born and raised an Episcopalian, Hiss occasionally attended Christ Church in Georgetown. Gilbert Armstrong, the rector of the church (and later Bishop of Pennsylvania), was a friend of Hiss's since Johns Hopkins days.

During the first trial Chambers related a story he had never before told the committee or the grand jury. In November 1937, said Chambers, either Mr. or Mrs. Hiss had lent him $400 in cash to help him buy a new, deluxe Ford sedan. He bought it, he said, in order to facilitate his break from the Communist Party. He freely admitted that he had not repaid the money or even made any effort to. Chambers further stated that he did not tell Hiss his reason for wanting a new car, only that he needed it for Communist Party work. As confirmation of Chambers' testimony the government then produced

[39] In an interview with the author, May 5, 1963 at the home of Isaac Don Levine (Waldorf, Md.); present also: Mandel, Wadleigh, and Levine.
[40] HUAC Hearings, p. 1201.

the records of the Hisses' bank account and clearly in evidence was an entry that Mrs. Hiss, on November 19, 1937, had withdrawn $400. The remaining balance was $40.46.

Throughout the House Committee hearings, the grand jury investigation, the Baltimore Deposition, Chambers did not mention such a loan, not, indeed, until the first Hiss trial. In fact, in November 1948, his wife testified that Whittaker's mother had helped pay for the car:

I cannot tell you that. [The extent of Laha Chambers' financial help] I don't know. But in the instance of the car, for instance, she did help on that.

In the second trial Mrs. Chambers' testimony underwent a considerable change:

Q. Did Mrs. Chambers—that is your mother-in-law—give the $400 to apply toward the purchase of the Ford car?
A. No, my husband gave me the $400.

Chambers, during the second trial, was questioned by the government prosecutor:

Q. Now you say that Mr. Hiss loaned you $400 at or about the time you bought this automobile in Randallstown?
A. That is right. . . .
Q. When did you remember it for the first time?
A. When I was going over this whole history with the FBI.
Q. 1949?
A. 1949.[41]

What enabled Chambers to "remember" belatedly this large loan occurred two months after his testimony at Baltimore and four months before the first trial. In late January 1949 the FBI obtained records of Hiss's bank account from the Riggs National Bank. Though Chambers assured Thomas F. Murphy, counsel for the prosecution, that he had not seen the Hiss bank records, he was collaborating full time during that period with the FBI. Chambers said, during cross-examination: "I had been in New York talking with the FBI every day except weekends for a matter of some months. . . ."

Q. Beginning when?
A. Beginning during the Grand Jury proceedings . . . of December 1948.
Q. And extending down to what period?
A. Extending to about some time in March, I believe, of 1949.
Q. And, of course, you have spent a considerable time with them since?
A. I have seen them from time to time.

[41] The three quotations here are from Baltimore Deposition, pp. 674–76; Trial Transcript, p. 1053, pp. 626–27.

Q. During that time would it be fair to say that you were spending some five or six days a week with them?

A. Five, I believe, would be a liberal estimate.

Q. The entire day?

A. From about ten-thirty in the morning until about four to four-thirty in the evening.

Q. Over a period of three and a half months?

A. Yes, with time out for lunch.[42]

"Such association must—at the very least—" wrote the Earl Jowitt, "give rise to the suspicion that the witness is being 'coached,' and must, as I think, tend to lessen the weight to be attached to his evidence. For example, if the FBI obtained a copy of the banking account for Hiss . . . from which they would have learned of the withdrawal of $400 on the 19th of November 1937, is it not a reasonable inference that this fact would have been mentioned to Chambers? And does not this inevitably reflect upon the independent value of Chambers' testimony?" [43] But although Hiss offered a rational counterexplanation the belated charge damaged him.[44]

Money was, according to Hiss, the cause of the termination of his brief relationship with George Crosley. Hiss told me that, to the best of his recollection, his last contact with Chambers, as Crosley, was a telephone conversation with him sometime in the fall of 1936, after not having seen him for some time. As Hiss best surmised the reason for the call, Chambers wanted to borrow another small sum. Hiss realized that he would be sponged on again, reminded Crosley that he had not paid him what he owed him, and told him that he did not want to see him again. This, according to Hiss's best recollection was the last contact he had with Crosley until he next confronted him at the Hotel Commodore twelve years later.

Would this parting be sufficient to inspire a lifelong grudge? Not, to be sure, in an ordinary man. But for Chambers, who was so deeply disturbed, so lost in the world of reality, so unsure of his own existence, tormented by the rejection of his homosexual love, it would indeed be sufficient. Chambers' opposing story of his last meeting with Hiss, rich in emotional content, only confirms this thesis.

It was early evening when I reached the Hisses' house, probably between six and seven o'clock. . . . I had to go to the bathroom. Priscilla followed me upstairs.

[42] Trial Transcript, pp. 434–35.

[43] The Earl Jowitt, *The Strange Case of Alger Hiss* (Garden City, N.Y.: Doubleday & Co., 1953).

[44] Hiss showed from his bank records other withdrawals of comparable sums which they had used to meet nonrecurring family needs. In this instance they testified that $400 was used for the purchase of furnishings for their new Volta Place house for which they had just signed a lease.

The bathroom was at the front of the house, facing the street. Directly to the right of the bathroom door, there was a bedroom door. A telephone was on a little table near the door. . . . I closed the bathroom door and thought: "This situation is tight." Before I washed my hands, I opened the bathroom door halfway. Priscilla was speaking in a low voice into the telephone. I walked directly up to her. She hung up. We went downstairs in silence. At that nerve-tingling moment, Alger Hiss came home.

There was, in fact, no upstairs telephone at the Volta Place house. Indeed, no extension anywhere. The only telephone the Hisses had was on a hall table at the bottom of the stairs immediately opposite the front door.

[Later, after supper] I asked Alger if he would break with the Communist Party. He shook his head without answering. There was nothing more to say. I asked for my hat and coat. Alger walked to the door with me. He opened the door and I stepped out. As Alger stood with his hand on the half-open door, he suddenly asked: "What kind of a Christmas will you have?" I said: "Rather bleak, I expect." He turned and said something into the room: "Isn't there. . . ?" I did not catch the rest. I heard Priscilla move. Alger went into the room after her. When he came back, he handed me a small cylindrical package, three or four inches long, wrapped in Christmas paper. "For Puggie," he said. Puggie is my daughter's nickname. That Alger should have thought of the child after the conversation we had just had touched me in a way that I can only describe by saying: I felt hushed.

The entire description is so mystical and romantic, the fantasy speaks for itself. One need only treat the psychic reality of Chambers' historic account as if it were a dream. The "small cylindrical package," Chambers explains elsewhere, was a child's rolling pin.

We looked at each other steadily for a moment, believing that we were seeing each other for the last time and knowing that between us lay, meaningless to most of mankind but final for us, a molten torrent—the revolution and the Communist Party. When we turned to walk in different directions from that torrent, it would be as men whom history left no choice but to be enemies.

As we hesitated, tears came into Alger Hiss's eyes—the only time I ever saw him so moved. He has denied this publicly and derisively.[45] He does himself an injustice—by the tone rather than by the denial. . . .

In the light of such different versions of their last meeting the following utterance by Chambers, made during the committee hearings, is indeed striking. McDowell, questioning Chambers about his last visit to Hiss's home, asked, "He cried?" Chambers replied, "Yes, he did. I was very fond of Mr. Hiss!" Could this be anything other than Chambers' own emotionalized, romantic involvement, his fantasied wish that Hiss would be so grieved over his absence?

[45] Hiss said: "The credibility of my being in tears is not likely to impress people who know me. I am not given to tears."

Chambers has repeatedly described his deep feelings for and against Hiss:

As I struggled to control my feeling, slowly and deliberately, I heard myself saying, rather than said: "The story has spread that in testifying against Mr. Hiss I am working out some old grudge, or motives or revenge or hatred. I do not hate Mr. Hiss. We were close friends, but we are caught in a tragedy of history. Mr. Hiss represents the concealed enemy against which we are all fighting, and I am fighting. I have testified against him with remorse and pity, but in a moment of history in which this Nation now stands, so help me God, I could not do otherwise.

In the completely silent room, I fought to control my voice.

In the light of Chambers' pattern of behavior and his fantasy system as we now know it, his account of his last alleged meeting with Hiss takes on special significance. It portrays, in his own system of thinking, Hiss's rejection of him. It is the final blow to his romanticized relationship with him. How ironic that Chambers, a few years earlier, should have translated a parallel situation in fiction. Compare Sebastian's recollection of Adler's slight of him in *Class Reunion*:

[Adler] drew himself up to his full height and said: "What is your idea, anyway? You presume a good deal for your size. You ought to be glad that we let you take part at all, and should wait till your own role is given you." . . . These words were destined to prove Adler's greatest sin in this world. They were more. They were his fate; for they let loose a devil in me. It may sound foolish, but I believe, and this belief burns in me even now like a scorching fire, that if Adler had never uttered that one sentence, he would not have been standing before me today, a ruined man.

After the Chamberses moved from the Hisses' 28th Street apartment, Chambers took along and kept in his possession certain objects that belonged to Hiss. Included among these were several pieces of furniture, which Chambers testified that Hiss had given to him, old things that Chambers stated Hiss had originally gotten "from his mother's house." Chambers' unusual treatment and retention of these objects are notable, for it conveys the fetishistic [46] meaning they had for him. Especially significant is his reference to an

---

[46] Psychological understanding of the meaning of a "fetish" is essential: "A fetish is a material object regarded as endowed with special magical powers. Literally it refers to an object of any kind (idol, charm, talisman) which embodies mysterious and awesome qualities and from which supernatural aid may be expected; . . . patients . . . who are unable to love a real person to whom they are attached may carry out all the pleasures of love through the agency of some object belonging to or associated with the love-object. . . . A fetish may be a part of the body such as the hair, foot, hand, or it may be some object owned by the loved one, such as a handkerchief, shoe, purse, etc. The fetish stands as a substitute for the loved person." (Hinsie and Shatsky, *Psychiatric Dictionary* [New York: Oxford University Press, 1953], p. 223).

"old, broken love-seat." With this in mind, let us consider the following testimony:

Q. Have you still got any of this furniture?
A. I have it.
Q. That the Hisses gave you?
A. I do.
Q. What do you still have?
A. I have the table, which I had refinished at a later period. I have the rug. And the wing chair I believe is stored around in the cellar somewhere. I also have a small child's rocker, which Alger and Priscilla Hiss gave my daughter at a somewhat later period. . . .
Q. Did Mr. Hiss give you anything else beyond the articles that you have described?
A. I have mentioned the rug, a wing chair, the table, and the chest that used to belong to Timmy. Yes, there was also a love-seat. . . .
Q. Do you still have the love-seat?
A. The love-seat was left in one of the houses on the property I sold a year or so ago, and it may still be there, for all I know. It was broken when we received it, and it was never very useful.[47]

Chambers testified in Baltimore that he and his wife had also received several gifts of books from the Hisses. Chambers alleged that he was given two books on birds by Alger and that his wife was given two on child care by Priscilla. How important it would have been if at least one of these books had some sign indicating it was a gift from the Hisses! But neither has any dedication, notation, or mark to indicate from whom it came. Not once was Chambers ever able to produce a letter, a personal note of any sort, written to him directly, which would be proof of his alleged close relationship with the Hisses. At a later date he added two other articles to the list, "Timmy's chair and table."

One last but most impressive confirmation of Chambers' fetishistic attachment to the former belongings of Hiss: Before the Hiss trials began, Edward McLean, counsel for Hiss, visited Chambers at his home in Westminster. He wanted to see at first hand the things Chambers stated Hiss had given him. Chambers brought up from a basement storeroom a small, folded, tattered piece of cloth. It was, he explained, the fabric which once covered the old wing chair. He had removed it, had it dry cleaned, and for thirteen years had kept it as a memento of a former friendship. Chambers volunteered that he had preserved it all these years but offered McLean no explanation for this.

But it was not by such fetishistic devices alone that Chambers strove to divert the repressed fraternal meaning of his love for Hiss. Just as in *Witness*

[47] Baltimore Deposition, pp. 1175, 1177–1178.

he places the blame for Richard's death on a "sick and dying" world, so he reacts with a feeling of "lethargy" and "despair" after his destruction of Hiss. Shifting from the personal to the political, he insists that the nation would not understand his plight:

The root of my lethargy, what filled me with despair, was the apparent hopelessness of making anything understandable to a nation that could so easily be misled into supposing that a struggle that involved its life and death was merely a grudge fight or a scandal involving two men.

Thus he leads himself and his reader away from the storm center of his conflict, but in so doing throws light into the area where he has attempted to cast a shadow. For it is his *own* life and death struggle he has generalized into a comparable struggle of nations. In his paranoia, Chambers behaved as though he were a nation.

12

Varieties of Revenge

EXTRAORDINARY as Chambers' behavior toward Hiss was, it was not an isolated case. There were many Hiss-equivalents—less publicized but no less significant—in the life of Whittaker Chambers. From his youth Chambers lived out a conflicted, episodic, masquerading existence. It was a harried and deprived mode of life in which he was wont to accept the largesse of colleagues or friends, then ultimately was driven to denounce or betray them. His actions, like his beliefs, were determined from within by the shiftings of his guilt-divided, tortured sense of his own being.

During the forty-odd years of his adult life Chambers crossed the paths of many different kinds of people. Some were blinded by his brilliance of mind; others, he enticed by fluency of language, extraordinary knowledge, or dramatic tales about his unusual personal experiences. And to others, his unkempt, needy appearance, the figure of the transient, impoverished intellectual, was appealing. On the whole, from the accounts of scores of people who through the years fell under his influence, it was discernible that the idealistic, romantic types were, for Chambers, the most gullible and responsive. The literati and liberal-minded intelligentsia of the thirties were especially susceptible to his devices. But beyond impressing those who entered his sphere and gaining some immediate advantage from them, Chambers secretly appraised and tagged them for possible future use as well. In his conspiratorial way Chambers collected and created suspects. In the event that he himself might be caught (either by the "secret police" or his own guilty conscience) and forced to confess, he would have stored away some kernel of fact or idea which had the potential of wringing confessions (true or false) from others.[1]

---

[1] In this pathological craving to expose suspects he was not alone. Allen Dulles, former head of the CIA, has written: "Every intelligence service makes use of people who work chiefly for money, or out of love for adventure or intrigue. Some people thrive on clandestinity or deception for its own sake, deriving a certain perverse satisfaction from being the unknown movers of events. Among Communist conspirators one frequently finds this trait. People who knew Whittaker Chambers claim that there was a definite

And so he kept mental and written dossiers on friends and acquaintances. He privately investigated the lives and habits of those men whose lives and careers interested him, even though he may never have met them. Julian Wadleigh, for example, whose own case is to be considered, testified and wrote how "amazed" he was when he discovered Chambers' fund of detailed information about Charles Darlington, Wadleigh's former superior in the State Department (assistant chief of the Trade Agreements Division in the thirties). Chambers' inordinate knowledge of Darlington's background—his career and "all the rest" that Chambers knew about him—came as a great surprise to Wadleigh. "When," said Wadleigh, "I asked Chambers, 'How come you know so much about Charlie Darlington?' Chambers answered, 'Well, we naturally like to know about a person who is your roommate so we have made inquiries from our friends in the State Department and that is how I got the information.' " [2]

One of the most striking illustrations of Chambers' conspiratorial style of life and the influence he wielded over others comes from Mrs. Chambers herself. Testifying at the Hiss trials, Mrs. Chambers stated that she was in sympathy with everything her husband did, never asked him what he was doing, gladly accepted work assignments and his every word without question. During the second trial when Prosecutor Murphy asked her, "If he [Chambers] told you that starting tomorrow we are going to Ypsilanti and your name was Hogan—" she interrupted, "We would go to Ypsilanti and we would be Hogans." [3]

As evidence of Mrs. Chambers' loyalty to her husband this is hardly worth noting. To be sure, under the circumstances most devoted spouses would testify in the same way. But the former Esther Shemitz was not just a meek helpmate. She had always been a forceful character in her own right, a

---

streak of this kind in him. In the upside-down world of espionage one also finds men driven by a desire for power, for self-importance, which they could not satisfy in normal employments. . . . The reader would be amazed to know how many psychopaths and people with grudges and pet foibles and phobias manage to make connections with intelligence services all over the world and to tie them in knots. Paranoia is by far the biggest cause of trouble. . . ." (Allen Dulles, *The Craft of Intelligence* [New York: Harper and Row, 1963], 185–86, 217–18).

The name "Hiss" found its way into the embellished testimony of such pathological informers. See, for example, the testimony of George Racey Jordan, an airplane and cargo inspector stationed at Great Falls, Montana, who reported that he had seen uranium shipments, plans of Oak Ridge atomic installation, and papers from the State Department marked "from Hiss" (and "from Sayre") on plane cargoes before they took off for Russia. (House Committee on Un-American Activities, *Hearings Regarding Shipment of Atomic Material to the Soviet Union during World War II,* 81st Cong., 2nd sess., December 1949–March 1950.)

[2] Julian Wadleigh, "Why I Spied for the Communists," *New York Post,* July 12, 1949; repeated to the author during a personal interview (Waldorf, Md.), May 5, 1963.

[3] Trial Transcript, p. 1063.

person deeply rooted in ideological convictions and early rebelliousness, who, before her marriage, led an openly nonconformist, self-assertive existence. But Mrs. Chambers sat or moved in the shadow of her husband's exploits. As a witness or wife she had more than once forsaken her true identity for an alias without questioning her husband's motives.

David Zablodowsky

The insidious quality of Chambers' revengefulness, more precisely his ongoing need to create an enemy out of a formerly admired friend, then ultimately to attack and destroy him, is apparent from a brief review of his relationship with David Zablodowsky. Zablodowsky was the Columbia classmate whom Chambers once impersonated and from whom he appropriated the name David for himself (a name he testified was his "favorite"). "David" later became Chambers' permanent "legal" name, either as David Chambers, Jay David Chambers, or Jay David Whittaker Chambers.

After graduating from Columbia (B.S., 1925; M.A., 1927), Zablodowsky continued his postgraduate studies there until 1928, when he joined The Viking Press. In the early thirties he, along with many liberals who made up the Popular Front, became interested in trade unionism and participated in some of the radical activities of the time.

Zablodowsky related to me the story of his experiences with Chambers, an intermittent series of unusual episodes beginning with a disturbing but innocuous prank against him when they were students at Columbia College and culminating thirty years later in a political travesty.

I had not seen Whittaker Chambers for about thirteen years, since our Columbia days. Then, sometime in 1935 or 1936, out of the blue, I received a call from Chambers. He told me that he was doing secret work for the Communist Party, and asked me if I would be willing to do him a "favor." In those days, Communism, to me, meant anti-Fascism and anti-Hitlerism. The word "underground" did not have the ominous ring it later acquired. Anything that would help the cause to fight Hitler I was in favor of.

Chambers told Zablodowsky that a person of unknown identity would telephone and then leave a sealed letter at his office. This letter would then be picked up by another person, whose identity would also be unknown to him. In short, Zablodowsky agreed to serve as a "mail-drop." Said Zablodowsky, "This was the sum and substance of what I did for Chambers. I never joined the Communist Party." Zablodowsky next saw Chambers again sometime in 1939, when I inadvertently ran into him at a preview of the movie *Grapes of Wrath*. I said, "Hello, Whittaker." Chambers was furtive, did not recognize me, and walked away. It was immediately evident to me that Chambers had changed and didn't want any part of me.[4]

Thirteen more years passed. During the war period Zablodowsky served with distinction in the OSS. He was stationed in Washington except for a few months at the Nuremberg trials. In 1945 he was on the organizational staff of the State Department at the United Nations Conference in San Francisco. He later became director of the Division of Publications of the Department of Conferences and General Services of the UN.

In April 1952 Zablodowsky had his first warning. He was called before a grand jury, which had earlier heard secret testimony from Chambers, and was interrogated by Roy Cohn, then a young government attorney, later to become Senator McCarthy's chief assistant. Then, on October 23, 1952, a coworker rushed into Zablodowsky's office and exclaimed, "Did you hear the news? Whittaker Chambers just testified before the Internal Security Subcommittee that you were an agent for the underground."

The substance of Chambers' testimony, printed in the *New York Times* on October 24, 1952, was:

Whittaker Chambers, once a courier for a Soviet spy ring, identified yesterday a United Nations editorial official, David Zablodowsky, as a member of the Communist underground in this country in 1936.

. . . Mr. Chambers testified that Mr. Zablodowsky had been assistant to a Soviet agent known as Richard, whose principal job was to procure fraudulent passports and other false identification papers for Russian agents.

The witness [Chambers] said he was introduced to Mr. Zablodowsky in 1936 by J. Peters, head of the American Communist underground, who described Mr. Zablodowsky as Richard's assistant. However, Mr. Chambers said he had known the United Nations official when both were students at Columbia College in 1923 or 1924.

"While we were undergraduates," Mr. Chambers told the subcommittee, sitting with Senator James O. Eastland, Democrat of Mississippi, as its only member, "Zablodowsky sometimes said he was a Communist. But in my opinion he was not an organizational Communist, though he had strong sympathies with the party."

. . . On two specific occasions Mr. Chambers identified Mr. Zablodowsky as a Communist. Once the witness was asked by Senator Eastland if he knew the United Nations employee and he replied: "Yes, I know him to be a Communist."

On another the Senator asked: "Was he a member of the Soviet underground in the U.S.?"

"I haven't the slightest doubt of it," the witness responded.

[4] Personal interview, May 12, 1963.

Mr. Chambers said it was Peters' idea in 1936, when he assertedly introduced Mr. Chambers to Mr. Zablodowsky, to "move" the latter into the "apparatus" in which Mr. Chambers was active, as a "letter drop." However, the witness added, nothing came of it. Later Mr. Chambers said that Mr. Zablodowsky, a former editor for the Viking Press, had established a "business cover, the Fawn Press," for Richard.

Mr. Chambers said Richard actually was Donald L. Robinson, also known as Robinson-Rubens, and that he had been recalled to the Soviet Union in 1936, and was never seen again.

On the same day, October 24, Zablodowsky appeared as a witness before the Senate Subcommittee and was questioned by Mr. Morris, its counsel, and by Senator Eastland.

MORRIS: Have you heard the testimony of Whittaker Chambers or heard about his testimony that you aided a man known to him as Richard, who subsequently became a public figure under the name of Robinson-Rubens?

ZABLODOWSKY: I have heard that name several times now in questioning before the FBI and before your committee and that is all I know about it.

MORRIS: Is it your testimony that you did not aid such a man?

ZABLODOWSKY: It is my testimony that I don't know who they are talking about.

MORRIS: Did you ever aid anybody who was conducting an illegal passport ring?

ZABLODOWSKY: If I did, I did so unknowingly.

EASTLAND: Well, did you?

ZABLODOWSKY: Here is the circumstance, Senator. I actually did agree to transmit an envelope, a letter, to somebody who called for it. It is now quite possible—

EASTLAND: Just give us the facts about it. Who was to get the letter?

ZABLODOWSKY: I was told that a certain person would call with a certain name and I was to give it to him.

EASTLAND: What was in the letter, do you know?

ZABLODOWSKY: I haven't any idea.

EASTLAND: Did you give him the letter?

ZABLODOWSKY: Yes, I did.

EASTLAND: Who called for the letter?

ZABLODOWSKY: This is a matter, a circumstance, that is sixteen years old, and I cannot pretend to remember the details. . . .

EASTLAND: Are you now or have you ever been a member of the Communist Party?

ZABLODOWSKY: I am not now and I never have been.

MORRIS: Have you been active in the Communist underground? . . .

ZABLODOWSKY: The point is this, that for a bunch of undergraduates to tag each other or get impressions of each other like that out of an incident that may have happened like this would be as wrong as if I were to accuse Mr. Chambers of being an anarchist or something like that, because in his undergraduate days he once showered me with a bottle of catsup. He did, and very nicely sent me a dollar for cleaning expenses. This is the sort of thing I am really surprised. I don't want to impute any motives, but I am really surprised that matters of this sort can be built up the way they are. Chambers made a statement about what he knew. I cannot say what he knew, but I know that I was not a Communist in that year. . . . At that time, three years later or whatever it was, I joined the Socialist Party and actually took part in one election day in watching the polls. This is the total extent of my political activities in the technical sense of political activities. All I want to say is this: When Mr. Chambers met me in 1936 he knew he was coming to a sympathetic person. . . . I got terribly excited about Adolf Hitler and Nazism. I had more reasons perhaps than other Americans to get excited about it, and anyway, I did, and a lot of others did, too. It triggered me off. I joined an organization known as the League Against War and Fascism, whose main concern and motive as far as I was concerned seemed to be to fight Hitler.[5]

It is difficult to ascertain to what extent Chambers used Zablodowsky as a "mail-drop" for the Communist underground or for Chambers' *private underground*—that is, his own fantasy system. There is little doubt, however, that under the guise of the Communist Party Chambers enlisted his friends as personal agents for carrying out his private schemes.[6]

Chambers had admired Zablodowsky at Columbia. His pathological envy of Zablodowsky's prowess as wrestler and student first erupted in an impulsive act against him in 1923 when he besmirched him by throwing the contents of a bottle of catsup at him. It will be recalled that immediately after he had given vent to his vengeful feelings by humiliating Zablodowsky in this way, Chambers' demeanor suddenly changed; he came back, apologized, and offered him a dollar for the cost of cleaning his suit. It was suggested that Chambers had acted out against Zablodowsky the love-hate he felt for his brother Richard. Chambers' subsequent actions confirm the psychological fact that Zablodowsky's image remained unchanged in Chambers' mind through the years. Indeed, Chambers' need to destroy him found fulfillment in the sinister denouncement of 1952, and his memory of him as "Richard's assistant" left, as convincing as if it had been his fingerprint, the hallmark of his fratricidal quest for an identity.

---

[5] *Hearings before the United States Senate, Subcommittee to Investigate the Administration of the Internal Security Act and other Internal Security Laws, of the Committee on Judiciary,* 82d Cong., 2d sess. (New York, October 23, 1952).
[6] Another former Columbia classmate, Dr. Nathaniel Ross (now a prominent psychoanalyst), told me he had known Chambers in his undergraduate days. He did not see him again until sometime during 1936 or 1937, when he happened to meet him on the street in New York. After a brief conversation Chambers told Dr. Ross he needed office space for some special work he was doing and asked if he could sublet part of Ross's office, with no questions asked. Ross, amazed, said, "What kind of a damn fool do you take me to be?" Whereupon Chambers turned on his heel and walked away. Dr. Ross never saw him again.

242) FRIENDSHIP AND FRATRICIDE

Note how gratuitously Chambers suggested to his interrogator that David Zablodowsky (rather than David Chambers) provided "Richard" with a false cover:

You must remember that Zablodowsky was, unless I am very much mistaken, employed by the Viking Press, and therefore probably the publishing cover which he secured for Richard. . . .

The true identity of "Richard" was, of course, never established. It came only from Chambers' account that "Richard" was the cover name for a real Communist agent by the name of Rubens (whose real name was Robinson).[7]

In accordance with Chambers' system of multiple identities, he first introduced the name of a well-publicized (Robinson-Rubens) Communist alias. He then ascribed to this alias his self-styled code name of "Richard." And then, in the context of his accusation of Zablodowsky, he named him as "Richard's assistant." But was it not Chambers himself who was in real life Richard's (Godfrey Chambers') "assistant" in a fratricidal act, and was it not Chambers again, years later, who (using his alter-ego, J. Peters) was the architect in creating another "Richard's assistant," by asking Zablodowsky to do him a favor and serve as a mail-drop, and ultimately, as he had his brother Richard, betraying him?

After Chambers denounced Zablodowsky, he concluded his testimony by asking permission to "make a small request" of the committee.

CHAMBERS: I would like the record to show clearly that I am testifying here today solely in response to subpoena power of the Committee; and that I myself solicited in no way this unpleasant privilege. . . . I raised my point because [of] one of the current smears against me—that I am continually advancing new names and making new testimony for sensational purposes. Of course, we would consider that preposterous probably, but then we are not left-wing educators or magazine editors or members of the intelligentsia.
EASTLAND: You have rendered very patriotic service, Mr. Chambers.
MORRIS: Thank you, Mr. Chambers.

Chambers' word was accepted without further question. Zablodowsky, his mythical but no less real victim, lost his job with the UN.[8]

---

[7] The Robinson-Rubens case was one of the most publicized spy cases of the thirties. Robinson, traveling in Russia under a false United States passport, allegedly a Communist spy, mysteriously disappeared. The significant part at issue here is Chambers' pathological accusation of a former classmate and his weaving together of the real and the imaginary.
[8] Mr. Trygve Lie, on accepting Zablodowsky's resignation, said in his letter of reply that Zablodowsky could take "real pride" in his contribution to the UN. (*New York Times,* January 8, 1953.)

Julian Wadleigh

The guilt of Zablodowsky remains in great doubt; Julian Wadleigh's guilt, as an aide to the Communist underground, has been established by his own admission. Nevertheless, it is interesting to see how Chambers' relationship with Wadleigh once again bears his personal stamp.

During the thirties Wadleigh was working in the Department of Agriculture and teaching an evening class in economic theory. But he was also, he has said, deeply disturbed about the world situation and drawn toward Communism.

I felt there was a need for me to help. . . . I suddenly decided to offer my services to the Communists and to do faithfully whatever task they might assign to me.[9]

Thus, through a friend, a Communist organizer, Wadleigh established contact with the Communist Party. At first he was asked to help simply by "supplying a sample of my work." Next, he was asked to turn over classified material about Germany and Japan, information that would be sent to Russia for use as background in evaluating the war potentials of those two aggressor nations. Wadleigh, who it seems was incredibly naïve, said he was "pleased and proud" to be of help but soon realized that what was wanted of him was not his ability as an economist but the use of his position in government for spying on other countries.

The procedure for Wadleigh's passing of State Department papers was arranged with great care. The system, said Wadleigh, was so methodical that no document going to the spy ring ever was out of its proper place in the State Department during working hours.

Wadleigh described how he was soon introduced to Chambers, through his first underground contact, by a party functionary with the code name of "Harold."

One day he [Harold] told me I was to go to Philadelphia to meet this new contact. There we met a plump little man with an air of great importance and authority. One of his front teeth was broken off and it gave him an odd appearance every time he opened his mouth.

Chambers insisted on Wadleigh's absolute silence while they were riding in a cab. Wadleigh and Chambers did not speak until after they arrived and

[9] The Wadleigh material in these pages is from personal interview, Trial Transcript, pp. 1107–1256 *passim,* and Wadleigh's "Why I Spied for the Communists," syndicated serial in the *New York Post,* July 12–24, 1949.

were seated in the appointed place, a restaurant. Then Chambers plunged into a conversation on world affairs. "I was enormously impressed with his fund of knowledge of events," Wadleigh said. "It pleased me very much to see that my briefer remarks were making a favorable impression on him." On the way home he was told that the name of "contact no. 2" (Chambers) was "Carl." Little happened during the next several weeks. Then, early in 1937, Wadleigh and Carl began having meetings—usually lunch or dinner appointments— about once a week. Wadleigh came to know Chambers well, and it is evident from his description that he fell victim to Chambers' worldliness and mystification:

I could scarcely mention a country in the world, but Carl would speak with an intimate knowledge of it, sometimes saying that he had been there, sometimes discussing it with such a wealth of detailed knowledge that I got the distinct impression that he must have seen it. . . . Carl had a prankish, boyish sense of humor that might easily have made him talk as if he had traveled in a country just for a lark and for the sheer fun of bluffing.

In his job at the State Department, Wadleigh felt insecure and unnoticed. He had a strong need for recognition. "I wanted to get out of the cloisters and into the world, so I had to work with the Communists." This was what motivated him to lead a double life, made him a perfect psychological target and scapegoat for Chambers' impressive tactics. Wadleigh felt like a shadow behind the brilliant group of economists and lawyers with whom he worked. He continued to be a visible eccentric, he "didn't bother to get a hair cut or have [his] shoes shined." He looked with envy and admiration at such men as Hiss, Dickey, Darlington—those clever young men who seemed to snub him and whom he didn't get to know socially or professionally. He felt he had to do something important in order to gain recognition. He tried writing a novel but nothing came of it.

In his clandestine meetings with Chambers, Wadleigh said, Chambers was always trying to get him to become "the kind of person who would get a promotion. But I just didn't want to be bothered. . . . I guess I should have been in a university."

In March of 1938 Wadleigh was sent by the State Department to Turkey "to help make a trade agreement with the Turks." He returned at New Year's, 1939.

I had not been back in the office many days when Carl (Chambers) phoned me to make a dinner date, or perhaps a lunch date; the news he broke to me on that occasion was so shocking that I am unable to remember the circumstances; . . . he told me two or three times that he had left the apparatus and the party. . . .

Here was Chambers' story: The authorities in Moscow were convinced that he

had become a Trotskyist and that he had converted me to Trotskyism. They had
ordered him to return to Moscow, clearly with the intention of executing him
when he arrived, as he told it. . . .

I realized that my underground work in the State Department was almost certainly ended, and I feared that Chambers, embittered as he was, might go to the
authorities and tell them of my activities.

Knowing that I could no longer trust this man, I feared him. . . . When we
parted, Chambers said: "Well, now I'm going to become a bourgeois." Then,
patting me on the shoulder, he added: "That's what you'll have to do, too."

I made no comment. I just said good-by.

From that day on, Wadleigh lived under the dread fear that Whittaker Chambers might turn him in to the authorities as a spy.

It is not surprising, in view of Chambers' shifting alliances, that he chose
to frighten and mystify Wadleigh by shocking him with his story (which may
or may not have been so) that he had become a "Trotskyist." [10] Having
effectively implanted in Wadleigh's mind the idea that Moscow now suspected
him, too, of being a Trotskyist, Chambers' psychological seduction of Wadleigh was complete.

Wadleigh next met Chambers in response to an unexpected phone call
from Chambers to Wadleigh's office. Asked to identify himself on the phone,
Chambers repeated several times, "in a very loud, hysterical-sounding voice,"
that it was "Carl." "He sounded desperate," said Wadleigh. "Do you want me
to starve," Chambers exclaimed on the phone and told Wadleigh to meet him
"immediately" in Jackson Place. (Jackson Place is in front of the White
House, and the State Department was then diagonally across an intersection
from it.) Wadleigh's reaction was, "Jackson Place? Was the man completely
crazy?" He imagined going there and seeing "Chambers flanked on either side
by an FBI agent, all three of them greeting me with a smile." But Wadleigh
hurried to the appointed spot and found Chambers waiting alone. Chambers
told him he was desperate for lack of money and asked Wadleigh to let him
have ten dollars. Wadleigh had a twenty-dollar bill and a one-dollar bill in his
wallet. He gave Chambers the twenty, fearing that otherwise he would be
blackmailed. As he walked away from Chambers he thought, "I hope I never,
never see that man again" (and he didn't, until 1948, nor did he ever get his
twenty dollars back).[11]

Wadleigh was left so shaken that he could not tell whether his fear of
Chambers was his own "hysterical fantasy" or whether Chambers might really
expose him. For months he lived in fear that Chambers would either do that

[10] Cf. Browder's statement on Chambers having been a Trotskyist, pp. 122–23.
[11] Yet, as late as 1963, Wadleigh, reduced to a life of obscurity and near-poverty, was
able to say to me, "I liked Whit, I really did! My grievance is against the world, for they
know me only because of the piddling things I did for the Communist Party."

or blackmail him. This last meeting, Wadleigh said, left him "limp and hope-less." His fear and disillusionment led him to the determination never to sub-mit to Communist discipline again.

For a brief period his State Department work seemed to be going well, he got one or two promotions, but he became discouraged again, feeling that his work was "a sheer waste of time." He was still hounded by the fear that his "ghastly mistake" would come to light, that Chambers might at any mo-ment expose him. In 1943 he applied for and was granted an assignment with the Allied Control Commission in Italy. But his anxieties and frustrations continued. In 1946 he obtained a position in the Food Division of UNRRA.

Though Wadleigh's acquaintanceship with Chambers extended over a period of several years, Chambers, by using a foreign accent when he talked with Wadleigh, deceived him as to his nationality. Chambers' speech, both its inflection and word order, created the impression that he was definitely not a native American. He sounded as though he had come from Russia. It was not until late in 1939, when, having decided to break from the party, Wadleigh was having his own last meeting with "Harold," that he first learned Cham-bers was not a foreigner:

. . . there was one point, involving Whittaker Chambers, on which my curiosity was still active. What was his nationality? Now I could ask.
  "Why, his family has been in this country for generations," Harold said.
  "Really? Then where'd he get that astonishing accent?"
  "I don't know. Must've cultivated it."
  "Do you know what he's doing now?"
  "He's working for a magazine."

Wadleigh's job with UNRRA soon terminated (April 1947) and he turned to free-lance writing for a livelihood. He then went to work as an em-ployee of the Italian Technical Delegation, an office of the Italian Govern-ment in Washington, "helping to get food for Italy."

It was then that Elizabeth Bentley's and Whittaker Chambers' sensa-tional charges appeared in the press. Chambers did not mention Wadleigh, who was surprised to hear him denounce Alger Hiss, "of all people." He re-garded Hiss "as a very moderate New Dealer with strongly conservative in-stincts." He was frightened and did not understand why Chambers made no mention of espionage and the transmission of government documents. In November 1948, after Hiss had sued him for libel, Chambers first produced copies of government documents and turned them over to counsel as evidence against Hiss. Then, early in December, Chambers produced and turned over to House Committee investigators additional evidence in the form of micro-filmed documents. Wadleigh was gripped with fear. "Possibly some of those documents had been furnished by me and might even be traced back to me," thought Wadleigh, even though Chambers at first insisted that he had received them all from Hiss. (This statement Chambers later recanted by saying that he "might" have received the documents from sources other than Hiss, of which, he said, there were four or five. It was characteristic of Chambers' testimony for him either to forget some previously known detail or spontaneously to volunteer some new fact with each successive telling of his story.)

In fact, Chambers did not mention Wadleigh's name until after later questioning by the FBI; at that time Chambers named Wadleigh as a member of an underground spy apparatus.[12] Confronted with this by the FBI, Wadleigh decided to tell them his story. Thereafter, he appeared before the FBI, the New York Grand Jury, and the House Committee, and testified at both Hiss trials. He admitted that among the State Department papers produced by Chambers there were some that he had seen and might have transmitted. He testified at the trials that he had transmitted as many as four to five hundred documents to Chambers alone (via Mr. Carpenter, the photographer who allegedly turned them over to Chambers). It is strange, indeed, that the one person whose espionage role was beyond doubt should have been "forgotten" by Chambers, a further indication that his selective remembrances and lapses of memory sprung less from his expressed ideological and political righteousness than from his personal needs and apprehensions.

Franklin Victor Reno

Whittaker Chambers' paranoia, particularly the destructive heel of his revengefulness, left its permanent impression on the psyche and life course of Franklin Victor Reno.[13]

[12] To remember Wadleigh as an "additional" source would have detracted from the strength of Chambers' accusation against Hiss. In the Baltimore Deposition Chambers could not remember Wadleigh until he was reminded of him by Isaac Don Levine. In February 1949, after Hiss had been indicted, the Deposition for the libel suit was resumed and Chambers was asked:

Q. Did you mention Wadleigh to Mr. Murphy? [State Department security officer]
A. I am not sure.
Q. What is your best memory on that?
A. My best memory on Wadleigh is that Wadleigh's name escaped my mind altogether. I remember that there was such an individual, but I had to call up Isaac Don Levine and ask him the name of the man whom I had originally mentioned to Mr. Berle.
Q. So your best recollection is that you did not tell Mr. Berle about Wadleigh?
A. No, I don't think so. (Baltimore Deposition, p. 1375.)

[13] Franklin Reno and his brother were on a list of people mentioned by Chambers in 1939 to Assistant Secretary of State Berle as having been members of the Communist

Reno was a gifted mathematician. An extremely shy and immature man, in 1935 he was working as a statistician in the Department of Agriculture. He had come to the department from the University of Virginia, where he had done graduate work.[14] During his years there he had joined the Communist Party and maintained his affiliation while in the Department of Agriculture. It was at this time—1935 or 1936—that he became known to Whittaker Chambers.[15]

Reno left Washington in 1937 to accept a better position as a civilian employee with the United States Army Proving Grounds in Aberdeen, Maryland. He was assigned to work on bombing tables for the Norden bombsight. Out of contact with the Washington Communist group, he decided to divorce himself completely from Communist activities. In his new job his genius as a mathematician did not go unnoticed. He came to know a new group of colleagues, who were appreciative of his extraordinary ability and sought to befriend him. Like many intellectuals of the thirties who had hoped to find in the Communist ideology the answer to their own life problems as well as the world's ills, Reno became disenchanted with Communism. Bent on advancing his career and anxious to divest himself of his former political associations, in the fall of 1938, shortly after he began work at Aberdeen, he severed all connections with the Communist Party.

But Reno had difficulty in loosening a particular tie with his past; he could not avoid the continuing intrusions of Whittaker Chambers, who had knowledge of his past personal as well as political activities. Reno had unwisely tried to keep the fact that he had once belonged to the Communist Party a secret from the government. Though he had been an open member of the party during his student years and had so stated on his civil service application when he first came to Washington in 1935, he later concealed this fact in his application for employment at the Aberdeen Proving Grounds in 1937.

Concurrently with Reno's move to Aberdeen and the beginning of a promising career for him as a mathematician there, Chambers left the Com-

---

Party during the thirties. The "official" account of Reno's case, briefly publicized by the press as a sensational atomic spy arrest, was, like the fate of Reno himself, hardly ever heard about again. Like another of Murray Kempton's "Monuments and Ruins of the Thirties," the facts of the case and the personal fate of Reno drifted into obscurity.

[14] In a combined course of mathematics and astronomy. Though he failed to receive his Ph.D. degree, one of his colleagues said that "Reno's thesis was brilliant, but it was too mathematical for the astronomers and too astronomical for the mathematicians."

[15] In 1937 Reno was "a party organizer during a brief tour in Cumberland, Maryland, using the name Lance Clark" (*New York Times*, November 14, 1951, from a statement by Bernard J. Flynn, United States Attorney in Maryland). Chambers stated that Reno was "an organizer for the Communist Party or the Young Communist League in Montana," using the name Lance Clark. "Toward the end of 1937," Chambers writes in *Witness* (p. 432), "David Carpenter introduced Reno to him as 'Vincent.' "

munist Party. During 1938 and early 1939 Chambers, unemployed, without money, harassed by fears of being killed, was frantically collecting "life-savers." His psychological hold on Reno was not unlike that which he exercised on Wadleigh. Because of his own disturbed sexuality and his fear of being discovered, Chambers kept track of and threatened to expose the habits of others, especially former associates or acquaintances on whom he had collected private dossiers. And Reno was an effeminate, ineffectual, and passively maladjusted person. He was for a time befriended and "mothered" by a woman many years older than he, but he never married. A close informant doubted whether Reno had "ever crossed the heterosexual barrier." He often drank excessively. But his way of life, both personal and political, seemed to be improving in his new setting at Aberdeen. According to those who knew him, he was making a sincere effort to shake off all his former Washington cronies and he had broken with the party. But Chambers maintained a personal "fix" on him, and even after the time of Chambers' alleged break with the Communist Party he did not lose track of him. He saw in Reno's emotional struggles and escape into alcoholism, as well as in his former Communist affiliation, an opportunity to exact from him another "life-saver" in the form of money. Thus Chambers exploited his knowledge of Reno's personal and political life. In need of money, Chambers brazenly demanded fifty dollars from Reno. Reno did not have that amount at the time. One of his former colleagues said: "We got together and chipped in to raise the fifty dollars for Chambers' blackmail money." Why Chambers went to such lengths to blackmail Reno was a deep mystery to several of Reno's close associates. But Chambers' exploitation of Reno was not limited to obtaining money from him. To one colleague, Herman Louis Meyer (later a mathematics professor at the University of Chicago), who lived just across the hall from Reno at Aberdeen, Reno intimated that "Chambers kept on asking him for something; insisted on getting from him some kind of government document." If Reno did not comply, Chambers threatened to report him to a federal agency. Chambers finally pressured Reno into giving him something. Reno put in an envelope some obsolete firing tables. But "there was nothing important or secret about these discarded sheets of firing tables—they lay around the Proving Grounds like toilet paper in a washroom." The papers Reno gave to Chambers, it later turned out, were those of a 1917 Browning machine gun.[16]

After 1938 or early 1939 Reno saw no more of Chambers. With the entry of the United States into World War II in December 1941, Reno developed into a steady government worker. He put to use his mathematical genius. The government was in acute need of certain bombing tables within six weeks,

[16] Personal interview with Professor John Wilkinson, July 25, 1962.

a computation task that under ordinary working circumstances should have taken a year's time to complete. Reno worked day and night and successfully completed his assignment, which resulted in the first modern bombing table. He worked with such diligence during the next eighteen months that he was acclaimed a local war hero by his associates and was commended as a civilian worker by the War Department and awarded a gold medal.

"During the war," Professor Meyer has recalled, "Reno's behavior was like that of a guilty man having to make expiation." This was the impression also of another close colleague in whom Reno had confided.

When the war ended, there began a round up of suspect characters at Aberdeen and a search for people who might be "security risks." Many of those who publicly denounced this agitation as "ridiculous" were fired. Reno, on the outskirts of this agitation, advocated a strategy of keeping quiet. He tried to help some of those who were fired by appealing to the Archbishop of Baltimore to intercede on their behalf. Always a heavy drinker, he began drinking to excess, was often drunk and became semi-doped. He was a very lonely guy and a very able one. I tried to take away his bottle, but he was too far gone. It was pathetic. His conversation was colored by reference to his mysterious, dark, unpleasant past. He talked about somebody taking an envelope from him and years later that person still had it. It was all factual, but disjointed. He was heavily ridden by something. He was a man with a monkey on his back.[17]

After V-J Day, Reno suffered a serious mental break. He was hospitalized and under psychiatric care in Baltimore during 1946–47 (Reno's psychiatrist characterized him as the most creative man he had ever met).

On November 8, 1948, in a routine loyalty check by questionnaire of all Aberdeen employees, Reno again concealed his former Communist Party membership. It was during this period that Chambers testified secretly before the House Committee that Franklin "Vincent" Reno had passed to him "confidential" military information (around 1937–38).[18] In December of 1948 Reno was called to testify before the New York Grand Jury. Following his appearance, Reno resigned from Aberdeen (1949). Meyer, who had left Aberdeen for the University of Chicago, got Reno a job at the University Observatory at Williams Bay, Wisconsin. Reno was there only a year, then left because of his drinking. Soon thereafter his case was brought up before a Baltimore Grand Jury, and on November 13, 1951, he was indicted. He was charged with fraud against the government, for having concealed his Communist Party membership on his application in 1937 and on the loyalty question-

---

[17] Personal interview with Professor Herman Louis Meyer, July 31, 1962.

[18] In *Witness,* Chambers states that he brought Reno into the special Washington apparatus "towards the end of 1937." This is hard to reconcile with the rest of Chambers' story that he was then preparing his break from the Communist Party, and it also was the time Reno left Washington for Aberdeen.

naire in 1948. Although in December 1948, as evidence against Reno, Chambers had produced a "government" document, the 1917 Browning machine-gun firing table, which he had kept in his possession for eleven years, Reno was not charged with espionage. The government did not pursue the matter of the "documentary evidence" Chambers produced.[19]

Three months later, on February 27, 1952, Reno, then living in Colorado, pleaded guilty in a Denver court to the indictment charge. He was sentenced on July 2, 1952, in the same court by Federal District Judge William Lee Knous and served three years at Leavenworth Federal Penitentiary.[20]

Since his release from prison Reno has been doing menial work as a job estimator, preparing bids for a plastering company. Together with his brother Philip, also named by Chambers in 1939 (to Adolf Berle) as the "head of an underground Communist group," he has withdrawn into a simple, nonprofessional existence.[21]

Jay Lea Chambers

Chambers' ingenious use of someone else's identity to serve a personal need took many forms. Another person victimized by Chambers, because he happened to share Chambers' name, was Jay Lea Chambers, a government employee who had never known or met Whittaker Chambers. In 1938, following his alleged break from the party, Chambers was living in Baltimore under variations of the name Jay Chambers. In the telephone directory he was listed as Jay V. Chambers; in the government files [22] he used the name Jay V. David Chambers. When questioned about this discrepancy during the

---

[19] The *New York Times,* November 14, 1951, reported Reno's indictment and stated that the FBI in Denver was asked to arrest him at his present home in Englewood, Colorado. The *Times* report went on to say that Chambers identified Reno in court as one of his sources of military secrets, and that Chambers testified that Reno had supplied bombsight secrets he had turned over to Russia.

In *Witness,* Chambers writes: "By the time I broke with the Communist Party, Reno had brought out material only two or three times. There was not much of it and none of it was on the bombsight. . . . When I came to testify about it, in 1948, I could not tell what material Reno had given."

The press, at the time of the investigation, sensationalized the story by picking up the refrain of the House Committee, which said (in connection with Reno's appearance before the New York Grand Jury) that testimony before the committee indicated that secret information on the Norden bombsight was leaked from Aberdeen to Soviet agents.

[20] At the time of the sentencing, Judge Knous gave Reno thirty days' freedom in which to finish work on a book on ballistics he was writing.

[21] The Reno brothers "have had a good many years of quite trying experience growing out of this matter. It is still followed whenever the occasion presents itself by widespread and near-hysterical publicity." (Philip Reno to the author, December 23, 1962.)

[22] Chambers had a government job for a few months in 1937–38. See p. 292 ff.

House Committee hearings he shrugged the matter off rather glibly. "At that time," he said, "I signed erratically." But a private investigator, employed by the Hiss defense counsel in 1948, discovered a more purposeful reason. In a routine investigation of the various aliases Chambers had been known to use [23] they came upon a credit application, in the Baltimore Credit Bureau, made out by Esther Chambers. Mrs. Chambers gave her occupation as teacher at the Park School, a job she had engaged in (without pay) and a reference she had used on other occasions. In her application she listed her husband as Jay Chambers, "Senior Administrative Officer, Treasury Department." A check of government files by the investigator revealed that there had been (and still was) a Jay Lea Chambers holding that position. His wife's name was Anna. According to the investigators' report, Esther Chambers, whose identity was established without question as the wife of Jay David Chambers, teaching at the Park School, had falsely used the name of the Treasury Department employee to obtain a good credit rating. She had given private information about his past life (former employment as a university professor, former residential addresses, and so forth), all of which had been the basis for establishing a good financial standing. It was later confirmed that the government dossier that contained the above data on Jay Lea Chambers had been stolen from the personnel files of the Treasury Department.[24]

This deception clearly bears the imprint of Whittaker Chambers' methods. It was a documentary form of imposture—using personal data from someone else's life. Its purpose in this instance was quite simple. He established a new, financially secure identity by setting up a false credit rating. Indeed, the matter probably went further: Anna Chambers and her husband had been troubled by the receipt of statements from Baltimore and Washington department stores for purchases made by another "Jay Chambers" and charged to their account. It is significant that this trickery happened after Chambers had broken with the Communist Party and after he had turned to religion. It cannot be explained away as part of the business of espionage or in any terms other than a symptom of Chambers' sociopathic behavior.

[23] Private investigator's report of Whittaker Chambers, alias Jay Chambers, J. W. Chambers, J. David Whittaker Chambers, Whittaker Chambers, D. W. Chambers, George Cantwell, Lloyd Cantwell, George Crosley, J. Dwyer, Vivian Dwyer, David Dwyer, David Whittaker Dwyer. (From the Hiss Defense Files, November 1, 1948.)
[24] Through his government job Chambers had known contacts with the Treasury Department, which helps to explain his mode of access to the personnel files. Mrs. Jay Lea Chambers was concerned that, because of the similarity of names, people might think she knew or was related in some way to the Whittaker Chamberses, who were, of course, total strangers. They had never known or heard of Whittaker Chambers until they were investigated during the Hiss trials, by both Hiss and FBI investigators. (Telephone Conversation—Mrs. Chambers and the writer, July 14, 1963.)

The O. Edmund Clubb Incident

Oliver Edmund Clubb was for most of his life an American diplomat in the Far East. On a single occasion, in 1932, he crossed paths with Whittaker Chambers. The encounter lasted only fifteen minutes but it was destined to change the course of his life.

Clubb entered the Foreign Service in 1928, at the age of twenty-seven. After serving his first year in Washington, D.C., he was sent to Peking, China, where he served as language attaché with the American Legation. Thus began a period of consular service in the Far East that continued uninterrupted for the next twenty-one years. Clubb advanced through the various echelons of the service. By 1947 he was the consul general in Peking. In April 1950, following the Communist takeover in China, all United States consular offices were closed. Clubb was the last United States officer to leave Peking. Recalled to Washington, he was promoted to the important post of director of the Office of Chinese Affairs.[25]

In 1948 Chambers testified before the House Committee that sixteen years before (1932) one Oliver Edmund "Chubb" had come to the offices of the *New Masses*. According to Chambers, "Chubb" was carrying a message to be delivered to Grace Hutchins. He was to give it first to Walt Carmon, editor of the *New Masses*. Carmon had left by that time; Chambers was his successor. When, according to Chambers, "Chubb" was informed that Carmon was not there, he talked for a few minutes with Chambers, left the message, which Chambers thought was in the form of a letter (converted by Clubb's Loyalty-Security Board into a "sealed envelope") for transmission to a third person, whom Chambers thought was Grace Hutchins, and took his leave. They never saw each other again.

In 1950, when Clubb returned to Washington to assume his new position as director of the Office of Chinese Affairs, his picture appeared in the newspapers, and Chambers relates that he recognized it as that of the young man

[25] Clubb held the following government posts in the Orient: 1931–34, vice consul at Hankow; 1934–39, 3rd secretary at Peking, 2nd secretary; 1939, 2nd secretary at Nanking; 1939–41, consul, Shanghai; 1941, assigned as consul at Saigon, detailed temporarily to Hanoi, Indochina; at the outbreak of World War II he was interned but was released in 1942 and returned to China after a call for volunteers to return there. For a brief period he was consul general at Vladivostok, and after the collapse of Japan he was detailed to Harbin. In 1946, after reopening the consulate general at Mukden, he was assigned to Harbin again. In 1947 he took up his position as consul general in Peking. (From HUAC Hearings, March 14, 1951, pp. 1964–66.)

who had once visited him in the office of the *New Masses* in 1932. Thus apprised of Clubb's promotion to a position of high importance in the State Department, Chambers, for reasons presently to be explained in his own words, repeated his story of having met Clubb in the offices of the *New Masses* to the FBI, the Senate Internal Security Subcommittee and the State Department's Loyalty-Security Board.

Chambers explains, in *Witness,* why he felt moved to report such a seemingly unimportant incident again to the government authorities:

. . . one day, in our local newspaper, I saw a picture of Oliver Edmund Clubb, a U.S. consular official in China who had recently returned to the United States after the Communists captured Peking. I said to my wife: "I know this man. He paid me a visit in the *New Masses* office in 1932. But they have his name wrong. It should be Chubb." I mentioned the fact because it amused me that my memory could retain an impression of someone of no particular importance (I then supposed) and details of a conversation held fleetingly almost two decades before. Out of the same sense of amusement, and for no other reason, I mentioned the incident *in a casual conversation with two FBI friends.*[26]

I was startled by their burst of interest in my memories of Oliver Edmund Clubb (for the newspaper had been right, and my recollection wrong about his last name).[27]

In this account Chambers fails to mention, among other things, the salient fact that two years before he had already brought to the attention of the House Committee the name of Mr. Clubb (as "Mr. Chubb"); and he omits the crucial part of his account, that Clubb had a "message" for Grace Hutchins, a Communist worker.

His "casual conversation" with the FBI was followed shortly thereafter by his signed statement, to the Loyalty-Security Board (May 1950), in which he deposed that Clubb had "delivered a message to me in the form of a letter, I believe, for transmittal to a third person."

On January 2, 1951, eight months later, Clubb received a written interrogatory from the Loyalty Board requesting his written answers to questions about his alleged pro-Communist sympathies.

The last two paragraphs of the interrogatory echoed Chambers' account:

It is alleged in 1932 you delivered a sealed envelope to the office of the editor of the *New Masses* magazine in New York City for transmittal to one Grace Hutchins, a reported Communist employed by the Labor Research Bureau, an alleged Communist organization.

[26] Italics the author's.
[27] And, futhermore, how disingenuously Chambers manipulates the reader (and the facts) by his statement, "When these lines were written some time in 1950, I had not intended to divulge the messenger's name," thereby leaving the impression of a pious considerateness for his victim.

Comment fully on this allegation, . . . how it was known to you that Grace Hutchins was the addressee, and how it was known to you to effect delivery at the *New Masses* office.

Clubb could not recall the occasion of his having visited the *New Masses* nineteen years before but informed the board that he was, however, taking measures to ascertain to what the reference could be. One of these measures was to procure his old diaries, which, under the circumstances of his departure from China, had been left for safekeeping with the British chargé d'affaires in Peking.

The board (as is customary in such cases) did not reveal the name of his accuser or the source of its allegations. A member of the board, at Clubb's request, did tell him that the name of the person on whom Clubb had allegedly called was Walt Carmon. On the basis of this information Clubb went to New York on February 27, 1951, to look up both Grace Hutchins and Walt Carmon. Two weeks later he told the House Committee:

I looked up Miss Grace Hutchins first and then I looked up Mr. Walt Carmon. Neither of them, according to their version, knew anything about the matter in point.

The interest of the House Committee, in their active investigation into the loyalty of government employees, was rekindled when they learned of the board's investigation of Clubb, and they subpoenaed him to appear before them again on March 14, 1951. His testimony on that day highlights the first phase of this story. He was questioned by Louis F. Russell and by Donald Appell, committee investigators.

RUSSELL: Have you ever been acquainted with David Whittaker Chambers?
CLUBB: No, sir; not to the best of my knowledge and belief.
RUSSELL: Did you ever know anyone who used the single name "Carl?"
CLUBB: As his last name you mean?
RUSSELL: As his only name.
CLUBB: Not to the best of my knowledge and belief.
RUSSELL: Did you ever have any association with a magazine, *New Masses?*
CLUBB: No, sir. . . .
APPELL: The person that you actually called upon [Chambers] has related that there was a conversation between you and he [sic] with respect to China, a detailed conversation. Could you have had a detailed conversation with someone in the offices of *New Masses* if you have never been there?
CLUBB: It seems—well, obviously if I had never been there, no. It seems to me unlikely that I should have had any detailed conversation with anybody connected with the *New Masses*. In the event that I met anybody at that time and they were interested in China, I might have talked in general terms on the subject of China, but I would not definitely have given up any confidential or clas-

sified information or anything in the nature of that. . . . I have no recollection of having visited the office of the *New Masses.*[28]

It should be said that such a visit would not have been unusual. Clubb, during those years, was political reporting officer for the State Department and his main field of contact was journalists. (Immediately prior to his return to the United States in 1932, Clubb submitted a 124-page report on the Communist movement in China.)

On May 29, 1951, Clubb's diaries arrived from Peking. Reviewing what he had recorded nineteen years past, he found under date of July 9, 1932, that he had indeed visited the office of the *New Masses.* Mr. Clubb showed me his diaries,[29] in which the following account had been recorded:

The most interesting meeting thus far was that with the *New Masses.* Their so-called "revolutionary organ" is a horrible rag, but Agnes had given me a letter of introduction to Walt Carmon and so I went to see. It was a ramshackle place to which one went by a rambling, rickety staircase. There were many *Masses* cartoons on the walls. A charming Jewess, typing, who acted as secretary. She introduced me to Michael Gold as "Comrade Clubb," and I talked to him awhile while waiting. He spoke of revolution but had no "hopes" of it for the United States at the present, bemoaning the lack of organizers when the field is prepared and the crops so ripe for the harvest. He asked of China, and then the successor to Walt Carmon, one Whittaker Chambers, a shifty-eyed, unkempt creature, who nevertheless showed considerable force and direction, asked me about the Red movement in China. In turn I asked him of conditions in the United States, but we didn't talk smoothly. I was, after all, out of my bailiwick, masquerading somewhat under false pretenses, so that I felt too much like a stranger to show the proper "revolutionary enthusiasm."

On discovering his own account of having, in fact, made a call on the *New Masses,* Clubb wrote to the Loyalty Board and presented them with his original account. He then further explained:

The "document" delivered to the office of the *New Masses* was a simple letter of introduction; the writer of that letter (or, "sender of the document") was Agnes Smedley; and the addressee was not Miss Hutchins, but Mr. Carmon; and, the ad-

[28] HUAC Hearings, pp. 1973–79, *passim.*
[29] The handwritten diaries consisted of two leather-bound volumes dated, respectively, January 5, 1932 through October 18, 1932, October 26, 1932 through June 30, 1933. (Personal interview with O. E. Clubb, May 7, 1964.)

In his testimony before the House Committee on August 20, 1951, Clubb explained how the diaries had been returned to him: "Eventually the British came into control and were able to send them to me pursuant to my request."

Chambers' version in *Witness* is quite different: "In the course of his hasty departure from China that diary had passed into the hands of the British authorities. Always great readers of diaries, the British read this one and found an entry to the effect that, in 1932, O. Edmund Clubb had had a coversation with Whittaker Chambers in the *New Masses. . . . This diary the British had turned over to the American authorities.*" (Italics the author's). This is not so. The diaries were sent directly to Clubb.

dress given me by the sender, and perhaps enscribed on the envelope, was presumably the office of the *New Masses,* where Mr. Carmon had been employed as Managing Editor, but in his absence, I met instead Michael Gold and Whittaker Chambers (the "successor" to Mr. Carmon).

He also sent a copy of the above memorandum to the House Committee, which found his explanation satisfactory. The Loyalty Board, however, did not consider the case closed and charged him with having been sympathetic toward Communism, echoing in a more sinister tone Chambers' story to them that,

In 1932 [you] delivered a sealed envelope to the office of the editor of the *New Masses* magazine, a Communist periodical, in New York City, for transmittal to one Grace Hutchins, an avowed Communist employed by the Labor Research Association, an affiliate of the Communist Party.

The board advised him that he was suspended from his position in the State Department. A hearing before the board began on July 31, 1951, and Clubb was questioned in detail about the various general allegations. The board quoted from Chambers' story of Clubb's visit to the *New Masses.* Said one of Clubb's examiners:

The informant [Chambers] has stated [to the FBI] that this whole matter sticks in his mind . . . because the delivery requested of the letter to Miss Hutchins . . . was his "first contact" with the Communist underground.[30]

On August 16, 1951, after Clubb had been suspended, Chambers testified again before the Senate Internal Security Subcommittee. Though his account was in essence the same as before, his memory had in certain areas become fuzzy and in other areas so enhanced as to remember new names and new facts:

While I was editing the *New Masses,* which is a Communist-controlled magazine, there came into my office a young man who asked to see Walt Carmon. . . . The man, the stranger, told me his name was O. Edmund Clubb. . . . I can no longer identify a picture of Clubb. If you realize that I spoke to him not more than fifteen minutes in the year 1932, I think it is simply impossible to make a positive identification. . . .

---

[30] Chambers has elsewhere described his "first contact with the Communist underground" in an entirely different setting: In *Witness,* referring to the period when he was working for the *Daily Worker* between 1926 and 1929 (three years before he met Clubb), Chambers writes: ". . . my first contact with a party underground cell . . . was in the Johnson and Johnson factory at New Brunswick, New Jersey." Chambers also states that it was in "June, 1932, while I was preparing my third issue of the *New Masses,*" that he received a call from "Comrade Bedacht," which resulted in his leaving the *New Masses* at six o'clock *for the last time,* entering the Communist underground the next morning. Yet, according to the entry in Clubb's diary, Chambers was still in the *New Masses* office in July 1932, when Clubb ran into him there.

The difficulty about my recollection of Edmund Clubb or Oliver Clubb is that I can no longer remember what that message was or even to whom it was to be delivered, but there has stayed in the back of my mind an impression which I will not testify to positively, that the message was written and that it was for Grace Hutchins. Grace Hutchins is an open Communist, a member of the open Communist Party, has run on the Communist ticket in various elections, and is well known to be a Communist. . . . But I cannot testify more positively to anything along those lines. . . . I have a further recollection, which I hesitate to make positive, that the message was from Agnes Smedley, but again I can't really testify to that positively.

This last recollection was a new addition to his story and was evidently appropriated from Clubb's own recent testimony. But what is most striking in his testimony is the reference to his inability to identify Clubb from a photograph, for in *Witness* he writes exactly the contrary, saying that it was his recognition of Clubb's picture in the newspaper that moved him to tell the FBI that he knew him.[31]

It is a critical fact that Chambers' testimony regarding Clubb's "message" for Grace Hutchins fell down completely. The letter of introduction was to Walt Carmon; Grace Hutchins was not involved at all.[32] Chambers said to the subcommittee:

I find it impossible, with the play of so many influences on my mind, because people are always asking me questions, bringing me information, *and there are actually areas of my experience where I can no longer distinguish between what I once knew and what I have heard and learned in the course of testifying.*[33]

After this gratuitous and startling display of confused memories on the part of Chambers, Clubb was never again questioned by the Loyalty Board; the matter of his visit to the *New Masses* was dropped. Meanwhile, however, the House Committee wanted to get the entire story. Clubb was subpoenaed to appear on August 20, and he went through his account once more, answering questions as to why he had had a letter of introduction to the editor of the *New Masses*. He explained again his official position and what had been expected of him as a political-reporting consular officer.

I have always understood that the desire of the State Department is that when we come back we acquaint ourselves with conditions in the United States, and it is for

---

[31] See p. 254.
[32] Regardless of Chambers' testimony, the facts and circumstances as Clubb recorded them in his diary were corroborated by Michael Gold (who in 1932 had been editor of *New Masses*). "In the absence of Carmon," explained Gold, "Clubb was first introduced to me, I talked with him for a while, *then* he met Chambers—as the successor to Carmon." (Personal interview with Michael Gold, January 11, 1964.)
[33] Italics the author's.

that purpose we are ordinarily called for consultation in Washington. . . . If I had come back and failed to learn what was happening in the United States, I would have considered myself derelict.[34]

To the committee's question as to whether the State Department, during the thirties, encouraged him, in forming his picture of conditions within the country, "to go to Communist headquarters or to an organization of such repute as *New Masses,*" Clubb responded:

I think it is clear from the character of my entry in my diary that I didn't spend much time there and I wasn't much impressed by those I met.

Four months later, on December 21, 1951, the Loyalty Board informed Clubb:

On the basis of all the evidence, the Loyalty-Security Board of the Department of State has determined that no reasonable doubt exists as to your loyalty to the Government of the United States . . . , but has determined that you constitute a security risk to the Department of State. . . . The recommendation of the Board was that you be separated from employment in the Foreign Service of the United States. . . .

There was no doubt that Chambers' testimony and the suspicions he had aroused were the cause of it all.

In accordance with established procedures, Clubb appealed to Secretary of State Dean Acheson, who designated Nathaniel P. Davis to consider his appeal. After consideration of all the evidence, Davis found

that no reasonable doubt exists as to your security risk to the Department of State and that therefore your removal from employment in the Foreign Service is not necessary or advisable in the interest of national security.

Secretary Acheson reviewed and concurred in Davis's findings. At long last Clubb was cleared of all charges and suspicions. But his position in the State Department could never be the same. With the consent of Secretary Acheson, Clubb retired from the Foreign Service.

I came to the realization [he later wrote], found by so many people in the twentieth century, how much easier it is to meet an enemy in strenuous contest, confident in the support of one's government behind him, than it is to face the slings and arrows of one's own people. The difference lies in what happens to the heart.[35]

In his letter of resignation, which appeared in the *New York Times* on February 11, 1952, Clubb gave public expression to his feelings:

[34] HUAC Hearings, pp. 1992–93.
[35] Quoted from "The Witness and I" (1952), an unpublished manuscript by O. Edmund Clubb.

It is with the deepest regret that I therefore have adopted the only appropriate course which apparently remains to me, and have exercised the option which is mine by reason of my age and years of service, and with the consent of the Secretary of State have retired from the American Foreign Service. I retire proud of my record of twenty-three years in that service, and confident that that record will stand by itself.

In juxtaposing these vignettes from the lives of Zablodowsky, Wadleigh, Reno, and Clubb, as biographical fragments extrapolated from Chambers' life, it has been my intent to highlight a common feature: the design, motives, and consequences of Chambers' role as a political informer. His deeply ingrained need to accuse others and witness their destruction represents a perverted confession of his own past sins. His compelling need to create scapegoats is both eminent and subtle, and in the recognition of its insidious quality lies the key to our understanding of his enigmatic and tortured existence. The incidents which have been cited are all illustrative of the chronic retaliatory quality of this facet of Chambers' paranoia, an ambulatory illness that harassed him throughout his life. The legal considerations of the "cases" described, that is, the question of guilt or innocence, is not the issue here.

Chambers characteristically employed as the central instrument of his schemes some document. He demonstrated an early mastery of this device as a senior in high school, when he plotted, in a literary way, to malign the president of the United States and to make derogatory forecasts about certain of his classmates on graduation day. When his plan was discovered, instead of relinquishing it, he submitted a false ("clean") version of his speech to the school authority, which, in retrospect, may be termed a forgery, for his secret intent was to deliver the original speech, which he did.

It was shortly after this incident that Chambers ran away from home. During this interval his use of the same device is discernible in the manner in which he mailed letters to his parents. Living under a false name, he gave no return address and his parents were helpless to find him. Thus he maintained a feeling of mastery over them (though in reality he was despondent, starving, and cast out). A year later came the episode of Williams College, and the experience with his roommate, Karl Helfrich, whom he used as a "mail-drop" so that at a later date he would have a document (his own letter) to "prove" he had posted it in Williamstown instead of New York. Then came his withdrawal from Columbia as the result of another denunciatory document (*A Play for Puppets*). And he reinstated himself with a simple lie to Dean Hawkes, as revealed in a letter to Mark Van Doren, a confession that in itself contained a subtle lie.

Then followed many incidents in which Chambers used his friends or

acquaintances as "mail-drops" for personal, political, or pseudo-political reasons. The outcome of his plots depended upon the degree of awareness, gulli-
bility, kindness, and many other personality factors of those he contacted.
Many responded, and many were, of course, immune to such invitations to
play-act with him. Note Jack Schulz's later reaction to Chambers, after having
been hurt by him:

I was however, no longer under his spell; I had to get back to my own work. Since
then (he was surely at that time in the party) it has occurred to me that he saw in
me a possible recruit.

Chambers was an engaging talker and clever prankster. His hidden motives were not recognized and he left people awed and mystified. The late A. J.
Liebling sent me a characteristic Chambers anecdote:

[In the early thirties] a reformed left-wing novelist named Edwin Seaver, a *New
Masses* literary light, . . . met Chambers at some Leftist powwow, . . . and
Chambers . . . invited him to dinner at Chambers' digs in Newark. Seaver was so
broke that Chambers had to provide him with round-trip fare on the Hudson
Tubes—two nickels. When Seaver arrived at Chambers' squalid apartment, he saw
a large, almost lifesize portrait of Hitler hanging in the most prominent spot.
Seaver expressed astonishment, and Chambers said: "Oh, that's just to throw *them*
off the track." Who the hell "them" was he didn't specify. He was always, in his
own fantasy, being pursued.
    After a scanty meal and some talk, Seaver started to go and Chambers asked
him to take some letters with him and leave them at some address in the Village, to
save postage. Seaver said he delivered the letters and so, unwittingly, became a
"courier" himself.[36]

By reducing others to the level of messenger boys, Chambers put himself
in a position of authority. His self-created world of reality was more real to
him than true reality, hence his conviction about his beliefs. By planting hard
facts into a relationship, he could later return and reap the harvest of revenge.
    When Chambers ostensibly shifted from poet to Communist agent, his
use of the false-document device served the same inner need; only the area of
external application changed. When as an editor of the *Daily Worker* and the
New Masses he "slanted" news, or when he later set up personal "mail-
drops," designed sealed letters, obtained false birth certificates, passports, and
business fronts, the underlying motives did not vary. His expanding system
transcended the personal and encompassed institutions—the New York Public Library, Government, Church, and God, but it remained essentially self-
serving.
    These manipulations helped him to translate his infantile fear of death

[36] A. J. Liebling to the author, May 17, 1962.

and wish to be reborn (suffering followed by salvation). Why this early child-hood fantasy failed to be replaced by realistic thinking cannot be answered simply. Certainly the ongoing conflict between Laha and Jay looms high as a basic reason, for the Chambers home was a continuing crucible of strife. And Vivian's envy and unconscious wish to destroy Richard persisted as the pri-mary by-product of his parents' way of life. In the complex skein of his later, more sinister plots and impersonations, one can still see the scarlet thread of his fraternalistic love-hate.

When parents are disaffected there is no greater hate than that which arises between two brothers ("The Sign of Cain"). Chambers was not entirely unaware of his own identification with Cain. In *Witness* he comments that as he watched those whom he had accused—"Alger Hiss, Priscilla Hiss, Donald Hiss, Julian Wadleigh and others"—entering and leaving the grand jury room, "each time that the door of the jury room swung shut, a single question formed in my mind: 'Where is thy brother, Abel?' "

On some occasions the design is more easily discernible than others. Consider, for example, his distortion of dates, entirely lacking in material pur-pose but serving his fantasy needs. In dates of events in his brother's life he either could not remember the year or, more often, he was off by exactly one year; for example, "my brother was eighteen or nineteen when he went off to college," or "he died in 1925" (instead of 1926), or, "I broke from the Com-munist party in 1937" (which he later changed to 1938). In his translation of *Class Reunion,* Chambers changed the age of Sebastian from seventeen to six-teen. On his New York Public Library employment record, Chambers' date of birth is recorded as April 1, 1900, instead of 1901. By moving back the year of his birth he began life over again, gave himself a second chance. Thus he would be disidentified from his former self, absolved from the guilty image of the monstrous child, who "weighed twelve pounds, measured fourteen inches across the shoulders," whose dry birth lacerated and almost killed his mother. He would, instead, be the sleek, gentle, lovable Richard, or David, or Adler, or Alger.

It is plausible to assume that Chambers' wish to be his brother probably originated in his mind during his third year of life when Laha's pregnancy be-came apparent to him. Fantasies of this order are commonplace in children at this age and under such circumstances. Vivian's wish to replace his infant brother achieved symbolic realization when Richard killed himself. It is postu-lated that Whittaker induced his brother to destroy himself so that he would remain his mother's only child. In the conception of the double death there are suicidal as well as homicidal components. In order to be his brother, he had to come close to destroying himself along with his brother, then be re-created.

The fantasy of being close to death was uppermost in Chambers' mental life. The idea spread into all areas of his life—political, literary, religious.[37] This helps to illuminate the destructivity and creativity in Chambers' life and provides a psychological answer to the most intriguing of all questions in this case: "What was Chambers' ulterior motive in his need to destroy Hiss?"

There is a psychological as well as a material reality in the legal interpretation of documentary evidence when used as testimony by a witness in a trial court. The laws of evidence insist that partial truths are not enough; for testimony to be valid it must be the *whole* truth. Wholeness of truth (credibility) from a human witness is dependent upon the psychic motivation that determines his state of mind. Hidden motives from inner recesses may thus govern the factual reliability of his memory and the validity of any documentary evidence he may produce. Chambers' conscious as well as self-deceptive methods of distorting the total reality involved the introduction of "pieces" of material reality that he astutely, almost instantaneously, put to use in the service of his belief system. His mind was a compendium of fact and fantasy. He kept dossiers of facts and foibles on his friends, colleagues, and many of those with whom, at any time, he had any dealings. These were his "life-savers." Some of them he actually hid or asked others to hide for him. But most he filed in the unwritten archives of his mind, a private storehouse of facts, ideas, real and fictional plots, gathered from readings, translations, and actual experience for future use.[38]

[37] At any moment a conflicted idea repressed in the unconscious mind may symbolically emerge or be re-enacted in meetings with persons or events which threaten or stimulate the return of repressed memories of the lost (destroyed) object.

[38] Chambers' life is replete with examples of such physical and mental caches. Most notable, of course, are the documents he asked Nathan Levine to hide for him, and which he himself later hid in a pumpkin. And, as impressive, is the plot of *Class Reunion*, which he hid in his mind and whose echo is clearly visible as the central theme of the Hiss-Chambers case.

13

"*I Am David Breen*"

LET US NOW, in the light of the foregoing, examine the facts as well as the implications contained in one of Chambers' more psychically revealing acts as a Communist. In 1935 Chambers obtained a false passport under the alias of David Breen. Let us assume that his external reason was, as he later claimed, that he intended to use the passport to travel to England, where, as part of a Communist underground operation, he was to help set up an apparatus.

When, either in real life or on the witness stand, Chambers found himself confronted with obvious evidence of his deceptions, he glibly and rather amusedly defied reality by "shifting his identify." During the second Hiss trial, for example, Claude Cross, the defense attorney, was determined to point up Chambers' fraudulence in his use of the David Breen passport. Caught up in his own design, Chambers simply "shifted his identity" by the use of rhetoric. Note the following colloquy:

Q. Now did you know David Breen?
A. Did I know David Breen? I *am* David Breen.
Q. You are David Breen?
A. Yes. I used that identity.
Q. You mean you are David Breen today?
A. I used—
Q. No. Are you David Breen today?
A. Obviously not.
Q. Now did you know the real David Breen that died three and a half years after he was born?
A. I never knew that David Breen.
Q. You came all the way up from Washington to the New York Office of the Passport division and signed this application for a passport, is that correct, about May 28, 1935?
A. I believe it is. . . .

Q. And you knew that that was a false statement, to represent yourself as David
Breen being born in New York City on April 28, 1900,[1] didn't you?
A. Certainly. . . .
Q. And you swore to this oath: "I, David Breen, a native citizen of the United
States, hereby apply to the Department of State at Washington for a passport. I
solemnly swear that I was born in New York, New York, April 28, 1900; that I
was married on April 3, 1929, and that my father, John Edward Breen, was
born at Rutland, Vermont, and died September 26, 1908." You knew every
statement in that was false, didn't you?
A. Yes.
Q. And you intentionally made this false statement?
A. Certainly.
Q. Did you make this oath: "Further I do solemnly swear that I will support and
defend the Constitution of the United States against all enemies, foreign and
domestic, and that I will bear true faith and allegiance to the same; that I take
this obligation freely without any mental reservation or purpose of evasion, so
help me God." You took that oath, didn't you?
A. I did.
Q. And you signed the name David Breen after it?
A. That is right.
Q. And then swore to it?
A. That is right.
Q. At that time what was your conception of what an oath is? . . .
A. I had the Communist conception of an oath which is that an oath has no bind-
ing force upon a Communist. . . .
Q. I say you knew that you were a traitor in fact of the United States?
A. I was a Communist and therefore I was.
Q. You were a traitor to the United States and you knew it?
A. That is quite correct.[2]

It is just as likely that Chambers' scheme of obtaining a fake passport
was as much in the service of his inner identity needs as it was to set up an
alleged Communist apparatus in England. In *Witness,* Chambers expresses his
amusement as he relates the cleverness of "J. Peters' " scheme of exploiting
the records of the Genealogical Division of the New York Public Library to
collate birth and death certificates. It is of more than passing interest, in light
of the author's formulations, that J. Peters, a real person and once head of the
Communist underground in America (deported by the Immigration Service
before the Hiss trials), was also used by Chambers as a fantasied image, a
secret double for himself. When Chambers was asked to state some of J.

---

[1] The correct date of the birth of David Breen as recorded on his birth certificate was
May 7, 1900. Note that Chambers' erroneous and false entry on his passport application
of "David Breen's" birth date as April 28, 1900, corresponds to the false birth date
noted on Chambers' New York Library Employment record, which also was April 1900.
Both are off a year from his real birth date, April 1, 1901.
[2] The testimony quoted in this chapter is from the Trial Transcript, pp. 313–16, 334–36.

Peters' pseudonyms he gave among many others the name J. *V*. Peters, making the secret resemblance to himself (Jay *V*ivian) even closer. In those important areas where Chambers introduced his so-called "hard" documentary evidence against Hiss, such as the certificate of title of the Ford car and the Baltimore documents, "J. Peters" was in each instance referred to by Chambers as the mastermind or figure of authority behind the scenes of these mysterious, still unproved transactions. These interchanges of real names and pseudonyms, though they may possibly have been the work of "J. V. Peters," bear the psychological fingerprints of his possible alter-ego, J. V. Chambers.

The satisfaction Chambers exudes as he relates this piece of illegality in *Witness* is reminiscent of the perverse pleasure of the arsonist who stands by, enjoying the fire only he knows he has set. With childish amusement he describes how "ghoulishly" simple was the system "Peters" used in procuring fraudulent birth certificates. It was, he says, "no problem at all for Peters." Chambers goes on to describe how Peters organized two teams of researchers who were planted in the Genealogical Division of the New York Public Library. One team studied infants' birth dates; the other, infants' death certificates. The names of infants who died shortly after birth, together with the names of the dead child's parents, were listed. Peters, explained Chambers, would then write to the Board of Health and request a certified copy of a birth certificate. The address given would be one of the secret letter-drops that Peters maintained around New York City. With these fraudulent birth certificates an American passport would be obtained. During the second Hiss trial Chambers was asked:

Q. Where did you get these birth certificates?
A. I got them from J. Peters.
Q. Where, I said?
A. New York City.
Q. Having gotten them here, do you think you studied them here?
A. It seems probable.
Q. But when you went to the passport office you only took the birth certificate of David Breen?
A. Yes.
Q. Well, did you see a death certificate?
A. I do not believe so.
Q. Well, you satisfied yourself he was dead before you used the name, didn't you?
A. J. Peters took care of all those details.
Q. I say, you satisfied yourself he was dead before you signed that application?
A. J. Peters satisfied me.
Q. And from whatever he knew, you accepted his statement and relied on the fact that the boy was dead when you posed as David Breen.

A. That is true.

Cross then read to the jury Chambers' testimony of August 3, 1948, before the House Committee on Un-American Activities:

MUNDT: I wish you would go into that in some detail because there have been many instances and it has become a veritable racket where these Communists get passports to visit Soviet Russia.

CHAMBERS: He [Peters] told me, with great amusement because of the simplicity of the scheme, he had sent up to the Genealogical Division of the New York Public Library a group of young Communists, I presume, who collated birth and death records; that is, they found that a child had been born, let us say, in 1900 and died a month or so later, or several months later. The party, through some members, then wrote to the proper authorities in New York for issuing birth certificates and asked for a birth certificate in the name of the dead child.

In this testimony Chambers selected as an explanatory example the date "1900," which, to be sure, was the date of his own (David Breen's) fraudulently obtained passport. Though he was ostensibly talking about someone else, the birth date was that of his own alias. Chambers often unwittingly betrayed himself with an account of someone else's activities, stories that reflected his own schemes and cleverness. Chambers' explanation as to how "a Communist" obtained a fraudulent passport was information he gave without reserve to the committee, in response to a leading, but not a direct, question. A careful examination of David Breen's original passport application in Chambers' handwriting, the psychic equivalent of a fingerprint, will show that it must have been Chambers, rather than (or posing as) Peters, who masterminded the selection and collation of the Breen birth and death certificates.

Let us first note a few of the following numerological facts: Richard Chambers was born in 1903; David Breen died in 1903. Was this Vivian's magical way of replacing Richard "on the record"? But let us look further into the realm of Chambers' fact-and-fantasy system. Richard was born on September 26; John Edward Breen (David Breen's father) "died" on September 26 (the imaginary death date Chambers could not explain but admitted having "invented out of thin air"). It is also notable that Chambers arranged for his own baptism into the Episcopal Church to take place on September 26 (1940).[3] And there is still another numerological observation: David Breen died on October 17, and Jay Chambers, his father, and Ellen, his daughter, were born on October 17.

It would appear that in taking over a dead person's identity (stealing a life), Chambers (or his alter-ego, "J. Peters") sought out from the genealogi-

[3] The circumstances of Chambers' baptism (a rebirth ritual) will be discussed in detail later. See p. 253 ff.

cal files, a source very familiar to him since he had worked in the Library for
several years, the name of a person who had died on the same numerical date
(day, month, or year) that his brother, father, and/or daughter were born.
Chambers did not have a generally poor memory. His errors of recall in one
area stand in significant contrast to an accuracy and consistency of this same
mental faculty in another. Chambers correctly remembered and recorded the
birth date (to the hour) of his daughter, yet the death date of his brother and
father were never accurately remembered. Chambers states in *Witness:*

The night of October 16, 1933, I reached home late, around eleven o'clock. At
seven o'clock in the morning, the baby still had not come. . . . At nine o'clock,
I called again. . . . The baby [had] been born.

Of course, Chambers could not have predetermined the date of his daughter's
birth. But he could well have selected documents with birth and death dates in
accordance with his birth and death fantasies, particularly if it was J. Chambers instead of "J. Peters" who searched in the files of the New York Public
Library during the time he, either as a member of the Communist underground, or for personal reasons, was in need of establishing a new identity
for himself.

   Shortly before the Hiss trials J. Peters, head of the Communist underground in America, faced charges by the Immigration Service for illegal entry,
was deported to Europe, and was never heard from again. Chambers, aware
of this, subsequently pinned many mysterious acts onto Peters. It was typical
of Chambers' design to ascribe to dead, deported, or mythical persons a role
in the fictionalization of his own reality. Chambers makes a special point of the
fact that J. Peters "stood high" on the list of those who "would be of interest"
to him if Hiss filed a libel suit against him. In a long footnote explanation in
Witness, he states that Peters "was suddenly permitted to leave the United
States" and that he (Chambers) drew "only the unhappiest inferences" from
the fact that Peters "was suddenly hustled from the scene."

   The obvious inference from this is that in Chambers' view the Immigration Department, in some alliance with the Department of Justice, deported
Chambers' "star" witness (even though he mentions the probability that if
Peters were called to testify he undoubtedly would have pleaded self-
incrimination). With Peters safely out of the country, however, Chambers
feels free to make his point: "Few knew so much about the Hiss case as he.
For Peters had been in charge of everything. He had known everybody."

   Chambers continues:

The head of the underground section of the American Communist Party had
clearly become one of the most dangerous possible witnesses against Alger Hiss, if

by any means he could be induced to talk. He had long eluded the efforts of the House Committee on Un-American Activities to locate him. Now, after years of surveillance (of which I had long known), he was suddenly picked up by the Justice Department and held for deportation.

While he was pondering why anybody could possibly wish to deport J. Peters at the moment when he had become important in the Hiss controversy, writes Chambers, "Congressman Nixon volunteered to enlighten" him. Chambers was called as a witness and identified Peters. Peters did not identify Chambers on the ground that his answer might "incriminate" and degrade him. After the House Committee hearing, Chambers waited to be called by the Immigration Service in the hearing against J. Peters, but Nixon told him, "They will never call you." "I [Chambers] asked why, since there were few men in the country who knew as much about Peters and his activities as I knew, and almost no one would testify to them."

Chambers quotes Nixon as having said to him, ". . . if the Government calls you to testify against J. Peters, it will have admitted that you are a credible witness. If you are a credible witness against J. Peters, you are also a credible witness against Alger Hiss. They will never call you." And, in fact, Chambers was not called by the Immigration Service.[4]

Chambers' conspiratorial character, the way he casts Nixon in the role of a co-conspirator against the Government of the United States (the concealed enemy), is exemplified by the above.[5]

Chambers assumed different names, manipulated them in the same way that he manipulated dates. They were interchangeable identity symbols. He used the name "David," for example, both "legally" and illegally. It was, he testified, his "favorite" name. At times he was Jay David Chambers, Jay David Whittaker Chambers, Jay V. David Chambers, or David Chambers.

---

[4] It is also possible that J. Peters might have refuted Whittaker Chambers' story of his participation in the underground, and, in preserving Whittaker Chambers as a witness, the reason for Peters' deportation might well have been the exact opposite.

[5] This account of remembered dialogue between Chambers and Mr. Nixon (along with other significant matters) could unfortunately not be checked by the writer with Mr. Nixon. In April 1961, shortly after being introduced to Mr. Nixon at a public meeting in San Francisco, I wrote to him, as he had suggested, and repeated my earlier request to talk with him about my study of the Hiss-Chambers case. Three and a half months elapsed (during this interval Whittaker Chambers died). On July 26, 1961, Mr. Nixon wrote me: "I wish that I could find time in my schedule to sit down and go over the subject with you as thoroughly as should be done if it is to be productive. Unfortunately, however, I am finding that the combination of an active law practice and the continuing responsibilities in the field of public affairs makes my schedule a very heavy one, particularly in view of the fact that I no longer have an official staff. I would, therefore, like to keep your interest in mind and try to let you know if I should find an opportunity to do this, as I would be most interested to learn the conclusions you have drawn from your study. . . . [Signed] Richard Nixon."

Despite a subsequent attempt by the writer to contact Mr. Nixon, the above letter represents the only word he has received from him.

Note the colloquy that ensued when Chambers was interrogated by counsel about the David Breen passport application:

Q. And you wrote in there the date of the death of John Edward Breen as September 26, 1908? [David Breen's father].
A. That is right.
Q. You did not get that from any birth certificate or death certificate, did you?
A. I don't remember. I should think that I would have.
Q. It certainly would not be in the birth certificate of May 7, 1900, would it?
A. No.
Q. And it certainly would not be on the death certificate of young David Breen who died at the age of three and one-half years October 18, 1903, would it?
A. No. I think you have a small point there.
Q. I beg your pardon?
A. I think you have a small point there.
Q. Irrespective of how big the point is, just answer the question.
A. It was either supplied me by J. Peters together with the birth certificate, or it was invented.
Q. Invented by you?
A. Yes. . . .
Q. Now, on the application there is a place for the name of your wife. "My wife's maiden name was Edna Rogers." That was false, wasn't it?
A. That was false up to the point where there was another birth certificate with that name on it.
Q. Mr. Chambers, your wife's name was never Edna Rogers?
A. My wife's maiden name was Esther Shemitz.
Q. And this statement that "My wife's maiden name was Edna Rogers" was false, wasn't it?
A. That is right.
Q. And you wrote in, in your handwriting, the name "Edna Rogers"?
A. That is right. . . .
Q. Will you look at this passport and point out to me a single true statement in the whole application?
A. Yes. . . . The true statement is that David Breen was born on April 28, 1900.
Q. That you had no knowledge of except you had a death certificate?
A. I had a birth certificate.
Q. A birth certificate. When you used that did you know that the boy had died in 1903?
A. I did.
Q. And were you posing yourself as David Breen, representing a grown-up man, when the boy had died in 1903?
A. That is correct.
Q. Where did you get the name Edna Rogers?
A. Edna Rogers was the name on another birth certificate given to me by J. Peters at the same time this one was given to me.
Q. Another birth certificate?
A. Yes.

Q. How many birth certificates did you have in your pocket when you went down
to the passport office in May of 1935 to get this passport?
A. One, I believe.
Q. Whose was that?
A. David Breen.
Q. Did you have the birth certificate of Edna Rogers?
A. Not with me.
Q. Not with you? But you just remembered it?
A. I had studied both of them carefully.
Q. You studied both of them carefully? Where?
A. Where?
Q. Yes.
A. That would be difficult to say.
Q. Where, would you tell his Honor and the jury; whether you made a careful
study of this birth certificate of David Breen and Edna Rogers in Washington or
Baltimore or New York or Philadelphia?
A. I certainly would not venture to say where I studied it.

No one during the trials recognized the coincidence in Chambers' testimony of a fantasy with a fact when Chambers told the court that he had invented the idea that his mythical father, John Edward Breen, "died" on September 26; this was, of course, the same day of the year that his real brother,
Richard Godfrey Chambers, was born.

Chambers lived for more than a year as Mr. Breen. He used the forged
passport, a "hard" document, as his presenting "card of identity" to the outside world. The passport privately served him as a magical "life-preserver," to
allay the fears of loss of his sense of self which arose from within. Though
Chambers' expressed mode of life underwent a complete change after he "sur-
faced" from the underground and was no longer a "faceless" man, his waver-
ing sense of identity remained. It is significant that he kept the David Breen
birth certificate and passport in a locked box for fourteen years.[6]

And his unconscious involvement continued even after the document
came to light. In *Witness,* Chambers again reverses "life and death" and
brings the image of David Breen back to life. Note that the following statement is contrary to all other evidence:

It was not until the second Hiss trial that I learned that David Breen was not the
name of a dead child, but that of a living man from whom permission to use his
birth certificate had been bought in another of Peters' operations.

A careful review of the transcript of the second Hiss trial reveals that
nowhere in the trial record is there any testimony indicating or even suggest-

[6] It is beyond the scope of this book to go further into the symbolic meaning of David
Breen's birth certificate and how it also represented a fetishistic object in Chambers'
fantasy life.

ing that David Breen was not the name of a dead child. As has been shown, defense counsel produced the death certificate of David Breen, and it was marked in evidence as an Exhibit. Chambers' guilt about using the life symbol of a dead person as a "life-saver" [7] accounts for his later assertion in *Witness* that David Breen was *not* the name of a dead child. Thus Chambers undoes his guilt by magically bringing David Breen back to life again in his last literary confession. In this involved fabrication he also magically saves himself from being identified with a dead person and thereby brings himself to life (another variation of his use of the "life-saver").

Careful analysis of his specialized mode of identity manipulation not only sheds light on the symbolic meaning of Chambers' acting out but explains the function of the lie in his bizarre behavior. On the surface he was (or posed as) a secret agent for the Communist underground. But in his own private world he was the omnipotent one. Chambers exploited the Communist Party, its technical resources and unique structure, for conspiratorial acting out. In this setting the Communist Party, like J. Peters, served as a private, secret "agent" for *him*. In his inner struggle, the stealing, copying (by typewriter or microfilm), withholding, hiding, and timely production of documents provided a "life-preserver" useful for any eventuality. Chambers' actions were equivocal. He had need to deceive almost everyone he dealt with, because he had need always to deceive himself. Chambers' sense of his own identity was so tenuous and unrealistic he required a "life-preserver" at all times to sustain him.

Except during his recurrent periods of melancholia, when he figuratively acted like a dead person, he otherwise maintained, by means of false identities, a hold on reality. This was aided by his perseverance and great capacity for work, which was his bulwark against the fear of loss of the sense of self. His fabrications were woven around certain provable facts and actual experiences, or, as was the case with some of his most dramatic stories, they were attributed to dead people. Beset with guilt, he was driven to confess by accusing others. Thus he became a professional informer (an anti-spy). Maintaining an alliance with a government security agency provided him with an outer protective shell, but he continued to be tormented within himself.

The same fears that drove Chambers in public life dictated the course of his family life. The childhood fantasy of having almost killed his mother when he was born was still evident thirty-five years later in his adult fear of, and wish for, children. His need to make restitution to his mother for his unforgivable crime is clearly transferred to his wife. In terms similar to those used

[7] The entire Chambers family lived under the name of Breen; his wife was Edna Breen, and his daughter, Ursula Breen.

in describing his own birth, Chambers tells how his wife bore their second child.[8]

Through her fog of anaesthetic, sickness and pain, my wife managed to whisper to me in the morning how happy she was that she had given me a son. . . . He was wrinkled and red and hideous. The instruments had sloped in one side of his head. The nurse assured me that it would grow back to the usual shape, and so it did, very quickly. But I did not venture to look at my son again until I was driving my wife back to New Hope. Then I parked in a quiet spot and gingerly lifted the blanket from the basket in which my son was sleeping on the back seat of the car. I hastily dropped it again. Nature has compensated John Chambers for his initial rough handling by man. Together with a very satisfactory set of features he has inherited his mother's character, gentle, generous, courteous.

The striking physical transformation, typical of the first three weeks of infantile growth, was, of course, quite normal. His safe return home with wife and newborn child ushered in also a reunion with his mother.

Our family was once more knit together at the stone house. . . . I drove up to Lynbrook and brought my mother down to spend the [Christmas] holiday with us at the stone house. She loved and was loved by my wife. With her grandchildren around her, the grief of the past began to thaw away, and all of us felt the continuity of the generations. Thereafter, my mother and I grew closer and closer together. . . .

And now a magical reversal of the ongoing stream of life occurs; time seems to flow backward, as though he is once again a child. He retreats from the political to the personal. It is precisely at this turning point in his family life when

. . . a subtle chemistry began its work, which if it were possible to trace it, would be found to have played an invisible part in my break with Communism.

That "subtle chemistry," Chambers' magical second chance to be an accepted member of his own family, opened the gates for his emergence from the Communist underground. And, indeed, from Laha herself, warmed by the new life, there began to flow a belated maternalism.

During the winter of 1936–37 Chambers moved his family back to Baltimore, leaving "the little stone house forever."

I had rented a house on Auchentoroly Terrace, opposite that Druid Hill Park, where, as he once told me, Alger Hiss, when he was a boy, had bottled spring water to sell to the neighbors.

Chambers' selection of this place to live, his nostalgic association with the site of Hiss's boyhood activities, is an interesting revelation. It shows

[8] John Chambers, born August 18, 1936.

again how Chambers acted out his own "family romance" when, after meeting Hiss and having been rejected by him, he chose a place to live "opposite" Druid Hill Park, one of Hiss's boyhood haunts.

But it would not be long before the shifting forces within him would drive Chambers back into those same conflicted areas from which he had been trying to escape.

14

Hidden Brotherhood

BUT WHAT OF HISS? I have endeavored to show that he was, to be sure, a victim of Chambers' fantasies. Still there is much in the meaning of Hiss's behavior toward Chambers, as George Crosley, in 1934–36 and later in 1948 that requires explanation. Why *was* he so readily victimized? Were there any specific psychic reasons that directed Hiss from within first to relate and later to react to Chambers the way he did?

The personal confrontation between Hiss and Chambers at the Commodore Hotel on the afternoon of August 17, 1948, was the most crucial event in the life of Alger Hiss. The outcome of this encounter, a dramatic meeting masterminded and set up during the early morning hours of that same day by Representative Nixon, was the turning point of Hiss's career. Any appraisal of this emotionally charged and widely publicized event must take into consideration the background of political forces, the objectives of the principal participants as well as of the protagonists, and, far from least, the public hysteria about Communist subversion and espionage that filled the atmosphere and encroached upon this event. The anticipated meeting of the protagonists had been built up by press and radio and condensed into a dramatized Moment of Truth. From this final showdown scene the long-awaited answer to the question, "Who was the greatest liar in America—Hiss or Chambers?" would be forthcoming. Yet, for my purpose, I must set aside these important external circumstances and concern myself with inner motivation in order to reconcile our understanding of Hiss, the person, and Hiss, the witness.

Let us, then, from this vantage point, peruse Hiss, re-examine his conduct and his manner as he confronted Chambers for the first time after an interval of twelve years. Let us also keep in mind the deeper motivations that determined Hiss's behavior, especially in regard to his belated recognition and identification of Chambers as a forgotten figure out of his past life.

It is impressive that from August 3, 1948, the day Chambers accused Hiss, until August 14, Hiss did not have even an inkling who Whittaker Chambers was. "The name," said Hiss, "means absolutely nothing to me." Yet, at the same time, several photographs of Chambers were shown to him which he described as "not unfamiliar." It was only after reading a leaked newspaper report of Chambers' secret testimony to the House Committee, to the effect that Chambers with his wife and child had stayed at the Hiss home for several days to a week, that Hiss's memory began to serve him and he first thought of George Crosley. After "cudgeling my brain during a four-hour ride on the train from New York to Washington, I thought of George Crosley and wrote his name on a note pad."

Then after careful scrutiny of Chambers' face and teeth and asking to hear his voice, Hiss in his lawyerlike, hypermethodical way at long last recognized and identified Whittaker Chambers as George Crosley, a man he had known during 1934–36. By his painstaking manner Hiss succeeded in giving the appearance of evasiveness and pettifoggery—so much so, that Representative Hébert was moved to comment, "Mr. Hiss, you are a very agile young man." And, to be sure, it is understandable that Hiss's unique behavior may have been conducive to the development of such suspiciousness. If the quasi-virtues of perfectionism, deliberateness, and ultra-caution were ever self-defeating to Hiss, they were clearly so on that crucial day of August 17. For by the manner rather than the substance of his testimony, Hiss enshrouded himself with suspicion, which, despite his efforts, has persisted through the years and hardened his image in the mold of history.

We are now in a position to appreciate how Hiss's compelling need for perfectionism and his inordinate objectivity characterized his extreme caution as a witness. Furthermore, earlier years of experience as a cross-examiner for the Nye Committee had made him especially skilled in examining "false statements" of witnesses.

Nevertheless, after a prolonged and intensive study of this matter, my analysis of Crosley's entry into Hiss' life, as Hiss described it from its very beginning "sometime in 1934–35," makes me believe that from its inception it contained elements of personal significance to Hiss of which he had no conscious awareness. In recollecting his initial feelings, Hiss said:

When Crosley first walked into my office in the old Senate office building, I received him as just another member of the press. Crosley showed an interest in the work of the Nye Committee and was therefore someone I wanted to be nice to.

Later statements made by Hiss and subsequent events indicated that Hiss must have felt more strongly drawn to Crosley, the itinerant journalist who purported to be "the stereotype of a Jim Tully or a Jack London." Crosley's engaging manner, his tales of world travel and personal adventure, his experiences with the unfamiliar, all beguiled Hiss. And Crosley's unkempt, harried, and poverty-stricken appearance struck a particularly appealing note.

For more than fifteen years Hiss has had serious and justifiable reason to search his past memories and reflect about this enigmatic man whom he once knew and then so completely forgot. Since Crosley's fateful re-entry into his life as Whittaker Chambers in 1948, Hiss has had countless occasions to re-call and reflect on his relationship with Crosley during the thirties. And peri-odically Hiss has, at my behest, gone over with me the course and meaning of this relationship many times, reiterating his feelings and memories about Crosley-Chambers.

First and foremost [said Hiss] I felt sorry for Crosley because he was so obvi-ously in need. Having been brought up in the Southern tradition, we were accus-tomed never to throw away any old or worn articles that might still be useful to someone else. If one had anything extra or unnecessary it was given to a friend who needed or could use it. In turn, one received from other people. There was no sense of humiliation in these gestures. Clothing, furniture, or other articles were freely given away to servants or relatives.[1]

It was in this spirit that he regarded Crosley as someone he could help and as one who could make use of things the Hisses no longer needed. When Crosley told Hiss he was planning to move from New York to Washington and needed a place to live and Hiss happened at that time to have an overlapping lease on an apartment on which he was then paying rent, Hiss offered to sublet it to Crosley. "It was," said Hiss, "a measure of economy to myself as well as a favor to Crosley." And when Crosley appeared at Hiss's home with his wife and baby but with no personal effects, because the moving van had not ar-rived, the Hisses took them in for several days. In the same utilitarian way he let Crosley have the use of his old Ford car. "I would have done the same thing for *anyone*," Hiss explained.[2]

But Crosley cannot be so summarily dismissed as a transitory figure in Hiss's life. Crosley was not just anyone, even though, at their first meeting, Hiss may well have thought of him as "just another member of the press that I wanted to be nice to." In an early conversation with Hiss I had noted the

[1] The Hisses gave their old piano to Timmy's music teacher. Personal effects left by deceased relatives were passed around to those who could use them.

[2] By the time of the trials one would have expected Hiss to have become more wary in his dealings with strangers. Richard Field, a former colleague and close friend of Hiss, told me about an incident that occurred during a period between the trials. The Hisses were staying at their summer home in Peacham, Vermont, when two unidentified young women turned up there and told Alger they wanted to talk with him about the case. Without any check of their identification, he invited them into his house, spoke freely with them, and, since it was late, invited them to spend the night there. They have not been heard from since. (Richard Field to the author, in a personal interview, October 13, 1963.)

similarity of the two names, Crosley and Bosley. As the saga of the Hiss family was unfolded to me I was impressed with certain remarkable resemblances in the personalities of Bosley and Crosley and with certain common features in their lives. I mentioned this coincidence to Hiss, and he reacted with pleasant surprise and a show of positive interest. The assonance of the two names had never occurred to him before that moment. He brought up a number of other personal similarities and adduced that Bosley and Crosley were much alike in their iconoclastic, adventurous, free-spirited ways. Both were gifted with irreverent wit; both were engaging, articulate, knowledgeable. They were both journalists. Bosley had been a staff reporter for the *Baltimore Sun* and aspired to become a more serious writer. Crosley had presented himself as a writer for the *American Magazine*. "Did you ever talk about Bosley to Crosley?" I asked Hiss. He had no direct memory of having done so, but now that I brought up the question, he believed it "likely" that he had, for he had always spoken readily about Bosley's talents and interests to many people. As we talked more about this, Hiss's feelings grew stronger: "I should be surprised if I had not mentioned Bosley; it was particularly likely that I had done so." Hiss went on to explain that when he first met Crosley it was not "too long after Bosley's death," and he used to visit his mother frequently. "All of which meant that I was keeping up my family ties more closely then, and Bosley was more on my mind." [3] Hiss recalled:

Moreover, Crosley's story to me of his having indeed worked in the wheat fields must have reminded me of Bosley's having done so at a similar time, and I think it most likely that I would have spoken of it. Crosley flattered me; he made me seem more important to myself.

Crosley talked about himself as a hobo, and this, too, "had a certain romantic appeal." Crosley mentioned Hannigan's book, *Merchants of Death*. This impressed Hiss with Crosley's sympathy for the work the Nye Committee was doing against the munition manufacturers. But Hiss's relationship with Crosley was not limited to the problems of the Nye Committee. He saw him about a dozen times, mostly at lunch. On one occasion (before he sublet the apartment to Crosley), Hiss mentioned to Crosley that he was driving from Washington to New York and gave Crosley a lift. The auto ride took them

---

[3] After Bosley's death Alger became his mother's favorite son . . . the one from whom Minnie expected great things.

Chambers, then living in Baltimore, knew about Hiss's achievements. When Hiss presumably told Crosley about his attractive brother Bosley, who died in 1926 (within a month of Richard Godfrey's death), Hiss unwittingly became a brother to Chambers. The story of Bosley may now be construed as having provided Chambers with a useful piece of reality for his magical system in which Chambers envisioned Alger as the coveted younger brother.

through Baltimore, and they drove very near to Hiss's home on Linden Avenue. Hiss reminisced with me about his childhood:

I think it was then that I must have told Chambers about the spring water route to and from Druid Hill Park and my interest in birds. It was then I very likely mentioned the prothonotary warbler.

The "baby brother," elevated to the higher echelon of the fraternal hierarchy, was now swapping stories and sharing the same experiences with the envied figure of Bosley. Listening to Crosley's escapades stirred in Hiss the memories of Bosley's free-spirited movements. Crosley's stories about his travels in Europe were reminiscent of the exciting things that had happened to Bosley on his European trips. Many of Alger's "interesting" contacts both at home and in Europe were people whom Bosley had previously met and befriended.

Despite Hiss's exceptional skills as an administrator and his wide experience with many character types, his appraisals of people are more idealized than worldly. Indeed, from a close study of him as a person one senses a lack of those very attributes of character—shrewdness and cunning—which characterize his public image. In his need to seek out the good in people, he unconsciously prevents himself from recognizing guile and deceit.

It took many months and repeated incidents before Hiss realized that he had been deceived by Crosley's promises and saw how gullibly he had accepted his stories.

Crosley never produced anything. I had made an investment in a virtuoso and I felt cheated. His articles about the Nye Committee which he said he was writing never appeared. He was going to produce excellent articles about the Committee's work and made me believe he would prove he was deserving. I had a wish to be kind to people in trouble. I thought of myself as sophisticated. I was a young bureaucrat and enjoyed being surrounded by journalists and press people. But his stories were part of the build-up, the stories got taller, and I finally decided he was drawing a long bow.

In his enticing way Crosley built up Hiss's interest in him, exploited and deceived him. Consciously Hiss was relieved to be rid of him; he had found him to be a "sponger." [4] And because of this, according to Hiss, Crosley disap-

[4] As a further clue to Hiss's "unrealistic sense of loyalty," in this instance, "sticking to his part of the bargain" with Crosley (that is, his agreement to let Crosley have the old Ford car as part of the sublease rental agreement on the 28th Street apartment), Hiss explained to me his reasoning behind this transaction: "Even though Crosley did not come through with the rent as he had promised, he left the rug at my house, which I accepted as payment in kind," since Chambers was hard up for money. Therefore many months later when someone, "probably a messenger from the Cherner Motor Co., appeared at my office with the certificate of title (for transfer) of the Ford and asking for my signature, I felt I was simply making good my original promise to Crosley."

peared from his life. Whatever meaning one may attach to Hiss's memory of this experience, it was an unpleasant episode, which he would understandably want to forget.

Reminiscing a quarter of a century after he first met Chambers, Hiss's memories about Crosley were still quite vivid. His feelings about him from the period 1934–36 had, however, become fused with later ones from the 1948–50 experience, when Crosley reappeared as Whittaker Chambers, his accuser. Our conversations and correspondence concerning the "unconscious relationship between Crosley and Bosley" extended over a period of four years. During the latter part of this period Hiss's positive associations that he had earlier expressed about the possible fraternal resemblance between Crosley and Bosley underwent a striking change. As he reflected and ruminated more and more on the idea that he may have unconsciously reacted to Crosley because of Crosley's hidden resemblance to Bosley, he progressively minimized the possibility of such an identification and ultimately negated the whole idea with increasing intellectual vehemence. Yet Hiss's discussion of this point remained as objectively "open-minded" as it was subjectively obstinate. But the vigor of his logic and his use of reason grew stronger. In 1963–64 the tone of his argument conspicuously changed in comparison to earlier feelings expressed during 1960–62.

Crosley was not *that* impressive, my efforts toward him stemmed *only* from a wish to be kind to him, for this was proper.

Hiss now emphasized the oppositeness of Bosley and Crosley.

Bosley was tall, slender, fastidious, graceful, and had a nice voice. Crosley was just the opposite, his teeth were bad, his clothes were rumpled. Yet [he conceded] all this was in line with the image of the writer and the transient intellectual, and I found Crosley more attractive than other writers.

Hiss's resistance to my interpretation was understandably protective; for I had equated the image of Crosley, a person Hiss had befriended and who became his accuser and arch enemy, with Bosley,

. . . my bright elder brother, who during my earliest years claimed and received most of my affection, yet from whose mistakes I later learned even more, for Bosley was undisciplined in habits of sleep, diet, and drink.

After a further lapse of time Hiss returned once again to my interpretation that he may have unconsciously harbored an indentification between Bosley and Crosley.

I have done my best to make an objective self-analysis of the validity of the idea. I recognize the evident assonance between the names but please note one is a first and one a last name. But, try though I have, I cannot find *any* emotional responses that are *remotely* similar in my attitudes towards the two. The assonance in names and the age similarities [they were a year apart] seem therefore not indicative of deeper equivalencies, but purely superficial and accidental.

Hiss continued:

Crosley really had no more attraction for me than literally hundreds of acquaintances I have known from college days on. On the contrary, I can think of many I knew no better and over no longer a period of time for whom I felt a quite real attraction. My interest in him was not in his personality but in the status of writer who might further the spread of sympathetic reporting about the Nye Committee in whose efforts I had an emotional as well as a career investment. Such interest as I could find in Chambers was based on the unfamiliar, a frequent source of my interest. I've tried to recapture in relaxed, most generalized form the respective emotional reactions I felt to Crosley-Chambers and to Bosley. I cannot find the remotest similarity, no déjà vu (in even a slight degree) feeling. I was aware of Crosley-Chambers' wide reading, but my response or interest was not akin to the influence of Bosley's infectious excitement in all cultural matters. But at no level do I find any equivalent. I felt sorry for Chambers, but only for his poverty, which he shared with many others I knew in those depression years—and this was not at all similar to the compassion I felt for Bosley's tragic illness and death. I was quite unaware of the self-destructive element in Crosley-Chambers' personality so I can't believe there was even that similarity in the images I had of each.

This lack of comprehension of psychic forces was, I felt, another exhibition of the same emotional blind spot Hiss had earlier revealed in himself when he related his account of the circumstances of his sister's tragic illness and death. It seemed to me that in his need not to blemish the image of Bosley in any associative way with that of Crosley, both of whom had, in their respective ways, elicited his admiration and disappointment, he ultimately dissociated *all* facets of resemblance between them.[5]

It is a truism that any meeting of two or more people evokes feelings on the level of the immediate, realistic awareness of one another's presence, but stirred also are many hidden memories in which there is no conscious awareness. It is characteristic of Hiss that when he is under emotional stress he thinks harder, more logically, and more objectively. It seemed likely to me that some hidden psychic association between Bosley and Crosley had occurred and been repressed. I have adduced also considerable evidence that

---

[5] It is noteworthy that the voluminous correspondence between Hiss and myself were handwritten serial responses. As far as I know, he kept no carbon copies. My own serialized questions to him, together with his written or spoken replies, were transcribed and filed. Thus they provided me with a continuous record of my own nuances or shifts of feeling, for comparison with Hiss's, over a period of about five years.

Chambers selected and tagged Hiss with the symbol of his brother Richard even before Chambers actually met him in person.[6]

Crosley and Bosley were similar in iconoclastic spirit. Both had rebelled early against domineering mothers; had several times run away from home and school. Each had lost his father; Bosley, by his father's suicide, when he was seven; Chambers, by his father's absenteeism since the time he was born. Bosley Hiss and "George Crosley" were both of high intellect; colorful and magnetic personalities. Both were knockabout, nonconformist character types. Both had lived unwisely. To Alger, the proper and obedient boy grown into the conventional gentleman, the "rough and tough" style was something he had always admired in others, a style of life he had pleasantly brushed but not really engaged in.[7]

To Alger Hiss and Richard Chambers, Bosley and Vivian were romantically elevated figures. And in the fall of 1926 the elder Bosley and the younger Richard died, two independent events whose only connection or even remote resemblance was the personal tragedy. But the aftermath of Richard's death exerted itself as a compelling pathological force in the life of his surviving brother. To Alger, Bosley's death was a bereavement of a different order. As a child he had looked up to Bosley's great freedom of spirit and action; in his youth, to Bosley's adolescent emancipation from Minnie's dominance; as a young adult, he emulated but never achieved Bosley's release. And so the figure of Bosley, after his death, remained fixed in a legendary way in Alger's mind.

In this fortuitous interplay of fantasies, the attractive figure of Hiss provided for Chambers the illusory image of the once admired, still envied Richard. And more fortuitously, but certainly no less crucially, Chambers' entry into Hiss's life stirred in him some romantic memories of Bosley. And neither was aware that each stirred in the other an unresolved residue of feeling for his dead brother.[8]

[6] Chambers' penchant for collecting dossiers makes it likely that he had some factual knowledge of Bosley's former existence when he first met Hiss. This presumption becomes more weighty after one scans the pages of the *Baltimore Sun* from October 1933 to March 1934. News articles and comments about Alger Hiss's work on the Nye Committee in the *Sun* during that period often alluded to Alger Hiss, "younger brother of Bosley," once a reporter for the *Baltimore Sun.*
[7] When he was in prison Hiss was regarded by his fellow inmates as a "legitimate square." Though this set him off from most of the prisoners he was in no sense a loner. When he left prison the windows of the wing where he had been confined were filled with cheering inmates. He developed lasting and diverse types of friendships and on occasion still sees some of these former convicts. Since his release from prison Hiss has enjoyed getting into conversations with bartenders about underworld characters he might have known. It makes him feel as though he, too, was just a knockabout guy.
[8] Combined in the above, also, is the more deeply repressed father-brother equation. Hiss had transferred much of his idealization of (and disappointment in) his father to Bosley.

It is known how such traumatic events become mentally fused and how the deep disappointment common to them both may be buried in repression. It is in this dimmed but still visible light that Hiss's difficulty in remembering, recognizing, and identifying Chambers as Crosley prior to their confrontation, and his difficult-to-understand behavior after they faced each other, becomes explicable. And let us not forget how angered Hiss was by the tactics of the House Committee. It is significant, also, that once Hiss had made up his mind that Chambers was Crosley, he felt suddenly relieved. "Any puzzlement as to identity," Hiss later explained, "was completely over and I felt a vast sense of relief."

Then followed an intense vehemence in the certainty of the identification:

McDowell: Well, now Mr. Hiss, you positively identify—
Hiss: Positively on the basis of his own statement that he was in my apartment at the time when I say he was there. I have no further question at all. If he had lost both eyes and taken his nose off, I would be sure.[9]

For by then the incontrovertible reality of Chambers' face, mouth, teeth, voice, and other features overshadowed completely whatever confusions Crosley's image may have stirred in him. It is significant, also, that until the moment of certainty Hiss was reluctant to voice the name "George Crosley," even though the memory of Crosley had come to him, lest the "real Crosley," if he proved not to be Chambers, might be unjustly brought into the picture. This inordinate show of loyalty (for if Crosley had not turned out to be Chambers he would have been guilty of nothing) is an integral part of Hiss's character.

Between his personal optimism and his altruism, Hiss sustained his self-image as a caretaker and contained his anger and hostility. But in so doing we shall see how he reinvited episodes that led to disappointment. Thus his altruism blended indistinguishably into his masochism.

Both in his private and public life Hiss reacts with saintliness rather than anger toward those who have hurt or defeated him. In a nationwide television program in 1962, after Nixon's gubernatorial defeat in California ("The Political Obituary of Richard M. Nixon"), Hiss was asked by news commentator Howard K. Smith, "Do you have any feelings of hostility toward Mr. Nixon?" Hiss replied:

Both had, in effect, failed to cope with the responsibilities of life. Thus the infantile "betrayal" which his father's death represented to him when he was two and one-half years old recurred nineteen years later when Bosley died.
[9] HUAC Hearings, p. 988. It is interesting to compare Nixon's version (*Six Crises*, p. 36) of what he believed was going on inside Hiss's mind at this crucial moment. His estimate was that Hiss, the master spy and liar, had capitulated. Nixon wrote: "Hiss finally gave up." Nixon's appraisal represented, too, the committee's attitude.

I don't think I have any feelings of hostility, . . . nor do I have any feelings of great personal warmth or affection. I regard his [Nixon's] actions as motivated by ambition, by personal self-serving, which were not directed at me in a hostile sense, so that I feel that what he was engaged in was something beyond his scope and size.

Hiss counters the aggressions of others by increasing his "objectivity." While he was in prison, for example, he received a letter with the news that his son (then aged eleven), while walking alone down Park Avenue, had been accosted by two teen-age boys who took away his money. Hiss wrote back:

Tony, my boy, that business on Park Ave. last Mon. must have been quite a shock. Actually, like most cases of aggression or hostility it will cease to bother you as soon as you understand what made those two boys pick on you. Once you understand why someone does something strange or unfriendly it ceases to be strange; and it even ceases to be unfriendly when you see it isn't really directed at you because you're you at all. It is caused by something sick in the other fellow or by his being mixed up about something. Actually, I have met in here a great many fellows who have done things just like what was done to you and almost all of them have, nevertheless, some very, very good qualities. If those two boys had known you, I'm sure they would have liked you so much that they would have wanted to be your friends and then they wouldn't have dreamed of doing anything against you. One thing I'm sure of—they certainly needed the money even more than you did, poor as we are! Another thing I'm equally sure of—there must be people, grown ups, who have been much, much meaner to them than they were to you. That's how they got that way, there's no doubt of it. So, seriously, I'm much sorrier for them than I am for you, though of course what I really mean is that I'm sorry people are so treated that they act that way. On the next visit you and I can compare our ideas of what they are really like and who or what taught them to be bullies, which is a very unhappy thing to be. x-x-x. [And to Priscilla] Thy Tues. letter came this evening. How lucky Tony is to have thee to help him understand that destructiveness is thwarted life and that forgiveness of those who know not what they do is the mark of health—it is only difficult for the whole man if he is so hurt by the aggression that his normal healthy outlook is impaired. But without an understanding of the causation of hostility it is not possible to depersonalize the incident by realizing that the aggressor knows not what he does. Thus, it is the level of understanding which is the key to preservation of the values of affirmation in the presence of destructiveness or hostility.

Despite the hard realities of Hiss's experiences in prison, his objectivity remained the primary line through which he observed and measured life. His letters from Lewisburg are remarkable in the way they consistently express the caretaker in him and his objectivity about matters subjective.

V

15

Death and Rebirth

AFTER THE MIDDLE THIRTIES the lives of Alger Hiss and Whittaker Chambers diverged until 1948. They have only one thing in common during this interval: for each of them it was a time of worldly success.

Hiss, with the diligence and precision he had demonstrated throughout his early life, rose quickly in the New Deal hierarchy. In 1935 he was still with the AAA, though he was working full time with the Nye Committee. In March of that year he resigned his former post and joined the Nye Committee staff officially. But the committee's work slackened, and he presently applied for a position in the Office of the Solicitor General. He was hired, largely on the strength of his AAA experience, to work on the Butler case.[1] He subsequently worked on the Trade Agreements Act and resumed his friendship with Francis B. Sayre, who had been a professor at Harvard, and was then Assistant Secretary of State in charge of trade agreements. Sayre offered him a job as his personal assistant in 1936, and Hiss accepted. By 1944 Hiss had become deputy director of the State Department's Office of Special Political Affairs, a specialist in the proposed United Nations plan, and in March 1945 he was made director. He was an adviser on UN affairs at the Yalta Conference, was named executive secretary of the American delegation to the Dumbarton Oaks Conference, and later was secretary general of the San Francisco Conference, at which the UN charter was written. In 1946 he resigned from the State Department and on February 1, 1947, became president of the Carnegie Endowment for International Peace, which then was largely devoting its resources to the United Nations.

Hiss's career cannot be dealt with adequately in summary, and we will return to it. But the focus of our attention in this period must necessarily be

---

[1] The litigation involving the constitutionality of the Agricultural Adjustment Administration. The Butler case was at that time before the Solicitor General's Office and was soon to go before the Supreme Court. This led Hiss in May or June of 1935 to apply for a position in the office of Stanley Reed, Solicitor General, because of his familiarity with the work of the AAA.

on Whittaker Chambers, because it was his actions—predetermined by his own psychic needs—that were slowly laying the groundwork for the Hiss case. By the late thirties, in Chambers' cyclical existence, the time had come for him to remove his mask of anonymity, emerge from the underground, and "establish an identity." There is only one choice, he often said: to be either a revolutionist or a counterrevolutionist. As we enter into this period of Chambers' life, tinged on the surface with the hopes for personal freedom—the anticipated rewards for his suffering—there is immediately apparent the resurgence of his infantile conflict, unchanged and unresolved. Though he reverses his politics, abandons Communism and atheism, and proclaims his allegiance to God and the United States, his lifelong yearnings and fears and his need to protect himself from them remain in full force.

It was during the year 1938, says Chambers, that

I . . . reached the division point of my life. . . . Up to this point, I have been painfully sketching the personal sins and follies of a weak man.

His politics (and his autobiography) now branched off into religion. The tremors of intuition in his thirty-seventh year gave way to a major convulsion that rededicated him to a new calling—God and Religion.[2] The transition from spy to informer, a complete reversal of his "outward image" (traitor to patriot), provided Chambers with a newly found "life-saver."

In his "crisis of the mind and spirit," Chambers describes how his conversion came about: "In 1935 or 1936, I chanced to read in the press a little item of some nine or ten lines. . . ." It was the story of Dimitri Schmidt, a general in the Red Army who had been sentenced and shot in Russia. Chambers points out that he had never heard of Dimitri Schmidt, nor had he learned anything about him since.

He is a ghost who appeared to my mind a few hours after his death, evoked by a few lines of type.

I do not know why I read and reread this brief obituary, or why there came over me a foreboding, an absolute conviction: Something terrible is happening. I felt this so strongly that I mentioned the item to J. Peters,[3] the head of the under-

---

[2] "All activities which men think of as 'Vocations' or 'Callings,'" writes Kubie, "are those for which men feel themselves to be in some special fashion chosen, and to which they feel dedicated. This somewhat exalted frame of mind has never been adequately studied despite its subtle flavor of discreet megalomania, a megalomania which may be masked by outward humility, poverty, chastity, religious devotion, or dedication to a life of scientific research. There is an aura of myth and legend about all such vocations, and about those who follow the Road. The acceptance of the Vocation is always pictured as a response to one of two forces. One is 'called' either by God or by the Devil; either for a church and its works, or for Beelzebub and his." (L. Kubie, *Neurotic Distortion of the Creative Process* [New York: Noonday Press, 1961], pp. 7–8).
[3] Again one can interpret "J. Peters" as Chambers' alter-ego.

ground section of the American Communist Party. He did not answer me at once. Then he said fiercely: "A comrade who has just come back from Moscow is going around saying that there is a terror going on there and that they are arresting and shooting everybody. He should be taken care of." This was Peters' way of saying that I should shut up. Then I knew that my foreboding was right.

The little item about Dimitri Schmidt meant, of course, that the Great Purge had reached the Red Army. . . . The purgees . . . had no possible chance to escape; they were trapped, arrested, shot or sent to one of those Russian slave-labor camps on which the Nazis modeled their concentration camps, substituting the gas oven for death by enforced starvation, hard labor and undoctored disease.

Chambers then goes on to describe Stalin's great massacre as "probably the greatest in history" and chides Western historians who, he alleges, described the Purge as a "drama of the Russian mind and soul" rather than the stark reality that it was. In effect, Chambers argues, it is not I but the historians (like the author of *Mission to Moscow,* whom he cites) who write "nonsense." But a careful reading of *Witness* reveals how its author uses history as a screen to cover his own inner conflicts. Why make the Russian Purge appear a worse massacre than the Nazi holocaust? They are basically no different. In the unfounded statement that the "Nazis modeled their concentration camps after the Russian slave-labor camps, substituting the gas oven for death by enforced starvation," Chambers circumvents the unprecedented horrors of death in the German gas ovens. Was this piece of history too reminiscent of his brother's death in a gas oven?

Chambers' explanation as to why it took him so long to recognize the evils of Communism is hardly convincing.

I had always known, of course, that there were books critical of Communism and of the Soviet Union. . . . I had never read them because I knew that the party did not want me to read them. I was then entirely in agreement with the European Communist who said recently, about the same subject: "A man does not sip a bottle of cyanide just to find out what it tastes like." I was a man of average intelligence who had read much of what is great in human thought. But even if I had read such books, I should not have believed them. I would have known that, in the war between capitalism and Communism, books are weapons, and, like all serviceable weapons, loaded. I should have considered them as more or less artfully contrived propaganda.

When one considers Chambers' wide reading and his known talent as a propagandist in his own right, one can hardly accept such self-appraisals. Had not Chambers devoted much of his time to reading about and embracing nonconformism, atheism, and profanism? His plea that he was a man of just "average intelligence" has a note of false self-mockery. Several American literary figures, including Malcolm Cowley, felt that Whittaker Chambers could have been the literary genius of this century. As Chambers allows, had he read anti-

Communist books, he could not have believed them (so great was his need to cling to the destructiveness inherent in Communist ideology)—until he had established an alternate outlet. And so he staggers on in his dilemma—"to kill or not to kill"—trying to resolve his ambivalence in terms of a mystic philosophy.

I can no longer retrace with certainty the stages of my inner earthquake or distinguish its successive shocks. . . . One thing I knew: I was no longer a Communist. I had broken involuntarily with Communism at the moment when I first said to myself: "It is just as evil to kill the Tsar and his family and throw their bodies down a mine shaft as it is to starve two million peasants or slave laborers to death. . . . I did not even know that with that thought I had rejected the right of the mind to justify evil in the name of history, reason or progress, because I had asserted that there is something greater than the mind, history or progress. I did not know that this Something is God.

"How could it be God?" he then asks himself. In the circle of his confusion he rationalizes, "It was evil because a violence had been committed against the soul (see *Witness,* p. 82)—the soul of the murderer as well as of the murdered." By prayer, he seeks God to save his soul.

I had tried to pray a few times before, in my boyhood and my youth. I had not been successful. . . . At the same time, I began to sense that the two mirages that had beckoned me into the desert—the mirage of Almighty Mind and its power to plan human salvation—were illusions.

And now Chambers experiences a profound transformation of his entire being, a disruption of his sense of self of such magnitude that there is no doubt about the severity of this psychotic break.

As I continued to pray raggedly, prayer ceased to be an awkward or self-conscious act. It became a daily need to which I looked forward. If, for any reason, I were deprived of it, I was distressed as if I had been deprived of some life necessity, like water.

Chambers' early childhood fear of death by impoverishment is clearly re-echoed during this period (1937–38). The force of reason has been supplanted by mysticism and the magic of prayer ("Man without mysticism is a monster"), which alone can keep the supply lines open, the manna from Heaven to keep him alive. It is a mirage in which prayer has produced nutriment and maternal love. In the throes of his struggle to translate himself into a new person, Chambers describes how

There tore through me a transformation with the force of a river, which, dammed up and diverted for a lifetime, bursts its way back to its true channel. I became what I was. I ceased to be what I was not.

With these powerful metaphorical devices and the imagery of physical violence and destruction, Chambers continues to dramatize the widening psychic split within himself in terms of other fundamental dualities: Mind versus God, Knowledge versus Wisdom, Death versus Life, Communism versus Freedom. And he goes on:

What I had been fell from me like dirty rags. The rags that fell from me were not only Communism. What fell was the whole web of the materialist modern mind. . . . What I sensed without being able to phrase it was what has since been phrased with the simplicity of an axiom: "Man cannot organize the world for himself without God; without God man can only organize the world *against man.*" The gas ovens of Buchenwald and the Communist execution cellars exist first within our minds.

Again we are justified in wondering whether this acute sense of generalized evil does not spring from his sense of personal guilt, whether the gas ovens of Buchenwald are not substitutes for the more painful gas oven in which his brother Richard died. Significantly, his despair leads him to thoughts of suicide.

I asked myself if I must not kill myself. And even when I answered: "No," not from force of reason, but from force of life, I felt that the answer should be: "Yes."

But once again he is rescued from his self-destructive guilt by a frankly hallucinatory experience, which climaxes the above episode. As he struggled to make what he calls "the impossible return," his fear of death, which he had tried to stave off in terms of an ideological world conflict, now recurred in the form of another religious experience, similiar to the one he went through in the fall of 1920 at Williams College. Note how vividly the auditory hallucinations are experienced:

Then there came a moment so personal, so singular and final, that I have attempted to relate it to only one other human being, a priest, and had thought to reveal it to my children only at the end of my life. . . .
    One day as I came down the stairs in the Mount Royal Terrace house, the question of the impossible return struck me with sudden sharpness. I thought: "You cannot do it. No one can go back." As I stepped down into the dark hall, I found myself stopped, not by a constraint, but by a hush of my whole being. In this organic hush, a voice said with perfect distinctness: "If you will fight for freedom, all will be well with you." . . . There was a sense that in that moment I gave my promise, not with the mind, but with my whole being, and that this was a covenant that I might not break. . . . The moment itself was something which to deny would be blasphemy. It was decisive for the rest of my life, and incomparable in that I never knew it again. . . .
    If I were asked to say, in terms of the modern mind: "What is the meaning of

this experience?" I should answer: "I do not know. Something happened in the hall at Mount Royal Terrace. I experienced something." From that hall, I walked into life as if for the first time. . . . Henceforth, in the depth of my being there was peace and a strength that nothing could shake. It was the strength that carried me out of the Communist Party, that carried me back into the life of man. It was the strength that carried me at last through the ordeal of the Hiss Case. It never left me [4] because I no longer groped for God; I felt God. The experience was absolute.

And so, Chambers undertook "the impossible return" from the underground and broke with the Communist Party.

To prepare the way and to safeguard his life he looked for a hideout near Baltimore that would "have a commanding situation so that we could see around us in all directions." They found two rooms in a large house—which also boasted a police dog—on the Old Court Road.

His persecutory fears and the urgency to establish an identity, "which for five or six years had been all but lost," together with a desperate need for money, prompted him to apply for a WPA job with the United States Government. Among his reasons for taking the job was his plan to implant a "life-preserver," which he would later use in the form of documentary proof that he had been a Communist:

If the Communist Party did not succeed in taking my life, I assumed that it would try to act against me in other ways. I could not foresee what they might be, but I could see that I might need weapons with which to fight back. If I should ever have to tell my story (and the problem of becoming an informer confronted me, as it does every ex-Communist, from the moment I began to break with Communism), it would also be important to have some proof that I had worked with the Communist Party in Washington. There could be no more official proof, it seemed to me, than to let the Communist Party get me a job under my own name in the United States Government.

Why should his superiors in the party believe that taking a government job under his own name would be helpful to their secret activities? It is understandable only in terms of Chambers' private belief system. Chambers' version in *Witness* casts great doubt on his actual role as an underground agent. The whole idea originated with Chambers, not with the Communist Party. In fact, he says that his superior, Bykov (alias Peter),[5] was not even informed about this important move.

[4] [Chambers' note:] "Except for one moment, which I shall relate, when I felt that God had left me."

[5] Just as "J. Peters" served as an alter-ego for J. Chambers, the evidence is equally strong that "Peter," code name for "Colonel Bykov," was also a figment of Chambers' imagination. And since the figure of Colonel Bykov is central to Chambers' entire story of Hiss's espionage, it is worthy of a proper note.

It was Bykov, Chambers' story goes, who ordered him in 1936 to give Hiss an oriental rug as a gift from the Soviet people. And shortly thereafter (January 1937), says

I instructed one of the apparatus men in Washington (George Silverman) to get me a job in the United States Government . . . without at first taking Colonel Bykov into my confidence. . . . I took that job under my name J. V. Chambers, if I remember correctly. Certainly J and probably V.[6]

Chambers, the way having been paved and on Bykov's orders, he arranged a meeting with Hiss. . . . I told Mr. Hiss that Peter wished to meet him—Peter, Colonel Bykov that is—that the meeting was to take place in New York. (Trial Transcript, p. 254.)

Accordingly, Hiss met Chambers at a "cafeteria on Chambers Street" and then Chambers "took Mr. Hiss . . . in Brooklyn to the Prospect Theatre, a movie house on Ninth Street. We went into the movie house and sat down on a bench on the mezzanine. . . . Colonel Bykov came out of the audience and I introduced him to Alger Hiss." Then, Chambers continues, the three walked away from the movie and went (either by taxi or subway or both) to a Chinese restaurant in Manhattan.

"The substance of the conversation was that the Soviet Union was acutely endangered by the rise of the Fascist powers; that it needed help, and that Mr. Hiss could greatly help if he would procure documents from the State Department. . . . Mr. Hiss agreed." During the conversation Bykov spoke only German and Chambers acted as interpreter. (Ibid., p. 257.)

At one point the conversation turned to Hiss's brother Donald: "Colonel Bykov asked Mr. Hiss' brother, Donald Hiss, could also procure documents, and Mr. Hiss replied that he did not know whether or not his brother was yet sufficiently developed for such work. Colonel Bykov said perhaps he can persuade him." Chambers remembers this well "Because Colonel Bykov spoke German with a very thick accent and the German word for persuade is 'uberreden,' and Colonel Bykov mangled the word so badly that I had difficulty in understanding him and I saw Mr. Hiss look at me curiously wondering why I could not understand the Colonel better." (Ibid.)

In the Baltimore Deposition, Chambers told the Bykov story with different dates: "In August or early fall of 1937, I arranged a meeting between Alger Hiss and Colonel Bykov."

Another item in the Bykov story is demonstrably false: Donald Hiss did not enter the State Department until February 1, 1938.

Apart from these, there are even more serious inconsistencies in Chambers' story about his "superior" Bykov. In an FBI report of an interview with Chambers on June 26, 1945, the FBI investigator wrote that Chambers had told him: "Other people whom he met while in the company of Peter included an individual who was later identified to him as Boris Bykov by Krivitsky. He recalled that during 1936 he met Peter one time in a theatre which he could not recall. Peter was accompanied by a man 5 feet 7 inches tall, red hair, slightly baldy, Jewish, very sloppy appearance, who spoke very little English and poor German, was apparently 36–37 years old in 1937." Chambers explained that Peter introduced him to this man, giving him some first name he could not recall. Chambers "sensed" that this man was connected with OGPU (Russian Intelligence) because he believed he had been introduced to the man so that the latter could size up Chambers. It was his impression that these men may have been secret agents of Peter who were instructed to check up on Chambers' activities and his personal life. (Trial Transcript, pp. 558, 559.)

In the FBI interview it was Peter who was in a theater with Bykov and there introduced Bykov to Chambers; in his later version it was Chambers who took Hiss to a theater and then introduced him to Bykov.

And there is further evidence, in Wadleigh's testimony, that Chambers story about Bykov and Hiss is a product of Chambers' imagination. Wadleigh testified that Chambers introduced him to "Sasha" and intimated that Sasha was Chambers' "boss in the apparatus." Chambers identified Sasha with Bykov as he had to do if he was to avoid attributing two heads to the same apparatus. (Ibid., p. 408.) The boss, whom Wadleigh met, had only one arm: Bykov had two.

[6] HUAC Hearings, pp. 1285–86.

When asked during the House Committee hearings what his salary had been, Chambers answered, "I think it was more than six thousand." "Than six thousand a year?" Nixon asked. "Yes," replied Chambers and voluntarily added:

I would say that this is a spectacular instance of the ease with which a Communist could at all times slide other Communists into practically any Government agency in which they had a foothold.[7]

Soon after he began working for the government, he says in *Witness,* he told Alger Hiss "and others" of his "cover" job, not mentioning his real purpose or that he was using his real name because

I thought that the knowledge might give them pause, if, after I broke, they were moved by zeal (or by others) to attempt reprisals against me. Hiss laughed when I told him: it was the capstone of the legend of "Carl's" Bolshevik daring. "I suppose you will turn up in the State Department next," he said. I kept the job only long enough to establish the fact that I had it, three or four months.

Upon leaving the government job, only "two or three weeks" passed, he testified to the committee, before he completely severed his relationship with the Communist Party and disappeared.

The government documents on Chambers' position with the National Research Project (a branch of the WPA) reveal a different story. On September 30, 1937, A. G. Silverman submitted to his superiors in the National Research Project a "Requisition for Personnel." The position was for a male editorial and research assistant, thirty-six years of age, with a suggested salary of $160 per month. Immediately thereafter Chambers filed an official application for a government position under the name of Jay V. David Chambers, in which he stated he desired a position, at once, as editorial and research assistant. As salary, he desired $200 per month, with a minimum of $160.

On the application he was asked to state his education and employment record. Under the former he wrote:

Lynbrook, L.I.?   1908–1915   Diploma: Yes
Rockville Centre, N.Y.   1915–1919   Diploma: Yes
Summer courses, University of Brussels, Belgium, 1920

Below this he listed his employment record:

	Employer		*Reason for leaving*
1935– 1937	Robert Cantwell Fortune Magazine,	Research for industrial articles on steel, rail-	$150

[7] *Ibid.,* p. 1287.

	Employer			Reason for leaving
	135 E. 42 St. NYC	roads, shipping, oil, etc.		
1930–1935	Maxim Lieber Publishers' Agent 545 5th Ave.	Complete editorial charge; Managing editor of American Feature Syndicate	$200	Business slack; syndicate failed
1926–1930	Elizabeth Nowell Publishers' Agent 114 E. 56th St. NYC	Complete editorial charge	$175	Left for better job
1923–1926	Reuben J. Shemitz 276 5th Ave. NYC	Personal investigator	$100	Distasteful job
1922	Unemployed			
1920–1921	Residence in Germany, Belgium France	Travel and Study		

Aside from the obvious falsifications, equally conspicuous, by their absence, are the facts that he studied at Columbia University intermittently from 1920 to 1925 and that he was employed at the New York Public Library from September 1923 to April 1927, except for a period of absence from July 1925 to January 1926.

On October 15, 1937, almost two weeks after he submitted his application, Chambers was approved for a position of "report editor," "to help in the preparation of manuscripts for publication and in other ways to facilitate the completion of the reports on the History of Technology." His salary was $2000 a year.[8] On October 17 he took his Oath of Office and began work the next day. He merely held a white-collar relief job, paid for from an Emergency Relief Appropriation. It was scarcely a case of Communists sliding into practically any government agency. And it could hardly have been of much interest to a man of his literary ability. As he later testified: "I sat in the offices and made up some kind of an index." [9]

---

[8] Immediately upon hearing Chambers' story for the first time, and before he was able to consult any of the official government records, Mr. McDowell of the House Committee felt moved to say: "As I recall the days of 1937, the country was in rather desperate straits. Millions were out of work. Hundreds of thousands of some of the finest people of the country were raking leaves for $50.00, $59.50, and so forth, and a Communist could slide in the Government on the feeblest, phoniest excuse for work at $6000. It is a curious thing." (HUAC Hearings, p. 1289.)
[9] HUAC Hearings, p. 1288.

Chambers remained at his job for three and a half months. However, he did not leave government service voluntarily, as he stated. Because of lack of work he was furloughed and then his position was terminated.

February 23, 1938

Mr. Jay V. David Chambers
2124 Mount Royal Terrace
Baltimore, Maryland

Dear Mr. Chambers:

Due to the reduction in volume of work you have been furloughed without prejudice from the position of Report Editor for the period February 1, 1938, to the close of business, June 30, 1938. If by June 30, 1938, no opening has occurred for which you are deemed qualified, your furlough status will be changed to a termination. Your last working day was January 31, 1938. . . .

Janet L. Wile
Senior Administrative Secretary
For the Director [10]

At the time he applied for the government job Chambers, by his own assertion, had undergone a transformation of mind and, within himself, was no longer a fanatical Communist. "I would describe myself as a deserter to [sic] the Communist Party," he said at the second trial. Furthermore, he had undergone a profound religious experience at Mount Royal Terrace, after which, he declaimed, "I no longer groped for God; I felt God." He had given his life to God and Freedom: ". . . I gave my promise, not with the mind, but with my whole being, and that this was a covenant that might not break."

In his quest to establish a new identity (another imposturous one, despite his use of the name Chambers) and to gratify his need for omnipotence, Chambers managed to deceive everyone—the United States Government, his Communist superiors, in later years, the readers of *Witness,* and, no doubt, himself.

Very shortly after the termination of his government job, he tells us, he broke from the Communist underground. He and his family left their house in

---

[10] In relation to the controversy over the date of his alleged break with the Communist Party, the date of this letter is indeed significant. Chambers' job terminated on January 31, 1938. At various times he testified that he left the party "two or three weeks" or "very shortly thereafter." In no way is this consonant with the testimony that he gave for the first time only in the *fall* of 1948, that the date of his break was April 15, 1938, two and a half months after he left his government job. On August 3, 1948, in a prepared statement and in subsequent answers to questions, he said that he left the party in 1937. It was not until August 28 that he said he left in "1938—early 1938." The date April 15, 1938, did not appear until either the grand jury testimony or the trial, at least not until after he produced the Baltimore documents, the last of which was dated April 15, 1938.

Mount Royal Terrace and moved to a small flat on Old Court Road near Baltimore. In fear of his life, he kept the shades drawn and sat vigil through the night. "We had somewhat the feeling of sitting in a sandbagged dugout," he writes. He carried a knife. In this hideaway he stayed with his family for about a month. There are discrepancies about the duration of this period, for, in another version, Chambers stated that for *a whole year* he sat with a shotgun in his lap every night. Having cut himself off as a paid functionary of the Communist Party, he was without any source of income. As always, when he was in dire straits, he searched for translation work. He remained at Old Court Road until he "had a translation job to do." This work he obtained in New York. Some time around March 1938 he called on his friend Meyer Schapiro, who introduced him to Paul Willert of the Oxford University Press. Willert gave him Gumpert's "Dunant—the Story of the Red Cross," and an advance.

And now the Chamberses were ready to move:

Our rooms were uncomfortable, our nerves were so raw that the sense of freedom, like a rebirth, that had possessed us when I broke with the Communist Party was wearing thin in furtive isolation. All of us needed a complete change. Tactically, too, perhaps, this was the moment to leave Baltimore and emerge somewhere else. It must be some miscellaneous place, where new arrivals make no stir.

And so, as he has testified, "as soon as I had the translation and the advance I went to Florida to Daytona Beach where I believe I finished the translation." [11]

They rented a bungalow on the beach. Mrs. Chambers watched over the children by day and "kept a hatchet under [her] pillow at night."

We resumed our security routine at once. . . . I sat up all night, translating. The very first night, I heard a sound of footsteps under the window. . . . I stopped work, put out the light and spent the rest of the night watching in the dark. This happened several nights in succession. I did not even know how to go about procuring a gun. I was desperate for one.

On the third or fourth day, my neighbor in the next bungalow knocked at the door. He was holding a revolver. "There are people prowling around these bungalows at night," he said. "Would you mind keeping this gun, and if you hear anybody, come out shooting and I'll come out shooting?" . . . I took the revolver with something more than gratitude to my neighbor. Thereafter, I worked with the heavy gun lying on the table beside my typewriter. . . . But the prowlers were not the G.P.U.

How easily Chambers thus dismisses the entire episode with no further anxiety or introspective curiosity of the great turmoil that had raged within

[11] Trial Transcript, p. 265.

him. He simply goes on to say that "some gang had been looting the nearby houses."

It is significant, also, that the four elements Chambers repeatedly stated were necessary as "life-preservers" are all represented here—a gun, money, the making of a document (a translation, a typewriter), and a car.

The Chamberses stayed in Florida "exactly a month" and then returned to their small flat on Old Court Road in Baltimore. Chambers had decided, after finishing the translation in Florida, that he was ready to come out of hiding. After their return to Baltimore they bought a house on St. Paul Street, moved from Old Court Road, and resumed the name of Chambers.

Mark Van Doren has provided a revealing glimpse of Chambers' frenetic movements during this period. Van Doren had not seen or heard from him for ten years.

Then in October [1938], back in New York, Whittaker Chambers showed up. He called from Pennsylvania Station one evening to say he must see me—alone, for he was in danger. What sort of danger? He would tell me when he came. Dorothy was at home, and Hedwig Koenig had been with us for dinner; but I must take him directly upstairs to my study on the third floor, where he would make everything clear. What he told me was that he had left the Communist Party, which because he had left it, and because he knew so many of its secrets—its plots, its murders, its misdeeds of every kind—was after him to kill him. What I could do for him was this: I could help him to become known again in the world out of which he had disappeared ten years before—from my sight, as I have said, and from the sight of everyone I knew. Now he was anonymous, so that if murdered he would not be missed. Even one review in a reputable paper would reinstate him in society; I must write a letter for him, recommending him to literary editors. He was so mysterious about all this, and overstated things, I thought, so laughably in the old way, that I teased him a little, reminding him among other things that as a result of his dark life for a decade I knew nothing about him. I ended up, however, by writing such a letter and giving it to him; he slipped downstairs; and I never saw his face again until it appeared in the photographs which every reader of newspapers was to be familiar with after ten more years had passed.[12]

Thus Chambers secured, with his familiar powers of conspiratorial persuasion, a document that he felt would permit his re-entry into the world. What use he made of it is unknown; it perhaps fulfilled only a magical function as still another "life-preserver."

Just after his break from the underground, so he tells us in *Witness,* the Communist Party made two attempts to track him down. One was a visit by Miss Grace Hutchins to the office of his brother-in-law, Reuben Shemitz, a lawyer in New York. (Miss Hutchins, a well-known member of the Commu-

---

[12] Mark Van Doren, *Autobiography of Mark Van Doren* (New York: Harcourt, Brace & Co., 1958), pp. 218–19.

nist Party, had been its official candidate in various election campaigns. Chambers describes her as a woman vitally connected with the underground even though she was a well-known political figure in the open party, and alleges that she had had several contacts with him in her capacity as underground worker.) Shemitz was not in his office, Chambers reports, and Miss Hutchins left a note. He continues:

I have never seen the note. My brother-in-law prudently never showed it to me. He turned it over to the FBI during the Hiss Case.

But I know that the note said something very close to this: "Tell Esther's husband to contact Steve at once. Very urgent." . . . Steve is Alexander Stevens, alias J. Peters, the head of the underground section of the American Communist Party.

With no word from Chambers, Miss Hutchins allegedly called again at Mr. Shemitz's office several mornings later. "If you will agree to turn Chambers over to us," she said, "the party will guarantee the safety of your sister and the children." When Mr. Shemitz explained that he had no idea where any of them were located, Miss Huchins stared at him and exclaimed, "If he does not show up by [such and such a day] . . . he will be killed."

On August 28, 1946, Chambers was interviewed by Ray Murphy, security officer of the State Department. Murphy's report records that Chambers had given a different account of this story:

After [Chambers'] break with the party, Grace Hutchins telephoned the mother of my informant (Mrs. Chambers) on Long Island one night and said that if he did not return to the party by the following Thursday it was a question of his death.

In *Witness,* Chambers makes no mention of this call, as in Murphy's memorandum there is no mention of Mr. Shemitz.

Miss Hutchins was interviewed in 1949, 1951, and again in 1957 about her contacts with Chambers.[13] Her story, like many others which have come directly from friends and acquaintances of Chambers, reveals an entirely different relationship from that described by Chambers.

Grace Hutchins knew Chambers through Esther Shemitz, with whom she had worked in the early twenties on the *World Tomorrow.* At Esther's request, Miss Hutchins was present as a witness at her wedding. Some months after Chambers had left the *New Masses* in 1932 and had been out of sight for some time, he appeared at Miss Hutchins' office, saying that he was doing "highly special underground work." Miss Hutchins said that she was completely taken in by him and didn't ask any questions. But the real purpose of

[13] From memoranda of interviews with Grace Hutchins by Elinor Ferry, October 20, 1951; and an interview with William Reuben, May 1957, and the investigative files of Chester Lane, January 21, 1949.

his visit was to borrow fifty dollars so that he could get his teeth fixed. Miss Hutchins recalled that his teeth were abominable, and Chambers told her that the importance of his work demanded that he make a good appearance.

They made an arrangement to meet again at Wanamaker's on Eighth Street for lunch:

I can see the very table at Wanamaker's where I met him and we talked. . . . In those days I did not have much money. My mother had not died and I had only a modest allowance. Fifty dollars looked like a lot of money. But I did lend him the fifty. He never made any attempt to return it or even mentioned it again.

At that luncheon, Miss Hutchins recalls, Chambers told her a horror story about a woman who had not cooperated with the underground. She remembers his zeal, how he "leaned over and looked at [her] very searchingly to see what kind of reaction [she] would have to this real horror story." It concerned a "comrade" who had betrayed the underground. The underground took revenge by putting her inside a wall of a building and cementing her in. In any event, Chambers again convinced her that at that time he was in the underground.

She did not see the Chamberses for several years. Wondering where they were and wishing to get her fifty dollars back, she did indeed pay a visit to Chambers' brother-in-law in an attempt to collect her money. But, she said,

I am almost certain that this was in 1937. When the FBI came to me and questioned me about it, they said they had a note I left. I asked if I might see it. I was not even sure if I had left a note, and wanted to see if it were my handwriting, and what it contained. They said, they didn't have it with them.

They never showed me the note. It is still in the possession of the FBI for all I know. There is something funny about that note. Clearly they did not want me to see it.

If I could see that note, it might be that it had a date on it, and that the date would prove that it was 1937, not 1938, that he made what he described as his break with the Communist Party. The question of the date is crucial, and that might provide a key.

Thus Chambers imposed himself on Miss Hutchins. By using real people and real events as material, he fused fact and fantasy. His purpose was to convince the reader, as he was convinced, that the Communist Party clearly intended to kill him.

In his account of how and why he later told his story of Communist activity in government to Assistant Secretary of State Berle, Chambers raises the question of whether an ex-Communist deserves immunity. In universal terms (war, history, the crisis of the twentieth century) he decides that an ex-Communist has the right to claim it, for his first task is to preserve himself.

Sometimes, he can even enjoy such immunity, if he is able to feel what is happening to him in the simplest terms, impersonally, as an experience of history and of war in which he at last has found his bearings and which he is helping to wage.

He concludes on a personal note:

I never asked for immunity. . . . What immunity can the world offer a man against his thoughts?
And so I went to see Adolf Berle.

Again, his story is at variance with the direct accounts of those with whom he dealt. Chambers stresses that he was acting out of conscience, that his real concern was duty, not immunity from prosecution. Both Herbert Solow and Isaac Don Levine were intimately connected with the events that led to Chambers' conversation with Berle, and I am indebted to them for their informative help in this area.

It was to Solow—a former Columbia classmate and a journalist—that Chambers first went with his combined confession and exposé:

[Chambers] sought me out, told me that he was breaking with the Party, and had a manuscript [14] he wanted me to market for him. It was always an ambigous matter with Chambers, i.e., about his Communist activities. Had I been asked to prove that he was engaged in underground activities, I would have been unable to do so. Either he was engaged in underground activities or he wished he was. He needed help and he wanted me to arrange a meeting with the President of the United States in order to make a deal with the President in which he would reveal secret information of a very important nature, the possession of which could get him in trouble, in exchange for which he wanted immunity. I did not know President Roosevelt, but felt "I must do what I can." I made several abortive efforts to contact people who might lead toward the White House. I hit upon Isaac Don Levine, who was then a well-known journalist, a strong person who did not just toy with ultra-rightism. I felt that Mr. Levine was savvy and would not blunder. I arranged the meeting with Isaac Don Levine.[15]

From this account it is clear that patriotic duty ranked low in Chambers' concerns. Solow also expressed some doubt about the reality of Chambers' fears of reprisal by the Communist Party.

The manuscript Chambers showed Solow was signed "Carl." This fact in itself was an indictment of Chambers' veracity. At the very time when he was

[14] During 1938 Solow was working on an article, published in 1939 in *American Mercury,* titled "Stalin's American Passport Mill." Chambers' manuscript, Solow states, was very similar to his story. But in Solow's article the people were real and the facts were documented. In Chambers' manuscript everything was disguised and pseudonymous. Solow said that his article owed nothing to Chambers and was based on independent work. When Chambers came to him wanting to sell his story, Solow told him that, though his facts might be true, no responsible editor would publish such an article unless the real names were given.
[15] Personal interviews, May 10, 11, 1962.

so afraid of being caught by the Soviet Secret Police after his "break," why would he want to market an article on Soviet espionage and false passports signed by his operational underground name "Carl"? As Solow pointed out, the whole idea of the manuscript and the pseudonym was an impractical one. People would of course ask, "Who is Carl?" It would, moreover, expose Chambers as an open target to those very forces from whom he was then hiding. But Chambers was in dire straits. He was in need of money and driven by persecutory fears. Unrealistic as it was, this was his private way of establishing an existence.

Isaac Don Levine confirms Solow's impressions of Chambers' motivations. Levine recalls that Chambers first came to his office (Levine was then editor of *Plain Talk,* a rightist, anti-Communist magazine) sometime in the "mid-thirties" with a story titled "The Disillusionment of a Communist."

Levine told Chambers that the manuscript was too vague (no real names were used) and it would be meaningless to publish it unless Chambers was willing to expose the conspiratorial activities of the underground in a definitive way. Chambers was too frightened to reveal whatever factual knowledge he had. He feared being arrested by the United States Government for his recent espionage activities. The period covered by the statute of limitations, after which time he would be immune, had not yet run its course. Levine stressed the fact that Chambers did not offer him any secrets or information important to the national welfare. Levine emphasized that the manuscript was not written out of any patriotic motive or deep sense of loyalty to the United States.

Within a few days after the signing of the Hitler-Stalin Pact, Levine realistically feared that secret State Department military or political information obtained by Russian spies prior to that time would be turned over to the Nazis. He therefore called again upon Chambers, who by then was working as a book reviewer on *Time* magazine, and implored him to reveal whatever information he had in the interest of national security. Chambers was triply threatened: he feared reprisals from the NKVD, he feared arrest by the Department of Justice, and he feared for his newly found identity with *Time*. It should be equally emphasized that Chambers' possession of highly secret knowledge—which he claimed was important for the national security—surrounded him with an aura of mystery and provided him with a feeling of self-importance.

Chambers said again that he would tell his story to the President of the United States. He later wrote:

It seemed to me that in a matter so grave, touching the security of the country at top levels of the Government, the President was the man who should first hear the facts and decide where to go from there. I told Levine that, if he would arrange the meeting, I would cooperate.

But it seems more than plausible that this was a bluff, that he knew that the chances of a meeting with the President were slight. Levine emphasized that Chambers' main concern was for his own safety; Chambers wanted reassurance that he would not be indicted. Levine did not arrange a meeting with Roosevelt, but he did contact Assistant Secretary of State Berle (then chief security officer for the State Department). Having earlier committed himself to Levine, in his need to sell a story at a time when he was destitute and in flight, Chambers had no recourse but to continue. In September 1939 Levine took a reluctant Chambers, as Levine described it, "by the arm" to the home of Berle. Had it not been for Levine's insistence (which included his own journalistic aspirations for a sensational scoop), one can only speculate whether Chambers might ever have told his story as he did.

As a result of his meeting with Berle, Chambers found himself in another crisis, for he had no way of knowing just what the Assistant Secretary of State would do with the information. His apprehensions returned:

The same night that I talked with Berle, I returned to New York. For the second time in two years, I had laid my life in ruins. I had only to wait for what would happen next. One of the things most likely to happen, it seemed to me, was my arrest.

And now Chambers was a harried man, no longer in fear of the Soviet Police but of the United States Government. He continues:

But nothing at all happened. Weeks passed into months. I went about my work at *Time*. . . . The thought crossed my mind that the story [that President Roosevelt had laughed on hearing Chambers' story from Berle] might have been put out to conceal the Government's real purpose. Surveillance and investigation were necessary. It might be some time before the Government was prepared to act. Meanwhile, it would watch and check.

I tried to believe that that was the fact. But I knew that it could not be, for if the Government were checking, it would not fail also to check with me.

And, to be sure, Chambers was visited by agents of the FBI as early as 1941.

A new suspiciousness and apprehension took root and grew in Chambers' thoughts in relation to President Roosevelt and the New Deal administration. This became the "concealed" enemy, for the United States Government, he felt, now controlled his fate.

And with astonishment I took my first hard look at the New Deal. . . . I saw that . . . the New Deal was a genuine revolution, whose deepest purpose was not simply reform within existing traditions, but a basic change in the social, and, above all, the power relationships within the nation. It was not a revolution by violence. It was a revolution by bookkeeping and lawmaking.

And after stating his political case, the unconscious motive of which is to prove to himself that there existed a concealed enemy ready to persecute him, he built up his personal case against the government.

I felt, too, that a persistent effort by any man to expose the Communists in Government was much less likely to lead to their exposure than to reprisals against him. That fact must be borne constantly in mind in understanding what I did and did not do in the next nine years, and indeed throughout the Hiss case, which was to prove on a vast scale how well-founded my fears had been.

One of my close friends, himself an ardent New Dealer, who knew my story in full detail, summed up the situation tersely. "I see," he said one day, "why it might not pay the Communists to kill you at this point. But I don't see how the Administration dares to leave you alive."

Having been examined at some length by the government during the early forties, Chambers was disturbed also by the thought that the government did not act on his information. It would seem that he had to account for this in *Witness,* hence the implication that the government was pro-Communist.

After Chambers' startling accusation—that people "high in Government" were members of a Communist underground cell in Washington—and his "shot-gun" naming of government employees, as recorded in Berle's notes, he lived in apprehension of the consequences of his act (and, apparently, was also apprehensive because there were no consequences). It would be highly unrealistic to assume, as Chambers did, that Berle, Assistant Secretary of State and security officer for the State Department, would do nothing about this matter. Later reports have shown that Berle took the information at once to President Roosevelt. Some time thereafter (exactly when is not known) the matter was turned over to the FBI. Just what Roosevelt said to Berle is not known; it has been variously reported, depending upon the political bias of the reporter. In his book *The Web of Subversion,* James Burnham states that the President "laughed it off." Chambers quotes the President's words (though he was, of course, not there) in more ominous language:

When Berle was insistent, he had been told in words (by Roosevelt) which it is necessary to paraphrase, to "go jump in the lake."

It is important to digress briefly from our continuing analysis of Chambers' use of literary rhetoric and his personal estimate of his own role in the "march of history" in order to point up some of Hiss's privately expressed and public statements which document his political posture and his opinions about international affairs during this same period (1938–39). It is revealing and ironical that, after the Hitler-Stalin Pact, while Chambers was privately accusing both Hiss brothers of being Communist Party members, Hiss was voluntarily preparing a memorandum for submission to Secretary of State Cordell Hull, dated September 26, 1939, written not as an assignment from that Department but on his own initiative (in answer to letters from Professor Charles C. Hyde and Professor Phillip Jessup of Columbia University to the *New York Times* in September 1939). In his memorandum Hiss advocated a "strict neutral position on the part of the United States." He took the position that "international law did not require the United States to take a position of neutrality as between the Allies and the Nazis," and that "the United States could, without violating international law, aid the Allies." This could hardly be interpreted as the political attitude of a Communist or fellow traveler, for American aid to the Allies was at that time anti-Russian as well as anti-Nazi.[16]

There is no official record available to confirm exactly when Chambers was first called upon by the FBI. According to his own account, it was not until 1941, when two special agents of the FBI visited him in his office at *Time*. Chambers had by this time established himself as a valuable staff member of *Time* ("a few days after my first visit by the FBI, I was made a senior editor of *Time*"), and were it not for what he collectively attributes to "my sins in the past," especially his most recent one, the "Berle failure," "he would have preferred," Solow emphasized, "to let by-gones be by-gones." But, on a deeper level, he had a private score to settle with his conscience, and, superficially, a recent political one with the United States Government. The former had to be appeased of its guilt, and to the latter he now owed a careful explanation of the wholesale accusations he had made in 1939. He

---

[16] William Marbury's close association and friendship with Hiss through the years have provided a continuing source of data regarding Hiss's opinions and ideology. From 1935 to 1940 Marbury and Hiss corresponded on various matters. They saw each other several times a year, either in Washington or Baltimore; on these occasions they had dinner at each other's home, went on to a concert or musical soirée. They were both very interested in the decisions of the Supreme Court affecting New Deal legislation and talked about these matters whenever they met. Marbury says, "Alger followed the Holmes line, but he was certainly not an extremist in his views. . . . I had a number of talks and correspondence with Alger on neutrality matters during 1938 and 1939. . . . I remember once his saying that he did not think that war would be the end of our civilization and that we must stand for collective security even at the risk of another war. At the time of the repeal of the Neutrality Act, I had some correspondence with him. This was shortly after the war in Europe had begun, and you will see from one of Alger's letters that he was not following the party line at that time."

Hiss wrote to Marbury, in one of their many exchanges: "I feel strongly that the whole concept of neutrality is inexactly defined. The word is used ambiguously and without the usual rigorous analysis. There are so few actual arbitral decisions that the development of neutrality is largely the product of text writers—and you know how inaccurate they can become." (Personal memorandum by William Marbury, December 1948).

needed a new "life-preserver." If only he had not gone to Solow and Levine in the first place to sell his spy stories! But he could not undo the consequences of his act. He had to seek refuge in the identity of the saint. He saw himself, as he now saw all men and women, "tortured by destiny."

Solow, who knew Chambers well during those troubled years, explains Chambers' predicament in 1948 in a more matter-of-fact way:

Chambers went to testify with utmost reluctance, having landed a good job at *Time* and making a big success and a good salary. He had a wife and two children, and the farm. . . . I think Chambers had resigned from the Messiah business. That's why he made no effort for nine years to do anything about this, and why he went reluctantly in 1948. So why didn't he refuse to testify, particularly about Hiss? Because he couldn't; he was hooked by the Berle memorandum and the knowledge that Levine had. He had to testify.[17]

Chambers had trapped himself with his own actions and his own embellishments of certain facts. He had interposed himself between the State Department and the FBI and assumed (for now Roosevelt and the New Deal had become the concealed enemy) that the FBI had never seen or heard of the Berle notes. When called upon by an FBI agent in the early forties,

I said that before I could answer his questions, I must first make a telephone call. The agent objected, but I insisted. I asked the *Time* operator to get me Adolf A. Berle at the State Department. The call went through at once. "Mr. Berle," I said, "there are two FBI agents in my office. Have I your permission to tell them what I told you in 1939?" There was a moment's pause at the State Department end of the wire. "Of course," said Berle, "of course."

"Thank you," I said. . . .

The FBI had not come to me because of my conversation with Berle, but for an entirely different reason. My old friend, Ludwig Lore, had denounced me—a fact that I did not learn from the FBI, but from another security agency of the Government.

It is significant that Chambers rationalized and brought out of his past an old Communist friend, Ludwig Lore (then dead), to blame as the reason for the FBI visit. Since he did not know exactly when or whether the information he had secretly given to Berle in 1939 had been turned over to the FBI, he preferred to believe that it was not Berle's talk with Roosevelt that had alerted the FBI—for this idea was not in accord with his need to regard the New Deal as the concealed enemy harboring Communists in government.

Once the FBI *had* contacted him, Chambers fortified his position with them by *further* informing:

[17] And, to be sure, Isaac Don Levine, an avowed rightist journalist, was "breathing down Chambers' neck."

I told Special Agent Smith [18] that in talking to Berle, I had omitted the names of Harry Dexter White and George Silverman. . . . In those days I did not know what degree of control the Administration exercised over the FBI, about which, in fact, I knew almost nothing. But by then I was certain that the Administration was more interested in suppressing my story than in discovering the facts. From what I knew of history and politics, I did not doubt for a moment that it would resort to any feasible means to suppress them. Therefore, I told Special Agent Smith that I would meet him at any time in my office, but nowhere else. . . .

Special Agent Smith promised to be back in a few days. I never saw those special agents again. In fact, I did not see another agent of the FBI for almost a year, and then only for a few moments. After that, I did not see another FBI agent for almost two years.

[18] A pseudonym used by Chambers in *Witness,* because, he explained, "I have forgotten his name."

16

Persecution

CHAMBERS WAS NOW BESET with fresh anxiety. He did not know what to expect from the FBI. Were they on his side or not? Did they regard him as a trusted informer or was he himself under surveillance?

Despite his apprehensions, by virtue of his great capacity for hard work and his skill in handling different assignments, his position at *Time* solidified ("I wrote with a new ease and authority"). The pressure of work and routine demands on his time and energies were indeed great. But equally, if not more taxing was the obsessive force within him, the guilt that directed his job at *Time* into a self-destructive campaign. Reports from former associates at *Time,* together with his own account in *Witness,* leave no doubt that Chambers, in and out of the office, was heading down a collision course:

But I found *Time*'s five-day week too short for my writing needs. I began the practice of working through a day, a night and the following day without sleep, that I was to follow (with one enforced interruption) throughout my years at *Time.*

And now he drew into the orbit of this killing schedule his "closest" friend and ultimate victim, the pliable Calvin Fixx:

As my immediate assistant, I had chosen my closest friend at *Time,* the late Calvin Fixx . . . one of the wisest, gentlest and mellowest souls I will ever know. . . . Often we ended our week at four o'clock in the morning after having worked for thirty-six hours, almost without stopping and wholly without sleep. We kept up the pace by smoking five or six packs of cigarettes and drinking thirteen or fourteen cups of coffee a day.

It was not long before Fixx suffered a physical collapse:

One night, some of our colleagues found Fixx wandering dazedly on the street. His heart had given out.

As Chambers reports, he exposes his own involvement and his feeling of responsibility for Fixx's destruction; he goes on to describe how

My turn came a few weeks after Fixx's. For some time I had suffered intermittently from pains that began in my chest and shot down my left arm. Friends
urged me to go to a doctor. I kept putting it off. But when at last pain forced me to
go, the doctor diagnosed angina pectoris and ordered immediate, absolute rest.

Chambers' period of physical incapacity was unduly protracted; the entire clinical picture and the course of his illness had some notable features.
Contrary to his own report in *Witness,* the basis of his symptoms, in the joint
opinion of his attending physician and a consultant, was essentially "nerves,"
caused by emotional strain and physical neglect. In a detailed clinical report
of her examination of Chambers, his physician noted:

I attended Mr. J. D. W. Chambers from Oct. 28, 1942, to May 1, 1943. The
angina-like sensations which he had . . . were probably not true angina. There was
no detectable aftereffect on the heart muscle or on any other cardiac component as
judged either by examination or by electrocardiography. I believe there is ample
explanation for this illness on the ground of extreme exhaustion, worry, overstrain
of every nerve and quite insufficient sleep. . . .
He began to work on his farm May, 1943, and was back in his office about
July 7, 1943.[1]

A Baltimore consultant concurred in the diagnosis. She alluded to his
emotional state and pointed up that Chambers was "very disturbed about the
future of the world." "Frankly," she concluded, "I do not believe he has
angina," and recommended, "Obviously, he should have his filthy mouth
cleaned up—I suggest 4 or 5 teeth be pulled with novocaine—and he was
given advice about dentures." [2]

In his own account in *Witness,* what he remembers was how critically
ill—in fact, how close to death—he was at that time ("my doctor's orders
were not to move my hands or arms even to shave"), and then unabashedly
notes, "a specialist later rejected the diagnosis of angina."

By juxtaposing his description of the circumstances of Calvin Fixx's
cardiac collapse and death from heart failure at a later date, Chambers
equates the reasons for his own collapse with that of his friend. In his mind
the two events were closely linked. His period of enforced immobility, ordered by his doctor, which, writes Chambers, followed by "a few weeks" the
breakdown of his "closest friend," has the clinical features of psychological
simulation. This entire episode is reminiscent of, if not identical with, an
earlier one—the "paralysis of the will" he suffered after his brother's suicide.
On both occasions his own collapse followed the death of someone he loved

[1] Report of Dr. E. Reese Wilkens, Westminister, Maryland, dated 2/14/44 (Hiss Defense Files).
[2] From a report by Dr. E. W. Bridgman, 11 S. Charles St., Baltimore, Md., dated 4/12/43
(Hiss Defense Files).

and in whose destruction he played a part. After a period of self-imposed suffering during which he acts out his own death, and with his conscience once again assuaged, he grants himself a reprieve.[3]

Chambers' affliction, from the time he first noticed the symptoms until his recovery, lasted nine months—August 1942 until May 1943 (corresponding to the period of gestation). Having passed through another symbolic death, was he ready to be reborn?

In retrospect, Chambers vehemently denied the possible role of any "nervous or mental" component in either his 1944 illness or in subsequent similar episodes. In any case, clinical reports both in 1942 and 1943 (and again in 1949 during the Hiss trials) revealed no evidence of heart disease.

Another physician who had treated Chambers for several months during the years 1949–50 told me of his experience with him during that period. Chambers had been referred to him by a colleague at *Time*. He had been having occasional bouts of lower chest pain. Physical examination and diagnostic studies showed no evidence of organic heart disease. Chambers' distress was not due to his heart (the EKG was normal). It was caused by overeating, too much smoking, and the stresses of a habitually irregular life. It was evident that Chambers was emotionally disturbed. "The most striking feature about Whittaker Chambers," said Doctor L.,[4] "was his compelling need to talk about the subject of Communism and its immediate dangers. He brought up this subject at every visit." Doctor L. recalled one Friday afternoon visit; Chambers was his last patient, and he allowed him to continue talking. The visit lasted for almost three hours. "It was easy to listen to him, though I was not particularly interested in the subject." The hour was late, but Chambers was reluctant to leave. He then invited Doctor L. to fly down with him to his Maryland farm for the weekend; the invitation was declined.

Doctor L. stated that Chambers saw him several times during the Hiss trials. He especially remembered one such visit during the second trial. The evening of the day Chambers had been to see him Doctor L. read a news report of the day's court proceedings in the evening paper. "I was startled," said Doctor L., "to read that Chambers had, on that same afternoon, within a few hours after he left my office, testified under oath that he had not seen a

---

[3] It is impressive that Chambers in *Witness* gratuitously comments, "He [Fixx] died while I was testifying during the Hiss Case." We know how Chambers put himself through a suicide ritual just prior to testifying (turning over the documents) against Hiss. And, again, as with his brother Richard, it was Fixx who "took the long journey alone."

Max Ascoli, in his review of *Witness,* titled it, "The Lives and Deaths of Whittaker Chambers" (*The Reporter,* July 8, 1952).

[4] My informant, a highly regarded New York specialist in internal medicine, asked that his name be withheld.

doctor for six months." He concluded: "I knew, of course, that he lied. How could I possibly believe any of the other things he said?" [5]

Chambers himself later adduced: ". . . it seemed impossible that I could have lived through the Hiss case if my heart had been ailing." Nevertheless he would insist that

There was no trace even of nervous breakdown, let alone mental collapse, so that it became impossible for the defense to use the story in court though it was fed out widely as a rumor.

After Chambers' first accusation before the House Committee on Un-American Activities, Hiss, on several occasions, asked whether they had looked into the matter of Chambers' mental competency. There had been several rumors that he had been a patient in a mental institution; none could be substantiated. But Chambers remained exquisitely sensitive to anyone's thinking that he may have had a mental illness. His fits of melancholia were for him a "paralysis of the will." Or else he thought of them in religious or mystical terms ("The world has lost its soul"). He shunned any hint, scoffed at the validity of any reference to him that might be construed as "psychiatric." During the first Hiss trial the question of the admissibility of psychiatric testimony to impeach or establish the mental credibility of a witness was argued. Chambers writes about this in *Witness,* alluding to a "syndicated news columnist" who "electrified his millions of readers" by asking, "Was that Whittaker Chambers who was seen leaving a Park Avenue psychiatrist's office?" There is vehemence mixed with his irony as he rebuts this remark: "At the time I was in Maryland, a fact that could have been checked instantly by telephoning me."

In his magical thinking it is quite conceivable for him to believe that millions of people would be electrified to learn that he had visited a psychiatrist's office, though the belief is hardly short of delusional. But such grandiosity is an integral part of Chambers' paranoia. At any rate, this readiness to protect the integrity of his mental state is self-evident.

In the life of Chambers each period of success had to be neutralized by a corresponding period of illness or failure. Suffering, deprivation, and creative work represented bribes to be paid to his threatening conscience. He imposed upon himself a physically exhausting, self-punitive work schedule. An ordin-

---

[5] As Chambers' private physician in 1949–50, Doctor L., for professional and other cogent reasons, did not wish to appear publicly in a celebrated political trial. After sixteen years of silence he feels that, for the historical record, he has no objection to the above facts being published about his former (and now deceased) patient. (Doctor L. to the author, June 29, September 29, 1965.)

ary writing assignment was geared so as to make it an emergency. He would physically exhaust himself to meet a deadline. Working strenuously against time, to meet each deadline, was one of his ways of repeatedly "killing" himself—a staggered suicide.

Though the symptoms of his illness (according to his medical records) began in August 1942 and lasted until May 1943, Chambers was not away from his *Time* office until November 11, 1942, and did not return until July 7, 1943. When he returned he immediately went back to editing seven sections. Within two months he was reassigned to Foreign News.

The tacit ban on Chambers' editing or writing of Soviet or Communist news had at last been broken. . . . I remained for more than a year [as editor of Foreign News] . . . one of the most strenuous years of my life.

Once again he gravitated back to the political and world arena, dealing with the problems of averting "World War III," and his differences with members of *Time*'s staff flared up:

. . . I had scarcely edited it so long [one month] when most of *Time*'s European correspondents joined in a round-robin protesting my editorial views and demanding my removal.

Chambers was beset by persecutory fears throughout his *Time* years. From the start, he felt that his colleagues still thought of him as a Communist. "We know," he quotes a *Time* writer as saying to him, "that you are a well-known revolutionist." Though Chambers recalls and quotes his direct denial —"You are mistaken, I have broken with the Communist Party"—the matter continued to harass him. "A few days later, the smear campaign against me was in full swing."

So many of Chambers' everyday concerns manifested themselves in the form of chronic suspiciousness. The concealed enemy lurked everywhere. Shortly after he began to work at *Time* he was asked by a colleague to join the Newspaper Guild, and he described in *Witness* how he watched

the Communists pop up here and there in the meeting to make their prearranged speeches about the points or people they wanted supported. . . .

In those days, I had a horror of uttering half a dozen words in public. But one night the spectacle of so much passive stupidity among so many intelligent people brought me to my feet. "Can't you see," I stammered, "that these speakers are simply Communists and that, in voting their way, you are voting the Communist line?"

He also claimed to have seen Nathan Witt (later named by him as one of the leaders of an underground Communist cell in Washington in the thirties) at one of the Guild meetings.

In the crowded hall, I became aware that someone was staring at me. I glanced into a face of undisguised hatred which at first I did not recognize. It was Nathan Witt.

In a private interview with Nathan Witt, his reply to my asking him about the above meeting with Chambers was a vigorous denial. "It was," said Witt, "a completely false statement." [6]

Though Chambers referred to the interval during which he worked at *Time* (1939–48) as "The Tranquil Years," his thoughts, actions, and mode of life revealed no tranquillity. His emotional life was in constant ferment; he was never free of the delusion that someone was after him. "The Communists only have to start the smear; the others keep it going for them."

Chambers' megalomania and his unconscious guilt were opposed to his outward need to get along. Because he had to impress everyone with the singularity of his experiences, he put himself in the awkward position of then having to support his previous embellishments. Once he gained the reputation of being a crank, unfair comments were more easily forthcoming, and actual injustices must have been done him, all of which whetted still further his feeling of being different and alone.

No sooner had the Communists discovered that I was a deserter than word rippled through the *Time* staff that Chambers was a crank on the subject of Communism. Specifically, he suffered from a delusion that the Communists were after his life. At *Time*, which in those days was in effect a big fraternity where people either intangibly belonged or they didn't, such gossip was poison, not so much because of what it might imply about my past, but because it made me ridiculous.

In this setting, as in the fraternity of his own family, Chambers sensed that he did not belong and felt as though he were an outsider. The vicissitudes of his childhood ("my past") had long since been replaced by more immediate threats. The difficulties he encountered with his colleagues at *Time* were, to be sure, a far cry from the family fraternity problems Chambers had had in relation to his brother Richard, and even more remote from the college fraternity incident that Chambers said was responsible for his brother's mental depression, but it is evident that Chambers was left with a conflict in all broader

---

[6] But Witt did say that he had met Chambers "socially" many times in the 1930s and knew him under the name of "Carl." "All political people were deeply involved in those years," he said, "and wanted to know what was going on. Carl was always ready to set them straight as to what was the party line. He was very eccentric and struck me as a man of mystery; . . . by dropping off hints he would try to give the impression that some deep or important stuff was going on. He was always 'hep' to something mysterious."

Witt knew Alger Hiss from their association in the AAA in the early thirties. "He was," said Witt, "one of the most attractive men I've ever known—warm, sensitive, with an aristocratic quality." (Nathan Witt to the author, December 6, 1962.)

areas of fraternal relations, ranging from personal friendships to the organized brotherhood of workers (for example, the Newspaper Guild).

The Communist whispers against me were abetted by other factors, as they always are; for the whole Communist smear strategy pivots on the knowledge that everybody is human, almost nobody can stand close scrutiny. For one thing, from the very first, I made no secret at *Time* of my Communist past (the Communists, of course, had the advantage of never admitting that they were Communists), and freely admitted that I had been underground . . . Then, too, I never missed an opportunity to jab at Communism in my stories.

From the start Chambers had wanted to write foreign news for *Time.* He was given a chance but soon became suspicious that the writer who edited his copy was, if not an active Communist, "at least a close fellow traveler." Chambers was assigned some Russian news to write and did so with a tone so unfriendly that his handling of the material displeased his superior.

T. S. Matthews, then managing editor of *Time,* first hired Chambers as a book reviewer in 1938. He told me that Chambers was "hipped on Russia" and so he avoided having him write Foreign News. Chambers, according to Matthews, believed that some of *Time*'s foreign correspondents were members of the Communist Party and that the West would capitulate to Communism. (In this regard, said Matthews, Chambers was "prescient to the threat of the spread of world Communism.") There was no doubt, Matthews pointed out, that Chambers had a pathological suspiciousness about all people.[7] And so thereafter he was not given any more Russian news to handle. But even the new assignments he did get, which he felt were stories that no one else wanted and were "least noteworthy," became a frequent topic of dissension. He was put back to reviewing books and noncontroversial subjects such as Art and Cinema. But as Chambers himself pointed out:

Even so, the forbidden subject sometimes crept in. My delighted review of the movie, *Ninotchka,* threw my fellow-traveling researcher into hideous gloom.

Though excluded from writing Communist news,

I saw no one around me (except the Communists, of course) who knew anything at all about the subject. But gradually I welcomed the ban. I began to see that the kind of sniping that I had been doing was shallow and largely profitless; *anybody* could do that.

Anecdotes relevant to his behavior during the period 1939–48 all have certain points in common. Especially remembered were his overweight, squat

[7] When in 1959 Chambers took a trip to Europe and visited Matthews at his home in London, Chambers' earlier feeling of "doom," said Matthews, had been lost. Chambers had profited with the purchase of some shares of stock and had become a "would-be capitalist." (T. S. Matthews to the author, August 29, 1965.)

appearance, and his badly neglected and missing front teeth. He always wore a disheveled black suit and a black tie.

His colleagues were all impressed with his strange manner of talking and his accompanying gestures. He spoke or whispered in low tones, the vocal sounds coming out of one side of his mouth. These mannerisms, like a signal that drew attention to his appearance, revealed his inwardly disturbed state of mind and his suspiciousness. While talking, he often looked over his shoulder, "casing" the room to be sure no one was lurking there. In his office he moved his desk to the far corner of the room, diagonally opposite to and facing the door, so that he could have a clear view at all times of anyone who entered. I have been told by several of Chambers' former colleagues who worked with him at *Time* and *Life* that he kept a notebook in which he recorded many facts about the daily habits and activities of friends and other office workers.

Chambers kept himself removed from the other members of the staff on all social occasions. Several of his colleagues who knew him well never met his family. The divisiveness that characterized his style of living is strongly reminiscent of his father's ways. When Chambers was away from the office, it was usually impossible for even the top members of the staff to get in touch with him.

A young woman staff writer who worked with Chambers when he was senior editor described how rude and arrogant Chambers was to a newly appointed staff member, a former university dean and a professor of chemistry. Time, Inc., had hired this reputable chemist as a consultant for articles on science. As his editorial superior, Chambers seemed bent on belittling him with derogatory comments about his writing.[8] Chambers had little use for experts in the physical sciences. He had himself avoided studying them (except in a cursory way) and no doubt felt threatened by the professor's knowledge.

During story conferences it was not unusual for Chambers to give a new writer a rough time. It was difficult to know whether Chambers was taking issue with the writer or his topic. "He was," said one informant, "a man less moved by conviction than the desire to disrupt." Louis Kronenberger, former drama critic at *Time,* who worked with Chambers for many years, confirmed this impression. "Whit was 'hammy' but not a ham," Kronenberger said. "A dramatizer who enjoyed frightening the young research girls in the office—but not the important staff members. Perhaps he knew he wouldn't be able to, so didn't try."

Far from trying to "frighten" his superiors, he could on occasion treat them with an ingratiating humility. The good graces of his employer were a lifeline that Chambers had to keep open. His editorial position at *Time* was

[8] Mrs. E. Rosner to the author, January 5, 1961.

the only long-time job he ever held. It provided him with a forum to dramatize his feelings of grandiosity and his literary skills, and enabled him to attain,
for the first time in his life, a measure of financial security. Dealing with
someone who controlled his position, he exhibited a facility for unabashed
flattery.

Harry,

    Listen, please, with Pauline patience and charity. I have made a few, a very
few, suggested changes in your speech. (They are indicated in pencil on the copy I
have sent to Tom). I am not evading responsibility when I say that I cannot do
more. Your speech is a simple, authentic testimony of the spirit. It is, if I understand that special field at all, almost perfectly attuned to its audience. It is a voice
with which I have seldom been privileged to hear you speak, and it moves me
deeply. I may not intrude upon it. Any flash of Chamberian prose would jangle in
this context like a false chord. Nor is "erudition" needed. I think it would be out of
place in a speech whose one rhetorical device is its dialectic suppleness. In short, it
is a good speech because it proceeds from the spirit, and the mode of the Christian
spirit is simplicity. God bless you, Harry.

                                                                Whittaker [9]

    But for the most part he maintained his conspiratorial guise. There was a
legend in the office—apparently begun by Chambers himself—that he had
once worked as a foreign agent in Europe, then quit, and that he was consequently being pursued. This was the reason, Chambers explained to his colleagues, that he had no fixed city address, moved from hotel to hotel, and periodically returned to his family in the country, when his work week was over.

    He had the reputation of prying into people's personal affairs and asking
embarrassing questions. One informant related hearing him accost a young
office boy and startle the young man by asking him some strange questions
about his student activities.

    On another occasion he felt threatened by a science writer, Jonathan
Leonard, who came back from a tour of the Los Alamos testing grounds with
a souvenir of an atomic explosion, a heat-formed piece of glass. It had, of
course, been thoroughly checked for any harmful radiation. Leonard hung up
his awesome souvenir on the wall of his office. Two doors down the hall was
the office of Whittaker Chambers. After some days the man in the middle
office came to Leonard and said Chambers was very fearful that radiations
were reaching him through the two walls and the intervening office and he
thought Leonard should take it out of there. Leonard did.

    Malcolm Cowley, writer, journalist, and authority on American liter-

─────────────────
[9] Chambers to Henry Luce, undated (Hiss Defense Files).

ature, has reported a telling experience with Chambers in 1940.[10] Shortly after the Hitler-Stalin Pact, *Time* planned to print a story about people who had recently become disaffected with Communism. Chambers wrote this story for *Time,* and Cowley was mentioned as one of those who had "jumped off the Moscow Express." A mutual friend [11] happened to suggest Cowley's name to Chambers as a knowledgeable person in political matters as well as a good candidate for employment by *Time* as a reviewer of books. Chambers' secretary phoned Cowley and a luncheon was arranged. Cowley commented: "Since I was one of the people mentioned in Chambers' article, a revealing conversation ensued." What Chambers said to Cowley during that meeting was so startling, Cowley recorded it in his journal as soon as he came home that day:

Friday, Dec. 13, 1940

He gave me a lot of dope on the CP underground. He said that it had its people all through the government service and that Nathan Witt of the Labor Board is the only one who has so far been forced to resign. Sayre, the high commissioner to the Philippines, is also connected with the underground movement. Chambers boasts that he tried to disrupt every underground activity that he knew about, after leaving the party, and that although he wants me to keep the information quiet he has turned it over to the proper sources. "The counter revolutionary purge is still to come," he said ominously. . . .

He is fighting now for "the Christian democratic counter revolution." He has joined the Episcopal Church. When I expressed some wonder, considering the formal and rather neutral quality of that church, he explained that it contained the worst enemies of the Comintern. There is utter sincerity in his hatred. But in his program for a Christian democratic counter revolution, all the accent is on the word "counter."

He is a short, stout, broad man with an apparently amiable soft face, and with very bad teeth—one of them only a metal bar from which the porcelain has been chipped. In spite of having a good job, he dresses rather badly. His eyes shift and he laughs on the right side of his mouth. He believes that conspiracies, traitors and spies surround us on every side and he is determined to wipe them out—and though he doesn't mention the word capitalism, that is what he is fighting for, quite consciously. At the same time, in his hatred, he gives you an impression of force and malign power.

Cowley's journal provides a fresh picture of Chambers in the grip of his persecutory delusions. His gratuitous accusation of Francis B. Sayre [12] (Hiss's former superior in the State Department) and his explanation that he joined

[10] Malcolm Cowley to the author, May 1, 1962. Cowley also testified during the Hiss trials.
[11] John Chamberlain, then a book reviewer for the *New York Times.*
[12] Son-in-law of President Woodrow Wilson.

the Episcopal Church because it "contained the worst enemies of the Comintern" stand out as new evidence of his extravagant need to defend himself
against imagined enemies. His conspiratorial confidences and his shifty-eyed
bearing were, even on a first meeting, clear intimations of the inner torment
that was driving him.

Chambers' family affairs at this period are revealing. His relationship
with his mother underwent some important changes. During the ten-year
period he was employed at *Time* he spent, as a rule, three days with his wife
and children on the farm and four days in New York—often with Laha in
Lynbrook. In her advancing age Laha grew increasingly dependent on her
only remaining son and kin. Her own mother had lived with her for a time,
but this had apparently been little comfort: Mrs. Whittaker had grown senile
and her disturbed behavior had permeated the house.

Subject to vivid auditory hallucinations, Mrs. Whittaker held animated
conversations with imaginary persons. At times she would break out in loud
and ribald songs, or start fires in her room, or stuff up the toilet bowl. A
neighbor reported that she brewed some foul-smelling mixture in her room,
which she peddled about the neighborhood as a panacea for numerous ail-
ments. She soon became well known in the town. Repeated attempts were
made to have her removed to a mental institution, which the old lady slyly
resisted. She was finally committed and died a few years later.

It was not long after her mother had been committed that Laha lost her
vigor and dynamic spirit. Laha's own mental deterioration followed a clinical
pattern comparable to her mother's. She gave up her theatrical and community activities and gradually withdrew into a shell. Formerly neat and well
groomed, she became sloppy, unaware of her appearance. She was often seen
walking on the street, wearing a new dress but an old pair of sneakers. In her
later years she seemed to want only to be left alone with her cat. She surrounded herself with the accumulations of the past and subsisted as a quiet,
eccentric old lady. Her haughtiness and domineering attitude shrank into an
enfeebled reliance upon her son, who, having reached the fifth decade of his
life, belatedly derived from her subdued presence some modicum or implied
proof of her love.[13]

The pattern of living part time with his mother at Lynbrook, part time
with wife and family at Westminster (and sometimes in Manhattan hotels),
satisfied Chambers' need to be both close to and separated from his mother.
His unannounced arrivals and departures (with friends as well as family),
since he first ran away from home, persisted as a way of life.

[13] Laha Chambers died on June 5, 1958, at the age of eighty-six in South Nassau County
Hospital, Oceanside, New York, of natural causes: cerebral arteriosclerosis, myocarditis,
nephritis.

A poem, "Braun," written in 1924, pastoral and plaintive, reveals Chambers' wanderlust, loneliness, and nostalgia; his feelings of having been cast out, and his itinerant search and wish to return home. A rather long poem in blank verse, it reflects clearly his own youthful yearnings and presages their hoped-for fulfillment. "Braun" begins:

> My father will scarcely know me this time
> He hasn't for the last five times
> That I've dropped in on him.
>
> I'm a strong man, but a man, and so
> I've been afraid of many things, and done them nearly all. . . .
>
> But in the end,
> I find myself returning to this place
> I am content to settle here
> And plow the ground and watch an old man die.

Braun's hope is that his father will find him acceptable; his self-image as a man is fortified against fear, and finally his ultimate wish is to return to his mother.

As one of the senior editors, Chambers' position as a writer and wage-earner was a secure one. During those years (1939–48) he became more productive than he had ever been. Yet his mode of life remained that of an itinerant. Much like Jay, his peripatetic father, he was away from home a great deal. During these ten years he commuted weekly between Lynbrook, Westminster, and New York City. He continued, as in earlier years, to be in constant flight and spent frequent nights in Manhattan hotels after working late hours. Though his external situation had improved, his fears did not abate. Past frights continued to intrude into his present. He warded off his deeper anxiety, the fear of death, by counterposing positive thoughts about new life (birth). He recalls how his daughter, Ellen, would find

Papa, with the light on, writing, with a revolver on the table or a gun against the chair. She knew that there were people who wanted to kill Papa and who might try to kidnap her. . . . [But] The farm was your kingdom. . . . There was the birth of lambs and calves. You remember how once, when I was away and the veterinarian could not come, you saw Mother reach in and turn the calf inside the cow so that it could be born.

Chambers deals with his fear of being killed and his child kidnaped in a redemptory way: he makes a savior out of his wife. To this end he elevates into significance her veterinary role as a deliverer of life and enlists her as an agent in his magical system. In his reminder of how she manipulated the position of the unborn calf he reverses the fate of the offspring—from death to life. By the use of such maneuvers in his thinking and his writing, and by the

heightened concern over everyday happenings and their outcome, he assuages
the guilt of his own birth.

It is significant to note the overevaluation and endearment that Minnie,
the favorite dairy cow, enjoyed on Chambers' farm. Patrick Skene Catling, a
Baltimore Sun staff correspondent, in describing an interview and visit with
Chambers at the farm on December 27, 1948, captioned his news report:

A COW BELLE IS MAIN ATTRACTION ON WHITTAKER CHAMBERS FARM

Christmas presents for Whittaker Chambers included jewelry for his favorite cow.
. . . And the cow is "Minnie," a svelte, beige, thoroughbred Guernsey, which was
pointed out by Mr. Chambers as a principal point of interest during a tour of his
place this afternoon.

Handsomest animal of a dairy herd 30 head strong, the placidly ruminating
"Minnie," comfortably installed on dry straw, is an embodiment of the rural at-
tractions which make Mr. Chambers wish he could spend all his time at his Carroll
County home. . . .

Chambers told the news reporter:

Much of the feed for the cattle is raised here—alfalfa, corn, barley and hay. We
grow our own vegetables and fruit, and preserve them in a large deepfreeze unit.
We have Aberdeen Angus beef cattle, chickens, and so on. . . .

Shortly before noon, Mrs. Chambers served tea and slabs of heavy fruit cake.
Luncheon consisted of roast turkey, macaroni, green peas (from the freezer);
cranberry sauce, pickles, milk, cookies, candy and coffee. Later in the afternoon,
after brief hilltop exposure to the wind, Chambers drank cups of hot chocolate.

While life in the farm revolves around the cows . . . [which are] practically
members of the family, life in the house is centered about the kitchen. . . .

The decoration of the dining room includes a glass case of stuffed birds,
reproductions of country scenes painted by Pieter Breughel, Sixteenth Century
Flemish painter, and a color print of "The Virginia Bunch Peanut," a plant with
complex underground roots.

The other ground-floor rooms are a small library and a large sitting room.
The library is lined with books from floor to ceiling; however, Mr. Chambers said
that he reads few books, but reads those often.

The plenitude of supplies, the overabundance of food and milk, the library
walls lined with books, all give a feeling of intense, compact coziness (the
antithesis of his inner emptiness).

By 1948 Chambers, working also for *Life,* was earning close to $30,000
and was enjoying a steady income for the first time in his life. He purchased as
much of the surrounding land as he could, accumulating about 340 acres at a
total cost of about $22,000 during 1940–47.[14]

[14] The records of his real-estate purchases show:
Gertrude H. Thomas & Frank Thomas to J. D. Whittaker Chambers and Esther
Chambers, his wife, 106¾ acres, on May 16, 1941, for $4500.

Yet despite his plenitude and the success of his long-dreamed-of dairy farm, his concern about death still predominated his thoughts:

In its soil and the care of its creatures, we bury each day a part of our lives in the form of labor. The yield of our daily dying. . . . A farmer is always half buried in his soil. . . . there was also death of animals, sometimes violent, sometimes slow and painful—nothing is more constant on a farm than death.

Chambers' paternalism toward his son, John, was overtly conciliatory. He did not wish to force or domineer the boy in the way he had been forced into an unreal world.

. . . as children, you experienced . . . the wonder of life within the wonder of the universe. Most important, you knew them not from books, not from lectures, but simply from living among them. Most important, you knew them with reverence and awe. . . .

Chambers' identification with his son is evident when he relates how

once, in place of a bedtime story, I was reading Shakespeare to John—at his own request, for I never forced such things on you. I came to that passage in which Macbeth, having murdered Duncan, realizes what he has done to his own soul, and asks if all the water in the world can ever wash the blood from his hand, or will it not rather

The multitudinous seas incarnadine?

At that line, John's whole body twitched. I gave great silent thanks to God. For I knew that if, as children, you could thus feel in your souls the reverence and awe for life and the world, which is the ultimate meaning of Beethoven and Shakespeare, as man and woman you could never be satisfied with less. I felt a great faith that sooner or later you would understand what I once told you, . . . "True wisdom comes from the overcoming of suffering and sin."

By inducing a reaction of horror in his young son with the selection of such a remarkable "bedtime story," Chambers, under the guise of paternal piety, endeavors to relieve himself of his own guilt.

The so-called "Tranquil Years" were the period of Chambers' apparent shift from destructivism to religious positivism. The significant point to be noted in the following is that whether his overt behavior was devilish or

---

Milton A. Feeser *et al.* to Esther Chambers, 10 acres, on May 14, 1940, for $500.

Woodrow W. Lepps & Carriemas Lepps to J. D. W. Chambers and Esther Chambers, his wife, 10 acres, on September 24, 1942, for $200.

Erman A. Shoemaker, Tax Collector, to Esther Chambers, 9⅞ acres, on November 25, 1942, for $95.00.

Elwood W. Hammett & Ethel B. Hammett to David Whittaker Chambers and Esther Chambers, his wife, 137 acres, on September 25, 1946, for $7500.

Herbert C. Bixler and Carrie M. Bixler to Jay David Whittaker and Esther Chambers, 14¾ acres, on September 8, 1947, for $1500.

Margaret Null *et al.* to Jay David Whittaker Chambers and Esther Chambers, 45 acres, on November 26, 1947, for $7500.

saintly, conspiratorial or contrite, his megalomania remained unaltered. His job provided an excellent forum for his exalted self-image.

It seemed to me that I had a more important task to do, one that was peculiarly mine. It was not to attack Communism frontally. It was to clarify, on the basis of the news, the religious and moral position that made Communism evil.

Religious articles became one of Chambers' specialities. The job shift from politics to religion is of interest to the psychobiographer. Is this a true "intrapsychic" alteration, and is the "deepening within himself," which Chambers describes, true insight? Or is this another transitory religious experience, not unlike his earlier ones at Williams and Columbia, another "life-saver" to assuage his guilt, bolster his sense of identity, and secure his existence at *Time*? He soon established a Messianic alliance with God against the evils of Communism.

A year later, by Henry Luce's personal order, I wrote the cover story on Pope Pius XII, and the Jesuits ordered several hundred copies of the essay to be used in their schools. I felt that I was beginning to carry out that command which I believed had been laid upon me in the hall at Mount Royal Terrace.

In the February 2, 1948 issue, *Life* published a piece by Whittaker Chambers called "The Devil," a strange allegory in which a personification of the Devil appears at a New Year's Eve celebration. It begins:

On New Year's Eve, a favorite occasion with the Devil, he visited a New York nightclub. There his conversation was overheard by Whittaker Chambers, one of the editors of *Time*.

What follows is a discourse on the collapse of the modern world. It takes the form of a dialogue between a party guest (called the "pessimist") and the Devil, who is characterized as "a massive and immaculate stranger with a rich Miami tan." The setting, "the Plutonium Room of Manhattan's swank hotel Nineveh and Tyre," is a caricature of materialistic excess, including—as the New Year is rung in—a balloon "crusted with diamond dust and labeled I'M THE ATOM—SMASH ME." The Devil looks with pleasure on the decadent scene as he confides in the "pessimist" that his urban garb is only a disguise and that he is in fact the representative of the "underground," Satan. He describes the horrors of the world for which he is responsible.

. . . leaning intently through the fires of a blitzed city, I listen, transfigured by that paralysis of pain which is half the pleasure of great music, while a child puddles in the stew of bones and shrieks, "Father," in a scream purged by pure terror of gross humanity.

Chambers ostensibly wrote the story as a act of piety, a plea for a return to God. But it is not difficult to discern that "The Devil," apart from its evangelic message, served an immediate, personal function for Chambers himself; another literary exercise that grappled with the problem of guilt and an unpardoning conscience. The Devil is both a mockery and a lamentation, a destructive fantasy about the world, under the guise of intellectualism or piety. Chambers' identification with the figure of Satan is evident not only in his grave vision of mankind but in his thinly disguised pleasure in enumerating the horrors of life in the present, in such macabre phrases, for example, as the "stew of bones."

In the final paragraphs of the story the Devil reveals his hidden motives, the source of false pride, envy, and his need to destroy. Perhaps nowhere else does Chambers come closer, using the Devil as his spokesman, to revealing the naked reason for his destructiveness. Chambers' inner emptiness, his tragic incapacity to feel, suffer, or love any human object come to the fore. In answer to the final question put to the Devil by the "pessimist," "Just what do you get out of it?" Chambers laments:

"My friend," said Satan, "you do not understand the Devil's secret. But since shamelessness is part of my pathos, there is no reason why I should not tell you. The Devil is sterile. I possess the will to create (hence my pride), but I am incapable of creating (hence my envy). And with an envy raised to such power as immortal minds can feel, I hate the Creator and His Creation. My greatest masterpiece is never more than a perversion—an ingenious disordering of Another's grand design, a perversion of order into chaos, of life into death."

"Why?" asked the pessimist.

"If I knew the answer to that one," said Satan, "perhaps I should not be the Devil. Perhaps it is simply, as every craftsman knows, that nothing enduring, great or small, can ever be created without love. But I am as incapable of love as I am of goodness. I am as insensible to either as a dead hand is to a needle thrust through it. . . .

"And yet it is at this very point that man, the monstrous midget, still has the edge on the Devil: he suffers. . . . Not one man, however base, quite lacks the capacity for this specific suffering, which is the seal of his divine commitment—this suffering which I cannot feel because of that light which in me is dark. Intellectually I can understand it since, by my origin, I share the intellect of angels. But I cannot feel it or I would not be the Devil. That is the source of my frustration and root of my rage against the breed. That is why I shall never cease working to entangle man in evil until the world becomes one universal graveyard whose lifeless peace is broken only by my shriek of triumph as I plunge into a deeper pit than Hell. For only one knows better than I that should I succeed in making man destroy himself, I will destroy myself with him, having destroyed my function. . . . Personally, as I glance around this room, I have never felt my chances to be so good.

"Happy New Year, young man."

Repressed in the psyche of Whittaker Chambers, the man, senior editor of *Time* in the year 1948, aged forty-seven, and disguised by the acquired skills of his craft and the brilliance of his intellect, there presided, paradoxically, the still frightened, impoverished Vivian. This developmental failure, which tied him to the fantasied guilt of his past, also imprisoned him as the pessimist of the future. Real or fictional characters were for him but symbols in the drama of his own moral conflict. And so, on this satirical note, he concluded this piece of unconscious autobiography, having used a "massive and immaculate stranger with a rich Miami tan" to characterize the Devil that was in him.

Much of Chambers' style, in literature or life, derives from his penchant for ambiguities. He leaves the reader always guessing and he remains the omniscient one. This is the essence of unconscious ambivalence, in which antithetical ideas exist side by side. A kind of unholy alliance is effected, as, for example, in Chambers' explanation:

> My need was to be a practicing Christian in the same sense that I had been a practicing Communist.

It is a paradoxical need. One has to disregard the meaning of his beliefs and actions and concern oneself only with the fact of his submission to something larger than himself for his statement to be congruous. And it is only in this sense that Chambers' facile yoking of the two opposite "Faiths" has any meaning. A deep disruption within his own sense of self was raging within him, for which both Christianity and Communism were havens of refuge. Chambers' need was magically to act out his role as a Christian in a properly ritualistic and convincing manner. To pose as a Christian was his way of being a Christian.

Chambers felt drawn to join the Religious Society of Friends (Quakers), but

> I hesitated because the Quaker rebuff to me in my youth, which I have also mentioned, lashing me at a moment of personal distress, and tender and naïve submission to the Quaker spirit, had left an unhealing scar.

Why does such a presumably minor incident (the Quakers refusal to send him to Russia in 1923) still fester in his memory as "an unhealing scar"? Chambers does not remind himself or the reader of the substantive facts and circumstances as to why the Friends had refused to employ him. The reason was that Chambers had just written and published his atheistic *Play for Puppets,* which had created a wide campus scandal, and as a result he had been forced to withdraw from Columbia University. But Chambers represses or omits this hard fact and remembers only the hurt feeling of having been cast out. And here the symbolic identity of Friend (Quaker) and Brother (Richard) in

Chambers' mind must be reintroduced. For his identification with Richard provides the key to our understanding of the act of his religious conversion.

Though Chambers professed a deep need to be a "Friend," he was directed by his inner ambivalence to reject them (him). And so, in 1940, he turned to the Episcopal Church:

But my need to be part of a community of worship was pressing. Chance threw me together at *Time* with Samuel Gardner Welles, who became my close friend and whose family became my friends. Welles was the son of a revered Episcopal clergyman and brother of a bishop. At the Cathedral of St. John the Divine, Welles introduced me to the Reverend William Dudley Foulke Hughes, who instructed and baptised me and presently assisted at my confirmation by the late Bishop Manning. My sponsors were Welles and my old friend Robert Cantwell, who had returned to the church just before me.

The symbolic meaning of baptism is, of course, that of rebirth, a ritual in which the original sin of creation is washed away. It fitted in with Chambers' own rebirth fantasies and represented a means of establishing a new identity.

I wrote to the Reverend William Dudley Foulke Hughes [15] for his account of the circumstances of the baptism and confirmation of Whittaker Chambers. His replies, sympathetic and gracious, were different from Chambers' account. The Reverend Mr. Hughes wrote:

Sometime in 1940, T. S. Matthews, who was editor of *Time* magazine in the 30's and 40's and is a close friend of mine, told me that there had come on the staff of the paper a man named Whittaker Chambers who had renounced Communism and who wished earnestly to make a full profession of Christianity. He introduced Chambers to me. I read *Witness* some years ago, but do not remember having noticed Chambers' mistake in saying that Welles introduced us. I knew Welles slightly, but knew Robert Cantwell very well indeed. . . .

Because of Chambers' obvious sincerity, deep conviction, and superior intelligence, it seemed proper to me to baptize him at once rather than to proceed in usual manner to a long period of preparation and instruction with baptism and confirmation together at the end. I baptized him after one or two meetings, and we then proceeded to a time of preparation for his confirmation. This was complicated by the fact that he lived in Maryland and came to New York for only one or two days each week to do his office work at *Time*. These visits were often omitted, I remember. And I left the cathedral in February, 1941, and went to Hastings-on-the-Hudson, a little distance out of the city. . . .

He was very modest and humble in his whole attitude to me, but I was somewhat in awe of his intellectual capacity and have wondered whether it was partly my inadequacy which led him to go on very soon after to the Quakerism of his early days. I imagine that Matthews and Cantwell were present at his confirmation.

[15] Then at St. Columba's Rectory, Middletown, Rhode Island. The Reverend Hughes died in 1964.

Once again, I found myself snared in the cryptic convolutions that characterized Chambers' interpersonal relations and his written autobiographical memories.

On discovering from the Reverend Mr. Hughes that it was T. S. Matthews, not Samuel Welles, who introduced Chambers to him, I wrote to Matthews and received an immediate, if abrupt reply:

. . . I can answer your specific question about Chambers' baptism and confirmation in the Episcopal Church. I had nothing whatever to do with it. I may possibly have introduced Chambers to the Rev. W. D. F. Hughes (who is an old friend of mine) but if so, I think it must have been at second-hand. Sam Welles and Robert Cantwell, I should think were the two who sponsored Chambers at his baptism—in any case, I wasn't the one.[16]

I informed the Reverend Mr. Hughes of Matthews' statement and received the following note:

My recollection is very clear that Chambers was originally introduced to me by my close friend, T. S. Matthews, in spite of his denial. One of us is in error [17]—it may well be myself. I have no way to refresh my memory as to the witnesses to Chambers' baptism or confirmation. It still seems to me that at the baptism were Cantwell and Matthews. I cannot confirm or disprove this.

A subsequent check through the Church Register showed that there may very well have been *no* sponsors at all at Chambers' baptism. On the page listing the record of Whittaker Chambers' baptism the column under "sponsors" is blank.

I wrote to both Welles and Cantwell. From Welles I received no answer. Robert Cantwell kindly wrote to me as follows:

. . . I should not like to leave you with the feeling that there was any mystery or confusion in the circumstances of Chambers' joining a church, or anything in any sense discreditable to those involved. In general, Chambers' account in *Witness,* which you find raises questions and is in part contradicted by the quotations in the letter of Father Hughes to you, is accurate. There are minor matters as to timing and individuals, but these could only be of importance to the individuals involved, rather than to Chambers, and scarcely related to the biographical facts of his career. You will doubtless have noted that Chambers' account is a singularly spare and factual recital, altogether lacking in the emotional prose and the rather strained reports of mystical ecstasy, which have become commonplace in books relating to conversion and monasteries in contemporary literature.

Chambers' baptism, Cantwell pointed out, was a dramatic and moving experience, one that he felt certain Chambers would have preferred to have dis-

---

[16] T. S. Matthews to the author, March 14, 1963.
[17] In a later interview (August 29, 1965) with Matthews at his home in London, his recollection was more definite: "I introduced Chambers to Reverend Hughes but was not present at his baptism."

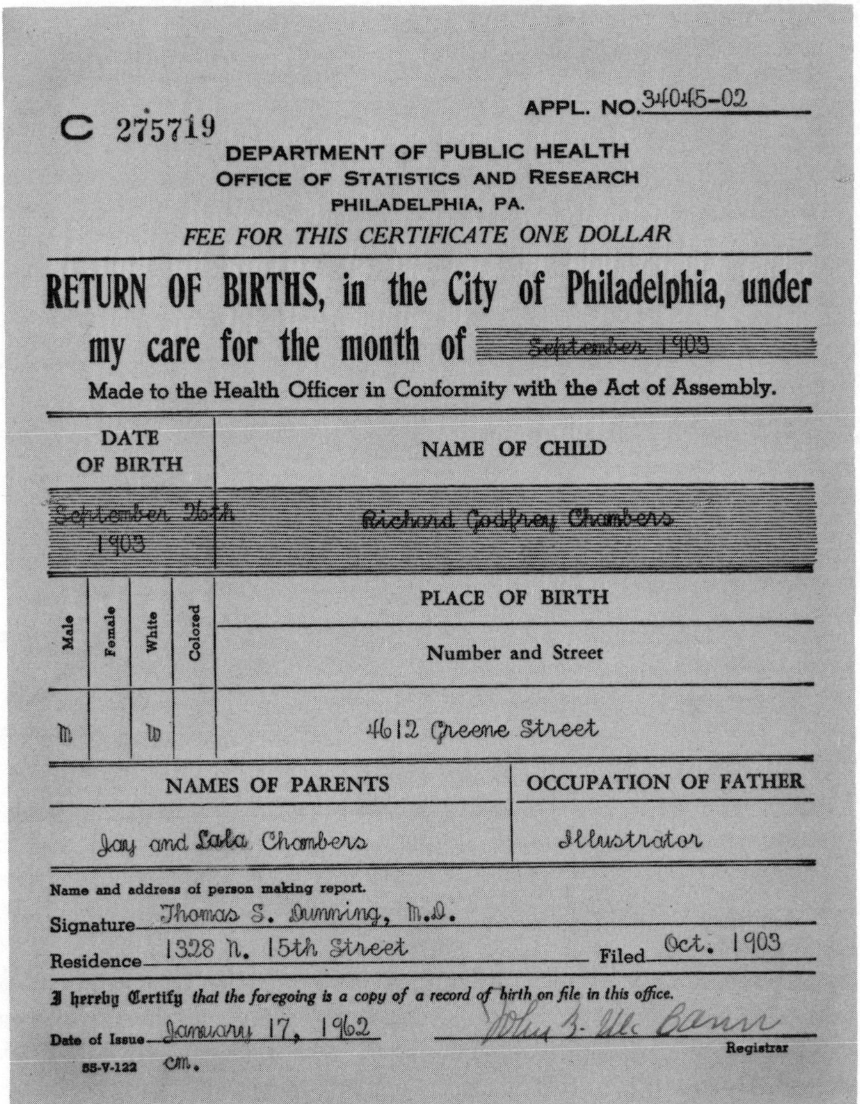

C 275719

APPL. NO. 34045-02

DEPARTMENT OF PUBLIC HEALTH
OFFICE OF STATISTICS AND RESEARCH
PHILADELPHIA, PA.

FEE FOR THIS CERTIFICATE ONE DOLLAR

RETURN OF BIRTHS, in the City of Philadelphia, under my care for the month of September 1903

Made to the Health Officer in Conformity with the Act of Assembly.

DATE OF BIRTH	NAME OF CHILD
September 26th 1903	Richard Godfrey Chambers

Male	Female	White	Colored	PLACE OF BIRTH — Number and Street
M		W		4612 Greene Street

NAMES OF PARENTS	OCCUPATION OF FATHER
Jay and Laha Chambers	Illustrator

Name and address of person making report.

Signature Thomas S. Dunning, M.D.

Residence 1328 N. 15th Street Filed Oct. 1903

I hereby Certify *that the foregoing is a copy of a record of birth on file in this office.*

Date of Issue January 17, 1962

CM.

Registrar

55-V-122

Birth certificate of Richard Godfrey Chambers.

86 *June 6, 1944*   **Cathedral Church of St. John the Divine, New York**
Official Department of Health Certificate of Birth Registration shows correct year of birth to be 1938, and not 1937. Certificate Number 7846 (91C. PK. W.)
Thomas A. Parks, Canon Pastor

BAPTISMS

1940

DATE OF BAPTISM	NAME	DATE AND PLACE OF BIRTH	PARENTS
Sept. 22	*Henry Mohandas Seenandan*	*April 18th 1940 New York*	*Henry Seena Agnes*
26 September	*Jay David Whittaker Chambers*	*1 April, 1901 Philadelphia Pa*	*Jay Chambers Laha Whitta*
14 October	*Rosann May Presbry*	*14 October 1939 New York City N.Y.*	*Peter Shaw Pre osborne Ward*

Baptismal record of the Cathedral Church of St. John the Divine, New York, showing the record of Whittaker Chambers' baptism.

cussed, if at all, in moral, religious, and philosophical language rather than in psychoanalytic terms.

Cantwell's independent appraisal that "there were minor matters as to timing and individuals," which he believed were unimportant to Chambers, and his expressed feeling that Chambers would not have wanted to have his baptism "discussed" in psychoanalytic terms, must regretfully be discounted by the analytic biographer. For the Register of the Cathedral Church of St. John the Divine yielded a startling piece of information: the date of Chambers' baptism was September 26 (1940), the *anniversary of his dead brother's birth.*[18]

In the timing of Chambers' baptism—his preparation for a symbolic rebirth and the establishment of a new identity—the Reverend Hughes was manipulated by Chambers into baptising him after "one or two meetings." As Chambers wrote (after deciding against becoming a Quaker), "my need to be part of a community of worship was *pressing*" (emphasis added). The baptismal date, September 26, is not mentioned anywhere; it does not appear either in his testimony or in his autobiography. It will be recalled that Chambers had, on several occasions used the date September 26—most significantly

[18] The space for "Residence of Parents," as well as that for "Sponsors," was blank. The name is given as Jay David Whittaker Chambers.

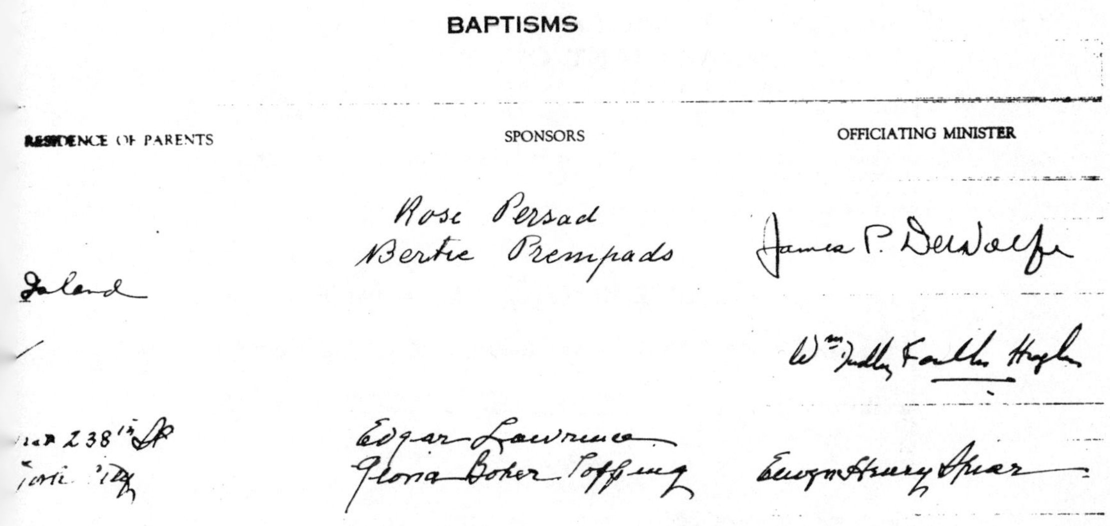

BAPTISMS

RESIDENCE OF PARENTS	SPONSORS	OFFICIATING MINISTER

[handwritten entries]

Rose Persad
Bertie Prempads

James P. DeWolfe

W.... Faulk Hugh

Edgar Lawrence
Gloria Baker Toffung

Ewyn Henry Spear

Zeland

238...

---

when he "invented" it (in 1935) and recorded it as the date of death of John Edward Breen, the mythical father of David Breen. Again, years later, when erroneously asked by counsel whether his brother died on September 26, he concurred in the error.

As to the question of who his sponsors at the baptism were, we are again confronted with a mystery. Why does Chambers omit from *Witness* his relationship with T. S. Matthews, with whom, as friend and colleague, he was closely associated for almost ten years? [19] And, conversely, Matthews does not mention Chambers by name in his own autobiography, even though the book contains many anecdotes about literary colleagues and is an otherwise richly revealing personal account of his twenty-four years at Time, Inc.[20]

There was apparently some falling out between them, as was almost always the case in Chambers' friendships or working alliances. As Matthew Josephson remarked about Chambers and his relationships, "something al-

[19] Matthew's name is mentioned once: "T. S. Matthews' contribution to the humanity of *Time,* both in the intellectual and personal sense of the word, cannot be overstated."

[20] T. S. Matthews kindly revealed to me the following single, cryptic reference to Mr. Chambers: "Nevertheless, one of them [referring to Chambers] had once said to me that journalism does more harm than good. That had shocked me; if he really thinks that, I said to myself, what the hell is he doing here?" (T. S. Matthews, *Name and Address* [New York: Simon & Schuster, 1960], p. 266; T. S. Matthews to the writer, October 12, 1963.)

SM-701 1M ——— 114

CITY OF NEW YORK .

DEPARTMENT OF HEALTH

BUREAU OF RECORDS AND STATISTICS

BOROUGH OFFICES:
MANHATTAN, 125 WORTH STREET
THE BRONX, 1826 ARTHUR AVENUE
BROOKLYN, 295 FLATBUSH AVE. EXT.
QUEENS, 148-18 ARCHER AVE., JAMAICA, N. Y.
RICHMOND, 51 STUYVESANT PLACE, ST. GEORGE, S. I.

New York. *NOV 16 1943* 19

This is to certify that a search was made
of the records of DEATHS in the Borough of........*Manhat'an*........

for the calendar years........*1908*........and........*1909*........for the

name of........*John Edward Breen*........

who is said to have died on the........*26th*........day of

September 1908........and the name was

Carl L. Erb...

NOT FOUND

Director of Bureau

ABRAHAM SINOVSKY
BOROUGH REGISTRAR

....
Borough Registrar.

By........

Information supplied by the applicant for the purpose of identifying the proper record.

Place of death........*Manhattan*

....

Order No.........Searched by........*FS*........Verified by........*RE*........

Department of Health report on the death of "John Edward Breen."

ways happened." The Reverend Hughes, in his last letter to me, confirmed this impression.

After his confirmation, I saw very little of Chambers, but often heard of him from my friend, Matthews. The latter was always very devoted to Chambers, but admitted that he was a difficult person to work with in an organization. [Chambers] would at times be responsible for getting out the paper when Matthews was away. Matthews said that on his return after an absence of a week or two he would find the staff divided into two camps with memoranda presented to him by each side charging the other with dire things. I gather that it was all quite unimportant but induced by Chambers' innate affinity for conspiracy.

It was not long before Chambers left the Episcopal Church and joined the Quakers. His "conversion" is variously explained by those who knew him. Chambers explains this abrupt shift in faith by saying that he had always felt himself to be a Quaker and had been held back only by the Quaker insistence on pacifism. (He shifts, here, from his previous reason—their rebuff in 1923—and offers a "patriotic" one instead.) He goes on to say, in a mystical vein, that the power of the Quaker faith was finally too great for him to resist: "The silence of Quaker worship continued to reach out and draw me irresistibly to it."

Perhaps one explanation of his conversion lies in his identification with his "close friends," the Hisses.

It is not at all chance that both the Chamberses and the Hisses, arriving over very different routes, should at last have found their way into the community of Quakers. For the simplicity inherent in the Quaker way of life must make an authentic appeal to the Hisses.

Chambers assumed for himself and his family what he believed to be the spiritual life of the Hisses. Chambers testified erroneously in 1948 that Priscilla Hiss was a "birthright Quaker"; she never became even a convert. Though the Hisses often used the plain speech, Hiss himself never was a Quaker—he was an Episcopalian. Chambers wanted to be Hiss, to live like him, and in that sense acted out a fantasied imposture of the Hiss family.

T. S. Matthews suggested that it was because Chambers "had a strong nose for the phoney" and that after Communism nothing less rigorous and mystical than Quakerism would do. He added that "some of us were surprised he didn't end up a Catholic." The Reverend Hughes laid Chambers' change of heart to the "tradition of his childhood," explaining that "his mother was a Quaker." So, apparently, Chambers must have told him, but Laha Chambers had, of course, never been a Quaker. Chambers made special point of the fact that his parents were "nominal Episcopalians" and that they had left him with scant, if any, religious tradition.[21]

If there was any religion in our home, I do not remember it. We never prayed or said grace at the table. I never heard my father mention religion in his life. My mother mentioned religion from time to time, but scarcely in a religious way. It was absurd, my mother sometimes said, for people to call themselves Christians when they did not practice Christianity.

After his conversion Chambers reports still another spiritual change. He describes how his office at *Time* became a kind of confessional, and he, a spiritual adviser.

Now a truly wonderful thing began to happen to me. . . . [Somehow] little by little people began to open my office door at *Time* which in my own need few had ever opened. They would sit down, and after a rambling preamble, suddenly confide to me some distress that was destroying their peace or their lives. . . . Sometimes there were personal confessions of the most desperate kind. They came from people at all levels of the organization, from top to bottom. Men and women both have burst into tears in my office while I rose to snap the lock on the door. . . .
    Why did they come to me? I think chiefly because, in ways that I do not understand, they sensed that I saw in each a subject to be consoled and not to be judged—the torment of destiny rules out judgment. From me they wanted not words, but the instinctive sense that I recognized what was peculiarly "that of God within them," and because I made them recognize it in themselves. And this was true even when they were godless. They felt, too, that I would not betray their confidence even to the point of never mentioning it again to them.

Having cast himself in the role of saint, and thus emotionally primed himself and the reader, Chambers psychologically sets the stage in *Witness* for what is to follow; he is getting ready to introduce the Hiss case. As a last thought before presenting the ostensibly hard facts of the "Great Case," he bolsters his own credibility as a witness by implanting in the reader's mind the following image of himself (taken from Charles Péguy):

"No one is so competent a witness to the substance of Christianity as the sinner; no one, except, perhaps, the saint."

---

[21] The only childhood exposure Chambers may have had to Quakerism was through his paternal grandmother. In *Witness* he refers to it. One Sunday, writes Chambers, his Grandma "was complaining that she could do nothing and that nobody paid any attention to her. . . ."
    "Why don't you sew, Grandma?"
    "Because it's Sunday," she snapped.
    "Why can't you sew on Sunday?"
    "Because my mother was a Quaker."
    "What are Quakers?" I asked.

She then described how the Quakers wore the "plain dress" and used the "plain speech."

17

Rumors

Having effected his own conversion from sinner to saint, Chambers proceeds to do the reverse with Hiss's image. Though Chambers did not see Hiss for over a decade, it is evident that Hiss was on his mind. Note how he ascribes to Hiss the conspiratorial role of a spy, an obvious projection of his own pathological suspiciousness:

. . . Hiss was able to keep a rather close check on me through friends and contacts at *Time,* and . . . he knew a great deal about me at a time when I knew almost nothing about him.

It was, of course, precisely this kind of surveillance that Chambers himself maintained over others. In his delusional way, his suspicions that "others" were watching him made it necessary for him constantly to be on the alert against "them." Chambers enlists the reader into the same game, never letting the name of Hiss slip far from our consciousness, for he is about to present the "Great Case." He tells the following anonymous anecdote, reinforcing the image of Hiss, a high State Department official, as the Communist spy at the Yalta Conference.

Chambers refers to "two visits from an officer of the State Department, one of the best-informed men on Communist matters":

On his second visit I asked him if he thought that Alger Hiss was still a Communist. Tito (still at one with Stalin) had just shot down an American military plane and captured or killed its crew. "I can answer like this," my visitor said. "We're having Alger Hiss draft the note of protest: one, to put him on the spot; two, so he will tell the Russians secretly that we mean business." It was this man, too, who first told me that Alger Hiss had been at Yalta. "Imagine," he said, "what kind of a deal we got with Hiss sitting five feet from Stalin." [1]

[1] A few pages later (*Witness,* p. 529) Chambers begins his presentation of "The Hiss Case." This consists of two lengthy chapters (11, 13) and comprises almost one-third of the entire book. Though these chapters are titled "The Hiss Case" and "The Hiss Case II," Chambers reports the House Committee Hearings (August 1948) as "The Hiss Case and the New York Grand Jury proceedings (December 1948) as "The Hiss Case II."

In answer to my query, Hiss replied this was "fiction" and stated that he never drafted any such protest. What is equally surprising is Chambers' claim not to have known from the press accounts that Hiss was at Yalta.[2] Chambers, indeed, wrote the *Time* story on Yalta, a characteristic piece, much like "The Devil"—allegorical, ironic, and, as journalism, highly irregular.[3] Chambers justified its form by citing the security restrictions on all "firm" news coming out of the Yalta Conference.

Yet *Time* had to report something about it. What it would have reported had I then known that Alger Hiss was sitting not far behind Franklin Roosevelt, I cannot say.

Although there was a "news clamp" during the conference on its location, personnel, immediate deliberations, and decisions of the conference, those who attended and its general decisions were made known immediately after the conference's conclusion. Furthermore, when Chambers wrote his story the security restrictions were already off, the conference was over, and he must have known the American personnel, all of whom were listed in the communiqué of February 12, 1945. That *Time*'s editor for Foreign Affairs would not have this information, as he later wrote in his book, seems highly doubtful. Chambers continued his description of the story's origin:

I decided to make the fantastic news blackout itself the take-off for a story . . . and wrote a political fantasy in which I put into the mouths of the Muse of History and the ghosts of the late Tsar Nicholas and the Tsarina . . . the hard facts about Soviet foreign aggression that I found it all but impossible to report in any other way.

Chambers begins his story:

With the softness of bats, seven ghosts settled down on the flat roof of the Livadia Palace at Yalta. They found someone else already there: a statuesque female figure, crouching, with her eye glued to one of the holes in the roof. . . .
    "Madam," said the foremost ghost, an imperious woman with a bullet hole in her head, "what are you doing on our roof?"

The proceedings and testimony of the two federal trials (*United States* v. *Alger Hiss*, May 31, 1949, to July 8, 1949, and November 17, 1949, to January 21, 1950, except for a few random references, are bypassed. In the last two pages of chapter 14 (pp. 793–94) Chambers mentions only the *result* of the trials. Thus he not only misleads the reader but avoids the many inconsistencies and ambiguities of his testimony, which were brought out under cross-examination during the two trials. This literary finesse is so cleverly camouflaged that I did not become aware of it until I was well launched in my study.
[2] On February 13, 1945, the *New York Times* published the "text of the report [communiqué] on the Big Three Conference." This report listed the names of those present (including Hiss) and in another list the thirteen participants "For the U.S.A.," and Hiss was again listed as one of the thirteen. The release was by the Associated Press, date line Washington, D.C., February 12. Thus news stories of Yalta appeared in papers all over the country.
[3] "Ghosts on the Roof," Time, March 5, 1945; reprinted January 5, 1948.

Clio, the Muse of History (for it was she), looked up, her finger on her lips. "Shh!" she said, "the Big Three Conference is just ending down there. What with security regulations, censorship and personal secretiveness, the only way I can find out anything these days is by peeping. And who are you?"

"Madam," said the male ghost (he also had a bullet hole in his forehead), "I am Nicholas II, Emperor and Autocrat of All the Russias. . . .

"Nicholas—how nice to see you again," cried History. "Wherever have you been? And the Tsarina Alix! Your four charming daughters, I presume—gracious, but those bullet holes are disfiguring. And the little hemophiliac—Tsarevich Alexei! Ah, yes, I understand—doomed for a certain term to walk the night. . . . Why, I've scarcely given you a thought since that time when the Communists threw your bodies down the mine shaft in Ekaterinburg (now Sverdlovsk). Whatever brings you here?"

It seems that the story springs as much from Chambers' private fantasy system as from the news blackout, for he must have known that Hiss was at Yalta. There is an evident symbolic equivalence between the character assassination of Hiss (the arch-traitor) sitting "five feet from Stalin" and shooting traitorous advice into Roosevelt's mind and the Czar and Czarina with bullet holes in their heads. The reversal of time and history in which the assassinated return to life (the ghosts on the roof) is equated with the implied traitorous act of Hiss, and Chambers' character assassination of him. For Chambers, Death was only a transcendental means to an end. By the use of such an allegorical device and a magical reversal of time and event, he resurrects the assassinated Czar with the same inventive ease that he uses to destroy Hiss.

The allegory continues:

. . . said the Muse of History, ". . . I am glad to see that Marxism has had the same psychotherapeutic effect on you as on so many neurotics who join the Communist Party. But your notions about Russia and Stalin are highly abnormal. All right-thinking people now agree that Russia is a mighty friend of democracy. . . . In a few hours the whole civilized world will hail the historic decisions just reached beneath your feet as proof that the Soviet Union is prepared to collaborate with her allies in making the world safe for democracy and capitalism. The revolution is over. . . .

"Death," said the Tsarina, "is a somewhat maturing experience. What Nicky means is that between two systems of society, which embody diametrically opposed moral and political principles, even peace may be only a tactic of struggle."

. . . said History, ". . . More is at stake than economic and political systems. Two faiths are at issue. It is just that problem which these gentlemen below are trying to work out in practical terms. But if they fail, I foresee more wars, more revolutions, greater proscriptions, bloodshed and human misery."

"Well," said the Tsarina, "if you can foresee all that, why don't you do something to prevent it?"

". . . in answer to your question, Madam," she said, glancing at the Tsarina,

"I never permit my fore-knowledge to interfere with human folly, if only because I never expect human folly to learn much from history. Besides, I must leave something for my sister, Melpomene, to work on."

During the August 1948 House Committee hearings, Hiss was repeatedly questioned about the extent of his influence and participation at this historic meeting of the three Big Powers. His role has been a much-talked-about subject since the Hiss trials. Many people came to believe that Alger Hiss was an important policy-maker at Yalta, that his role was on a par with such senior members of the delegations as Winston Churchill, Anthony Eden, James F. Byrnes, Edward Stettinius, Averell Harriman, and the leading military figures of both Britain and the United States. But however one appraises the Yalta agreement, a careful study of the event demonstrates that Hiss had a decidedly minor part in it.

In *Roosevelt and Hopkins* by Robert E. Sherwood, which treats Yalta at length, the name of Alger Hiss is not mentioned. Sherwood apparently did not regard Hiss's function at Yalta as having historical significance. His book was published in 1948, prior to the summer hearings of the House Committee and the Hiss case.

Edward Stettinius's book, *Roosevelt and the Russians,* published in 1949, praised Hiss's work at Yalta. In Stettinius's account, written just after Hiss had been publicly accused by Chambers, the former Secretary of State made a particular point of Hiss's loyalty and integrity. Stettinius had worked closely with Hiss, was aware of the caliber of his work, as he was of his other two State Department experts, H. Freeman Matthews (director of the Office of European Affairs) and Wilder Foote, who shared equally in an advisory capacity to Stettinius.

Shortly after I became Undersecretary of State—October 1943, [wrote Stettinius] . . . with the approval of the President and Mr. Hull I called in the FBI to conduct a security examination of the State Department. Assistant Secretary of State, G. Howland Shaw, served as liaison with the FBI during this examination. I never heard of any questioning of Mr. Hiss's loyalty from anyone inside or outside of the State Department or from the FBI during my time of service in the Department.

Hiss performed brilliantly throughout the Dumbarton Oaks conversations, the Yalta Conference, the San Francisco Conference, and the first meeting of the United Nations Assembly in London. I always had reason to believe that Hiss acted honorably and patriotically in the performance of his duties at these conferences.[4]

[4] Edward R. Stettinius, Jr., *Roosevelt and the Russians* (Garden City, N.Y.: Doubleday & Co., 1949), p. 31.

Stettinius relates this significant anecdote:

Hiss, our representative on the subcommittee, told me as the [plenary] meeting was coming to order that he had just asked Eden for a copy of the report drafted by the subcommittee, which the British representative had agreed to have typed. When Eden had somewhat reluctantly handed him a copy, Hiss noticed that it expressed American support for the extra votes, which had not been in the draft which he as American representative on the subcommittee had approved. He protested to Eden that the United States had not approved the extra votes,[5] but Eden replied, "You don't know what has taken place." It was obvious from Eden's remark that the President had had a private talk with the British after the subcommittee had adjourned and before the plenary session had convened.[6]

James F. Byrnes has written at two different times of the Yalta Conference. In the first volume of his memoirs, *Speaking Frankly,* published in 1947 before the Hiss trials, Byrnes discussed the conference in detail. There is no mention at all of Hiss.[7] In 1958 Byrnes' second book appeared. And now he pondered over Hiss's role at Yalta:

I have previously expressed my doubt that at Yalta Hiss exercised any influence directly upon President Roosevelt in the decisions he and Churchill made on the Far East. . . . Whether Hiss, through Hopkins and Stettinius, influenced the President on any matters other than the United Nations proposals is pure speculation and a point upon which partisan opinion will never agree.[8]

Despite all the accounts of the Yalta Conference by high government officials who participated in the proceedings, the names "Hiss" and "Yalta" have become mixed in the crucible of "guilt by close association," fused and confused in the political mind with "traitor" and "sell-out." Hiss himself wrote an article in 1955 (shortly after his release from Lewisburg) about Yalta, in which he attacked the "legend" that surrounded the agreement:

The Yalta legend has it that there a failing President, incompetently or malevolently advised, betrayed stricken Poland and our ally China; . . . the legend explains the vast social upheavals of Europe and Asia as resulting from the faltering or cynical appeasement of Stalin by Roosevelt. . . . The "Myth of Yalta" is related only in name to the historical event it purports to recount. . . . Its destruc-

---

[5] Stettinius here refers to the United States' agreement to support Soviet Russia's application for votes in the Assembly and membership in the United Nations Organization for Byelorussia and the Ukraine.

Questioned about this controversial point, Hiss later explained to the House Committee: "I opposed the particular point [that the Chairman referred to]; I did not oppose the Yalta agreement as a whole—quite the contrary. I still think the political agreement was a very valuable agreement for the United States." Said Mr. Mundt, "I congratulate you on your opposition to that particular section. . . ." (HUAC Hearings, pp. 656–57.)

[6] Stettinius, *op. cit.,* pp. 195–97.

[7] James F. Byrnes, *Speaking Frankly* (New York: Harper & Brothers, 1947).

[8] James F. Byrnes, *All in One Lifetime* (New York: Harper & Brothers, 1958), p. 322.

tive ghosts will be laid only as the American public learns again to face the problems of the real world with rationality and fortitude. . . ." [9]

At Yalta, President Roosevelt, on the advice of Secretary of State Stettinius, designated Hiss as interim Secretary General of the San Francisco Conference, which was to open on April 25, 1945. By then, Hiss had succeeded Edwin Wilson as director of the Office of Special Political Affairs.

After the Yalta Conference, Hiss lectured to the public about the forthcoming plans for the United Nations. Along with Archibald MacLeish (then Assistant Secretary of State), and John Dickey, they devised a plan of having consultants from forty private national organizations attached to the United States Delegation at San Francisco.

(While Hiss was preparing for the UN Conference, Whittaker Chambers had a private conversation at his Westminster farm with Ray Murphy, security officer for the State Department, in which Chambers repeated his earlier charges against Hiss and others.)

Hiss's work at San Francisco placed him suddenly in the public eye; the press was without exception favorable. Of special interest is *Time*'s report on May 28, 1945:

In a class by himself was young, handsome Alger Hiss, a U.S. State Department career man functioning as international secretary general. Relaxed and alert amid innumerable annoyances, Hiss was master of the incredibly complicated conference machinery. The wheels turned. A charter of world organization was taking shape.

On July 16, 1945, after the conclusion of the San Francisco Conference, the picture of Alger Hiss appeared in *Life* magazine as "Picture of the Week." During the first Hiss trial, Chambers was asked if he had read the articles. His first response was startling, "I believe I wrote that." He later denied it. The point of the Hiss defense was that if Chambers had "real" knowledge that Hiss was a Communist—as he stated privately to Ray Murphy and to the FBI (who saw fit to do nothing about it)—or that Alger Hiss was "planted" by the Kremlin to destroy State Department policy, how could he remain silent? Furthermore, why would he condone or, perhaps, write laudatory articles about Hiss? [10] And why would he not press his case with the State Depart-

[9] Alger Hiss, *Yalta: Modern American Myth* (New York: Pocket Books, Inc., 1955).
[10] When Chambers, in 1948, appeared on "Meet the Press," a similar question was raised.

REYNOLDS: As a professional newspaperman, Mr. Chambers, I have some curiosity about one matter. As I recall it, you were foreign editor of *Time* magazine during the war.
CHAMBERS: I was.
REYNOLDS: The correspondents for foreign news around the State Department had as one of their better sources Alger Hiss. I am quite sure that is true, because I was told

ment? But Chambers seems to have had an irrational, equivocal attitude toward the State Department.

During the very period when he was naming Hiss and other high State Department officials as members of an underground Communist cell, Chambers published an article and several book reviews (under the pen name "John Land") in the *American Mercury* (January through May, 1944) in which he praised the State Department for its wariness of the Russians.

If there is one agency of the United States Government that has a precise, factual and even statistical knowledge of Russia's multiplex political activities in all parts of the world, including North America, it is the State Department. Secretary Hull was no doubt gratified by his reception in Moscow, but there is no evidence that he was fooled by it. Nor does anything that the Department has done or left undone suggest that it does not have a knowing grasp of Russia's postwar plans. Thus its tactful but firm refusal to let Bolshevism migrate into Italy and France, as a stowaway of the Allied politics of liberation, has made the State Department a target for covert and overt Communists. It must have been icily clear for some time in the Kremlin that the American State Department, as at present constituted, must go.

Thus while he is privately saying that the State Department is infested with Communists, Chambers (under an alias) is assuring the reading public that it isn't so. This contradictory behavior seems explicable only in terms of Chambers' private necessity to repeat the endless cycle of doing and undoing, sinning and repenting.

Chambers' secret charges did, to be sure, reach the top officials of the State Department before they became public knowledge, but they came indirectly.

In February 1946 (by which time Chambers had already made one of his two secret reports to Ray Murphy) Secretary of State Byrnes called Hiss into his office. Byrnes told Hiss that several congressmen, "members of the House Committee on Un-American Activities or the House Military Affairs Subcommittee," had been told by a former FBI agent then working for one of those committees that Hiss's name was on several subversive lists and that the congressmen were threatening to make speeches calling Hiss a Communist. Hiss vehemently denied that there was any truth in such accusations, and Secretary Byrnes advised him to go immediately to the FBI and talk directly with

at times he talked in confidence to them. Did you use material from Alger Hiss in *Time* magazine during the war years when you were foreign editor?
CHAMBERS: Not to my knowledge.
REYNOLDS: Not to your knowledge? How could you escape that knowledge if the memorandum came in marked "from Alger Hiss"?
CHAMBERS: I recall no such memorandum.

("Whittaker Chambers Meets the Press," *The American Mercury*, February 1949, p.154.)

J. Edgar Hoover. Hoover did not see him, but Hiss talked with an FBI aide. The talk lasted little more than a quarter of an hour. Hiss reported his conversation with Byrnes, stated that he wished the FBI to make a full and free inquiry to get to the root of the matter. He denied he was or ever had been a member of the Communist Party or had ever had any association with it. Hiss stated the names of the organizations to which he then and in the past had belonged. He described three or four occurrences that could possibly have caused reports that he was a Communist. Asked if he knew Lee Pressman, he described, as he had to Byrnes, his associations with Pressman. Several other names came up in the course of the conversation, but the name Whittaker Chambers was not mentioned.

Some months later, on August 28, 1946, Whittaker Chambers had a second "conversation" with Ray Murphy, and again, except for certain additions and variations in Chambers' story, Murphy's memorandum follows the general lines of his previous interview of March 20, 1945. *But Chambers' story of his personal relationship with Alger Hiss* (the latter now a well-known national figure by reason of the publicity and commendations for his work as Secretary General of the San Francisco Conference) *had changed from the mere mention of Hiss's name among a list of others to that of a close personal friend.* In the final paragraphs of the memorandum Murphy said: "My informant [Chambers] asked Alger Hiss personally to break with the party in early 1938, but Hiss refused with tears in his eyes and said he would remain loyal to the Party."

During 1945 (before he heard his loyalty questioned) Hiss began to consider leaving the State Department.

I had always thought of myself as a lawyer (the reason I was not interested in teaching when that had been proposed). I liked the freedom of action and the financial independence of a private lawyer and the subject matter was congenial.

In January of 1946, while aboard ship en route to London to attend a preparatory meeting of the United Nations, he had an informal talk with John Foster Dulles. It was then, Hiss recalls, that Dulles asked him if he intended to stay on indefinitely in the Department. When Hiss indicated that he did not, Dulles thereafter considered him as one of several men eligible to fill the recently vacated position of president of the Carnegie Endowment for World Peace. Hiss's initial reaction to this idea was negative. He still planned to leave government service to go into private law practice, but the Endowment's interest in the UN changed his mind.

My interest in the UN and foreign policy was paramount and when Mr. Dulles, John W. Davis, Arthur Ballantine and Mr. Wadsworth—the Endowment's nominating committee—agreed that if I accepted the presidency I could make the Endowment's chief activity the study and support of the UN, I accepted late in 1946.

In December of that year Hiss was elected president of the Endowment. Rumors about Hiss were then sufficiently current to prompt speculation that he was leaving under fire.

The *Christian Science Monitor* on December 14, 1946, reported Hiss's resignation and spoke to that point:

Acting Secretary of State Dean Acheson announced with evident regret this week the resignation of Alger Hiss, able chief of the Department's Office of Special Political Affairs, to become President of the Carnegie Endowment for International Peace. . . .

Mr. Hiss, it can be said positively, is not retiring because of any pressure or criticism of him for leftist leanings. That he was the subject of much propaganda on that score is public knowledge. More than one Congressman, whenever the subject of leftist activity in the State Department was mentioned, pulled out a list of suspects that was invariably headed by Mr. Hiss.

The choice of Hiss as president (and Dulles as chairman of the board), said George A. Finch, secretary of the Endowment, "serves to emphasize the decision of the Trustees to concentrate the Endowment's efforts as much as possible upon the success of the United Nations as the instrument best adapted at the present time to promote the purposes for which the Endowment was founded." [11] As president, Hiss was responsible for the administration of the staff, for the formulation of the organization's policies, which were subject to the approval of the board of trustees, and for effecting those policies and programs. The Endowment had lagged during the war and was in need of new energies and reorganization when Hiss came into office. He felt that the foundation had "reached a stage in which new plans for the future should be drawn up" and changes should be made so that the Endowment could pursue more efficiently the objectives which Carnegie envisioned when he created it. Three months after Hiss took office, on May 8, 1947, at the annual meeting of the board of trustees, he submitted his first formal report, titled "Recommendations of the President," in which he formulated his plans:

I recommend . . . that the Endowment construct its program . . . for the support and assistance of the United Nations . . . that this program be conceived of as having two objectives. First, it should be widely educational in order to encourage public understanding and support of the United Nations at home and abroad. Second, it should aid in the adoption of wise policies both by our own government in its capacity as a member of the United Nations and by the United Nations organization as a whole.[12]

[11] *Annual Report of the Secretary,* dated January 31, 1947, pp. 32–33.
[12] "Recommendations of the President," *Carnegie Endowment Yearbook,* 1947, pp. 16, 17, 18.

Since 1911, when the Endowment had been established, it had been organized into three divisions, two in New York and one in Washington.[13] The Washington branch was run independently. Not only was efficiency impaired with this system, but the expenses, Hiss felt, were considerably greater. Hiss eliminated the three divisions, created a single, unified staff. He recommended an increase in salaries for Endowment personnel.

Anne Winslow, editor-in-chief of the Carnegie Endowment, informed me that when Hiss first came into the office of the Endowment he and the staff were mutually wary of each other, but it was not long before Hiss had won his staff over (with the exception of Malcolm Davis, director of the Division of Intercourse and Education, a department Hiss abolished). Hiss soon was acquainted with everyone—even messenger boys and telephone operators. They "adored his recognition of them and his consideration for them, yet at the same time he had an uncanny way of remaining aloof, without ever being snooty." As president, Hiss engendered a cohesive spirit among the staff and kindled a new excitement in the work and aims of the Endowment. This was a time of considerable public acclaim for Hiss. He was awarded an honorary degree by his alma mater, Johns Hopkins, and was commencement speaker at Haverford College and at Wells College. He gave over much of his time to speaking on other occasions—to business associations as well as to college groups—and he wrote several articles and papers. His subject was always relevant to the "Prospects for Peace" (the title of his address at Haverford) and the role of the United Nations.

But the rumors of his alleged subversion did not stop. It was very soon after Hiss's election as president of the Carnegie Endowment was announced in the press that Dulles received a communication from a man, later identified as Alfred Kohlberg, alleging that Hiss was or had been a Communist. Kohlberg was the publisher of *Plain Talk,* a magazine edited by Isaac Don Levine. Hiss later testified (during the second trial) that sometime in December 1946 Dulles called him on the telephone from New York and said, "What shall I say in answer to a letter from some man who claims you are a Communist?" Hiss replied that he thought "that subject had been laid to rest; did Dulles know the background?" Dulles said that he had discussed the whole matter fully with Justice Byrnes, but what he wanted was an appropriate answer to the individual who had written to him. Hiss said that he could only suggest that Dulles ask for any possible basis for such a charge, any possible evidence or information. Dulles said he thought that was a good idea, and that concluded the conversation.

[13] Division of Intercourse and Education; Division of International Law; Division of Economics and History.

Murky rumors which had been floating around Washington regarding Hiss's loyalty and political affiliations continued to crop up. On June 2, 1947, two FBI agents called on Hiss at the Washington offices of the Carnegie Endowment to question him about a long list of people, several of whom he had known and worked with in the government. As in all his previous statements, Hiss denied being or having ever been a Communist. He repeated to the FBI agents the fact that he had once belonged to the International Juridical Association and recalled for them several contributing members of its journal. He was asked about his associations with Harold Ware, Charles Krivitsky, Henry Collins, John Abt, Victor Perlo, Harold Glasser (names cited by Whittaker Chambers as Communists). He told them about his relationship with these men. He reiterated in detail his friendship with Lee Pressman while at Harvard and during the days of the AAA. He was asked whether he knew Nathan Perlow, Nathan Gregory Silvermaster, and said that he did not. For the first time he was asked if he ever knew a man named Whittaker Chambers. He said he did not. The FBI prepared a detailed summary of the interview, which Hiss read and signed.[14]

On March 16, 1948, Hiss was asked to appear before the New York Grand Jury. The statements he had made to the FBI in June 1947 were read back to him. He was asked whether they were his, and he affirmed that they were. He was asked whether he had any corrections of dates to make, and he did not. He was asked whether he knew Whittaker Chambers, and he stated that he did not.

On that same day John Foster Dulles, having recently received two additional communications accusing Hiss of being a Communist, asked Hiss to come to see him.

As soon as I had left the Grand Jury I went to see Mr. Dulles and told him of my appearance. . . .
On that occasion he told me that the first letter he had received in December 1946 he had replied to along the lines that I had suggested, and had received a reply from the man, whose name he then told me for the first time, a Mr. Kohlberg, who . . . had replied he had no facts, and the matter had thereupon been dropped. On this occasion in March 1948 Mr. Dulles said he had received another . . . communication. . . . I told him of my testimony before the Grand Jury; . . . and of people about whom I had been interrogated, and I remember specifically telling him that from the time Mr. Byrnes had first spoken to me in March 1946, that the name of Mr. Pressman had figured. Mr. Byrnes had mentioned it to me; the FBI had asked me about it when I went to see them in March of 1946; they had again asked me about it in May or June of 1947, and it was contained . . . in my statement written on that day which had been read just before I saw Mr. Dulles, at the Grand Jury.

[14] For Hiss's "Statement to Federal Bureau of Investigation," June 2, 1947, see Appendix.

Mr. Dulles said that the last person who had written to him had mentioned Assistant Secretary Peurifoy of the State Department in a way that had led Mr. Dulles' correspondent to feel Mr. Peurifoy had some question about me. I urged Mr. Dulles to communicate directly with Mr. Peurifoy. . . .

He subsequently told me he had seen Mr. Peurifoy and talked to him, and Mr. Peurifoy said any such implication was a complete misunderstanding and he had said no such thing and had full confidence in me.[15]

From a review of the early rumors, the private, then public charges against Hiss, Chambers' exclusive role as the agent of the scandal is clearly evident.

The rumor that Alger Hiss was a Communist, echoed and re-echoed about Washington since 1939, all stemmed from a single source: Chambers' original statement to Isaac Don Levine in 1938, which, as we have seen, was followed in 1939 by Chambers' visit, through Levine's insistence and help, to Assistant Secretary of State Berle. On May 1, 1963, in a note to me, Berle wrote:

Mr. Chambers did not tell me the truth on the evening you mention [in September 1939], and later testified that he did not. . . . My own impression of the man [Chambers] is a matter of record and you have it, and I do not think I can add much to that record now.

Chambers' accusation of Hiss, true or false, once told, then relayed by Berle to the FBI, thereby became converted into a "substantive suspicion," recorded in some form in Hiss's official dossier. Once incorporated into the investigative labyrinth of the FBI, it could not be retracted. In 1941, 1942, 1944 (as far as is known), the FBI had repeated private interviews with Chambers. In 1945 and 1946 Chambers had interviews with Ray Murphy, security officer of the State Department, and from 1946 to 1948 FBI agents, Chambers tells us, were "frequent visitors." The public, as well as the Hiss defense counsel both before and during the trials, never could find out the frequency of Chambers' contacts with the FBI during the period prior to the time Hiss appeared before the House Committee in August 1948.

Sometime in 1939, the year Chambers visited Berle (entirely unknown to Hiss), Hiss was investigated under the Hatch Act. His reaction to this was: "I think most everyone I knew was investigated. We regarded it as routine."

"The very first happening, which," says Hiss, "came to me out of the blue," was early in 1946—this was when Secretary Byrnes told him that members of Congress were going to attack him on the floor and that he should see Hoover. Hiss immediately made an appointment with the FBI. Then, on June 2, 1947, came the FBI call during which Hiss was presented with a long

[15] Personal memo from Hiss to author.

list of names, including the name Whittaker Chambers. Yet Hiss was remarkedly undisturbed:

. . . with the background of Byrnes' statement in February 1946, and *my call on* the FBI at that time, the 1947 Kohlberg rumor plus Dulles' talk with me at that time, the call by the FBI *on me* in the spring of 1947 seemed merely a rehashing of old tales and not very important. Undoubtedly there were other rumors that I didn't then know of and probably some I still haven't heard of.

But these rumors all led back to Whittaker Chambers. For example, after the trials Hiss learned that Arthur Schlesinger, Jr., had told friends of his during the trials that he had seen "documentary" evidence that Hiss was a Communist. When Schlesinger had written an article for *Life* magazine on "Communists in Government," the FBI had shown him an affidavit (that is, a "document") by Chambers saying this.

Then, in the winter of 1947–48, Hiss heard that a man named Chambers had called him a Communist but on challenge had declined to repeat it. Hiss did not, at the time, recognize this name as one of the many he had been asked about eight or nine months earlier. Before the House Committee in 1948 he told the story of this attack:

. . . a friend of mine attending a dinner party had heard a fellow guest at the dinner party say that Alger Hiss was a Communist and had been when he was in Government service.

This friend of mine had challenged this fellow guest and the fellow guest said, "I know it, because a man named Chambers said so."

The friend, according to the report as I got it, had followed it up, and had been told several days later by that same person that the person had checked back, and the person had been told that Chambers had been talking too much and was not saying [that] now; so that I paid no further attention to it.

A lot of people, Mr. Hébert, have been called Communists in recent years.

Hiss's appearance before the New York Grand Jury in March 1948 also stirred little or no anxiety or concern in him:

At the time, many former Government officials were being called to testify on technical matters. I was present very briefly. The questions seemed routine (did you know so and so, where did you work?) and I assumed and still do that I was called merely in an attempt to describe my knowledge of or acquaintance with a number of people whose names would naturally in one fashion or another be brought up in such an enquiry. I didn't assume it affected me to any extent.

Afterward, "as a matter of normal judgment," he told Dulles about it. Dulles had just received another communication regarding Hiss, and they discussed the whole matter.

There was yet another rumor, which *seemed* to come from an independent source. Back in 1939, just after Hiss had taken up his position in the office of Stanley Hornbeck, State Department adviser on political relations, former ambassador William C. Bullitt, in a conversation with Hornbeck, said he had heard Hiss called a Communist. Hornbeck had brushed the matter off, and Hiss did not hear of the accusation until the summer of 1948. But Ambassador Bullitt's charge to Hornbeck also came, via Isaac Don Levine, from Chambers. "When no results were forthcoming from Chambers' interview with Berle, I sketched [to] Bullitt the whole thing, and gave him some additional bits of information that I knew from Krivitsky; thus the whole story was put before Bullitt." [16]

From a study of the texts of Hiss's FBI interviews and the repeated stories told to Levine, Berle, and Ray Murphy by Whittaker Chambers, it is evident that the questions asked of Hiss by the FBI all sprang from Chambers' story. In Hiss's interview with the FBI in the spring of 1947 he was asked whether he knew anyone by the name of Sayre. He mentioned two: Francis B. Sayre and a Dan Sayre of Princeton, neither of whom, to his knowledge, was a Communist. Only Whittaker Chambers had mentioned Francis Sayre's name to Malcolm Cowley and Berle in connection with Communist affiliations.

Ironically, it was the charges of another ex-Communist—against other government officials—that fanned the long-smoldering embers.

On July 31, 1948, the late Elizabeth Bentley appeared before the House Un-American Activities Committee. She said she had been a courier for a Communist spy ring. Her testimony inaugurated a series of hearings before that congressional body which was officially titled by the committee, "Hearings Regarding Communist Espionage in the United States Government." Miss Bentley's accusations were brought quickly to public attention by a series of sensational articles in the *New York World-Telegram,* revealing that a "red spy queen" had successfully operated an espionage ring in Washington, D.C., during the war years. Her accusations were followed three days later by those of Whittaker Chambers, subpoenaed in the heat of the "exposé" to repeat in public what he had said before only in private. It was on the eve of

---

[16] Isaac Don Levine to the author (personal interview, January 5, 1962). Levine later co-authored a series of sensational articles in the *Saturday Evening Post* with General Walter Krivitsky, a former Russian military intelligence officer and GPU agent, entitled "In Stalin's Secret Service."

On August 18, 1948, Levine testified to the House Committee:

NIXON: Mr. Levine, did you convey this information that Mr. Chambers had given to Mr. Berle to any other persons in the Government?
LEVINE: Yes, sir; I did. I conveyed it some three months later to former Ambassador Bullitt, a friend of the President's, at breakfast with him in his Anchorage Hotel apartment. (HUAC Hearings, p. 1008.)

that occasion—which we have described at the outset—that Chambers felt the extraordinary anguish, which we will now call guilt: "What I felt was what we see in the eye of a bird or an animal that we are about to kill, which knows that it is about to be killed. . . ." [17]

[17] See p. 4.

18

Documents

D ESPITE THE SENSATIONAL EFFECT of Chambers' charges in August, they
were, by September, in danger of backfiring. Chambers had been unable
to offer further substantiation for his claims; dissent over the House Committee's tactics was appearing in the press, and Hiss had threatened a libel suit
against Chambers. Of all the figures Chambers named in his appearance before the House Committee, Hiss was the only one who would choose to challenge Chambers in the courts. It was a costly decision; by the end it would
cost him his career.

He could not sue, however, until Chambers repeated his accusations in a
public situation; the House Committee hearings were privileged sessions. The
opportunity came when Chambers appeared on "Meet the Press" on nationwide radio. The questioning began:

Mr. Chambers, in the hearings on Capitol Hill you said over and over again that
you served in the Communist Party with Alger Hiss. Your remarks down there
were privileged; that is to say, you were protected from lawsuits. Hiss has now
challenged you to make the same charge publicly. He says if you do he will test
your veracity by filing a suit for slander or libel. Are you willing to say now that
Alger Hiss is or ever was a Communist?
    Chambers said, "Alger Hiss was a Communist and may be now."
    The matter was raised a second time: "Does that mean that you are now pre-
pared to go into court and answer to a suit for slander or libel?"
    "I do not think Mr. Hiss will sue me for libel," Chambers answered.[1]

Hiss says he now felt that the advantage had shifted to him. At last he
could initiate an effective course of action. In his mind there was no alternative but to carry out his threat and proceed with the libel suit. And in the mind
of the public, for him to remain silent would have been tantamount to an

---

[1] "Whittaker Chambers Meets the Press," *loc. cit.*

admission of guilt. Nor would it have been feasible for him, as president of the Carnegie Endowment, to carry on his work there unless he was cleared of the cloud of suspicion that surrounded him. He decided, however, to confer with some of his friends before making his move. Professor Richard H. Field of Harvard Law School, a colleague and close friend since their student years, has described how Hiss came to Cambridge, sought his advice and the opinion of several other faculty friends as to whether he should bring the suit. "Indeed," said Field, "I recall his attitude at that time as an added voucher of his innocence. . . . I have talked again with Henry Hart, Paul Freund . . . and Harold Rosenwald. . . . Hart remembers having given the advice that a suit should be brought." [2]

William Marbury was chosen to conduct the suit. He was then in Europe on government business and was not due to return for another month. The delay gave rise to some suspicion that Hiss would not take action. But he had no intention of letting the matter subside. By way of encouragement he was receiving hundreds of letters expressing confidence in his loyalty and hope for his vindication.

The costliness of such an action, added to what Hiss had already spent in his defense before the House Committee, became a pressing reality. Field and several others, realizing the large sums required for such an undertaking, offered financial help, which Hiss initially did not want to accept. Once the suit had been filed and Hiss realized the financial burden it entailed, he decided to accept Field's advice. Eventually more than $50,000 was contributed.

On September 27, 1948, Marbury, of the legal firm of Marbury, Miller and Evans of Baltimore, instituted legal proceedings and claimed damages in the amount of $50,000 for defamation of character. When, about a month later, Chambers received a summons to defend himself in court, he made a public statement. "I welcome Alger Hiss' daring suit. I do not minimize the ferocity or the ingenuity of the forces that are working through him. But I do not believe that, ultimately, Alger Hiss, or anybody else, can use the means of justice to defeat the ends of justice."

"By the forces that are working through him," he later explained in *Witness,* "I meant, of course, the Communist Party."

The following day Hiss's attorneys, as a reaction to this statement, felt their client's reputation had been further injured and raised the amount of the suit to $75,000. Chambers, represented by Richard Cleveland and William MacMillan, Esq., of the firm of Semmes, Bowen and Semmes of Baltimore, formally defended his statements as the truth. Counsel for Hiss, in accordance

[2] Richard H. Field to the author, October 15, 1963.

with legal procedure, then began a private and what proved to be lengthy pre-trial cross-examination of Chambers on November 4.[3]

Meanwhile the House Committee's interest in the case continued, and the New York Grand Jury investigating Communist activities called Chambers. It will be remembered that in his first public appearance Chambers had said that the Communist "apparatus" to which Hiss was allegedly attached was not involved in espionage. He was repeatedly questioned on this crucial point. On October 14, before the New York Grand Jury, Chambers was asked:

Could you give one name of anybody who, in your opinion, was positively guilty of espionage against the United States?
CHAMBERS: . . . I don't think so but I would like to have the opportunity to answer you tomorrow more definitely. Let me think it over overnight.

The next day he testified:

CHAMBERS: . . . I assume that espionage means in this case the turning over of secret or confidential documents.
JUROR: Or information—oral information.
CHAMBERS: . . . I do not believe I do know such a name.

Three weeks later, November 4, Marbury asked Chambers to produce any letters or papers he had in his possession that he had received from the Hisses. And the next day Marbury repeated his request:

Yesterday, at the close of the hearing, I asked you if you would produce any papers or notes or correspondence from any member of the Hiss family this morning. Have you got any such papers with you, Mr. Chambers?

Chambers replied, "No, I do not." Later that same day Chambers testified that he ". . . never transmitted a State Department document from Mr. Hiss to the Communist Party." [4]

Thirteen days later Chambers inexplicably contradicted this definite testimony. On November 17 Chambers produced sixty-five typewritten pages of copied State Department documents and four small slips of paper with penciled notes in Hiss's handwriting.

This dramatic coup was like a transfusion of life blood into an otherwise dying case. The unexpected introduction of documents served to cover the doubts in many people's minds about Chambers' credibility. Where had they come from? In *Witness*, Chambers later described how he found his "life-preserver" hidden in the apartment of Nathan Levine, his wife's nephew.

---

[3] The typed transcript (never published) of this testimony (1382 pages), referred to in this study as the Baltimore Deposition, included also testimony of Mrs. Chambers.
[4] Baltimore Deposition, p. 317.

Levine led me up to the second floor. By then he was laughing at what seemed to him a somewhat absurd business. He led me to a bathroom, where, over the tub, a small window opened into a dumbwaiter shaft that had long been out of use. Inside the shaft was some kind of small shelf or ledge. There Levine had laid "my things."

He climbed upon the tub, opened the little window and half disappeared into the shaft. When he reappeared, he handed me an envelope that was big, plump and densely covered with the clotted cobwebs and dust of a decade. As I took it from his hands, the accumulation slid to the floor.

In surprise, for I had supposed that the envelope was a small one, I carried it to the kitchen, which was at the end of the hall, and laid it on a white enamel table top. Levine's chief concern was for the mess that I had made on his mother's floor, for she was a somewhat implacable housekeeper. He took a broom and dustpan and went back to tidy up.[5]

In his absence, I opened the envelope and drew part way out the thick batch of copied State Department documents. At a glance, I saw that, besides those documents, and Hiss's handwritten memos, there were three cylinders of microfilm and a little spool of developed film (actually two strips). By a reflex of amazement, I pushed the papers back into the envelope. Then I held on to the edge of the table, for I had the feeling that the floor was swinging around me and that I was going to fall to it. That passed in an instant. But I continued to grip the edge of the table in a kind of physical hush that a man feels to whom has happened an act of God.

I was still standing there—it had all taken only a few moments—when Levine came back with his broom and dustpan and asked me, as nearly as I remember, if I had found what I was looking for.

My answer was more to myself than to him. "Good God," I said, "I did not know that this still existed."

What followed is a familiar story. According to Chambers' account, with the manila envelope and its packed contents safely in his possession, he returned at once to his farmhouse in Westminster. Then, in the secrecy of his remote surroundings, he carefully examined the material he had with such remarkable prescience caused to be hidden ten years past. With his flair for the dramatic end, as we shall see, a clearly designed plan, he divided the paper documents and the microfilm. Then on November 17 the former was shown to Marbury, Hiss's counsel, who immediately notified Alger Hiss. Hiss had them turned over to the Justice Department. The Justice Department took them to Washington, imposing secrecy on all. Chambers, however, discreetly got word—through an intermediary—to the House Committee that he not only had produced sensational evidence but that there was still more to come.

[5] "I was more concerned," Levine explained to me in a recent interview, "with what I then felt would be my mother's annoyance with the 'schmutz' [dust] that had fallen on the white tile floor of the bathroom, than I was curious about what was in the manila envelope which Chambers took into the kitchen and opened during my absence." (Nathan Levine to the author, December 1964.)

Bert Andrews, reporter for the *New York Herald Tribune,* who had been close to Chambers, informed Nixon that Chambers had "produced something important at the Baltimore hearing," adding, "I have a hunch that he may have another ace in the hole. Why don't you try to find out?" Whereupon Nixon and Robert Stripling drove to Chambers' Westminster farm.

We didn't even have to open the subject. Chambers knew why we were there. . . . He said he could not talk in detail because he had been warned he might get held in contempt of court if he did. I asked him: "Did you drop a bombshell at the Baltimore hearing?" . . . He said that he did and implied he had still more information, but didn't want to get in contempt of court.[6]

Following Andrews' advice, Nixon had Robert Stripling serve a blanket subpoena on Chambers to produce "anything and everything he still has in his possession."

The next morning, December 2, despite the turn of events, Nixon departed on a planned Caribbean cruise, well aware that Chambers was to be served with a subpoena which might well produce further evidence against Hiss. That evening, following receipt of a subpoena issued by the House Committee, Chambers, accompanied by committee investigators William Wheeler and Donald Appell, returned to his Westminster farm. Andrews later wrote a dramatic account of Chambers' actions and the exact sequence of events:

It was about 10 p.m. The night was dark. Chambers did not enter the house at first. He walked to a pumpkin patch, stooped over, and looked around. Then he returned to the two investigators and said he couldn't find what he was seeking. He went to the house and turned on some yard lights. They gave slight illumination to the pumpkin patch. Chambers picked up one pumpkin, examined it, and dropped it.

Then he picked another one.

It was like a pumpkin prepared for Hallowe'en. The top had been severed in a circle. The pumpkin had been hollowed out and dried, as had been the top. The top had been replaced. Chambers lifted off the top . . . reached inside and brought out three small aluminum cylinders. Each was wrapped in adhesive tape. Two more rolls were brought out. They were wrapped in oiled paper. One of them had been slightly crushed. Chambers said he didn't think the film inside the crushed one was any good, adding, "I think it has been lightstruck." He put the pumpkin back in its place.

Wheeler and Appell got into their car and started back to Washington. On the way they stopped at a café to mark the cylinders for identification. They delivered the films to Bob Stripling on the morning of December 3.

[6] The Andrews quotations are from Bert and Peter Andrews, *A Tragedy of History,* (Washington, D.C.,: Robert B. Luce, 1962).

Robert Stripling immediately sent a telegram to Nixon aboard the *Panama,* announcing the new developments. When he received no answer Bert Andrews sent one that read:

Information here is that Hiss-Chambers case has produced new bombshell. Chambers has been questioned in libel suit brought by Hiss. Indications are that Chambers has produced new evidence. All concerned are silent. However, Justice Department practically confirms indications, saying case too hot for comment. Inference is new information in Justice Department hands. May lead to reopening of New York Grand Jury's inquiry and more intensive perjury inquiry here. In view of your committee's role, can you tell me whether committee will reopen its investigation. Also who will be called and when. Any other details appreciated. Please rush answer collect.

Nixon answered in this way:

Have advised Stripling to investigate and advise me regarding new hearings. Will reopen hearings if necessary to prevent Justice Department cover-up. Will advise date, witnesses, etc., upon hearing from Stripling.

Again Andrews sent a message:

Documents incredibly hot. Link to Hiss seems certain. Link to others inevitable. Results should restore faith in need for Committee if not some members. New York Jury meets Wednesday. Could you arrive Tuesday and get a day's jump on Grand Jury. If not, hold hearing early Wednesday. My liberal friends don't love me no more. Nor you. But facts are facts and these are dynamite. Hiss's writing identified on three documents. Not proof he gave them to Chambers but highly significant. Stripling says can prove who gave them to Chambers. Love to Pat. (Signed) Vacation-spoiler Andrews.

On receiving the above, Nixon asked the committee to make arrangements for him to return immediately to Washington. By direct order from Secretary of Defense Forrestal, Nixon's immediate return by special plane was arranged.[7]

On December 3 the New York Grand Jury, whose tenure was due to ex-

[7] William Reuben describes Nixon's return with heavy irony: "On December 5, Nixon, with photographers somehow miraculously able to record every phase of the drama, was picked up at sea from a cruise ship by a Navy crash boat and then rushed to a waiting sea plane and flown back to Washington. His first word on the 'pumpkin papers' was issued as he sped back to Washington. With no need to even look at the documents, or to ask Chambers a single question for an explanation as to how their existence had never previously been mentioned or even hinted at, Nixon held his first press conference aboard a speeding Navy crash boat. The AP quoted him as saying that, 'it is no longer just one man's word against another's'; and that: 'The hearing is by far the most important the Committee on Un-American Activities has conducted because of the nature of the evidence and the importance of the people involved. It will prove to the American people once and for all that where you have a Communist you have an espionage agent.' " (William A. Reuben, *The Honorable Mr. Nixon* [New York: Action Books, 1958], p. 78.)

pire on December 15, was hurriedly reconvened to examine the sensational evidence contained in Chambers' "Pumpkin Papers" and other documents. On December 6 the jury received blown-up copies of the microfilm from the House Committee. From December 7 to 15 Hiss appeared daily (except Sunday) before the grand jury.

Grand jury proceedings are secret, hence no official transcript is available for study. However, after each of his daily appearances, Hiss dictated a complete memorandum of the questions he was asked and the answers he gave.

After his first appearance on December 7 Hiss noted:

Mr. Whearty showed me the originals of the handwritten documents. . . . I explained the circumstances under which I made notes of this general kind for use in reporting orally to Mr. Sayre and explained my general procedural duties with respect to the voluminous material coming to Mr. Sayre's office.

The four handwritten documents in Hiss's handwriting were memos on ordinary $3'' \times 5''$ note pad, two on scratch paper and two were small sheets from which the letterhead, "Department of State Assistant Secretary," seemed to have been torn off. Regarding these chits of paper, Chambers' story was that

From time to time Hiss also gave me small handwritten notes. These notes were about documents which had passed under his eyes quickly, and which for some reason or other he was unable to bring out, but which he thought were of some importance.

It is interesting that Chambers, in describing these documents, referred to them as "the handwriting specimens of Mr. Hiss."

Hiss explained these chits quite simply. They were samples of rough notes he made for his own use as he read over the scores of dispatches and cablegrams, many of which were not important enough to present in their entirety to Sayre. In examining these chits, one sees that words are abbreviated, and in three of the chits two types of pencil have been used. In two of these Hiss has written the top part in blue crayon and the bottom with lead pencil. In the third, he has overwritten with lead pencil certain parts of the original blue script. Hiss explained that on going over such notes, before reporting their contents to Sayre, he would sometimes clarify or expand them on the same slip of paper. After his sessions with Sayre were over, Hiss would then either leave them attached to the cables from which they were derived or, detaching them as he completed his report, would drop them in the wastebasket.

An explanation for the typed documents and the microfilm was harder to come by. Chambers described the microfilm as being made from documents Hiss would bring home from the State Department at night.

> I would then take the documents and take them to Baltimore where they were photographed. . . . After they were photographed I would return them to Mr. Hiss at his home . . . that same night.[8]

Chambers' story was that at the start he picked up documents only once every week or ten days. After a while a new system was devised to expedite the transmission of greater quantities of material: Hiss was to bring documents out every evening and Mrs. Hiss would copy them on the typewriter the same night. Chambers would then pick up these typed copies for the week as well as the originals for that day and have the whole batch microfilmed. He would return the originals to Hiss later that same night or during the early morning hours and destroy the typed copies. Some of these, he explained, he did not destroy but kept as "life-preservers." The typed documents that Chambers produced as evidence against Hiss were dated from January 1938 to April 1, 1938.

Hiss's notes read:

> With respect to the typewritten documents, I was asked . . . if they appeared to be copies of State Department material and I replied that some of them appeared to be complete copies . . . and some . . . summaries of State Department material.

Shortly after Chambers had turned over the typed documents, stating they had been typed on the Hisses' machine, Hiss's attorney began making inquiries to find out what make of typewriter the Hisses possessed in the early thirties. Priscilla's father had given them a typewriter around 1930, and on December 4, 1948, Mr. Fansler's office informed them that the machine was a Woodstock. In the meantime the House Committee investigators and the FBI were making a countrywide search for samples of the Hisses' typing.[9] Hiss wrote to many of his friends asking if they had samples. Richard Field still remembers Hiss asking whether he had any letters that might have been written on the typewriter. Field did not, but several letters written on the Woodstock were finally located by the FBI and the Hisses. An FBI expert examined them, compared the typing of the Baltimore documents with the Hiss samples ("Hiss standards"), and concluded that both had been typed on the same machine.

[8] Trial Transcript, p. 258.
[9] A total of 263 FBI agents worked on the case in forty-five of the fifty-two FBI field divisions. In Washington alone, about thirty agents were engaged in the search for the typewriter.

What was Hiss's reaction to the judgment of the government expert? "Alger seemed to be so serenely untouched by all this," Field recalls. "he was cool, collected and unruffled, while Edward McLean was tearing his hair." Field says that McLean came to him, saying, "For Heaven's sake, you're closer to Alger than I am—please talk with him, and tell him it is the coldly objective judgment that on the basis of what the Government has, an indictment is inevitable." Field talked with Hiss at the Harvard Club. Hiss said he "expected it" [the indictment, it would seem]. But he had great faith in the judicial process of the court and didn't see how a jury could believe Chambers. "It was," says Field, "either the attitude of a man who knew he was innocent or [a man who was] foolhardy."

On the afternoon of that same day Hiss appeared again before the grand jury. He was questioned at length about a number of typewriters the Hiss family had used in their house. His memorandum of the day noted:

Mr. Whearty asked me about our typewriters. He wanted to know for what we used typewriters in our house and I said that my first recollection of any extensive use of typewriters was when Mrs. Hiss was working on the book for the Carnegie Corporation. . . . I said that I thought that book was probably the occasion for Mr. Fansler having given us his old office typewriter. I said in answer to questions that I thought we had had one or more portables and that we had never bought a new typewriter, that one or more of the portables could have been purchased secondhand or could have been given or lent to us. I said that I had little interest in typewriters; I did not make use of them myself. The jurors themselves asked several questions including what use we would have for portables or other typewriters. I replied that Timmy's recollection is that he had had a portable in his own room and that I thought he used it for school papers and just for amusement. I was asked how early he had used a typewriter and I said perhaps as early as seven or eight as far as playing with it was concerned. I said that he had had a typewriter at boarding school and that he has one now.

I was asked if we had any specimens of typing that had been done in our house and I said we had found three which had been turned over to government officials.

One of the jurors asked me how Chambers could have gotten any papers from the State Department. I said there were to my mind two ways:

1) He could have walked in and taken them himself during office hours.

2) He could have had a confederate. I was asked if I had any suspicion as to who might be his confederate. I said that I had no suspicion but that it was relevant to the question to say that Mr. Wadleigh,[10] in the course of a casual conversation in the waiting room, had told me that he had given some documents to Chambers. . . .

[10] Wadleigh at first refused to testify, but later admitted passing as many as four to five hundred documents to Chambers. Were not some of them dated at a time he was absent from the State Department, he might have been thought the source of all Chambers' documents.

One of the jurors asked me how Chambers could have got the four handwritten notes. I said that I thought one of them was not in my handwriting and he rephrased his question to refer to the three which appeared to be in my handwriting. I told him that I did not know but that the normal disposition of such notes would be for me to tear them up and throw them in the wastebasket. . . .

I was asked if I could have made notes at home. I said I could have as I sometimes brought work home. One juror asked me if it wasn't forbidden to bring work home. I said not at all, I had never heard of any such rule, we all brought work home as necessary. I said that I was more given to bringing work home in later years when my responsibilities were greater and I had less time in the office for reading material. I was asked if I made any distinction in the material I brought home and said yes, that I would normally in those days have brought less confidential material home rather than the more confidential. I was asked to distinguish between such types of material and said that the bulky typewritten copy of the report from Manchuria was a good example of the kind of material which was not at all confidential.

A juror asked me who would have access to my personal office as distinguished from the reception room. I said that many people could have access to the office whether I was present or not, that people were going and coming in the department constantly. I remembered one occasion when I found a stranger in my office when I returned. I said that someone could easily have come into my office and claimed to be a friend or there on business and would probably be told to wait if I were out.

In Washington on that same day (December 10), the House Committee held another public hearing. On this occasion Nathan Levine [11] told his story of having received a sealed envelope from Chambers about ten years past, which he hid in his mother's home in Brooklyn in a dumbwaiter shaft. After Levine had testified, Nixon made a series of comments in behalf of Chambers and concluded:

I for one wish to say that Mr. Chambers, apart from the disservice that was rendered to the country and a disservice which was rendered only because there were people in this Government who gave him the information that he was able to turn over to the Communists and which he couldn't have rendered without the cooperation of those people, that apart from that, that Mr. Chambers has willingly and voluntarily, with no necessity at all upon his part to do so, rendered a great service to the country by bringing these facts before the American people at this time. [12]

At the close of this public hearing other members of the committee expressed their personal opinions. Congressman Hébert said:

I believe Mr. Chambers has done a splendid service to this country. At the opening

---

[11] Mrs. Chambers' nephew; not to be confused with Isaac Don Levine.
[12] The remarks of House Committee members quoted through these pages are from HUAC Hearings, pp. 1461–74 *passim*.

of these hearings I made the remark that the only way you could find criminals and have a successful police department was through the use of stool pigeons.

I do want to comment, however, and bring out the fact that Mr. Chambers did not tell this committee the entire facts in the case when he was brought before us the first time; and if it had not been for Mr. Alger Hiss filing a suit against Mr. Chambers which forced Mr. Chambers to produce evidence to protect himself in a slander suit, we probably would not have gotten as much as we now have.

I don't want to commend Mr. Hiss for bringing a libel suit. I say that in an objective fashion in order to keep the record straight.

I appreciate what Mr. Chambers has done, and I don't appreciate the fact that he may be used as the goat of the situation. . . .

Then Congressman Mundt added:

Had it not been for the existence of this committee and the functioning of this committee in open hearing, Mr. Alger Hiss would never have brought suit against Mr. Whittaker Chambers, so the documents would never have been brought into existence up until this very moment.

Parenthetically, it is to the point to mention an incident that I shall discuss in detail later. In order to check the dates, code markings, and other identifying features of the film, Nixon asked the Eastman Kodak Company to examine it. The report came back that that type of film had not been manufactured until after 1945. This fact alone would have collapsed Chambers' entire story. Confronted with this dilemma, Nixon made a hurried phone call to Mr. Keith Lewis, manager of the Washington office of the Eastman Company. At Nixon's request, Lewis immediately communicated with his firm's "headquarters" to determine once again the year in which the film was made. He phoned back a possible explanation. The kind of film that Chambers had used was manufactured up through 1938, then discontinued until 1945, when its production was resumed. So, to Nixon's great relief, Chambers' story could still be valid:

I had no need to hear the answer. Stripling put the receiver down, let out a Texas rebel yell, grabbed me by the arms, and danced me around the room.[13]

Congressman Rankin appraised the situation in a somewhat different light. Though his concern about Chambers' credibility and loyalty to the United States was grave and he still distrusted Chambers, he nevertheless saw fit to accept Chambers' story about the documents as true and used it to praise the committee for its work:

I am not yet convinced that Mr. Chambers was not a Communist during the time he was on the staff of *Time* magazine. I cannot join in any exuberant commenda-

[13] Nixon, *op. cit.*, p. 55.

tion of a man who knew all during the war, according to his own testimony, that this man Wadleigh, who had been passing out, according to his statement, secret documents from the State Department, was still in that position and probably carrying on the same conduct while our boys were dying by the thousands on every battle front in the world, and many of them perhaps as a result of this treachery; and knowing also at the time that this man Hiss, who he says was also perpetrating this treason, was still in the State Department—all that throws many question marks with me, but there is one thing that is definitely certain . . . if it had not been for this committee, this conspiracy would never have been uncovered. If we did not have the ocular proof, I would still have grave doubts, but we have these microfilms, copies of the documents that were stolen from the State Department at that time, and nobody has ever been able to explain those documents or those microfilms away.

On Saturday, December 11, Alger Hiss again appeared before the grand jury. He was questioned about his wife, her former husband, Thayer Hobson, and

I was asked between now and next Monday to think about and talk with Mrs. Hiss about persons from whom we might have borrowed or bought typewriters.

That same day Nixon announced that he would take the microfilm to New York and personally appear before the grand jury in order to "assist them in bringing to justice those who fed this information to Chambers." The next day the Sunday papers carried reproductions of many of the microfilmed documents and Chambers' account that he had received them from Alger Hiss.

Monday, December 13, Hiss appeared for the sixth time before the grand jury:

I was asked whether I had ever been in Mr. Harry White's house and I said I had not and I had not known Mr. White socially. . . . I was asked if we had used the rug right away and I said I thought so and continuously since then.

On that same day, December 13, Nixon appeared before the grand jury. There is no record available of what he told the jury. His views were by then well known, and he stated to the press that "the indictment of Chambers for perjury without anybody else would constitute a whitewash because it would be impossible to bring out the truth regarding other people."

On December 14 Hiss made his seventh appearance before the grand jury. On that day the jury also interviewed Julian Wadleigh, Adolf Berle, Isaac Don Levine, Mr. and Mrs. Chambers, and others. In the notes of his testimony that day, Hiss says:

I was called in about 4:30 p.m. and stayed until after 5:30. Mr. Donegan spent a good deal of time getting me to identify a letter of early September 1936 in my handwriting to Mr. Banfield, the head master of Landon School. . . .

Mr. Donegan then said with great emphasis that positively the typewritten documents produced by Chambers on November 17 had been typed on the same machine that Timmy's application [enclosed in the handwritten letter to Mr. Banfield] which had been shown me had been typed on.

Before testifying that day Hiss had been summoned by Alexander Campbell, assistant attorney general. In their brief talk Campbell made such prejudicial declarations to Hiss that Hiss requested permission to relate them to the jurors:

I then told the Grand Jury that at noon today, Mr. Campbell had asked to speak to me and had told me that I would be indicted. I said . . . that naturally I did not know all of the evidence which the jury had but that I did know that much damaging evidence had been produced by my own direct efforts and had been turned over to the government officials at my direction. . . . I said that whatever the evidence, I knew that I had done nothing that was a breach of trust or a dereliction of my duty, that I was proud of my years of government service.

At this point Mr. Whearty said, hadn't Campbell said I would *probably* be indicted? I said no, I was confident that he had not. . . . Mr. Whearty asked if Mr. McLean, my lawyer, had not been present. I said that he had. . . . I then testified from the notes I had made as to the conversation as follows:

Mr. Campbell said in practically these words, "The FBI has cracked the case. You are in it up to your eyes. Your wife's in it. Why don't you go in there and tell the jury the truth?" I said that I had replied that I had continuously told the truth and that I will continue to do so. Mr. Campbell had then said, "You are going to be indicted. I am not fooling. There are five witnesses against you." . . . Mr. Campbell then said, "This is your government speaking." That concluded the very brief interview but later Mr. Campbell had called me back in again and had said, "I want to make it plain, your wife will be included." . . .

I said that I thought Chambers was a person of unsound mind and not normal, that he had for some reason which I did not pretend fully to understand, acquired a grudge against me and was trying to destroy me. I said that I considered that he had deliberately tried to frame me.

While Hiss was testifying, McLean was having a private conversation with Assistant Attorney General Campbell. What Campbell told him was so startling, McLean later drafted a sworn affidavit quoting Campbell's statements to him that Whittaker Chambers was an "unstable and abnormal" person and that he [Campbell] had "expected for several days to pick up the paper in the morning and read that Mr. Chambers has jumped out the window."

On the next to the last day of the grand jury's session (December 14) the House Committee held its final public hearing. It called as a witness Mrs. Marion Bachrach, a writer employed in the national office of the Communist Party. What reasons the committee had for linking Mrs. Bachrach with

Chambers' accusation of the Hisses is not clear. Mrs. Bachrach claimed her constitutional privilege in refusing to answer whether she knew Alger or Priscilla Hiss, had ever been in their home, and if she had ever seen a typewriter in the Hiss home. Asked whether she ever copied any documents removed from the Department of State, Bureau of Standards, or Navy Department, she responded that she had not. She denied ever having lent a typewriter to Mrs. Hiss or ever having delivered one to her.

Mundt climaxed the end of the hearings with the judgmental announcement that he, the chairman,

would like to state that the crime involved is very definitely a capital crime. It is either treason in wartime or treason in peacetime.

Thus the public hearings provided last-minute items for the grand jurors in the morning news of December 15. The committee reiterated their agreement with Nixon that an indictment of Chambers would "give the greatest encouragement to the Communist conspiracy in this country."

The final day of the jury's existence, December 15, had arrived, but no definite decision as to who would be indicted had been reached as the jury went into session that morning.

When the proceedings had started in December, it seemed that Chambers, regardless of Hiss's fate, would certainly be indicted for perjury since he had previously denied under oath his involvement in any espionage activity. However, it was obvious to both the House Committee and the Justice Department, as represented by Assistant Attorney General Alexander Campbell, that if Chambers was indicted, without a doubt no more ex-Communists would come forth as informers for the government. The grand jury was made to understand, by the House Committee and the Assistant Attorney General, that it was imperative not to indict Chambers and it was equally imperative that Hiss be indicted.

In the last few hours of the grand jury's existence Campbell personally appeared before them and exhorted the jurors to indict Hiss. In discussing Campbell's transgression of his role, as a United States attorney, Hiss in his legalistic way quoted the opinion of the late Judge Augustus N. Hand:

The proper functions of a Federal attorney in presenting material to a grand jury . . . is that he may question the witnesses, advise as to the law, and explain the relation of the testimony to the law of the case. In doing this, he may review the evidence. He must refrain from the slightest coercion of the grand jury and take every pains to have a fair inquest. . . .[14]

[14] (*United States* v. *Rintelen,* 235 Fed. 787, 794) (Alger Hiss, *In the Court of Public Opinion,* p. 192)

In the light of Campbell's statement to McLean the previous day, in which he expressed his serious doubts about Chambers' reliability, this action bespoke the influence of the political forces of the time.

On December 15 Hiss was again asked for a possible explanation of how the typed documents produced by Chambers in Baltimore on November 17 could have been typed on his old Woodstock machine, and he repeated the possible explanations that he had given before—that Chambers got access to the typewriter by entering the house or obtained the machine after the Hisses had disposed of it. Hiss noted:

Four or five of the jurors appeared very frankly to be completely skeptical of my testimony with respect to the possibility of Chambers' having had access to the typewriter. . . . I said that I felt his use of the typewriter, if the identity of the typed exhibits were established, was simply a form of forgery less easily detected than an attempted forgery of handwriting and was part of the pattern of attempting to frame me.

Hiss was then dismissed from the jury room. Two hours later he was recalled and questioned exclusively about the typewriter, his habits of dictating letters at the office, and about how Chambers might have got the State Department papers and access to the machine.

A juror asked me to explain what I meant by my reference to Chambers' trying to frame me. . . . I said that for some psychological reason that I did not understand, he was trying to destroy me.

Then Hiss was asked:

Q. At any time did you . . . turn any documents, or copies of documents of the State Department or any other Government organization . . . over to Whittaker Chambers?
A. Never. Excepting, I assume, the title certificate to the Ford.
Q. Can you say definitely that you did not see him after January 1, 1937?
A. Yes, I think I can definitely say that.

On the basis of these two questions and these two answers, the grand jury indicted Hiss on two counts of perjury. (Despite Campbell's prediction, Mrs. Hiss was not indicted.) It was a divided vote, one more than a majority.

A member of the grand jury told me in an interview:

Hiss' indictment was a close vote, not a unanimous one. I was never convinced that Hiss was guilty of the crime we indicted him for. Chambers perjured himself many times, but the final decision of the jury was, "He's our witness, we are not going to indict him." It was a politically inspired matter.[15]

[15] Juror to the author, December 4, 1962.

On December 31 the House Committee dealt its last damaging blows to Hiss. In two official reports [16] the committee reviewed its work of the past two years, "the most active and productive period in the history" of the committee and described: "The most startling disclosures . . . which should rock our national complacence to its foundations. . . . Testimony taken by the Committee has definitely shifted the burden of proof from Chambers to Hiss. . . ."

On the eve of Hiss's trial [17] the reverberations of these reports made widely available to all prospective jurors that the committee was of the opinion that the burden of proof had shifted to Hiss (who was not worthy of belief), and the committee vouched for the credibility of Chambers.

On January 16, 1949, the widely publicized trials of Communist leaders —Eugene Dennis and others—began in the same courthouse where Hiss was to be tried. Their trials continued until October 14. When Hiss's trial began in May 1949 (after repeated postponements), the two trials were daily reported on parallel columns as front-page news. In March 1949 Judith Coplon, a government employee, was arrested by the FBI and charged with espionage. Miss Coplon's trial ran almost concurrently with the first Hiss trial. After her conviction on June 30 (which was later reversed), the *New York Times* printed a special article with the headline, "Coplon Verdict Spreads Fast in Hiss Trial Room." On May 11, three weeks before the start of the first Hiss trial, Gerhardt Eisler, a well-known Communist awaiting trial, jumped bail and escaped the country aboard a Polish ship. Such, in brief, was the atmosphere and sensational setting in which Alger Hiss endeavored to prepare and carry on his legal defense. Often during the trial the courthouse was surrounded with Communist pickets protesting the trial of their leaders.

But more detrimental to Hiss than the surging crowds that surrounded and infiltrated the courthouse was the inflamed atmosphere that branded liberals and Communists alike with the marks of espionage and treason. What had started as a presumption of guilt by association was fanned into an epidemic of guilt by contamination with concurrent and remote events.

---

[16] *Annual Report of the Committee on Un-American Activities to the United States House of Representatives,* December 31, 1948, 25 pp.; *Soviet Espionage within the United States Government* (Second Report), December 31, 1948; 129 pp., with appendix and exhibits.
[17] Hiss's libel action was postponed, and though the Baltimore Deposition of Mr. and Mrs. Chambers was resumed on February 17, 1949, the suit was, because of the impending federal trial and the subsequent conviction of Hiss, never reinstituted.

19

Woodstock Number N230099

THREE DAYS before the indictment Hiss offered his resignation as president of the Carnegie Endowment. The offer was not accepted; he was granted a year's leave of absence instead, and he gave himself over to his self-defense. Advised that he would need a criminal lawyer, he chose Lloyd Paul Stryker. Other members of the defense counsel included Edward C. McLean, Harold Rosenwald, and Harold Shapiro. As they launched their investigative efforts, Hiss continued his own. Much of his correspondence with family, friends, and former associates—searching for details of his past life that would help him rebut Chambers' story—is extant. It suggests a man honestly attempting to discover any fragment of truth, confident that it would vindicate him. One illuminating example of Hiss's diligence is a lengthy analysis he prepared of the Trilling novel, *The Middle of the Journey,* which had been recommended to him as a psychological portrait of Whittaker Chambers. One of the novel's central characters, Gifford Maxim, clearly is based on Chambers, and several passages that Hiss selected from the book offer precise psychological understanding of him. The novel describes Maxim's paranoid behavior, his constant search for a "new existence," and even uncannily presages his attack on his "closest friend." [1] What is just as significant as the book itself is the fact

---

[1] Indeed, Chambers refers to himself as the "main character" of the novel in *Cold Friday.* Trilling and Chambers attended Columbia at the same time and knew each other during the thirties. Trilling regarded Chambers in his youth as having had great literary possibilities, which he never realized. He recalled two of Chambers' early poems "written with elegant simplicity, dash and importance," different from anything Chambers later did and wholly unlike *Witness,* which Trilling called "souped-up and sentimental." Though Trilling was fascinated with Chambers, he had little to do with him in college: "I was far too conventional a person, especially during my student years," he said. "Chambers was out in the world in a way that differentiated him from others. His extramural activities frightened me, and I did my best to stay away from him." After their undergraduate days they did not meet again until 1930, at a writers' conference of which Chambers was chairman. The topic was the "relation of literature to Marxism"; Trilling was at that time "on the fringes" of the Communist movement. Chambers subsequently asked to use the Trillings' address as a "mail-drop," though this was refused. Trilling and most of his group became disaffected with Communism in the early thirties, but he re-

that during January 1949, when Hiss was busily engaged in his own legal defense, he exerted considerable effort in an attempt to understand the psychology of the man who had accused him. He submitted his analysis of *The Middle of the Journey* to his lawyers, hoping this would shed light on his accuser.[2] There is little doubt, from a study of Hiss's efforts during those weeks, that he was unable to explain to himself, or others, Chambers' accusations against him.

But by far the most significant find that came out of all the investigations and searches that went on in preparation for the trial, *U.S.* v. *Alger Hiss,* was the discovery by Hiss investigators, on April 16, 1949, of the Woodstock typewriter that had apparently belonged to Hiss. Although more than thirty-five FBI agents had also been looking for the machine, it was found by the relatively sparse efforts of Hiss's counsel, Edward McLean, in collaboration with Donald Hiss. It was an irony, indeed, hardly mentioned at the time, and forgotten by most through the years, that it was the Hisses and their investigators who discovered and introduced into court the material evidence that was eventually to damn him.

Hiss was tried twice. The first trial began on May 31, 1949. Presiding over the Court was Judge Samuel H. Kaufman. The jury, chosen by counsel in a little over two hours, consisted of ten men and two women.

Hiss chose Lloyd Paul Stryker as his trial lawyer. After the shock of his indictment, Hiss was advised by Felix Frankfurter and other Washington friends that he needed an experienced criminal lawyer. Stryker was regarded as the finest and most suitable for such a task. Hiss shrank from the idea of being represented by a "criminal lawyer." This was the first time Hiss had ever been in a criminal court. He had never been before a jury. (Hiss's inexperience in the field of criminal law is complemented by his academic lack of interest in the subject. Though he graduated *cum laude* from Law School, he received his two lowest grades in courses in Criminal Law and Evidence.) His administrative skills, his knowledge of corporate law, and his experience in diplomacy and world affairs had lulled him into a false sense of security.

Philip Jessup (at present a member of the International Court of Justice at The Hague), a friend of Hiss who knew Stryker well, assured Hiss

---

marked that everyone seemed to "know Chambers was an underground agent." (Lionel Trilling to the author, personal interview, September 11, 1961.)

[2] On January 25, 1949, Hiss sent the following letter to members of his counsel, Edward McLean and Harold Rosenwald, and to Dr. Carl Binger: "Several friends have suggested that I should read a novel called *The Middle of the Journey* by Professor Lionel Trilling of Columbia, in which one of the characters, according to Trilling, is partially based on talks Trilling had with Chambers. I have now got around to reading the book and have prepared a memorandum quoting several passages which it occurs to me may possibly be of some interest to you. I have sent copies to Mr. McLean and to Harold Rosenwald."

of Stryker's integrity. Though Stryker's courtroom style was dramatic, he was not the ruthless type. Jessup told Hiss that he would find him a warm, liberal, cultivated person with a deep sense of justice.

The government prosecutor was Thomas F. Murphy, an Assistant United States Attorney. He made this claim:

Now, if we prove to you, as Mr. Chambers will, that he got the documents from Hiss, and we prove that they were typed on a typewriter in his possession or control, and that the documents themselves came from the State Department, and some of them right from his office, I daresay you will be convinced that Hiss lied in the grand jury.

The government, he said, would present witnesses to corroborate Chambers' story. Murphy ended his opening with the admonition to the jury that "if you don't believe Chambers then we have no case under the federal perjury rule."

Stryker took up this challenge and agreed that the entire case hinged on "whether or not you believe Chambers." He would base his argument on Chambers' credibility.

The Hiss defense, he said, would show what kind of a man Whittaker Chambers was. They would confront the jury with the inconsistent testimony Chambers had given before the House Committee and the grand jury, and in the pre-trial libel-suit deposition. The defense would show what a mysterious life Chambers led in contrast to the openness of Hiss's life. The strategy proved effective to a point. Distinguished public figures, former associates, and friends, testified as to Hiss's excellent reputation,[3] while Stryker hammered away at inconsistencies in Chambers' testimony. But the fact of the documents remained. The Hiss defense could say only that Chambers must have secured them from other sources, and indeed he admitted during the course of the trial that he had no less than "five" sources in Washington. There were, Chambers testified, "Hiss, Wadleigh, and three others." But he insisted that the Baltimore documents all came from Hiss, though in their interdepartmental circulation they had passed many desks and

---

[3] Justice Frankfurter, one of the character witnesses presented by the defense, when asked by Stryker:

"Can you state . . . whether the reputation of Mr. Alger Hiss for loyalty to his Government, integrity and veracity is good or bad? . . ."

Answered:

"I would say it was excellent."

Fifteen years later, in a letter to the author dated May 8, 1963, Justice Frankfurter wrote:

". . . All I have had to say about Hiss I said on the witness stand and I have not since then added or subtracted anything I there said."

been initialed by many other State Department officials.[4] The government expert, Ramos Feehan, testified that the typed documents and samples of Priscilla Hiss's typing had been done on the same machine. The type face of the Woodstock that the Hisses introduced as their former machine seemed to duplicate the peculiarities of the documents. It was essentially this evidence against Chambers' demonstrable unreliability in the past. The jurors could not agree; after hours of deliberation they were still divided eight to four for conviction. The trial ended in a hung jury on July 9, 1949.

Hiss's second trial was scheduled to begin sometime in October 1949 but was postponed to mid-November. On the basis of the wide and heated publicity his case had received in New York City, defense attorneys, on October 4, presented to the court a motion for a change of venue to Rutland, Vermont. On October 14 Judge Coxe denied it.

There were several changes in the second trial, which began on November 17. There was a new judge, Federal District Judge Henry W. Goddard. Hiss had a new criminal lawyer on the defense counsel, Claude Cross of Boston.[5] This was largely due to the anticipated change of venue. Cross was expected to be more effective in rural Vermont than the rather flamboyant Stryker. Judge Goddard admitted witnesses who had formerly been denied; for the first time psychiatric testimony was permitted. But perhaps the most significant change was that Thomas Murphy, who continued as prosecutor, altered his strategy. He did not warn the jury at the outset, did not admonish that "if you don't believe Chambers then we don't have a case under the federal perjury rule." His former assertion that "a searching cross-examination" of Chambers would be more than welcomed by the government was now

---

[4] Charles Darlington, Wadleigh's superior in the State Department during the period in question, wrote to me:

> During the first trial, Wadleigh, who was then protected by the Statute of Limitations [sic] readily admitted having taken papers from my desk. This he could more easily have done because we had virtually no security arrangements in the Department at that time. . . . It would have been the easiest thing for Wadleigh to have taken carbons of any number of papers from my desk, or from others' desks, for such use as he might wish. . . . On several occasions I recall having returned from lunch to find him in my room reading some of my papers.
>
> It is curious that Wadleigh, although admitting having taken many papers from my desk and having passed them to Soviet agents, said under oath in Court that the paper on German Trade Policy which turned up in the pumpkin he did *not* [sic] take. My feeling is that his recollection on this point must have been faulty. We have no other easy explanation as to how the German paper was removed from the Department other than to attribute this act to Wadleigh. At the time, this paper did not seem to be of unusual importance, even though the press gave it a great play ten years later, and so I am inclined to think that Wadleigh probably did take it along with many others and then later forgot that he had handled this one.

(Personal communication, Charles Darlington to the author, February 28, 1964)
[5] Harold Shapiro, assistant attorney for the defense, was replaced by Robert von Mehren.

shifted to the argument that the "immutable documents themselves" would prove that Hiss had lied and Chambers had spoken the truth. And thus he directed the jury's attention to the question:

. . . do the documentary exhibits prove beyond a reasonable doubt that Whittaker Chambers is telling the gospel truth from that chair? And if you resolve that, as I think you will, I am going to ask you when the case is in, to bring in a verdict of guilty.

This claim, emphasized and re-emphasized throughout the trial, would carry the day.

But were the documents "immutable?" The answer, insofar as it can be determined, centers on the typewriter.[6] Many features in the story of "Defense Exhibit UUU," seemingly the old Woodstock typewriter which the Hisses had in their home during the thirties, remain unexplained and unproved.[7] To the professional investigator, trained to detect fraud and forgery, Woodstock N230099 remains one of the most intriguing, baffling pieces of evidence in the Hiss case.

The Woodstock, factory serial #N230099, was found at the home of its then owner, Ira Lockey, a truckman, after it had been passed from servants who formerly worked for the Hisses through a series of other persons. McLean purchased the typewriter from Lockey for fifteen dollars.[8] Six weeks later, when the first Hiss trial began, the Hiss defense brought the old Woodstock into court and presented it as their most important defense exhibit. It was with the hopeful expectation that the machine's presence in court would enable its typing samples to be compared with the Baltimore Documents and thus show that it was *not* the "murder weapon." During the trials Hiss and his counsel assumed the authenticity of this inanimate witness—an assumption they later repudiated. Furthermore, they accepted the judgment of Mr. Feehan, the government expert, who said that the Baltimore Documents and samples of Priscilla Hiss's typing ("Hiss Standards") had been typed on the same machine. Only after the trials was the idea that a duplicate typewriter could have been fabri-

---

[6] The source of the four original, small (3″ × 5″) note-pad pieces of paper, State Department memos, in Hiss's handwriting that Chambers produced along with the typed copies of government documents could be simply explained by the defense as a wastepaper basket pick-up either by Chambers or one of his agents.

[7] This machine was given to the Hisses shortly after their marriage by Thomas Fansler, Priscilla's father, after having been used for several years as an office machine for the Northwestern Mutual Life Insurance Company, of which Mr. Fansler was a general agent.

[8] For a detailed summary of the vicissitudes encountered in the search for the Woodstock, see: Alistair Cooke, *A Generation on Trial;* Fred J. Cook, *The Unfinished Story of Alger Hiss;* Alger Hiss, *In the Court of Public Opinion;* The Earl Jowitt, *The Strange Case of Alger Hiss;* Herbert Packer, "A Tale of Two Typewriters," *Stanford Law Review,* May 1958.

cated and the possibility of this kind of forgery by typewriter seriously investigated by Hiss counsel.

There have been significant developments regarding the typewriter which have kept Hiss's still lingering confidence alive. Such, for example, is Nixon's statement in "Six Crises": "On December 13 [1948], FBI agents found the typewriter." And in an official report prepared by the House Committee, titled *The Shameful Years—Thirty Years of Soviet Espionage in the United States,* dated December 30, 1951, their reporter wrote, in regard to the Hiss case:

The Committee wishes to commend the Federal Bureau of Investigation for its work in bringing this case to a successful conclusion when all the odds were against it. *The location of the typewriter* and certain pieces of other evidence needed during the trial of the case was amazing.[9]

In a communication of April 5, 1962, Claude Cross wrote me:

Because of some comments about Mr. Nixon's recent book *Six Crises* in our newspapers lately referring to the Woodstock typewriter, particularly as to whether the FBI ever had it, Mr. Nixon now says that a researcher made the mistake, but this sounds awfully unconvincing. One would think that he would have read the book before it was published and readily picked up any error, particularly since it related to a matter as to which he had personal knowledge.

Our Attorney General [Robert Kennedy] said a recent check has been made and finds the FBI never had the Woodstock typewriter. In my mind there is still a mystery connected with this typewriter and its whereabouts for the period just prior to the trial.

In another communication Cross wrote:

I wanted to cross-examine Mr. Feehan, but my associates advised against it and I followed their advice. I think it was my biggest mistake.

I could never understand why Mr. Feehan did not have someone type from the Woodstock typewriter in the courtroom and make his comparison with the Baltimore Documents. Instead, in rebuttal, Judge Murphy had a typist type something with the Woodstock typewriter in the courtroom, marking the typing as exhibits, and then in his argument told the jury that they did not need an expert; that they could tell for themselves whether the typing just made was the same as the Baltimore documents. He practically requested them to send for the typewriter as soon as they got in the jury room, which they did.

As to the examination of Mr. Feehan, my judgment then, and now is, that I think an examination of all of his working papers would be illuminating.

After Hiss was convicted in January of 1950 Chester Lane took over as investigative counsel for Hiss. Initially, Lane felt that the Baltimore Documents and the Hiss Standards had been typed on the same typewriter. This concession had been made when Mr. Feehan had asserted that the documents

[9] Italics the author's. *Loc. cit.,* p. 58.

and the Hiss Standards contained similar typographical errors in ten characters.[10] Nonetheless, Lane, suspecting a forgery of the machine, set out to
determine whether it might be possible to build a machine that could sucess-
fully duplicate these errors. He contacted a typewriter engineer named Martin
Tytell and gave him samples of the typewriting from N230099. In a sworn
statement Tytell said:

I have constructed a machine which I believe meets Mr. Lane's specifications. Neither I nor any of my associates in the work have had any access whatsoever to the
original machine during the course of the experiment. . . . So far as I know, this
is the first time such a machine has ever been made except possibly for forgery or
other illegal purposes. With the experience I and my associates have gained
through this experiment I am confident that we could now create other duplicates
with an even higher degree of fidelity in a fraction of the time which this machine
has taken.

Then a professional examiner of questioned documents, Miss Elizabeth
McCarthy,[11] was called in and, after careful examination of the samples, concluded:

. . . it is my opinion, based upon my long experience in methods of questioned
document explanation, that the duplication has progressed to such a degree that an
expert in the field, however highly qualified, would find it difficult if not impossible
to distinguish between samples from the two machines. . . . In particular, the success of the experiment shows that any such testimony as that given by the Government's expert, Mr. Feehan, at the second trial, basing his conclusion of identity of
machines on the identity of only ten characters in the two sets of documents, is
absolutely worthless.

Another expert, Mrs. Evelyn Ehrlich,[12] was called in to give her opinion. After a detailed study Mrs. Ehrlich stated:

. . . In my opinion, N230099 cannot be the same machine that typed Government Exhibits 37 and 46-B and Defendant's Exhibit TT (Hiss Standards). I base

[10] In the affidavit in support of a motion for a new trial on the grounds of newly discovered evidence, Lane said: "But after extended reflection it occurred to me that the
method employed by Feehan and other experts rested on an assumption that if two
typed documents contained a certain number of *similar* deviations from the norm—a
repetition of similar peculiarities in a certain number of the typed characters employed
in the two documents—the laws of chance would preclude the possibility that two different machines had been used. This assumption, while doubtless sound enough in the ordinary type of case, appeared to neglect altogether the possibility—if it was one—that a typewriter might be deliberately created, or adapted, so as to duplicate some, if not all, of
the peculiar characteristics of another. (Notice of Hearing of Motion for New Trial—
United States District Court, Southern District of New York, p. 9.)
[11] Miss McCarthy was an attorney-at-law and document expert for the Police Department
of the City of Boston and for the Massachusetts State Police.
[12] Mrs. Ehrlich was, from 1934 to 1951, on the staff of the Fogg Museum of Art, Harvard
University, as an expert in the technical examination and conservation of prints, drawings,
manuscripts, and typography. She developed visual techniques of presentation to illustrate technical details in the detection of deceptive imprints and typography.

this opinion upon certain differences in type impression between many of the letters in the two sets of documents, these differences appearing with such a high degree of regularity as to preclude the possibility of their being due to variations of ribbon, typing pressure, or other peculiarities of operation, and being of such a nature that differences in imprint cannot be due to age or wear on the machine.

Mrs. Ehrlich concluded:

. . . the observable peculiarities in the type of the Baltimore Documents in my opinion more nearly resemble the peculiarities in the typing from N230099 than they do the peculiarities in the Hiss Standards which I used for comparison.[13]

Lane did not base his theory of forgery on document comparison alone. Proceeding along other lines of investigation, Lane examined further into the identity of N230099. He hired Daniel P. Norman, an expert chemist, president of Skinner and Sherman, Inc., of Boston, Massachusetts, a firm that specialized in the chemical analysis of metals and papers for the Armed Services, for federal, state, and municipal departments, as well as for major industrial firms. Mr. Norman concluded that N230099

. . . shows positive signs of having been deliberately altered, in that many of its types are replacements of the originals and have been deliberately shaped.

Mr. Norman also stated:

The solder used for the replacement types has a different metallic content from that used on the types which apparently have not been altered, and from that used on other contemporary machines.

Lane also found out that

. . . a Woodstock typewriter bearing the serial number N230099 would have been manufactured in or around August 1929, and certainly no earlier than the first week of July 1929. At the same time the best available information indicates that the typeface style on our machine (N230099) was a style used by the Woodstock Company only in typewriters manufactured in 1926, 1927, and 1928, and possibly the early part of 1929. These inconsistencies point to the conclusion that N230099 is a fabricated machine.

The machine given to the Hisses by Mr. Fansler

. . . was in use in Mr. Fansler's office at least as early as July 8, 1929, and therefore could not have been the typewriter now in the possession of the defense— N230099.

[13] In a recently published book, *Room 3603* by H. Montgomery Hyde (New York: Farrar, Strauss) the author cites two references to the feasibility of forgery by typewriter. In the first (p. 135) Hyde quotes from E. Maschintz's book, *No Chip on my Shoulder*. Maschintz speaks of work at "Station M" with people who "could reproduce faultlessly the imprint of any typewriter on earth." Again (p. 145) Hyde says, ". . . a typewriter was rebuilt to conform to the exact mechnical imperfections of the machine upon which the General's Secretary had typed the original letter."

On January 2, 1952, when Hiss was in prison, the motion for a new trial on the ground of newly discovered evidence was filed in the United States District Court by Hiss counsel, Chester T. Lane and Robert M. Benjamin. The government was represented by Myles Lane, United States Attorney, and Stanley Robinson, Assistant United States Attorney. The motion came before District Judge J. Goddard, the same judge who had presided during the second Hiss trial.

In reply to the above, Judge Goddard stated:

It is evident that McCarthy, Ehrlich and Defense Counsel have proceeded on an erroneous elementary assumption when they say that Mr. Feehan based his opinion, that the Baltimore Documents and the Hiss Standards were typed on the same machine, solely upon a comparison of the characters and his examination was therefore inadequate. For in Feehan's affidavit he states that " I examined and compared *each typewritten character*,[14] appearing on Baltimore Documents #5 through #9 and 11 through 47, the known standards, taking into consideration style of type, alignment, horizontal and vertical spacing, footing, variations and defects."

At the trial Feehan was asked to point out "*some* [15] of the evidence which you discovered which made you come to that conclusion." Feehan was not cross-examined regarding his testimony. Judge Goddard, in brief, concluded that the "defense experts were unable to show that Feehan of the FBI was wrong . . . and that a jury could not reasonably find that Chambers constructed a duplicate typewriter or that #N230099 was not the Hiss machine." He held to the opinion that "After a full consideration of all the defendant has offered, there is no newly discovered evidence which would justify the conclusion that if it were presented to a jury, it would probably result in a verdict of acquittal." [16] On the basis of this and other subsidiary arguments, it was Judge Goddard's opinion that the defendant was not entitled to a new trial and the motion was denied.

In a legal study based on a review and analysis of the public record of the Hiss trials, Professor Herbert Packer, not unlike many others before him, ponders over the probability and motives of forgery by duplicate typewriter:

The implied conclusion, of course, is that 230099 was acquired as a reasonable facsimile of the Hiss machine by the forger or forgers, who altered it to conform either to the original Hiss machine or to samples of typing from that machine, used it to produce the Baltimore Documents, and then left it where it would eventually be discovered and mistakenly identified, as it was, as the Hiss typewriter. . . . How and when was this done? . . . It is likely that if forgery was commit-

---

[14] Italics the author's.
[15] Italics the author's.
[16] Federal Supplement, vol. 107, pp. 128–37 *passim*. July 22, 1952.

ted, it was done when Chambers still had at his beck and call the services of the underground Communist operatives, skilled in all the black arts. . . . If the typewriter was forged at some time during Chambers' days in the Communist movement, it could have been planted *before* the Hisses disposed of it, and the *original* Hiss machine could have been taken away and used to type the Baltimore Documents. There would then be no problem of two typewriters turning up, for one would be in the hands of the conspirators (i.e., of Chambers). However, that one would not be 230099, as has been generally assumed, but would be the Hiss machine. It would presumably be destroyed after it had served its purpose. And the forged typewriter, 230099, would be left to go through the vicissitudes that were described at the trial.[17]

If this was the case, as Packer suggests, the disparity between the Hiss Standards and the typing samples produced on 230099 becomes perfectly understandable.

The above theory, as Packer then points out, which the Hiss defense did not use, fits the forgery hypothesis "far more neatly" than the "1948 theory" —that Chambers somehow manufactured in three months a forged typewriter from samples of typing he had in his possession—which the defense adopted in support of the motion for a new trial.

Chambers' need to collect "life-preservers," [18] especially pieces of someone else's identity, lends credence to the theory of forgery by typewriter sometime during the thirties, when the Hisses still possessed the typewriter. The thesis that Chambers first discovered Alger Hiss from reading about him in the *American Magazine* and the *Baltimore Sun* and was drawn to him before he actually met him is consistent with Chambers' life style. Once he had insinuated himself into Hiss's life, the usual involvements of everyday living followed. Their relationship soon developed enough of a core of reality to rekindle his fratricidal fantasies, and the gentle personality and attractive physique of Alger Hiss were reminiscent of his brother Richard. Thus the psychological mold was cast. And Hiss's typewriter caught Chambers' fancy as an object he could put to use. It would have been easy enough for him to have switched the old Woodstock machine when he first came across it in 1935 (either at the 28th Street apartment or the P Street house)—or prepared typing samples from the Hiss machine, from which, at a later date, he could duplicate the original machine. Thus Chambers had easy and unsuspected access to the Woodstock at that time. Furthermore, he might have had it to himself from May to July 1935 in the 28th Street apartment, left furnished by the Hisses.

[17] Herbert Packer, *Ex-Communist Witnesses* (Stanford, Calif.: Stanford University Press, 1962). Published earlier in the *Stanford Law Review* as "A Tale of Two Typewriters."
[18] A "life-preserver" for Chambers consisted of money, an automobile, a gun, and some type of document.

Hiss could not recall whether he moved the typewriter from the 28th Street apartment to the P Street house before or after the Chamberses (Crosleys) occupied the apartment. If he moved it before, it could still have been available to Chambers, for the Woodstock was sometimes kept in a storeroom next to the third-floor guest room of the P Street house, where the Chamberses stayed for several days. Either in the service of his personal underground or whatever "special work" for the Communists he was allegedly engaged in then, Chambers could have used the technical implements for forgery by typewriter, to which he presumably had access as a member of the Communist underground.[19] He could, at any time between April 1938 and December 1948, have typed the documents from the microfilmed State Department documents.

The old typewriter had been with the Hisses since the early days of their marriage. It was a family possession—an object that had once belonged to Mrs. Hiss's father. As a potential piece of Hiss's identity, it was something Chambers could secretly use in the service of both his erotic fantasies and his destructive schemes. Armed with either typing samples or a duplicated machine, Chambers had in his possession the makings of a "life-saver," a magical (yet real) weapon which he could use at some future time against a friend who, like most of the friends in Chambers' paranoid system, was destined to be transformed into a concealed enemy.

A typewriter, whether it was Hiss's Woodstock machine or some other one, certainly carried a special meaning for Chambers. Note his remarkable testimony during the second Hiss trial when, in response to interrogation by counsel about his own typewriter, he told of the bizarre way he came to possess and later got rid of what he freely admitted was a *guilt-laden* typewriter:

MURPHY: Did you have a typewriter during say the period from 1934 to 1945 or any number of typewriters?

CHAMBERS: I had a Remington portable typewriter during that period, or part of it.

MURPHY: Remington portable?

CHAMBERS: Remington portable.

MURPHY: And what is that period of time?

CHAMBERS: I believe it is roughly 1934 until some time in 1940.

MURPHY: And do you remember how you got it?

CHAMBERS: It was given me by Uhlrich.

MURPHY: And who is Uhlrich?

[19] It is important to keep in mind the diverse activities and multiple identities Chambers was concurrently engaged in during this period (1934–36). As David Breen he wore a mustache (Hiss never saw him with one). As Lloyd Cantwell he leased an apartment in Baltimore. And as Whittaker Chambers he visited and stayed in the New York home of his friend Meyer Schapiro.

CHAMBERS: Uhlrich, as I think I mentioned last week, was the head of the first Soviet apparatus to which I was attached.

The following day (November 22), Chambers was interrogated further by Cross regarding the fate of the typewriter:

CROSS: Did you dispose of it at some time?
CHAMBERS: I did.
CROSS: When?
CHAMBERS: Either in 1940 or thereabouts.
CROSS: How did you dispose of it?
CHAMBERS: I left it on a streetcar or on an elevated train.
CROSS: Where?
CHAMBERS: In New York City.
CROSS: Where were you living at the time?
CHAMBERS: I was living on my farm in Westminster, Maryland. . . .
CROSS: Well, is it fair to say that you came up by train with this typewriter and got on either the New York subway or the elevated or a streetcar in New York City and then left the car or subway or elevated and left the typewriter behind?
CHAMBERS: That is quite fair.
CROSS: Now was the reason for disposing of that typewriter in that manner because it reminded you of the past and you wanted to dispose of it?
CHAMBERS: That is right.
CROSS: And you wanted to dispose of it in such a way that it could not be traced to you, didn't you?
CHAMBERS: No, I do not think it could have been traced to me.
CROSS: Well, you knew that when you disposed of it in this manner.
CHAMBERS: That was not the thought in my mind. I wanted to get rid of it.
CROSS: You knew that at that time, didn't you?
CHAMBERS: I certainly must have known it, yes.
CROSS: And this abandonment of this typewriter was planned before you left your farm in Westminster, wasn't it?
CHAMBERS: I believe it was.
CROSS: In just this manner?
CHAMBERS: Perhaps. I am not sure about that.[20]

Like the arsonist who returns to the fire, Chambers deliberately brings to the attention of his adversary and the courtroom a compelling fact: his past need to get rid of his typewriter. In his mind his past life is interchangeable with the symbol of his guilt—the typewriter. To forget his past he gets rid of the typewriter. Yet on a more realistic level, if an examination of *his* (conceivably the Hiss Woodstock) typewriter would expose his past actions, it is not just an innocuous fetish but an incriminating piece of hard evidence that he had need to get rid of.

If the "Remington portable" that Chambers testified he had to dispose of

[20] Trial Transcript, pp. 279; 456–57.

"in 1940" was, in fact, the Hisses' Woodstock on which he himself copied the stolen government documents, then Chambers' actions, were he to have switched the Hiss machine in 1935 (that is, kept the original and left the fabricated one with the Hisses), would be consistent with both the design and motive of other known acts of forgery he committed. Such an interpretation would be consistent with both his fantasy system and the physical vicissitudes the Woodstock N230099 went through before it was finally found by the Hisses in 1949.[21]

It was sometime during the year 1936, according to Hiss, that he had his last contact with Crosley. Chambers had phoned and asked for a loan and Hiss told him that he did not want to see him any more because he had shown himself to be a sponger. Cast out by someone he had earlier admired and envied, Hiss was thereafter tagged as his "concealed enemy." Thus, I submit, the first seeds of revenge were implanted in Chambers' mind, and it happened at a time when the Hiss typewriter could already have been appropriated by Chambers (either switched with a duplicate or typing samples taken). It was, in any case, available as a retaliatory weapon.

Revenge is a two-edged weapon. Out of his sense of guilt, Chambers feared that, in a talionic way, he would be destroyed. He had to protect himself against this retaliatory dread. And so he needed versatile "life-preservers" to serve his ambivalent future needs, as aggressive weapons or as creative instruments. He stored a revengeful plot in his memory just as he forged a "card of identity" or hid a document or a roll of microfilm; both the idea and its material implementation were buried for future use.

Chambers states in *Witness* that he searched his memory but could not remember what it was he had hidden away or what he might come up with. This significant piece of forgetting, which Chambers was quite explicit about (that is, he did not forget to remind the reader that he had forgotten the contents of the envelope), was his way of making it appear that he was not acting specifically against Hiss. Actually the documents could have been used, though less convincingly, as a weapon of accusation against any number of government employees who had occasion to see the documents. More specifically, Chambers probably had not yet sifted through what must have been great masses of material he had stored away, probably in many places, and

[21] How ironic that the factual circumstances surrounding Chambers' statement of such a significant act as disposing of a typewriter neither stirred the curiosity of the court nor was more incisively probed by the Hiss defense. It should be noted that the central idea of Chambers' taking over Hiss's typewriter is psychologically equivalent to his gaining possession of the piece of farm land in Westminster, Maryland, on which Hiss had earlier put a deposit. Comparable, also, is Chambers' claim that some tools, which Hiss left with Mr. Case, belonged to him (Chambers).

had not yet selected his evidence or worked out a precise plan as to how he could adapt and use the evidence for the specific situation which then confronted him.

Chambers' explanation of his delay in unearthing the documents is rich in psychological meaning. Before he sets out on his plan to destroy Hiss, he must (in his private ritual) first put *himself* through a death equivalent:

I had not gone to look for Hiss's memos for two simple reasons. I did not believe that they were of much importance, and I was overcome with a deep inhibiting lethargy. I had realized from the tone and the maneuvers of the pre-trial examination how successfully the Hiss forces had turned the tables with the libel suit. The issue had ceased almost completely to be whether Alger Hiss had been a Communist. The whole strategy of the Hiss defense consisted in making Chambers a defendant in a trial of his past, real or imaginary, which was already being conducted as a public trial in the press and on the radio. . . . I saw that I might well lose the libel suit, though it was not in my nature to lose it without a fight.

My sense of loneliness drove me to keep all the more to myself. My lethargy made any effort seem futile. The idea of making the long trip to New York City to reclaim some scraps of paper that I had left there ten years before, seemed an unendurable effort. I wanted only to be with my family and not to leave the sanctuary of the farm.

For ten silent years this "life-preserver" lay hidden in the back of Chambers' mind, dormant, but alive. Whether the envelope, allegedly taken from the dumbwaiter shaft in Mrs. Levine's home in Brooklyn, as Chambers testified at the Hiss trials, actually contained the particular typed documents *and* the rolls of microfilm or whether this scene was staged and the story fictionalized by Chambers, using Levine as a dupe, is still open to question. In this envelope Chambers allegedly stored sixty-five pages of typed documents, together with three undeveloped cans and two strips of developed microfilm. But, according to Claude Cross, defense counsel for Hiss during the second trial, the envelope was too small in size to contain all of these items. Unfortunately, during the trial, in the tension-packed courtroom, Cross failed to ask Chambers, as he had indeed intended, to reinsert the papers and the microfilm into the envelope as they allegedly were when Nathan Levine handed the package to him. After many years of reflection about the case, Cross said that he could have "knocked the government's case into a cocked hat" if he had had the presence of mind to do this while Chambers was in the witness box. The documents, plus the film, were far too bulky. When Cross later tried to insert them into the envelope, he proved to himself that his suspicion was true. It was physically impossible to do so without tearing the envelope.

Chambers' entire account of how and why he put away the stolen State

Department documents in 1939; his story that he forgot about their existence and content, then remembered enough to recover them;[22] his actions in dividing the evidence—using the paper documents in the Baltimore Deposition and later inserting the microfilm in a hollowed-out pumpkin—privately and secretly carried out, is an act as rich in symbolism as it is cunning in purpose. This uniquely designed set of (life-or-death) circumstances is reminiscent of Chambers' fateful birth fantasy and his clinical story of Dr. Dunning's role in saving his mother's life when he was born. Before delivering the handwritten slips, the typed papers, and the microfilm, Chambers describes how he went through a suicidal act in which he "almost" killed himself, a symbolic re-enactment of the way he "almost" killed his mother when he was born. By substituting idea for fact and *suffering out the idea* in a Dostoevskian way he played pranks with the idea of his death. In his subsequent struggle to live (shall I destroy the evidence and myself?) he re-enacted his mother's strength and power to stay alive (identification with her omnipotence). In effect, his delivery of the microfilm to the House Committee, arrogated into an act of patriotism to save his country in a crucial moment of history, was a symbolic acting out of the suffering and trauma he felt his mother had gone through when she bore him forty-seven years before. The infantile fantasy—that he had almost killed his mother—was repeated, like an obsessional ritual, throughout his entire life. It was characteristic of Chambers' life that all events, personal or historical, were molded into a stereotype of agony, suffering, and close calls with death. Miraculous self-rescues were effected to follow periods of self-torture. Only by translating the unconscious meaning of Chambers' fantasy system can his bizarre behavior be made meaningful. In the symbolic act of hiding the microfilm for ten years (gestation), then transplanting (inseminating) it to the inside of a pumpkin from which he had first scraped out the natural seeds (aborted), and then "delivering" his self-created "life-preserver" to the committee investigators, there is discernible the recapitulation of his death-and-rebirth fantasy.

Chambers says there were "rumors that strangers were prowling around the farm." He feared they were investigators for Hiss and that they "might well force my wife to let them ransack the house." He decided to hide the film so that "experts couldn't find it," and he thought of classic examples of concealment. At this moment he recalled an old Soviet moving picture in which underground Communists had transported arms and ammunition inside a

[22] All this without anyone else's knowledge. Even Mr. Levine, an attorney, who put the package away for him, then recovered it, knew nothing of the contents or importance of the manila envelope; nor did he at any time see the contents. There is no testimony but that of Chambers as to what was in the envelope. (Trial Transcript, pp. 728, 729.)

number of papier-mâché human figures. One of these, the Chinese god of Fate, was a "seated, pumpkin-shaped idol."

How magical, and personally revealing of his own self-rescue fantasies is this dreamlike memory of a pumpkin-shaped idol (Fate) inside which there had been hidden "arms and ammunition." And how pleased Chambers was with his idea: "A hollow pumpkin was the perfect hiding place for the microfilm. Investigators might tear the house apart. They would never think to look in a pumpkin lying in a pumpkin patch."

But an additional source for the animation of a pumpkin into a human figure and the symbolization of a birth may have been a poster drawn by his father, Jay Chambers, in 1925.[23] Like Chambers' translation errors, use of parables, allegories, or alteration of documents, the pumpkin poster painted by his father provides another possible source for a "life-preserver." The symbolism of Jay Chambers' sketch of an animated pumpkin in the form of a clown standing behind the footlights on a theatrical stage bears a striking resemblance to what we know of Whittaker's own fantasy system. Since this originally colorful picture presumably was one which hung in the Chambers' home it would have been unusual for it not to have attracted Whittaker's attention. And with Chambers' talent for appropriating the ideas of others, it is not implausible to assume that he may well have mentally stored the theme for use as a future "life-preserver."

The microfilm, delivered directly into the hands of the House Committee's investigators, was handled with all the care accorded a new-born infant. To insure its survival, it still required a favorable climate. Nurtured by the news media at a time when the public mind had been primed to the highest pitch of excitement, it was not long before Chambers' brainchild developed into an impressive legal witness. Government Prosecutor Murphy would within a few months characterize it as an "immutable" piece of evidence at the second Hiss trial. And Chambers, having delivered himself of the microfilm, would be saved and in his fateful way regard himself (as many, too, would regard him) as the savior of the country. Sinner turned saint, Chambers emerged overnight as a public figure. He had, once again, established a new identity.

The whole episode of the "pumpkin papers" made superb news copy. It was so unusual a plot that it captured the imagination of the public and has remained to this day one of the most remarkable of political coups. He shifted

[23] This poster was printed by the Marchbanks Press (New York) for the Japan Paper Co. Emily E. Connor of the Marchbanks firm still had a copy displayed in the office in 1961. She had known Jay Chambers for many years, for he had, on occasion, drawn sketches and painted posters for the Marchbanks Press. She stated that Jay Chambers was the artist. (E. Connor to the author, June 1961.)

The Pumpkin poster.

the burden of suspicion from himself to Hiss at a strategic moment during a period of legal conflict and public political turmoil. Chambers wrote:

No act of mine was more effective in forcing into the open the long-smothered Hiss Case than my act in dividing the documentary evidence against Hiss . . . placing the microfilm, separately, in the pumpkin. It was my decisive act in the Case. For when the second part of the divided evidence, the microfilm, fell into the hands of the Committee, it became impossible ever again to suppress the Hiss Case. . . . [without an understanding as to why he divided the evidence] the heart meaning of the case is blurred.

The Hiss case could hardly be regarded as "long-smothered." It was one of the most publicized cases in American history. What, then, is Chambers really saying? For Chambers, the Hiss-Chambers case was a double-death pact in which both participants should have been destroyed, but by a clever division of the evidence, Chambers alone was able to carry out his plan of destroying Hiss and, by aligning himself with the House Committee, save himself. And thus Chambers unwittingly speaks from the depths of his fratricidal problem when he refers to the pumpkin as the "heart meaning" of the case. His selection of the pumpkin from which he produced his "brain-child" has all the symbolic features and materials of a rebirth.

Chambers reminds us that he had been trained in photography during the thirties when he was an espionage agent in the underground, and he volunteers the fact that he was capable of developing the microfilm himself. When he turned over the sixty-five pages of typed documents to Marbury in November and, two weeks later, the microfilm to the House Committee investigators, Wheeler and Appell, he, of course, knew exactly what each contained. It would appear that if his real aim had been to expose the Communist conspiracy, he would not have taken the precaution of examining the film, dividing the evidence himself, and using one part to defend himself in the pre-trial examination for the libel suit and turning the other part over to Richard Nixon of the House Committee. If he had come forward at once with all the evidence, before the pre-trial examination, and made it all available to the FBI, then all of his other alleged sources would, if his claims were valid, have been brought to light. It is interesting to note how many of those whom Chambers named as sources or co-conspirators were one of a "pair of brothers": the Hiss brothers, the Reno brothers, the Pigman brothers, the Coe brothers; also Laurence Duggan, brother of Stephen Duggan, Francis Sayre, brother of Nevin Sayre, and Harry Dexter White, brother of Nathan I. White.[24] Because Chambers' sense of self was a divided one, he was similarly divisive

---

[24] Author of *Harry D. White—Loyal American,* written in defense and memory of his dead brother; privately published by his sister Bessie (White) Bloom.

in his relations with others. He was wary of the helpfulness of Herbert Solow and Isaac Don Levine. As he privately "confided" to Berle (to whom he did not tell the truth under any interpretation), he distrusted Roosevelt. In his alliance with Nixon or the House Committee, the Department of Justice became the concealed enemy.

If we keep in mind Chambers' inner need for omnipotence we can better understand his reasons for having to withhold some part of the truth. After he had repeatedly testified under oath that he had told all, it turned out that he had withheld still another trump card, or "life-preserver." He obviously knew much more than he testified to and his withholding may represent his own "compromise," a tacit (psychological) agreement with the Communist Party.

Having (once again) effected a symbolic rebirth and been given a second chance, Chambers was faced with the problem of fortifying his new image in its transformation from underground spy to public informer. He now felt more secure under the protective wing of the FBI, and the possibility of his indictment appeared less likely.

But it was very soon thereafter that Nixon, in response to his inquiry about the date of manufacture of the microfilm, received the startling reply from a representative of the Eastman Kodak Company that their examination of the film showed "that it had been manufactured in 1945." Nixon, understandably angered by the realization that he might, after all, have been duped by Chambers, telephoned him and demanded an explanation. Chambers' "life-preserver" had suddenly deflated. In *Witness,* Chambers recounts Nixon's call:

"The Eastman Kodak experts," said Congressman Nixon, "have just reported that the film in those undeveloped rolls was manufactured in 1945. If you got them in 1938, how do you explain that?" "It cannot be true," I said, "but I cannot explain it." . . . "God is against me," I thought. . . .

How could I dispute the opinion of an expert? If the expert said that the film had been manufactured in 1945, that was what the world would believe.

That was what the world wanted to believe, anyway. For, in fact, the world's instinctive feeling was against the little fat man who had stood up to testify for it, unasked. The world's instinctive sympathy was for the engaging man who meant to destroy it, was for Alger Hiss. He, and not I, personified the real values of a world that could not save itself, and it was he, and not I, that that world felt that it understood. "God is against me."

I toted my frozen core about the streets of the financial district. I was not going anywhere. Kierkegaard had, of course, been right: "Between man's purposes in time and God's purpose in eternity, there is an infinite qualitative difference." . . . By informing against the conspirators, I had misunderstood God's purpose, and God was making clear to me in the one way that reduced my error to the limit of absurdity. . . . I knew absolute defeat.

Chambers sinks into a mood of despair and suicide. On the surface this is a most paradoxical reaction. Why should he feel betrayed by God—unless God is the retaliatory force of his own destructiveness? The appropriate reaction to such a report, if his story were true, would have been immediate insistence that it was utterly impossible for the film to be dated 1945.

As Chambers pondered his fate, the realization of the meaning of his conflict—that is, the wish to destroy Hiss—threatened him. He panicked at the thought that his secret plan had collapsed. He would now be publicly exposed as a fraud and a character assassin. Without his "life-preserver" he would have to face his murderous self-image, his lifelong denial of his role in the death of his brother. The panic that shook him in 1948 was caused by an eruption of forces far more devastating than the date of manufacture of the microfilm.

Then, within a few hours, Chambers was informed that the Eastman Kodak representative had called back. "An error had been made." Further investigation showed that the film could have been manufactured in 1938 after all. Despite the favorable turn of events Chambers' guilt persisted.

But my mood did not change. . . . I went into a seed store and looked for a while at the seeds. Then I strolled among the sprays and insecticides. . . . I was looking for that poison one of whose ingredients is a cyanide compound. At last I asked a clerk if they stocked it. From some hiding place, he brought me the big round, tan-colored tin. I paid for it and went out.

I went to another seed house. Again the poison was not displayed. I had to ask for it. "Is there any danger in using it?" I asked. "Be very careful," said the clerk, "if you breathe enough of it, it will kill you." I thanked him.

I took my two wrapped tins to the Pennsylvania Station and put them in a lock box. Then I got ready to meet the Committee.

Despite the crucial turn of events, the change of date on the microfilm —symbolically a new birth date and a second chance—Chambers had brushed too closely against the highly charged significance of his actions. The threatened upheaval had been so disruptive and its momentum so great, he had to undo the situation by acting out his death. Note how impressively he puts himself through a near-suicide:

. . . I had suffered a spiritual exhaustion . . . a drought of the soul, a sense of estrangement and of being discarded. . . . I was alone in an absolute sense.

It is evident that his struggle is with symbolic figures, not real persons. He does not know why he has to destroy those he loves.

I could not undo what I had done, nor did I wish to. But there was one act that I could perform which would still spare the others. I could spare the others by re-

384)   FRIENDSHIP AND FRATRICIDE

moving myself as the only living witness against them. As men and women, they would then be free of my charges.

In the same manner that he uses a dead person on whom to center the blame (for example, Harry Dexter White), he now contemplates using himself as the silent witness, once again a substitution of the thought for the act.

One night I went to my room [at his mother's house in Lynbrook]. My mother had already retired. . . . Then I wrote a letter addressed simply: To All. In it I said that, of course, my testimony against Alger Hiss was the truth (time would certainly bear me out), but that the world was not ready for my testimony. I wrote that, in testifying, my purpose had always been to disclose the conspiracy, never to injure any individual man or woman. That I had been unable to do. But I could spare them the ultimate consequences of my actions and their own, by removing myself as a witness against them. My act was not suicide in the usual sense, for I had no desire to stop living. It was self-execution. . . .

I unwrapped the tins of chemical. It was a substance that liberated a lethal gas in the presence of moisture. The instructions for use were printed on the side of the cans in blocks of small black type. I had the same difficulty that I had had at the Commodore Hotel confrontation: I could not make out the type. The letters were blurred. But I thought that I understood the principles involved.

I poured some of the chemical in the cover of each tin. . . . I moistened the chemical. The fumes began to rise. . . .

I awoke abruptly and painfully in the early morning. . . .

The physical and chemical causes of my failure are simple. They involved a mistake in moistening the chemical. I do not care to go into the details. Had I been able to read the instructions, I should not have made the mistake. . . .

I no longer felt absolutely alone. I no longer felt estranged. I felt a sense of gentlest solicitude playing around me. . . .

Still, no one who has been through such an experience can be expected to be quite the same man again. He is both freer and stronger, because he is, ever after, less implicated in the world. For he has been, in his own mind at least, almost to the end of everything, and knows its worth.

He has put himself through a death and rebirth ritual. In a near act of suicide (although this whole story may have been a piece of expiatory fiction), he repeats, by inhalation of poison gas, the death pact and thus absolves his guilt. In his description of his attempt to end his life the "near miss" serves as a "suicide equivalent." Chambers elaborates on the difference between an act of suicide and "self-execution." In the sense that suicide is total homicide, Chambers shuns the idea and fears the act. But to the end that self-execution is the prerequisite for rebirth of a new self, he acts it out. Chambers' inner division allows him to experience, as though it were real, the difference between death of his body and death of his soul. The distinction, then, between suicide and self-execution is between the choice of death as an escape from an intolerable situation and the imposition of death as a punishment.

In the shiftings of Chambers' dissociated mind, he vacillates between suicide and homicide. To protect himself against his own self-destruction he confesses his guilt (in words), but as he does so he converts his confession into an accusation. This shifting of his identity sense and the manner in which he related to others explains his conversions of the personal into the political and religious.

The inner motivations of his behavior demonstrate the common root of his fears about the fate of the world and his anxiety about his personal survival in that world. His past conflicts govern his future actions. The unconscious mind has no sense of the present, no differential sense of time: a vast storehouse of repressed thoughts and events from the past surge up (as in dreams) and are experienced as immediate threats and remobilize apprehensions about the future. A repressed, unconscious death wish against a hated and loved person may be transformed into anxiety about one's own death.

Chambers' testimony during the Hiss trials about his strange life was highlighted by the defense counsel. The many episodes in his itinerant and vagabond existence were linked in a long chain of clinical evidence presented by counsel to show Chambers' sociopathic personality, his amoral behavior, and his unreliability as a witness. Although the government objected, such historical material was relevant and essential to the case. For the central issue boiled down to the single fact: one of the two, Hiss or Chambers, was lying. The testimony of Dr. Carl Binger, a New York psychiatrist, and Dr. Henry Murray, a professor of psychology (also a psychiatrist) at Harvard, called as experts by the defense, was scholarly indeed. But the effectiveness of their opinions was considerably reduced by the restrictions of trial procedure and the pitfalls of cross-examination techniques. One brief excerpt, typical of the medico-legal joustings that characterized Prosecutor Murphy's courtroom tactics in his cross-examination of Dr. Binger, should suffice to make this clear:

MURPHY: Now, Doctor, you told us that when Mr. Chambers . . . was about 17 or 18 he left home, he ran away from home, and he worked in Washington for a street railway company and used the name Charles Adams, and you said that he was playing a game and you thought that that was evidence of pathological lying. Is that correct, Doctor?

BINGER: Well, I think taking on a role that you wish to assume is evidence of pathological lying.

MURPHY: What facts did you rely upon from which you drew the conclusion that he was playing a game?

BINGER: Just the fact that he would at random pick a name that suited his fancy.

MURHY: Well, did you say as a doctor then that you came to the conclusion that he was playing a game because he used a fictitious name?
BINGER: A name of his own choice that suited his particular fancy, yes. . . . Acting out a fantasy.
MURPHY: You have used the word "fantasy" a couple of times. What facts in evidence are there that you have relied upon from which you can say as a doctor that Mr. Chambers had fantasies? What facts in the hypothetical question or in your observation of him do you rely upon as a doctor to prove or to say, for that matter, that Mr. Chambers had fantasies?
BINGER: Well, I think you must misunderstand me when I use that word "fantasy." Everybody has fantasies. Every human being has imaginations. And when a man selects a name because it suits a certain role, I call that a fantasy. You may call it imagination. . . .
MURPHY: Fantasies are the workings of the mind, are they not, Doctor?
BINGER: Yes, imaginative workings.
MURPHY: Imaginative workings. You can't see them?

As Murphy's cross-examination of Binger extended into other areas, Binger exceeded the prescribed boundaries of the "hypothetical question" and was reminded of his legal limitations as a witness:

MURPHY: I only ask you to use the facts I gave you.
BINGER: All right. I am sorry I mentioned that. I can't always divorce things that are in my mind. I am not trained to do that. I am trained to include them, not to exclude them.[25]

Despite the existing strictures of the law, which limited the admissibility of such expert testimony, I still find it difficult to understand how the reliability and credibility of Chambers could have been accepted or given serious courtroom consideration once his clinical picture had been portrayed. Unfortunately the law did not provide or even allow for a direct clinical psychiatric examination of the litigants by a panel of psychiatric experts. Furthermore, the substance of the analysis that Dr. Binger and Dr. Murray were permitted to present to the court was continually broken down, and the many characteristics which, when viewed together, showed Mr. Chambers' psychopathic pattern of behavior throughout his life were isolated and dealt with separately. The tone of the prosecution, moreover, was, without a doubt, derisive. When, for example, Dr. Binger gave his opinion that the theft of some fifty-six books by Chambers from the Columbia Library was evidence of his psychopathic personality, Murphy retorted: "Doctor, did you ever take any hotel or Pullman towels?" Binger replied, "I can't say whether I did or not."

In the face of the seemingly "immutable" evidence—and the jury, it must be remembered, had no knowledge of the ambiguities about the origin of

[25] Trial Transcript, p. 2738.

Woodstock N230099—Chambers' clinical history (so far as it was known) bore little weight. Alger Hiss was convicted of perjury on January 20, 1950. In his final statement before the court Hiss said:

I would like to thank your Honor for this opportunity again to deny the charges that have been made against me. I want only to add that I am confident that in the future the full facts of how Whittaker Chambers was able to carry out forgery by typewriter will be disclosed.

Thank you, sir.

VI

20

Prisoner

DURING THE YEAR 1950, following the jury's conviction and Judge God-dard's sentence of five years' imprisonment, Hiss and his lawyers were occupied with the task of preparing a brief for appeal. Hiss was bitterly disappointed when the verdict was returned, but his energies did not wane. Diligent and hopeful in his way, he worked on the preparation of his legal brief.[1] "My spirits and confidence remained high," said Hiss, "I felt sure that the appeal would be granted and worked until 3 or 4 a.m. searching for new evidence." Though the Hiss appeal, which was argued on October 30, 1950, was not widely publicized, partisan lines were drawn and the vehemence the case had aroused did not subside.[2]

On December 7, 1950, the United States Court of Appeals denied his appeal. In the opinion written by Judge Harris B. Chase, and concurred in by Judges Augustus N. Hand and Thomas B. Swan, the complex matter of Chambers' psychological motivation was summarily disposed of. The Court said:

It seems abundantly clear that the jury was amply justified in believing that those circumstances (the taking of State Department documents and their transcription on the Woodstock typewriter) did not indicate some ulterior motive to harm the

[1] After Hiss's conviction, Chester Lane succeeded Edward McLean as defense counsel, and the firm of Beer, Richards, Lane and Haller became Hiss's "attorneys of record," succeeding the firm of Debevoise, Plimpton & McLean.

Chester Lane was assisted in his investigations by attorneys Robert Benjamin, Harold Rosenwald, and Kenneth Simon. Benjamin, in his preparation of the argument for the appeal and writing of the legal brief ("Brief for Appellant," 125 pp.) was also assisted by attorneys Rosenwald, Simon and J. Lowenthal. But, in the last of many communications I was to receive from Mr. Benjamin (ten days before his death on January 17, 1966), he wrote: "In the preparation of the appeal, Alger helped me even more." (Robert Benjamin to the author, January 7, 1966.)

[2] The cast of characters was pretty much the same as at the second trial. The "Oyster Bay Roosevelts," including Mrs. Longworth (the extreme rightist contingent of the family and political adversaries of President Franklin D. Roosevelt and the New Deal), were present in the courtroom in full political battle array.

appellant at some future date but in believing that they pinned the abstractions and deliveries fast to the appellant himself.[3]

The Earl Jowitt, on the contrary, in his review of the trial testimony, expressed a plea for clarification of this crucial matter.

I must admit that I am sufficiently impressed no longer to be influenced in my judgment by the apparent absence of motive on the part of Chambers.[4]

On the day the adverse decision was announced by the Court of Appeals, Hiss wrote his stepson:

. . . let me say that in spite of much anger we are not in the slightest broken up (or down). And basically our calmness comes from the same analysis you make, so I assume your anger will also have a good stout layer of calm under it. When fear leads to a willingness to believe what you want to believe—which is true of a great many more people than usual—then those who are willing to stop at nothing to get their own selfish ends served will ride high and injustice will become so frequent that it will breed its own cure. We've got social poisons at large today among the people which will have to develop their own anti-bodies. In such a situation those who resolutely oppose injustice will be serving others more than they can see now.

In March 1951 review was denied by the Supreme Court. Hiss prepared to go to prison. In his methodical way he made plans to leave his family, home, and friends. Since the outset of the first trial in May of 1949 Priscilla had stopped teaching at the Dalton School. In search of a job for Priscilla, the Hisses went to see Ken McCormick, editor of Doubleday & Company.

After the trial [wrote McCormick] he and Priscilla came to see me in the office and sat across the office from me on the davenport, holding hands and almost in a state of transfiguration. The whole resolution of matters seemed to relieve them and the fact that he was going to prison gave the whole atmosphere a crusade-like quality. He didn't have any naïve notion that he was going to have a picnic there but the fact that he was going to prison seemed to exhilarate him and excite her.[5]

Hiss, with characteristic practicality, got in touch with Austin H. Mac-Cormick, head of the Osborne Association for prison reform, who talked to him about prison life. Anxious to know what to expect, as well as what to be able to tell his nine-year-old son, Tony, about where he was going, Hiss

[3] From the Opinion of the United States Court of Appeals for the Second Circuit in *U.S.A.* v. *Alger Hiss,* December 7, 1950, p. 254.
[4] Jowitt, *op. cit.,* p. 223.
[5] "We talked about a book Hiss might write," McCormick continued, "or think of writing while in prison. He was reasonably sure that he couldn't write anything there, but he was equally sure that he could do a lot of research towards a book, so I urged him to let me know any books I could send him. He pointed out that this would have to be done very carefully through the prison librarian, so as not to seem to give him any privileges." (Kenneth McCormick to the author, January 3, 1964.)

listened carefully to MacCormick. He was advised how best to conduct himself in prison ("Never start a conversation . . . wait for the man next to you
to speak"), told of the hazards of certain types of prison jobs (the prison hospital, for example), and what types of convicts he would meet.

On the morning of March 22, 1951, in the company of three members of
his defense counsel, Hiss appeared at the courthouse to surrender himself to
the United States Marshal. Taken to a detention cell, he was routinely finger-
printed and searched. Then, his right wrist shackled to the wrist of a mail
thief, he was led from the courthouse through a crowd of newsmen and
photographers and entered the sheriff's van. Together with seven other prisoners, Hiss was removed to the Federal House of Detention, where his suit was
changed for prison clothes—a gray flannel shirt and blue denim trousers—and
where he remained until his transfer to Lewisburg Penitentiary.

While in prison, Hiss worked as a stock clerk in the prison warehouse.
Immediately tabbed as a "Commie" by a certain clique of prisoners, he refrained from any discussion of his case and did not fraternize with any particular group. He sought no favors, asked for no soft job. Following Mac-
Cormick's advice, Hiss avoided taking a job in the prison hospital or getting
into any situation where he could be subjected to demands from the narcotics
addicts. Though Hiss was careful he was not a loner. He became friends with
many of the inmates, but of them all he found the Sicilian gangsters the most
appealing. He admired their close family ties, was impressed by the affection
they displayed toward their wives and children. The missionary spirit in him
found an outlet with prisoners of little education. He taught several illiterate
inmates to read and write, wrote letters for others, talked over personal problems with some.

Of the scores of people with whom I talked during the course of this
study, two of the most enlightening were Hiss's former fellow prisoners. Both
had come to know him well. They were quite different from each other—one
was an underworld character, the other a conscientious objector. The former,
in a long, intimate communication which he recorded on a reel of tape and
sent me, noted, among other things:

Hiss was denied a lot of privileges in Lewisburg. He couldn't debate because he
would win all his debates with Bucknell University and in time the officials stopped
him from that.[6]

He didn't receive any . . . "meritorious good days" because the officials were
afraid of public opinion.

Hiss never complained. . . . This man wore old clothes while he was there,
never got new clothes, wore old shoes. And, although you're entitled to two pairs

[6] Debating with nearby colleges was one of many activities, along with organized games,
concerts, and so on, which was part of the rehabilitation program at Lewisburg.

of new shoes a year, he never received these. The homosexuals that worked in our clothing issue used to cut his trousers one leg higher than the other when he'd send his clothes to the laundry. Hiss would never go to the officials to complain . . . and the officials that worked in the clothing issue knew this was going on. The only way it could be straightened out was by cons like myself and others that liked Hiss. . . .

I know of one case where he took an illiterate, taught him to read and write on his own time, during Hiss's recreation hour. He spent two hours a day with this boy for months, till he could read and write fairly well. . . .

Hiss always had something good to say about everybody. He could always see the good things in everybody and that's why a lot of fellows like myself accepted Hiss. . . .

All the top Commies in the country that were in jail at that time came through Lewisburg. They stayed there a while, Hall, Winters, all of 'em. Hiss never fraternized with these people. Always spoke to them, which we all did. . . . In there we all run in what you call "packs." Hiss never joined one. . . . Hiss went about his own way, had nothing to say to nobody, good or bad, about them and said very little about his own case. He seemed to just let it rest, "Here I am, think what you want." And that's what makes me say that this man is not guilty. . . .

I don't think Hiss was a Communist. My reason for saying this is that while I was in jail with him I had time to observe and study this man. He is a very liberal man. He sees only what is good in people. . . .

Most all of us there respected Hiss for what he was. A few fellows, the so-called "flag-raisers," called him a Commie. . . . While they were in jail, they became great Americans. . . . These were the only ones they would try to harass Hiss and in time they quit this. . . .[7]

The other informant, the conscientious objector, wrote:

Mr. Hiss and I worked together for a while, and then I was transferred to the library. Mr. Hiss remained in the storeroom (a very lonely, depressing place) for the rest of his stay at the club, though after a couple of years he was offered a transfer to the kitchen, which he turned down. . . .

I can't say I was one of Mr. Hiss's best friends at Lewisburg, though he is one of the few people there who helped make my stay a relatively pleasant one, kept my mind operating by discussions of mostly art and literature. We lent each other books, and Mr. Hiss introduced me to and lent me the weekly *New Statesman & Nation* (London), a real breath of fresh air in that milieu, for some reason. . . .

Mr. Hiss at Lewisburg quickly got the respect of most of the staff and in the end I would say very, very nearly 100% of the inmates. . . .

Mr. Hiss showed great adaptability. At one time we were both in a large dormitory. . . . The noisiness and lack of privacy made it very difficult. . . . Mr. Hiss however took it all in stride, and seemed quite happy, though the noise, etc. could not have been entirely what he would have liked. . . . Mr. Hiss from there went to the Honour Block . . . which was really very nice, because one could stay in one's cell and read or study, or go out into the corridor and talk with people.

[7] Personal communication, A. Rocco to the author (tape), February 1964.

Mr. Hiss once prepared and gave a lecture. . . . I remember seeing him in the library working on it for some days, in his spare time. . . . I was struck by the perfection of the thing. Very, very simple language—more simple than Mr. Hiss habitually uses—and this combined with a simple, quiet delivery gave me an impression of great beauty.

Because of the visually monotonous environment . . . art books and art postcards were important. Mr. Hiss got a steady diet of art postcards from his family, mostly 19th century European works. . . . Mr. Hiss had a large reproduction of a Cezanne landscape taped to the wall [of his cell in the Honour Block] for a long time. It got rather faded after a while, but remained there. . . .[8]

Hiss made of his life in prison a positive, challenging experience. He dealt resourcefully with the many hazards that surrounded him, and the record of his forty-four months at Lewisburg was without untoward incident. However, it was not easy, and Hiss earned the affection and respect he received from the other inmates. "When he went out of the gates on November 27, 1954," Brock Brower has noted, ". . . there were rousing cheers from the bleak prison windows. Hiss's success in prison derived from human qualities that it would be hard to fake. Possibly for some days, or some weeks, but not for almost four years." [9]

The role of caretaker in Hiss was not limited to fellow inmates. Hiss's letters to Priscilla, Tony, and Timothy offered support and reassurance. In closely written pages, three times a week he strove to keep their spirits buoyed with a dutiful flow of lighthearted chatter, humor, and intellectual stimulation. His earnest endeavor to hold together the family morale is evident in the tone, style, and newsiness of all his letters to his family.

The bolstering, pedantic tone of the letters are characteristic of his manner in life. Several months after his imprisonment Hiss wrote to his stepson:

Your letters have been absolutely wonderful, very concrete and vivid, full of T.H.'s best quick wit (which is high praise) and permeated with the sense of purpose you have about your new field. They have given me much pleasure.

Commenting on a poem Timmy had written, Hiss wrote:

Editorial comment on the versifying effort is necessarily "restrained" in view of the smallness of the submitted sample: promising? skillful? Aren't these the appropriate words for a reviewer? *Fatherly* comment, however, is quite unrestrained: good work, try several more, great stuff; but especially pleasure that you sent it to me.

The dichotomy of feeling toward such an everyday human experience is striking. Is he editor or is he father? Yet it is this quality of objectivity balancing his affection that characterizes Hiss's adaptive, formal informality and sets the tone for a polite but perplexing style.

[8] Personal communication, A. Bergdoll to the author, February 1, 1964.
[9] Brock Brower, "The Problems of Alger Hiss," *Esquire,* December 1960.

Do you have time for any of the Stadium concerts? The only music here is the NBC orchestra on the Steel Hour Sundays 8:30–9:30 p.m.—I am listening as I write (via earphones) to waltzes from *Der Rosenkavalier*. The programs err on the "popular" side but as there is *no* other music I accept them gratefully nonetheless. I'd get some vicarious enjoyment out of your going (and describing) the much richer fare of the Stadium. . . .

Prisons have their own jargon: joint for prison, hack or screw for any officer (one newcomer thought, the first time he was in jail, that this must be the officer's name who first had charge of him. He told me with chagrin for his great faux pas that he had, therefore, addressed said officer—this was years ago, in Mass.—as "Mr. Hack"), play it cool—meaning take it easy, rat for a bearer of tales to the officials, rap for a sentence (bit is a synonym but there the emphasis is on the time meted out, not the conviction), etc. etc. So much more to say but. . . .

Much love,

Alger [10]

The absence of self-pity (and the hint of pleasure) echoed through the many letters Hiss wrote from prison. His story at Lewisburg was another experience on which, despite the deprivation (or because of it), Hiss seemed to thrive.

Regulations restricted Hiss's correspondence to a total of seven relatives and friends (excluding married women). He was permitted to write three letters a week; the amount of incoming mail was also restricted. Visitors were limited to once a month. Subtler hardships affected his family. The public suspicion prevalent after the trials made life especially difficult for Priscilla and the two boys. And Hiss's absence (an ironical re-enactment of his own paternal loss), despite his distant efforts, added its toll to an already burdened situation between Priscilla and her two sons.

Timmy, then in his mid-twenties, had been through a stormy adolescence and an extended period of psychological revolt that estranged him from his parents. His father's trials and imprisonment had a shocking, salutary effect. After five years of a rather aimless existence, Timmy sought and received psychiatric help. He returned to college as a premedical student. His major interest was psychology, and he was deeply involved in the therapeutic unraveling of his own emotional life, particularly his conflicted feelings toward Alger, Priscilla, and his younger brother.

In November 1951, after eight months at Lewisburg, Hiss wrote to Timmy:

I was tickled and touched by your writing so fully about what's on your mind . . . especially about so personal and important a matter as your relationship to Pros.

[10] Alger Hiss to Timothy Hobson, July 29, 1951.

I remember a much younger Tim saying vehemently to me: Why don't you stop psychoanalyzing everybody. . . . we seem to have reversed roles. I *now* . . . believe nothing is less productive of good psychic health than amateur analysis. . . . So, on the issue of your analysis of Pros I shall be Alger the Silent. . . . As all relationships are two-way, some of the imbalance stems from within your own personality. You cannot for the present do anything constructive about the confusions toward the relationship in Pros' mind; but you—and only you—*can* do something about those you bring to the relationship. My advice, since you ask it, is that you work on those. . . . I know and love you both and I'm sure that the relationship can and will eventually be made what it should be. You can, of course, and should show this letter to anyone you consult as, obviously, our own relations are themselves a very important part of the whole family psychic picture —and they, too, need working on from both sides.

More particularly and immediately, since the Tony-Pros relationship has, in the nature of things, for better or worse, to be primarily their responsibility and mine . . . leave that and like questions to me. What the heck, I may be physically hobbled but I'm not dead! . . . Thus and here endeth this disquisition which I hope won't discourage you from writing (again, again, and again) equally fully and candidly whenever you are moved to do so. If you don't want comments on same just say so and I'll observe the injunction. This time I took it you wanted my views on the same forthright basis as your own.

Timmy's vehemence toward his family subsided. He became engrossed in the study of medicine at the University of Geneva and gradually effected a comfortable distance between himself and his family.

My letters to you [Hiss wrote to Timmy on his twenty-sixth birthday] have become precisely as infrequent as your birthdays, I'm afraid. . . . Your last letter contained the statement that you feel you have nothing much to write about because your "activities seemed to be more or less similar week around." . . .

You are unerringly accurate in your recognition that values give life its meaning and that maturity is the conscious formulation of values. But unconscious, unrecognized values are for most people today, as they have been heretofore, so warped by societal maladjustments that the acquisition of rational values, as opposed to *rationalized* ones, is halting. They (prevalent unconscious values) lead many psychiatrists and sociologists, as a writer in the *New Statesman and Nation* put it, to be more concerned with morale than with morals, with amelioration of symptoms than with making men whole. A more recent *NS & N* author expressed the same concept when he noted: "The Fabian criticism of society was fundamentally a criticism of machinery, not a criticism of the upper middle-class spirit [i.e. values]." And Dostoevsky lamented in his dark culture that (his) "society is [was] organized so meanly that man cannot help but perpetuate villains."

Today, for the first time, we have all the verifiable knowledge needed for fulfilling man's potentialities, the vision that specially marks each radiant figure in the company of the great liberators of man's spirit. A grand time for a 26th birthday! Much, much love,

Alger.[11]

[11] Alger Hiss to Timothy Hobson, September 15, 1952.

"Alger," Hobson has commented, "is a combination of a beatitude and an IBM machine."

In writing to his wife, Hiss used the plain speech ("thee," "thy"), as had been their custom in conversation. Each letter included a special section in carefully printed script for easy reading, to his young son Tony, with whom he carried on a continuous narration about nature, art, music, and a mythical bedtime-story hero, known to them only as "SLB."

During his forty-four months at Lewisburg, Hiss wrote more than five hundred letters to his wife and family. Though a detailed analysis of this voluminous correspondence would in itself constitute a definitive document about him, it is beyond the scope of the present study. A few excerpts will, however, provide some cross-section of his thoughts and feelings in many areas of his interests during this period of his incarceration.

April 17, 1952

The facts of daily life include much more regular activity at the storeroom. . . . We have been moving drums of oil to new positions, taking down metal shelving and shifting paint from one location to another. As . . . my colleague is a devout Jew, and as he is not supposed to work during Passover I have tried to take most of the jobs.

April 13, 1952—Easter morning

At church this morning we sang two of my favorite alleluia hymns: "Christ the Lord is risen today" and "Come, ye faithful, raise the strain." And the chaplain spoke wisely and gently of the ever-living nature of the spirit of love which Jesus understood so well and had within himself in such great measure that it overflowed into those about him and has lived on in human hearts (those that are healthy and strong enough to nurture it).

April 22, 1952

Form in art is largely determined by cultural conditioning. . . . Form, therefore, necessarily proceeds in styles and reflects the preoccupations and concepts of current civilization. But the emotional impact . . . of art (as opposed to expertise in writing or painting or music) derives, I feel certain, from the sincerity, intensity and maximation of the artists-and-their-respondents' visions of man's perfectability.

May 17, 1952

A grand, vigorous and alert letter from Chester [Lane] came on Friday. He pointed out, with his usual objectivity, "the vested interest in many quarters in having this false conviction stick" and "Chambers' talents for perjury [and] the resources which he and his friends might be able to call on to produce additional fabricated evidence." . . .

Mimmy's regular Sun. letter was terrific in its account of her energy, e.g., last Wed. she was away from home from 8.30 a.m. till midnight—at the bank, a 10.00 a.m. meeting of the College Club, a tour of duty all afternoon at the annual

Flower Mart selling pony ride tickets, and that evening the Annual Meeting of her Church! All this at 84!

May 20, 1952

Will thee see if thee can find words of affirmation, outreach and aspiration which I have overlooked? Remember thy remarking on the paucity of psychiatric thought about the nature of the emotionally healthy man?—he appears only as one free of various mental ills, a most negative fellow indeed!

May 22, 1952

This feeling of certainty in counting on others, of knowing that they will always be the same (except for constantly growing in sweetness and understanding) is one of the most wonderful things that people can give each other, isn't it? . . .

The Friends have the healthy ability to give for the sake of the giving, with no twisted rationalization that directly or indirectly it will "protect" or "advance" the giver. The uncomplicated joy of helping others for *their* sakes, of enjoying the enjoyment of others, is so natural a human trait that it is sad to think how much perversely employed energy has been and is spent in frustrating it so that in today's loveless, causeless confusion of values the Friends seem rare spirits.

June 9, 1952

As long as you have to be in the city in hot weather, it is worthwhile planning to be as comfortable as possible—don't exercise so much you get excited and steamy, get to the parks when you can in the early morning or late evening, wear as little as possible especially indoors where shorts are enough, eat cool foods, don't "fight" the heat and get tense but relax and do the pleasant things (like picnics, quiet indoor games) that you have time for with school over and rest a lot. Save a few treats like an aircooled movie or restaurant meal for the worst days, etc. I'm sure you can think of lots better ways than I can to keep from feeling "bothered" by the heat before you go to camp.

June 14, 1952

The saga of our "public robin" has taken a new turn. He had so many foster fathers that one of them, worried for his health, spirited fledgling and nest to some hidden spot and dug worms furiously for him until the agitated mother found the new location. He is ready to fly anyway so his "kidnapping" would not have been much of a separation from Mama even if she hadn't found the transplanted nest. But there was a lot of excitement on the part of all the other foster fathers who thought at first that some harm had been done to their pet.

June 22, 1952

Yesterday morning I saw a charming and amusing thing. A mother song sparrow was energetically seeking food. She popped in and out of a border of iris leaves, quickly (almost nervously) picking here and there in the ground. Now and again she would suddenly hop about this way and that on the nearby lawn—always intent solely on food. She was a pale tan-brown, trim, abrupt, precise. The whole time she was followed by a roly poly, slow, unsure baby who had the silliest stump of a new tail. I was watching a lesson in getting lunch. The much darker, muddy colored little fatty was NOT a very good pupil (probably too well fed by mama to be hungry). He watched mama pretty closely—most of the time and now and then he would take a slow and lazy peck at the ground. Every now and then his atten-

tion would wander and when he came to, mama would have moved off a couple of
feet. Then he would run-waddle (he hadn't learned mama's abrupt quick hop)
after her as fast as he could until he was only about a foot away. Two or 3 times
mama darted into the iris stalks while he was daydreaming and was nowhere to be
seen when he woke up. Then he was panicky until he caught sight of her again and
would pay much closer attention—*for a few minutes*. Once she bounced out of the
iris with tubby left behind—probably woolgathering again. Suddenly he came
scooting out as if he were being chased by a bull elephant, but as soon as he
caught sight of active efficiently busy mama he slowed his hurrying pace and once
more began his dawdling imitation of his mother, with frequent lapses of attention
and occasional anxious scurryings to catch up again with her.

July 5, 1952

A full article (in the *Times*) warns all auto drivers "for safety's sake" to give no
stranger a lift. The Auto. Club of N.Y. pipes shrilly: "No matter how innocent or
pathetic the hitchhiker may appear, the best bet is not to take a chance." J. Edgar
Hoover again aids divisiveness and isolation of spirit by an official warning of "the
danger of attack by criminals who may be posing in the guise of innocent hitch-
hikers along the highways of the nation." Hitchhiking is now illegal in 20 states
(including N.Y. and Pa.) and the D. of C. The Auto. Assoc. is trying to banish
Good Samaritans in all other states, but Vt. and N.H. still permit the friendly lift
to the wayfarer!

July 24, 1952

You have probably heard by now that in spite of all of Chester's wonderful work,
Judge Goddard on Tues. denied the motion for a new trial. As you know from our
last few visits I expected this result in view of Judge G.'s attitude. We will, of
course, keep right on trying and as soon as we decide on the next steps I'll let you
know.

During his nearly four years of confinement Hiss had ample time to reflect on the meaning of his life, his values, and his fate. It was, he said, an
opportune period for self-analysis. To my unrelenting proddings about deepening insights, self-realizations, and other possible discoveries that may have
advanced his understanding of himself Hiss responded:

I don't mean to inflate the significance of my efforts by suggesting an analogy to a
real psychoanalysis. . . . All I did was to use the time presented for prolonged
. . . and undistracted concentration to examine my major goals, tolerance for
types of strain, ethical standards, capacity for affective relations, self-control, willingness to assume responsibility, sense of affirmation, ability to live in and savor
the immediate, historical outlook, relations between the individual and society
(with me as the individual), spontaneity, forthrightness, consideration for others,
and other areas in just these non-technical and amateur terms. Next I sought to
discover the sources of my attitudes in my early family relations and atmosphere
and training; church, school, neighborhood, summer farm life, the Scouts, camp,
college and professional influences; and the impact of my own marriage and being
a parent. Also I tried to examine and understand in the light of these inquiries my
emotional responses as I could recognize them in consistent patterns over periods of

time: anger, affection, pride, pleasure, serenity, euphoric states, boredom, recurring illnesses, response to pain, to intensive work, to long hours of work night after night. The time available for these reflections resulted from the prison routine of "lights out" at 10 p.m. (whereas I had long been conditioned to much later hours) and from the not infrequent periods when I was left alone in the storeroom in times of inactivity with no books or other reading matter.

I don't know that there were any particular results of this self-analysis. I wasn't seeking over-all results except that I wanted to know better what my capabilities were for the immediate future (in Lewisburg) and for later on. There was the occasion for a reconsideration of first principles, of values, of objectives and I welcomed the occasion. I had lived so actively that the reflective side of my nature had had only occasional chances to assess basic directions and motivations. As my experience had been quite extensive and I was in middle life (I was 46 when I went to Lewisburg) this seemed a splendid chance to devote concentrated attention to re-examining and extending my personal philosophy.

One other point—the analysis was not done *in vacuo,* depending only on memory, examination of my dreams and my sensations. I was able to observe my daily reactions to my fellow prisoners and the guards and officials. I read, as widely as the uneven library permitted, in ethics and social customs (for example I read the Bible more intensively than ever before and for the first time primarily as history, ethical formulation and psychological insight; I also read considerably in the Babylonian Talmud and for the first time read *Totem and Taboo*), in history and psychology. And the considerable reading and thinking about such matters that I had done for many years were a basis for my starting in on a continuing and intensive self-examination.

As a result of this prolonged period of introspection Hiss's intellectual insight deepened. He became more knowledgeable about psychic forces, and it brought him closer to an understanding of his emotional self and illumined to some extent the existence of some of his deeper motivations. All in all, however, his sense of objectivity and overriding rationalism remained unchanged. On November 27, 1954, sixteen days after his fiftieth birthday, Hiss was released from prison. The three years and eight months he had served represented the adjusted maximum time of his five-year sentence. After his release he was subject to the usual parole restrictions for ten months. Once every month Hiss reported to his probation officer. During this period he was prohibited from making any public appearance, was not allowed to leave New York, except, on occasion, to visit his aged mother in Baltimore.

As a convicted felon, for the rest of his life (unless he receives a Presidential pardon) Hiss remains deprived of his right to vote, the right to practice law or hold public office. By a special act of Congress, the Hiss Act, he has been cut off from any government pension.

Hiss found, however, that the passage of time had softened many things. The hostility and public hysteria had subsided. He moved about New York, went to the theater, concerts, visited museums and other public places. His code of honor, sense of privacy, his cultural and idealized values had undergone no apparent change. Though his image has hardened in the public mind, "I have always insisted," said Hiss, "on living my life as an individual, and not as a symbol."

In 1955 he began work on his book, but his initial effort was interrupted by several months of illness, during which he underwent gall-bladder surgery.

In a long interview with Chester Lane in 1951 Timothy Hobson aired his thoughts about his stepfather:

I have never understood Alger's reticence to use legal fire to fight fire as far as that case went. Alger always thought it was not only more dignified, but absolutely demanded that everything be done in a completely justifiable, honorable way, and the fact that he felt that the opponents were using other techniques did not influence his judgment. But that was not surprising to me in view of the fact that I have known him for so many long years, when he would do things because he thought they were honorable and worthwhile, in spite of the fact that other things would bring him more fame, fortune and income. I am sure that he has already felt that his life has amounted to a great deal of constructive good in the State Department, the Carnegie Endowment for International Peace, the U.N. I'm sure that when he gets out [of prison] he'll find ways to make his life even more constructive and good.

He's supposed to write a book, but when the book comes out I am absolutely convinced that it will not be a book in personal vindication, but a book on the evils of civil rights, perjury in general, and the atrocities that are committed by the civil rights investigating committees and the Attorney General.

After Hiss's release from prison he tried to write a philosophical dissertation on civil liberties, the limits of court procedures in times of public hysteria, and so forth. It was hard going, for Hiss tried to use his case as the skeleton of an academic analysis. After some helpful suggestions from literary friends, Hiss restricted himself to writing of his own case rather than a generalized commentary on law in social action. The book, when it appeared in 1957, was not the general study that Hobson predicted, but neither was it the book of "personal vindication" that his supporters hoped for.[12] *In the Court of Public Opinion* was a discussion of the case in the same detached, objective

[12] Ken McCormick of Doubleday confirmed that Hiss intended "not to argue the case, nor write another *Witness,* but to write a book about what happens to a society in which this sort of thing is possible. I assured him," said McCormick, "that when it was ready to see, I wanted to have first look to consider it for publication. There was no commitment. When the manuscript did come in, it was quite a disappointment. It seemed to us evasive and talking all around the point. We finally regretfully had to say no. Ultimately Alfred Knopf said this book should be published as a document and went ahead and published it. I thought that this was a very splendid thing of him to do, but regretted that we hadn't been the ones with that kind of guts." (Kenneth McCormick to the author, January 3, 1964.)

terms that had characterized Hiss as a person and as a witness. He chose to set forth and discuss the facts and evidence and offer his legal rebuttal, referring to witnesses and exhibits where they bore directly on Chambers' charges. He omitted the color and drama of the hearings and the trials, and he did not include the laudatory statements by high-ranking government officials who testified about his life and character.

But Hiss was on sound, if not popular, ground in the way he set the tone for *In the Court of Public Opinion,* and in this regard he was encouraged by his attorney, Robert M. Benjamin, to

keep it accurate, recognizing at the same time that that would make it dull for anyone who was looking for sensation.

Indeed I think that most of the people who found it dull would have been satisfied only by a confession of guilt or of covering up for someone else who was guilty. I don't see how one who has been convicted of perjury could have proclaimed his innocence with flourishes and expected the public to believe him (especially against the extraordinary emotional qualities of *Witness*).[13]

Hiss introduced the startling new evidence that Lane had uncovered, but his report was so methodical and precise that its impact was dulled. Most important, Hiss suppressed the bitterness or outrage that an innocent man imprisoned for nearly four years would be expected to feel; he showed hardly a trace of indignation. As a result he bypassed the main avenue of communication and failed again in his own forum, his own Court of Public Opinion, to reveal himself as a person and as a defendant. And so he did not erase the doubts or dispel the aura of guilt in which Chambers' accusations had encased him.

Herbert Packer has observed:

"What the book is not appears more readily . . . than what it *is.* . . . Very little of Hiss the man comes through, except a kind of stereotype of folk-image of the "smart lawyer"—austere, precise, a little picayune. We got no glimpse of the charm of manner or the distinction of mind that won and kept for him so many distinguished friends.

Yet it is clear why Hiss could have written only the kind of book he did. A subjective account to the world of his private life was utterly contrary to the values and principles by which he lived. It would have violated his taste, style, and sense of objectivity. He has repeatedly pointed out:

My book was written as a lawyer's brief. It says all I have to say about the case. I'm not going to write an autobiography, and I'm not going to write about my experiences in prison, because I hold certain strong views about privacy. I see no reason why my personal life should be compared with my case.

[13] Robert Benjamin to the author, January 7, 1966.

Hiss's credo of objectivity and personal privacy pervades all discernible areas of his life. Virtue or defect, it characterizes Hiss, the man, and is the key to understanding his image and character. He feels strongly that the validity of an opinion or judgment becomes correspondingly reduced as it is infiltrated with sentiment. His need to suppress and eventually to drain feeling out of emotionally charged situations has developed in him a quality of detachment to others, which is often as offensive as it is misunderstood. He wants to set the record straight, but his inordinate sense of self-restraint renders him helpless. The thought of espousing his own cause by the use of self-acclaim or the plaudits of others makes him cringe. The facts must speak for themselves, not someone for them.

Hiss remains in the strange position of a man who is held in contempt by most of his country and yet esteemed by almost all who know him well. Most of his friends recognize the contradictions within his personality that have made this paradox possible.

One of Hiss's close friends described to me how Alger received the encouraging and praise-filled letters that came in from people all over the country during the trials. Hiss showed him the carbon copies of his replies. They were stiff, courteous, formal State Department letters. Why such formality? he asked Hiss, and he pointed out that these people had "gone all out for him." Alger's replies were like "a bucket of cold water on their heads." [14]

Another of Hiss's friends said that she was appalled at Hiss's behavior when, years later, she read over the printed House Committee record of his first confrontation with Chambers on the afternoon of August 17, 1948, at the Commodore Hotel. She referred to Hiss's unusual request to examine Chambers' teeth as

the let-me-see-your-mouth part. Alger sounded so foolish, so phony, so unlike him. . . . It was apparent he was in a rage and since it is so rare for him to openly show anger, I knew how very angry he must have been throughout the hearing. He has always been arrogant, proud and stubborn. If anyone tries to order him about, he gets inwardly mad, turns cool and stubborn ("How dare you do this to me!").

Professor Edward M. Morgan, Hiss's former teacher at Harvard Law School and long-time family friend, wrote that he would

not believe Hiss guilty even if he confessed. . . . The real cause of Alger's difficulty in his relations with others is that he believes that they will act rationally in controversies which involve their emotions and preconceptions.[15]

[14] D. Tilghman to the author, August 1961.
[15] Edward M. Morgan to the author, February 4, 1963.

Many others have expressed their support of Hiss, though the case remains troubling to them. Dean Acheson asked to be excused from any interview about Hiss. The subject, he wrote, was too deeply distasteful to him.[16] Francis B. Sayre, Hiss's former superior in the State Department, wrote:

. . . no sound proof of these preposterous charges have ever been brought to me. Until, if ever, such proof can be made, I shall remain unconvinced of the disloyalty of Alger Hiss.[17]

Some bow to the court's decision while continuing to support Hiss, the man. Jack Sutro, former Harvard Law School classmate, member of a prominent San Francisco law firm and a distant relative (by marriage) of Alger Hiss, served under Hiss during the United Nations Conference in San Francisco. He described Hiss with a mixture of fondness and perplexity:

Hiss was one of the most charming men I ever met; the last person in the world I would suspect of being a traitor to his country. Still the House Un-American [Activities] Committee had its job to do, and the United States Government doesn't prosecute idly. I thought Hiss was a loyal American, but the jury convicted him of perjury and I believe in the American system.[18]

Stephen Farrand, a former colleague in the Department of Justice, wrote:

I have always had a feeling that the result of his trial was wrong and that somehow, some time, something would occur to prove him innocent. . . . I have always considered Alger a good friend, one whom I had liked and admired, who showed absolutely no indications whatsoever of being anything other than a hardworking, loyal government attorney.[19]

Toward the few of his friends who believed him guilty as the evidence unfolded, Hiss bears no apparent ill will. The most painful disaffection, the direct result of Chambers' attack, was the loss of William Marbury's friendship. Marbury, though he felt Hiss to be innocent of Chambers' charges, suspected Priscilla of some kind of involvement in the case, which he felt that Hiss was concealing out of loyalty to her. He felt, when the documents were revealed, that Hiss had not told him "the whole truth." [20] Hiss wrote me in regard to this:

I *did* communicate to him the whole truth. Unknown to me until his recent letter (Dec. 1963), he erroneously suspected Priscilla of actions which he further be-

[16] Dean Acheson to the author, February 25, 1963.
[17] Francis B. Sayre to author, September 19, 1963.
[18] Personal interview, July 29, 1963.
[19] Stephen Farrand to the author, April 3, 1963.
[20] Marbury interview with the author, May 6, 1964.

lieved I must have known about. Bill Marbury remains a man of honor, if of limited psychological perceptiveness, because he remains true to his own formulations of fact. That he is factually erroneous doesn't affect that. I, of course, replied to his letter that he was wrong in his assumption of fact but until he recognizes his error there is nothing more I can do, though I am saddened by the loss of his friendship.

Hiss's reaction to the disaffection of his lifelong friend is a paradigm of his behavior toward the entire tragedy of the case. He once again takes refuge in "objectivity," in lieu of exposing his feelings. A hint of arrogance, to be sure, shows through in his suggestion that Marbury is "of limited psychological perceptiveness"; it is the same show of superiority that tainted his behavior in the hearing rooms and in the courts. But it is perhaps little enough emotion for a man to allow himself when he might feel betrayed, resentful, deeply hurt. And there can be no doubt that he means his appraisal of Marbury as a "man of honor" with complete sincerity: for to let himself feel otherwise would be to betray his own ideals.

Marbury's suspicion that Hiss might be shielding his wife was shared by others. Some felt that Timmy might be involved as well, since he did not testify. For this reason I undertook a comprehensive personal investigation into the lives of Mrs. Hiss and Timothy Hobson. I should like to say, without equivocation, that any theories suggesting that Alger Hiss was protecting some member of his family,[21] contained only this essential truth: Hiss did not want to subject his wife and Timmy to any embarrassment on his account. Why Hiss refused to allow Timmy to testify (in order to impeach Chambers' story that he had visited the Hiss home regularly over a period of several years) has been a mystery and questioned by many writers. Hiss was protecting his stepson from something quite remote from Chambers or his charges. During World War II (1945) Timmy had enlisted in the Navy. He failed to complete Naval Officer's training because of an acute emotional upset. His father did not want to subject him, not long thereafter, to the emotional strain of appearing as a witness in a public trial. Hiss's undue caution and overprotectiveness of his stepson not only proved to be a mistake in defense strategy but added fuel to certain rumors that Timmy in some way had been involved with Chambers and that Hiss was protecting him because of it.

After Hiss's conviction the question of Timmy Hobson's possible role was carefully gone into by Chester Lane. In his privately conducted post-trial exploration into some of the still unanswered aspects of the case, Lane did not leave a single stone unturned. One of his investigations included a specially

---

[21] Hiss did not even want his brother Donald to testify; only at the insistence of his counsel was he overruled in this.

arranged interrogation in depth of Timothy Hobson,[22] during which Hobson said:

> . . . I know only one thing, and that is I feel quite sure that he [Hiss] doesn't think I had anything to do with it [the case]. . . . If he had been willing to let me testify in his behalf, which I think would have been strong testimony—it's been a feeling more than any other that's made me want to come down here today and answer any questions you might have as I've felt that I haven't been able to contribute enough to the case.[23]

Because of Hiss's overprotectiveness the Hiss defense was deprived of its most important witness. For if the relationship between the Hisses and the Chamberses was as close and as long lasting as Chambers claimed (from 1934 to 1938), surely Timmy (from the age of eight to twelve), the only other member of the family, would have remembered Chambers' alleged visits. What did Timothy Hobson remember and what would he have testified?

He recalled "the family that once stayed with us on the third floor of the P Street House." [24] He remembered the "mother and baby" but could not remember the "man." He remembered that he had been at home recovering from some mild illness those few days and the woman had painted his picture. "I would certainly," Hobson told me, "have testified that Chambers was *not* a close family friend, did *not* visit our house every two weeks for two years, and that, in fact, Chambers was a liar on this score." Hobson had been thoroughly investigated by the FBI and questioned by the House Committee (August 23, 1948) and the New York Grand Jury (December 13, 1948) in secret session.

In a recent interview Hobson elaborated for the writer the circumstances that precluded his being called as a witness in his stepfather's defense:

> Two FBI agents visited me early in 1949. I was then living in a cold-water flat in New York. They were polite with me, regarded me as being on Alger's side rather than their side. They were not interested in whether or not I knew Chambers and did not ask me anything about him or the case. They let me know that they already knew a great deal about me and my personal life. They read to me a list of names of all my friends. They had already talked with all of them and had encompassed all of my activities. The FBI had dug completely into my life. My friends later informed me that they had been interviewed by the FBI. I was told by the

[22] This included a tape-recorded interview of Hobson, conducted under deep sodium pentothal narcosis. The drug was administered by a reputable psychiatrist in the presence of Mr. Lane and Dr. Henry Murray, the interrogators.
[23] Excerpted by permission (Hobson to the writer, April 20, 1962) from taped record of interview (Hobson to Lane, May 1953).
[24] It will be recalled that Hiss had testified that the Chamberses had spent several days at the P Street house; this should not be confused with Chambers' story that he also stayed with the Hisses at their 30th Street house.

FBI agents that my Bohemian way of life was all part of the case and would be brought out during the trial. It was polite blackmail.[25]

When asked by a member of Hiss's counsel whether he would be willing to testify, Hobson said that he certainly would. But Alger responded, "I'd sooner go to jail than have them embarrass Timmy on the stand."

On May 7, 1957, the book section of the *New York Times* printed an announcement of the publication of *In the Court of Public Opinion*. In one corner there was a boxed profile of its author. It was through this "ad," said Hiss, "that I got my first job after my release from prison."

R. Andrew Smith, president of a small company engaged in the manufacture of a new type of ladies' haircomb, Feathercombs, Inc., offered Hiss a position in his company. Feathercombs was then in the midst of a patent fight with some of the large manufacturers and needed an executive with organizational ability. Hiss was hired at a salary of $6000 a year, a sum considerably less than what Smith would have had to pay any other competent executive.

The main purpose of Hiss's employment at Feathercombs, Inc., his first venture as a business executive, was to rescue that organization from business failure. The day Hiss began work, Andrew Smith turned over to him the many problems of the company and departed for Europe. According to Smith,

When I got back six weeks later, he knew more about the office than people who'd been there five years. . . . Everyone eventually had a run-in with Alger because he was such a driving perfectionist, knew everybody's job better than they did. But after the blow-up, they either liked him—or found a way to get along with him." [26]

This was the kind of challenge Hiss liked and was temperamentally suited for. He worked for two years (1957–59) reorganizing the company, knowing from the outset that he would not share in its future success. "I told Andy from the beginning that the best thing I could do for him was to work myself out of a job." Smith's adventurous and mercurial ways were a magnet for Hiss's steadfastness and caretakerism. Before Smith entered the business world he was an art student. A colorful and attractive personality, he exuded knowledge and a worldliness that stemmed from having been brought up in a foreign country (Japan). In any case, Andrew Smith attracted Hiss, who discounted Smith's lack of business experience and minimized his unpredictability as a businessman. It was not long before Hiss found himself deeply involved in the rescue of Feathercombs, Inc. The company's patent rights had been encroached upon, and competition with big business threatened its survival. A difficult and costly legal battle ensued, into which Hiss let himself be

[25] From personal interviews, 1960–64.
[26] Brower, "The Problems of Alger Hiss," *loc. cit.*

drawn far beyond the realistic demands of his job and above the prudent limits of his meager financial assets.

When Minnie Hiss died in 1958 she left her son a legacy of $15,000. Though this represented his total assets, Hiss withdrew $3500 from his savings account and lent it to Andrew Smith to help defray expenses incurred by the legal suit.

After a year's work at Feathercombs, Hiss foresaw that the business would not warrant two top executives and told Smith then that as soon as the company was out of the state of incipient bankruptcy he would look for another position. In March, Hiss took a voluntary salary cut (his initial salary had subsequently been increased). "We got on an even keel by August," Hiss later wrote, "but so barely that I never got paid after August 15. My past arrears (at one time, 6 months' salary) and the $3500 I had put up in January to keep us from losing the injunction (that had already cost $11,000 or more and that alone saved the ship) I got back in late August and September, just before I finally left. I couldn't afford to work full time for office space and a telephone." In August, Hiss told Smith he would like to stay on till November, if it took that long for him to find another job. But Smith couldn't afford any further salary for Hiss. Smith's plan was to sell out quickly since he owned most of the stock. "I didn't so much quit," said Hiss, "as the job disappeared."

But Hiss's inordinate need to be a rescuer transcended the business bounds of Feathercombs, Inc., and spread to the role of being father to Andrew Smith's college-age son, Chris Smith, who, since the age of twelve or thirteen, had shifted about from one school to another; then, in his later teens, had drifted in and out of California and New York night clubs as a volunteer singer. After an unsuccessful return to school, Chris went to work for his father at Feathercombs. Hiss took him to art museums, lectures, and recitals (reminiscent of the way Minnie used to take him). They spent much time talking—about everything, "from poetry to politics to Proust," but particularly about what was wrong with Chris's life. Alger showed him how he wasn't doing anything to develop himself.

Chris came to the office unshaven and without a jacket. He usually had on a T-shirt, khaki trousers, and tennis shoes. His appearance, next to Hiss's attire (usually a gray herringbone or blue pin-stripe suit), became a subject for pleasant banter between them and a challenge to Hiss, who dealt with it by changing the desks in the office so that Chris was placed in the front of the office where everyone saw him in his dirty T-shirt. The strategy got Chris to shaving again and spruced him up a bit, but he still kept his collar and cuffs unbuttoned on principle.

Hiss has made very few public appearances since the trials. He was asked on one occasion to do a telecast from Providence, Rhode Island, on the United Nations. He took Chris along as his "publicity agent." In a humorous vein, Chris related to Brock Brower a few highlights of his trip with Hiss:

. . . the TV station happened to be over a big department store, and [around mid-night] Alger suddenly decides he has to go all through this empty store. . . . I thought we were going to get arrested. He was trying to find where the Feather-combs display was, you see. The night watchman finally came up, and Alger asks him, "Do they carry Feathercombs?" . . . Then he gave the watchman his card. . . . Alger was just being a sort of cutup—you could tell he'd never had a chance to be one before.[27]

I have cited this anecdote because it brings out clearly Hiss's hidden need to behave prankishly. It was a form of mischief he had observed and envied in others but had not allowed himself to enjoy.

Hiss left Feathercombs in 1959. In retrospect, he remains grateful to Andrew Smith for having given him a job when he needed one. But more significant was the really good time Hiss had during those two years. He enjoyed pulling a staff together (something he hadn't done since his Carnegie Endowment days), and he enjoyed the direct relations with the office staff and with the working force who packed combs by hand, affixed costume jewelry, and so forth. He also enjoyed the responsibility for supervising legal problems, such as the choosing of counsel, assisting in preparations for trial, and general management of financial problems. As part of his consolidative plan for Feathercombs, Hiss brought attorney Walter Beer (Chester Lane's partner) onto the board of directors, found a sales manager, took part in corporate negotiations, and the like.

That kind of practical day-to-day business experience [said Hiss], was new to me—quite different from the contact with business issues and people I'd had as a young lawyer, in the Government or with the Carnegie Endowment. The contacts with Japanese businessmen and bankers added to the interest for me.

Until the latter part of my stay I had good relations with Andy, an interesting . . . and off-beat person. And my relations with Chris were close and cordial despite the difference in our ages.[28] I certainly don't regret the experience at all.

Hiss had singlehandedly saved the firm from bankruptcy and organized it into a going concern, yet the ironic reward for his efforts was his return to the ranks of the unemployed. For the next five months he searched for a new job and subsisted on unemployment insurance. As he approached friends or strangers in the role of job seeker his celebrated name and appearance served

[27] Brower, "The Problems of Alger Hiss," *loc. cit.*
[28] By the time Hiss left Feathercombs, Chris seemed to have achieved some direction in his life. He decided to go back to school and prepare for a singing career.

as a reminder of his fallen public image and his enshadowed past. But Hiss was not embittered. He has remained as interested in other people's problems as he always has been.

Alger is like a Pied Piper [said a close friend] and people gravitate to him. Especially youths . . . eager for someone to listen to their interests or problems. Parents constantly report back to him, "My, did you make a hit with my son!"

It is not an unusual sight to find Hiss, during a social evening at the home of one of his friends, withdrawn into a corner of the room, listening to and answering the questions of the teen-age sons and daughters of his host. For Hiss to be so given over to the interests and need of others, "whether they be waifs, bores or others" is, said a close friend, "typically Alger. People fasten onto him because he doesn't rebuff them. Coupled with his tolerance, his modesty and belief in himself, this makes him so saintly, he's almost Christlike."

During the two-year period in which Hiss was taken up with the organizational and legal problems of rescuing Feathercombs, and with being a friendly father (or older brother) figure to Chris, his life with Priscilla was going through a deepening estrangement. The belated recognition of this marital breach came neither as surprise nor shock. It was the ultimate emergence of a subliminal fact: for many years, he then saw, their marital partnership had been wearing thin, and in his opinion they were left with a paucity of the essential ingredients of a good marriage. Chambers' accusations against them had the salutary effect of drawing them closer together in a protective alliance. This was true of the entire Hiss clan and of Priscilla's relations, the Fanslers.[29]

As an extension of their having been thus drawn together, after his return from prison Hiss lived in hopeful expectation of a closer and more meaningful marriage. But the painful vicissitudes of separation, the emotional stresses of rehabilitation following his release, weighed heavily on a marriage that had been sustained but had not consolidated through the years. A collapse of this kind, explained Hiss, has early beginnings and does not build up like a sudden storm.

Despite their separation in 1959 Hiss retains only respect and concern for Priscilla. Though he has grieved over the death of their joint hopes and sharings, he feels "it is possible to recognize that death and build separate new lives—as we would have had to do had either of us died five or more years ago."

After the marriage "died" Hiss moved to a cold-water flat. He left with

[29] During the period of preparation for the trials, after Hiss's indictment, all the Hisses and Fanslers were closely united in their unquestioned allegiance to Alger and Priscilla.

Priscilla all his worldly possessions—books, furniture, money—symbolically reminiscent of the $50,000 life-insurance policy Charles Hiss had provided for his children. He realized that living alone in a furnished room or cold-water flat was much easier for a man, so Priscilla kept the apartment and furniture. He also left his savings account with her and whatever they had in the checking account.

His generosity and self-sacrifice are reminiscent of his father's failure. But whatever similarity there may be in Alger's own image and that of his father's, the hard fact is that he did not succumb.

In February 1960 Hiss took a job as salesman with Davison-Bluth, Inc., a small and long-established stationery shop in New York. He took it as a "stop-gap" measure, something that would allow him to make contributions to Priscilla's expenses. Despite the job's financial shortcomings and the obvious drudgery of being an ordinary salesman Hiss showed neither embarrassment nor remorse as he called on former colleagues as a sales representative. In fact his attitude toward this work seemed in some way reminiscent of Bosley's youthful enthusiasm.

It will be interesting for a while [said Hiss] to see a part of the huge selling area of American life. After that I can say I've seen EVERYTHING. I'm also angling for some free-lance editorial work to do at nights—one job already, another possible. These will be taken on *only* because of intrinsic interest or as likely to lead to something.

Alger and Priscilla were deeply tormented following their separation. For months they kept in daily touch with each other and were careful to avoid any embarrassing social situations with mutual friends. Hiss subsisted on fifty dollars a week, allocating the rest of his earnings to Priscilla and Tony.

Despite this self-imposed stringency Hiss has achieved a certain peace of mind. He looks forward to frequent weekends in the country, usually spent at the homes of friends. During the week in the city his appointments are closely scheduled, often far ahead, and punctiliously adhered to. Hiss lunches regularly with newly formed friends, former associates, or foundation members, in whose work he continues to have an active interest (such as the Religious Freedom Committee, Osborne Association for Prison Reform, Carnegie Endowment). He continues to receive a considerable amount of mail, which he answers by hand, punctually and conscientiously. While unemployed he took a course in speedwriting, hoping it would help him get an executive assistant's job.

The Hiss case has run its legal gamut, but Hiss still hopes that some governmental commission of inquiry may yet be appointed to re-examine the "new evidence." Though Hiss has learned a great deal about psychological causation, and his understanding of himself and of Whittaker Chambers has deepened, he looks back on the trials in the same detached lawyer-like way. He disagreed strongly with the way the government conducted the case against him, yet quickly added, "Murphy had a job to do and he just went ahead and did it." Though Hiss did not approve of Judge Goddard's conduct of the second trial, he viewed with legal objectivity Goddard's later denial of a motion for a new trial. Hiss compared Goddard's decision to Holmes' refusal to issue a stay of execution to Sacco and Vanzetti.

Alger Hiss lives on, cherishing an image. He continues to measure himself against his ideal of "objectivity," even though it is his adherence to this precept that, more than any other action, cost him his public life.

As one of the last questions of the many hundreds I had put to him since the beginning of my study, I asked Hiss whether, in retrospect, he had any misgivings about the way he had dealt with Chambers' accusations against him in 1948. Hiss replied:

While I was in prison in Lewisburg I had much time to reflect about the entire case. I kept thinking, would I do this over again? There was no moral alternative. Though, in part, my behavior was motivated by real anger, that is, that someone I had befriended would turn on me like this—I would defend my name and honor in the same way if I had to do it over again, despite the tragic consequences of my actions.

From other conversations it was clear that when Hiss said "in the same way," he meant quite literally that he would not change his method or his style of self-defense. But there is little doubt that his insistence on maintaining his rational distance on the events in which he was fatally entangled caused the greatest misconceptions. His objectivity pervades all discernible areas of his life. Virtue or defect, it characterizes Hiss, the man, and is the key to understanding his image and character. To Hiss, the subject of his innocence is a very matter-of-fact, easily expressed matter.[30]

Hiss still maintains the same dedication to standards of friendship, loyalty, and objectivity as he did before his fall from public grace. His stoicism about his defeat has, however, added a quietly crusading note to his present existence. Despite the drastic disruption to his life Hiss does not regard the loss of the case as a personal failure. His image of himself is more important to him than the public reverberations set in motion by the jury's verdict. This sense of propriety, deeply etched into his character by the events of his child-

[30] Mrs. Helen Buttenwieser, Hiss's present legal representative, has condensed Hiss's attitude into a few words: "Hiss went into the first trial with the firm conviction that his word would be taken. He saw it as a credible story versus an incredible story. He simply can't get over the fact that he wasn't believed." (From personal interviews with the author, 1960–65.)

hood, antedated the lawyer-like sense of logic about life. Neither his demeanor nor his values have changed since he was convicted. With an unfettered conscience and an abiding optimism that history will prove him innocent, Alger Hiss, the person, remains superfluous to his case and immune to the public image it cast up. Hiss's attitude has been likened to the last words of Enid Bagnold's martyred heroine in *The Chalk Garden*: "What I have been listening to in Court," she answered, "is not my life. It is the shape and shadow of my life with the accidents of Truth taken out of it." [31]

[31] Cited by Brower, *op. cit.*

21

The Prodigal Son

CONCURRENTLY with Hiss's imprisonment, Chambers retreated to his West-minster farm. There, in an unconscious identification with the man he had once loved and had now destroyed, he lived out his parallel fate of self-imposed seclusion and silence, in a prison of his own making. This period, the last decade of his life, has all the clinical features of pathological grief, a symbolic return to the underground.

After Hiss's conviction Chambers wrote to a friend, Ralph de Toledano:

The days that will diminish the echoes of the trial already reveal that I have an all but incurable wound. My good, intuitive friend, Marjorie Kinnan Rawlings, wrote during the first trials "When this is over, I believe that you are planning to kill yourself." In the literal sense, this is not true, but it was so close to my feeling from the beginning that I have never trusted myself to answer her. At the end of that day of turmoil in which I decided to put the Baltimore papers in evidence, I thought "Because of Esther and the children, I cannot pray to God to let me die, but I cannot keep from hoping that He will." Now this feeling dogs me through these beautiful, unseasonable days and in the hours of the night when I wake. There keep running through my head two epitaphs that Byron saw in an Italian graveyard: "implora eterna pace," "implora eterna quieta." "All they ask for is peace," Byron noted. "And that they implore."

Add to this the feeling that it was all for nothing, that nothing has been gained except the misery of others, that it was a tale of the end and not of the beginning of something. . . . You cannot save what cannot save itself. These things happened because our sector of the world could not understand what was happening to it. It does not understand yet, nor does it understand this Case.[1]

Though Chambers emerged victorious from the trials and was lionized as a patriot, he found no peace of mind. The conviction of Hiss roused over again the residues of guilt that lay buried within him. He found no respite from his conscience, which tormented his very existence.

[1] Cited by De Toledano, "Let Only a Few Speak for Him," *National Review,* July 29, 1961, p. 50.

One need only recall the letters that Hiss was writing from Lewisburg at this time to realize that Chambers, though legally the free man, was psychologically the imprisoned one. As Chambers' despondent thoughts turned to death, Hiss maintained a balanced optimism about his future and the possibility of vindication. He wrote to his wife and son on May 1, 1952:

Dearest Pros and Tony,

This will be a rushed letter, for I have spent most of my evening (after an hour in the cool and gray yard) writing Chester [Lane] to tell him how superb the new affidavit is. I received it this afternoon. By now thee has undoubtedly read it and has seen how far beyond thy Sat. understanding of its contents it goes. No wonder Chester is so delighted with the results of his brilliantly conceived and executed investigations. There is little that is more cruelly disheartening than disappointment in great hopes and the last thing I would want to do is to raise thy hopes and Tony's unjustifiably. I know the bitter winds that are blowing in this loveless and causeless era and I know that the dust they raise can obscure reality and values for the time being. So I make no predictions, and honestly abstain from judgment in my own mind, as to the near term outcome. But this I *know*—that Chester's work has exposed the fabricated story and documents for all who in a calmer time will care to examine the record for themselves. And *that* is a great and stirring accomplishment.

Chambers struggled with his guilt in many ways; in seclusion in the hinterland of his farm, close to nature and the fertility of the ground, he not only lived out a self-burial but attempted a rebirth. It was during the first years of this withdrawal that Chambers wrote *Witness*.[2] His need to be a witness was deeply determined. His autobiography, like his life, was the product of a harassed and guilty mind. It was a compilation of massive emotional discharges, fusions of fact and fantasy repressed and then selectively remembered. It was, in essence, a self-destructive, re-creative autobiographical myth. And to be sure, *Witness* reads like an account of a lifelong dream. Be-

---

[2] The sensational tone of the publicity that surrounded the case and the political hysteria of the early fifties can quickly be brought back by a glance at the chapter titles in the *Saturday Evening Post's* prepublication serialization of Whittaker Chambers' *Witness:*

February 9, 16, 23: "I Was the Witness."
March 1, 1952: "How Alger Hiss Gave Our Secrets to Russia."
March 8, 1952: "Why Did Hiss Think He Could Get Away With It?"
March 15, 1952: "How Hiss Got Trapped in His Own Lies."
March 22, 1952: "How Hiss Lost His Temper and Betrayed Himself."
March 29, 1952: "Hiss Is Cornered and Fights Back."
April 5, 1952: "The Last Warning and the Film in the Pumpkin."
April 12, 1952: "I Was the Witness: The Tragedy of Alger Hiss."

From these advance chapters, it is reputed that Chambers netted about $80,000. Profits from the book (a Book-of-the-Month-Club selection for May 1952) were more than twice as rewarding.

fore presenting the (imagined) "fact" of his physical birth, Chambers portrays himself in a heroic rebirth (at the age of thirty-six), as if he were
Lazarus returning from the dead. In Chapter I, he writes:

In 1937, I began, like Lazarus, the impossible return. I began to break away from
Communism and to climb from deep within its underground, where for six years I
had been buried, back into the world of free men. "When we dead awaken. . . ."
I used sometimes to say in those days to my wife, who, though never a Communist,³ had shared my revolutionary hopes and was now to share my ordeals:
"When we dead awaken. . . ." I felt a surging release and a sense of freedom, like
a man who bursts at last gasp out of a drowning sea.

He prefaced his autobiography with a twenty-two-page "Letter to my
Children," which sets an immediate confessional tone. By telling all with apparent contriteness, from the outset he imposes upon the reader an idealized
image of himself. But, as we have seen, his self-sanctified confessions are so
formulated and directed that someone else ends up bearing the punishment;
the causes of his personal torment—his brother's death, the Hiss case, and
so on—are blamed on the world, the "tragedy of history." He dramatizes himself as the Man of Destiny over whose self-sacrificial decisions (that is,
accusations) the future of all mankind depended. Although *Witness* is an
apologia to his own conscience, it is in itself another destructive act for which
Chambers would have to go on trying to absolve himself. His autobiography
has proved to be the opposite of what Chambers wanted it to be—that is, a
heroic saga of his life. He resolved nothing in writing it.

Witness is a skillful composite of a distorted confession and accusation,
an amalgamation of the real and the unreal. Chambers wrote it during
1950–52, an agonizing period in which he had a wearisome and all-important
score to settle with his conscience and the world. He had just consummated
one of the most significantly destructive acts of his life—the ruin of Alger
Hiss. In writing *Witness* he drew freely from the vast storage of his imaginative and creative mind, tapping every memory, anecdote, and experience. He
cunningly fictionalized or reconstructed facts, fantasies, personal and historical events. He identified himself with Shakespearean tragedy and Dostoevskian crime. Poetic forms, literary devices, plots borrowed from his prolific reading of history, biography, psychological fiction and from books he had
translated, were all part of his armamentarium. These mental cumulations
were his "life-preservers," his magical defenses to combat the fear of loss of
identity. Through the years his childhood fears and strivings became indistinguishably fused in his mind with external happenings. Early memories and

---

³ Cf. *Witness*, p. 267, where Chambers refers to Esther Shemitz's being controlled by the
Communist Party in relation to her marriage to Chambers.

unresolved residues of inner conflicts pervaded his knowledge of external events and directed his real-life experiences.

Despite the excesses of *Witness* in its published form, it is a mild document compared to what appears to have been its first version. Early in 1950 Chambers submitted a manuscript to Doubleday.[4] It was rejected, but its contents were revealed by chance to Robert Crichton, a young writer then living in Connecticut. Crichton, who was expecting a manuscript of his own, one day discovered in his mailbox a "bulky" package from Doubleday, which turned out to be Chambers' manuscript, in the form of a diary. Crichton describes his surprise:

I opened it and was stunned to see the personal papers of Chambers. At this time, if I am correct, the second trial was on or just over. The name of Whittaker Chambers was impressive to say the least.

Crichton goes on to say that he could not resist the temptation to read the papers and expresses his shock at what they contained.

What I read, as I recall, was ridiculous, absurd, incredible, frightening, sad, disillusioning, weird. . . . The pages were old and grimy and dirty and stained. The papers had evidently been around.[5]

Against my better judgment, . . . I began copying extracts from here and there. They had no sequence and I don't think anything I copied had any real political or news value in the sense of shedding new light on Chambers' revelations. I copied them because they were so exaggerated, so obviously lunatic. . . . But I copied extracts, finally, because they revealed to me a Chambers so far gone beyond the line of being able to see reality that it made me incredulous. . . .

Certain background sections of Chambers' life, which I recall appear in *Witness,* have been nicely cleaned up, brightened up and given the face of sanity. Had the details been put down in the way I recall them from the papers, right or wrong, the man would have been laughed out of contention.[6]

Unfortunately Crichton subsequently lost his copied extracts, and one can only speculate as to the significant differences between the unpublished and "cleaned up" versions of *Witness.* Of great interest, however, is Chambers' compulsive effort to publish his book immediately after the Hiss trial in a desperate flight from the guilt that threatened to engulf him.

[4] Kenneth McCormick, editor of Doubleday & Company, confirmed the receipt of Chambers' manuscript and Doubleday's rejection of it.
[5] This raises the question whether the manuscript that Chambers first tried to market in 1938, the one he submitted to Herbert Solow and then to Isaac Don Levine (see p. 301 ff.), titled "The Disillusionment of a Communist," might have been an earlier draft or part of these "papers."
[6] Robert Crichton to the author, July 1963, November 16, 1963; personal interview, December 1964. Robert Crichton, son of Kyle Crichton (Robert Forsythe), is author of *The Great Impostor—The Amazing Careers of Ferdinand Waldo Demara* (New York: Random House, 1959).

Chambers' affliction with guilt during this period is evident in another way from a speech he made on January 25, 1951—six weeks after the Court of Appeals upheld Hiss's conviction—to a joint Rotary-Kiwanis meeting in Towson, Maryland. Chambers was introduced as "the Prodigal Son," and he turned the parable into a political allegory in which he was "the Prodigal Son" come home to warn the "Father" (President Roosevelt) about the subversive threat to his "house." Chambers referred to himself as "the Prodigal Son" throughout, avoiding the word "I." Though his text is not available, we have an abridgement of it by Chester Lane, who attended the meeting and made extensive notes. The speech, as he summarizes it, alternates between broad irony and solemn philosophical discourse. In the extracts that follow, quotation marks are Lane's and indicate his "best memory of precise words used."

The Prodigal Son went away from his father's house, and into the depths—not of high living and debauchery, but of deep moral conviction (for reasons he would explain later) among the Communists. Learning finally the wickedness of their ways, he left them and sought a new life. He found it, with happiness and satisfaction in accomplishment, with his loving family and his work.

After some rehabilitation, the Prodigal Son paid a visit to his Father and was shocked. The old man was doddery; his establishment was completely overrun by Communists. His estates ("which may for convenience be called State Department") were being run by six of them; the family finances (Treasury) were looted by two more; and "scores more of the rascals" were scarring the paint and stealing the knives and forks.

Concerned, he sought out the Old Man, to warn him of the waste of his substance. But the Old Man waved him away, with: "Look, son, don't you see I'm busy reading this new book, called 'Russia, the World's Greatest Experiment in Democracy.' " "But, Pop, this is serious!" "O.K., son, go see my security officer."

So, the Prodigal Son went to see the security officer "whose name is Adolf A. Berle, then Assistant Secretary of State, now leader of the Liberal Party in New York." The Prodigal Son gave him a list of forty or more of the faithless stewards; and "the security officer, being an honest man," went in great perturbation to the Old Man.

"Look, security officer," said the Old Man, "can't you see I'm reading this most fascinating new book 'Russia, the World's Greatest Experiment in Democracy'? Don't bother me."

"But, sir," said the security officer, "this endangers your whole estate, your whole life. You must attend to it."

The Old Man replied to the security officer with "a phrase which cannot be repeated here, and should not be repeated anywhere—the general purport of which was: 'Go jump in the lake.' "

So the security officer, being disillusioned, "put his notes in a safe, where they were not found for five years."

And the Prodigal Son returned to his own home, where he became a "leader of his profession," loved his wife and children more and more, made plenty of money, and waited for a chance to do something.

He waited "nine years, and then his chance came. Bit by bit, he made it, and finally produced evidence."

He knew, when he appeared before that great body in Washington, that he must surrender the good things he had earned. When he stood up to identify Alger Hiss, "by far the most important of the enemies in his father's house," all the wise, well-educated, good-looking people "sniggered." And he said to himself, "My good people, it is yourselves that you are sniggering at. You made this thing."

And those forces then set out to destroy the Prodigal Son. They invented charges so wild and disgusting as to have been themselves only the products of a diseased mind. But their power was not enough to meet the effect of three things which then happened:

(1) The power of prayer.
(2) The smartness of the FBI.
(3) The integrity of Thomas F. Murphy, who fought for the right.

And so, when after two long years Alger Hiss was finally brought to conviction, three other things happened:

The New York Herald [sic]
The Baltimore Sun
The Washington Post

wrote editorials regretting that Alger Hiss had been framed.

And the New York Times, not to be caught short, ran a full page of carefully selected letters accusing the Prodigal Son of villainy.

And Thomas Murphy, who had been successful in the most important case of the first half of the Twentieth Century, was pushed aside, and finally resigned to become Police Commissioner of New York.

So the Prodigal Son, as a witness and aide, was destroyed. Another arose. "I was called from my garden to answer a phone call from a Baltimore Sun reporter: "What did I think of Senator McCarthy?" Panting from my run to the phone, I answered in six words "I hand my mantle to him"; "I doubt that the Baltimore Sun ever printed them."

The rest of the speech consists of a discourse on the nature of Communism. But it is evident that the real subject is Chambers himself, heroically self-portrayed as the sinner turned saint. And what is most impressive is the power of his belief system, the conviction with which he presents himself as "the Prodigal Son." In this near-psychotic identification with the Biblical figure, he magically rescues himself, for a moment, from his guilt. This device recalls not only his previous literary deceptions but his actual impersonations of people. In a word, this behavior can be described as imposture.

Dr. Phyllis Greenacre has provided the clearest definition of the impostor:

An impostor is not only a liar but a very special type of liar who imposes on others fabrications of his attainments, position, or worldly possessions. This he may do through misrepresentations of his official identity, by presenting himself with a fictitious name, history, and other items of personal identity, either borrowed from some other actual person or fabricated according to some imaginative conception of himself.[7]

The success of the impostor, Dr. Greenacre emphasizes, depends on the need of his audience to be deceived, "to believe in the fraud." When the impostor perpetrates his hoax, he experiences "a seemingly paradoxical heightening of his feeling of integrity and reality" by virtue of being believed by other people. Tracing the infantile origins of the need for imposture, Dr. Greenacre concludes that the impostor's gratification, in the form of public adulation, is a replacement of his mother's love, and that his fraud is an act of hostility directed at his father, sometimes mediated through a brother. Chambers' role as "the Prodigal Son," ridiculing the "Father" for his stupidity and denouncing his brother surrogate, Alger Hiss, for his treachery, is an enactment of this syndrome. One remembers also his fantasy of Hiss's contempt for Roosevelt.[8]

The personality of Whittaker Chambers—who exchanged his name for perhaps a dozen aliases and his identity for at least as many roles, and who emerged as a hero to his country—clearly falls into the clinical category of impostor.

But Chambers' accumulated guilt took its constant toll. In November 1952, on Election Day, he suffered what his doctor diagnosed as "a true coronary attack." [9] Dr. Wilkens said that he had come into the town of Westminster to vote ("for Eisenhower and Nixon") and that, leaving the polls, he was stricken with chest pain. After summoning her, he was forced to sit down on some steps nearby. Dr. Wilkens relieved his distress with a hypodermic injection and took him home. She arranged to have him hospitalized. A friend

---

[7] Phyllis Greenacre, "The Impostor," *Psychoanalytic Quarterly* (1958), Vol. 27, p. 359.
[8] See p. 210.
[9] Dr. Elizabeth Reese Wilkens to the author, May 1962. Dr. Wilkens, a general practitioner now in her mid-seventies, had been a devoted friend and doctor to Chambers for many years. She described to me how Chambers first came into her office on Main Street in Westminster in 1937 for treatment of a laceration of the arm, which he incurred while trying to pry open a jammed window. Chambers at that time told Dr. Wilkens about his break with the Communist underground. This was in *1937,* and she recalled that someone had remarked on that occasion: "Did the Communists shoot him?"
For her first professional services, Chambers sent her a five-pound box of candied fruit and a note of gratitude. Dr. Wilkens, who lived for many years as a medical missionary in the Orient, came strongly under the aegis of Chambers' thinking since she first treated him in 1937. He was "the savior of his country," said Dr. Wilkens, "a gifted writer and a wonderful mind, it is a pity the world had to lose him." Dr. Wilkens commented to me: "If a psychiatrist were to have examined Chambers he would have regarded him as being mentally sick." She insisted, therefore, that she would never have allowed this to be done, because Chambers was not "sick, sick, sick; he was strong, strong, strong."

of Chambers in Baltimore, an "important government official," quickly managed to get him a bed in St. Agnes Hospital in Baltimore, where, according to
Dr. Wilkens, "they rolled out the red carpet for him as everyone was expecting him. He made a rapid recovery," Dr. Wilkens concluded, "and has been
active and well all these years."

22

The Last Death

ALGER HISS was released from prison in November 1954. The knowledge that Hiss was free and was resuming an open, civilian life had a devastating effect on Chambers (as though brother Richard had come back from the dead to haunt him) and stirred again the painful residue of feelings and memories of his crime against him. It rekindled his guilt and remobilized his need for self-punishment.[1]

As Hiss gradually rehabilitated himself, unequivocally reiterating his innocence, Chambers felt progressively persecuted and helpless. His accusations against Hiss, though still vehement, had lost their public audience and found private expression in letters to his friends. In 1954 he wrote to William F. Buckley, Jr.:

Alger came out more fiercely than even I had expected. . . . His strength is not what it was. But that it exists at all is stunning. Every time that, in the name of truth, he asserts his innocence, he strikes at truth, utters a slander against me, and compounds his guilt of several orders. . . . It is this which squirts into my morale a little jet of paralyzing poison.[2]

Once again he accuses Hiss, but these are the words of a man who is destroying himself with the most noxious of self-administered poisons: psychological guilt. He is enraged and overwhelmed by his helplessness to provide a new scapegoat for his guilt.[3] He can no longer manipulate surrogate

---

[1] How clearly this echoes Sebastian's fear in *Class Reunion:* ". . . but suppose he (Adler) came back? No, he was not a man to come back. He would be lost forever. And I should be free from the guilty occasion of my torment and my crime."
[2] William F. Buckley, "The End of Whittaker Chambers," *Esquire,* September 1962, p. 168.
[3] His reaction to another guilty man is of interest. After the television quiz-show scandals he wrote to his old friend Mark Van Doren, whose son Charles had admitted to his role in the deception. Chambers enclosed a note to Charles, which said in part: "You will never get over this. The world will never leave you alone until you die." The note is almost certainly a projection of the guilt that Chambers—unlike Charles—carried, unconfessed, within himself. (Mark Van Doren to the author, December 6, 1960.)

figures to "take the long journey" for him. Hiss has not succumbed to Chambers' omnipotent wish that he (Hiss) destroy himself, as brother Richard had done. In an agony of unrealism Chambers complains to his friend because Hiss will not ease his (Chambers') conscience by confessing at this stage to an act, the denial of which had already cost him his career. And failing this, he shifts the area of conflict, displacing it from the personal to the historical.

The Hiss Case remains a central lesion of our time. That is why, ultimately, I cannot say . . . that Alger Hiss had paid any effective penalty. For precisely he can end the lesion at any moment that he chooses, with half-a-dozen words.[4]

Chambers grew more and more weary. Despite his daily efforts and accustomed pattern of hard work, fatigue and an increasing obsession about his death seriously curtailed his productivity. On his fifty-fifth birthday, in 1956 (five years before his death), he wrote to De Toledano:

I hope you have my obit ready. What fun the yappy little dogs will have. I don't even begrudge it them, rest seems so welcome.[5]

Along with his longing for death, he remained occupied with farm problems. But even his lighthearted moments reflect his central concerns, which are especially evident in his interest in animal birth, the vicarious manifestation of a rescue fantasy re-enacting his own mythical birth. He wrote (around 1951):

After several days of warm fine weather we had cold and sleet last night, so Willett's Lillian, having carefully watched the weather, decided to lamb. Esther found the shivering lamb early this morning. Willett's Lillian is the grand champion of Maryland. Therefore she would have to have her lamb on the coldest day, and to have the weakest lamb. I have been working over it for an hour or so, filling it with warm milk and Haig & Haig. I've rigged it an incubator on the gas stove. It has got over its drunk and is now warm, sassy and baaing like an Ingersoll watch being wound. It is also doing its best to upset the incubator.[6]

In 1957, during an interval of rebound ("I had touched bottom and was rising again to the surface"), he felt moved to write and joined the editorial staff of the *National Review*. Although he was encouraged by William Buckley, the editor, to contribute articles of his own choosing, and although he apparently wanted to write, Chambers turned his anger and hatred against himself and became his own victim. He had grown so distraught, he now became a rival and destroyer of the products of his own creativity. He diligently wrote and rewrote: letters, articles, a book; then burned what he had so laboriously created. He wrote to Buckley:

[4] Buckley, *op. cit.*
[5] Cited by De Toledano, *loc. cit.*, p. 49.
[6] *Ibid.*, p. 48.

To your gladdening letters, I wrote a close-set, three-and-a-half page reply, which I have just had the pleasure of setting a match to. . . . I have burned a book half the size of *Witness,* and consider it one of my best deeds.

Buckley then adds:

As soon as he regained consciousness after one coronary attack, whose relative ferocity he was sure would end up killing him, he groped his way down to the basement to destroy another great pile of manuscripts.[7]

Was the book Chambers had written and then burned, which he says was "half the size of *Witness,*" his true confession—a second *Witness* impeaching *Witness*? [8] He was in the throes of indecision—to do or undo. Should he recant and absolve himself? Or should he continue to mystify, remain magically omnipotent, and act out the accompanying guilt. This, in oversimplified terms, is the meaning of the ongoing struggle within him.

Several years before Chambers' death he was not only advised but "begged and beseeched" by Dr. Wilkens to sell his fine herd of cows and slow down his working pace, but he refused.[9] In 1957 a fire broke out in the attic of Chambers' home. They managed to remove most of Chambers' books, papers, and many other things from the house to the barn. For a while after the fire they stayed with neighbors to recuperate. And then they returned to live in the small, rustic, century-old house they had originally purchased through Mr. Case in 1937 and had lived in before buying the additional acreage and the large house. Chambers now devoted the greater part of his physical energies to landscaping the hillside. He planted flowers and trees, dug a large artificial lake near the house, cleared the thicketed brush on the hillsides.

The final period of retreat to Nature and his lonely rural isolation marked Chambers' last symbolic return to the underground and to the Good Earth, Mother of All. During the last ten years of his life he remained a near recluse. His feeble attempts to resume an urban existence and re-enter the world brought on an overwhelming physical fatigue. For a brief period during the last months of 1958 he did travel fortnightly to New York, where he wrote an occasional piece for the *National Review.* After three months another apparent heart attack struck him down. Then in the summer of 1959 he

---

[7] Buckley, *op. cit.*

[8] An interesting remark relevant to this speculation is found in *Cold Friday.* In a letter to Duncan Norton-Taylor he remarks: "If I do not get my meaning down on paper I will die with *Witness* as my whole meaning. It is not my whole meaning. . . ." (Norton-Tayor refrained from quoting further.)

[9] Dr. Wilkens stated that Chambers was a person who wanted to "die with his boots on." Though he was receiving medication for his heart he never tried to take care of himself as he should have.

made a trip to Europe with his wife. This, too, ended in illness, and he returned to the refuge of his farm.

In the fall of 1959 Chambers, at the age of fifty-eight, decided, startlingly, to return to college. He enrolled as an undergraduate student at nearby Western Maryland College and for the next two years he attended classes faithfully. After nearly thirty-five years he returned to make amends by trying to complete the college education he had set aside in 1925 in order to join the Communist Party. In this symbolic return Chambers also made restitution for his brother's ill-fated college career. It was a part of his preparation for death. Chambers attended classes and carried on his academic assignments with diligence, devoting all of his time to his studies. His courses, according to Lowell S. Ensor, president of Western Maryland College, were mostly "in language, both classical and modern, and his grades were usually A, with a small smattering of B's." [10] At this stage of his life he also began to study the sciences. His instructors all agreed that "although much older, of course, than the other undergraduates in his classes, he adjusted very well and took his part without any attempt to dominate the class." Thus in his last two years of life, by attending classes regularly every day, doing his homework conscientiously, and achieving good grades in all his work, he magically undid the guilt of his earlier academic failure and the responsibility for his brother's failure.

But his weariness and wish for death hung heavily over him, and it soon became an overwhelming obsession, for only in death would he be free of the guilt that was haunting him. In a letter to Buckley he expressed his mood:

Weariness . . . you cannot yet know literally what it means, I wish no time would come when you do know, but the balance of experience is against it. One day, long hence, you will know true weariness and will say: "That was it." My own life of late has been full of such realizations. [11]

In another letter Chambers had been quite explicit about the meaning of Death as salvation, the publication of *Witness* as his last act, and his resignation to mark time in this world until his son John reached his majority. Chambers said:

John's parents live for John, and for little else. In 1952, I sat and reckoned—so many years I must live to get John to his majority. It seemed an impossibly long course. Now each day is subtracted from the year that is left. . . . The day I finished the last section of *Witness,* I took the copy into town and put it in the mail myself. Then I returned to the little house at Medfield, where, for about two years, I had written alone. I sat down at my now needless table and thought that now, perhaps, God would permit me to die. I did not really wish this—much less, I now

[10] Lowell S. Ensor to the author, January 30, 1962.
[11] Cited by De Toledano, *loc cit.,* p. 47.

know than I then supposed. And I could not pray for it because of the children. I thought that I must live until they reached their majority, at least, so that they would be beyond the reach of men in the legal sense. They would be their own man and woman. In John's case, this meant some five or six years. It seemed to me an almost unendurable span of time. In the past year I have found myself inwardly smiling because only a few months of that span are left. I have been saying to myself: I am free at last.[12]

Of particular interest is Chambers' concern with living until his son comes of age. In Chambers' unconscious mind, his "closest" friend, Hiss, his only son, John, and his only brother, Richard, are symbolically interchangeable objects. Consequently John's majority was, for Chambers, a critical age, because it was the age beyond which Richard had not survived. When John passed that period he would free Chambers from the unconscious fear that John might suffer Richard's fate.

"Each day is subtracted from the year that is left," Chambers writes. By numerically offsetting the diminishing days of his own life with a commensurate portion of his son's life, Chambers arranges his own death in order to insure his son's survival.[13] In this fanciful way Chambers strives to pay with his own life, to be rid of his unresolved guilt for his role in his brother's death. John's survival will then represent the redemption of Richard's death and his reincarnation. Then Chambers' conscience "will be free at last," pardoned by his own devices for his complicity in the death of his brother. However, once John does come of age, he becomes identified, in Chambers' mind, with Whittaker and his own survival after Richard's death. Chambers then wishes to postpone his own death, so that he can see John married in order to "carry on the line." This is clearly reminiscent of Chambers' earlier expressed need, after the death of his brother and father, to replenish the family line: "No need was so strong in me as the need to have children." [14]

John Chambers was married on June 8, 1961, at the age of twenty-five —Whittaker's age when his brother Richard killed himself. The marriage, held at Washington's Statler Hotel, was completely secret. Only Chambers' closest friends were present, and he was extremely apprehensive lest any members of the press discover the event. Having established a filial substitute for himself, he relinquishes to his son his own paternal prerogatives; now John can procreate and live for him. On a deeper level he also effects— through his unconscious equation of John and Richard—a magical resurrec-

---

[12] Buckley, op. cit., pp. 77, 80.
[13] This kind of magical thinking stems from Biblical times. It appears in various mystical and religious forms; a "bargaining with God" on an interpersonal level, which belies the individual's own identification with God's omnipotence to reverse, exchange, or redeem Death.
[14] See p. 102.

tion of his dead brother. Symbolically, Chambers is now ready to fulfill, within his self-created world of fantasy, his role in the unfulfilled death pact with Richard.[15]

A month later, on July 9, 1961, death came to Whittaker Chambers. Three days afterward the *New York Times* released the following:

Whittaker Chambers died of a heart attack at his farm house near Westminster at 7:00 a.m. Sunday.

The family of the 60-year-old confessed former Communist spy courier let the news be known today through a funeral director, John Myers, only after Mr. Chambers had been secretly cremated in Washington today. His wife, the former Esther Shemitz, was reported to have collapsed after his death. . . .

That same day the *Times* covered the reactions of Nixon [16] and Hiss:

"His book *Witness*," said Nixon "is the most penetrating analysis of the true nature and deadly appeal of Communism produced in this generation. It should be required reading by every American who is concerned by the threat of Communism."

Mr. Hiss declined comment on the death of Whittaker Chambers. He has steadfastly vowed confidence in his "eventual vindication." He charged Chambers "fabricated the evidence against me."

The stark fact of Chambers' death seemed to obscure for the moment the peculiar circumstances that surrounded it. The press and radio gave wide coverage to the event, but no one, to my knowledge, felt moved to find out why Whittaker Chambers was cremated secretly three days after he died and why the fact of his death was only then made public. Curious about the clinical diagnosis of Chambers' last illness and the specific cause of his death, I wrote

---

[15] It is important in this context to recall Chambers' sexual behavior after his father's death in 1929. He brought Ida Dales to his mother's home, where he lived with her in an illicit "Communist marriage" for two years. During this time Ida became pregnant and miscarried. Within a month after this event Chambers left Ida Dales, entered into a dramatic ("life and death") courtship, and impulsively married Esther Shemitz. There are, of course, many psychic determinants to this piece of sociopathic behavior: Chambers took his dead father's place and moved back into his mother's home after his father died. And, like his father before him, he acted out his contempt of his mother for having frustrated him all his life, by defying her rigid, moral values and carrying on sexually in *her* home with *another* woman. He then repeated this theme by acting out his revenge against Ida, the mother substitute. After she became pregnant he abandoned her and married Esther Shemitz, the subservient, idealized mother figure.

[16] Nixon and Chambers maintained their alliance, begun in 1948, to the end. Nixon concludes the *Six Crises* (p. 425) by citing a letter he received from Chambers several months before his death. It was, Nixon explained, the last letter Chambers was ever to write him, received at the end of February 1961. Chambers wrote: "It seems possible that we may not meet again—I mean at all. . . . I do not believe for a moment that because you have been cruelly checked in the employment of what is best in you, what is most yourself, that that check is final. It cannot be. . . . Great character always precludes a sense of come-down. . . ." (Chambers refers here to Nixon's defeat in the 1960 Presidential election.)

to the Department of Health of the State of Maryland for a copy of the death certificate. The request was denied.[17] This was strange; of the scores of comparable documents requested in the course of research for this book, Chambers' death certificate is the only vital statistic that was not made available.

The denial had come from the Chief of the Vital Records Section; I wrote next to the director of the department. Again the request was refused, this time with the remark that

We appreciate that high professional standards will be brought to bear on your study . . . [but] our policy does not permit the issuance of a certified copy of the death certificate *in this case*.[18]

Only by local telephone, after my arrival in Baltimore to investigate the circumstances of Chambers' death, was I told that the cause of death as recorded on the certificate read "coronary occlusion." My informant added that the diagnosis was "presumptive." I was not allowed to see the certificate but was informed that it had been signed by Dr. Wilkens, who had not seen Chambers for several days prior to the time she pronounced him dead. Dr. Marsh, deputy medical examiner (coroner) in Carroll County, had not been informed of Chambers' death until almost seventy-two hours after it occurred, and by then the body had been cremated. Dr. Russell C. Fisher, Chief Medical Examiner for the State of Maryland, wrote that the matter "puzzled me too." [19]

It was evident to me that some kind of clamp had been placed on this event. This, together with Mrs. Chambers' unexplained and equally mysterious collapse on the night after her husband died, moved me to go to Westminster to investigate further. There I spoke with Dr. Wilkens, Mr. Myers (the local mortician), and others. Dr. Wilkens told me that she had received a call around midnight on Saturday, July 8, from Mr. Chambers, who said he did not feel well. She offered to come out to see him, but he said that he did not wish to inconvenience her and would have Mrs. Chambers keep vigil for him during the night. Dr. Wilkens said Mrs. Chambers sat at his bedside but dozed off until the early morning, and when she awoke she saw her husband's body lying unconscious on the floor. He had apparently fallen between their two beds. Mrs. Chambers called Dr. Wilkens, who arrived at the Chambers' farm at 7:30 a.m., at which time she pronounced him dead. Dr. Wilkens presumed he had died of a heart attack. Mrs. Chambers' directions about the funeral arrangements were very explicit. Her husband's death was to be kept completely secret; "she did not want to face any newsmen." Mrs. Chambers

---

[17] By J. Charles Judge, Chief, Vital Records Section.
[18] Arthur S. Kraus, Sc.D., to the author. Dr. Kraus wrote in behalf of Dr. Prather, director of the department. Italics the author's.
[19] Dr. Fisher to the author (via Dr. L. Kubie), March 20, 1962.

requested that Mr. Myers be called and the body be removed immediately by him for cremation. It was specified also that there would be no funeral service. In accordance with these instructions, Mr. Myers drove out to Chambers' house in a station wagon rather than a hearse and in it transported the body to the mortuary in Westminster. From there it was to be taken early the next morning (Monday) to Fort Lincoln Cemetery in Washington, D.C., for immediate cremation. But on Sunday night, July 9, Mrs. Chambers sank into a deep coma. Dr. Wilkens was again called, this time by Chambers' son, who had that day been summoned from his home in Washington, D.C. Under Dr. Wilkens' instructions, Mrs. Chambers was taken by ambulance to the Annie Warner Hospital in Gettysburg, Pennsylvania.[20]

Mr. Myers informed me that John Chambers had told him that his mother had "oversedated" herself with barbiturates. Because of Mrs. Chambers' precarious state, the plan to take Chambers' body to Fort Lincoln crematory early Monday morning had to be postponed. And so, from Sunday morning, July 9, to Tuesday, July 11, Chambers' corpse and the fact of his death lay secretly hidden in a Westminster mortuary. However, under state law, Mr. Myers knew that he was not permitted to withhold burial or cremation of a body for more than seventy-two hours unless the coroner was notified. Accordingly, on Tuesday morning, accompanied by John and Ellen Chambers, he removed their father's corpse to the Fort Lincoln crematory in Washington, D.C., where it was immediately cremated. No funeral service was performed, a surprising betrayal of Chambers' religious avowals. That afternoon, after the cremation, Mr. Myers made his report to the Maryland State Department of Health that Chambers had died and was already cremated. Within an hour after his return to Westminster, Mr. Myers found himself surrounded by a group of news reporters, the center of an impromptu press conference.

There is a startling discrepancy between the facts of Chambers' last hours and the story as revealed to the world. Dr. Wilkens said that around midnight on Saturday, July 8, Chambers had telephoned her to say that he was not feeling well: the *New York Times* stated that "he refused to telephone Dr. Wilkens." The following morning, after his death, a second call was placed to Dr. Wilkens, this time by Mrs. Chambers. But these calls could not have been made from the Chambers' farm. The telephone company had disconnected Chambers' phone several days prior to his death. This fact,

[20] Transferred to the care of Dr. Sheely of Gettysburg, Mrs. Chambers remained deeply unconscious for seventy-two hours with complications of pulmonary congestion and beginning cardiac failure. After eleven days of hospitalization Mrs. Chambers was able to return home.

originally told me by Isaac Don Levine, later was confirmed in an article by William Buckley. Buckley related that he tried to reach Chambers by phone the day before he died but was unable to do so. When he inquired about this from Chambers' daughter, she explained, "Poppa and the phone company are having a little tiff, and the phone is disconnected. They wanted him to trim one of his favorite trees to take the strain off the telephone line, and he put it off. So . . . they turned off the phone." [21]

How was the midnight call to Dr. Wilkens placed? For Chambers to drive several miles to a neighbor's home at midnight, when ill, make a call to his doctor, and then insist that she *not* come to see him would be incomprehensible behavior indeed.

The mystery that surrounds Chambers' death demands some explanation. Certainly the clandestine nature of the event was contrary to the public interest. It precluded a post-mortem examination, which would have established beyond a doubt the exact cause of Chambers' death. An autopsy was clearly appropriate; this was truly a coroner's case.

But in the absence of an official investigation we have the elements of the mystery itself, which lend themselves to speculation. It is apparent at once that the reason we cannot know the cause of Chambers' death is that Chambers did not want us to have that knowledge. He specified the secret terms of his cremation and by so doing insured that he would only have to be pronounced dead by his sympathetic doctor. But he did more; he made a telephone call, from somewhere other than his own house, announcing that he was ill but asking Dr. Wilkens not to come. Inexplicable if he was really ill, this call could, however, have been part of a suicide plan. It could later be taken as evidence that he died a natural death. "Any fool can commit murder," Chambers has pointed out, "but it takes an artist to commit a good natural death." [22] Chambers was, by his own admission, weary of life and waiting for death in order to find peace of mind. But to end his life, and to let the world know that he had, would have been tantamount to an admission of his guilt. The anguish of Chambers' mental state in his last years, the psychic pattern of his entire life, and the mystery of his death all suggest that Chambers' final act was self-destruction. He was ending a lifetime of ever-increasing guilt, whose burden had at last grown intolerable, paying in a single act for a

[21] Buckley, *op. cit.,* p. 172.
[22] The quotation is from *Witness,* p. 485, in reference to the mysterious death of Walter Krivitsky in 1941, who was either murdered by the Soviet Secret Police or committed suicide because of his fear that he was being tracked by them.
    The date of Chambers' death, July 9, 1961, was twelve years, to the day, after the end of the first Hiss trial, July 9, 1949.

multitude of real and fantasied sins, above all for his two equivalent crimes: the psychological murder of his brother and the destruction of his brother surrogate, Alger Hiss.

On the evening after her husband's death Esther Chambers took an overdose of barbiturates, which kept her in a deep coma for seventy-two hours and in the hospital for eleven days. This near-death is strikingly reminiscent of Whittaker's unresolved death pact with Richard in 1926. Did Chambers have a similar death pact with his wife? There is no doubt, at least, that a double death was his wish. He closes *Witness* by reciting the Greek fable of Philemon and Baucis, the old couple who are granted their wish to die together, and then states:

. . . my wife and I have no dearer wish for ourselves—when our time shall have come, when our children shall be grown. . . .[23]

There is ample reason to believe that Chambers did indeed expect to enter death with his wife. Then his death takes on deeper meaning: he would be symbolically achieving a reunion with his mother, the dream of rebirth that had dominated his lifelong fantasies.

The cloak of secrecy that Chambers drew about his own death was his final deception, his last tragic gesture, a dramatically disguised ending to a life whose hallmark had been mystery. And in this way he freed himself, at last, from the lifelong tortures of his inner self. By the very nature of his own end he magically elevated himself beyond life and in his last agony strove to perpetuate into legend the image of himself as savior and martyr.

The personal tragedy of Chambers' life cannot be understood by blaming Communism, atheism, or the political and social anxieties of his generation. Nor was it in any sense a tragedy of history. From the night of his birth on April 1, 1901, to the morning of his death on July 9, 1961, Whittaker Chambers' life must be viewed as one prolonged span of psychic conflict. The fears and fantasies that filled his earliest years inexorably predetermined his future thoughts and actions. His childhood frustrations embroiled him in a lifelong pattern of ambivalences of thought and feeling. The deep turmoil within him

[23] Chambers lends direct confirmation to his earlier expressed wish for a double death in his posthumously published book, *Cold Friday* (p. 30): "The only thing about dying," wrote Chambers sometime during his last years, "that seems to me really insupportable is that my wife should not go with me. Ultimately, it is perhaps simply incredible. I could face eternity—or nothing—without a qualm if her hand were in mine at the moment we slipped into it. It is curious. I took her hand as we walked through the yard to go mushrooming the other day; and I had the strange sensation that we were walking toward death together, with great contentment, hand in hand. The image at the end of *Witness* is completely literal, like the whole passage, not, as I have reason to think some people suppose, a matter of prose."

never abated. It kept him in a state of emotional ferment, directing his loves and hates, driving him to destroy and to re-create. Finally, it seems, he could destroy nothing less than himself, giving his life in the mystical hope of re-union and rebirth.

Epilogue

IN MAY 1962, ten months after Chambers' death, I called on Mrs. Chambers at her Pipe Creek farm in Bachman Valley, a few miles outside Westminster. I was accompanied by the Reverend Mr. Kirk, minister of the Church of Christ in Westminster. Our visit was unexpected and was understandably a surprise to Mrs. Chambers. The Reverend Mr. Kirk, a mutual friend, introduced me at the door. (I had written to Mrs. Chambers some months earlier and received no reply, but I had spoken to her by long-distance telephone.) On hearing my name, Mrs. Chambers asked, "Are you the doctor from California who is writing about my husband?"

Mrs. Chambers was dressed in work clothes: old dungarees and a tattered sweater. She spoke to us at the door in a cordial but guarded manner. After several minutes we were invited to sit in the living room. Mrs. Chambers remarked that she was not her husband and therefore could not speak for him. Besides, she said he had already told the whole story in *Witness*: "It is all there in his book." She spoke poignantly and reverently about her late husband, implying his greatness and his role as savior of his country. Though she viewed the purpose of my study and my visit with suspicion, she discussed with us some of her husband's early writings, particularly his poems and short stories.

As our visit ended, Mrs. Chambers walked outside with us to show us the beautiful landscape. Her loneliness and sense of bereavement were clearly apparent as we walked about the grounds. She showed us the lake her husband had dug out of the land. Tears welled in her eyes as she told us how he had toiled with his bare hands to clear the overgrown land and how he had replanted the rocky hillside with lawn and many dogwood trees, which were then in full bloom.

We drove back to Westminster, moved by the afternoon visit. Chambers had worked hard to enrich the land, but he was not there to reap the rewards of his labors. And it was evident that Mrs. Chambers could not enjoy it without him.

The visit was as enlightening as it was affecting. It was so clear now, how the once vigorous Esther Shemitz, now gray and bowed beyond her sixty years, had become intertwined with and engulfed by her husband's life and was lost in the living world without him, how she was living out this role after his death, worshiping and sustaining his image as martyr, savior, and hero. In a sense, it seemed that the force of Chambers' fantasies of omnipotence had not been stilled, not even by death.

In the spring of 1965 Alger Hiss visited San Francisco. In anticipation of his trip he wrote me (our interviews and correspondence were by now drawing to a close) that he expected his visit to be "a succession of pious pilgrimages, as this will be the 20th anniversary of the UN conference." I met him in the city and spent part of his "pilgrimage" with him.

He had not been in San Francisco since 1945, and one had to reflect on the vastly altered circumstances of his return. He arrived anonymously this time, for now his face only occasionally stirs the memory of a passer-by. He reported, with evident pleasure, a commotion at the airport as he disembarked, and he said that a man had approached him and asked, "Have you seen the Attorney General? He's supposed to be here." The local newspaper learned of Hiss's presence but on his request made no mention of it. It was not considered a big story.

Hiss's face showed all of the twenty years that elapsed since he was prominently pictured in the papers as the efficient but gracious Secretary General, who "gave the impression of great youthfulness." Yet he has maintained the dress and the bearing of the figure he once was: his gray flannel suit and wing-tipped shoes appeared just faintly dated; his manners were as elaborate as always.

As we walked near the Civic Opera House, where the United Nations Charter was signed, he was silent. I thought not only about the fate of the young man who had helped to found the United Nations but of the world organization itself. There seemed to be a sad analogy. The brightest ambitions of both had been checked; one could only wonder about their futures.

But as we resumed our conversation I realized that this was unnecessary gloom. It was a disappointed but not an unhappy man who walked next to me. Despite his fall from public grace, he behaves much as he always has. We talked of his interests, which have not changed: art, literature, the theater, national and international affairs. We talked about some newly discovered facts about his case; he was hopeful, even optimistic. His faith in his eventual vindication has not diminished.

APPENDIX

ACKNOWLEDGMENTS

BIBLIOGRAPHY

INDEX

Chronology of Whittaker Chambers

April 1,	1901	Birth of Jay Vivian Chambers.
Sept. 26,	1903	Birth of Richard Godfrey Chambers (brother).
June	1919	Graduated from South Side High School, Rockville Centre, L.I.
	1919	Ran away from home. Used name Charles Adams.
	1920	File clerk at Frank Seaman Advertising Co., N.Y. Used name Charles Whittaker.
Sept.	1920	Entered Williams College. Used name Whittaker Chambers (?).
Sept.	1920	Entered Columbia University. Used name Whittaker Chambers.
Nov.	1922	Publication of *Play for Puppets* under name John Kelly.
Jan.	1923	Withdrew from Columbia.
Summer	1923	Trip to Europe.
Sept.	1923	Employed at New York Public Library.
Sept.	1924	Readmitted to Columbia University.
Feb. 17,	1925	Joined the Communist Party.
	1926–29	Worked for *Daily Worker.*
Sept. 9,	1926	Death of Richard Godfrey Chambers.
April 13,	1927	Discharged from New York Public Library.
	1929	Living with Ida Dales.
	1929	Out of Communist Party for a short period.
	1928–29	Translated *Class Reunion.*
Oct. 29,	1929	Death of father, Jay Chambers.
	1931–32	Editor of the *New Masses.*
April 15,	1931	Married Esther Shemitz.
	1932	Left *New Masses* and "entered underground." Pseudonyms: "Carl" and "Bob."
Oct. 17,	1933	Birth of daughter, Ellen Chambers.
Spring	1934	Moved to Baltimore. Used name Lloyd Cantwell.
June/July	1934	Met Alger Hiss under the name of "Carl" (Chambers' account).

April 15–July 1,	1935	Moved to Washington, D.C. Lived at 28th Street apartment of Hiss. Uncertain under what name.
May	1935	Obtained passport. Used name David Breen.
Oct. to spring	1935 1936	Lived at Eutaw Place, Washington, D.C. Used name Lloyd Cantwell.
	1935–36	First received documents from Julian Wadleigh.
Spring	1936	Alleged trip to Westminster, Md., with Alger Hiss.
Spring	1936	Lived with Maxim Lieber at New Hope, Pa. Used name David Breen.
July 23,	1936	Certificate of title of motor vehicle (Ford).
Aug. 18,	1936	Birth of son, John Chambers.
Fall	1936 (?)	Lived at 3310 Auchentoroly Terrace, Baltimore. Used name Jay Chambers.
Spring	1937	Purchase of Westminster, Md., farm.
Oct.	1937	Employment with National Research Project. Used name Jay V. David Chambers.
Late	1937	Date of break with Communist Party (this date given at first months of testimony and in statements to government between 1939–48).
Nov. (or prior, to April 1938)	1937	Lived at Mount Royal Terrace, Baltimore.
Jan. 21,	1938	Furloughed from job with National Research Project.
Spring	1938	Date of break with Communist Party according to later testimony.
June	1938	Purchased 2610 St. Paul Street, Baltimore, under name David Chambers (summer 1939, sold this property).
Dec.	1938	Alleged visit to Alger Hiss to persuade him to break with Communist Party.
Sept.	1939	Visited Adolf A. Berle, Jr.
Sept. 26,	1940	Baptism in Episcopal Church.
March 20,	1945	Interview with Ray Murphy, security officer of State Department.
Aug.	1946	Another interview with Ray Murphy.
	1939–48	Employment with *Time* magazine.
Jan.–May	1944	Book reviews for *American Mercury*. Used name John Land.
Aug. 3,	1948	Accused Alger Hiss before House Committee on Un-American Activities in public session.
Aug. 17,	1948	Confrontation with Alger Hiss in executive session.
Aug. 25,	1948	Confrontation with Alger Hiss in public session.
Aug. 27,	1948	Repeated his accusation on "Meet the Press."

Oct. 14,	1948	First appearance before New York Grand Jury.
Nov. 17,	1948	Gave Baltimore Documents to Mr. Marbury in pre-trial examination in libel suit.
Dec. 2,	1948	Production of pumpkin microfilm.
Dec. 10,	1948	Resigned as senior editor of *Time* magazine.
	1951	Returned to Westminster farm at termination of trial.
	1952	Publication of *Witness*.
	1957	Joined the *National Review*.
Sept.	1959	Enrolled as undergraduate student at Western Maryland College.
June 8,	1961	Marriage of John Chambers.
July 9,	1961	Death of Whittaker Chambers.
July 11,	1961	Cremation in Fort Lincoln Cemetery.
July 11,	1961	Release of news of death, after cremation.

APPENDIX B

Chronology of Alger Hiss

Nov. 11,	1904	Birth of Alger Hiss (Baltimore, Md.).
April 7,	1907	Death of Charles Alger Hiss, Alger's father.
	1909–17	Attended Baltimore Public School 14.
Sept.	1917	Entered high school, Baltimore City College.
June	1921	Graduation from Baltimore City College.
	1921–22	Attended Powder Point Academy, Duxbury, Mass., and Maryland Institute of Art.
Sept.	1922	Entered Johns Hopkins University.
Summer	1924	Summer trip to Europe. Met Priscilla Fansler.
June	1926	Graduation from Johns Hopkins.
Summer	1926	Spent in Rye, N.Y., with his brother Bosley.
Sept.	1926	Entered Harvard Law School.
Nov. 3,	1926	Death of Bosley Hiss (brother).
May	1929	Death of Mary Ann Hiss (sister).
June	1929	Graduation from Harvard Law School.
Summer	1929	Trip to Europe.
Oct.	1929	Started year as secretary to Justice Oliver Wendell Holmes. Lived on Connecticut Avenue, Washington, D.C.
Dec. 11,	1929	Marriage to Priscilla Fansler Hobson.
Oct.	1930	Employed by Boston law firm of Choate, Hall and Stewart.
Spring	1932	Employed by New York law firm of Cotton, Franklin, Wright and Gordon. Lived first on Claremont Avenue and then on Central Park West.
May	1933	Joined Agricultural Adjustment Administration. Lived at 3411 O Street, Georgetown (Washington, D.C.).
June	1934	Moved to 2831 28th Street, Washington, D.C.
July	1934	Lent to Nye Committee.
Dec. (or Jan. 1935)	1934	First met Whittaker Chambers under the name George Crosley (Hiss's account).

March 2,	1935	Resigned from AAA, went on payroll of Nye Committee.
April to June	1935 1936	Lived at 2905 P Street, Washington, D.C.
August	1935	Joined Solicitor General's Office.
March	1936	Argued case of *U.S.* v. *Knott* in Supreme Court.
Spring	1936	Contracted for purchase of Westminster, Md., farm.
July to Dec.	1936 1937	Lived at 1245 30th Street, Washington, D.C.
July 23,	1936	Signed certificate of title of Ford car to Cherner Motor Company.
September	1936	Joined the Department of State—office of Francis B. Sayre, Assistant Secretary of State.
Dec. 29, to Oct.	1937 1943	Lived at 3415 Volta Place, Washington, D.C.
	1939	Investigated under the Hatch Act.
August 5,	1941	Birth of Anthony Hiss.
	1943–46	Moved to 3210 P Street, Washington, D.C.
Sept.	1939–44	Assistant to Stanley Hornbeck, adviser on political relations.
Spring	1944	Joined State Department Office of Special Political Affairs.
Aug.–Oct.	1944	Executive Secretary (of the American delegation) to Dumbarton Oaks Conference.
Oct.	1944	Became Deputy Director of Office of Special Political Affairs.
Feb.	1945	Adviser to Stettinius at Yalta Conference.
Early	1945	Became Director of Office of Special Political Affairs.
April 25–June 26,	1945	Secretary General of San Francisco Conference for United Nations.
Jan.	1946	Attended first meeting of General Assembly in London as principal adviser to American delegation.
March	1946	Interview with FBI.
Dec.	1946	Elected president of Carnegie Endowment for International Peace.
Jan.	1947	Left government service.
Feb. 1,	1947	Took office at Carnegie Endowment.
Feb. 21,	1947	Awarded Honorary Degree from Johns Hopkins.
June	1947	Interview with the FBI.
Sept.	1947	Moved to New York, 22 East Eighth Street.
March 16,	1948	Appeared before New York Grand Jury.

Aug. 3,	1948	Accused by Whittaker Chambers before the House Committee on Un-American Activities in public session.
Aug. 5,	1948	Denied Chambers' accusation before House Committee in public session.
Aug. 16,	1948	Testified before House Committee in executive session.
Aug. 17,	1948	Private confrontation with Whittaker Chambers.
Aug. 25,	1948	Public confrontation with Whittaker Chambers.
Aug. 27,	1948	Accused by Chambers on "Meet the Press."
Sept. 27,	1948	Sued Chambers for libel.
Nov. 4,	1948	Pre-trial deposition of Chambers began.
Nov. 17,	1948	Chambers presented Baltimore Documents in pre-libel suit deposition.
Dec. 4	1948	Interviewed by FBI in Baltimore.
Dec. 6–15,	1948	Appeared before New York Grand Jury.
Dec. 13,	1948	Resignation as president of Carnegie Endowment tendered.
Dec. 15,	1948	Indicted for perjury by New York Grand Jury.
May 31–July 9,	1949	First Trial
Nov. 17,	1949	Second Trial
to Jan. 21,	1950	
Jan. 25,	1950	Sentenced to five years in prison. Released on $10,00 bail pending appeal.
Dec. 7,	1950	U.S. Court of Appeals denied appeal.
Jan.	1951	U.S. Court of Appeals denied petition for rehearing.
March 12,	1951	U.S. Supreme Court refused writ of certiorari to review conviction.
March 22,	1951	Began prison term, most of which was served at Federal Penitentiary, Lewisburg, Pa.
Jan. 24,	1952	Counsel filed motion for a new trial.
July 22,	1952	Motion for a new trial denied.
Nov. 27,	1954	Released from prison—10 months' parole period.
Nov.	1955	*Yalta: Modern American Myth* by Alger Hiss, Pocket Books, Inc.
May	1957	Publication of *In the Court of Public Opinion*
	1957–59	Employed by Feathercombs, Inc.
	1959–60	Unemployed.
	1959	Separation from Priscilla Hiss.
Feb.	1960	Employed by Davison-Bluth, Inc.
	1963	Publication by Atheneum of abridgment of Holmes-Laski correspondence.

APPENDIX C

Statement to Federal Bureau of Investigation, signed by Alger Hiss, June 2, 1947

Washington, D.C.
June 2, 1947

I, Alger Hiss, make the following statement to Charles Cleveland and Edward L. Grampp whom I know to be Special Agents of the Federal Bureau of Investigation. No threats or promises of any kind have been made to me to induce me to make this statement. I have been advised that I need not make this statement and I know that it can be used against me in a court of law.

When I first went to New York City to practice law I became associated with the International Juridical Association. When I became associated this association was a small group which published a pamphlet on labor law mainly. I was one of the editors of the Association's journal. The following men according to my recollection contributed to this publication: Jerome Hellerstein, Nathan Witt, Lee Pressman and Isador Polier whose wife was Justine Wise (ph). This group was not connected with the International Labor Defense, the National Federation for Constitutional Liberties, or the Lawyers Guild to my knowledge. To my belief Earl Browder did not use the International Juridical Association to advertise the "New Masses" or to use the mailing list of the Juridical Association to increase the subscriptions to the "New Masses." I left this association when I came to Washington, D.C. I do not believe that any of the individuals in the Juridical Association were or are Communists but have heard a number of individuals state the belief since my association with them that Lee Pressman and Nathan Witt were Communists. I have also heard allegations that Polier was a Communist.

I have never been a member of or associated with the Committee for Democratic Action or the Young Communist League. I have never been nor am I now a member of the Communist Party. Neither am I personally acquainted with any member of the Communist Party, to my knowledge.

I can recall only two individuals by the name of Sayre—Francis B. Sayre with whom I was associated in the State Department and Dan Sayre who was formerly with the C.A.B. and is now teaching at Princeton University. To my knowledge neither of these individuals were Communists.

My brother Donald Hiss, a local lawyer, never worked for Harry Bridges and to my knowledge was never considered for employment for or on behalf of Bridges.

I am sure my brother was not and is not now a member of the Communist Party.

I am not acquainted with an individual by the name of Whittaker Chambers. No individual by that name has ever visited my home on any occasion so far as I can recall.

I became acquainted with Harold Ware while I was in the Department of Agriculture. Also I am acquainted with Charles Krivitsky, who is now known legally as Charles Kramer, having met him while he was employed at the Dept. of Agriculture. Lee Pressman and I have known each other since my attendance at Harvard Law School. Pressman and I were associated on the Harvard Law Review at which time I wrote a "note" for the law review on the subject as well as I can remember of "Yellow Dog Contracts." I have known Henry Collins since childhood and consider him a close personal friend. I cannot recall any person by the name of Nathan Perlow. I knew Alice Mendham quite well when she was running a children's school in 1933 or 1934. Her husband's last name was Powell but I can't recall his first name. I know no one by the name of Post in connection with the above individual, neither do I know Nathan Gregory Silvermaster.

I have never met with any group at the home of Henry Collins or any other place where government information was discussed when people who had no right to the information were present. Nor do I know of any group of individuals which met together without authority to make government information available, orally or written, for the use of the Soviet Government.

I first met John Abt at the Agriculture Department in an official capacity. I have never attended any meetings of the foregoing type where John Abt was present neither have I visited at his apartment. I also met Marian Bachrach at the Department of Agriculture through her husband.

I have never been known to my knowledge by the name of "Gene" or "Eugene." I know of no individual by the name of "Gene" or "Eugene" Hiss having been employed by the State Department.

I met Victor Perlo back in 1934 but I can't recall him too well. I have had no further contact with him since approximately that time and do not know of his whereabouts at this time.

I met Harold Glasser in an official capacity as an official of the Treasury Department. I have never placed Glasser in touch with a Russian representative in order that he might furnish government information to this individual.

The foregoing represents summaries prepared by Mssrs. Cleveland and Grampp of oral answers. [sic] I had previously given to questions asked orally by them in a call at my office made at their request on June 2, 1947. I have read the foregoing four pages and to the best of my knowledge they are true and correct. I was asked by Agents Grampp and Cleveland if I would give them a signed statement on the information I had given them orally.

ALGER HISS

Witnesses:

EDWARD L. GRAMPP, F.B.I.

CHARLES G. CLEVELAND, F.B.I.

Acknowledgments

The long course of research and composition of this book was an arduous undertaking. The challenge posed by the problems of gathering facts and collating and organizing large masses of personally collected data into a readable account was an enriching experience. The knowledge gained during the period of preparation of this book has extended my horizons and brightened my perspectives. I should like to express my gratitude to all sources, personal and institutional, who contributed to these enhancements and who provided information and assistance.

In the preparation of such an intimate, closely documented work, one becomes acquainted with and in various ways indebted to many people for many reasons. During the past six years I have gleaned all manner of "live" data—a fact here, an anecdote there, a personal reminiscence or revelation, a document, translation, some undiscovered item or literary reference. Though I have kept careful files, I may nevertheless have failed to set down every source to whom I owe some acknowledgment. My gratitude to all those who in one way or another were helpful and who, either inadvertently on my part or by their own request, are not listed, is indeed great.

For personal recollections and biographical material, heretofore unpublished and generally unknown, concerning Whittaker Chambers during the approximate period 1920–40, I am grateful to many of his Columbia classmates, former colleagues, and other associates who responded to my queries. Many of their names have been cited or alluded to in the text and are listed in the bibliography. I should like here to express my gratitude to David Cort, Guy Endore, Clifton Fadiman, John Gassner, Meyer Schapiro, Dr. Jack Schultz, the late Herbert Solow, Mark Van Doren, Dr. Nathaniel Ross, and Lionel Trilling for their accounts of Chambers' activities during the twenties and thirties.

For documentary material, personal reminiscences, or other information regarding Whittaker Chambers during his later years (about 1930–60) I am obligated, among others, to Dr. Nathan Adler, Earl Browder, Robert Cantwell, Edward W. Case, Esther Chambers, Mrs. Jay Lea Chambers, Robert Crichton, Malcolm Cowley, Bishop Horace W. Donnegan, Lowell Ensor, Michael Finn, Harry Freeman, Dr. Russell Fischer, Michael Gold, the late Rev. William Dudley Foulke Hughes, Martha Greene, Langston Hughes, the Rev. Bradford W. Ketchum, Matthew Josephson, the late Alexander King, the Rev. and Mrs. Nevin Kirk, Arthur S. Kraus, Louis Kronenberger, Nathan Levine, the late A. J. Liebling, Leon Herald, T. S. Matthews, Felix Morrow, John E. Meyers, Jr., the Rt. Rev. James A. Pike, James Reston, Elsie Rosner, Samuel Roth, the Rev. Edward West, Dr. Elizabeth M. Reese Wilkins, and Nathan Witt.

I am indebted to Elinor Ferry for information related to me orally, and for making available to me memoranda of several of her interviews during the early fifties with Whittaker Chambers' associates.

To Alger Hiss I owe special thanks for his diligent responses to my endless queries over a period of six years, for all the information he gave me orally and in writing, for making available the Hiss defense files, for his personal recollections, letters and speeches, fantasies and opinions. I should like to express my appreciation also for the original memoranda and calendar appointments of Hiss's daily activities during 1946–48, when he was President of the Carnegie Endowment. These records, kept by the late Elizabeth B. Sayre, Hiss's private secretary at the Carnegie Endowment, were turned over to me by Hiss through the kindness of Anne Winslow, to whom these papers had been entrusted.

To the members of Hiss's immediate family—Priscilla Hiss, Anthony Hiss, Dr. Timothy Hobson, Hiss's stepson—I am grateful for their help and for their tolerant attitude toward my probings.

To Alger Hiss's relatives, who generously supplied me with historical data and family lore obtainable from no other source, my deepest appreciation. These were: Elliot Emerson, Ruth Emerson, Anna Hiss, Donald Hiss, Charles Alger Hiss, Edna Hiss, John A. Hiss, Lillian Hiss, Mary C. Hiss, and Elizabeth Hiss Hartman.

Many of Hiss's former classmates, colleagues, and legal, governmental, and other associates from diverse walks of life furnished important factual information and background material. These were: Alfred Bergdoll, Hanson Baldwin, George Boas, Burns Chalmers, Edward Chandler, Charles Darlington, Constance Ducey, Thomas Fansler, Stephen Farrand, Mr. and Mrs. Richard Field, the late Justice Felix Frankfurter, Don Freeman, Erwin Griswold, Loy Henderson, Thayer Hobson, Charles Horsky, C. Ridgeley Howard, the late Moses Huberman, Gardner ("Pat") Jackson, Dr. Hugh Jewett, Isabel Johnson, Mr. and Mrs. Harding Lemay, William Marbury, Edward M. Morgan, the late Edward R. Murrow, Kenneth McCormick, Charles Ford Reese, Arthur Rocco, Dr. and Mrs. Allen Roos, Francis B. Sayre, Jesse Slingluff, the late Adlai E. Stevenson, John Sutro, Gerard Swope, Telford Taylor, Donnell Tilghman, Rexford Tugwell, Julian Wadleigh, and Charles Willard.

I owe a special debt to the members of the Hiss defense counsel and to his present attorney. Without their help and encouragement over a period of six years and the development of a working relationship which extended beyond the bounds of friendship, this project could not have been accomplished. I am grateful beyond measure to the late Robert Benjamin, Claude Cross, Edward McLean, and Harold Rosenwald. Mrs. Helen L. Buttenwieser, Hiss's present attorney, granted me unrestricted access to the Hiss files and gave generously of her time and energy from beginning to end.

There remains still a host of others who furnished information and gave assistance of various kinds or acted as intermediaries. Among these were: George Altman, Carolyn Anspacher, Donald Appel, Walter Beer, Adolph A. Berle, Jr., Dr. Viola Bernard, Scott Buchanan, Huntington Cairns, Morris Ernst, Dr. John Frosch,

ACKNOWLEDGMENTS   (449

Mary T. Heathcote, Paul Jacobs, Dr. Edward Joseph, Professor Frank Kelly, the late Dr. Robert Knight, Dr. Lawrence Kubie, Geoffrey Levy, Manice de F. Lockwood, III, Benjamin Mandel, Marchbanks Press (Emily Connor), Abe Mellinkoff, Professor Herman Louis Meyer, A. G. Nelson, Edward Osgood, Richard H. Popkin, Philip Reno, William A. Reuben, Arnold Rogow, Leo Rosten, Mark Schorer, Dr. and Mrs. Herman Serota, Carl Spero, Ruth Stevenson, the late Dr. Sidney Tarachow, Martin Tytell, and John Wilkinson.

I am indebted to the registrars and librarians of Baltimore City College, Columbia, Harvard, Johns Hopkins, and Colgate Universities, and Williams College.

I owe a singular debt of gratitude to Dr. Carl Binger for his early encouragement and moral support when my doubts were great and my interest far outweighed my knowledge. I want to thank him also for his thoughtfulness in sending me his entire file of personal and documentary material, books, letters, and other paraphernalia relevant to his participation in the Hiss trials.

I am grateful to Isaac Don Levine for his several accounts to me of his experiences with Whittaker Chambers and for his helpfulness in arranging a joint meeting at his home in order for me to talk with Donald Appell, Benjamin Mandel, and Julian Wadleigh.

To Oliver Edmund Clubb and David Zablodowsky, my thanks for their extended accounts and for their permission to use them.

I wish to thank Margaret Burton, former secretary to the late Chester T. Lane, for making available to me certain memoranda from Mr. Lane's post-trial investigation of the Hiss Case.

I am obliged to William Marbury for his informative oral account to me of his relationship with Mr. Hiss and of his role as Hiss's lawyer in the libel suit against Chambers, and for the use of material from his personal memorandum of 1948 regarding Hiss.

I have left until now my special acknowledgment to Margaret Brenman, Ph.D., George Klein, Ph.D., and attorney John Lowenthal. All three became involved with this project and were my stanchest and severest critics, yet bolstered me when I was full of frustration. For their understanding and especially for their careful readings, editorial comments, and cogent criticisms of several working drafts I shall remain beholden.

Dr. Leo Rangell and Dr. Bert Lewin kindly read through one version of an early draft and made helpful comments.

I have not yet mentioned those who worked closely with me as typists and provided secretarial assistance. From inception to completion of this book Karin S. Armitage has remained steadfastly diligent and loyal as part-time secretary and typist. For two years Miss Vasanti Ferrando labored full time deciphering and transcribing handwritten copy and typing endless revisions. Mrs. Elsa Hickey and Miss Jean Carter typed portions of the manuscript. My thanks to them all.

I come, finally, to my wife, Elizabeth Winifred, and my children, whose daily lives were encroached upon and whose pleasures were invaded by the demands of this book. All weathered with me the excitements and disappointments of this under-taking. Were it not for my wife's faithful presence and devotion, her loving manage-ment of home and brood, to say nothing of her great knowledge of language and lit-erature (which I constantly tapped), this work could not have been finished.

All have been helpful and contributory. In the final analysis, however, I alone remain responsible for whatever errors of fact or citation this book may contain, and I alone am accountable for its assertions, interpretations, and omissions.

Bibliography

PUBLISHED MATERIAL:

Alsop, Joseph. "Miss Bentley's Bondage," *Commonweal,* Nov. 9, 1951.
———. "The Strange Case of Louis Budenz," *Atlantic Monthly,* April 1952.
Altman, George T. "The Added Witness, New Doubt on the Hiss Case," *The Nation,* Oct. 1, 1960.
Andrews, Bert and Peter. *A Tragedy of History.* Washington, D.C., Robert B. Luce, 1962.
Ascoli, Max. "The Elections," *The Reporter,* Nov. 22, 1962.
———. "The Lives and Deaths of Whittaker Chambers," *The Reporter,* July 8, 1952.
——— and Robert Bingham. "The Case of Alger Hiss," *The Reporter,* Aug. 30, 1949.
Baltimore Sun. Obituary of Charles Alger Hiss, April 8, 1907.
Beirne, Francis F. *Baltimore—a Picture History, 1858–1958* (compiled under the auspices of The Maryland Historical Society). New York: Hastings House, 1957.
Bentley, Elizabeth. *Out of Bondage.* New York: Devin-Adair Co., 1951.
Bergler, Edmund, M.D. *The Writer and Psychoanalysis.* New York: Robert Brunner, 1954.
Berle, Adolf A., Jr. Memorandum of interview with Whittaker Chambers, Sept. 1939.
Birnbach, Martin. *Neo-Freudian Social Philosophy.* Stanford, Calif.: Stanford University Press, 1961.
Boorstin, Daniel J. The Image—or What Happened to the American Dream. New York: Atheneum, 1962.
Brower, Brock. "The Problems of Alger Hiss," *Esquire,* Dec. 1960.
Brown, Stuart Gerry. *Conscience and Politics—Adlai E. Stevenson in the 1950's.* Syracuse, N.Y.: Syracuse University Press, 1961.
Buckley, William F., Jr. "The End of Whittaker Chambers," *Esquire,* Sept. 1962.
——— & the Editors of *National Review. The Committee and Its Critics: A Calm Review of the House Committee on Un-American Activities.* New York: G. P. Putnam's Sons, 1962.

Burnham, James. *The Web of Subversion*. New York: John Day Co., 1954.
Busch, Noel F. *Adlai E. Stevenson of Illinois*. New York: Farrar, Straus & Young, 1952.
Byrnes, James F. *All in One Lifetime*. New York: Harper & Bros., 1958.
———. *Speaking Frankly*. New York: Harper & Bros., 1947.
———. "Yalta and Hiss and the Atom Bomb," *Look,* Oct. 14, 1958.
Chambers, Whittaker.

ARTICLES:

"Deep River," *Time,* Dec. 18, 1945.
"The Devil," *Life,* Feb. 2, 1948.
"End of a Dark Age Ushers In New Dangers," *Life,* April 30, 1956.
"Ghosts on the Roof," *Time,* March 5, 1945.
"Herring and the Thing," *Look,* Dec. 29, 1953.
"Sanity of St. Benedict," excerpt from "Saints for Now" (ed. by C. B. Luce), *Commonweal,* Sept. 19, 1952.
"What Is a Communist?" *Look,* July 28, 1953.

BOOK REVIEWS:

By "John Land" (Whittaker Chambers), *The American Mercury,* January through May 1944. See especially "The Future and American Foreign Policy," a review of Joseph M. Jones's *A Modern Foreign Policy for the United States* (The Macmillan Company) and Carl L. Becker's *How New Will the Better World Be?* (Alfred A. Knopf), May 1944.

BOOKS:

Cold Friday. New York: Random House, 1964. (Edited posthumously by Duncan Norton-Taylor.)
Witness. New York: Random House, 1952.

PLAY AND POEMS:

A Play for Puppets, The Morningside, Nov. 1922.
"Before the End," *News Magazine Supplement,* July 9, 1927.
"Braun," *The Morningside,* Dec. 1924.
"Lothrop, Montana," *The Nation,* June 30, 1926.
"October 21st, 1926," *Poetry,* Feb. 1931.
"Poems," *The Nation,* April 7, 1926.
"Quag-Hole," *The Nation,* Dec. 31, 1924.
"Rosedale Trestle," *The Morningside,* Dec. 1924.
"Spartacus' Song," *The Morningside,* Nov. 1922.
"Tandaradei," *Two Worlds,* June 1926.

SHORT STORIES:

"Can You Hear Their Voices," *New Masses,* then International Pamphlets, 1932.
"The Damn Fool," *The Morningside,* March 1922.
"The Death of the Communists," *New Masses,* 1932.
"In Memory of R.G.," *The Morningside,* Dec. 1924.
"Our Comrade Munn," *New Masses,* 1932.
"You Have Seen the Heads," *New Masses,* 1932.

TRANSLATIONS:

Edschmid, Kasimir. *The Passionate Rebel (Life of Lord Byron).* New York: A. & C. Boni, 1930.
Gumpert, Martin. *Dunant, The Story of the Red Cross.* New York: Oxford University Press, 1938.
Mann, Heinrich. *Mother Mary.* New York: Simon & Schuster, 1928.
Regler, Gustav. *The Great Crusade.* New York: Longmans, Green & Co., 1940.
Salten, Felix. *Bambi* (1928); *Fifteen Rabbits* (1930); *The City Jungle* (1932). New York: Simon & Schuster.
Tralow, Johannes. *Cards & Kings.* New York: R. Long & R. R. Smith, 1931.
Weirauch, Anna Elisabet. *The Scorpion.* New York: Greenberg, 1932.
Werfel, Franz. *Class Reunion.* New York: Simon & Schuster, 1929.

OTHER:

"Il Faut le Supposer Heureux" (excerpts from the last letter William F. Buckley, Jr., received from Whittaker Chambers), *National Review,* July 29, 1961.
"Whittaker Chambers Meets the Press," *American Mercury,* Feb. 1949..

Childs, John. "The Hiss Case and the American Intellectual," *The Reporter,* Sept. 26, 1950.
Cleckley, Hervey. *The Mask of Sanity.* St. Louis: C. V. Mosby Co., 1941.
Cook, Fred J. *The FBI Nobody Knows.* New York: The Macmillan Co., 1964.
———. "Ghost of a Typewriter," *The Nation,* May 12, 1962.
———. "Nixon Kicks a Hole in the Hiss Case," *The Nation,* April 7, 1962.
———. *The Unfinished Story of Alger Hiss.* New York: William Morrow Co., 1958. (See the *Saturday Review* of May 31, June 21, July 12, 1958, for Victor Lasky's review of this book and the author's answer.)
Cooke, Alistair. *A Generation on Trial.* New York: Alfred A. Knopf, 1952.
———. "The Nagging Doubts about the Hiss Case . . . ," *Look,* July 15, 1952.
Costello, William. *The Facts about Nixon.* New York: The Viking Press, 1960.
De Toledano, Ralph. "The Alger Hiss Story," *American Mercury,* June 1953.

De Toledano, Ralph. *Lament for a Generation*. New York: Farrar, Straus & Cudahy, 1960.

———. "Let Only a Few Speak for Him," *National Review,* July 29, 1961.

———and Victor Lasky. *Seeds of Treason*. New York: Funk & Wagnalls Co. for *Newsweek,* 1950.

Dos Passos, John. "Mr. Chambers' Descent into Hell," *Saturday Review,* May 24, 1952.

Dulles, Allen. *The Craft of Intelligence*. New York: Harper & Row, 1963.

Erikson, Eric H. *Young Man Luther*. New York: W. W. Norton & Co., 1958.

Ernst, Morris L. & Loth, David. *Report on the American Communist*. New York: Henry Holt & Co., 1952.

Fiedler, Leslie. *An End to Innocence: Essays on Culture and Politics*. Boston: The Beacon Press, 1955.

——— "Hiss, Chambers, and the Age of Innocence," *Commentary,* Aug. 1951.

Freeman, Joseph. *An American Testament*. London: Victor Gollancz, 1938.

Freud, Sigmund. "Dostoyevsky and Parricide" (1928), *Collected Papers.* London: The Hogarth Press, 1950. Vol. V, pp. 222–42.

Fund for the Republic. *Bibliography on the Communist Problem in the United States*. New York: 1955.

———. *Digest of the Public Record of Communism in the United States*. New York: 1953.

Gitlow, Benjamin. *I Confess; the Truth about American Communism*. New York: E. P. Dutton, 1940.

Greenacre, Phyllis, M.D. "The Impostor," *The Psychoanalytic Quarterly,* vol. 27 (1958).

———. "The Relation of the Impostor to the Artist," in *The Psychoanalytic Study of the Child*. New York: International Universities Press, 1958. Vol. XIII, pp. 521–41.

Gunther, John. *Roosevelt in Retrospect*. New York: Harper & Bros., 1950.

Halsey, Margaret. "The Natives Are Restless Tonight," *The Reporter,* Jan. 13, 1955.

———. *The Pseudo-Ethic*. New York: Simon and Schuster, 1963.

Harney, Malachi L., and Cross, John C. *The Informer in Law Enforcement*. Springfield, Ill.: Charles C. Thomas, 1960.

Henderson, D. K., M.D. *Psychopathic States*. New York: W. W. Norton & Co., 1947.

Hiss, Alger. *In the Court of Public Opinion*. New York: Alfred A. Knopf, 1957.

OTHER:

"Basic Questions in the Great Debate," *New York Times Magazine,* Nov. 16, 1947.

"The General Assembly of the United Nations," *Illinois Law Review,* Jan.–Feb. 1947 (vol. LXI, no. 5).

"Maybe So," column in the *Johns Hopkins Newsletter,* 1923–24.

"The Prospects for Peace," *The Friend*, June 19, 1947. (Haverford Commencement Address.)

"Two Essential Elements of Policy for European Reconstruction," *Christian Register*, March 1948.

"Yalta: Modern American Myth," *Pocket Book Magazine*, Nov. 1955.

Hitschmann, Edward, M.D. *Great Men—Psychoanalytic Studies*. New York: International Universities Press, 1956.

Hook, Sidney. "The Faiths of Whittaker Chambers" (review of *Witness*), *New York Times Book Review*, May 25, 1952.

———. *Political Power and Personal Freedom*. New York: Criterion Books, 1959.

——— (ed.). *Psychoanalysis, Scientific Method and Philosophy*. New York: New York University Press, 1959.

House Committee on Un-American Activities. *Hearings Regarding Communist Espionage in the United States Government*, 80th Cong., 2nd sess., July 31–Dec. 14, 1948. (For Hiss Testimony, see Aug. 5, 18, 24, 1948.)

———. *Annual Report to the United States House of Representatives*, Dec. 31, 1948.

———. *The Shameful Years—Thirty Years of Soviet Espionage in the United States*, Dec. 30, 1951.

———. *Soviet Espionage Within the United States Government*, Dec. 31, 1948.

Howe, Irving. *Politics and the Novel*. Cleveland: World Publishing Co., 1962.

Joseph, Edward D. "Identity and Joseph Conrad," *The Psychoanalytic Quarterly*, vol. 32 (1963).

Jowitt, The Earl. *The Strange Case of Alger Hiss*. Garden City, N.Y.: Doubleday and Co., 1953.

Kempton, Murray. *Part of Our Time: Some Monuments and Ruins of the Thirties*. New York: Simon and Schuster, 1955.

Koestler, Arthur. "Complex Issue of the Ex-Communist," *New York Times Magazine*, Feb. 19, 1950.

Krivitsky, Walter. *In Stalin's Secret Service*. New York: Harper & Bros., 1939.

Kubie, Lawrence S., M.D. "The Fostering of Creative Scientific Productivity," *Daedalus*, Spring 1962.

———. *Neurotic Distortion of the Creative Process*. New York: The Noonday Press, 1961.

———. "Research in Judicial Administration; A Pychiatrist's View," *Boston University Law Review*, Spring 1959 (vol. xxxix, no. 2).

Lesser, Simon O. *Fiction and the Unconscious*. Boston: The Beacon Press, 1957.

Levine, Isaac Don. *The Mind of an Assassin*. New York: New American Library, 1960 (a Signet Book).

———. "The Inside Story of Our Soviet Underground," *Plain Talk*, Sept.–Dec., 1948.

———. "Sequel to Chambers' Story," *Plain Talk*, Jan. 1949.

———. *Stalin's Great Secret*. New York: Coward McCann, 1956.

Liebling, A. J. *The Press,* Rev. ed. New York: Ballantine Books, 1964.

Lofton, John. "Trial by Fury," *The Nation,* Nov. 25, 1961.

Lyons, Eugene. "Lattimore, Dreyfus or Hiss?" *New Leader,* Sept. 2, 1950.

McCarthy, Mary. *On the Contrary.* New York: Farrar, Straus & Cudahy, 1961.

Massing, Hede. *This Deception.* New York: Duell, Sloan & Pearce, 1951.

Matthews, T. S. *Name and Address.* New York: Simon & Schuster, 1960.

Matusow, Harvey. *False Witness.* New York: Cameron & Kahn, 1955.

Mazo, Earl. *Richard Nixon.* New York: Harper & Bros., 1959.

Mises, Ludwig von. *The Anti-Capitalistic Mentality.* Princeton, N.J.: D. Van Nostrand Co., 1956.

Morris, Richard B. "Chambers' Litmus Paper Test," *Saturday Review,* May 24, 1952.

————. "The Case of Alger Hiss," *Fair Trial.* New York: Alfred A. Knopf, 1953. Chap. XIV, pp. 426–79.

Murrow, Edward R. (and Friendly, Fred). Columbia Record ML4261: *I Can Hear It Now,* "Chambers and Hiss," appearance before the House Committee on Un-American Activities, Aug. 25, 1948.

Nixon, Richard. "Plea for an Anti-Communist Faith," *Saturday Review,* May 24, 1952.

————. *Six Crises.* Garden City, N.Y.: Doubleday & Co., 1962.

Norton-Taylor, Duncan. "Wisdom Is the Most Terrible Ordeal," *National Review,* July 29, 1961.

Packer, Herbert L. *Ex-Communist Witnesses.* Stanford, Calif.: Stanford University Press, 1962.

———— and Cutler, Lloyd. "Make Them Tell Congress the Truth or Take the Consequences," *Harper's,* March 1952.

Pilat, Oliver. *The Atom Spies.* New York: G. P. Putnam's Sons, 1952.

————. "Report on Whittaker Chambers," *New York Post,* June 14, 15, 1949.

Pritt, D. N. *Spies and Informers in the Witness Box.* London: Bernard Hanison, 1958.

Reik, Theodor. *The Compulsion to Confess.* New York: Farrar, Straus & Co., 1959.

Reuben, William A. *The Atom Spy Hoax.* New York: Action Books, 1960.

————. The Honorable Mr. Nixon. New York: Action Books, 1960.

Schlesinger, Arthur, Jr. *The Age of Roosevelt.* Boston: Houghton Mifflin Co., 1959.

————. "Whittaker Chambers and His 'Witness,' " *Saturday Review* (symposium), May 24, 1952.

Senate Internal Security Subcommittee of the Committee on the Judiciary, *Hearings to Investigate the Administration of the Internal Security Laws,* 82d Cong., 2d sess., Oct. 23, 1952. (Case of Zablodowsky.)

Sherwood, Robert E. *Roosevelt and Hopkins.* New York: Harper & Bros., 1948.

Shirer, William L. *Stranger, Come Home.* Boston: Little, Brown & Co., 1954.

Stettinius, Edward R., Jr. *Roosevelt and the Russians.* Garden City, N.Y.: Doubleday & Co., 1949.

Stone, I. F. "Will There Be a Third Trial for Hiss?" *Daily Compass,* June 5, 1952.

Stripling, Robert. *The Red Plot Against America.* Drexel Hill, Pa.: Bell Publishing Co., 1949. (Edited by Bob Considine.)

Tarachow, Sidney. "The Beloved Executioner," *Psychoanalytic Quarterly,* vol. 29 (1960).

Taylor, Telford. *Grand Inquest—The Story of Congressional Investigations.* New York: Simon & Schuster, 1955.

Trilling, Diana. "Memorandum on the Hiss Case," *Partisan Review,* May 1950.

Trilling, Lionel. *The Middle of the Journey.* New York: The Viking Press, 1947.

Valtin, Jan. "Communist Agent," *American Mercury,* Nov. 1939.

Van Doren, Mark. *The Autobiography of Mark Van Doren.* New York: Harcourt, Brace & Co., 1958.

Wadleigh, Julian. "Why I Spied for the Communists," syndicated articles, *New York Post,* July 12–24, 1949.

Wechsler, James A. *Reflections of an Angry Middle-Aged Editor.* New York: Random House, 1960.

———. *The Age of Suspicion.* New York: Random House, 1953.

Werfel, Franz. *Class Reunion.* New York: Simon & Schuster, 1929. (Translated by Whittaker Chambers.)

———. *Der Abituriententag.* Berlin: Paul Zsolnay Verlag, 1928.

———. *Twilight of a World—Collected Short Stories.* New York: The Viking Press, 1938. (Translated by H. T. Lowe-Porter.)

West, Rebecca. "Whittaker Chambers," *Atlantic Monthly,* June 1952.

Weyl, Nathaniel. "I Was in a Communist Unit with Hiss," *U.S. News & World Report,* Jan. 9, 1953.

———. *Treason—The Story of Disloyalty and Betrayal in American History.* Washington, D.C.: Public Affairs Press, 1950.

White, E. B. "Noontime of an Advertising Man," *The New Yorker,* June 25, 1949.

White, Victor. "The Analyst and the Confessor," *Commonweal,* June 23, 1948.

Whitehead, Don. *The FBI Story.* New York: Random House, 1956.

Williams, Edward Bennett. *One Man's Freedom.* New York: Atheneum, 1962.

Wilson, Colin. *The Outsider.* Boston: Houghton Mifflin Co., 1956.

LEGAL DOCUMENTS:

United States District Court, for the District of Maryland, Baltimore, Md. (Civil #4176). Deposition of Whittaker Chambers and Esther Chambers in the case of Alger Hiss (plaintiff) *vs.* Whittaker Chambers (defendant), Nov. 6–7, 1948, Feb. 17–18, 1949, March 25, 1949. (Stenographic copy of Baltimore Deposition.)

United States District Court, Southern District of New York; *United States of America against Alger Hiss;* Transcript of Record [First Trial], May 31-July 8, 1949. (Stenographic copy.)

United States Court of Appeals for the Second Circuit; no. 78, October term, 1950. *United States of America against Alger Hiss:*

    Appeal from a judgment of the District Court of the United States for the Southern District of New York. Affirmed.

    Transcript of Record [Second Trial], Vols. I–X. On appeal from the District Court of the United States for the Southern District of New York.

    Brief for Appellant.

United States District Court, Southern District of New York; *United States of America against Alger Hiss:*

    Affidavit submitted in opposition to the motion of defendant for a third trial.

    Memorandum in support of defendant's motion for a new trial under Rule 33 on the ground of newly discovered evidence.

    Motion for a new trial based on the ground of newly discovered evidence, Jan. 24, 1952.

    Supplemental affidavits in support of motion for a new trial.

    Federal Supplement, 1952, vol. 107.

United States Supreme Court; October term, 1952; No. 629. *Alger Hiss against the United States of America.* Petition for a writ of certiorari to the United States Court of Appeals for the Second Circuit, March 1953.

UNPUBLISHED MATERIAL:

Acheson, Dean. Statement for the Press, Dec. 10, 1946 (cited by *Christian Science Monitor*); personal communication, Feb. 25, 1963.

Adler, Nathan. Personal interviews, June, Oct. 1963, and correspondence, Oct. 1963.

Attman, George. Personal interview, June 17, 1961.

Appell, Donald. Personal interview, May 5, 1963, at Waldorf, Md.

Baldwin, Hanson. Personal communication, Oct. 12, 1962.

Baltimore City College, Registrar. Scholastic records and memoranda of Alger Hiss, February–March 1963, from Henry T. Yost, principal.

Bedacht, Max. Interviewed by Chester T. Lane, May 14, 1957.

Beer, Walter. Personal interview, Dec. 1963.

Benjamin, Robert. Personal communications and correspondence, 1959–66.

Bergdoll, Alfred. Personal communication, Feb. 1, 1964.

Berle, Adolf A., Jr. Personal communication, May 1963.

Bernard, Viola, M.D. Personal interviews and correspondence, 1959–65.

Binger, Carl. Cumulated papers on the Hiss case, memoranda, correspondence, fan mail; personal interviews and correspondence, 1959–63.

Boas, George. Personal interview, Feb. 5, 1963; correspondence, March–April, 1963.

Brenman, Margaret, M.D. Personal communications and interviews, Oct. 1963.

Bridgman, E. W., M.D. Medical report on Whittaker Chambers, April 12, 1943.

Browder, Earl. Personal communications, Oct. 18, 29, 1963.

Burton, Margaret. Personal communications and interviews, May–Oct. 1963.

Buttenwieser, Helen. Personal interviews and correspondence, 1959–65.

Cairns, Huntington. Personal communication, March 27, 1963.

Cantwell, Robert. Interviewed by Edward C. McLean, Nov. 2, 1948; personal interview, May 10, 1963, and communications, March 23, 30, 1963.

Carmon, Walter. See Ferry, Elinor.

Case, Edward W. Personal interview at Westminster, Md., May 8, 1962.

Chalmers, Burns. Personal communication, March 25, 1963.

Chambers, Esther. Personal interview at Westminster, Md., May 8, 1962.

Chambers, Mrs. Jay Lea. Personal communication (telephone), July 14, 1963.

Cowley, Malcolm. Interview with Whittaker Chambers, Friday, Dec. 13, 1940. Personal interview, May 1, 1962, and correspondence, May–June 1962.

Chambers, Whittaker. "The Prodigal Son," speech delivered at Joint Rotary–Kiwanis Meeting, Towson, Md., Jan. 25, 1951, notes taken by Chester T. Lane.

Clubb, Edmund O. Unpublished MS., "The Witness and I," 1952. Personal interviews and correspondence, 1963–66.

Colgate University, Registrar. Personal correspondence, Jan. 11, 1962.

Columbia University Assistant Registrar, Mr. Ellis, and Librarian. Correspondence, Dec. 31, 1961–Aug. 2, 1962.

Cort, David. Personal interview, Nov. 30, 1964, and correspondence, 1964.

Crichton, Robert. Memorandum regarding Chambers' early MS. of *Witness,* Oct. 16, 1963; personal communications, 1963–64; personal interview, Dec. 7, 1964.

Cross, Claude. Personal interview, Sept. 13, 1961, and correspondence, 1961–62.

Darlington, Charles. Personal communication, Feb. 28, 1964.

Dickey, John. Memo of interview by Hiss defense, Jan. 15, 1949 (Hiss Defense Files).

Dirba, Charles. Statement for Helen Buttenwieser, June 13, 1957 (Hiss Defense Files).

Ducey, Constance. Personal communication, Nov. 12, 1962.

Edstrom, Edward. Interviewed by Hiss Defense, Oct. 1948; see also Ferry, Elinor.

Emerson, Ruth. Personal communication, Feb. 18, 1963.

Endore, Guy. Personal interviews and correspondence, 1962–64.

Ensor, Lowell S. Personal communication, Jan. 30, 1962.

Ernst, Morris. Personal communications and interviews, July–Aug. 1961.

Fadiman, Clifton. Personal communication, Oct. 1963. Memorandum of interview with Fadiman by Harold Rosenwald, Oct. 15, 1948 (Hiss Defense Files).

Fansler, Ralph. Letter to Priscilla Hiss, Dec. 24, 1948 (Hiss Defense Files).

Fansler, Thomas. Letters to Priscilla Hiss, Dec. 26, 30, 1948 (Hiss Defense Files).

Farrand, Stephen. Notes from his diary regarding activities of Alger Hiss, 1936–37. Personal communication, April 3, 1963.

Ferry, Elinor. Memoranda on Levine–Shemitz household, Jan. 8, 1953; notes on *Saturday Evening Post* serialization of Witness, Oct. 15, 1952. Memoranda of interviews with Walter Carmon, Oct. 1952; sister of Ida Dales, June 15, 1954; Edward Edstrom, Oct. 1952; Harry Freeman, Oct. 21, 1952; Sender Garlin, Oct. 1952; Grace Hutchins, Oct. 20, 1952; A. B. Magil, Oct. 7, 1952. Personal interviews and correspondence, 1960–63.

Field, Richard. Personal communications, Oct.–Nov. 1963, and interview, Oct. 13, 1963. Copies of letters regarding Hiss Fund.

Finn, Michael. Personal communications, Jan. 12, Feb. 15, 1961, Aug. 23, 1962.

Fisher, Russell, M.D. Letter to Dr. Lawrence Kubie regarding Chambers' death, March 15, 1962.

Frankfurter, Felix. Personal communication, May 8, 1963.

Freeman, Don. Personal interview, July 1962.

Freeman, Harry. See Ferry, Elinor.

Garlin, Sender. See Ferry, Elinor.

Gassner, John. Personal communications, Sept. 30, Nov. 7, 1962.

Greene, Martha. Personal communication, Jan. 30, 1962.

Griswold, Erwin. Personal communication, May 3, 1963.

Hartman, Elizabeth Hiss. Personal communications, Feb. 7, March 8, April 26, 1963.

Harvard University Law School, Registrar. Academic record and data sheet on Alger Hiss, May 1963.

Helfrich, Karl. Interviewed by Edward C. McLean, Jan. 19, 1949.

Henderson, Loy. Personal interview, May 8, 1963.

Herald, Leon. Personal memoranda, Feb. 1963. Personal communications and interviews, May 10, 1963, Oct. 1963.

Hiss, Alger. Analysis and comments on Whittaker Chambers' testimony before the House Committee. Memoranda of testimony before the New York Grand Jury, Dec. 1948. Statements to the FBI, March 1946, June 1947, Dec. 4, 1948. Personal correspondence and memoranda of interviews, 1959–66.

S P E E C H E S :

"The Development of International Organizations," delivered at a meeting of the American Society of International Law, Washington, D.C., April 24, 1947.

"The Meaning of Geneva," Whig-Clio Club, Princeton, N.J., April 1956.

"The United Nations, May 1948," Commencement Address, Wells College, May 24, 1948.

"United Nations to Date," Louisville, Ky., April 12, 1948.

Hiss, Anna. Personal communication, Oct. 17, 1962.

Hiss, Anthony. Personal interview, May 7, 1964.

Hiss, Charles Alger (cousin of Alger Hiss). Personal communication, Feb. 22, 1963.

Hiss, Donald. Memorandum of testimony before the New York Grand Jury, 1948. Memorandum of interview with Donald Hiss by Harold Rosenwald and Claude Cross, Oct. 25, 1949. Personal interview, Feb. 3, 1963, and correspondence, 1962–63.

Hiss, Edna. Personal communication, Feb. 12, 1963.

Hiss, Lillian. Personal communication, March 10, 1963.

Hiss, Mary C. Personal communications, March 20, May 2, July 4, Sept. 28, 1963.

Hiss, Priscilla. Memorandum of testimony given before the New York Grand Jury, 1948. Memorandum of interview with Mrs. Hiss by Lloyd Paul Stryker, Feb. 1949. Personal interviews, 1960–63, and correspondence, 1959–63.

Hobson, Thayer. Personal communication, Nov. 26, 1961, and interview, Nov. 8, 1961.

Hobson, Timothy. Personal interviews and communications, 1960–64.

Horsky, Charles. Personal interview, May 7, 1963.

Howard, Ridgely. Personal communication, Feb. 21, 1963.

Hughes, Langston. Personal communication, April 24, 1963.

Hughes, the Reverend William Dudley Foulke. Personal communications, Feb. 22, March 1, April 6, 1963.

Hutchins, Grace. Interviewed by Hiss defense, Jan. 21, 27, 1949; telephone conversation with Hiss defense, Nov. 3, 1948. See also Ferry, Elinor.

Jackson, Gardner. Personal communication, April 15, 1963, and interview, May 6, 1963.

Jewett, Hugh, M.D. Personal communication, March 5, 1963.

Johns Hopkins University, Irene Dani, Registrar. Data sheet, academic transcript of Alger Hiss, and other memoranda, March, Aug. 1963; academic transcript of Bosley Hiss, March 29, 1963.

Josephson, Matthew. Personal communication, July 16, 1962, and interview, May 1964.

Kelly, Frank. Personal interview regarding Franklin V. Reno, July 31, 1962.

Ketchum, the Reverend Bradford W. Personal communications from the Diocese of New York regarding Chambers' baptism, Feb. 21, March 26, 1963.

King, Alexander. Personal interview, May 1961.

Kirk, the Reverend and Mrs. Nevin. Personal communications, April 1962, and interview, May 8, 1962.

Klein, George, Ph.D. Personal interviews and correspondence, 1962–65.

Kronenberger, Louis. Personal interview, May 1963.

Kubie, Lawrence S., M.D. Correspondence with State of Maryland Chief Medical Examiner. Personal correspondence and interviews, 1960–64.

Levine, Isaac Don. Personal correspondence and interviews, 1961–64.

Lewin, Bertram, M.D. Personal communications, May 1961, May 1963, and inview, May 5, 1962.

Liebling, A. J. Personal communication, May 17, 1962, and interview, May 5, 1962.

Lockwood, Manice de F. III. Personal interviews and correspondence, 1960–65.

Lowenthal, John. Personal interviews and correspondence, 1960–66.

McCormick, Kenneth. Personal interview, Oct. 1963, and correspondence, 1963–64.

McLean, Edward. Personal interview, Dec. 6, 1962.

Magil, A. B. See Ferry, Elinor.

Mandel, Benjamin. Personal interview, May 5, 1963, and communications, May 8, May 20, 1963.

Marbury, William. Memorandum of relations with Alger Hiss, Dec. 30, 1948, including correspondence between Marbury and Hiss. Personal interview, May 6, 1964, and correspondence, 1963–64.

Marchbanks Press. Personal communications from Emily Connor, June 1, 1961, and interview, Dec. 7, 1961.

Maryland State Department of Health. Personal communications from Charles J. Judge, Chief, Vital Records Section, Jan. 18, 1962; Arthur S. Kraus, Sc.D., Chief, Division of Statistical Research and Records, Feb. 1, 1962. Personal telephone conversation with Dr. March, deputy medical examiner, Carroll County, May 7, 1962.

Matthews, T. S. Personal communications, March 14, Oct. 12, 1963, and interview, Aug. 1965.

Meyer, Herman Louis. Personal interview regarding Franklin V. Reno, July 31, 1962.

Mills, Mr. (of Longmans, Green). Copy of correspondence regarding Chambers' translation of Regler's *Great Crusade,* July 9–Dec. 28, 1938. Memorandum of conversations with Mr. Mills by Harold Rosenwald, Nov. 12, 1948, (Hiss Defense Files).

Morgan, Edward M. Personal communication, Feb. 4, 1963.

Morrow, Felix. Personal communications, April 25, May 9, 1963. Copy of unpublished letter, dated August 13, 1962, to John Berendt of *Esquire,* regarding William F. Buckley's article, "The End of Whittaker Chambers," in *Esquire,* Sept. 1962 (Morrow to the author, May 9, 1963).

Murray, Henry A. Interview with Timothy Hobson, May 1953 (taped).

Mussey, Barrows. Unpublished ms., What Makes Whittaker Chambers Tick Like a Bomb? (Hiss Defense Files).

Myers, John E., Jr. Personal interview, May 8, 1962.

Nixon, Richard. Personal communication, July 26, 1961.

Peters, Paul. Memorandum of interview by Harold Rosenwald, Nov. 19, 1948.

Popkin, Richard H. Personal communication, Oct. 20, 1962.

Reese, Charles Ford. Personal communications, Feb. 18, March 14, 1963.

Rangell, Leo, M.D. Personal communications and interviews, 1962–63.

Reno, Philip. Personal correspondence, Dec. 23, 1962, Jan. 11, 1963.

Reston, James. Personal communication, Oct. 10, 1962.

Reuben, William A. Personal interview, May 11, 1961, and correspondence, 1961.

Rocco, Arthur. Personal communication (taped), Feb. 1964, and correspondence, March 1964.

Roos, Allan, M.D. Personal interview, 1960.

Roos, Beatrice. Personal interview and correspondence, 1960.

Rosenwald, Harold. Personal interviews and correspondence, 1960–63.

Rosner, Elsie. Personal communication, Jan. 5, 1961.

Ross, Nathaniel, M.D. Personal interview, Dec. 9, 1960.

Roth, Samuel. Personal communication, Oct. 2, 1963, and interview, Oct. 18, 1963.

Sayre, E. B. (former secretary to Alger Hiss). Notes and memoranda regarding Alger Hiss and the Carnegie Endowment, 1946–48.

Sayre, Francis B. Personal communications, Sept. 19, Oct. 10, 1963.

Schapiro, Meyer. Personal interview, Dec. 9, 1961, and correspondence, Dec. 1961. Interviewed by Harold Rosenwald, Nov. 22, 1948.

Schlesinger, Arthur, Jr. Memorandum, Jan. 4, 1949, regarding statements alleged to have been made by Chambers to Schlesinger, who was preparing an article on Communism in America.

Schorer, Mark. Personal interview and correspondence, Aug. 1963.

Schultz, Jack, M.D. Personal communication, Sept. 1962.

Slingluff, Jesse. Personal communication and memorandum of relationship with Alger Hiss, May 15, 1963.

Solow, Herbert. Personal interviews (New York), May 10, 11, 1962, and correspondence, May–Sept. 1962.

Spero, Carl. Personal interview, Dec. 4, 1962.

Stevenson, Adlai. Deposition taken at Springfield, Ill., 1949. (From transcript of first Hiss trial.)

Stone, Brinton. Letter to Alger Hiss, June 4, 1949. Signed affidavit of relationship with Alger Hiss, June 4, 1949.

Sutro, John. Personal interview, July 29, 1963.

Sversky, Leon. Interviewed by Harold Rosenwald, Sept. 8, 1948.

Swope, Gerard, Jr. Personal communication, Aug. 7, 1963.

Taylor, Telford. Memorandum of conversation with Alger Hiss, Oct. 9, 1948. Personal interview, Oct. 17, 1963, and correspondence, 1963.

Tilghman, Donnell. Personal interview, Aug. 5, 1961, and correspondence, May–July 1961.

Trachtenberg, Alexander. Interviewed by William Reuben, 1957.

Trilling, Lionel. Personal interview, Sept. 11, 1961.

Triplett, William (assistant headmaster, Landon School for Boys). Statement regarding character and background of Alger Hiss, Oct. 1948 (Hiss Defense Files).

Tytell, Martin. Personal interview, Dec. 8, 1960, and correspondence, 1960–61.

Van Doren, Mark. Personal interview, Dec. 7, 1960. Interviewed by Harold Rosenwald, Nov. 15, 1948.

Wadleigh, Julian. Personal interview, May 5, 1963. Interviewed by Edward C. McLean, Dec. 11, 1948, Jan. 17, March 12, 1949.

Weiss, John. Conversation with Earl Browder, Dec. 31, 1948. Memorandum of interview by Harold Rosenwald regarding Earl Browder and Whittaker Chambers, Sept. 8, 1948.

Willard, Charles. Personal communications, Nov. 15, 1963, Jan. 12, 1964.

Wilkens, Elizabeth Reese, M.D. Personal interview (Westminster, Md.), May 18, 1962.

Wilkinson, John. Personal interviews, July 1962.

Winslow, Anne. Personal interview, May 1963.

Witt, Nathan. Personal interview, Dec. 6, 1962.

Yost, Henry. See Baltimore City College.

Zablodowsky, David. Personal interview, May 12, 1962, and correspondence, 1962–63.

Zepp, Calvin. Personal interview, Westminster, Md., May 8, 1962.

Index

Abt, John, 6, 8, 189, 343
Acheson, Dean, 259, 341, 405
Adams, Charles, *see* Chambers, Whittaker
Adams, Franklin P., 163
Adams, John Quincy, 50
Adler, Nathan, 123, 125, 217
Agricultural Adjustment Administration (AAA), 8, 188, 189, 190, 191, 192, 193, 195, 196, 197, 206, 286, 313, 343
Alger, Russell Alexander, 136
All in One Lifetime (Byrnes), 337
Allard, John S., 195
Allied Control Commission, 246
Alpha Delta Phi, 160, 164
American Friends Service Committee, 69, 154
American Magazine, 218, 278, 373
American Medical Association, 28
American Mercury, 301, 339
American Testament, An (Freeman), 107
Andrews, Bert, 352, 353
Andrews, Peter, 352
Annie Warner Hospital, 430
Annual Report of the Committee on Un-American Activities to the United States House of Representatives, 363
Appell, Donald, 12, 16, 228, 229, 255, 352, 381
Arnault, Christine, 146
Arundel Club, 142
Ascoli, Max, 310
Associated Press, 334, 353
Astor, Mrs. Vincent, 173

Atlas Stores Corporation, 110
Autobiography of Mark Van Doren, 298

Bachrach, Marion, 191, 360, 361
Bagnold, Enid, 414
Baldwin, Hanson, 154
Ballantine, Arthur, 340
Baltimore City College, 158, 159, 164
Baltimore Credit Bureau, 252
Baltimore Deposition, 100, 108, 121, 207, 208, 221, 222, 223, 230, 234, 247, 293, 350, 368, 369, 371, 372, 373, 378
Baltimore Friends School, 153
Baltimore Polytechnic High School, 157
Baltimore Sun, 139, 141, 147, 160, 167, 168, 217, 278, 282, 320, 373, 420
Barber, Alvin, 63, 64
Barnstormers, The, 163
Baruch, Bernard, 195
Beadle, *see* Chambers, Whittaker
Bean, Louis, 218
Bedacht, Max, 120, 121, 122, 257
Beer, Richards, Lane and Haller, 391
Beer, Walter, 410
Benjamin, Robert M., 372, 403
Bentley, Elizabeth, 6, 246, 346
Bergdoll, A., 395
Berle, Adolf A., Jr., 4, 247, 251, 300, 301, 303, 304, 305, 306, 307, 344, 346, 359, 382
Binger, Carl, 114, 365, 385, 386
Bixler, Carrie M., 321
Bixler, Herbert C., 321